CALIF...

A Guide t...
Tavern... ...Inns on the West Coast

Written by

Robert Wlodarski and Anne Wlodarski

CALIFORNIA GHOSTS

A Guide to the Most Haunted Restaurants, Taverns and Inns on the West Coast

G-HOST PUBLISHING

8701 Lava Place | West Hills, California 91304-2126
Phone/Fax: 818-340-6676 | E-mail: robanne@ix.netcom.com

Other books from authors **Rob and Anne Wlodarski** (Southern Fried Spirits; Spirits of the Alamo; Dinner and Spirits; California Hauntspitality, Louisiana Hauntspitality and, A Texas Guide to Haunted Restaurants, Taverns & Inns); are available through: www.prairieghosts. com; www.amazon.com; www.sdparanormal.com; www.sandiegoghosthunters.com; www. sgvps.com; www.sandiegoghosthunters.com; www.barnesandnoble.com; www.fetchbook. info/search; and www.invink.com

G-HOST PUBLISHING is proud to offer the following books: The Haunted Queen Mary ($13.95); Haunted Catalina ($12.95); Haunted Alcatraz ($13.95); Spirits of the Leonis Adobe ($14.95); Louisiana Hauntspitality: A Ghostly Guide to Haunted Inns, Restaurants and Taverns ($15.95); Haunted Whaley House II ($15.95); Ghosts of Old Town San Diego State Historic Park ($14.95); and Fullerton Ghosts ($14.95).

If you purchased this book without a cover, the book is probably stolen property. It was reported as "unsold and destroyed" to the publisher and neither the authors nor the publisher has received any payment for this "stripped book." The stories appearing in this book are factual. The information presented herein does not necessarily reflect the views or opinions of the individual owners or establishments listed herein.

The authors would enjoy hearing from readers about their paranormal experiences in California. The most interesting of these stories may be included in future printings. Please write or e-mail your stories to G-Host Publishing. The authors take no responsibility for the veracity of each story except that we believe the storytellers. We have attempted to detail the encounters as accurately as possible.

Although the publishers have made every effort to ensure that the information was correct at the time the book went to press, they do not assume and hereby disclaim any liability to any party for any loss, damage, or injury caused by information contained in this book. The publishers also disclaim any liability resulting from the use of this book.

All rights reserved. No part of this book may be reproduced or transmitted in any form by any means, electronic or mechanical, including photocopying, recording, or by any informational storage or retrieval system in English or in any other language that has been invented or is yet to be invented (except by a reviewer who may quote brief passages in a review to be printed in a magazine or newspaper) without written permission from the publisher.

Thanks to Mrs. M.B. Wlodarski for taking time to edit this tome.

Special thanks for their help in researching the stories in this book go to the San Diego Ghost Hunters (Maritza Skandunas, Dawn Gaudette and Vinnie Skandunas), psychics Ginnie McGovern, Deann Burch, Victoria Gross, Robin Collier and Alma Carey of the International Paranormal Research Organization (IPRO), and fellow paranormal investigators and friends, Alex, Lonnie, Nicci and Natasha Sill, Richard Senate, Diane Melvin, Chad Patterson, Peter James, Jack Rourke and Peggy Stahler.

© Copyright 2007 - G-HOST PUBLISHING, ITF: Robert J. Wlodarski and Anne P. Wlodarski
- All Rights Reserved

G-HOST PUBLISHING, Limited Edition

ISBN: 1-4243-2735-0/ 978-1-4243-2735-5 – Softcover

All photographs are provided courtesy of the authors unless otherwise noted under a particular photograph.

Printed in the United States by M & M Quality Printing, Woodland Hills, California

Design & Layout by Celine Luk | www.CelineLukDesigns.com

Though terrified, curiously I was never afraid. It must have been a child's delight in terror. And to the degree that we remain child-like, the supernatural not only continues to intrigue but very much seems a real possibility. And so to this day, I remember the stories. Such lasting power must make them true. And those voices, although the same that spoke of Santa Claus, they would never lie. I believed.

Walter Nicklin, Editor & Publisher -
Foreword in, Virginia's Ghosts by L.B Taylor (1995)

"There are no experts in the field of paranormal investigation, no matter what anyone says or who claims to be one."

Troy Taylor

"Eliminate the impossible and whatever remains, however improbable, must be the truth."

Sir Arthur Conan Doyle

Then stand to your glasses steady and drink to your comrade's eyes; here's a toast to the dead already, and hurrah to the next who dies.

Popular drinking song at the Whitechapel Club in Chicago

Assemble a group of almost anybody from any profession or walk of life, pose a question if spirits of the dead really exist, and at least one individual will come forward with an anecdote. It may be something they've heard somewhere or perhaps an incident that occurred to a friend or relative. That person might not even believe in elusive spectral phenomenon, but he or she still delights to relate the tale.

Hilber H. Graf, Visiting Haunted Southern California (2005)

They come at night often. And often they come into your most private, intimate time: sleep. It is as if unconsciousness--like madness--is some sort of in-road to where they live and play. But they also show themselves in broad light, making their appearance even more mysterious by not being so mysterious as to use darkness for a cover. They manifest themselves in many guises, using all your senses. Auditory apparitions seem to be the most common, accounting for about 60 percent of the experiences; but all the senses are involved, including that unnamed sense that simply tells you something is not quite right by sending that special chill. And they manifest themselves just about anywhere---at the foot of your bed, across a sun-showered field, through a window or door, or sometimes as just light or shadow.... "They," of course, are "ghosts." "Spirits" may be a better, less volatile term, but we're talking about the same thing. A sound, a smell, of something that is long gone; a vision, a touch out of time and beyond reason, of someone who is dead. And perhaps "dead" isn't the right word either, with its connotations of Final and eventual decay. If the spirit is the very essence of the person, and the body is something it just lives in and breathes out of for a while, then maybe the word for the moment of cessation of the living body in terms of what the spirit does is "to move on. "

Over the years, I have read a number of books based on paranormal investigations and various places that were investigated around the United States. Although most of these were interesting, only a few caught my attention, to which I remember thinking, Yes I'd like to investigate that particular actively haunted place. After reading numerous books written by Rob and Anne Wlodarski on related subject matter, I felt as though I was there with them. I actually had the good fortune of participating in one of their investigations at the George Gershwin/Rosemary Clooney House in Beverly Hills. After reading their books and having a first hand experience working with them, I heartily recommend reading their most recent book.

Peter James, author, psychic and paranormal investigator

"There are no other authors who can capture the 'spirit' of California the way that Rob and Anne Wlodarski can. In their previous books, they have managed to present the history and hauntings of the region in a manner that captivates not only ghost enthusiasts, but history buffs and the casual reader as well…. This book is the essential travel guide… Don't miss this compelling --- and chilling --- read!"

Troy Taylor, Founder, American Ghost Society

I'm sure you will enjoy reading [this book], which is filled to brim with history and haunted destinations. I have had the pleasure to work with Rob and Anne Wlodarski and look forward to many future investigations.

Diane Melvin, Founder and Director of the San Gabriel Valley Paranormal Researchers (SGVPR)

Assemble a group of almost anybody from any profession or walk of life, pose a question if spirits of the dead really exist, and at least one individual will come forward with an anecdote. It may be something they've heard somewhere or perhaps an incident that occurred to a friend or relative. That person might not even believe in elusive spectral phenomenon, but he or she still delights to relate the tale.

Hilber H. Graf, Visiting Haunted Southern California (2005)

Most who come searching for spirits find more than their share of the unexplained. Rob and Anne Wlodarski are adept at not only researching haunted locations, but in writing about their encounters. Their books blend… ghostly tales… with a crisp look at the history of the legendary structures in this setting. I believe this is the quintessential book on the area, and as such is a "must read" for those who have heard the local ghost stories. It is both easy to read and clears away the myth from the real story of the historic structures. This book not only reveals the scary tales but also the history behind them. I recommend this book and leave you with only this admonition: Don't read it at night before going to bed!

Richard Senate, renowned paranormal investigator, lecturer and author of: Hollywood Ghosts: The Fabulous Phantoms of Filmdom, Ghosts of the Haunted Coast, Haunted Ventura, The Haunted Southland, Ghost Stalker's Guide to Haunted California, The Ghosts of the Olivas Adobe, Ghosts of the Ojai, and Ghosts of the Camino Real

Table of Contents

Acknowledgements

Every creative work has passion, inspiration and cooperation as its sources; this book is no different. Researching this book and compiling the stories took us over 10 years to put into print. Completion of this work involved parts research, patience, perseverance and otherworldly guidance. Our initial book, *California Hauntspitality* and this updated version was a wild investigative ride we will never forget. The fact that it is completed is due in large part to the numerous individuals who contributed their time, energy and knowledge to this undertaking. Without their help this updated would never have come to fruition. Therefore, special thanks are due to our many good friends, acquaintances and family members helped along the way.

To Troy Taylor, friend, author, paranormal investigator, founder and president of the Ghost Research Society, editor of Ghosts of the Prairie Magazine, creator of the Ghosts and Hauntings web site, founder of Bump in the Night Tour Company, Illinois Hauntings Tour Company, Alton, Springfield and Chicago Hauntings Tours and Whitechapel Productions Press for originally publishing *California Hauntspitality*, which has now, sadly gone out of print. We closed one chapter with Troy and opened another under our own publishing company. We've always admired Troy's work ethic: He has his own ghost tours; is a regular guest on television and radio; continues to publish book after book, and lives the life most of dream of; working full time uncovering the mysteries of the afterlife. His Website and data base is peerless and he is one of a few writers and researchers who continues to produce quality material for other paranormal enthusiasts around the world to emulate on a regular basis. Troy can be reached at E-mail: ttaylor@prairieghosts.com or his Website: www.prairieghosts.com)

To Richard Senate, a long-time friend, well-known author on the subject of ghosts, lecturer, and renowned paranormal investigator who graciously provided input about haunted California locations. Richard, (who we like to refer to as the Huell Howser of the paranormal in California, is pure "California Ghoul(d)"He has always been there to answer questions regarding haunted locations and willingly share his research data. Check out his paranormally potent website at www.ghost-stalker.com or E-mail: hainthunter@aol.com. Senate was the first investigator to have a website dedicated to the paranormal. Richard and his gifted wife, Debbie, continue to investigate haunted locations.

Dennis Hauck - Renowned, lecturer, paranormal investigator, alchemist, and author of the ultimate ghost hunters guide to the United States, the National Director of Haunted which has inspired numerous like ourselves to continue in his footsteps (www.haunted-places.com/E-mail: DWHauck@poetic.com).

To Arthur Myers - For his informative trilogy on haunted destination across the United States: the Gazetteer, Register, and Ghosthunter's Guide, and his input along the way (www.globalpsychics.com).

To local author, Carol Biederman (carolb@sonnet.com) who provides ghost tours of City Hotel, Fallon Hotel, Fallon House Theater, Rehm House, Harlan House and a residence on Fulton Street; Call for reservations at 209-532-1479.

To Ron Smith and Martha Chacon of the Queen Mary, for their help in obtaining documentation and photographs of the Queen Mary which is considered the most haunted ship in the world.

To Sally Fowler of Banta, California, for helping us obtain photographs, and for sharing the history of the Banta Inn.

To Sally Hamilton, for providing us with a copy of her very interesting book on the history of the Hotel Willow, and in providing photographs of the haunted Willow Steak House for our book.

To Nancy Bradley for her excellent reference works on Gold Rush Ghosts. Bradley is a gifted psychic, lecturer, and author (Phone: 530-622-0977 or write P.O. Box 911, Diamond Springs, California 95619. Web: www.bizarre-n-stuff.com and E-mail: bizarrenstuff@sunset.net).

To our dear friends, Marc, Kharla, Marcus and Kinsey Lundin for their spirited help in obtaining information for our Pleasanton listings including the Gay 90s Pizza, the Pleasanton Hotel and Vineyards Restaurant.

To Shannon LeClair and owner Dave Parker of the Spadra Restaurant in Fullerton for their ghost stories and for an incredible visit to their very haunted restaurant.

To Matthew B. Wlodarski for his enthusiastic support, and tireless efforts while helping to document Heroes Bar and Grill, The Cafe Hidalgo, the Brownstone Café and the Cellar in Fullerton, the White House Restaurant and Paris Restaurant in Anaheim, Mrs. Knott's Chicken Dinner Restaurant in Buena Park, the Royal Hawaiian Restaurant in Laguna Beach, the Victorian Manor Tea Room and Rutabegorz in Orange, the El Adobe Restaurant in San Juan Capistrano, and the Holly Street Bar and Grill in Pasadena --- Thanks so much, Dad, for believing; and thanks Mom, for letting Dad attend! Also, thanks, Mom, for editing this manuscript, which needed your kind attention to detail and your patience in completing this tome.

Dan Larson, long-time friend, fellow archaeologist and researcher, for his spirited help with the Big Yellow House, Bella Maggiore, Landmark No. 78, Stagecoach Inn and Holly Street Bar and Grill listings as well as helping to map the Leonis Adobe for an investigation and aid in the Saddle Peak Lodge research project.

Jim Dorsey, photographer, writer and balloon pilot for his excellent photograph of the Braken Fern Manor in Lake Arrowhead.

To Cathy Thomas, Curator, Launer Local History Room of the Fullerton Public Library for her assistance during our research in Anaheim and Fullerton and her help in obtaining historic photographs for our book, *Fullerton Ghosts*.

Jane Newell and Ann Erlich of the Elizabeth J. Schultz History Room of the Anaheim Public Library for their valuable assistance pertaining to the Anaheim White House Restaurant and Paris Restaurant.

Aimee Aul, Education Coordinator, Fullerton Museum Center, who administers the fantastic Haunted Fullerton Ghost Tours and who prepared the informative booklet: Haunted Fullerton, A Guide to the Ghostly Downtown. Aimee, with her knowledge of spirited Fullerton, helped along the way, particularly with our Fullerton haunts listed herein.

We would like to thank our friend, gifted medium/psychic and spiritual consultant, Ginnie McGovern (Malibu/New Mexico), for her help at the Bob Morris Beverly Hills Barbecue, Victorian Manor Tea Room in Orange, Leonis Adobe in Calabasas, the Holly Street Bar and Grill/Turner and Stevens Mortuary in Pasadena and numerous investigations in Los Angeles, San Diego, Orange and Ventura counties. Ginnie also authored the foreword for this book.

To our friend, gifted psychic and healer Victoria Gross, who began conducting paranormal investigations with the International Paranormal Research Organization in 2000. She also founded the North Orange County Tarot Society in 2003. You can visit her at her web site at www.noctarot.com or contact her at E-mail: thecrescentmoon@adelphia.net. Her insights, research skills and investigative participation greatly aided in completing this book.

To, Deann Cutright Burch, a fellow IPRO researcher, a gifted Astrologer and the Metaphysical "Dear Abby" -- e-mail questions regarding aromatherapy, stones & crystals, meditation, divination, paranormal activity, cleansing, rituals, healing, pagan/Wicca studies, etc., etc. You can reach her at dburch@adelphia.net.

To our other gifted psychic friends Robin Collier, Palah Sandling, Dan Smith and Christy Flowers for utilizing their special psychic gifts to provide valuable assistance during our paranormal investigations.

Profound thanks to the San Diego Ghost Hunters (Maritza Skandunas, Dawn Gaudette and Vinnie Skandunas). We worked side by side during numerous investigations referenced herein. They also helped with follow up work on genealogy that in some cases, helped identify the spirits we encountered. We highly recommend their Website at www.sandiegoghosthunters.com.

Additional paranormal research information was provided by the following outstanding local groups, which we have had the pleasure to work with in the past: The California Society for Ghost Research (CSGR – Chad Patterson) - Website: www.csgr.us/; the San Gabriel Valley Paranormal Researchers (SGVPR – Diane Melvin) - Website: www.sgvpr.org; and San Diego Paranormal (Bonnie Vent) - Website: www.sdparanormal.com.

To Alma Carey, an internationally renowned psychic and dear friend who has worked with us on numerous other investigations including, Greystone Mansion, The Gershwin-Clooney House; the Sharon Tate murder scene; Banning Residence Museum; Linick-Weisman House; Leonis Adobe; Workman-Shadow Ranch; Glen Tavern Inn; the Whaley House and many more locations. Alma has a unique talent and gift of insight that adds significantly to the haunted history of a location. We encourage you to contact Alma Carey at 818-972-2953 for psychic readings or special events (Website: www.almacarey.com).

To archaeologists and friends, Dennis Gallegos, Karen Hovland, and investigators David Gallegos, Tony Love and Nick Doose for their help during our

Old Town San Diego State Historic Park investigations. With the help of Debbie Valdez, Bob Wohl and Elizabeth Allancorte of the State Park system, we were able to access the Casa de Estudillo, Robinson-Rose House, Theater in Old Town, Casa de Machado y Stewart, U.S. House, the Commercial Store and several destinations in Heritage Park. Dennis runs a successful archaeological consulting firm in San Diego (Gallegos & Associates, Environmental Services, 5671 Palmer Way, Suite A, Carlsbad, California 92008-7256 – 760-929-0055).

Thanks to David Deelo and Donavan McDougle from Take 3, LLC for accompanying us and documenting several of our investigations.

To Bonnie Vent of San Diego Paranormal for her respected metaphysical and paranormal work in the region and her highly regarded Website that continues to enlighten and inform (www.sdparanromal.com).

In memory of Peter James, who always, graciously gave of his time and knowledge when called up for help. We count ourselves lucky to have known Peter James was world-renowned authority when it came to ghosts and hauntings. Many regarded him as the quintessential paranormal researcher and an accomplished clairvoyant medium; he provided private consultations when his active schedule permitted. Be sure to check out his book, "*Heaven Can You Hear Me?*" and his video, the Mysterious Spirit World that documents his research aboard the Queen Mary. We will truly miss you Peter.

To Kathy Sneed of the Amargosa Hotel for her great photographs and spirited insights into their hotel hauntings.

To producers Joel Lipman, Sara Hutchison and Ali McCallister (Greystone Productions) who believed in our Dinner and Spirits concept and allowed us to work alongside them as consulting producers during the production of "Haunted Restaurants" for the Food Network. Two of the television stories (Sir Winston's Restaurant aboard the very haunted Queen Mary, and the Anaheim White House Restaurant) appear in this book.

Owner Bruno Serato of the Anaheim White House Restaurant for allowing us to investigate his five star establishment. Bruno also worked with us on a television special for the Food Network, entitled, "Haunted Restaurants."

To Ellen Zehna of the Cutting Horse in San Juan Bautista, who researched her own building and its spectral history.

Glen and Kim Rhynes, Chris and Tyler for allowing us to conduct an investigation in the Brownstone Cafe (Villa del Sol) in Fullerton, and assisting us in the process.

To DanaLee and Pablo at the former Bob Morris Beverly Hills Barbecue for taking care of our physical needs while we helped them out with their otherworldly clientele during an investigation.

Marsha Gibbs, a landscaper at the Cliff Crest, who with the owners Constantin Gehringer and Adriana Gehringer Gil of the Cliff Crest Bed and Breakfast Inn in Santa Cruz, diligently compiled their ghost stories for our book.

To those who participated in the Turner and Stevens Mortuary/

HoweMarketingGroup/Holly Street Bar and Grill Investigation including: Matthew Wlodarski, Ginnie McGovern, Patricia Bryan, Peggy Stahler, Victoria Gross, Karen Camus, Matt Cope, Alfredo Vargas, Sadie Carver, Traci Gunn, Carla Bowen, Kevin Locarro, and Paul Gadd.

The Orange County Society for Psychic Research (OCSPR - P.O. Box 3692, Orange, California 92857 - Phone 714-637-5822), and in particular Peggy Stahler, Veral Pitsenbarger, Patricia Bryan and Almeta Womack for their help during the investigations of the California Hotel, Brownstone Cafe and Cafe Hidalgo in Fullerton; Veral Pitsenbarger, Patricia Bryan, Julee Donahue, Almeta Womack and Diane Enders during the investigations of the Paris Restaurant and Anaheim White House in Anaheim, California; Patricia Bryan and Peggy Stahler for their excellent work at the Victorian Manor Tea Room in Orange; and Peggy Stahler and Pat Bryan for their eventful work at the Holly Street Bar and Grill/Turner and Steven Mortuary in Pasadena -- may the spirits be with them!

Matt Cope, friend, cameraman and film editor for his help at the Victorian Manor Tea Room in Orange, the Whaley House in San Diego, the Leonis Adobe in Calabasas, and the Turner and Stevens Mortuary in Pasadena.

Thanks go to fellow archaeologists Wayne and Diane Bonner, Dan Larson, Jon Brady, and Matthew Conrad for their assistance along the way.

To Matt and Hank Wlodarski who raised us with open minds, instilled in us a desire to learn, explore, and continually question what we see and who we are. They encouraged us to leave something for the next generatio. Hopefully we have done this, and will continue to do so by writing these books.

To the owners and managers of the establishments listed herein, who provided the facts, list of paranormal events, and photographs which gave life to this book; we thank them profusely, and hope they enjoy the book.

To those who helped along the way that we may have inadvertently forgot to give thanks. We apologize and hope that our brain cells don't fail us if we are fortunate enough to revise this edition.

To those who wrote and published the books referenced herein, and whose prior efforts helped bring the past into the present for future generations to enjoy... a profound, Thanks!

To the next generation of readers and storytellers of folklore and history which expand our horizons and contribute to our own growth and development as individuals and as part of a greater universal force, keep the magic of creativity that inspires, flowing; always follow your dreams and never give up on them. May our children and our children's children continue the legacy of keeping the spirits alive as an integral part of our heritage?

And finally, to the spirits who roam this physical dimension. May those who are having trouble crossing over find the impetus to walk into the light and find true peace and happiness; that is, unless they are content to be where they are in the physical moment, a place they still call home.

We are riding on our rainbow, it's nearly at an end
It was given as a promise to each and every man
It's a long time since we started and the days left now are few
It seems the words sent long ago are true

Life goes on forever, and it changes like the tide
There's a meaning for existence, no need to run and hide
We are fighting for our freedom, we are searching for a way
And we live in hope of some eternal day

We are waiting, we're impatient, we're unfaithful, we are true
There's a lesson in the learning of the different things we do
As it is in the beginning, it shall be at the end
We will come full circle to begin again

Search your heart before you die, is the cost way to high
To explain all the tears we have caused throughout the years
When everything is finished and we've done all that we can
Will we come full circle to begin again?

When everything is finished and we've done all that we can
Will we come full circle to begin again?
Will we come full circle to begin again.

Birtles, Shorrock, Goble – *Full Circle*

About the Authors

Robert James Wlodarski

Born in Los Angeles, California, Wlodarski has BA's in history, anthropology, and an MA in anthropology from California State University, Northridge. As the President of Historical, Environmental, Archaeological, Research, Team (H.E.A.R.T.) and Cellular, Archaeological, Resource, Evaluations (C.A.R.E.) since 1978, Wlodarski has administered over 1400 archaeological and historical projects for federal, state, county, city agencies and private companies, and has authored and co-authored over 20 articles for journals and magazines throughout California and the Southwest. Mr. Wlodarski, the President of Mayan Moon Productions, has co-authored seven screenplays: The Crawling Eye, Cities of Stone, The Cool Change, Illusion, No Innocents, Ghost Glass, and The Palace of Unknown King. Mr. Wlodarski has served as a consultant for: *Catalina, A Treasure from The Past* for Ironwood Productions; the History Channel/Greystone Productions on their *Haunted History* series; and Consulting Producer with the Food Network on *Haunted Restaurants*; The Travel Channel/Indigo Productions on their *Most Haunted America* series; Authentic Entertainment /TLC on their *Haunted Hotels* series; Mike Mathis Productions/The Travel Channel on the *Mysterious Journeys* program; and USA TV Special: *Weekend before the Movie – The Whaley House.*

Anne Powell Wlodarski

Born in San Antonio, Texas, Ms. Wlodarski is a registered art therapist. She received her MA in behavioral science from the University of Houston, and has published several articles including a chapter in California Art Therapy Trends. She has been an exhibiting artist and is the president and founder of HEARTWORLD Arts Center for Children, a non-profit organization for abused and disadvantaged youth. Ms. Wlodarski served as an education outreach coordinator and gallery assistant for the City of Los Angeles' Artspace Gallery from 1989-1993 and has been featured in the media for her work with children and the arts. She was honored as a "Sunday Woman" by the Daily News, and was a J.C. Penney Golden Rule Award nominee. She is also a member of the Daughters of the Republic of Texas (DRT), and the Southern California Art Therapy Association (SCATA). Ms. Wlodarski is Vice-President of Mayan Moon Productions, and has co-authored six screenplays: The Crawling Eye, Cities of Stone, The Cool Change, Illusion, No Innocents, and Ghost Glass.

Rob and Anne Wlodarski

They founded G-Host Publishing, and have authored and published the following books: *A Guide to the Haunted Queen Mary: Ghostly Apparitions, Psychic Phenomena, and Paranormal Activity; Haunted Catalina: A History of the Island and Guide to Paranormal Activity; The Haunted Alamo: A History of the Mission and Guide to Paranormal Activity; The Haunted Whaley House: A History and Guide to the Most Haunted House in America; Haunted Alcatraz: A History of La Isla de los Alcatraces and Guide to Paranormal Activity; Spirits of the Alamo; The Haunted Queen Mary, Long Beach, California; Southern Fried Spirits: A Guide to Haunted Restaurants, Inns, and Taverns; Dinner and Spirits: A Guide to America's Most Haunted Restaurants, Taverns, and Inns; A Texas Hauntspitality: A Guide to the Most Haunted Restaurants, Taverns and Inns of the Lone Star State; California Hauntspitality: A Ghostly Guide to Haunted Inns, Restaurants, and Taverns; Spirits of the Leonis Adobe: History* and Hauntings in Calabasas, California; Louisiana Hauntspitality: A Ghostly Guide to Haunted Inns, Restaurants, and Taverns; Haunted Whaley House II; Fullerton Ghosts; and Ghosts of Old Town San Diego State Historic Park.

Foreword

We asked our dear friend, IPRO member and gifted medium Ginnie McGovern to provide us with an opening that we could use in our book that would provide some insight about what we do from the perspective of a medium. She obliged as follows:

As a member of a paranormal investigating team, I'm often asked if I ever get frightened. I find that I'm more afraid of the living. I've only screamed twice on investigations. Once, when a flesh and bone busboy almost collided with me around the corner of what I thought was a deserted restaurant. The other time was when a huge cockroach scurried over my foot at the Whaley House in San Diego, California. When I'm tuned in to work with the dead, things like this happen because I tend to not be as aware of the living.

Every medium I know has their own style of investigating. Some will tell you they open their third eye, the chakra or energy point between the physical eyes. Some just tune in naturally by asking spirit to come close. Spirit will never come into your body. They may move close and influence your senses in many ways by impressing various thoughts into your energy or etheric field, but they will never move into your body and take over. That is Hollywood.

I state my intentions. I tell them who we are, why we're there and what we hope to accomplish. The spirit world is all around us and perfectly capable of hearing what we say, as well as communicating with us on other levels as well. Our team (The International Paranormal Research Organization – IPRO) has a statement of intention we read at the beginning of every investigation as well as a thank you or closing statement for the end. I then shut down all of my chakras and step into my God light. Spirit recognizes us as light and frequencies or vibrations. When I intensify my God light it stands out more as a beacon than my normal level would.

A universal truth is that like attracts like. Therefore, my philosophy is that those in spirit, working with the light, will be attracted to me and willing to converse, or at least commune. Those not working in the light will scatter. That works for me. I really don't want to talk to them anyway.

I've learned two important things about investigations. The first, from Judith Seaman, President of the Spiritualists' National Union in England, is that you never, ever enter into a discussion with evil. The second, from my good friend Victoria Gross, fellow investigator and great teacher, is that if you wouldn't spend your time in this life talking with nasty people, why would you seek them out on the other side? Don't go there.

Please keep in mind that just because someone is in spirit doesn't make them spiritual. Spirits are just us without bodies. Or, looking at it from another angle, we are just spirits with bodies.

If Uncle George or Auntie Sue were crabby and miserable human beings, chances are that they may be similar on the other side. Now, I do think eventually they'll get the hang of it and lighten up, but it may take a while. There is no time in spirit. There's no rush.

Some people that were narrow-minded in the physical will probably cross over being the same way. It often takes a lot of work from others, on both sides of the veil, to get them to open up to other realities. Once this happens, they do change. They will often come through a medium to apologize or make amends. However, we don't suddenly sprout wings and a halo when we cross over. We stay us to a larger degree.

I often liken our paranormal investigating team to Mission Impossible. Rob Wlodarski is our Mr. Phelps. He handpicks the team for each investigation. For most of our investigations we, the mediums, are told as little as possible about the place we are going. Sometimes we are just given an address. This helps keep our own minds out of the picture and allows us to be clearer communicators. Our team consists of mediums and technical members to do the scientific bits.

Communication is the key. Spirit will communicate in many different ways. They may send a thought, a smell, a feeling, or even a taste. They may touch you gently. All mediums have their own way of receiving information.

On our team we have sensitives who are open to emotions and feelings, or clairsentients. Some see and are clairvoyant. Others hear and are clairaudient. Most mediums work with a combination of all or some of these abilities.

When you are communicating with spirit and are unsure of something, there is a simple rule to follow. Ask them. Go back to your communicator, the spirit you're conversing with, for more specifics. If you get grandmother, ask "Maternal or paternal? ". If you feel a constriction in your chest, ask them to clarify it. Is this how they died, or a condition from which they suffered, but died in a different way? Always go back to your communicator for clarification or details.

Be respectful. These are people, not trained seals. They deserve the same considerations that you would give anyone with whom you were conversing.

This in no way implies that they have a right to be rude to you either. If you don't like the way a discourse is going, or something doesn't feel right, correct it or cut it completely. If spirit will not comply, end the communication. Tell them why. I have usually found spirit polite, if sometimes a bit overexcited to be able to communicate.

Lastly, I want to talk a bit about ghosts vs. spirits. In my opinion, ghosts are those who have not yet passed into the light. This occurs for various reasons. Ties to material things, control issues, and fear of religious judgments are common factors.

Ghosts sometimes are not even aware they have died. They will follow familiar patterns, sometimes for centuries. Part of what I feel is my responsibility is to offer them the chance to choose to leave if they'd like.

Sometimes it's difficult to get their attention. Once I have it, I let them know that they have total free will to leave or not. If they're not ready that's their choice. If they are, there are various techniques I use to help them pass.

Spirits are those who have crossed and come and go at their own whim. They are not stuck anywhere. They exert their own free will and are fully aware of the different realms.

These are the friends we communicate with when doing readings for people. They sometimes return to a place they loved, and are thought to be haunting it just like a ghost would. However, they are there because they choose to be.

So there you are; Mediumship 101 in a nutshell. I hope these basics help to give you some insight into the world of spirit. Enjoy the adventures and investigations in this book.

Ginnie McGovern, Medium, Malibu and New Mexico

Why Ghosts?

One of the questions that a paranormal investigator frequently gets asked is why there are ghosts. It's a difficult answer because it's hard for people to admit that such a thing even exists. If we can agree that there are ghosts or spirits, then we can begin offering definitions and even postulate reasons why this phenomenon exists. If there is an agreement that spirits exist and that by existing we, the living, can actually make contact with their energy, whether it be imprinted (passive energy) or interactive, then we can delve into the "why"!

Our opinion, which is one of thousands that float through the pages of myriad ghost books that have been written, centers on one defining principle, that Ghosts "R" us. That is to say, they do everything we do, except without a physical body. Essentially, the living and the dead are all energy-based, separated only by the constructs of time and space. Just because spirits belong to an unseen universe or another dimension doesn't mean they don't exist. It's primarily a matter of belief rather than proof. Just because you can't see something doesn't mean it doesn't exist. However the timeless pursuit of scientific proof has done little to prove or disprove the reality or illusion of ghosts. For those who believe, no proof is necessary and for those who don't, no proof is possible; and simple yet apparently true construct of how spirits or ghosts are perceived by us humans and fellow life forms. Maybe that's the way it should be left; that you either believe or not. Even skeptics are open to the possibility that there is life after death, but die-hard disbelievers will never accept the possibility; for them, you live, you die and that's it.

Even among believers, there are varying degrees of believability or healthy skepticism. Then there are those simply in it for the science. They search for absolute proof in a world where absolutes are hard to come by; even the most contentious issue, what happens after death is an unresolved debate that is as old as mankind. Those seeking scientific proof oftentimes miss the underlying purpose of investigating; that is, to make contact and try and help the energy they've contacted either resolve an issue or simply communicate a message to the living. We wouldn't have spirits crossing dimensions unless there was a reason, a purpose behind the encounter.

Waving gaussmeters and EMF meters about in the air, getting anomalous registrations on IR thermometers, talking into space to try and get a voice from beyond, using our senses to know that something extraordinary is occurring, is not a means to an end. You don't just record data and leave with a simple notation, that the place is haunted. What does this really accomplish? So you found what you think is a ghost. You wandered around, got something, wasted a spirit's time and energy to reach out and touch us, and then leave. Self satisfying, maybe, but that approach certainly leaves the poor soul who came to the table to interact, in the dark. There is more to this process, or at least there should be; it's like saying I know you are here and then abruptly walking away.

If you are trying to find a spirit, and use all the means at your disposal to convince yourself or your groupmembers that there is something unexplainable out there, then you must go the distance and attempt to communicate. We must ask questions using a tape recorder, dowsing rods, or other means, and see if you can get more information on the energy you made contact with; not simply leave them floating. Remember, you spent a lot of time and energy getting to that point and so did they. At least give them the courtesy of sitting down as a group and try to listen, or even better, to try and help. Maybe all they want to do is know that someone cares enough to initiate contact. It's not a game just to get a thrill or a chill, it also about caring and helping. Remember, all spirits were someone like you in life; some good, some bad, some lonely, some confused, but every one of them has a story to tell or a riddle to solve, or an unfinished conversation. It's all about communication once a spirit has been identified; otherwise, what's the point. It's certainly not about collecting a hundreds of pictures of orbs, apparitions, or sound bites of EVP, apparitions. It can't be about collecting evidence of anomalies and filing it away for a book or personal research. It shouldn't be about hunting ghosts for media exposure. If it is solely for science, then it's a waste of energy. If it is about listening, researching and trying to help where compassion, caring and helping are a critical goal, then what paranormal investigators do, may have some emotional, physical and metaphysical utility for the greater good of all concerned.

Ghosts co-exist with us, perhaps in a parallel universe, which intersects the physical plane when, the cosmic clickers connect or our energy frequencies are in tuned. They seem invisible to us most of the time, and perhaps visa versa, yet our paths cross more frequently than most are willing to admit. Do they walk along side us, occupying the same space yet exist at a different energy frequency? Although the phenomena of ghosts and hauntings may seem complex, most paranormal investigators will attest to the fact that interacting spirits are habitual, compulsive and often dysfunctional creatures who have feelings and emotions, and can do everything we can do under the apparent guise of invisibility.

Call them what you will: Phantasm, wraith, phantom, spook, specter, supernatural being, manifestation, haunting, paranormal phenomena, haint, shadow, wisp, mist, apparition, poltergeist, spirit, but a rose by any other name... still spells a ghost. The fact is, the living and deceased do make contact, and have been doing so for thousands of years. It is a cross-cultural phenomenon and transcends race, color, religion, philosophy, politics, etc. Do we see ghosts because we believe in them, or is it perhaps belief that makes seeing possible. Many a skeptic "wants" to believe and therefore see.

Ghosts can be encountered anywhere at any time by any person. They have been witnessed in taverns, pubs, bars, diners, restaurants, fast food outlets, markets, retail and outlet stores, hotels, hostels, inns, bed and breakfasts, cemeteries, burial grounds, mausoleums, crypts, graveyards, mortuaries, morgues, hospitals, sanitariums, asylums, battlefields, churches, missions, monasteries, nunneries, theaters, auditoriums, schools, dormitories, fraternity houses, sorority houses, prisons, jails, penitentiaries, houses, office buildings, apartment and tenement buildings, bowling alleys, historic buildings, museums, caves, amusement parks, pyramids, archaeological sites, ruins, roads, bridges, trains, ships, lighthouses, automobiles and airplanes. In other words, wherever there was human contact, there is likelihood for encountering ghosts.

According to renowned paranormal investigator and writer Troy Taylor in his book The Ghost Hunter's Guidebook (1999), 90% or more of the cases he's involved in have perfectly natural explanations behind the phenomena that is reported. However, he aptly concludes that it is the small percentage of "unexplained" phenomena that keeps all of us coming back for more. Taylor suggests that there are several different types of ghosts, and related paranormal activity. Two types of activity however, seem most prominent; the intelligent spirit and the residual haunting. The intelligent spirit is a lost personality that for some reason did not pass over to the other side at the moment of death. It shows intelligence and a consciousness and often interacts with people. Sometimes they manifest themselves as a rush of cold air, a chill or an overpowering presence. Their physical interactions can be a little more startling through sight, sounds, contact and even smells. Residual hauntings occur at a specific site, and represents an imprint left on the environment, marking an event or series of events that happened in the past. These events were usually traumatic ones, but not always, and are often likened to videotape playing repeatedly; a moment in time that is on instant and constant replay mode.

Furthermore, Taylor suggests that one part of the human perception use our five senses while the brain processes the information. The brain only allows us to see what it thinks we can handle. Some individuals are simply on a different "wave-length", and act as "receivers" to an energy field that most of us cannot, or "will not" see. Taylor does not believe that ghosts are seen by people as they really are, which is why photographs sometimes show balls of light, orbs and strange mists which is more in character with how psychical energy is probably manifested. Taylor does believe that when people see ghosts wearing clothing they are actually witnessing residual impressions because they are not conscious spirits, merely imprints left behind. Conscious spirits will sometimes appear in clothing because people are sensitive enough to see the spirit as it once was. They see the spirit as it still visualizes itself.

According to L.B. Taylor in **The Ghosts of Virginia Volume III** (1994), stories of hauntings go back thousands of years. What are ghosts? Taylor suggests that the only real definitive and indisputable answer is, simply, no one knows; however, experts attempting to label and explain ghosts for centuries, concluded that:

- Ghosts are the disembodied spirits or energy that manifests itself over a period of time, generally in one place.
- Ghosts are the souls of the dead.
- A ghost is the surviving emotional memory of someone who has died traumatically, and usually tragically, but is unaware of his or her death.
- A ghost is a person who has died and is stuck in a kind of limbo existence.
- Apparitions are the super-normal manifestations of people, animals, objects and spirits.
- Most apparitions are of living people or animals that are too distant to be perceived by normal senses.
- Apparitions of the dead are also called ghosts.

Some experts believe that a ghost is a manifestation or recordable occurrence of persistent personal energy, or is an indication that some kind of force or energy is being exercised after death which is in some way connected with a person previously known to have existed on the earth. A number of studies and investigations suggest that spirits appear:

- To communicate with the living in a time of crisis such as sickness or death.
- To provide a warning to the living of some impending tragedy or disaster.
- To comfort those who are grieving or lamenting as serious loss.
- To transmit or communicate to someone in particular valuable personal information.

- To complete a vocation, mission, or duty that was left incomplete while on earth.
- To right a wrong that was done to them, essentially seeking justice for a wrongdoing or transgression.
- To ask the living for help, guidance, or understanding. Sometimes, ghosts seek out individuals to help them complete a specific task such as find their missing body and give it a proper burial, or pinpoint the location of an object that must be given to someone in particular.

L.B. Taylor (1994) implies that a majority of ghostly manifestations involve sound and noises, unusual smells or odors, extreme cold, the movement or disappearance of objects, visual images, tactile sensations, and disembodied voices. While the most common perceived image of a ghost is a filmy apparition, in actuality, visual images are seen only in a small percentage of reported cases. Such figures are always clothed, and most often appear in period costume.

The term "haunt" comes from the same root as "home," and refers to the occupation of houses by the spirits of deceased people and animals who lived there. Other haunted sites seem to be places merely frequented or liked by the deceased, or places where violent death has occurred. Some haunts are continual; others are active only on certain dates that correspond to the deaths, or major events in the lives of the dead.

Are ghosts real? That question has remained unanswered through the ages. It is, ultimately, up to each individual to decide. A Gallop poll reported that 14 percent of Americans said they have had a ghostly experience, in Great Britain, and other parts of Europe, the percentage is much higher. Certainly, most reported supernatural happenings are usually explained by scientific or rational means. But not all! As psychic expert Hans Holzer once said, "There are theories, but no proof, as to why (hauntings) happen. But that the incidence of such happenings exceeds the laws of probability, and that their number establishes that there is some-thing to investigate, is beyond dispute."

Regardless of one's personal feelings, there is, unquestionably, an innate longing in human nature to "pierce the veil" which hides the future after death. Thus, the origin and nature of ghosts have popularly appealed to mankind at all times and in all places, and will doubtless continue to do so until the craving to know some-thing of the unseen world is satisfied.

According to Shadowlands, Ghosts and Hauntings (www.ttheshadowlands. net), "One of the greatest hindrances when investigating the paranormal is the popular disbelief ingrained into the general population by mainstream science. This stems mainly from the common tenant of science that a given phenomenon must be objectively measurable to be given credence. From this basic precept one can immediately witness the great hypocrisy of science, because this precept is rendered null if a given phenomenon is either mathematically possible, or the phenomenon is proposed by someone with a known scientific background.... Current science is dismissing many classical assumptions with the advent of Quantum Theory and Chaos science. Both state reality as a subjective experience based on belief, a tenant of astrologers, alchemists, and priests for millennia. With these new precepts finding their way into traditional science, the study of the paranormal may be taken seriously within the next few decades, with the likely result that the prefixes para- and super- shall be removed and only the natural shall remain. When the first shift of these areas into modern science occurs, new equipment, methods, and ideas will be available for use in determining the nature of reality, and it is possible that the energies discovered could be harnessed for the good of all mankind. For now, though, the methods of researching the paranormal and supernatural remain stunted."

According to Dale Kaczmarek (1999), after being involved with many investigations both into private and public buildings, restaurants, churches, cemeteries, Indian burial grounds, historic locations, battlefields and murder sites, he has found that no area is totally free of ghostly activity. Most areas seem to begin to produce phenomena after a sudden, violent, emotional, tragic or traumatic death such as a murder, suicide, or tragic accident like a car or plane crash. The current theory is that because of the way that the people met their demise; energy is released at that location and can be seen, felt, smelled or sensed in some way by people passing through the area. Other times a location where a person might have spent a great deal of their time such as a house, restaurant, church or tavern could become haunted by the deceased simply because the ghost might come back to "check in" once in a while to see loved ones or the structure itself.

So, what is a ghost, and why does its energy continue to intrude on our time and space reality? Is it because something in their life remains unresolved? Is it because a habitualized behavioral pattern is replaying itself like a motion picture rerun? Is it someone who is still watching over a living relative or friend in an angelic capacity? It is an angry person in life carrying those traits into the afterlife or someone who dies so suddenly he or she doesn't even know that their physical life has ended? Maybe ghosts or spirits are all of the above. It really all boils down to belief or in a perception that death is not something final, but rather, part of an eternal process where, like the seasons, we are recycled or continually transformed to complete a series of tasks in the school of life.

We may not know why ghosts exist, but we know they do. This book is not intended to resolve philosophical or metaphysical issues regarding ghosts. Instead, it intends to provide the traveler searching for unusual getaway locations and the seekers of spirits by providing myriad places in California where ghosts or paranormal phenomena have been reported. Perhaps, at one of these destination spots, under the right circumstances, you might feel, hear, or see the other-worldly. Furthermore, you may even be the one to come home from an unusual holiday adventure with proof about the existence of ghosts that will stand the test of scientific scrutiny, and fill in yet another missing piece of the puzzle about the nature of ghosts. Until we meet again through our ghost books, and paranormal adventures; May the spirits be with you and

Happy Haunting!

Dedicated to those we loved in the past, cherish in the present, and will meet again in some other dimension...

Matthew and Henrietta Wlodarski
David and Emma Lou Powell
Adam and Victoria Rokita
Boyce and Jesse Walker
Zigmond and Regina Wlodarski
Cader B. and Kate Powell
They gave us love and friendship, the spirit of adventure and an insatiable desire
to unravel the greatest mystery of all...what happens after we die!

A brief candle; both ends burning. An endless mile; a bus wheel turning.
A friend to share the lonesome times. A handshake and a sip of wine.
So say it loud and let it ring. We are all a part of everything.
The future, present and the past. Fly on proud bird, you're free at last.
Charlie Daniels - written en route to the funeral for his friend,
Ronnie Van Zant of the band, Lynyrd Skynyrd.

For everything there is a season, and a time for every matter under heaven:
A time to be born, and a time to die; a time to plant,
and a time to pluck up what is planted;
A time to kill, and a time to heal; a time to break down, and a time to build up;
A time to weep, and a time to laugh; a time to mourn, and a time to dance;
A time to throw away stones, and a time to gather stones together;
A time to embrace, and a time to refrain from embracing;
A time to seek, and a time to lose; a time to keep, and a time to throw away;
A time to tear, and a time to sew; a time to keep silence, and a time to speak;
A time to love, and a time to hate, a time for war, and a time for peace.
Ecclesiastes 3:1-8

I wanted a perfect ending. Now I've learned, the hard way,
that some poems don't rhyme,
and some stories don't have a clear beginning, middle, and end.
Life is about not knowing, having to change,
taking the moment and making the best of it,
without knowing what's going to happen next. Delicious Ambiguity.
Gilda Radner

Tell me not, in mournful numbers, life is but an empty dream!
For the soul is dead that slumbers and things are not what they seem.
Life is real! Life is earnest! And the grave is not its goal;
Dust thou art; to dust returnest, was not spoken of the soul.
Henry Wadsworth Longfellow

The gods conceal from men the happiness of death, that they may endure life
Lucan

Death--- the last sleep? No the final awakening
Walter Scott

I look at life as a gift of God. Now that he wants it back, I have no right to complain.
Joyce Cary

I am ready to meet my Maker! Whether my Maker is prepared for the great
ordeal of meeting me is another matter.
Winston Churchill

Do not seek death. Death will find you. But seek the road,
which makes death a fulfillment.
Dag Hammarskjöld

Here is the test to find whether your mission on earth is finished:
If you're alive, it isn't
Richard Bach

Death-the last voyage, the longest and the best
Thomas Wolfe

Because I could not stop for death; he kindly stopped for me. The carriage held
but just ourselves and immortality.
Emily Dickinson

Nothing you can lose by dying is half as precious as the readiness to die, which
is man's charter of nobility.
George Santayana

There is but one freedom, to put oneself right with death.
After that everything is possible. I cannot force you to believe in God.
Believing in God amounts to coming to terms with death.
When you have accepted death, the problem of God will be solved...
and not the reverse.
Camus, Albert

When you were born, you cried and the world rejoiced.
Live your life in a manner so that when you die the world cries and you rejoice.
Native American Proverb

If God hath made this world so fair, where sin and death abound, how beautiful
beyond compare, will paradise be found!
James Montgomery

Drink and be merry, for our time on earth is short, and death lasts forever.
Amphis, 330 B.C.

Dream as if you'll live forever; Live as if you'll die today.
James Dean

Disclaimer

The stories appearing in this book are based on factual accounts of people who have owned, worked, or visited a particular establishment listed herein; some of those people have chosen to remain anonymous. The authors take no responsibility for the veracity of each story except for the fact that we believe the storytellers.

We have researched the 184 establishments listed in this book in order to obtain the most updated paranormal encounters. Some of the stories have been passed down as urban legends or folklore, while other stories have appeared in various books and newspaper articles. We have tried to portray the haunting as accurately as possible and in a non-sensational manner... after all, why should we have to embellish a perfectly good ghost story just to scare someone.

Recent movies such as House on the Haunted Hill, 13 Ghosts and The Haunting have tried to re-create a wonderful old story with special effects that significantly detract from the original version. The fabric of the story becomes lost in the effects, and what was scary to begin with, has often become laughable or forgettable. Then there are the classics like the original Haunting, The Changeling, The Others, The Sixth Sense, The Uninvited, Ghost Story, Blithe Spirit, The Ghost Breakers, The Canterville Ghost, and Lady in White, that rely on the story to frighten; not special effects; that's the essence of a good ghost tale.

The most frightening aspect of true ghost stories is that it can happen to you, because it "did" happen to someone else. True ghost stories hold accurately to the actual event without the need to embellish. The ghost story is by all rights, a home spun, honest version of someone's encounter with the unknown. If you need more than a jolt of reality to have your hair stand on end; embellishment and showmanship, then this book isn't for you. This book is strictly about paranormal encounters of everyday people who have had unexplainable encounters in places where the average person can stroll in and perhaps have a brush with the unknown. You can draw your own conclusions after reading the stories in this book. We have no desire to modify a story to create a greater impact on one's psyche

Although we have made every effort to ensure that the information was correct at the time the book went to press, we do not assume and hereby disclaim any liability to any party for any loss, damage, or injury caused by information contained in this book, as well as any liability resulting from the use of this book. We ask that you please check with each establishment before visiting if you plan to do any ghosthunting. Always obtain permission to photograph, tape, or otherwise intrude on the normal activities of any establishment. Never enter a place illegally, and never put you or others in harms way while conducting your research. Always use common sense in approaching the paranormal.

Once again, we area adamantly against drinking and driving. Please act responsibly and within the law when consuming alcohol when you visit any bar or tavern; communing with spirits doesn't mean you have to consume them. Since this book is about bars and taverns, and there is a chance that you might imbibe while visiting or investigating a haunted establishment. We recommend that you find someone in your group who does not drink and make sure that they or a taxi, if need be, gets you safely home; we do not want to be investigating you in the future due to a lapse in judgment.

We apologize if there is inaccurate information presented herein, and will attempt to rectify future additions if we are contacted by mail, fax, or e-mail, and provided with the correct information. Given the nature of businesses, and the fact that many change ownership, names, phone numbers, go out of business, or become some other type of business; we also wish to hear from those establishments where these changes have taken place.

If you do find mistakes in this publication, please consider that they are there for a reason. In an effort to publish something for everyone, we realize that some people are always looking for mistakes; therefore have gone out of our way to please those individuals.

The authors would love to hear from our readers about their paranormal experiences at an establishment mentioned in this book, or from those of you who know of other "haunted" locations. Address all inquiries, or story submissions for future editions to G-host Publishing, 8701 Lava Place, West Hills, California 91304-2126; by Phone or fax to: 818-340-6676; or by E-mail to: robanne@ ix.netcom.com.

Hauntingly yours!

California Facts

The following historical information was excerpted from the California Trade and Commerce Agency, Division of Tourism, 801 K Street, Suite 1600, Sacramento, California 95814 - Phone: 916-322-2881 /Fax: 916-322-3402 http://gocalif.ca.gov/index/history

California is so culturally diverse that within metropolitan Los Angeles, San Diego or San Francisco you can sample traditional cuisine of Maine, Texas, Mexico, Asia, The Middle East, Europe and Native Americans, or regularly hear foreign languages from just about every part of the world being spoken simultaneously. You can find Jazz, rock, heavy metal, classical, hip-hop, blue grass, country and ethnic music played within a few miles of one another. The threads that bind all cultures are intricately and sometimes subtly interwoven into the diverse physiographic landscape of California that reaches from the Sierra Nevadas and the Mojave Desert, to the Pacific Ocean. From the first migration into California over 20,000 years ago, people have been flocking to this richly diverse state with a mild climate, and matchless splendor. From the days of the 49ers to the present, people have made their way here with abundant hope and boundless courage and energy. California's sons and daughters have charted new beginnings in aerospace, biotechnology, electronics, music, entertainment, art, literature and fashion to make this one of most important states in the Union with world reaching influence.

<u>20,000 B.C.to 15,000 B.C.</u>: Humans cross the Bering Straits from Asia and inhabit California. At the time of Spanish exploration in the 18th century, more than 300 distinct tribes and language groups exist in the state.

<u>1769</u>: California is settled by Spain. Mission San Diego de Alcala is founded by a Franciscan monk, Junipero Serra.

<u>1781</u>: The City of the Angeles is founded by a small band of 11 families of European, African and of Native American heritage.

<u>1822</u>: The era of Spanish ranchos reaches its peak. Following the Rancho era, the mission system declines, and the Spanish ranchos become Mexican land grants. Legal battles over land continue for generations.

<u>1847</u>: Yerba Buena becomes San Francisco. From a few hundred pioneers in 1847, the city becomes the 10th largest in the U.S by the early 1870s.

<u>1848</u>: The discovery of gold at Sutters mill in Coloma draws 300,000 daring men and women from around the United States to California.

<u>1850</u>: California becomes the 31st state, all 158,706 square miles of it. Four years later, the state capital moves from Benicia to Sacramento.

<u>1853</u>: After his efforts to sell canvas tents to the '49ers fail, Levi Strauss creates the hard-wearing denim trousers that become the prospectors' work uniform. Still in family hands today, Levi Strauss & Co. of San Francisco is the largest clothing manufacturer in the world.

1857: Agoston Haraszthy, an adventurer and viticulturist whose aristocratic family produced the Tokay wine in Hungary, finds in Sonoma the perfect location for growing his European vine stock. There he establishes the Buena Vista Winery, still producing quality wines today.

1869: The Central Pacific, begun in Sacramento, and the Union Pacific, begun in Omaha, join at Promontory, Utah, forming the first transcontinental railroad.

1888: Lick Observatory established. California enters into the forefront of exploration of the heavens, beginning the state's technological legacy.

ca.1900: Arts & Literature. Writers such as Jack London, Frank Norris, and Gertrude Atherton begin to give California a literary voice. A young girl from San Francisco, Isadora Duncan, will reinvent dance.

1906: Great San Francisco Earthquake. Some 300,000 people are left without homes; then with courage and optimism, they rebuild the city.

1908: Motion picture production begins in California as Colonel William Selig calls for "action" on, In the Sultan's Power, the first complete film made in Los Angeles.

1927: "The Spirit of St. Louis" is built in San Diego. Ryan Airlines, San Diego, constructs the plane that carries Lindbergh on the first solo trans-Atlantic flight.

1930s: Dust Bowl spurs immigration. Route 66, from America's heartland, brings 10,000 new settlers per month by 1938.

1933/1934: The first mass-produced commercial aircraft is built. The DC-2 is built by Donald Douglas in Santa Monica.

1935: A statewide irrigation system is begun, transforming the Central Valley from semi-arid to green. Citrus groves dot the Southland. Today, California is the leading agricultural economy in the United States.

1962: California becomes the most populous state in the Union. From the eve of World War II to 1962, the state jumps from 9 to 22 million. Today, there are over 32,344,000documented persons living here.

1977: The personal computer is successfully taken to market. In the classic "two-guys-tinkering-in-a- garage" story, the Apple II is developed in Silicon Valley.

The threads that bind all cultures are intricately and sometimes subtly interwoven into the diverse physiographic landscape of California; one that reaches from the Sierra Nevada's and the Mojave Desert, to the Pacific Ocean. From the first migration into California over 20,000 years ago, people have been flocking to this richly diverse state with a mild climate, and matchless splendor.

From the days of the 49ers to the present, people have made their way here with abundant hope and boundless courage and energy. West Coast Ghosts, the ultimate parnamormal travel guide for Califoria visitors or natives, takes you on an unforgettable journey through the highways and byways, big cities and backroad towns of the state in search of spirits. From Albion to Ventura, you'll meet the ghosts of California's most haunted restaurants, taverns and inns, up close and extremely personal.

This paranormal journey will take you from the haunted hot spots of San Diego such as America's Most Haunted House, the Whaley House and the equally spirited Hotel Del Coronado, through Beverly Hills, Hollywood, Catalina, Malibu, Long Beach, San Francisco and into the heart of Gold Rush ghosts.

Along the way, you'll learn about the history and hauntings of places where you can dine or slumber in the company of otherworldly guests. Take a look inside this phantom-packed book if you dare; then take a journey to your favorite California Hauntspitality spot. Remember to keep your senses peeled for signs of afterlife activity; and may the spirits always boo with you. Enjoy and happy haunting.

Alameda
Croll's 1883 Restaurant & Bar

Particulars
1400 Webster Street,
Alameda, CA 94501
Phone: 510.748.6075

History
The Croll Building, in Alameda, California, was the site of Croll's Gardens and Hotel, famous as training quarters for the some of the greatest fighters in boxing history from 1883 to 1914. James J. Corbett, Bob Fitzsimmons, Jim Jefferies, Jack Johnson, and many other champions all stayed and trained here. The building is registered as California Historical Landmark [#954] and is listed on the National Register of Historic Places (NPS-82000960). Croll's Bar was a local watering hole for visiting sailors and locals alike. From the early 1880s until circa 1998 when the building closed for business, the bar served drinks to men from five wars, from the Spanish-American War through the Vietnam conflict due to its location near the Alameda Naval Air Station. Local lore supports the generic history of numerous fights, robberies and even shootings that took place in or near the bar; historically, nothing can be confirmed to date about any deaths.

Hauntspitality
We are including this building because it has closed and reopened several times and there is a good chance that it may materialize once again. It seems historic haunted restaurants have a way of going in and out of business, and just when you think its over, they suddenly return from the dead; so-to-speak. The age and look of the building certainly conjures up spirits, and when you ask around, the building apparently doesn't disappoint when it comes to spirited clientele. There are numerous reports of apparitions inside, as well as locals reporting noisy parties taking place inside when the building is unoccupied.

Those inside have reported phantom men dressed in Period uniforms; cold spots everywhere; disembodied footsteps; sounds of phantom parties when the building is closed for business; and an occasional spirit or two seen gazing out the windows during off hours. Its history certainly creates the potential for haunting, and the building does not disappoint. The ghostly figure of a lone male spirit standing at the front door, has been spotted by onlookers before suddenly vanishing in front of their eyes. Sensitive people who walk by the building often pick up on the spirited clientele inside, still celebrating before going to war. Sounds of laughter, glasses clinking, brawling and such, are just part of the ambience at this haunted Alameda establishment.

When the building reopens, you can bet that the restless spirits will be the first to greet the new owners and carry on its ghostly tradition.

Albion
Fensalden Inn

Particulars
33810 Navarro Ridge Rd.
Albion, CA 95410
Phone: 707-937-4042
Fax: 707-937-2416
Toll Free: 1-800-959-3850
E-mail: inn@fensalden.com
Website: www.fensalden.com

History

Fensalden, "Land of the Mist and the Sea," commands a magnificent view of the ocean from the 400-foot elevation on Navarro Ridge Road. Located 150 miles north of San Francisco, it's a beautiful drive through the wine country of the Anderson Valley, and the Redwood Forest. Overlooking the Pacific Ocean, this former stagecoach stop offers warm hospitality for the traveler. The building was constructed in the 1850's when lumbering was a huge industry in Albion. At that time, the Pacific Coast Highway did not exist, and the driveway was the main route between Eureka and San Francisco. Serving as a stage stop, it was later a farm, saw mill, hippy commune, and a haven for struggling artists under Terry Ault's ownership. Each time the place changed hands, the new owner made renovations. Eventually the place became a Bed & Breakfast. Lynn Hamby bought the place in 1997 from Scott and Francis Brazil who owned the establishment for 10 or so years. She come from New England, and always owned old houses; although this is her first place occupied by a ghost.

Spirits

The spirit of Fensalden is named Elzabeth. At one time the building was a house of ill repute and Elzabeth was one of the "ladies of the night". She made the unfortunate mistake of falling in love with one of her clients. When he prepared to leave, she tried to go with him; he said, "Oh, no, honey. This was strictly a business deal. Good-bye." The story goes that she went up to the attic and pined away her life. Their have been numerous reports that confirm that the attic is always cold and exudes unhappiness upon entering.

The attic is now the Hawthorne Suite, named after Innkeeper, Lynn Hamby's great-great grandfather, Nathaniel Hawthorne. Her father painted his portrait, which hangs over the fireplace. Hamby added a queen canopy bed to the bedroom. It is now a very romantic and cheery room. Hamby thinks that it's possible that Elzabeth and old Nathaniel have gotten together, because the room is now a very happy place.

Elzabeth has taken to effecting pranks. She will take something that belongs in a certain place, remove it, then always bring it back to its proper place either a short time later, or within a few days. Guests have reported hearing footsteps on the stairway, but no one is there when they go to investigate. One guest said he was sure someone was behind him as he prepared to go upstairs to bed. When the owner told him of Elzabeth, he said, "Oh that explains it." Fensalden is a quiet, relaxing retreat with all the amenities a person could ever need, including a spirited, non-paying guest named Elzabeth.

Amador City
Hotel Imperial

Particulars
Post Office Box 195,
Amador City, CA 95601
Phone: 209-267-9172
Fax: 209-267-9249
Toll Free: 800-242-5594
E-mail: info@imperialamador.com
Website: www.imperialamador.com

History

Located an hour from Sacramento, and 2 1/2 hours from San Francisco, The Imperial Hotel, a brick building, was originally constructed in 1879 by a man named B. Sanguinetti, to serve exclusively as a mercantile store providing homeless miners with the basic creature comforts. Sanguinetti eventually renovated the building and expanded his business interest to include a hotel and boarding house. A second story was added in 1880, and the hotel/boarding house continued to prosper. The hotel remained in operation until 1927. Current Innkeepers Bruce Sherrill and Dale Martin began restoring the building in 1988, and a new chapter in its illustrious history was initiated---it would once again become a prominent hotel. When the restoration began, the spirits became restless, no doubt uncertain the direction their dwelling spot was headed. The restoration turned out fine, and the spirits seem very happy with the way things have turned out.

Spirits

A number of unexplained events have taken place inside the Imperial Hotel. Guests have reported having their order taken by someone, only to find out that person never existed. Their have been numerous reports of a phantom waitress who looks very much like a portrait of a lady handing on the wall in the dining area. Just who this woman is still remains a mystery. The portrait was said to have originally come from San Francisco. Could the spirit have attached itself to the painting and found a home at the Imperial? Whoever the mysterious lady is, she is sighted wearing period clothing similar to the dress exhibited in the portrait, and she is described as friendly, and courteous.

There have been reports by the owners and staff of the constant feeling of being watched by unseen eyes in various parts of the building. There are also accounts of personal items disappearing, and then reappearing in other parts of the hotel; lights suddenly turning on by themselves when the hotel was shut down for brief periods; apparitions being sighted in certain rooms; doors that will lock by themselves, then suddenly open; and electrical appliances that will turn themselves on, unassisted.

The kitchen and basement areas also have been hotspots for paranormal activity, where unexplained footsteps can be heard when no one else is in that part of the hotel; as well as sounds as if someone is dragging something across the floor. The lively and friendly spirits of the Imperial Hotel are awaiting your visit to this historic spot, where guests and ghosts co-mingle.

Mine House Inn

Particulars
P.O. Box 245, 14125 Highway 49
Amador City, CA 95601
Phone: 209-267-5900
Fax: 209-267-5703
Toll Free: 1-800-MINE-HSE
E-mail: minehse@cdepot.net
Website: www.minehouseinn.com

History
Enduring beauty and structural integrity are only part of what make Amador City's Mine House Inn one of the Gold Country's most unique Bed & Breakfast. Centrally located in the "Heart of the Mother Lode," it is within a 10 to 40 minute drive of more than 30 Amador wineries; 45 minutes from Sacramento and 2 1/2 hours from San Francisco.

The Mine House Inn, a brick Victorian structure was built in 1858. The original building was designed as eight, well-equipped offices for the Keystone Mine, of the largest gold producing enterprises in Amador County. It was such an important enterprise, that upon opening for business, a grand party was held for the officials, employees, and the local inhabitants. The offices were designed to perform every aspect of gold production. Gold mining in the county finally declined, and eventually, the building was abandoned for its intended use.

The Keystone Mine and the offices were closed in 1942 due to the wartime Conservation of Precious Metals Act. The house was purchased in 1954, remodeled in 1957 by Peter and Anne Marie Daubenspeck, and opened as a Bed & Breakfast. In 1993, Rose and Allen Mendy, engineers in the Bay area began the painstaking and tireless work of restoring the old building for a second time. The Mine House has been restored to its former splendor with period antique furniture and accessories added. The Mendys later purchased the adjacent 1930's era house, which was converted to three luxury suites. The newest building, the Victorian House, contains two more suites, a Victorian parlor, and a dining room where gourmet dinners are served on weekends.

Each room is named after their original mining function. The Vault Room contains the original vault where the gold was stored, after making the trip upstairs on a dumbwaiter from the Assay Room. The dumbwaiter method of moving the gold upstairs helped keep the gold safe from robbers. The Vault Room and the Inn were recently featured on Home & Garden TV's "Restore America" show hosted by Bob Vila. The rooms in the main building of the Inn are furnished with nineteenth century antiques purchased within a ten-mile radius of the Inn.

Spirits
At the Mine House, people have sometimes witnessed a very stern-looking elderly woman scolding her alcoholic husband---the problem is, both are dead. The spectral female constantly locks her phantom husband out of the house, along with the owners. Neither the ghostly duo knows that they have left the physical plane. The spirited woman does enjoy company in the mine house, as

long as it's not her deceased. The only time she seems to get perturbed, is when someone makes or leaves a mess.

The Mendys got something extra when the bought the Mine House--ghosts! They first noticed something strange in the downstairs bedrooms. They would hear footsteps pacing around the building, even in the kitchen area on the other side of the house. There was never anyone there when a search was made to find the source of the footsteps. Additionally, there were times when the water in the sinks in some of the bedrooms would be on when they were unoccupied. The center of paranormal activity seems to be focused on guests who tended to be sloppy. The spirit would leave water running, or move things around to let the guest know that the mess was an irritant to the otherworldly guest and would not be tolerated.

Legend has it that in the 1800s, a caretaker and his wife occupied the building. They were hired to ensure that no one would come on the grounds without authorization when everything was closed down while the gold was locked up safely. The caretaker apparently drank heavily, but this did not diminish his ability to perform his duties. His wife would occasionally cook for the employees, clean the offices, and take care of the offices and grounds. The woman was reliable and compulsive in having to keep things neat and tidy. She did not like her husband's sloppiness, and drinking habits. The men respected her, which she in turn used to get back at her slovenly, ever-imbibing husband at every opportunity.

A psychic was able to obtain the name Sarah, for the woman who looks out a second floor window for her husband's approach, and potential guests who might need her assistance. The spirited woman has also been sighted holding a pet cat that has been known to rub up against startled guest's legs, and as a shadowy image that prances around the building. The psychic also picked up on a young girl who enjoys staying in the Director's Room. Speculation has it, that the girl may have been injured in a freak accident involving a horse, and was brought to the building where she eventually died from her injuries. The phantom girl has been spotted wearing a white pinafore-type dress and black buttoned-up shoes. The youthful, female spirit loves to tease the ghost cat, unmake beds, and play with the doors and electricity.

The Mine House is not only a beautiful historic building where you can enjoy the scenery, but it contains several spirits, one of which is very finicky, and demands that you keep your room neat. A brief listing of recent paranormal events include: Footsteps when no one is there; lights going on and off for no reason; water faucets turning on by themselves; and, tables in the upstairs room that move by themselves

The place is certified as being "haunted" by psychic Nancy Bradley who visited the inn with another psychic. As Nancy Bradley states in her book *The Incredible World of Gold Rush Ghosts*, that a ghost named Sarah, the stern wife of an alcoholic caretaker in the 1800s, haunts the upstairs. Sarah gets upset when things are messy (the water faucets seem mostly to turn on in rooms of guests that are sloppy)." At the Mine House Inn, Sarah and her white cat will be keeping close tabs on you. This is a "Purr"-fect place to relax and get away from everything…. But friendly ghosts!

Anaheim
White House Restaurant

Particulars
887 South Anaheim Boulevard,
Anaheim, CA 92805
Phone: 714-772-1381
Fax: 714-772-7062
E-mail: twhouse@earthlink.net
Website: www.anaheimwhitehouse.com

History

There are eight different dining areas and the menu features fresh seafood and specialties influenced by owner Bruno Serato's frequent trips to his hometown of Verona, Italy. The restaurant is included in Epicurean Rendezvous' "100 Best Restaurants in Southern California" and received three stars from the Mobil Guide. The wine list features nearly 200 Californian and European wines. Guests have included everyone from Madonna and President Carter to George Burns and Danny DeVito. The restaurant is included in Epicurean Rendezvous' "100 Best Restaurants in Southern California" and received three stars from the Mobil Guide. The wine list features nearly 200 Californian and European wines.

The Anaheim White House occupies a lovely home built in 1909 for Dosithe and Alberta L. (Penney) Gervais and their three children, Violet, Dorothy and Galdys. Dosithe, born in Illinois, came to Los Angeles and worked for the Southern Pacific Railroad in 1894. He came to Anaheim in 1903, and raised strawberries and had a nursery with 35,000 orange trees and 15,000 other plants. He belonged to the Orange County Growers Association and the Modern Woodmen of Anaheim. Alberta Penney was the daughter of early California pioneer named A. Penney. The Gervais family lived in the home until 1916 when Mr. and Mrs. George Waterman purchased it.

In 1919, Dr. John Wenceslaus Truxaw and his wife C. Louise (Wallberg) Truxaw bought the showcase home. Truxaw was born in Nebraska in August 1883 and moved to the area in 1910. After he and Louise were married in Long Beach in August 1913, the Truxaws raised eight children in the house including: Robert E., Mary Ellen, Robert, Louise Ann, Joseph, Joan, Jean and Carol. Dr. Truxaw who had his office at 130 East Center Street (Lincoln) delivered over 3500 babies. He was known throughout the area as a kind and generous man who never refused help to those in need, and died in 1952. Carol Truxaw never married and lived with her mother until she passed away in 1969. The house was bought by the Stovalls in 1980, renovated, remodeled and converted into a restaurant, and then bought by Bruno Serato and opened in 1981.

Spirits

A young girl, several children, and a woman haunt this charming restaurant. Some believe that Dr. Truxaw lost one of his daughters to a tragic car accident in front of the house. It seems the young girl while playing in the street was struck by an automobile or truck. She was quickly taken upstairs where she died from the injuries she sustained. Recent research could not substantiate this fact. However, through research, we did find out that a car hit Robert Truxaw at the age of 17, while playing in the street; he did not die.

Who then are the spirits of the White House Restaurant? Perhaps the Gervais family, the original owners had a child who died in the house; or, a member of the second family, the Watermans who might have suffered a family tragedy, which forced them to leave after only three short years. Or, perhaps it is one or more of the members of Truxaw family, the third owners. Another possibility is that there may be spirits representing all three families who still remain in this structure, reliving memories of a happier time.

The female spirit could be a Gervais, Waterman or Truxaw matriarch who still walks the halls and rooms of her former home. Current owner Bruno Serato is the only person to date who has seen the phantom female, but without pictures of the earlier occupants, it is impossible to specifically identify her. There are also indications that spirited children also call the restaurant home. Voices of children have been heard in the hallways, and psychic investigators have confirmed that at least two youngsters from beyond play inside the former residence.

During one investigation, the chandelier in an upstairs room began swinging and twirling around as if someone was hanging on it or spinning it around; something children might do. There are times when staff hears the sound of footsteps running back and forth between the upstairs rooms when the area is unoccupied. Although the name of the spirit or spirits presently eludes us, one thing is certain, that when the house was remodeled into a restaurant, a ghostly clientele emerged. There are also strange noises, unexplained footsteps, and items that are moved by unseen hands that are attributed to the spirits who seems to enjoy the upstairs Blue Room and hallway the most.

Staff has frequently heard footsteps making their way up the stairs or back and forth down the hallway connecting the Green Room to the Blue Room when the upper floor is unoccupied. A waiter working alone on the second floor watched one time as the handle on a balcony door suddenly turned, and the door opened, although there was no one outside at the time. Lights have been known to suddenly dim, or go on and off on both floors, although it happens more frequently on the second floor.

A waiter working in the Main Dining Room ran into what he called a wall of cold energy that prevented him from moving for a few seconds. He described the feeling as if someone unseen has passed right through him. This area used to be the living room when the house was a residence. A woman standing behind the bar once reported being pinched by an unseen force as she was pouring wine. A day later a noticeable bruise appeared on her leg. There was no one standing anywhere near her at the time.

Owner, Bruno Serato states that a woman was here dining in the restaurant several months ago when she told Serato that he had three spirits in the house. The woman said that one spirit belonged to an elderly lady who frequents the downstairs and is very pleasant. In fact, several guests have reportedly witnessed this same woman while dining in the downstairs area. The woman then reported that a beautiful, slim, blonde-haired woman in her mid-to-late 30s roams the upstairs area along with her four or five year old daughter. The Mother and child appear to be very happy in the house, and seem to frequent the hallway and Blue Room.

Serato also had an unusual encounter with his spirited clientele. As he was closing the restaurant one evening he stated, "It was very late and just before I was walking out, someone like a kid was running up stairs. I was little scared because the alarm was on and if someone would have been upstairs it would show." As Serato cautiously ventured upstairs he noticed a bluish light coming from in the Blue Room. He never did find out the cause of the strange light nor did he see who was responsible for the running sounds that came from upstairs, but he is sure that the spirits love what he's done to the place. The restaurant was recently featured on a Food Network/Greystone Communications presentation of Haunted Restaurants, which revealed a few more paranormal tid-bits about the phantom clientele.

Additional research or paranormal investigation may turn up a name or a reason why the restaurant is haunted. Until then, the great food and ambiance are enough to lift anyone's spirits in this five-star gem that is a favorite for locals and at least one otherworldly guest. Bon appetite!

Paris Restaurant

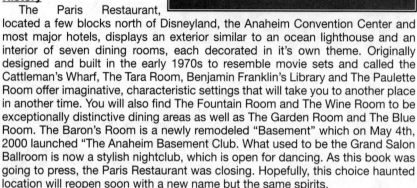

Particulars
1160 W. Ball Road,
Anaheim, CA 92802
Phone: 714-535-1622
Fax: 714-635-3074
E-mail: ParisRestaurant@earthlink.net
Website: www.parisfrenchrestaurant.com

History
The Paris Restaurant,
located a few blocks north of Disneyland, the Anaheim Convention Center and
most major hotels, displays an exterior similar to an ocean lighthouse and an
interior of seven dining rooms, each decorated in it's own theme. Originally
designed and built in the early 1970s to resemble movie sets and called the
Cattleman's Wharf, The Tara Room, Benjamin Franklin's Library and The Paulette
Room offer imaginative, characteristic settings that will take you to another place
in another time. You will also find The Fountain Room and The Wine Room to be
exceptionally distinctive dining areas as well as The Garden Room and The Blue
Room. The Baron's Room is a newly remodeled "Basement" which on May 4th,
2000 launched "The Anaheim Basement Club. What used to be the Grand Salon
Ballroom is now a stylish nightclub, which is open for dancing. As this book was
going to press, the Paris Restaurant was closing. Hopefully, this choice haunted
location will reopen soon with a new name but the same spirits.

Spirits
As their web site states, "The Paris Restaurant is the prime destination for
a dining experience to remember and one to bring you back again and again!
We have a warm welcome waiting for you!" What's unique about this dining
experience, it is also includes several spirits. Although of recent construction,
there are spectral visitors who seem to come from a much earlier period. To date,
research has turned up maps, which indicate that possible structures existed on
the property as early as 1894. Two buildings appear in proximity to where the
present restaurant is now situated. Two families have been identified in 1899-
1900 as owing adjoining property in the area of the current building formerly the
Cattleman's Wharf. A William Neubauer, his wife and a Bert H.W. Neubauer and
J.C. and J.V. Schutz are listed in the Orange County directory as farmers owing
adjoining 10 acre parcels on the south side of Ball Road between Magnolia and
West streets.

The paranormal events reported inside are too numerous to report them all
here, however, staff and guests have reported seeing three Victorian ladies stroll
through the 2nd Floor lounge, bar, office and locker rooms, vanishing before they
reach the elevator. On one occasion, an employee carried two boxes up the back
steps to the office door, when he realized that he forgot the key. He scurried back
down, went in the front door, climbed the stairs and as he turned the corner on
the third floor, noticed that the boxes were now inside! There was no one else on
the third floor at the time, and no one knew that the boxes were on the other side
of the door to bring them in anyway. It was a case of phantom assistance for the
stunned staff person. Numerous times there have been reports of sudden gusts
of cold breezes as well as the feeling of being watched when certain areas are

unoccupied.

There are several "haunted" dining rooms, including the Wine Room, Paulette Room, Garden Room and Library room where the chandelier over table 22 will often start swaying or jumping around as if someone unseen is playing with it. There have been reports of a spectral female in the Paulette Room who likes to play pranks on the unsuspecting staff around tables 42 and 43. There is an energy spot on the left side of large chandelier as you enter the room from the main entrance. A male presence (a man was rumored to have died from a heart attack) visits the Wine Room and has been felt near tables 72/73 and 77 in the corner. The Garden Room near tables 61 and 64 also seems to be a paranormal hot spot where a female presence is felt and sighted. In fact, there doesn't seem to be a dining area in the place that is without some sort of anomalous occurrence.

The upper floor contains seating for guests and ghosts. There have been numerous reports of people laughing, drinking and dancing coming from the upstairs area while it is unoccupied, the same area where the Victorian ladies frequent. Every time the noises or voices echo downstairs, someone runs up to check and see if guests are touring the area. There is never anyone that can be seen, in the room. One of the most haunted hot spots in the building is the former Grand Salon Ballroom that used to be reached by a slide, and is now a stylish nightclub venue. A young child around eight, an elderly woman, and a very suspicious and sometimes angry male spirit has been identified in this area. Most employees do not like to venture down to the basement area alone. The sounds of children playing, people mixing drinks or talking or party-like sounds frequently emanate from the basement area when it is unoccupied. The information we obtained through interviews is only the tip of the paranormal iceberg for this establishment. There have been times that sofas were overturned, tables and chairs moved and bar accouterments scattered around the room just after it was cleaned.

A hunch at this point, until additional research information comes to light, is that an earlier building (perhaps more than one) was constructed on this spot and was torn down in the 1940s or 1950s. This area was vineyards and farmland until the 1950s when Disneyland and development impacted the environs. The energy from the 1890s-1950s was still strong when the present building was constructed and a number of spirits still remain inside, perhaps wondering what happened to their original surroundings.

An investigation by the authors and the Orange County Society Psychic Research on January 21, 2001 resulted in the recordation of a few unexplained events and apparent contact with two young girls, a farmer, and two women. Other events that took place during the investigation, included a chandelier swaying in full view of the researchers, napkins that were resting on a table in the Wine Room suddenly whisked from their positions and tied to the ceiling rafters; a food container being moved from one location to another; suddenly manifesting cold spots in a number of areas; audible growls picked up through EVP coming from the downstairs area (this location produced the most chilling results. We would later find out that a day after an exorcism took place in the basement, all of the furnishings were found stacked against the eastern wall. The restaurant was closed shortly thereafter. We found out later that a woman had a fatal heart attack in the Library Room and a man choked to death in the Wine Room.

A séance produced six distinct spirits: two young girls (Mary and Margaret); a farmer; one young and one middle-aged woman; and a very male presence, which seemed to control the others. The three Victorian ladies that frequently appeared to the staff were not contacted however several of the psychics present picked up on a "Victorian" element in the restaurant. The psychics all felt that the basement was a focal energy point and that something tragic had occurred on the spot of the present-day restaurant at the turn-of-the-century. The psychics picked up on a stagecoach stop or pony express route running in front of the building; an disturbed farmer; a murdered woman; a young child killed by farm equipment; Native Americans on the land; a noxious zone in the cellar; a murder in the outside parking lot; and, a general sense of foreboding in the basement, The group focused on sending the two children into the light and appeared successful. Video and audio equipment recorded the event.

A few weeks later we were told that the activity had increased so much after the investigation, especially the manifestation of a very negative male presence in the basement, that a priest from the Vatican, who was visiting the owner, was brought in to perform a cleansing. The staff was in such a state of frenzy over the recurring events such as misty apparitions, strange voices, moving objects including the swaying chandelier in the Library Room, that drastic measures were necessary. The initial results of the cleansing indicated that the malevolent force had dissipated and perhaps moved on, and that the kinder, benign energy remained. Only time will tell if the cleansing was successful. In the meantime, we recommend a visit to this unique restaurant where spirits come with the excellent food --- at no additional charge!

Aptos
Bayview Hotel and Ristorante Barolo

Particulars

8041 Soquel Drive,
Aptos, CA 95003-3928
Phone: 831-688-8654
Fax: 831-688-5128
Toll Free: 1-800-422-9843

www.baroloristorante.com | www.bayviewhotel.com | E-mail: Lodging@bayviewhotel.com

History

This Victorian hotel is the oldest operating inn on the Monterey Coast. The National Register building was constructed circa 1878 by Joseph (Jose) Arano for his wife Augustia Castro. Augustia's grandfather, Joaquin Castro, and her father, Rafael, received Rancho Aptos in 1833 as the county's first Spanish land grant. Jose Arano, a cultured Basque who was raised in New Orleans and spoke four languages, built a grocery store that still stands at Wharf Road and Soquel Drive in 1850. In 1851, Jose became the first postmaster of Aptos, with the office at his store. Jose Arano, who intended his grocery store to mark the heart of Aptos, was now bypassed by the railroad. In 1878, he constructed a 28-room hotel at Aptos Depot, where he moved his store and post office and added a saloon. His New Orleans-bred taste for French culture led to installation of marble fireplaces from France and massive furniture from his native Spain. Its original name was the "Anchor House," but it was changed to Bayview Hotel.

Peter Larsen bought a 100-acre spread from Jose and Augustia Arano for $3,000 in 1890. The property had been gift-deeded to Augustia by her parents in 1866. Jose Arano never made it to the bank with the $3,000. He abandoned his family and hotel business and he was found 10-years later, living as a hermit in Ventura. Returning in 1896, his wife had died and their children, Amelia and Ed were running the hotel. As Arano became an invalid, he was cared for by daughter Amelia, who ran the hotel. The fortunes of the Bayview Hotel diminished when the lumber industry began its demise. In 1915, Amelia converted the hotel into a boarding house, where Joseph resided until his death in 1928 at the age of 91. That year, the service wing in back of the hotel caught fire, and all local firemen could do was cut it loose from the main building and let it burn.

Amelia sold the Bayview in 1942 to hardware merchant Fred Toney and his wife, "Babe." They moved the hotel onto the formal gardens, and constructed a hardware store in its place. Toney converted the hotel's grocery store into a popular local restaurant, and Babe added an antique and gift shop. Fred Toney suffered health problems in the 1970s and leased the hotel to several people who carefully restored the building. Fred and Babe were killed in a car accident in 1979 and their daughters ran the

hotel until 1989 when it was sold to Bayview Partners, who now operate this historic structure as a bed-and-breakfast and restaurant.

Hauntspitality

The spirits of this delightful National Register building are well known to locals and those in the paranormal community. Local writer Ross Eric Gibson in his article entitled "The Spirit of Aptos: 116-year-old Hotel to become landmark", and our friends, paranormal investigators and writers Mark Jean and Terry L. Smith in their book, "Haunted Inns of America", discuss the haunted nature of this historic building in detail.

From the demeanor of the spirited population reported inside, the identity of the ghosts are believed to be Jose Arano, who built the hotel, his wife, Augustia Castro, and possibly Fred and Babe Toney who died in a tragic automobile accident. The haunted aspect of this building continues to impress psychic visitors and paranormal investigators. Guests are also amazed at what they have seen and heard. Some of the stories that have been reported over the years include:

1   A visiting psychic who saw a woman in Period clothing appear on the staircase, stare for a few seconds and then vanish into thin air.
2   A staff person recalled watching in disbelief as a ghost waived at him while he was in the kitchen, standing at the end of the counter and facing the door.
3   Another time a dishtowel in the kitchen rose up and down on its own.
4   Guests have reported that room lights turn on and off by themselves and cold spots materialize out of nowhere.
5   The heavy pendulum on an antique clock that must be manually push started began to sway back and forth on its own before anyone had a chance to activate it.
6   The big-screen television has been known to turn on by itself for no apparent reason. There have also been times when someone unseen will change channels on unsuspecting clientele or staff.
7   Some hotel guests swear that they have witnessed a female and her child suddenly manifest in their bathroom.
8   Others patrons have reported hearing footsteps and singing coming from unoccupied hallway. There are other reports of phantom children playing and laughing, although upon inspection there is never anyone there.
9   There are frequent reports of sudden manifestations of sweet perfume scents that will appear out of thin air, engulf a guest and then simply go away.
10 Room 14 has its share of the unexplained as guests have had items disappear right in front of them. They have placed an item down on a table, turned away for a second, looked back, and the item has vanished. It usually turns up in another part of the hotel by the time they leave.
11 Pictures on walls are found tilted, ghosts music is heard, doors will open on their own, and occasionally a lucky guest or staff person will actually see a ghost.

At Bayview Hotel and Ristorante Barolo, the unusual is the usual. People come from all around with the hope of having a paranormal encounter, seeing an actual manifestation or they simply come to enjoy the very best in Aptos hauntspitality.

Arcadia
Derby Restaurant

Particulars
233 East Huntington Drive,
Arcadia, CA 91007
Phone: 626-447-8174
Phone: 626-447-2430
E-mail: thederbyarcadia@aol.com
Website: www.thederbyarcadia.com

History

The general area was once part of a 13,000 acre land grant established in 1845, known as Rancho Santa Anita. By 1875, after changing ownership three times, Elias J. "Lucky" Baldwin bought 8,000 acres of rancho land for $200,000. Baldwin later subdivided the land into the Santa Anita tract that would later become the City of Arcadia. At the height of Baldwin's ownership tenure, his holdings encompassed the current day cities of Sierra Madre, Arcadia, Monrovia, El Monte, and Baldwin Park. Rancho lands were used to grow oranges, lemons, grapes and walnuts and sustain herds of cattle, sheep and horses. Baldwin's horses were also bred to race all across the United States. When the town was officially incorporated in 1903, Baldwin became its first mayor. During 1904 Baldwin's built the Santa Anita Race Track. The short-lived venture closed in 1909 when horse racing was banned in California. "Lucky" Baldwin died the same year; his luck ran out. When Route 66 was completed in 1931, the Army, who owned the land on which the original racetrack stood, transferred it back to Los Angeles County and it was developed into Arcadia County Park. After horse-racing bans had been lifted in California, the present Santa Anita Race Track was opened to the public on Christmas Day, 1934. Arcadia grew and soon hotels and restaurants sprang up along Route 66.

The Derby Restaurant was purchased by jockey, George Woolf, who became co-owner in 1938 with his partner. Bill Peterson. Woolf who rode Seabiscuit to victory over War Admiral (when the scheduled jockey, Red Pollard, was injured) in the "Race of the Century," envisioned his restaurant as a place where jockeys and race fans could enjoy each others company. Prior to Woolf, Hudson M. Proctor owned the establishment (called the Proctor Tavern) when it operated in 1922. During 1931, it moved to its present location. Woolf planned the establishment as a source of retirement earnings.

When Woolf purchased The Derby in 1938, he was at the top of his game. Each wall, adorned with memorabilia of prestigious horses and races, would cause diners to revisit glorious wagers and harrowing photo finishes. George Woolf was fatally injured on January 3, 1946, when he was thrown from his mount "Please Me" during the running of the fourth race at Santa Anita.

During 1952, Dominic and Lorene Sturniolo, bought The Derby from Woolf's widow, Genevieve, who let them have her late husband's scrapbooks, the silks Woolf was wearing when he was killed, some of the whips he used in his greatest races, and Phar Lap's saddle (all are on display in the restaurant's trophy cases).

Spirits

The restaurant that was so dear to George Woolf may well contain his spirit. This is where he witnessed his greatest achievements and sadly the area where he rode his last race, which took his life. It's natural for some spirits to remain in a place where so many memories abound. The ambiance is much the same as when Woolf took over the establishment and made it into a local hangout. Woolf, who earned the reputation as the "iceman," a jockey able to carefully select the right moment to make his move, giving him the greatest advantage, seems to return occasionally, letting people know he is there by generating a icy breeze.

Some guests and even management believe that the spirit of George Woolf, continues to drop by "his" place to revisit all the racing memorabilia. It still packs in throngs of Santa Anita regulars prior to major races like the Breeders' Cup, including the spirit of a former jockey. The current owner is among those who believe his establishment is haunted. Others also sense the presence of Woolf as they gaze at all the old scrapbooks and photos. There have been numerous times when someone standing near the display areas will feel someone breathing down their neck. When they turn around, they are alone.

As their website states, "Perhaps the ghost likes to admire the Calumet Farm silks the 36-year-old Woolf was wearing on Jan. 3, 1946, the day he suffered fatal injuries when Please Me threw him at Santa Anita. Possibly he inspects the saddle Woolf was given in 1932 by Billie Elliot, the jockey of Phar Lap, the great New Zealand champion whose career-and mysterious death was the subject of a 1983 movie. Or maybe he looks wistfully at the photos of Kentucky Derby winners. Could the gentle breeze that works its way through the restaurant be a ghostly sigh over the fact that Woolf never won the Derby in nine tries from 1932 to 1945?"

The Derby's appeal is the spirited setting, the great selection of food and wonderful service. George Woolf would be proud of the Derby legacy he began back in 1938. The "Iceman" still visits his former establishment, perhaps awaiting one last shot at winning the Kentucky Derby through an afterlife miracle. An odd fact about Woolf, according to William F. Reed in his Sport Illustrator article, "The Iceman's Watering Hole", dated October 18, 1993, is that both times Woolf finished second in the Derby, the race he wanted most to win, he was beaten by a horse from Calumet, the farm whose silks he was wearing during the fatal accident (the ones on display in the restaurant). The room upstairs where Woolf lived is usually off limits. But when the place is overcrowded, the living is allowed a rare opportunity to co-mingle with a racing legend.

Here at the Derby Restaurant in Arcadia, we are not horsing around when we say that the afterlife is constantly jockeying for a better position with the living.

Arroyo Grande
Crystal Rose Inn

Particulars
789 Valley Road,
Arroyo Grande, CA 93420
Phone: 805-481-1854
Fax: 805-481-9541
Toll Free: 1-800-ROSE-INN
E-mail: stay@callamer.com

History
This venerable "Painted Lady" is located roughly half way between Los Angeles and San Francisco just off Highway 101. The Crystal Rose Inn was built about 1890 by Charles Pitkin, who moved to the Arroyo Grande Valley from the east coast. In 1905 when Edgar Conrow and his family got off the train in Oceano, his wife Abbie gasped, "Why have you taken me to this God forsaken place?" She was only willing to stay if Mr. Conrow bought the Pitkin house, which he did.

The Conrows raised their four children in the home, and Mary Conrow lived there until her death in 1952. In 1957, Ben and Mary Colburn bought and renovated the home, adding an intimate restaurant featuring a floor-to--ceiling fireplace. In 1981 Diana & Ross Cox acquired the home, which they renovated and opened as the Rose Victorian Inn. The Inn was purchased by Crystal Properties in September 1994, and renamed Crystal Rose Inn. Partners Dona Nolan and Bonnie Royster now add their special touch of hospitality.

Spirits
The ghost of the Crystal Rose is named Alice, a seven-year-old girl who reportedly died in the Queen Elizabeth Tower Suite, which was to be her bedroom--she never moved in, at least in the flesh. Some people believe that Alice died by accidentally falling out a two-story window, while other people are convinced that she died of Scarlet Fever. Although her sudden demise still remains a mystery, her otherworldly presence is not. Alice is often heard sobbing within the building and she also likes to play tricks on the staff and guests. This benign child spirit has never tried to hurt anyone; she just enjoys the company of strangers.

Alice keeps the staff busy by ringing the doorbell, which is unusual, since the doorbell rings off of batteries that have been long since removed. Also, one afternoon while cleaning out the refrigerator in the basement, a staff person felt a tapping directly under her feet. At first she didn't think too much about it, but she asked another employee if anything like that had ever happened to her, and the person replied that it had. Neither could explain it, unless---it was a ghost. The two employees decided to check out the basement together. As they were standing in the spot where they had felt the tapping, a space now occupied by a broom, something made the broom handle fall to the floor. They left the basement without missing a beat.

One woman claimed to have had no knowledge of the ghost before staying at the Inn; yet after her visit, she told the innkeepers about her encounter with Alice. The woman described her encounter with Alice as a very playful tug-o- war with a throw pillow on the bed. An invisible guest was holding onto one end, while the woman was holding tight to her end. As the ghost guest let go, the woman watched in amazement as a young girl with pig tails ran through the restroom and up the stairs to the tower room and vanished. Another event involved a music system in the restaurant. One evening, while two waiters were closing up, the system came on, but instead of music, a child's voice echoed through the speakers. The child was trying to speak, but it seemed to get frustrated at being unable to communicate; then the music came right back on.

Richard Senate investigated the establishment when it was the Rose Victorian Inn. With his wife Debbie, a gifted psychic, the Senates entered the house and faced the main staircase. Debbie was able to see a little girl standing on the staircase, and proceeded to describe the young child, as being about nine-years-old, wearing pigtails, a long dress, and a small apron. After a few seconds, the child looked at Debbie then ran upstairs. The child eventually told Debbie that her name was Alice. In pursuit of the phantom child, the Senates entered what used to be her room (the Tower room). The little girl said she loved cats; doesn't know she's passed on; and is waiting for her mother to come to get her. Alice told Debbie that she liked one of the ladies who takes care of the house.

When paranormal researcher Gordon Ting, and his wife, Sylvia, visited the inn, they stayed in the "haunted" Tower Room. Before going to sleep, they locked the door leading to the tower. At 1:00 a.m., Gordon woke up out of a sound sleep. He heard the lock at the door clicking, as if someone were trying to gain entrance. This was followed in short order by their bed shaking with tiny vibrations, accompanied by the feeling of someone else in the room with them. Ting then became experiencing what he described as something like a small child trying to climb into bed with him and his wife. Then, the feeling dissipated, and the area became cold. As he looked toward the window, he witnessed a greenish white light at the top left-hand corner. It would appear for several seconds, and then vanish, only to reappear a few moments later. There was a rounded look to the image, but there were no discernible features. Ting finally dozed off.

Journal entries kept at the Inn include feelings by a number of guests that the place is haunted, including the fact that the ghost likes the lights left on, and that an unseen someone is in the room with them. On one occasion, a writer and his wife spent the night in the Queen Elizabeth Room. During the night, the wife was awakened by the feeling that someone was crawling in bed with her and her husband. She also thought she heard a child's voice call out for her mother. The startled woman, who had entered the house a skeptic concerning ghosts, had a quick change of heart.

Does Alice still haunt the inn? From the continued sightings, the answer would have to be a spirited --- "Yes!" Visit the Crystal Rose Inn, and spend the night in the Tower Room, and see if Alice pays you an otherworldly visit.

Auburn
Latitudes Restaurant

Particulars
130 Maple Street,
Auburn, CA 95603
Phone: 530-885-9535
E-mail: patandpete@latitudesrestaurant.com
Website: www.latitudesrestaurant.com

History
The Victorian house was first built around 1880 by Mr. And Mrs. White across from the Historic Placer County Courthouse. Mr. White was a blacksmith. The original walls are the brick walls. During World War II, a family with three children owned the home in this exclusive neighborhood. The youngest child developed a deadly strain of the influenza virus. The teen-age daughter, entrusted with the care of the baby while the parents were out, shirked her duties, left with her friends and the baby died. The girl was so distraught that she left home, not returning until she was in her late 20s. According to local stories, the girl would sit in front of the stain glass window, rocking back and forth until one day she simply vanished from history. Fact or fiction, it's hard to say. However, if true, a double tragedy would leave a lasting imprint.

In 1980 the house was added onto and designed for a restaurant on the middle floor, a bar on the basement floor and with offices on the top floor. Latitudes and Pat & Pete's World Kitchen, is sole-owed and operated by Pete and Pat Enochs. The restaurant was first opened as "The Kitchen" at another location in Auburn in March of 1978 and closed there January 24, l992. Opening day at 130 Maple Street as "Latitudes Restaurant and Gallery was on February 4th, l992. In September of 1998 Pat and Pete purchased the ABA Bar, located on the floor below their restaurant, becoming "Latitudes Restaurant, Gallery and Bar-Café.

Spirits
According to their website, "There are stories of ghost sightings in the small meeting room in the historic dining room and downstairs in the bar." A story by Chuck Butler in the Auburn Journal dated January 22, 2002, goes into more details about the paranormal past of this historic building. When it was opened as a restaurant in 1980, the spirits became restless, and sightings as well as paranormal events became commonplace. The expansion of the original building was designed to accommodate a restaurant on the middle floor, a bar in the basement and offices on the top floor. Latitudes wasn't opened until twelve years later by Pat and Pete Enochs.

The small meeting room, the historic dining room, and the bar area seemed to bear the brunt of the spirited shenanigans. On numerous occasions, staff and guests who passed the alcove area glimpsed a hooded figure sitting at the table next to the stained glass window, staring out. The encounter was always brief.

As the person did a double take and refocused to get a better glimpse of the mysterious figure, it would vanish. Could this be the teen-ager who abandoned the baby and came back to look for forgiveness? No one knows for sure.

Another ghostly tale involves a tunnel that was supposedly excavated beneath Maple Street to connect the White's House to the Courthouse across the street. Rumor has it that a prior owner used the bar area to hold prisoners who were waiting to appear in court. The tunnel was apparently used to transport the prisoners underground and keep them out of the publics view during their trial. Stories of tearful ghostly sounds, balls of light, and mysterious shadows began to surface in the bar area.

There are quickly manifesting cold spots, sounds of a baby crying, disembodied footsteps, shadowy figures, orbs and streams of lights, and other unexplained events associated with the building. This is truly a building that serves up delicious food and menu of history and hauntings.

Banta

The Banta Inn

Particulars
22563 South 7th Street,
P.O. Box 34,
Banta, California 95304
Phone: 209-835-1311
E-mail: bantainn@aol.com

History

The Banta Inn was operated for many years by Juanita "Jenny" Gukan, with her daughter Lucille "Sis." A descendant of the early Spanish dons, Jenny Gukan came to Banta from Pleasanton in 1895, when her father, Frank Gallego went to work on a San Joaquin City ranch as a vaquero. The family moved to Banta in 1899 when Gallego bought the Banta Inn. The original building was replaced in 1937 after a fire destroyed most of the building. The present structure was designed and built by Tracy contractor Jere Strizek. The Banta Inn, which serves meals in a dining room and outdoor patio, has been operated for the past two decades by Joan Borland.

Spirits

Two permanent ghost guests have been sighted over the years at this quaint inn. One spirit is believed to be that of former owner, Tony Gukan who had a heart attack behind the bar in 1968. His apparition has been sighted as well as blamed for playing with glasses, chandeliers, coins, ashtray, and furnishings in the Inn. He occasionally enjoys playing with the guests as well. Paranormal Investigator Loyd Auerbach came to the Banta Inn as part of a Sightings investigation in May of 1992. Witnesses have reported a number of strange events that have taken place over the years at the Inn including:

1 A door to the kitchen which suddenly opened, followed by an apparition that floated out, and then vanished in front of startled staff;
2 A figure appearing in a mirror standing behind an unsuspecting staff member, only to vanish as the shocked individual whirled around;
3 A women claimed that someone ran their finger down her leg, only to turn and find no one there;
4 A beer bottle on the bar abruptly turned on its side and spun around three time;
5 Patsy Cline songs will come on the jukebox when no one else is around and the plug disconnected;
6 Money is found stacked in neat piles after being thrown in the cash register only seconds before;
7 A prior owner's favorite table showed marked anomalies in equipment used to measure energy fluctuations;
8 A bartender, who escorted two inebriated men out of the bar, tried to get back in. Unfortunately, the door had been locked from the inside, even though he was the only remaining person in the bar;
9 The apparition of a young woman has been sighted floating through the bar area;
10 One of the spirits reportedly levitates and throws objects in a tantrum-like manner across the bar room;
11 The chandelier will suddenly begin swaying, unassisted.

The Banta Inn continues to be a favorite watering hole for locals, tourists, paranormal investigators, the curious who come for the food and the spirits, and most importantly, the spirits who liven things up here.

Benicia
Captain Blythers

Particulars
123 First Street,
Benicia, CA 94510
Phone: 707-745-4082
Fax: 707-745-9327
E-mail: info@captainblythers.com
Website: www.captainblythers.com

History

The building that houses Captain Blyther's Restaurant was originally built as a home for Captain Samuel Blyther, his wife Anne, and their children sometime circa 1879. Their first house on Lot 5 of Semple Slips was between 1859-1861. Samuel Blyther was a native of Maine and a mariner. Anne emigrated from Ireland to Philadelphia. In 1858 she moved to San Francisco, that same year she came to Benicia where she met the Captain and married him. Samuel Blyther, like his neighbor up the street, Captain John Paladini, operated a local freighting business between Benicia and San Francisco. Blyther operated his steamer, the Sophie Hager, for many years, hauling merchandise between Benicia and Bay ports.

Samuel and Anne had four children, two boys, and two girls, their oldest son, Samuel C. died in 1864 at the age of three. The oldest child Julia was married in 1905 to Thomas McDermott, an employee of the Southern Pacific Railroad. They held their wedding reception in the Blyther home. Unfortunately, Thomas would lose his right leg five years later in an accident on the Solano Train Ferry when a section of train No. 15 struck him and the wheels passed over his right leg. Annie, the Blyther's third child, was born in 1871, and their fourth child George, was born three years later in 1874. Five years after the birth of George, in 1879, Captain Blyther died, leaving his widow with three young children to raise.

When Anne Blyther died in 1909, Annie and George continued to live in the home, which they converted to a rooming house in 1910. George Blyther was a bartender who at one time worked at the saloon which was on the site of the present railroad station, though little is known about George, he does have the dubious distinction of having been arrested in September 1923 for a minor liquor-law violation. A year later in 1924, George's sister Annie died leaving only himself and his sister Julia, who lived with her husband in Oakland. George died in 1934 bringing the Blythers in Benicia to an end. This building has been home to a rooming house; purportedly during the war converted to a bordello "The Alamo Rooms" of which we have been told was one of eleven active bordellos in Benicia at the time. In 1982, the eight small rooms upstairs were gutted and replaced with the bar and dining area that is now there. Over the years it has been several types of small shops, but for the past 30 years or so it has been home to three restaurants, the latest, Captain Blyther's Restaurant, was established in 1991.

Spirits

According to locals, staff and psychics who have visited this historic building, the place is filled with spirits. Considering its history, especially that it functioned as a bordello, it's not a far stretch to assume the place would be spirited. The stories are far from generic in nature. Sure there are the manifesting cold spots, disembodied footsteps and occasional anomalies with lights and doors opening and closing on their own. However, the active spirits have also been responsible for pictures flying off the wall and security alarms going off when the place is unoccupied.

The police have reportedly frequented the place when the alarms have gone off. When they arrive and search the place, there is never a soul to be seen; at least no one from this dimension.

Psychics who have entered the building have immediately picked up on the otherworldly vibrations that create the unique ambiance inside. The immediate impression is that there are numerous spirits including a male, female, children and women of the night who frequent the building. The psychic sense is that the building is still home to Captain Samuel Blyther, his wife Anne, a child (possibly Samuel who died when he was three) and at least two women from the time the place served as a bordello. There's nothing threatening inside, just a few spirits who seem for the most part content to share their space with the living. Occasionally, one of the spirits throws a tantrum, perhaps because he or she is being neglected or because something that has changed inside does not meet with their approval.

A visit to this historic home turned rooming house, bordello and finally a restaurant is sure to wet your whistle when it comes to dinner and spirits. You get both for the price of one when you visit.

Union Hotel

Particulars
401 First Street,
Benicia, CA 94510
Phone: 707-746-0110
Fax: 707-745-3032
Toll free: 866-445-2323
E-mail: unionhotel@msn.com

History

The Union Hotel is the only surviving hotel from Benicia's nineteenth century past. The exact date when the Union was first built is not known, but estimates are that the hotel was constructed in the mid-1850's. Because of it's proximity to the bay and downtown Benicia, the Union most likely had important figures register as guests because Benicia was a State Capitol at the time. The Union Hotel was also an important inn for lodging guests during the Gold Rush. It is rumored that there is gold hidden in the walls somewhere in the Union Hotel. There are also tunnels underneath the Union Hotel. Over a hundred years ago, these tunnels were used to transport gold from the bay to the hotel. The finest room at the Union Hotel is the Coast Lotus room. It is said that Humphrey Bogart stayed in this room and left a cigar burn in the wall after he checked out (The cigar burn has been painted over since then).

Spirits

At the historic Union Hotel, on certain windy nights, one can hear the sound of voices from the past echoing through the unoccupied hallways. Some individuals have mentioned that they can sense a lot of happy spirits and energy in the hotel, behaving as they did when they frequented the building. According to the current owners, once in a while, a guest riding the elevator hears the sound of voices, even though they are alone at the time. Others have reported hearing phantom conversations coming from unoccupied rooms and corridors.

During renovations, items would disappear in one part of the hotel and end up in a completely different location. Workers would complain about feeling uneasy working in certain areas of the building, and often felt as if they were being watched. A child entered a room during remodeling, stayed a few minutes, and then ran out saying that there was a ghost in the room. While visiting the hotel, a psychic claimed to have witnessed a couple of spirits sleeping in one of the hotel rooms; even though no one was staying in the room at the time.

A friend of the current owner and former employee who used to work at the Union Hotel would have to wake up at four in the morning to get the hotel ready for guests. The woman said that on one staircase between the second and third floors, the lights would often flicker when she was alone.

In the Beach Primrose Room, one closet door refuses to stay closed and guests have commented that it seems like someone does not want them to close the door; however, the guests are more curious about the event than frightened. There are other areas of the building where various strange and unexplained events have been frequently reported and continue to occur. If you want to know more about their amicable spirits, you'll have to pay a visit to this historic establishment and ask the owners about the "other stories" that make the Union Hotel in Benicia, a sought-after haunted travel destination.

Berkeley
Claremont Resort

Particulars
41 Tunnel Road,
Berkeley, CA 94705
Phone: 510-843-3000
Toll Free: 1-800-551-7266
E-mail: reservations@claremontresort.com
Website: www.claremont.com

History
Frank Lloyd Wright called The Claremont, "…one of the few hotels in the world with warmth, character and charm." A Kansas farmer named Bill Thornburg struck it rich in the gold fields and with his wife and daughter, built a castle and several stables. It was later sold to the Ballard family. On July 14, 1901, the castle burned to the ground. Won in a game of checkers, the property then fell into the hands of Frank Havens, who with his partner Eric Lindblom, opened The Claremont in 1915. In 1937, Mr. and Mrs. Claude Gillum virtually rebuilt the Claremont from the foundation up. The Claremont's Garden Room hosted Count Basie, Louis Armstrong and Tommy Dorsey.

Around 1940, the Claremont was painted white, the roof was fireproofed, and the shingles were turned a whitish-silver color. In 1954, Mr. Harold J. Schnitzer of Harsch Investment Corporation bought The Claremont property and leased it to Mr. Murray Lehr. By 1959, The Claremont was the largest convention resort in the Bay Area. Harsch Investment Corporation took over management in 1971. In April of 1998, KSL Recreation Corporation bought The Claremont. Renovations over the years have continued to make this resort hotel a must visit vacation destination.

Hauntspitality
Within this stately, historic California structure, in Room 419, a benign spirit is rumored to play tricks on staff and guests. On numerous occasions, a nameless phantom has turned on lights, opened and closed doors and stood at the foot of the bed as unsuspecting guests awakened to a misty, fog-like specter.

Housekeeping has reported that after making the bed in the room, they work another area only to return and find that someone has been sleeping on the freshly made bed. Other times, people in adjoining rooms will report loud noises coming from the spirited room. When staff goes to investigate, there is never anyone in the room, except an occasional cold spot. Who is this pesky phantom? No one seems to have a clue so far. There have also been occasions when a phantom has been sighted in the hallway outside the room before suddenly disappearing in front of startled witnesses.

On your next visit to this beautiful resort destination, we suggest that you focus all your psychic powers and see if you can come up with the identity of the Claremont spirit. There's always the possibility that more than one after-life guest frequents this fabulous resort hotel. Come see the unseen for yourself.

Beverly Hills
Love's Wood Pit Barbecue

Particulars
9740 W. Pico Boulevard,
Beverly Hills, CA 90035-4711
Phone: 310-553-5513

History
Formerly, Bob Morris' Beverly Hills Barbecue, the current establishment is situated along Pico Boulevard in Beverly Hills. With a stunning view of Westwood as the sun dips below the horizon, this restaurant can truly boast great food in a casual atmosphere with a bevy of spirits to keep you company. There doesn't seem to be an area inside the establishment that is without some kind of unexplained activity. Its history dates back to 1938 and it's former incarnations as Loves and Noonan's restaurants, may hold a key to it's haunted past and the spirited clientele who now frequent the building.

Hauntspitality
Several tragedies have occurred in this building over the years. A woman was murdered while sitting in one of the booths facing Pico Boulevard and a male guest who frequented the establishment died of a heart attack while enjoying his last meal inside. These events may account for two of the most frequently sighted and sensed afterlife guests, but there are a number of other friendly spirits roaming this establishment.

The after-life clientele are so friendly in fact, that Pablo and Danalee, former restaurant staff, invited us inside to see if we could tell them who might be responsible for all the unusual disturbances that were taking place in various parts of the building. It wasn't that they were fearful, it was more a matter of constant apprehension that the staff felt, especially working late at night or closing up. Many of the employees felt that the spirits seemed to be trying to tell them something and that this would ultimately translate in pestering the "living" clientele.

A visit to this barbecue establishment when restaurateur Bob Morris (who also owned Gladstone's 4 Fish and the equally spirited Paradise Cove Beach Cafe in Malibu) owned the building yielded some interesting investigative results. The authors, accompanied by psychic, Ginnie McGovern and a "sensitive" named Daniel Smith, spent roughly five hours inside, taking readings and experiencing the afterlife ambiance.

Upon arriving at the restaurant, the group (my wife and I included) entered the front door and was immediately drawn to the bar area, which was located to the right of the entrance fronting Pico Boulevard. We all picked up a tingling sensation or strong energy vibration and feeling of being watched as we entered the bar area. The group spread out with their equipment that included dowsing rods, an EMF meter, a Gauss meter and digital thermometer, and within twenty minutes, found four, "strong" hot spots in the bar area.

These four "hot" spots coincided with feelings or sensations suggesting the presence of a woman with long, flowing brown hair. The phantom female seemed right at home while occupying the second stool in front of the bar after entering the area. This woman may be the murder victim who was killed in the other room, and our general feeling was, that although she likes to check up on the staff and float around the restaurant, she prefers the company in the bar area where the activity seems to suit her quite nicely. This phantom lady has been sighted by guests and staff on several occasions, particularly in the bar area. On one occasion, a patron watched as a spectral lady made her way through the bar and out the entryway to the bar room, before vanishing in the main part of the restaurant. Her sudden disappearance was followed a few seconds later by a male energy that entered the bar and slowly dematerialized; and this person was sober!

The investigators also picked up on an elderly Jewish couple who came to the restaurant for years, and enjoy watching people from the booth to the immediate right upon entering the bar area. A short wall hides the booth as you enter and is tucked away in the corner. Here, the instruments, including the EMF meter, dowsing rods and digital thermometer picked up on numerous anomalies. The elderly couple, who are in their 60s-70s, love "their" spot, and will, also come an go from this location, as if dropping in as they did in life. The male presence was stronger than the female energy, here. The staff remarked that on several occasions, they have felt cold spots and have seen the nylon cords that allow the window shades to be drawn, suddenly move in unison along the seating area fronting Pico.

Another hot spot was the end of the bar as if wrapped around and became an entryway into a corridor which serviced the kitchen, storage area and men's and women's bathrooms. This was a very strong energy spot that registered drops in temperature of up to 15 degrees. Everyone picked up on a male presence that used the entire restaurant as his personal playground. He seemed to favor this location, and may be the man who died of a heart attack inside the building. T his energy has been frequently heard as disembodied footsteps and as a cold gust of air passing through the corridor that connects the restaurant to the back of the bar.

There were several other locations inside that gave pause to the investigators. One was the second booth fronting Pico upon entering the restaurant, unmistakable because of the bullet hole still visible in the window. This is where the phantom lady of the restaurant was apparently murdered. People have reported that they feel a "prickly" energy engulfs them when they pass by or sit in the booth.

There is also a lone booth way in the back of the restaurant facing the alley and back parking lot that is also very active. This is where the employees often sit while taking breaks. A former manager named Fernando also used to sit at the table balancing the daily receipts and just relaxing during a break. Two days before conducting the investigation, Fernando, in his early 30s, met an untimely death on the Ventura Freeway. Danalee and the other employees were still mourning his loss when we arrived. His energy is still attached to the building. In fact, Danalee, while in her office the day after Fernando was killed, felt something grab and gently pinch her arm as she was conducting business. Ginnie McGovern told Danalee that the energy pinning her right arm belonged to Fernando and that he was letting her know that he was okay. Even with his traumatic death, he was sympathetic to the worries and concerns of his friends and fellow employees. We all felt his energy in the restaurant as if watching over or checking up on those he used to work with.

The list of other unexplained events included: Place settings being moved by invisible hands; apparitions that floated through certain areas of the restaurant before vanishing; disembodied footsteps that came from unoccupied areas of the building; rapidly manifesting cold spots; bottles breaking by themselves; lights that would suddenly turn on and off without human assistance; an occasional door opening or closing by itself; and people's names being called out by someone unseen.

After the walk through, the group met with manager Danalee and Pablo, and after exchanging impressions and stories, concluded that all of the spirits are here because they want to be and that they seem to enjoy the action inside. The consensus was that one of the spirits seemed lost and confused (the female who was shot) and that Fernando had reached out from beyond the grave to let his friends know that he was fine and not to worry about him. A majority of the energy felt inside was curious, playful and loved mingling with the living. The spirits also seem content with the way things are being run. So, when you drop in on the newly named establishment to have a barbecue feast, a drink at the bar or a cup of coffee, remember that at this eatery, dinner and spirits are the main course. In addition, if you feel as if unseen eyes are watching you, they probably are.

Brookdale
Brookdale Lodge

Particulars
11570 Highway 9, P.O. Box 903,
Brookdale, CA 95007
Phone: 831-338-6433
Fax: 831-338-3066
E-mail: manager@brookdalelodge.com
Website: www.brookdalelodge.com

History

The Brookdale has hosted a number of notable guests, including movie stars, music celebrities, and President Herbert Hoover. Joan Crawford, Tyrone Power, Rita Hayworth, Howard Hughes, Henry Ford, Marilyn Monroe, Hedy Lamarr, and many other celebrities have visited the Brookdale during the heyday of motion pictures. Judge J.H. Logan built the original lodge in 1890 at the site of the Grover lumber mill (others say that Horace Cotton was the original builder).

Over the years, the Brookdale Lodge has hosted a number of notable guests: movie stars, music celebrities and a U.S. President. Brookdale opened in 1900 when Judge J.H. Logan, the originator of the loganberry, purchased the Grover lumber mill. The landholding became campgrounds and summer cabins, with the mill's lodge headquarters from 1870 converted into a hotel. A bridge over Clear Creek led to a small dining hall. In 1922, Dr. F.K. Camp bought the land after the river changed its course, and built the beautiful dining room with the brook running through it, which was featured in "Ripley's Believe It or Not."

Famous bands and singers of the Swing Era often performed here. The fireplace, dance floor, bandstand and tables were to the left of the brook and the original owner didn't allow alcohol on the premises. The advertising slogans included: "In all the world, nothing like it" and "In the heart of Big Tree Country... Come linger with us and listen to the brook singing merrily through our dining room." Gangsters frequented the place in the 1940s, and several murders were said to have occurred at the Lodge. The hotel burned to the ground in 1954 but it was completely restored to its former splendor using the original building specifications.

Hauntspitality

Based on Historical Memories Haunt Brookdale by Ross Eric Gibson, the following paranormal information was provided by the Brookdale Lodge: A girl in a formal dress runs across the lobby, then disappears into thin air. In an empty Mermaid Room, voices and music are softly heard. Hidden rooms and secret passages are mysterious vestiges of Brookdale Lodge's rich past. Brookdale, two miles south of Boulder Creek, opened in 1900 when Judge H.J. Logan, originator of the loganberry, purchased the Grover lumber mill.

The extensive acreage became campgrounds and summer cabins, with the mill's log- lodge headquarters from 1870 converted into a hotel. A bridge over nearby Clear Creek led to the small dining hall, which overlooked Minnehaha Falls. After Dr. F.K. Camp purchased the site, the river changed course in 1922, cutting a channel through the hotel grounds. Embankments were needed to keep the creek in its place, but Camp felt they shouldn't detract from  the streambed's natural appearance. The resulting terraces lined with granite boulders suggested a marvelous setting for dining, and Camp envisioned a dining hall straddling the fern-lined creek. This vision was carried out by architect and landscaper Horace Cotton, whose design gained critical acclaim among architects for so deftly integrating a rustic structure into the very fabric of the forest. It was ranked with Yosemite's Ahwahnee Lodge as that rare example of serious "rustic style" architecture. The barn-like structure resembled a redwood log cabin, with whole-log verandahs decorated in sticks of "tanglewood gingerbread." Inside, the terraces were supposed to protect the lodge from rising water. For 70 feet, the creek passed through the dining room, under a large atrium skylight that allowed continued growth of the woodwardia and other ferns. Trees growing through the roof formed a natural canopy.

In a back wall above the rustic bridge over the falls was a round window, lit at night to look like moonlight through the trees. Here a woman sang "Indian Love Call" opening day, on what became known as the Honeymoon Bridge. Horseshoes from the old mill were welded together as lanterns. Even the stream was lit, with colored underwater lights (a device perfected by architect Cotton), and people could watch trout swimming by as they dined. And the kidney- shaped pool (lit from below) later had an underwater window behind the Mermaid Room bar. Cotton also remodeled the 1870 lodge into a lobby and reading room. (The undated post card to the right shows the lodge) New entry doors went up, each, four inches thick, 51 inches wide and weighing 300 pounds. Their ornamental hinges were cut out of the mill's scrap boilerplate. The river-rock fireplace had a 6-foot tall opening, and the chandeliers were rounds of polished burl hung with lit clusters of pinecones.

Camp, a Seventh-day Adventist physician, was a strict prohibitionist. Even the end of Prohibition didn't end his habit of sniffing the customers' drinks, and pouring out liquor into the brook. Yet in spite of his idiosyncrasies, Camp's era from 1924 to 1945 was the golden age for the lodge. He ran it as a first-class retreat, attracting international celebrities, Hollywood stars, presidents and kings. Shirley Temple and Johnny Weissmuller had homes nearby. Herbert Hoover visited often, and enjoyed fishing off the dining room bridge. And during the San Francisco conference establishing the United Nations, world leaders and diplomats came to the lodge to relax.

Brookdale was also a popular host of famous bands and singers of the swing era. At least three songs were written about the lodge, such as "My Brookdale Hideaway," "A Place Known as Brookdale" and "Beautiful Brookdale Lodge." The last was an Ink Spots tribute, which will be performed at an upcoming Actors Theater revue in Santa Cruz. The lodge changed hands in 1945, shortly before

Mist and orbs at the Brookdale (courtesy of Alex Sill, West Hills, California)

Camp's death. The twin evils which Camp had successfully kept out during his ownership -- booze and gangsters -- now became familiar fixtures in a lodge falling rapidly into disrepair. Secret passageways and hidden rooms filled the lodge, and there were rumors of mobsters having buried a body under the floor. The topper for this shady era was when the niece of the lodge owner drowned in the dining room creek. Sightings of her ghost have been reported ever since.

Barney Morrow bought the lodge in 1951 and remodeled it after a 1956 fire destroyed the dining hall. He called his design a "Hansel & Gretel theme motel," transforming the redwood buildings into a mock French Tudor and "Santa's Village Swiss" hybrid. Most of the campground was paved for a massive parking lot, bordered by a barracks-like motel wing, the only one built of five planned cinder-block wings. Current owners are conducting a more sympathetic restoration of the lodge. In 1990, real estate investor Bill Gilbert bought the lodge and the surrounding eight acres.

The Brookdale Lodge has been called the Mother Lode of ghosts in California along with the Queen Mary. At least 49 separate entities have been identified floating around the Lodge. A child named Sarah is the most notable spirit. She was the blonde-haired, six-year-old niece of a former owner who drowned in the creek running through the Lodge during the 1920s. During the early 1970s, a teenager drowned in the swimming pool.

The spirits of the Brookdale have been known to clink glasses during phantom celebrations; play spectral music from bygone days which can be heard echoing through the halls; there are repeated reports of shadowy figures, and apparitions which appear out of thin air, and vanish within seconds; and there is the scent of gardenia cologne, a favorite perfume in the 1930s and 1940s, which can be smelled from time to time in parts of the Lodge. Everyone from the managers and

Mist and orbs at the Brookdale (courtesy of Alex Sill, West Hills, California)

staff, to the guests have seen or heard unexplainable things over the years.

The strange tales associated with the Brookdale have made it a celebrity haunted house for those visiting the area, as well as for locals who continue to tell their tales. Doors have frequently slammed shut for no apparent reason.

The television and jukebox will start playing oldies but goodies when no one is around the jukebox. Cold spots and icy drafts will suddenly occur in parts of the establishment. Laughter will be heard in the conference room when it is empty (it used to be a game room), and upon investigation, the balls on the pool table will be scattered about as if someone was shooting a game of pool--no one is ever found to be responsible for the ghostly billiard game.

One time, when the Lodge was closed, big band music was heard coming from the Mermaid Room. In the past it was a notorious place where call girls were available, and mobsters frequently hung out. A young girl, probably Sarah, has been sighted a number of times, laughing, playing, and running through the Lodge. After a reported cleansing, the spirits became angry, ripping wooden planks off the walls. A woman in 1940s formal attire, with long hair has also been seen running through the main lobby before vanishing through an office window.

Psychics and paranormal investigators who have studied the Brookdale have unanimously concluded that this spirited place will continue to provide after-life thrills for the living clientele who make the Brookdale one of their favorite haunts.

Buellton

Pea Soup Andersen's Restaurant and Inn

Particulars

376 Avenue of the Flags,
Buellton, CA 93427
Phone: 805-688-5581
Fax: 805-686-5670
Toll Free: 1-800-PEA-SOUP
E-Mail: info@peasoupandersens.net
Website: www.peasoupandersons.net

History

The story begins with Anton and Juliette Andersen. On June 13th, 1924, Danish born Anton Andersen purchased a piece of land on the former Jose Maria Covarrubias and Joaquin Carrillo land grant. The property was later sold to the Buell brothers in 1865. R.T. Buell ran a horse and cattle ranch and dairy farm named Rancho San Carlos de Jonata. R.T. Buell married Miss Emily Budd in 1892 and they had five children. When Mr. R.T. Buell died in 1905 he was buried in the family plot, now the parking lot of Pea Soup Andersen's Hotel. His body was moved to Oak Hill Cemetery in Ballard.

William Budd, brother of Mrs. Emily Buell, opened a post office and it became an official United States Post Office in 1920. When the highway was diverted through Buellton in 1924 and electricity was brought to the valley, Anton and Juliette Andersen purchased a small parcel of land and a building from William Budd and opened a restaurant. Anton, wearing his trademark tuxedo in his wife, Juliette, called their business venture "Andersen's Electric Cafe," in honor of their new electric stove. They began by serving simple, foods such as hot cakes and coffee, ice cream sodas to salesmen, tourists and truck drivers who drove the main highway between Los Angeles and San Francisco. Hearst's newspaper writers and reporters developed the habit of stopping at Andersen's. Their praise of excellent food and hospitable atmosphere was carried in their newspaper columns throughout the entire country.

In 1928, the Andersen's sank a well and built a hotel and dining room for their now quite popular cafe. They named their new establishment the "Bueltmore." Anton was famous for his capacity to remember faces and names without error. Soon celebrities stopped for a meal on their way along the coast. Juliette a devout Catholic, was a gracious woman, warm and friendly to all those around her. Juliette, from the east of France was an expert cook, so she prepared many of the recipes she had brought with her; the most popular with the customers was her split pea soup. Ultimately the name of the restaurant changed to reflect the success of her soup. Anton had to order one ton of peas for their successful recipe and proclaimed in the window of the establishment, "The Home of Split Pea Soup," a slogan that continues to this day. In recognition of the restaurant's pre-eminence as probably the world's foremost pea purchaser, the pea growers of Idaho have named Andersen's the location for the start of the annual "National Split Pea Soup Week" every November, to honor the pea and the delicious soup it makes.

Son Robert returned to the family business after graduating from Stanford in the 1930's. A very forward-looking man, Robert established the billboards, a famous cartoon showed the occupation of splitting peas for pea soup, with two comic chefs standing at a chopping table, and he even adopted his nickname "Pea Soup," the eventual trademark and official name of the family business. In 1941, Robert married Rosemary Mohan, who immediately became active in the family business and opened a gift shop which remains today filled with wonder for children and adults alike. Their only son, Rob, was born in 1942.

During World War II, the restaurant closed to the public. The hotel rooms were used to house military personnel stationed locally and meals were served to servicemen and their families. During 1947, the new coast highway was rerouted through the center of Buellton. The same year the name of the restaurant was officially changed to "Pea Soup Andersen's" and Buellton was nicknamed "The Home of Split Pea Soup".

Robert Andersen sold the Buellton restaurant to Vince Evans in April 1965. Vince and his wife Margery moved to a 900-acre ranch south of Buellton in 1959. They raised cattle, grew alfalfa and operated a feed store. The business thrived under Evans' hand. By then the restaurant was purchasing 50 tons of peas each year. He installed a train for children to ride that went from the restaurant to the area where the motel now stands, and even had a miniature wild animal park for two years. The park was discontinued in 1970 to make way for the addition of a Danish style motel in 1970. On April 23, 1980, Vince, his wife Margery and their 21-year-old daughter, Venetia, were tragically killed in small plane crash just minutes from the Santa Ynez Valley airport.

Hauntspitality

Psychic researcher Brian Cloninger stumbled on the ghosts of this popular restaurant in 1993. At the time, the gift shop and banquet room (the Juliet Room) were reportedly haunted. Numerous unexplainable events took place inside according to the wary staff. Music was heard echoing through the darkened hall late at night, lights would go on and go off unassisted, and doors would mysteriously open and close.

The night crew recounted how the furniture would be moved around by unseen hands and sometimes heard heavy pieces of furniture were being guided across the floor in unoccupied areas of the building. The rooms where the activity was the strongest happened to coincide with the original living quarters of Anton and Juliette Andersen.

The renowned ghosthunting/psychic duo of Richard and Debbie Christenson Senate decided to pay Buellton and Pea Soup Anderson's a visit. Knowing nothing of the ghost stories, Debbie had her meal and toured the second floor gift shop. Strangely silent as they walked through the restaurant, Debbie finally said out of the blue, that something was in there with them. To be exact, it was a woman with big sad eyes who is looking for someone. She went on to say that the woman worked there a long time ago, and for some reason continues to return. The Senate's confirmed that the restaurant is haunted, and at least one spirit remains behind. Perhaps it is Juliette Andersen making sure her recipe for split pea soup continues to meet with her approval.

There are other sensitives who believe that additional spirited clientele occupy the building, including the Evans family who loved the restaurant and who died tragically nearby. Some mediums have sensed a young girl and a man they call Vinnie, who seem to like the gift shop and Pavilion Room.

A place with such happy memories, and so much love and dedication filling its walls to the brim, seems to contain the spirits of those who worked to shape the building and the history of Buellton. After all, who wouldn't want to haunt this place with its otherworldly soup and spirited delights? Try some the next time you are in Buellton, and see if you can sense one or both of the Andersons standing or floating proudly behind their world famous recipe.

Buena Park
Mrs. Knott's Chicken Dinner Restaurant

Particulars
8039 Beach Boulevard,
Buena Park, CA 90620
Phone: 714-220-5080
Reservations and Information:
Toll Free:1-800-422-4444

History

Knott's Berry Farm is located in Buena Park, California along Beach Boulevard. The park is on one side of the street and free parking on the other side with an underpass connecting both areas. The California Marketplace offers shopping and dining outside of the park, including that World Famous chicken dinner restaurant where they're still serving the chicken that made Mrs. Knott famous. Back in 1920, Walter and Cordelia Knott came to Buena Park and started a 20-acre berry farm. It became Knott's Berry Place in 1928 when they built a permanent building to serve as a berry stand and tea room. Despite some success in the propagation of the boysenberry, money got tight as the depression hit and they needed another source of income, so, in 1934 Cordelia reluctantly began serving chicken dinners in the tea room on her own wedding china. The chicken was a hit. By 1937 they built a full-fledged restaurant, and soon they had thousands of customers lining up to get in -- so many that Walter began to look around for some way of keeping them entertained while they waited. In 1940 he moved the Old Trails Hotel to the Farm from Prescott, Arizona -- the first of many old buildings that he would relocate or replicate to form his own ghost town. He added "The Covered Wagon Show," a cyclorama, to the hotel's lobby and the farm had its first themed attraction.

In the 1950's more buildings and more shows were added to what was now known as Knott's Berry Farm. In 1952 Walter bought the entire the Denver and Rio Grande railroad and moved it to the farm where it was reborn as the Ghost Town & Calico Railroad, the park's first ride. Since then the park has continued to grow, developing into one of the world's premier theme parks (Knott's Berry Farm won the Amusement Business/Liseberg Applause Award in 1988, only the fourth park so honored.) After the deaths of Cordelia and Walter, the Knott family carried on as managers until 1997 when the park was acquired by Cedar Fair, L.P., which has continued to expand and improve it.

Hauntspitality

Cordelia Knott loved her restaurant. When she passed away in the early morning hours of April 23, 1974 at her home near the restaurant, her spirit seemed to remain behind in the place she and her husband spent most of their lives tending to. The restaurant is rumored to have a friendly spirit in one of the empty, windowless back dining rooms.

Those who have witnessed the apparition describe the form as resembling an elderly woman who floats through the room as if tending to invisible clients and then suddenly vanishes. A busboy claimed to see a fog-like image in the dining area before the image disappeared. Those who knew Mrs. Knott believe that she loved the place so much that even after death should refused to go anywhere else. There are ghostly footsteps, shadows on the walls, and an occasional inspection of the kitchen by the spirit believed to be Mrs. Knott. Sensitives who have walked into the restaurant have immediately sensed a proud, hard-working woman who seems to dominate the place. She is strict yet tolerant of her earthly clientele. She wants to make sure her recipes and hard work continue to be properly administered by the current staff. She has been known to move place settings, call out the names of some staff, and is probably responsible for quickly manifesting cold spots and unexplained footsteps that can be heard late at night in the kitchen area as if performing an inspection.

When you sample the great food at this original family run business, you can thank Cordelia in spirit if you're lucky, for establishing the tradition of fine food and country ambiance in Buena Park that continues to lure the living over 30 years after she passed away.

Calabasas
La Paz

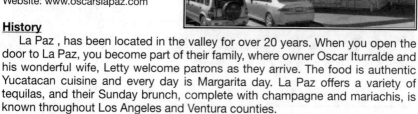

Particulars
4505 Las Virgenes Road
Calabasas, CA 91302
Phone: 818-880-8076
Fax: 818-880-0844
E-mail: lapaz@charter.com
Website: www.oscarslapaz.com

History

La Paz , has been located in the valley for over 20 years. When you open the door to La Paz, you become part of their family, where owner Oscar Iturralde and his wonderful wife, Letty welcome patrons as they arrive. The food is authentic Yucatacan cuisine and every day is Margarita day. La Paz offers a variety of tequilas, and their Sunday brunch, complete with champagne and mariachis, is known throughout Los Angeles and Ventura counties.

Entering La Paz Restaurant is an unforgettable experience. On the left is a collection of historic tequila bottles from throughout Mexico. On the right is the welcoming booth and reservation area. Charismatic, charming, friendly and an incredible chef, Oscar is La Paz. He came to America in 1966 and began his career as a chef for the Beverly Hilton Hotel. He furthered his career in Boston at the Sheraton Prudential Center. In 1979 Oscar opened his first La Paz, in Canoga Park and in 1986; he opened his second restaurant in Woodland Hills. In 1989, he moved La Paz to Calabasas. The staff at La Paz is friendly, loyal, many having served at the Calabasas location since it opened.

Hauntspitality

According to psychics who have visited La Paz, and those who have worked here over the years, the place is definitely haunted. Although the number of spirits is in question, the consensus is that two spirits call the restaurant home, at least on a temporary basis. They seem to come and go as they please, not stuck here by any means. According to archaeologists and historians, the area on which the restaurant and business complex now stand, was once home to the Chumash Indians, with a major campsite dating back several thousand years, located across the street where a new housing development has just been completed. The nearby stream would have provided at least seasonal water for the Native Americans occupying the area, and Las Virgenes Road was a major trade and access route for the Native Americans and early settlers to commute between Malibu and the El Camino Real (Highway 1). Early Plat Survey maps from 1860-1890 also suggest that an early homestead may have existed on or near the current La Paz property, tapping into numerous springs that dotted the landscape. Given the extensive history of the land from Native Americans and Spanish land expeditions, to early settlers, is it any wonder that this building is spirited.

There are two areas where people most often sense spirits inside the restaurant. One is in the back, eastern portion of the restaurant when a younger Hispanic woman in white is occasionally sighted and often felt, and the bar area near the restrooms. Here, a male energy is periodically seen as shadowy figure, gliding along the row of booths before vanishing in the bathroom area.

The younger female is sighted as what best can be described as a white dress with hand sewn colored stitching around the fringes of the dress. She is friendly and often smiles at patrons who spot her. She seems to be checking in on the establishment and may be related to the owners or someone who works there. She is known for causing rapidly manifesting cold spots and for materializing and dematerializing at will. As one psychic stated, "The woman loves the restaurant and pops in from time to time, just to see how things are going." There have been occasions when patrons report smelling a sweet fragrance in this portion of the restaurant. The scent is there one minute and gone the next. She is a friendly and happy energy that fits the place perfectly.

The male energy seems to have a past tie to land. One person remarked that the man looked like an early settler, while another person said he looks like a cowboy. No one has really had a good look at this specter, who is a quick as a bullet, passing through the building. He is sensed by psychics as having died on the property, probably in the late 1800s. Some people have remarked that while going to or coming back from the bathroom, or even sitting at one of the booths, they have felt a cold rush of energy pass through them, sending chills up their back.

Psychics point to another male energy and a child also occupying the building, but there is little confirmation of these energies. Most of the sensory paranormal experiences seem to take place during the quieter times, when the restaurant is minimally occupied. When you visit La Paz, you are in for a culinary treat, where haunt cuisine is at its best. It's so popular that it has a friendly after-life clientele as well.

The area where is female spirit is sometimes spotted.

Saddle Peak Lodge

Particulars
4l9 Cold Canyon Road,
Calabasas, CA 91302
Phone: 8l8-222-3888 I 3l0-456-7325
Website: www.saddlepeaklodge.com

History
The lodge is in the Malibu Hills along a creek that flows through Las Virgenes Canyon, standing under the fabulous Saddle Peak, a majestic rock formation. According to local legend, this formation was made when God's first horseman sat upon the Santa Monica Mountains. At one time, it brought a colorful mix of cowboys, hunters, fishermen, oil riggers and miners bound for the gold fields of Piru Creek and Upper Ojai, who would stop at the Lodge, a one-room cabin, to swap stories, take on supplies or quench their thirst with a brew called "Hillbilly Punch."

In the last century, the Lodge has been a roadhouse, Pony Express stop, hunting lodge, European tavern, and bordello. It remains a place of enchantment. Memorabilia covers three levels of walls, including objects of fine art to relics of the Old West, along with vintage hunting and fishing gear, stuffed birds, animals, fish, and items to inspire every sort of story. One is of the ghostly woman with long dark hair who occasionally appears at Table 41, upstairs. Rumor has it that mayhem was committed by a jilted rancher in that exact spot.

Hollywood's infamous Rat Pack used to feed coyotes with buffalo bones thrown from the back terraces at night. When old Hollywood discovered the lodge, it had been a dry-goods, beer and sandwich shop. But it was soon featured in many movie classics, serving as a road-house for stars from Warner Brothers, Paramount, and Twentieth Century Fox. Errol Flynn and Clark Gable, and starlets were constant visitors, as were Mary Pickford, and Charlie Chaplin.

The restaurant has three dining floors, outdoor patios, and layered terraces; with rustic scenic beauty and waterfalls in a woodsy remoteness. Native rock walls, massive timbers and a mixture of fantasy and excellent service make it a great spot for intimate dinners, power-meetings, banquets and special events.

Hauntspitality
The following information is taken from their website, "There is a story of a ghostly woman with long dark hair who occasionally appears at Table 41 upstairs. Rumor has it that mayhem was committed by a jilted rancher in that exact spot." This is just the tip of the paranormal iceberg for this establishment. The International Paranormal Research Organization (IPRO) performed a series of paranormal investigations on 11/20/2002, 11/23/2002, 2/22/2003, 3/18/2003, 11/8/2003 and 12/13/2003. Psychics Ginnie McGovern; Robin Collier, Deann Burch, Victoria

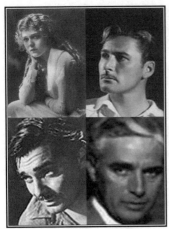

Gross, Alma Carey, Daniel Smith, Tony Charness and Palah Sandling, and investigators from the San Gabriel Valley Paranormal Researchers and the San Diego Ghost Hunters as well as Matt Cope (Sacred Mesa Productions); Karen Camus (EVP Consultant), JoJo Wright (DJ from KIIS FM); Matthew Wlodarski, Lonnie, Nicci, Alex and Natasha Sill, Ed, Paul, Stephanie and Mallory Wehan and friend Vanessa, and Dan Larson, spent time inside this very haunted locations. With the help of Gerhard Trattier, Mariah Shaw, Tracy Levine and Gwen Davis, we were also able to perform a séance. Based on several investigations of the property by paranormal investigators and psychics to date, the following conclusions are presented.

There are at least five strong interacting energies present in the restaurant and there are numerous other energies that are either imprinted by events of the past, or flow through the building at various times:

1. There is one female presence that we call Edith. This may or may not be her name, but one psychic was able to come up with this. Edith is in her 40s, and enjoys the third floor, although she also visits the second floor. She has dark hair with a hint of grey; is about 5'4", and lived on the property or nearby. She is an early inhabitant of the area (probably 1880s-1910) and lived here with her family. Her favorite spot is the westernmost chair at Table #41, one with arms, and she enjoys looking outside as well as watching guests come upstairs. She will come in the room from the area of the office and stay close to the table and stair area. She infrequently makes her way to the second floor. She may be responsible for some of the movement of items, and noise which are heard by staff in this area, although our feeling is, that there maybe another spirit or two that are more mischievous. This is a rather content and benevolent being who watches over the building and grounds.

2. There is a rather gruff, rugged, and standoffish male who frequents the second floor and occasionally the third floor. There was no sense or feeling that this individual spirit was aware of the female called Edith. He seemed to have his own energy plane, or dimension, so-to-speak, and interacted with other spirits of like energy; but not Edith, unless she simply dismissed him. The man did not seem to trust people at first, although after getting acquainted with our energy, he seemed to open up a little. He was very curious as to who we were and why we were here, but did like being acknowledged. He was about 5'7"-5'8" tall and wore rather rugged, period clothing, indicating a rancher, cowboy, or western-type. He's husky, but not

Orb above Haunted Table 41 (courtesy of the International Paranormal Research Organization – IPRO)

heavy; a very sturdy and strong man. He comes off as hostile or angry, but it's a protective front. When he lets his guard down, he's a decent person. A psychic picked up the name, Zachariah, and that he was a very good poker player. He could be responsible for some of the noises, movement and spilling of things related to liquor consumption; he is perhaps protective over what is still taking place in the other-dimensional, saloon-like environment on the second floor. He loves the piano, cards, smoking and drinking.

3. A female about 5'2", who seems to stay only on the first floor. She may be the Lady in White occasionally spotted near the kitchen and bar area. She has dark hair and wears a white blouse. There is a sense of being lost or confused when she is spotted by staff. Her suggested time period is 1930-1940s and she may have something to with the place when it was a popular hang-out during Prohibition, or when it was a Hollywood inn-place. Tragedy or trauma; lost love, broken heart; something keeps her stuck in this place. There is little indication that she was raised on the land, but something did happen to her on or near the restaurant. She is not mean, or mischievous, and always seems to vanish when shown the front door.

4. This is an interactive, young male around 19-20. He is described as being over 5'7" and rather handsome. He prefers the second and third floors, and may have died as a result of a robbery, where he was dragged from his horse and a pouch full of money taken from him. He's is not unhappy, but is tied to the land. He is dressed in the clothes he was buried in and is rather well-dressed, with nice pants and a vest. He is inquisitive, likes women, and may be responsible for touching people, playing pranks, and otherwise trying to get people's attention. He is not harmful or malicious. A psychic picked up the name Jim (James) Brodie when contacting him. He is aware of other energies in the building. He likes the outdoor, third floor patio.

5. A young girl who according to a psychic, goes by the name of Claire or Clara, also frequents the building and is not confined to one floor. She does have other children for playmates, and is afraid of Zachariah. She sees a lot and knows most of the other spirits. The girl said that she drowned during a flood in back of the building which near her favorite water hole. She has light-colored hair and may be a tom-boy. She is very playful and loves to play pranks on people. She can be heard in the building late at night and enjoys music. She is befriended by one of the female spirits in the restaurant. She smiles and sings, and is very tied to this place.

6. There is a strong female energy in a portal area on the second floor where a mirror hangs from the wall facing the rest rooms. This is not a kind energy according to the psychics and she is confined to the mirror, to keep her in check. She is responsible for odd smells and closing doors on this floor. Her energy is being held in check by the other energy in the building that will not allow her to harm others. She told the psychic that a mirror has two sides; the

Spirit drawings made by former restaurant manager, Mariah Shaw based on psychic descriptions.

41

back side leading into the woman's bathroom. So, people should take note if unexplainable things happen in the bathroom area. She may be responsible for the feeling of imbalance some of us felt going up the stairs from the first, to the second floor and on the landing and entry into the second floor dining area.

7. There is quite a bit of imprinted or passive energy on the second floor of the restaurant. It is a place where numerous energies still call home. There are hints of partying, gambling, a brothel, card games, sounds of music, shadowy figures, strong fluctuations in the energy fields, and movement of objects from 1900-1940s. Whatever is playing out in this area is strong and manifests frequently. This is the heart of the building, and with the books, spoon collection, animal heads, and other artifacts, it contains a flowing, constantly changing, atmosphere that makes it a very lively, after hour spot. The energy on this floor is vastly different, than the first and third floors. This area had by far, the highest EMF readings of anywhere in the building except Table #41 on the third floor.

8. There is a strong, unidentified energy near the server's station on the second floor. This active energy field will not hesitate to contact people. It is seen as a shadow and will also speak, as we heard "Get out" when we entered the area near the screen that leads to the back servers station. The energy seems to feel that the area belongs to it, and is reluctant to share the space. This force isn't always there for some reason; consider it like a cranky relative who comes to visit and expects to be treated like royalty when he/she arrives! The bark is worse than the bite in this case.

9. The energy of the place hits an in tuned person from the moment they set eyes on the building and set onto the parking area. This is very active, flowing energy; some of which comes and goes with the change in weather, time of the year and other elemental fluctuations. The energy is stronger during some periods than others. There is little doubt that late and night and early in the morning, this place rocks. Also,

Huge orb above the two investigators (Courtesy of the San Diego Ghost Hunters)

the less people inside, the more you are able to notice the slight nuances of each spirit and the personality each room exudes. The first floor is the greeting area, the grounding energy for the place. The second floor is the heart of the building where the activity is the strongest. The third floor is the cerebral portion of the place where the quieter and more relaxed energy waits. It's almost like a therapy room compared to the other places in the building.

The investigators were able to capture voices on tape (EVP); record orbs and strange balls of light shoot through the restaurant; smell perfume, alcohol and tobacco smoke; hear voices and footsteps in unoccupied areas of the restaurant; had a chair inexplicably pushed out from a third floor table; witness shadowy figures, and have a napkin resting on a table end up on a chair, tied in a pattern resembling a dove that illustrated in a nearby painting. In addition, the EMF meters picked up numerous anomalies and sudden drops in temperature (5-10 degrees) on the second floor. There was so much paranormal activity taking place throughout the building that it was difficult to focus on a specific area. Just when you settled into on location and began taking readings, you would hear a knocking sound coming from somewhere else or another investigator call for assistance.

At the Saddle Peak Lodge, you get the very best in haunt cuisine. The ambience is unrivaled, the food impeccable, the wine list is to die for, and the spirits are plentiful. Who wouldn't want to haunt this incredible lodge where dinner and spirits is taken to the next level?

Mist on first floor (Courtesy of the International Paranormal Research Organization (IPRO)

Orb in the middle of the room (Courtesy of the International Paranormal Research Organization (IPRO)

Orbs on the stairs (Courtesy of the International Paranormal Research Organization (IPRO)

Sagebrush Cantina

Particulars
23527 Calabasas Road,
Calabasas, CA 91302-1367
Phone: 818-222-6062
Website: www.sagebrush.com

History
Calabasas was once a part of Mission San Fernando situated along the famous El Camino Real. The restaurant lies next to the haunted 1840s historic landmark, the Leonis Adobe. Calabasas was once a stop on the Flint, Bixby and Butterfield coastal stage line route. During its formative years, Calabasas was known as one of the toughest and wildest spots in California. A dance hall and a saloon stood on the south side of the Calabasas jail.

Alongside the jail was the famous hangman's tree. The oak that grew beside the former Kramer store, according to old-timers, was used for expeditious frontier justice. What is now the Sagebrush Cantina was originally a group of small stores built by Lester Agoure, Sr. in the early 1920's. The parking lot once was the local jail. Outside was the famous hanging tree, dead, but still standing today. It is the identifying logo of the Calabasas Chamber of Commerce.

Old Jail circa 1902 (Courtesy of the Leonis Adobe Museum, Calabasas)

Hauntspitality
Over the years, at least four spirits have been reported by staff and patrons, and they are not the drinks served at the bar. One phantom lady, two phantom gentlemen and a young boy have been sighted inside the building since 1974. Of course, the history of the area dates back to the time when the Gabrielino and Chumash occupied the area. Historically, the Leonis Adobe, which lies adjacent and to the west of the current Sagebrush Cantina, occupied the grounds on which the restaurant now stands. It wasn't until the 1920s that local landowner Lester Agoure Sr. constructed a series of stores on the restaurant land. In addition, the parking lot was the site of the Calabasas jail and the famous hanging tree, a local landmark once stood proudly on the Sagebrush property. It's only a remnant of its former self, but even in death, it stands as a grim reminder of the days when Calabasas was a notoriously rowdy town. Perhaps the spirits at the Cantina are tied (so to speak) to the earth, remaining in the area where they lived and died. Although the landscape has changed since the 1800s-early 1900s, the ghosts continue to make their rounds inside the building. One phantom gentleman has

been described as a cowboy-type, gruff looking and wearing western garb. He is sometimes spotted near the bar and kitchen area, standing around for a few heartbeats before vanishing into the walls.

A second spirit is that of a woman in her 40s, who may be tied to one of early stores that once occupied the grounds. She is seen wearing

Kramer Store (Courtesy of the Leonis Adobe Museum, Calabasas)

period clothing, including a bib or shawl. She materializes in the back portion of the building near the women's bathroom before vanishing. A third spirit reportedly belongs to either a bus boy or cook.

Psychics who visited the building sensed a young man who worked in the building but who may have died elsewhere, comes to visit and check up on things. More of a transient energy, he apparently hangs around the kitchen and back seating area. Another spirit may be a young boy who appears to be (according to psychics) from the late 1880s-early 1900s and may be associated with another building that once occupied the property.

Orb near the ceiling of the bar to the left of the post (courtesy of the International Paranormal Research Organization –IPRO)

There are frequent cold spots on warm days that suddenly manifest and times when objects have been known to move on their own. The door to the kitchen sometimes has a mind of its own and will suddenly swing open. Glasses on the bar have been known to move by themselves and sometimes staff report seeing people out of the corner of their eye. When they look, no one is there. The back portion of the building where there is seating and bathrooms appears to be the focal point for much of the activity as well as the kitchen and bar areas.

Orb on the ceiling in the bathroom area (Courtesy of the International Paranormal Research Organization (IPRO

There's nothing negative about the experiences, it's just that several spirits have chosen to remain behind and enjoy the spirited, party atmosphere of the Sagebrush.

Large orb on table in the center of the picture (Courtesy of the International Paranormal Research Organization - IPRO)

45

Calistoga
The Elms

Particulars
1300 Cedar Street,
Calistoga, CA 94515
Phone: 707-942-9476
Fax: 707-942-9479
Toll Free: 888-399-3567
E-mail: info@theelms.com
Website: www.theelms.com

History

A.C. Palmer, the first circuit judge in the area, built the house in 1871. Palmer and his bride went to Europe on their honeymoon. While in France, they picked up the seedlings to the French Elm trees, then came home and built the French style Victorian. The Elm trees are now the tallest and oldest elms in the Napa Valley. There were originally eight "great" Victorian houses built in Calistoga; the Elms is the last one standing today.

Hauntspitality

The owners assume that a couple of their spirits are A.C. Palmer and his wife. Recently, a female guest who grew up in an English Tudor home came to visit the Elms. She reportedly told the owners that ever since she was a little girl, she could "see ghosts." Friday night while she was sleeping, she awoke to a woman kneeling next to the side of the bed, sitting face-to-face as the guest was on her side. She woke up, looked at the ghost, and the ghost said "get out!". The guest said that the woman's name is Ruby, and that she used to be a servant at this house. The guest was staying in the carriage house in a room that was added to the property about ten years ago. The owner asked her why the ghost would be out there, and she said that there was probably some sort of servant's quarters on that area of the lot at one point and that's where Ruby lived. The guest said she could tell Ruby was a servant by what she was wearing. She only knew her name because she could "sense it," not because she was told the name. The guest also said that she felt other spirits in the main house, but didn't run across them on her visit,

There is a room on the third floor of the house called "Blithe Spirit", and since the owner has been there, she has always felt like someone or something is in the room. One day one the maids was vacuuming that room, and the vacuum turned off. The maid walked over to the wall to check the plug, and the vacuum came back on. This happened three times. Finally, the maid yelled (in Spanish) "Please let me finish! I have guests coming to check in!" at which point the vacuum remained on for the duration of her work. The owners spoke to a woman who owned the place back in 1992, but the woman would only say that she had also always heard that the Blithe Spirit room was haunted, but had no specific stories to share.

La Chambre, which is the original master bedroom of the house, has had two incidents occur since September 2001. One-night guests were sleeping in there and the overhead light came on by itself. One of the owners was sleeping in there in early November, and the same thing happened to her. Again in mid-November, one of the owner's was in the house, alone on the third floor. As she came down the stairs, she could hear running water. She proceeded to walk into La Chambre, and the faucet in the sink was turned on. No one had stayed in that room for two days.

If there are any questions about whether friendly spirits haunt this establishment they can be put to rest. Come visit and you may get a glimpse of the past in the form

Carmel-by-the-Sea
La Playa Hotel and Cottages by the Sea

Particulars

P.O. Box 900, Camino Real at Eighth Avenue,
Carmel, CA 93921
Phone: 831-624-6476
Fax: 831-624-7966
Toll Free: 800-582-8900
E-mail: info@laplayahotel.com I Website: www.laplayahotel.com

History

The original building, a part of which still stands today, had a star-shaped stained glass window facing the street, and steps leading to a non-existent bell tower, a facet inspired by the early missions.

Surrounding the building were potato fields that have long since vanished. A commanding view of the countryside that still exists today brought guests from all over the country to this magical retreat.

The following historical tid-bits are provided by the hotel Website: 1905-The original building was designed in 1905 by artist Christopher Jorgensen as a luxurious home for his bride, a member of San Francisco's famous Ghirardelli chocolate clan;

1   1906-After a few years, however, the Jorgensen's chose to leave Carmel and leased their former home to Agnes "Alice" Signor;

2   1920's-La Playa remained in the Signor family many years, adopted by the sons of Alice's favored niece - Harrison and Fred Godwin;

3   1930's-In those days, La Playa guests would frequently arrive by train in Monterey, to be met by Fred Godwin with a pickup truck large enough to transport the steamer trunks filled with enough clothing for a six-week visiit.

4   1940's-While Carmel grew up around the property -- streets becoming paved, more houses being built -- the Godwin's continued to expand the hotel;

5   1952-Godwin leased La Playa to Ashton Stanley, son of Carl Stanley of California Hotel fame and a successful hotelier in his own right;

6   1968-Howard E. Bud Allen, who had known the hotel as a child growing up in Carmel, had his eye on the Grande Dame for years before he purchased it in 1968;

7   1983-when the Cope family of San Francisco bought La Playa, the hotel had become somewhat run-down. The original mansion from which this time-honored Carmel luxury hotel had evolved was connected to a second building. The second building was constructed in the 1920's and housed most of the guestrooms. A two-level brick patio was installed and its wrought-iron gazebo replaced with a larger one. The surrounding gardens and landscaping were upgraded, expanded and replanted. The guestrooms of this classic Carmel-by-the-Sea hotel were repainted and refurbished to complement the stunning views of the ocean, garden, patio and residential Carmel. Many pieces from the Cope family collection of European antiques, artwork and California memorabilia were imported to enhance the property's decor. La Playa reopened on July 15, 1984.

8   The Cope Family has owned this unique property since May 1989, at which time a major renovation of the cottages and the gardens took place. It is now like a brand-new facility with the same old-fashion charm.

Hauntspitality

Rumor has it that the famous La Playa Hotel is haunted by Christopher Jorgensen's wife, Angela Ghirardelli, a member of San Francisco's famous Ghirardelli chocolate clan. Jorgensen built the stunning house for her. Angela supposedly drowned in the nearby waters shortly after moving in to her new home, and her restless spirit is said to still wander the hotel grounds, a place she loved so much in life.

Other permutations describe the phantom as Angela's cousin as the unfortunate victim of a watery death. An interesting observation that may add credibility to the rumor that it was Angela, who fell victim to a watery death, is the fact that Jorgensen left the house after living there only a few years. Jorgensen leased his home to Agnes "Alice" Signor. The Signor family continued to occupy the house for many years.

A phantom woman has been occasionally spotted on the hotel grounds, before suddenly vanishing in front of startled witnesses. Is this the spirit of Angela Jorgensen, who is forever tied to the house that her husband built just for her? Did Angela or another, as yet unidentified woman drown near the hotel? Historic research may eventually provide some answers to this riddle.

Another question also remains to be answered; Are there more spirits associated with this historic hotel other than Angela Ghirardelli? Some sensitive individuals, including psychics who have visited the hotel, also sensed the presence of a male energy from the Prohibition era that has been sighted in the older portion of the building. His apparition is rare, yet he has not only been sighted, but felt as a gust of cold air and the smell of tobacco.

There are also disembodied sounds of children playing, the smell of sweet perfume, an occasional door that will open and shut on its own and the fact that several psychics sensed a strong female presence with the letter "A" attached to the place. Could this be Angela or Agnes?

Time, research and additional investigations may provide the key to unraveling the mystery regarding the spirited clientele in this amazing resort. Even if you don't see of feel a spirit here, your stay will be heavenly.

Catalina Island
The Burning House Lodge

Particulars
P.O. Box 2530,
Two Harbors, CA 90704-2530
Phone: 310-510-2800
Fax: 310-510-1354
Website: www.catalina.com/banning

History

With breathtaking views of the Isthmus Cove and Cat Harbor, the Banning House Lodge gives its guests access to all the activities and facilities in the island village of Two Harbors. The Banning House, completed about 1910, was used as a family summer home by the children and grandchildren of pioneer Phineas Banning until 1919.

At this time, Santa Catalina Island was purchased by William Wrigley. Jr. From the 1920's until the start of World War II, the Banning House was used as a hotel for the stars and celebrities filming on location for the movies shot at the Isthmus. Wallace Beery, Clark Gable, Charles Laughton and Dorothy Lamour are but a few of the famous people that have stayed here.

Joseph Brent

In 1987, the Banning House was restored to its former rustic charm. Today, the Banning House Lodge offers eleven rooms, each with private bath. Oak and brass fixtures, antique accents and rooms individually decorated, give the Banning House Lodge turn-of-the-century charm. There are also rumors that this famous lodge caters to an after-life clientele who refuse to budge from the comfortable surroundings and heavenly view.

William Banning

Hauntspitality

Along with the Rinehart House, and the Civil War Barracks the Banning House is another haunted location within the confines of the Isthmus Cove.

The structure is built on an archaeological site that dates back at least 1,000 years and is related to the Gabrielino Indians who

Hancock Banning

worshipped at the Isthmus. There have been frequent sightings of an elderly gentleman reported in the recreation room that contains a fireplace and stairway to a second floor observation area. The accounts of this spectral gentleman are all similar. The apparition is of a man in his 40s-50s who wears an overcoat, hat and sports a beard has been witnessed walking up the stairs or standing near the large window directly across from the fireplace. The man seems to be gazing out toward Cat Harbor and has been described as a "fisherman" or "sailor"; someone who looks as if he is heading out to sea, or wishing he was already there. Another man has also been sighted walking slowly down the corridor that leads to the recreation room, on a repetitious, otherworldly journey.

There have also been reports of cold spots that materialize out of nowhere

From Left to right
Wallace Beery, Clark
Gable, Charles Laughton
and Dorothy Lamour

and just as quickly dissipate. Guests and staff have reported a strong "tobacco odor" whenever the ghostly presence is around, or about to manifest. Unexplained footsteps have also been frequently heard late at night or early in the morning, climbing up or down the staircase, or pacing outside some of the guestrooms. This male ghost may also be responsible for haunting several of the rooms at this hostelry, as if checking in on the clientele.

One guest was awakened in the middle of the night to the sound of numerous people talking and laughing outside her cottage door. Since it was around three in the morning, she was tired and in no mood for noisy guests carrying on at that hour. She put on her robe, got up and opened the door to her cottage. She was ready to let the boisterous group have a piece of her mind. As soon as she stepped out the door, the calamity ceased. She peered into the darkness, looked around, listened and waited for the noisy neighbors to show themselves. There was absolute silence. She shook her head, went back to bed and within a few minutes the noisy neighbors began again. She quickly jumped out of bed, without her robe, hoping to catch the group before they disappeared. Upon opening the door, the noise immediately ceased. Frustrated, she yelled out into the darkness to please be quite and let her sleep. She slept the rest of the night without incident.

On another occasion, a couple staying in one of the rooms that line the main corridor heard a couple of people talking outside of their room late at night. Their room faced the courtyard and when they peered out, they could see two men standing near the rock-lined wall in a heated discussion. The odd thing was, that the men were dressed in clothing (suits to be exact) from the early 1900s and smoking cigars. As they looked at each other, as if to say, "Are you seeing what I'm seeing" they turned back toward the scene and the men had vanished. They were looking at an empty courtyard. The next day, they asked if any gentlemen fitting their description were staying at the lodge. The reply was matter-of-fact. Their description of the men fit two of the Banning Brothers perfectly (the men resembled photographs of Joseph Brent and William Banning). The Bannings used this as a summer home when they came to the island, and the brothers would love to stand outside and talk well into the night. The other brother, Hancock Banning and his family had a house at Descanso Beach outside of Avalon.

While filming the documentary, "Catalina Island Treasures of the Past", on the island in the mid-1980s, the crew was housed at the lodge. On at least two occasions, there were instances of cast and crew hearing phantom footsteps ascending the stairs to the observation level in the recreational lounge. One person witnessed a middle-age man standing near the window, looking out before vanishing. There were also reports of tobacco and perfume smells wafting through some of the rooms, although no one smoked or was wearing that particular lilac scent. There were also reports of phantom people talking outside their rooms between one and three in the morning and a young woman who was standing in front of one of the guest beds for a few beats, before vanishing.

The International Paranormal Research Organization (IPRO) performed a preliminary investigation of the lodge and came away with high EMF readings in the kitchen area, rooms 6 and 10, in the recreation/lounge area by the fireplace and impressions of at least five strong energies,

Early photographs of the Civil War barracks (courtesy of the Santa Catalina Island Company)

primarily related to the Banning family. Since the Banning family owned the island and used the building as a summer home they would have left a strong imprint on the landscape. Perhaps a brother or two chose to remain at the place they cherished in life.

Recent reports also suggest a feminine presence that frequents the building. Psychics who have visited the lodge sense a betrayal or tryst that took place involving the Bannings. The female they sensed was young, with curly short hair and the initial "K". Could this be Katharine Stewart Banning who was married to Joseph Brent (and his first cousin) and shares the house with the ghostly sailor or fisherman. Guests also report smelling women's perfume, or hearing what they refer to as a long dress rustling in the corridor, although they don't see anyone when this occurs. Sometimes a female voice can be heard calling out a name along the darkened corridors and in some of the rooms. She has never been sighted; at least not yet!

Maybe with time and a paranormal investigation the identities of the spirits of this historic lodge and unforgettable vacation destination will materialize. The spirited population in this building is extremely friendly and non-threatening. The energy in this place is playful and for the most part, happy. This was a retreat for those who came to visit over the years; and it remains that way to this day. Those who stay are welcomed not only by the current staff but also by the prior owners and guests who still love to call this place home in the afterlife.

Early photographs of the Isthmus Cove (courtesy of the Santa Catalina Island Company)

The Catalina Beach House Hotel

Particulars
200 Marilla Avenue, P.O. Box 64,
Avalon, CA 90704
Phone: 310-510-1078
Fax: 310-510-1573
Toll Free: 1-800-974-6835

History
Constructed originally in the late 1880s, history reports that Captain Joseph McAfee sailed his flat-bottom houseboat from Venice Beach to Santa Catalina Island in the early 1900s, with the intention of making Avalon his home. The Captain purchased a parcel of land with a wonderful view of the bay. Maintaining a strong attachment to his houseboat, as well as the desire to have a home overlooking the bay, Captain McAfee devised an ingenious plan to haul his houseboat up the hillside to his newly acquired property. Using only horses, logs, ropes and sheer determination, the Captain and a group of friends hoisted the boat inch by inch up the dusty road to its new location. Captain McAfee's houseboat was now referred to by one and all as "the Captain's Beach House."

Captain McAfee loved the sea, and came up with a clever idea that would enhance his income. He was fascinated by the unusual sight of flying fish leaping gracefully above the ocean's surface, so he built and operated the island's first Flying Fish boat, the *Catalina Flyer*, and began taking out passengers on nightly excursions along the Catalina coastline. The boat was equipped with a powerful searchlight that would attract and capture the beauty of these unique fish in its hypnotic beam. As the years passed, the enterprising Captain added rooms to take advantage of the booming tourist trade. These rooms were attached to the original houseboat and tiered down the hillside. The houseboat hotel initially was known as the Driftwood Inn, but was renamed in the early 1960s the Catalina Beach House Hotel.

Hauntspitality
According to owner Diane Boultinghouse, she always felt a strong attachment to the place. When she came over to the Island in the early 1980s to visit, she made friends with the owners. She and her husband eventually purchased the hotel from them, when they retired, along with the ghost of the deceased Captain, who was still watching over his house. Boultinghouse said that as soon as the family moved in, strange things began to happen in the area where Captain McAfee was said to have died. According to various sources on the Island, although still in the prime of his life, the Captain suddenly passed away in the back of the house on the upper deck.

When Boultinghouse first moved into the place in December of 1986, she and her brother-in-law, who also lives at the Beach House, both felt the presence of something in the room. In Room #2 below the hotel entrance, the lights would turn themselves on for no apparent reason. Several times when everything would be turned off, and the room secured, the electricity managed to be turned back on. In addition, the doors would open on their own. Other times, Boultinghouse would be sleeping in the room where the Captain slept, and would hear someone walking around the room at night. The floor boards would creak, but she was always too frightened to get up and investigate. She had heard the stories of the ghostly presence, and reasoned it might be the Captain. Fear played a big part in her choice to remain snugly tucked in bed, while the ghost was free to wander around. Sooner or later she would either fall asleep, or the noises would subside.

There were also a couple of occasions during the first year or two when Boultinghouse actually felt the Captain's presence in the room, sitting on the edge of her bed. Too frightened to attempt communication, she waited nervously until she was convinced the presence had gone. Her intuition told her that the Captain meant her no harm; he was just checking up on the new owners, ensuring that they were going to take care of the house he had spent his life building.

Boultinghouse claimed that the ghost actually helped her and her husband when they attempted to buy the building. She wanted the building the first time she saw it; however, there were a lot of stumbling blocks to overcome. They were young, had never owned a hotel, and would have to put a lot of money into the property. Diane felt that as long as they had the Captain's best intentions at heart, he would approve of their ownership, a process that transpired without a hitch.

The Captain's presence was felt frequently during the winter months, when Avalon was quiet. When the summer came, and with it a hectic parade of visitors, the Captain seemed to disappear; however, Boultinghouse and her brother-in-law had strong sensations that the ghostly Captain was never far away from his beloved creation. The entity was less mischievous than other ghosts they had heard stories about, and Boultinghouse could not remember a time where objects were thrown, or someone felt the least bit threatened. The Captain was always courteous to visitors, although a little unnerving at times.

A woman named Ruth, who lived in the Hotel in the middle 1960s, visited with Diane and confirmed Captain McAfee's presence. She shared several interesting tales about the Captain's ghost, haunting the houseboat. Her most vivid recollections centered on the room above where she stayed (where Diane's encounters occurred). Also, there was the usual assortment of mysterious lights and sounds that occurred at night.

The Beach House still caters to tourists while still keeping the welcome mat out for its original owner, Captain McAfee, just in case he returns from an otherworldly fishing excursion.

Clubhouse Bar & Grille

Particulars
1 Country Club Drive,
Avalon, CA 90704
Phone: 310-510-7404
310-510-7400 ext.12 for meetings & banquets
Website: www.scico.com/cirs/mainclub.html
menus at: www.menu4u.com

History

Following the lines of Early California architecture, the Country Club House consisted of a cloistered patio, fountain and gardens of tropical plants. The structure was originally intended to service the patrons of the golf course, and the clubhouse dominates a pitch-and-putt green. It was also used as a temporary facility for the Chicago Cubs while they trained on Catalina, and a restaurant/sports bar. The structure was built between 1927 and 1929, over the original Country Club House that was constructed in 1894.

William Wrigley, Jr. brought the Chicago Cubs to the island for spring training in 1921, an event that brought the team and a legion of writers and followers from the east, to Catalina for 26 seasons. The writers were as fascinated with the charm and beauty of the island as with their team. The Cubs personnel used a portion of the Club for lockers and training facilities while staying at another facility on the Island. Rogers Hornsby, Joe McCarthy, Gabby Hartnett and Charlie Grimm were a few of the notable ballplayers who managed the team over the years the prepared on the island.

Several individuals operated the Country Club over the years, and a wine cellar was built for the restaurant. Closing down for periods of time, Morand reopened the club in 1989. He retained the original name for the restaurant, but renamed the lower dining room the Palms Room, while the upper patio level bar was called Silky's Sports Bar after the beloved golf pro, Silky Reyes. The building has recently been retrofitted and restored by Paxson Offield Enterprises, and is once again a beautiful dining spot for islanders and tourists alike.

Chicago Cubs training facility (courtesy of the Santa Catalina Island Company)

Hauntspitality

When the Cubs finally ceased their spring training activities, going elsewhere to train, they appeared to have left someone behind---perhaps a player or coach who continues to visit the spring training facilities at the County Club. Additionally, discussions with several individuals, including former operator Dudley Morand, indicate that there may be several spirits who haunt the recently restored building.

One evening, Morand was closing up what was then called Silky's Sports Bar, which was part of the Country Club that also served golfers. It was approximately 11:00 p.m., and his last nightly duty entailed taking out the trash. Exiting onto the patio area, something caught his attention. Out of the corner of his eye, he noticed movement in the darkness. Pausing, he watched as an indistinguishable figure emerged out of the shadows and slowly came toward him. Still clinging to the trash bin, he focused for a moment, thinking it might be an intruder. Even though he had locked all the access doors to the patio area, there were still times when people climbed the fence to sneak in. He assumed that this was one of those rare occasions, and prepared for a confrontation. That's when Morand realized that this was no ordinary intruder, but a tall, thin man dressed in a baseball uniform and cap. Any person walking in a baseball uniform at that hour would have been unusual in itself, but this person was wearing a uniform seemingly from the 1930s.

Interior courtyard (Courtesy of the Santa Catalina Island Company)

Dumbstruck, Morand watched the uniform-clad figure move diagonally across the courtyard toward another dining room area on the other side of the patio. Still thinking it could be some kind of prank, he lowered the trash can, and taking his eyes off the man for a few seconds to move the trash can into the doorway. When Morand looked up, the figure had vanished. He wondered how someone could have disappeared so quickly. He later noticed the strange- looking man walking toward an adjacent dining room area, so he went back there, reasoning that he had to get the man out before he could go home. Morand recalled that the man seemed in no hurry while sauntering through the patio area. Practical joke or not, he gave chase, pursuing the elusive stranger into the adjacent building, formerly a banquet room. The door was unlocked as he approached the entrance.

By the time Morand entered the building and turned on the electricity, he was a bit apprehensive. Was someone hiding inside trying to scare him? Perhaps it

Area where the spirit of a baseball player was sighted (courtesy of the Santa Catalina Island Company)

was it something else that made him feel uneasy. His desire to get home overcame his anxiety and fear, and he followed the only path the man could have taken into the building. He thoroughly searched every room and corridor---there was no other way in or out of the building, and all the windows were locked from the inside. It began to sink in that what he saw may not have been a prankster or intruder, but something else entirely---a ghost. A sweep of the building revealed no one inside. Whoever, or whatever it was, had vanished. Morand wasted little time in locking up and leaving the premises.

Employee Alphonso Hernandez had a frightening encounter of his own in the basement while working for Morand. Morand had sent Hernandez to the basement to get a few things for a party that was being held in the main area of the clubhouse. After a few minutes, Hernandez, ran up from the basement, white as a sheet, eyes as big as saucers, shouting that there was something down in the basement, and he would not go back down there alone. It was an extremely hectic time, and this news didn't sit well with Morand. Between Morand's limited Spanish and Hernandez's "Spanglish," Morand understood that something unusual had taken place in the basement---something that prevented Hernandez from going downstairs again. Unfortunately Morand didn't have time to deal with his employee's fears. The immediacy of the dinner party required that they immediately obtain the necessary items from the basement. Morand convinced a reluctant Hernandez to return to the basement with him and another employee.

The three men quickly made their way to the basement, which had once served as the boiler room, and obtained what they needed. Hernandez was constantly looking around for whatever had frightened him, but the other men saw nothing as they gathered party items. Hernandez never forgot the incident and never returned to the basement alone---it seems that what Hernandez experienced, was not his imagination. Hernandez's father worked for the previous owner and would sometimes spend the night on a cot in the building. The elder Hernandez related many strange tales about securing the building, and finding doors open after being locked for the evening, lights turned on after they had been turned off, cold spots, shadows, and a sensation of being watched. The elder Hernandez knew the place was haunted.

The authors also had a strange experience at the Country Club. While in the kitchen area of the complex, discussing the baseball player sighting with Morand, they were accompanied by Morand's two-year-old son Alex and daughter Alicia in July 1995. While walking through the structure containing Silky's bar, as Morand explained the history, everyone walked through the kitchen area. Mid-way through, Alex, who had been very quiet, began crying without cause. The room was musty, with its share of cobwebs and darkened areas, and as everyone passed through the kitchen, Alicia began to feel a little uneasy, and Alex cried until the group entered another room. At that point, the boy's demeanor completely changed, and he smiled once again. Morand said his son rarely cried like that. The incident was summarily dismissed, and the personalized tour continued into what used to be the main dining room.

While attempting to reach the lower level of the building where Hernandez had his encounter, the lights wouldn't turn on (was it a breaker gone awry?). Since we didn't have a flashlight, we were out of luck. As everyone proceeded back through the kitchen area, Alex began crying at the exact same spot that he had earlier upon entering the room. This time, everyone got the chills, and felt uneasy, as if some unseen person were watching the light. With that, the group scurried to reach the light of day, and Alex stopped crying immediately. Everyone was more than curious about what Alex was able to see that the others in the group could not.

As an experiment, using Alex as kind of "ghost-hunter," everyone prepared himself or herself for a third walk through. As co-author Rob Wlodarski stood with his back to the kitchen, facing Morand, Alex, and the other co-author, Anne Wlodarski, the expression on Alex's face changed from contentment to what can only be described as terror in a matter of a heartbeat. He began wailing as if he were looking at someone or something that would have been standing right in back of Rob Wlodarski. That was enough for the group as they left the building post-haste! Once outside, Morand locked up the former bar, and Alex regained his smile. What had Alex witnessed in the kitchen? Morand believed that the haunted areas of the building were used as locker rooms for the Chicago Cub's players. He also speculated that over the years, perhaps a few people died and returned to a place that brought them much pleasure, or perhaps to play an extra paranormal inning! Although the spirits still appear to be restless at the Clubhouse Bar and Grille, they are playful, and won't bother you while dining at this beautiful restaurant.

The Glenmore Plaza Hotel

Particulars

120 Sumner Avenue,
Avalon, CA 91304
Phone: 310-510-0017 | Fax: 310-510-2833
Toll Free: 1-800-422-8254
E-mail: glenmore@glenmorehotel.com
Website: www.glenmorehotel.com

History

The Glenmore Plaza Hotel has been around since the 1890s. It has beckoned visitors from the mainland for over one hundred years with its beauty and charm; a reminder of a bygone era. Clark Gable slept there, Theodore Roosevelt told stories in the garden courtyard, and Amelia Earhart enjoyed the ocean panorama from the hotel's cupola.

The hotel, which is four stories high, has undergone renovation over the years, yet through it all, has managed to retain it's charm. In fact, there are still some of the older rooms available for tourists to rent. The older rooms do not date back to the original hotel, since the fire of 1915 destroyed them. However there are some rooms that date back to the period right after the Hotel was rebuilt. Essentially, the existing Hotel was constructed over the remains of the original Glenmore Hotel.

Hauntspitality

Former employee, Michael Gruber, recalls working at the hotel. Not all of his routines were what one might consider normal, and they definitely weren't dull. According to Gruber and others, the most haunted parts of the Hotel are the lobby area, which contains a comedy club, and certain areas on the upper floor. There are some rooms which are more haunted than others, including Room 17, and Room 401. Room 401, the largest room, is named after Clark Gable often stayed there when visiting the island.

Guests who have stayed in some of the rooms, have reported smelling smoke and insisting that a fire was taking place next-door to their room. Calls to the fire department always resulted in false alarms. Across the street from the Glenmore, numerous witnesses swore that smoke and flames were coming from the upper rooms of the Glenmore. Each time there was an investigation, nothing was found; not even a hint that a match had been lit. Perhaps this is a psychic imprint from the devastating 1915 fire that is replaying itself over and over for a select few who may be sensitive or attuned to psychic phenomena.

Gruber recalled an incident in 1994 while working behind the front desk. As a night clerk, he would sometimes hear the sounds of the Comedy Club in full swing. The club is a wall away from the front desk. One night, as a comedian entertained, several of the audience rushed into the lobby and looked around as if they were searching for someone. When Gruber asked if he could help, they wanted to know if there was a door in the wall behind the stage in the club.

They went on to explain that several members of the audience had seen the figure of a strange, almost transparent man standing behind the performer. Shortly after the figure disappeared behind the curtain, which is used as a backdrop against a wall (not a normal curtained stage) the group came rushing into the lobby in search of the strange looking man, thinking the curtain area led to the lobby. When Gruber showed them that a wall separated the stage from the lobby, they were completely baffled. How could the man have simply vanished into thin air in front of a captive audience; unless, of course, he was a ghost?

On another occasion, Gruber was finished with his shift, and watching a routine in the adjacent comedy club, when something unusual happened, as the comedian was using a small pocket- size flashlight in his act. As soon as the comedian raised the light, and turned it on, all the lights in the club instantly went out. The startled performer and the patrons wondered what was happening. When he lowered the flashlight, all the lights went back on. The performer jokingly remarked that he had his own remote control device; this occurred several times before the lights stayed on for good. No one had been standing in the area of where the lights were regulated, and no one could understand "what" was responsible for making the lights go off and on, only during that portion of the show; a ghostly performance, perhaps?

Late one Sunday night while Gruber was stationed behind the front desk, guests called to complain about a noisy party taking place in an adjoining room; Room 17. It was wintertime, and the Hotel was usually quiet. The impatient guests had come to get away from it all, and they were in no mood to tolerate a loud party. Gruber first attempted to call Room 17. When this proved unsuccessful, he went up to room 17, to see what he could do about quieting the boisterous guests. Reaching the second floor room, he heard loud noises coming from the room. As he knocked on the door, the noise immediately ceased inside. Curious, he tried to enter with his passkey, but noticed that another key had broken off in the door. There was no way to extract the broken key, and no one came to the door, so he rushed back down to the main desk.

Reaching the lobby, Gruber told a clerk and the night manager what had happened. Realizing that the room was listed as unoccupied, both men immediately reached the conclusion, that some kids had managed to break into the room to party. Gruber and the night manager rushed upstairs to check on the condition of the room. When they arrived, there was no broken key in the door. Gruber swore that a key had been jammed in the keyhole preventing his entrance; that guests had complained of loud noises; and that he heard noise coming from inside, but no one would come to the door when he knocked. When both men entered the room, there was no sign of a party, or that anyone had ever been in the room. It was immaculate, looking as if the maids had just cleaned it. Gruber knew what he had seen and heard, The night manager was doubtful, until the guests confirmed the commotion next door. No one could figure out what had happened, unless it was a ghost party!

The history of this hotel is steeped in romance and tragedy. This is evidenced by the long list of movie stars that have graced its rooms as well as the pre-dawn fire of 1915 that swept through Avalon destroying most of the establishments. There is also the unsettling fact that the hotel is situated on the spot of a former Native American village. Although the hotel has been extensively upgraded, the charm and mystery of a bygone era are still indelibly imprinted on the Glenmore. Only a chosen few are allowed to experience the paranormal events that manifest from time to time in various parts of the hotel---maybe your visit to this historic hotel will conjure up some spirits. At the very least you will certainly have a truly unforgettable stay.

Hotel Catalina

Particulars
129 Whittley Avenue, P.O. Box 365,
Avalon, CA 90704
Phone: 310-510-0027
Fax: 310-510-1495
Toll Free: 1-800-540-0184

History
The following information was provided by Sherrie Walker of the **Catalina Islander** (from a story by Antoinette Teglovic). The Hotel Catalina was one of the first hotels on the island. Dating back to 1898, it was destroyed by the pre-dawn fire of November 29, 1915. The owner at the time, William H. Gill, vowed that his hotel would be the first to be reconstructed after the fire. True to his word, and with the help of the Milwaukee Building Company, the Hotel Catalina reopened on June 16, 1916. Two years later, and with an eye toward the continuing growth of the Island, the Hotel was closed for three months of renovation.

When the Hotel reopened on April 4, 1918, there was an enlarged lobby, an added wing and the now- familiar sign on top. With room rates listed at $3.50, the Catalina was advertised as the only hotel with hot and cold running water and steam heat in every room. John Windle, a long-time local resident, remembers his first job as a water delivery boy for the hotel. His weekly task was to carry five-gallon jars up to the roof to the tank that provided running water. The job required 40 trips to fill the tank. In 1918, Gill expanded the hotel with the acquisition of the lot on the ocean side of the property where a hot tub currently exists.

Hauntspitality
Servicing the rich and famous from the mainland, the century old hotel attracted its share of psychic energy. Prior employees and managers discuss a variety of unexplainable occurrences over the years. In particular, cottages C and D have had distinctive events, which continue to occur with regularity, particularly during the winter months. The cottage with a kitchen is the host to friendly spirits who seem content to focus around the area of the table and chairs. Several guests have reported hearing the table and chairs being moved across the floor, when no one else was present. It's as if mealtime may have been important to ghostly visitors. Although it's a little unnerving at first, most of the live folks just let their ghost guests "do their thing" for the duration of their stay.

According to other guests, the small cottage closest to the hot tub has had other mysterious things happen. There have been times when the cottage doors opened and closed on their own, much to the surprise of the cleaning and maintenance personnel.

Several guests, though not frightened, have reported that the bathroom has been visited by friendly spirits who play tricks by turning the lights on and off after first using the toilet and the faucets---Evidently the spirit world also has its standards for cleanliness. This type of pattern is seen frequently in other

hauntings. The benign spirit or spirits seem to enjoy playing with the electricity and water in the cottage---then vanish.

In the main hotel area, several guests have stated that winter is the most active period for haunting activity to manifest. Although no one has actually seen a ghost at the hotel, there are constant sounds of disembodied footsteps, doors opening and closing by unseen hands, and lights that have a mind of their own, which turn themselves on and off during off-season when few guests are staying at the hotel. This is especially true on the second floor near the end of the hallway next to room 205.

Add to these strange occurrences, the occasional sounds of voices coming from unoccupied rooms, frequent cold drafts that chill staff persons and guests to the bone, and the uneasiness of feeling like your being watched or followed, and you have all the ingredients for a haunted hotel.

The Hotel Catalina caters to the people from all walks of life, as well as a neighborly ghost or two.

The Inn on Mount Ada

Particulars
398 Wrigley Terrace Road, P.O. Box 2560,
Avalon, California 90704
Phone: 310-510-2030
Fax: 310-510-2237
Toll Free: 1-800-608-7669
Website: www.innonmtada.com

History
Their Website states: William
Wrigley Jr. bought 99% of the island of Catalina in 1919 and chose the setting, 350 feet above the town as his home because it received first sunlight in the morning and the last rays at sunset. The building of the Wrigley's home was started in 1920 and finished in 1921. The hilltop was named Mt. Ada after Mr. Wrigley's wife, Ada. The couple enjoyed the home together between the years of 1921 and January 1932 when Mr. Wrigley died.

Mrs. Wrigley continued to visit until 1947, when she suffered a stroke and lingered in a coma in Pasadena for 11 years. She died in 1958. From 1921 to 1932, the Wrigley's entertained a number of famous guests at their island home, including President Calvin Coolidge, Warren Harding and the Prince of Wales. Mr. Wrigley also owned the Chicago Cubs professional baseball team, and invited them to hold their spring training on the island. Following Mrs. Wrigley's death, the home was owned by the Santa Catalina Island Company and used as a tourist attraction.

In the 1970s, the home was given to the University of Southern California to be used as a conference center. In 1985, the present innkeepers secured a long-term lease of the property and created the business known today as The Inn on Mt. Ada. For the past 14 years in a row, the Inn has been awarded the Mobil Travel Guide 4-Star rating, a rating awarded to only the top 2% of lodging properties in the entire state. The building is listed on the National Register of Historic Places.

Hauntspitality
Spectral noises, unexplained footsteps, and phantom shadows that roam the historical home and the adjoining grounds occasionally break the peaceful atmosphere of this spectacular house. Former employees have seen strange lights and heard disembodied footsteps coming down the stairs. They have also heard tapping noises and voices in the middle of the night that no one has been able to explain.

One former employee saw a ghostly woman where the road from the Inn junctions with the main road. The shadowy figure appeared briefly near the entrance to the Wrigley mansion, then vanished instantly in front of the startled on-looker. Other rumors about Room #4 include a ghostly apparition of a young woman who appears out of nowhere, looks at the guests in their bed, pauses, walks toward the closet door and vanishes. This would have originally been a guestroom or the children's room.

Occasionally, people claim to see shadows moving down the hallway on the second floor, up the stairs, or in certain rooms. The shadow seems to float in one direction, and then slowly dissolves. Lights in the former residence will occasionally turn themselves on and off, and cold spots will suddenly appear in various parts of the house.

Myriad stories continue to be told about the spirits of the Wrigley Mansion, none of them negative in connotation. During the winter months, and especially during Christmas, strange sounds and sightings have been rumored to occur with increased frequency. In one instance, a Christmas tree was seen levitating slightly above the floor, as if someone were moving the tree for a better placement in the room. The tree was relocated from its intended spot to a better location--better, that is, for the spirits. Christmas is a very important and emotional time for the living---and the spirits.

It seems likely that residual energy from past family memories and experiences of good times have remained imbedded in the very fabric of the former Wrigley residence. To date, all of the paranormal events, which have been documented, have been friendly in nature.

Whatever spirit or spirits remain at the former Wrigley Mansion, it or they represent benign energy. The feeling inside is one of warmth, family, of relaxation and peace. The spirits are as much a part of the house as the frequent visitors who come to enjoy all that was good about this special place that some call a slice of heaven on earth. Perhaps the spirits are reliving their happiest times at the mansion house as well as checking up on the guests to ensure they have a pleasant stay. At the Inn on Mount Ada, the fine line between the past and present is all but gone. While the living partakes of the magic of this place, the spirits are busy doing their own thing and sometimes, by chance, their paths cross.

Old Turner Inn

Particulars

232 Catalina Avenue, P.O. Box 97,
Avalon, CA 90704
Phone: 310-510-2236
Website: www.catalina.com

History

The house was constructed in 1927 by Mrs. Matilda Joughin "Tilly" Murdock as a summer residence. Since then, owners have included: Esther Barnes; Oma and Kelsey Turner (the current name associated with the Inn) who rented out rooms; the Bob O'Guin family who called the place, "The haven"; and Gary and Kathy Brown who completely remodeled and refurbished the structure Today, it is run by Bill and Jeanne Hill, and is considered by many, as the best B&B in Avalon. The Hill (Bill Hill) and Sook (Jeanne Hill's maiden name) families have been associated with the island since 1887 and 1906 respectively. When Avalon was known as Timm's Landing, Matilda Joughin and three other sisters came to Catalina by rowboat. Each sister had a house on the island as well as their mainland home at Arlington and Adams Boulevard.

Hauntspitality

Perhaps Matilda "Tilly" Murdock haunts her former home. A recent guest and his wife came to visit Catalina and at the last minute decided to stay at the Inn. Fortunately, the Garden Room was available and after wandering around beautiful Avalon, they came back to the room and settled in for the night. The lone downstairs guest bedroom was a perfect fit for the exhausted couple; cozy and relaxing. Little did the man know how cozy it was going to get. Around 5:30 in the morning, the sound asleep gentleman was awakened to an odd encounter. Standing at the foot of the bed and looking not at him but rather his slumbering wife was a misty form that the man readily assumed was female. For the briefest of moments, he thought he was dreaming, but unfortunately, that was not the case. As he sat up in silence, looking at someone staring at his wife, the phantom form levitated off the bed and floated out of bedroom where the window is located. The startled guest told his story to the Hills in the morning and the first thought was that the original owner "Tilly" was still checking up on her house and those who come to visit.

Other guests have reported disembodied footsteps making their way up the stairs, doors opening and closing by themselves, occasional unexplained drafts and cold spots, an a gentle feminine voice that is sometimes heard downstairs when a guest is alone. On one occasion a guest was sitting by the downstairs fireplace reading a newspaper when he heard footsteps coming down the stairs. Thinking it was his wife, he waited until the footsteps had reached the bottom of the stairs. When the footsteps stopped, he looked over his shoulder. As he was about to say good morning, there was no one there. His wife came down a few minutes later and the startled witness told his wife what had happened. The event added a little something extra to their trip.

If its relaxation and ambiance you're after, then the Old Turner Inn is the place to be; and, if you're looking for a little spirited excitement, a stay in the Garden Room may put you in touch with the original owner!

Zane Grey Hotel

Particulars
199 Chimes Tower Road, P.O. Box 216,
Avalon, CA 91304
Phone: 310-510-0966
Fax: 310-510-1340
Toll Free: 800-3-PUEBLO (California only)
E-mail: zanegrey@catalinaisp.com
Website: www.zanegreypueblohotel.com

History

The Zane Grey Pueblo Hotel is situated high above Avalon with a spectacular view of the bay and surrounding hills. The hotel was once the home of the famous western writer. Zane Grey, author of over 80 books including western novels, baseball stories, boy's adventures, and fishing books, was born Pearl Zane Grey in Zanesville, Ohio in 1872. He accepted a scholarship at the University of Pennsylvania where he studied dentistry and played baseball. After graduating, he took up dentistry, but confinement to an office left him restless.

Within a few years he realized he wanted to travel, dream and write about his adventures. Fortunately, his wife, Lina Roth Grey, saw the romantic dreamer in her husband and encouraged him to explore and write. Grey became one of the most prolific writers of his time. His robust, imaginative and romantic stories made him the foremost writer on the American West, and his books are still read by many today.

Grey's first novel, *Betty Zane*, resulted from an invitation to travel. Buffalo Jones, a plainsman, invited Grey to accompany him to Arizona and experience the Wild West. The journey began Grey's love affair with the desert which would translate into an endless stream of stories. When Grey was in his late 40s, he and his family moved to Altadena, California.

Zane Grey spent most of his later life in Avalon, writing and fishing until his death in 1939 at age 67. The pueblo, now a hotel, was constructed in 1926, when Grey was in his mid-50s. On the cactus-covered hillside just above the Avalon Casino, is the sprawling Hopi-style pueblo. In his book, *What the Open Means to Me*, he expresses his feelings about Catalina with the words, "...It is an environment that means enchantment to me. Sea and Mountain! Breeze and roar of Surf! Music of Birds! Solitude and tranquility; a place for rest, peace, and sleep... I could write here and be at peace..."

Grey's original home had a long hall dividing the bedrooms overlooking the ocean, and those overlooking the hills. A fireplace with a long mantle, open beam ceilings, a hewn plank door graced

a large living room and dining room, and an oak dining table brought from Tahiti on one of his fishing trips graced the home. At the time of construction, workman reported that goat's milk was added to the mortar. Later workmen, who replaced some small windows with picture windows, attested to the strength of the walls. To please the Greys, the men hewed an upright piano. A former dirt patio, now a beautiful pool separated the home from that of his brother Romer C. Grey.

Hauntspitality

According to a former manager, a number of strange things have happened, and continue to occur at the hotel. Nothing harmful or frightening, just shadows and sounds---which many believe, belong to Zane Grey. Shehabi's background in electrical engineering compelled him to check for logical explanations for the various *"unexplainable things"* that have, and continue to occur at the Hotel; his courses in parapsychology cause him to question what can't be explained away by science. Shehabi maintains a very open-minded attitude about the paranormal. He reasons that, if science can't explain it away, then *something* must be there.

Other witnesses concur that the activity appears to be centered in selected areas within the hotel. Unaccountable footsteps have been heard, ghostly shapes are frequently seen and cold gusts of air are felt near the entrance to the Office. Directly across from the office, separated by a long, narrow hallway, was Grey's study, located in the *Desert Gold* room (each room was named after one of Grey's western books).

Adjacent to the study, was the *Purple Sage* room where his wife slept. There are times when a shadow is seen emerging from the room, which then moves down the hallway corridor toward the original living room area, also one of Grey's favorite rooms. Oftentimes, the fog-like image is accompanied by footsteps, or there are simply sounds of footsteps and no manifestation.

Hotel sources say that no matter how late Grey came in the night before, he would always awaken bright and early and go out on the balcony to watch the sun rise. He would spend most of his time at his southwestern-constructed hideaway between the living room and his study (which has been remodeled), and write. Shadows, the sound of footsteps, unexplainable cold spots and various unaccountable electrical problems have been reported at the entrance, along the main hallway, in the living room area and balcony, and some of the rooms.

Another area of activity is the room where Shehabi lives while managing the hotel. The room he occupies, *The Stairs of Sand*, and the adjacent room, *Drift Fence*, are located across from the main building in an area built for his brother, Romer. Ghostly activity includes footsteps, dark shadows that pass through the room and disappear, cold spots, and pungent smells (possibly tobacco odors). As with the other sightings, they are benign occurrences, and no one has felt uneasy about witnessing any of the strange events, which occur at all hours of the night.

The authors spent a night in Romer Grey's former room and had several unexplained events take place. Shortly after going to sleep, we were awakened by the smell of tobacco and then what smelled like fish being cooked. The smells were followed in short order by tapping sounds from inside the walls and then footsteps as if someone was pacing in the rooms. When the footsteps ceased, an unearthly cold filled the room and then everything returned to normal. This all took place within a three hour period from around midnight until three in the morning. Since this is what we write about and enjoy, I suppose you can say we were blessed by the unusual series of events that took place while we were writing our haunted Catalina book.

Chatsworth

Los Toros Mexican Resturant

Particulars

21743 Devonshire Street
Chatsworth, CA 91311
Phone: 818-882-3080
Fax: 818-882-9553
E-mail: lostoros@lostoros.com
Website: www.lostoros.com

History

This local hangout is situated two blocks East of Topanga Canyon Blvd in the City of Chatsworth. Los Toros Mexican Restaurant has been serving up great Mexican Food since 1967. Los Toros provides a fun, family atmosphere. Located in Chatsworth, Los Toros is great for all occasions: a family night out, birthday parties, etc... Come in and try one of the delicious Mexican delicacies. As one restaurant review states, "The hand-crafted doors have hinges and handles made in Mexico and the entryway boasts a colorful, tiled floor reminiscent of the work of Mexican artisans. Hand-painted lighting fixtures were also imported from south of the border for that truly authentic feel. Be sure to sit on the patio with its fountain, large tables and brightly painted chairs in various colors -- it offers a cool breeze in the warmer months and is heated in winter." That's only the beginning of your unique dining experience here... there's also a spirit or two floating around.

Hauntspitality

Numerous unexplained things have occurred in this building since it opened as a restaurant. Visitors have spotted a man in his 50s and a woman in her 60s in the southeastern portion of the building that fronts Devonshire Boulevard. They are spotted independently and several individuals have stated that spotting the phantoms is usually preceded by cold chills that completely engulf them.

A staff person behind the bar the older portion of the building watched in disbelief as a well dressed Hispanic man walked by the bar, and before reaching the end, vanished. Another staff person in the back portion of the building near closing time, walked in on a woman who appeared to be cleaning a table. The trouble was, that portion of the restaurant was closed, no one was at the table and as the lady turned to look at the startled waitress, she vanished

Orbs on the ceiling and wall (courtesy of the International Paranormal Research Organization - IPRO)

67

Orbs on the wall (courtesy of the International Paranormal Research Organization - IPRO)

into thin air.

During one seating, a couple sitting in the outside patio area, witnessed the lantern hanging above them literally fly off the nail that was anchoring it to a overhead wood beam, drop down and begin swinging back and forth above their heads. It turns out a waiter was also watching in amazement. He shook his head and blamed the whole thing on the restaurant spirits.

Around the bar area, people have reported having someone unseen brush by them as they were holding a drink. They quickly turned to say something the rude person, and no one was anywhere near them.

There have been sightings in the back area of the room where an elderly woman has simply vanished through the wall. Glasses have been known to move unassisted, table settings are mysteriously rearranged and some people hear their name called out by someone unseen. The cold drafts that suddenly materialize and the sense of being watched by someone invisible are common occurrences in this famous restaurant. It has been drawing people because of its authentic food, great margaritas and its spirited clientele. A visit to this establishment is sure to quench your appetite for dinner and spirits.

Chico
Goodman House

Particulars
Address: 1362 Esplanade,
Chico, CA 95926
Phone: 530-566-0256
Fax: 530-566-0256
E-mail: proprietor@goodmanhouse.net
Website: www.goodmanhouse.net

History

The Goodman House was built in 1906 by Horace Goodman, a Butte County rancher and "Chico civic leader," so that his five children could attend school in town, according to the Chico Heritage Association's 1983 Historic Resources Inventory. Horace Goodman was born in Peoria, Illinois, on November 27, 1863, to John Goodman of New York and Mary Hill. He attended school in Peoria and Bondville. On April 6, 1887, he married Ella Cade of Seymour, Illinois, the daughter of Simon Cade (England) and Sarah Ashcroft (Ohio). He traveled to California and toured California, eventually buying 964 acres north east of Butte City. As a farmer, he was noted for having the most modern machinery; a 75 H-P Caterpillar engine and a combined harvester. Desiring to give his five children, Howard, Elmer, Brian, Ira and Hubert, the advantage of city schools, he moved to the Chico Vecino and erected the house at the corner of 4th and The Esplanade. As a resident of Chico, he was progressive and a leader in having the Phone line built and in securing the new county road by giving a strip 60 feet wide and a mile and a half long and in working to have the Chico Vecino annexed to the City. He was a member of the Presbyterian Church, and a supporter of Democratic candidates. While in Illinois he was the Postmaster of Bondville and township school treasurer. He died in Chico on May 5, 1917. Following his death, Ella Goodman continued to look after the Goodman interests and operated the ranch demonstrating keen business ability.

George Vogelsang was born in Fulton, New York, September 16, 1867, the youngest of eight children of Frederick and Margaretta Vogelsang. He came to California at the age of seventeen. He lived in Stockton for a short time; moved to San Francisco and worked on streetcars; he then moved to Tehama County where he worked on the Rhiland Ranch. When the Stanford Vina property was subdivided he purchased part and farmed it for twelve years. Thereafter he retired, moved to Chico and in December, 1919, purchased the property at 1362 The Esplanade from Ella Goodman. He was married to Erin Porter and had four daughters; Retta Vogelsang, Helana Vogelsang Newmann, Eleanor Vogelsang Lucas, and Estella Vogelsang Boyd. He died on May 19, 1958, at the age of ninety from a fall at home. Then in 1974, the house was sold to M. Brooks Houghton, who transformed the building into professional offices. The Grahams, the current owners, bought the building in 2002 for use as a bed and breakfast and as their residence.

Hauntspitality

According to the current owners, the Goodman House is reportedly host to the ghost of George Vogelsang. Legend has it that the 92-year-old Mr. Vogelsang, a retired rancher who used to own the house, fell down its stairs and died from the injuries on May 19, 1958. For the last 30 years, while the building was used as a law office, there were rumors of the wanderings of his restless spirit. According to the current owners, a lot of people say to us, that they are haunted.

After the current owners moved in, Mrs. Graham felt a little nervous sleeping in the house alone while her husband was away. A branch would brush the house and she didn't sleep too well. However since the Grahams began transforming the place into the Goodman House Bed and Breakfast last spring, Mr. Vogelsang's spirit has quieted down. Apparently the spirit did not like attorneys, and seemed to bother them on a regular basis.

There are other stories about the spirited house. People working inside have reported mysterious happenings. One woman told of being in the kitchen and the door unexplainably flying open and shut. Another woman said the hot water was found running full blast in the sink all night, yet no one had turned it on. One attorney who often worked late at night would hear distant muted tingling noise. Another lawyer had problems with his desk nameplate being turned over, thrown on the floor and then completely missing.

After the purchase of the house in 2002, the current owners were surprised by people stopping in to see the renovations they were undertaking, but to also tell haunting stories. A man who had been painting the house for the law firm told of being in the basement at night and hearing footsteps upstairs. He would go up to see who it was and no one would be there. He also told of turning off lights and having them come back on, yet he was alone. Another woman told of the attic door being stuck and she couldn't get files she needed early one morning before anyone else was in the office. She went to answer a phone and came back to find the door wide open. No one else was at work yet. One woman reported that she woke up in the middle of the night with the feeling that someone was trying to wake her by bouncing the bed. Another woman explained that she smelled fresh cigarette smoke in the room she was in by herself. No smoking is allowed, we don't smoke, and there were no other guests that particular night. However, there were stories that former owner Retta Vogelsang did sneak cigarettes. Another morning when a couple was having breakfast and told that there hadn't been any ghost activity lately, the top to the waffle iron dramatically flew open.

The current owners contacted a noted San Francisco Bay Area Medium/Psychic.

Marge Cuddeback, author of Vanishing Veil, stayed in the B&B overnight. She reported that she definitely felt a strong spirit presence, but that there was a man and a soft feminine presence as well. She said that on two occasions during her stay, when she was 5 to 6 steps from the bottom of the main staircase, she felt an ominous sense that someone was there. She actually turned to see if someone was there. After telling Marge about the stories we had heard, she said that all of the incidents were consistent with spirit activity in haunted houses. Marge said that the male spirit was a gentle man and we had nothing to fear. She also felt that the spirits were probably happy that this was a home now and not a business

Margo and Tom Graham will be glad to share their latest encounters with you as long as you do them the service of first spending a night or two inside and see what you sense. Even if you don't see or feel one of their guardian energies, and you don't experience the Goodman House hauntspitality, you will most certainly be treated to loving

and caring hospitality by the current owners of the historic inn.

Clayton
La Cocotte Restaurant

Particulars

6115 Main Street,
Clayton, CA 94517
Phone: 925-672-1330

History

Thanks to the Clayton
Historical Society archives (http://
claytonhs.com/chsLaCoc.html) the following information was obtained for the
building. The restaurant is comprised of two buildings constructed in the late
1800s that were moved back from Main Street and joined to become a restaurant.
Jack Duncan built the structure on the left (west) side in the 1870s as a home,
possibly for his sister. In 1898, Judge Gus Goethals purchased the property. His
brother Jack operated a barbershop in this house. In 1909-1910, Mr. and Mrs.
LeClaire purchased the building; somewhere between 1908 and 1910 a façade
was added and the building became a store.

Mr. LeClaire probably installed the Shell gas pump that can be seen in early
photographs. During the early days of automobile travel the LeClaires operated
a roadside stand selling gasoline, candy, soft drinks, etc. According to Clayton
pioneer, George Frank, Mrs. LeClaire also ran a post office, he thinks in the
adjacent building. George also remembered that the LeClaires were horse traders
and kept corrals on a Center Street property. He remembered seeing many, many
horses there for sale and trade. Later, a saloon known as "The Growler" was
added to the complex of buildings. The building served as a real estate and
insurance office, where patrons could "bank" valuables in his safe.

In the 1970s, Joe L. and Marie Pastor and, Mr. and Mrs. Edward G. Minadeo,
entered a partnership; they purchased the Growler and were intent on keeping the
historical integrity of the building. After restoration, the Growler Tavern opened on
February 24, 25, 1973. The Pastors and Minadeos purchased the adjacent green
building that had been Judge Gus Goethals' real estate office. The buildings were
later sold to Joseph and Marjorie Salas, who converted what, had been The
Growler and the adjacent building into what later became La Cocotte.

The restaurant had two major dining areas, a reception room and bar, and
three smaller dining coves. In 1976, Rudy and Ingrid Hempell purchased La
Cocotte, and developed it into a cozy French café that has become a Clayton
landmark, known throughout the bay area for its fine meals. In June 2002, Ingrid
Hempell retired and sold to Sharon and John Johnston, a husband and wife team
from Northern Ireland who plans to continue La Cocotte's long tradition of fine
dining.

Hauntspitality

From miners to ordinary citizens, the buildings forming the current restaurant
are filled with spirited former clients. A folk story about a gunfight gun awry resulting
in the death of a little girl is said to be responsible for one of the restaurant spirits.
The little girl was reportedly shot in the street by a stray bullet from a gunfight
and died on the floor of the bar area. The young innocent girl was mourned by all

who witnessed the tragedy, and her restless spirit is often sighted or heard in the building.

Numerous individuals have reported hearing mournful cries and desperate moans coming from inside the building when it was unoccupied. The misty form of a girl has also been sighted wandering through the building or standing outside looking in.

The girl is not the only specter reported inside. Some claim a man from the early 1900s and a woman and child are also resident spirits. Disembodied footsteps have been heard coming from unoccupied rooms. Several employees have felt something unseen brush by them while working and one person heard their name called out by a female spirit. The lights will sometimes flicker or turn on or off unassisted and cold spots will suddenly manifest in various portions of the building.

There are times when people see things move out of the corner of their eyes, and an occasional door will open without human assistance. A couple of psychics

once visited the building and came away sensing that tragedy was behind the hauntings. Without knowing anything about the history, they sensed a young person who died tragically and a middle-aged woman who were somehow tied to the tragedy, haunting the establishment. They also felt that a man, possibly an early bartender or owner, also makes the building his afterlife home.

There is a lot more than meets the eye in this fine local dining establishment, so while you settle into a scrumptious dinner, you should be aware that you may be catered to by more than a waiter or waitress or those from this dimension.

Clovis
Andelberry Estate

Particulars
2603 Clovis Avenue,
Clovis, CA 93611

History
We are including this location
in the book, because a recent
City Council meeting stated, A
haunted house that scared thousands of visitors every Halloween for seven years
is being brought back from the dead as a new Clovis Hotel. Clovis Planning
Commissioners approved the hotel plan in a 4-0- vote Thursday night. Todd
Wolfe, owner of the property at 2604 Clovis Avenue plans to turn the former
haunted house into a unique hotel that will feature rooms furnished with antiques
as well as memorabilia from the historic hospital and sanitarium that first opened
on the site nearly 100 years ago". A plaque on the side of the house reads,
Andleberry Estate, established in 1871.

Hauntspitality
Numerous paranormal groups have
visited this very haunted building including
our friends and fellow researchers Diane
Melvin of the San Gabriel Valley Paranormal
Researchers and Chad Patterson and his team
from the California Society of Ghost Researchers
(CSGR). Both groups came away convinced
that there were several disembodied spirits still
occupying the building. Some of the results from
the CSGR investigation follow: Gifted psychic Virginia Marco remarked, "On my
first visit to psychically investigate the Andleberry Estate house I touched the
walls of the inside of the house and I saw two houses in one dimension, I felt that
it was something else before it was an asylum." I saw a male ghost in the living
room. He does not speak, he observes and follows us around; in the kitchen I
saw three ghosts, Bertha, Paul and the last one could not speak. This last male
ghost could not speak because his body had deteriorated when he was alive; in
the cooking area, I saw a male ghost. He was 65, overweight and tall, his named
was William and he was the cook. This male ghost is very active in haunting the
place; on the second floor, I saw the ghost of an old woman named Mary sitting
in a rocking chair; in the basement there were three rooms. In one of the rooms,
they punished there. There was a feeling of misery in the basement.

Through questions and answers via Electronic Voice Phenomena (EVP), the
following information was gleaned:
- There is a ghost who calls himself Ahmel.
- He is a male ghost, around 70 years of age.
- The spirit is African-American.
- The male energy had three front teeth missing.
- He was homeless and he died in the attic of a heart attack in 1975).

Other spirits who responded during the investigation, included Mary Haloway who was 71, and William C. who was 65. The spirit population said that they were all in the house and not going to leave.

Another investigative group (www.invisiblerealms.com) also visited the house with the following results:
- Upon entering the premises the investigators were immediately struck by the heaviness of the atmosphere;
- One investigator heard the sound of crying in the pantry in the kitchen;
- The dining room contained the energy of a woman who was a cook, and very anxious to please;
- Heading into the basement an investigator saw the partial manifestation of a male figure from the knees down. The phantom man was wearing clothing and his shoes. Entering the room directly in front of the steps the group was met by a baby swing going at a high rate of speed. The owner swore that no one had been down there prior to the inspection;
- The group encountered an energy anomaly in the second story of the house and in the dining room.

A third investigative group (www.ghosttrackers.com) visited The Andleberry Estate and Sanitarium and their investigation produced the following results:
- Upon entering the heavily steel gated driveway, the energy emanating from the house was very heavy;
- The lead investigator felt a heavy pressure to my chest, his knees became wobbly and he felt lightheaded;
- One group smelled an old fashioned type of rose fragrance;
- In the kitchen, a curtain covering a small pantry-type area fluttered in one direction only. There were no windows in that closet and no vents;
- Two measurable cold spots were found in different bedrooms;
- While in the basement a stuffed animal hanging from the ceiling by a string began revolving counter clockwise. Five other stuffed dolls surrounded this animal but no other doll was moving. Orbs turned up in the photographs;
- Entering the sanitarium portion of the building, there were about 21 rooms. There were measurable lasting cold spots and cold drafts that filtered passed the investigators;
- Two investigators were pushed; Shadows were seen crossing hallways;
- Doors were closing without help;
- Through the rest of the night the group heard banging sound and felt cold drafts of air although it was over 100 degrees during the day. Every window in this house was boarded and double sealed, inside and out. There were no open vents and the thick, heavy, steel doors did not allow any air to filter through.

Generally speaking, it seems that the Andleberry Estate still contains a tremendous amount of energy from the days when it served as a sanitarium. Groups who have ventured inside have all come away with measurable EMF readings and personal accounts of apparitions and encounters with the numerous energies inside. The range of experiences includes rapid temperature changes, orbs, disembodied footsteps, and apparitions, moving objects, unexplained voices, EVP, moving shadows and spikes in EMF meters.

When the house opens as a hotel, you can bet that the spirit population is going to make itself known; after all it is still their afterlife home.

Coloma
The Argonaut (the Schulze House)

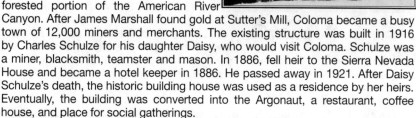

Particulars
8928 Hwy 49
Coloma, CA 95613

History
The town of Coloma lies in a densely forested portion of the American River Canyon. After James Marshall found gold at Sutter's Mill, Coloma became a busy town of 12,000 miners and merchants. The existing structure was built in 1916 by Charles Schulze for his daughter Daisy, who would visit Coloma. Schulze was a miner, blacksmith, teamster and mason. In 1886, fell heir to the Sierra Nevada House and became a hotel keeper in 1886. He passed away in 1921. After Daisy Schulze's death, the historic building house was used as a residence by her heirs. Eventually, the building was converted into the Argonaut, a restaurant, coffee house, and place for social gatherings.

Today, Coloma has a population of 175 with a tinsmith, blacksmith's shop and a gunsmith still operating in town. The old schoolhouse bell still rings as visiting children go to class. In Coloma, another hangout is Argonaut Café on Main Street where people drop in for a cup of coffee and some homemade pie.

Hauntspitality
The former home turned café, is a local hangout, where the living and deceased still congregate. There are so many unexplained events that have taken place inside that its common knowledge the building is haunted. The owner, guests and psychically inclined persons all agree that the building has a few otherworldly guests inside. Several people have reported hearing footsteps come from unoccupied areas of the building. Sometimes there will be loud footsteps on the front porch making their way to the front door. Thinking it's a tourist or friend, the owner will rush to the front door to see who it is, only to find no one anywhere around.

Sensitive people, who walk in, immediately sense that a spirit or two enjoys the hauntspitality of this building. Perhaps it is none other than Mr. Schulze and his daughter Daisy who choose to remain behind and watch over their former home. Several people have spotted or sensed a robust female and a heavy-set elderly gentleman making themselves at home inside the building

A sensitive individual claimed that one of the spirits was a robust woman who was lonely, while another individual spotted a hefty elderly man would float across the floor and walk over and end up looking out of a window before vanishing. There are cold spots that will manifest suddenly and engulf an unsuspecting individual. Some people have witnessed apparitions, while others sense the energy inside.

Coloma once boasted a living population of 12,000 miners and merchants, and although the living population is under two hundred, you can bet that the spirit population greatly outnumbers the current merchants and residents. On your next visit to the area, come visit the former historic Schulze House, now the Argonaut, which is filled to the brim with good eats and friendly spirits in a town where the past and present co-exist.

Sierra Nevada House

Particulars

835 Lotus Road, P.O. Box 457,
Coloma, CA 95613
Phone: 530-626-8096 I Fax: 530-626-8565
E-mail: info@sierranevadahouse.com
Website: www.sierranevadahouse.com

History

The historic Sierra Nevada House was built on the banks of the American River, just down river from Sutter's Mill and right next door to the first Wells Fargo Depot in Northern California. In the early days of the Gold Rush, the Sierra Nevada House was a way station for miners and tradesman. Throughout its heyday, the hotel was owned and operated by Robert Chalmers, a successful businessman who held 'fancy' parties in the Coloma area.

The hotel remained in operation until 1902 when it was destroyed by fire. It was rebuilt shortly thereafter and became a silent movie house as well as the local Community Hall. Many local elders still remember times from their childhood spent in and around the Sierra Nevada House. The structure burned again in 1925 and was rebuilt and restored to its current standing. The Lodge, Restaurant, and Inn are gems from the past. One walk through the grounds or one meal in the old dining hall will take you back to a time that, even now in our modern world, sings quite uniquely to our imaginations. The building is surrounded on all sides by the beauty of the rivers and mountains, and inside, the spirit of the past truly comes to life.

Hauntspitality

A spirit called Christopher is blamed for the myriad paranormal events that have taken place inside this historic hotel over the years. He has been blamed for moving pots, pans, and utensils, hiding objects, moving furniture, opening doors, and turning lights on and off. Another spirit, called Mark, was apparently released through psychic intervention. Christopher, or whatever his real name is, is still very active in the building. Then, there is the spirit of a former proprietor named Isabelle, who seems attached to the large mirror that hangs in the House.

According to management, around 3:00 a.m. or 4:00 a.m., the bartender staying in one of the back hotel rooms, heard screaming and moaning sounds coming from everywhere. He looked around but never found the source. Later, he found out that about 150 yards behind the house, in the 1870s, 17 Chinese laborers, working in a mine, were killed when the mine collapsed. To this day, many guests and staff reports the eerie screaming, moaning, and wailing sounds come from the area in back, although the sounds seem to engulf the building.

During a wedding reception in the ballroom, a couple and their child went upstairs to spend the night in Room #4. The restless father couldn't get to sleep, so he went back downstairs to join the party. When he finally returned to the room, he found the sink filled with hot water. His wife awoke and he thanked her for filling the basin. She denied having anything to do with filling up the sink; saying that she had been asleep the entire time and just awoke. At that moment, their three-year-old daughter bolted up in bed, pointed to a red, antique, hanging lamp and yelled "Fire" two times; then went peacefully back to sleep. The interesting thing was that in the past, the Sierra Nevada House had burned down twice!

A cocktail waitress once witnessed a bearded old sea captain, wearing a captain's hat and attire from the 1800s; appear as if he just stepped off a fishing boat. He wasn't seen alone, either. When the apparition appeared, he was holding the hand of an 8-10 year-old, blonde-haired child wearing a very pretty Sunday school dress. Both apparitions were observed walking across the hallway from the ballroom to the kitchen. The little girl has also been spotted in other buildings in Coloma. Perhaps the young girl occasionally hooks up with other spirits in Coloma in her never-ending quest to find someone she misses.

There is a huge mirror at the Sierra Nevada House that weighs over 600 pounds. The gargantuan mirror has survived two fires. Sometimes, right after the mirror is cleaned and wiped; it immediately fogs up. The strange mist will suddenly appear and then just as quickly vanish; and it has nothing to do with the window cleaner they use.

On another occasion, when the mirror was hanging in the bar area, the alarm would occasionally go off. The sheriff would cautiously make his way into the building; but nothing would ever be found out of place. The only alarms in the building that would do this were the ones nearest the bar. The Isabelle was credited with bringing the gold mirror (now in the ballroom) from Gold Hill, California to Coloma. Her spirit has been blamed, along with the others occupying the Sierra Nevada House, for all the paranormal activity that continues to take place inside the building, and around the establishment.

It's a great place to visit if you really want to get away from it all--all that is, except benevolent spirits who seem to enjoy the "fleshy" guests.
past and present co-exist.

The Vineyard House

Particulars
P.O. Box 501,
Coloma, CA 95613-0501
Phone: 530-622-7050

History

Robert Chalmers built this historic house in 1879 at a cost of $15,000 furnished. The main building consisted of 18 rooms including a 25 by 90 feet ballroom. Under the ballroom were the dining room, kitchen, pantry wood shed and toilet. The basement consisted of two large storerooms, a bar or wine room and reading room, which was used as a band room. The cellar was converted into an auxiliary jail, and at least two prisoners spent their last night on earth in the basement of the house, and were hanged the next day.

Ulysses S. Grant once made a speech on the porch of the house. Louise (one spelling is Louisa) Allhoff married Robert Chalmers after her first husband, a successful vintner, committed suicide in a Virginia City Courthouse. Louise had a penchant for business, and Chalmers was elected to the State legislature. They were a dynamic social duo.

A year after the house was completed; Robert Chalmers reportedly lost his mind. For his own protection, his wife Louise reportedly chained him in the cellar where he died a lonely death in 1881. The story goes that Chalmers starved himself to death, because he feared that his wife was trying to poison him.

After Chalmer's death, the family's grapevines mysteriously died, and Louise was forced to close their winery and take on boarders to make a living. She even rented out the cellar as a jail, and allowed hangings in her front yard. She died in 1913, and was buried next to her husband in the cemetery facing their home.

Hauntspitality

According to numerous books and articles, subsequent residents of the house have been so frightened by apparitions, rattling sounds, voices and doors opening and closing by themselves, that eventually people refused to live in the mansion. The house was made into a hotel in 1956, and since then, Vineyard House has been the sight of hundreds of unexplained phenomena witnessed by staff and guests.

Glasses have moved by themselves in the basement bar and the sounds of someone being murdered in the adjacent room frightened one couple enough that they failed to make it through the night. A guest once reported seeing the spirit of a small boy being beaten in Room 5, the same room where other guests have heard screaming. Drinks were served in the cellar jail where thieves as well as original owner, Robert Chalmers once languished. Unexplained footsteps were often heard on the stairs and a doorknob in the bar in the cellar jail was occasionally seen turning when no one was on the other side. Once, a freshly made bed became unmade, leaving the impression of a person on the sheets. A stack of old coffins that was found under the front porch shortly after one owner bought the place, added to the macabre history of the building.

Guests frequently reported hearing the sound of chains rattling, rustling skirts, heavy breathing, and brisk footsteps across the floor. A couple heard a rambunctious group enter by the front door, laughing loudly as they climbed the stairs. Going to the door to quiet the revelers, they saw three men dressed in Victorian clothing abruptly fade before their eyes.

One night, a bartender watched in disbelief as two wine glasses slid across the bar on their own, coming to rest in front of the startled man. A Ouija board spelled out the name "George," who reportedly is the spirit of a small boy still remaining behind in the house. Room 5 on the second floor seems to have tragedy etched on its walls. Many individuals have felt fear, sadness and overwhelming pain while occupying the room. The spirits of Robert Chalmers and his wife, Louise is also spotted in the cellar bar areas. Louise has been sighted walking across the road from the Pioneer Cemetery opposite the hotel, where she and her husband are buried.

The third ghost is a child known as George. His figure has oftentimes been sighted in the window of Room 3 when the room is unoccupied. A rumored murder took place in Room 5 and Room 1, Louise's old room, and Room 2, Robert Chalmer's room, have also has their share of unexplained phenomena. A photograph taken by a guest showed a shadowy female figure perched on the roof-at the top of a ladder that had no rungs.

A few people have even attested to witnessing a gray, bearded figure, dressed in a black suit and looking like Ulysses S. Grant, materialize in the bar behind a group of drinkers, then walk towards a solid brick wall and vanish. Local police officers once held a party in the Vineyard House, and stayed around to see if there were any ghosts. They all heard the sounds of people talking and laughing come from Rooms 2 and 6. Each time they went to check the rooms, no one was there. This haunted house, though currently not operating as an overnight sleeping venue, is definitely worth a visit, even if it's just to browse and see what you can sense, or what senses you! At the Vineyard House you can have the pick of the spirits.

Columbia
The City Hotel of Columbia

Particulars
The City Hotel Corporation,
22768 Main Street, P.O. Box 1870,
Columbia, CA 95310
Phone: 209-532-1479
Fax: 209- 532-7027
Toll Free: 1-800-532-1479
E-mail: info@cityhotel.com
Website: www.cityhotel.com

History
The City Hotel, a two-story brick building, was constructed in 1856. The hotel ultimately fell into disrepair but was reopened in 1975 as a museum and inn. The historic City Hotel and its sister, the Fallon Hotel are restored 19th century country inns.

Hauntspitality
The story goes that a wealthy gentleman from the Midwest came to Columbia with a large, carved bedroom set for his bride who was coming to meet him. The bedroom furniture arrived but the bride never did. She apparently caught a fever on her journey west and died along the way. The distraught man had the unused furniture stored in a San Francisco warehouse where it remained until the man passed away and his treasured, unused newlywed bed was donated to a museum. The furniture ultimately made its way to the Balcony Room (Room 1) in the City Hotel, and with the furniture came a spirit.

Guests who spend the night in the room often report the sensation of being watched. There are cold spots that suddenly materialize, and unseen hands often move items. Perhaps the gentlemen from the Midwest or his bride managed to attach to the furniture and are now joined in the afterlife within the cozy confines of the hotel. Another possibility is that the man continues to wait by the bedside hoping that his lost love will make her way over to their wedding bed to be finally joined for eternity.

The spirit at the hotel is named Elizabeth. This name was given by the staff and has no historical reference that we can determine. It is my personal theory that she is a woman who lost a child - tried to nurse it to health, but was unable to save it. Others tend to think she is a woman who died in childbirth. Both theories hold some validity. There are a number of instances of guests being awakened to moaning and crying; a member of the night staff saw her in the parlor, crying and calling for her baby; a psychic as well as staff remark on the sadness that permeates the parlor; guests report a presence in the parlor and in some of the rooms, a photographer took a picture in which appear the faces of an adult and a child on the headboard of the bed in Room 1. Most of the activity at the hotel reportedly takes place in Rooms 1 and 6 and the parlor. At the City Hotel of Columbia they charge for the rooms but not for the spirits.

Local author, Carol Biederman (carolb@sonnet.com) gives ghost tours which last about 1 1/2 hours, a walking tour which includes a walk up to the Columbia Cemetery, and ghost stories (and history) of City Hotel, Fallon Hotel, Fallon House Theater, the Rehm House, Harlan House and a residence on Fulton St. For reservations call 209-532-1479.

Fallon Hotel, Theatre & Ice Cream Parlor

Particulars

PO Box 1870, 11175 Washington Street,
Columbia, CA 95310
Phone: 209-532-1470 I Fax: 209-532-7027
Toll-free: 1-800-532-1479
E-mail: info@cityhotel.com
Website: www.cityhotel.com

History

The hotel was constructed in 1857 during Columbia's Gold Rush days and restored in 1985. James Fallon built the theater in 1886. The establishment is listed on the National Register of Historic Places. Enjoy an evening in this restored Victorian hotel featuring rooms from the small and intimate to the grandeur of the bridal suite. Management is pleased to share the Fallon Theater, which has productions throughout the year (call: 209-532-3120. Treat yourself to a hot-fudge sundae or banana split at the ice cream parlor.

Hauntspitality

A youthful phantom boy at the Fallon is quite active according to management and staff. He has been sighted by a medium and a four-year-old girl spoke to him. The child likes to borrow the toys of the children who stay at the hotel and when he tires of them he discards them in places other than where they originated. Recently, this spirit has taken apart a child's toys -- once while the child slept and the other time while the family was out for dinner -- in the latter case, the spirited boy scattered the pieces all around the room. These latest incidents took place in Room 3 of the hotel.

On another occasion, while in Room 3, a startled housekeeper watched as a small rug in the room slid across the floor and under one of the beds; needless to say, the room was not cleaned that day by that housekeeper. A mysterious furniture mover has also been busy in Room 1 and Room 6. Also, recent guests in Room 1 reported waking up from a deep sleep to see a man walk through their room and out the doors that lead to the balcony. There is no information as to who the male energy might be.

Parapsychologists visiting the theater (which is attached to the hotel) speculate that the man in Period clothing roams the theater is none other than James Fallon who built the theater in 1886. Perhaps he visits the hotel to rearrange furniture and ensure that everything is as HE wants it.

To this day, there are frequent reports of unexplainable noises; disembodied voices which call to staff and guests or carry on animated, other-worldly conversations; and overpowering smell of smoke that drifts through certain areas of the theater; the smell whiskey in one room; a female spirit who materializes in rooms 9 and 13; theater lights which mysteriously go on and off; and dark shadows or misty forms that suddenly confront people at the hotel.

Local author, Carol Biederman (carolb@sonnet.com) gives ghost tours which last about 1 1/2 hours, a walking tour which includes a walk up to the Columbia Cemetery, and ghost stories (and history) of City Hotel, Fallon Hotel, Fallon House Theater, the Rehm House, Harlan House and a residence on Fulton St. You can call for reservations at 209-532-1479. At the Fallon Hotel you never know exactly what awaits you. Perhaps an excellent theater show, comfortable room, ice cream and even spirits which love to entertain without adhering to a schedule.

Corona del Mar
Five Crowns Restaurant

Particulars
3801 E Coast Highway,
Corona del Mar, CA 92625
Phone: 949-760-0331
Website: www.lawrysonline.com/fivecrowns

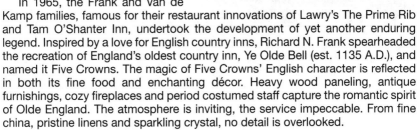

History
In 1965, the Frank and Van de Kamp families, famous for their restaurant innovations of Lawry's The Prime Rib and Tam O'Shanter Inn, undertook the development of yet another enduring legend. Inspired by a love for English country inns, Richard N. Frank spearheaded the recreation of England's oldest country inn, Ye Olde Bell (est. 1135 A.D.), and named it Five Crowns. The magic of Five Crowns' English character is reflected in both its fine food and enchanting décor. Heavy wood paneling, antique furnishings, cozy fireplaces and period costumed staff capture the romantic spirit of Olde England. The atmosphere is inviting, the service impeccable. From fine china, pristine linens and sparkling crystal, no detail is overlooked.

Hauntspitality
Over the years, those who have working inside have reportedly sensed at least one female presence roaming the building. There have been reports of sudden cold spots which engulf guests and staff alike; disembodied footsteps making their way up the staircase; doors that open and shut by themselves; and lights that occasional flicker on and off without human assistance. Some people report the feeling of being followed or as if someone unseen is watching them in certain parts of the building. No one has ever felt threatened, and over time, people have come to accept the benign spirited play inside as if they were regular paying customers.

One employee reportedly came face to face with a misty apparition. Although there were no identifying features, the staff person felt as if the energy was feminine, as the warm, soft cloud-like energy engulfed the individual. The staff-person not only did not feel threatened, but rather, sensed a caring, kind spiritual energy fill the room. No matter what direction the person decided to head in, the energy followed. After a few minutes, the feeling dissipated as quickly as it had arrived.

Other individuals have actually spotted more than one female figure floating around upstairs area, which served as a former bordello. Unexplained footsteps, odd noises, rapidly materializing cold spots and feelings of being watched, are common inside. The nameless female phantoms, who continue their afterlife service in a place that many must have called a second home, are still sighted or felt inside this Orange County establishment. If this keeps up there may come a time where there is a spirit for each crown.

Coronado Island
Hotel del Coronado

Particulars

1500 Orange Avenue,
Coronado, CA 92118
Phone: 619-522-8000
Fax: 619-522-8262
Toll free: 1-800-HOTEL-DEL
      (1-800-468-3533)
E-mail: delinquiries@hoteldel.com | Website: www.hoteldel.com

History

The world-renowned Hotel del Coronado, southern California's only oceanfront resort, graces 26 seaside acres along the sun-swept Pacific coast. A National Historic Landmark, The Del Coronado has enchanted guests for more than a century with its spectacular setting, lavish service, world-class facilities, and easy-going charm. Visited by celebrities, foreign dignitaries and 14 U.S. presidents, beginning with Benjamin Harrison in 1891, the Hotel del Coronado has remained the Grande Dame of the Pacific since 1888.

In the 1880s, the Coronado (then known as North Island and South Island) was merely sagebrush and sand. But two men, H.L. Story and Elisha Babcock, envisioned a grand hotel. Babcock and Story purchased the entire Coronado peninsula for $110,000. In 1888, The Del became the largest electrically lit facility west of the Mississippi. It made headlines around the globe. Before the Hotel del Coronado opened its doors in February 1888, developers tirelessly promoted the grand opening. When sugar magnate John D. Spreckels sailed into quiet San Diego harbor in the late 1800s, he invested heavily in The Hotel, and soon purchased "the talk of the Western world." He undertook a renovation to transform The Del into an even more opulent hotel, and it was closed from June to December of 1900, and guests were put up in tents on the beach. After the renovation was complete, the tents remained and became a popular summer resort known as Tent City.

In 1911, Glenn Curtiss successfully flew the first hydroplane launched from a ship anchored just off the hotel's shores. The Prince of Wales visited the hotel in 1920. In 1904, The Wizard of Oz author L. Frank Baum visited the hotel, and some readers suggest that the "Emerald City" he describes in his later Oz books bears an amazing resemblance to The Del Coronado. Charles Lindbergh was honored with a gala dinner on September 21, 1927, to celebrate his historic transatlantic flight. The Spirit of St. Louis was built in San Diego, and Lindbergh flew from North Island to St. Louis and then to New York, the starting place for his flight across the Atlantic. President Franklin D. Roosevelt visited the hotel several times during his presidency.

Tent City continued to thrive until it closed in 1939. In 1948, the hotel was sold to Robert Norblom, who sold it 48 hours later to Kansas City hotelier Barney Goodman, who undertook a restoration project until his death in 1951. The hotel went through a period of neglect until 1960, when the hotel's owner, John S. Alessio, began a renovation. Soon Hollywood began filming at the hotel. Perhaps the most famous of all is Some Like it Hot. In 1963, Chicago developer M. Larry Lawrence purchased the hotel, and began an ambitious $80 million construction and renovation project that nearly doubled the number of guestrooms and added convention space. In 1970, the Hotel del Coronado was the site of the first state dinner held outside Washington, D.C., when Mexican president Gustavo Diaz Ordaz was the guest of President Richard Nixon. The Hotel del Coronado was made a "National Historic Landmark" in 1977 by the U.S. Department of Interior. Ronald Reagan followed Nixon's lead with a mini-summit meeting in 1982 for Mexican president Miguel de la Madrid.

Hauntspitality

The "Del" is one of the most frequently used locations for television shows dealing with the paranormal, joining the Myrtles Plantation in Louisiana, the Winchester House in San Jose and the Whaley House in San Diego as one of the most well-known haunted locations in the world. The primary spirit of the Del Coronado is Kate Morgan. Many old buildings have a ghost story or two; but few tales have as many interesting twists and turns as the Kate Morgan story. Morgan arrived at The Del to meet her estranged husband, Tom, in November 1892. She waited three days and, on the fourth day, Kate was found dead on the beach with a gunshot wound to her head. Although the San Diego coroner's office declared the death a suicide, many believe Morgan was murdered. San Francisco lawyer Alan May became interested in the story, and during his visits to the Del Coronado, he encountered enough ghostly happenings to make him a true believer. May discovered that as a young woman, Morgan had kept house for a minister in San Francisco. During that time she gave birth to a son and left the child in the minister's care. The minister later adopted the baby and was rumored to be his father. May was amazed to find out that the minister was his great-grandfather!

May wrote a book about his findings entitled "The Legend of Kate Morgan: The Search for the Ghost of the Hotel Del Coronado." May looked through old records from the time of Kate's death. He came to the eventual conclusion that Kate did not kill herself, but was murdered by her husband. There are several pieces of evidence supporting this theory, the most compelling of which is the fact that the bullet in Kate's head was of a different caliber than the ones in the gun she bought. Also, the position her body was found in was not consistent with a suicide.

The room Kate checked into was 302, which is now room 3312. Room 3502, is also considered haunted. Both rooms have experienced oddly functioning electrical equipment (lights turning on and off, etc.) and cold breezes. Maids report that unseen hands move around objects. Guests in the rooms (those who were brave enough to stay the night!) have experienced oppressive feelings and curtains that move even though the windows are closed. Other people swear they have heard murmuring coming from somewhere in the room.

Kate's ghost has been seen walking down hallways of the hotel and standing at windows. According to Alan May, an electrician told him that the light over the steps where Kate died would not stay lit. The bulb is replaced constantly, but the light always winks out. May also claims that while he was staying in one of the haunted rooms (the sources I have do not make it clear which one), he saw a face on the television (which was, of course, turned off at the time). One or two hotel employees verified this sighting.

HOTEL DEL CORONADO,

E. S. BABCOCK, Manager.   Coronado, California.

Money, Jewels, and other valuable Packages, must be placed in the Safe in the office, otherwise the Proprietors will not be responsible for any loss.

NAMES.	RESIDENCE.	ROOMS.	TIME
Thursday Nov. 24th 1892			
Mark F. Williams	N.Y. City	300	L.
Henry Pereira	Pawtucket R.I.	157	"
Mrs R.M Gage	Pawtucket R.I.	153	"
Mrs M.E French	Pawtucket R.I.	153	"
Geo Nest	Detroit M	113	
Mrs R. Irwin	Denver Colo	315	"
Grace Irwin	Denver Colo	315	"
Miss Lottie A. Bernard	Detroit	300	
Jos Jones	Boston	371	"
Ira Clark + wife	Coronado	cottage	"
Fran E Clark	"	"	"
H.C. Moon	New Mex	196	S

85

Coulterville
Hotel Jeffery

Particulars
1 Main Street, P.O. Box 440,
Coulterville, CA 95311
Phone: 209-878-3471
Fax: 209-878-3473
Toll Free: 800-464-3471
E-mail: info@hoteljeffery.com
Website: www.hoteljeffery.com

History
Nestled in the foothills of the Majestic Sierras is the three-story, Hotel Jeffery. The hotel's 30-inch adobe and rock foundations date to before 1850, when it was a Mexican store and fandango hall. A glass case in the lobby contains a guest book signed by President Theodore Roosevelt on May 15, 1903, when he stayed overnight on his way to meet John Muir in Yosemite National Park. Many other luminaries have stayed at the comfortably furnished hotel in days gone by, including gold miners, gun fighters and adventurers from every continent.

Among the famous that have stayed at the Hotel Jeffery were John D. Rockefeller, John Muir, Mark Twain, Carrie Nation, and the last king of Hawaii.

Infamous guests have included Black Bart, Frank James and Joaquin Murietta. The Hotel Jeffery, family owned since 1851, is located in Coulterville, the whole of which is a state Historical Landmark.

Hauntspitality
The Hotel Jeffery website begins, Are we Haunted? Over the past century-and-

a-half, strange things have occurred at Hotel Jeffery. Many of these incidences have been documented and some simply remain as legends passed down through the years. Hotel Jeffery is listed in the book "California Ghost Notes, Haunted Happenings throughout the Golden State" by Randall A. Reinstedt, and today new 'experiences' occur quite often. Come in and see for yourself."

According the hotel, a number of ghost guests have been sighted in the structure. Appropriately, the ghost that is most often observed in the saloon is that of a miner. The restaurant, on the other hand, seems to cater more to ghosts of the female variety. One such entity - thought to be the ghost of a maid who worked at the facility in the early 1900's - delights in rearranging silverware after tables have been set. In particular, knives are mysteriously moved from their customary spots and placed horizontally above the place settings. Other dining room incidents occur in the dead of night, when objects are turned upside down.

Finally, the ghostly figure of a female guest has been observed both in the restaurant and on the hotel's second floor. (Incidentally, the maid who rearranges the silverware is also said to frequent the hotel. Usually her image is spotted on the staircase leading to the second floor. If you happen to visit the Jeffery, check the fourth or fifth step from the top.)" You can find more exciting stories about the Hotel Jeffery in the book "California Ghost Notes" for sale in the lobby of the Hotel.

At least one former occupant reportedly frequents this fabulous old hotel. Staff and guests frequently report paranormal events inside particular hotel rooms, which have a reputation for spirited activity. The haunted Magnolia Saloon, with its long, hand-carved wooden bar serves up great food amongst an eclectic collection of local characters and memorabilia from the Yosemite and Mother lode areas.

There are numerous reports of an older spectral gentleman in his 50s and a younger phantom female in her 30s. If you're looking for the ghosts, ask to stay in room 22. A parapsychologist who worked for the Los Angeles police department visited the hotel and said that the ghosts are friendly and mean no harm. The Hotel Jeffery has been featured on An American Moment with James Earl Jones in a segment titled "Haunted Hotel" which aired on July 13, 1998.

Additional reports of paranormal activity, which have occurred over the years are fairly benign and include:
• Lights will inexplicably turn on and off by themselves;
• Doors will open unassisted, or suddenly close in front of startled guests or staff;
• Unexplained sounds including footsteps and voices come from unoccupied rooms;
• Occasional apparitions are spotted in the hotel corridors; and,
• Items will manage to disappear and reappear in other areas of the building.

At the Jeffery you never know if you will be talking to or sleeping with your companion or one of their ghostly guests.

Crystal Bay
Cal-Neva Resort Hotel & Casino

Particulars
2 Stateline Road,
Crystal Bay, NV 89402
Phone: 800-CAL-NEVA
Fax: 775-831-9007
E-mail: Reservations@CalNevaResort.com
Website: www.CalNevaResort.com

History

The original Lodge was built in 1926 by wealthy San Francisco businessman, Robert P. Sherman, who used the Lodge as a guesthouse for his friends and real estate clients. The Lodge was designed after Frank Bacon's log cabin in the hit Broadway play "LIGHTNIN," starring Will Rogers. The Cal Neva Resort quickly became the playground for celebrities and socialites who wanted to escape from the public eye. During 1928 The Cal Neva Resort came into the hands of Norman Biltz, known as "The Duke of Nevada.". Then in 1930 Biltz married Esther Auchincloss Nash, granddaughter to the founder of Standard Oil and aunt of Jacqueline Kennedy-Onassis. The original Cal Neva Lodge burned to the ground on May 17, 1937 and was rebuilt in just over thirty days by Norman Biltz and Adler Larson, both early Tahoe pioneers and developers. Over 500 men were employed to work around the clock to finish the new building which is seen today in the Indian Room, Circle Bar and main casino area.

The Cal Neva Resort earned the nickname "Lady of the Lake," weathering heavy snowfalls and the remodeling of a succession of owners including serious gamblers with names like "Pretty Boy," "Bones," and "Baby Face" during the 1940's and 1950's. During the Frank Sinatra ownership years of 1960 to 1963, along with his associates "Wingy" and "Skinny," Sinatra built the now famous Celebrity Showroom and installed a helicopter pad on the roof in an attempt to make access easier for his colleagues and guests appearing at The Cal Neva Resort during the summer months.

Hollywood followers were enamored with Sinatra and the "Rat Pack". Dean Martin, Sammy Davis Jr., Juliet Prowse, and Marilyn Monroe (among others) "sang for their suppers" in the Celebrity Showroom and the Indian Room while politicians and Hollywood stars played at the tables and in the private cottages overlooking Lake Tahoe.

When the presence of one particular guest, Sam Giancana of Chicago, was noticed by authorities, it finally cost Sinatra his gaming license in a losing battle with the Nevada Gaming Control Board. The "Lady of the Lake" suffered tremendously from neglect for nearly twenty years before she was purchased in December of 1985 and was given a new life by owner, Charles P. Bluth who operated the resort until February 15, 2005 when it was purchased by Namwest, LLC and went through a complete renovation and restoration program intended to position the resort as the leading destination in Lake Tahoe with services and accommodations that will meet the needs of the most discriminating traveler.

Hauntspitality

If walls could talk, and some say that the walls inside this historic building do, the stories this place could tell could fill several books. The Cal-Neva is the oldest standing casino in the US. Dignitaries, celebrities and figures from organized crime frequented this building, and many people think that their spirits or energy still converge on the hotel from time to time. Rumors of mob killings, overdoses, illicit and secretive affairs, excessive gambling and drinking parties, and high level bribes and payoffs are only part of the history and mystery of this place.

A week before her untimely suicide, Marilyn Monroe was rumored to have overdosed in her private cabin after Robert Kennedy visited her here. Her final suicide occurred a short time later, but her spirit is said to frequent her hideaway here. Marilyn was born Norma Jeanne Mortenson on June 1, 1926 in Los Angeles and died on August 5, 1962 at 36.

Secret tunnels, private rooms, gossip and untold secrets always mark a good haunted location, and this resort is no exception. Most of the ghost stories materialized after the hotel went through its thorough renovation process. Immediately after reopening to the public, a security guard saw a filmy, sobbing figure in the hallway that he described as Marilyn Monroe. Guests and staff have reported seeing a hearing her ghost in various parts of the building. The sad and forlorn figure seems to be seen or heard one minute, and will then vanish into thin air. Other apparitions have been sighted downstairs and in parts of the hotel. There are often seen as filmy or misty images that float by, sometimes oblivious to the onlookers, and then they vanish.

Frank Sinatra is said to also wander the hotel, particularly in the secret tunnel area. Sinatra was born Francis Albert Sinatra on December 12, 1915 in Hoboken, New Jersey and died in Los Angeles, California on May 14, 1998. Having frequented the resort over the years, and having had a vested interest at one time, this place no doubt harbored quite a few good memories for him, enough to still draw his spirit back for occasional visits. Other reported phenomena include doors opening and closing without human assistance; rapidly manifesting cold spots and unexplained gusts of freezing air; disembodied footsteps; animated conversations coming from unoccupied areas of the building; disembodied footsteps; people being touched by unseen hands, and shadowing figures that suddenly vanish into thin air. At this resort, the dead famous still make occasional appearances; you can bet on it!

Death Valley
Furnace Creek Inn

Particulars
P.O. Box 1, Death Valley, CA 92328 and
Highway 190, Death Valley, CA 92328
Phone: 760.786.2345
Fax: 760.786.2514
Toll-free: 800-236-7916
E-mail: info-fc@xanterra.com
Website: http://www.furnacecreekresort.com

History

The complex was constructed by the Pacific Coast Borax Company in 1927 and was finished in 1935. Its adobe brick walls were made on site by Paiute and Shoshone laborers. The Furnace Creek Inn rooms are clean, well-appointed and provide modern comforts without sacrificing historic character.

Hauntspitality

According to those in the paranormal "know", "Room 199 at the Furnace Creek Inn at Death Valley National Park is reputed to have been visited by ghosts! This room is so popular that advanced reservations are required! Check it out!" According to the Legends of America: Sleeping with Ghosts Website (http://www.legendsofamerica.com/CA-HauntedHotels2.html) The Furnace Creek Inn & Ranch Resort lies on the glittering salt flats of Death Valley National Park; an oasis in the desert. The mission-style inn with its thick adobe walls, opened in 1927, and not only continues to retain its vintage atmosphere, but also a vintage era ghost. This friendly phantom is thought to be that of Chef James Marquez, who worked at the hotel from 1959 to 1973. Forced to quit due to illness, he died three years later. But, Chef Marquez evidently liked his job so much, he continues roam "his" kitchen and dining room, mysteriously opening and closing doors, rearranging equipment and tools, and making all manner of odd noises in the middle of the night.

Psychics who have visited this historic structure confirm that as many as five spirits may inhabit this building. The feeling in the paranormal community is that several former borax company employees, a chef and a female who may have helped with the house cleaning duties are still hanging around the building, mingling with the guests and keeping an eye on the staff.

The unexplained events at the inn are numerous and include doors that open and close by themselves; disembodied footsteps; lights that mysteriously turn on and off in some of the rooms; noticeable changes in temperature in some areas of the inn that chill people to the bone even on the hottest days; misty forms and shadowy figures; items being moved or rearranged by unseen hands; and a rare apparition or two.

At the Furnace Creek Inn, luxury and relaxation compliment the enthralling desert environs that surround your senses at every glance. The seasons may come and go, but there is one constant at this slice of heaven; its spirits who seem to enjoy communing with the living all year around.

Death Valley Junction
Amargosa Hotel

Particulars
P.O. Box 608,
Death Valley Junction, CA 92328
Phone: 760-852-4441
Fax: 760-852-4138
E-mail: amargosa@kay-net.com

History

Death Valley Junction was built by the Pacific Coast Borax Company, with construction completed by 1924. The town has gone through many ups and downs and passed through many owners as it spiraled to Ghost Town status after the Borax Company pulled up stakes. Moving the majority of the buildings to a new location in the 1940's the company left behind the currently existing adobe structures which were immovable. Before the Borax Company constructed the town, the only sign of life was a ramshackle tent/shack area called Amargosa.

During 1981 Marta Becket's Amargosa Opera House, Inc. (a non profit Corporation) purchased the town of Death Valley Junction. In 1968, Marta Becket leased the current Amargosa Opera House building from the then owners. It was named Corkgill Hall, used as a multi-purpose building over the years until it was abandoned. Marta resurrected the old hall and turned it into a beautiful Opera House. The Hotel building served a dual purpose in the old days. Half the structure served as a working hotel, while the other half served as a dormitory for single miners. The hotel is being restored. The dorm has not yet been revitalized. The south wing of the building housed a grocery store, post office, payroll offices, cafe, and small dorm.

Hauntspitality

Many orbs, mists and streamers of ectoplasm are photographed in the south wing of the building, as well as the Hotel and Opera House. According to Becket and Novak, some days you will hear doors opening and closing in the hotel all day, while other days the doors actually do open and close. There are unexplained knockings on walls and doors; people's names being called out by an invisible someone; lights turning off and on by themselves; a lady wearing a long blue dress will occasionally run down the length of the colonnade, always north to south, and disappear at a gate at the end of the colonnade; voices, like a large crowd of people, are often heard coming from the abandoned old cafe; the sound of a baby crying emanates from a wall in one of the hotel rooms; one room has a shower curtain which sometimes slams closed when one sits on the commode; things are frequently moved to another location or disappear for several hours before reappearing; moans, groans, mumbling sounds come from various unoccupied locations; singing and, or, sounds of music emanate from areas that are not being used; the noise of chains being dragged are sometime heard; the sounds of two men fighting have been heard on Becket's roof; horrible cries of a cat fight come from Becket's bedroom where she and one cat sleep, and; the sounds of furniture crashing and glass breaking have been heard coming from the downstairs area in her house. Several tragedies occurred over the years in the hotel, especially when it was used as dormitory, including a hanging that was shrouded in mystery.

During a Fox Family Channel Special that aired in October 2002, called **America's Scariest Places**, Hotel Manager, Lori Novak called the Amargosa Hotel the most spirited place she has ever been in. Owner Marta Becket considers her place the Times Square of the spirit world, while Tom Willett, Marta Becket's stage partner who appears in the Ballet, pantomime and comedy productions presented at The Amargosa Opera House is more frank in his appraisal of the place, "I know damn well it's haunted." Add housekeeper Ann Sherrell Gray's frequent contact with the dead in the form of sightings and various moans and groans, and you have a hotel located in an area which ties in perfectly with its clientele, Death Valley Junction. Novak adds that there are times when it sounds like doors are being kicked in, glass is falling to the floor and unseen hands are rearranging furniture.

One staff person while staying in Room 9, during November 1998, went to her room to get things ready to enter the dorm after the office closed at 10:00pm. Another staff member, who was to join her, was writing dates on a cassette tape since there was no power in dorm. The woman at the dresser writing in front of a mirror got an odd feeling that she was being watched. Turning to look up and over her right shoulder, she was stunned to see a lady propped up on the pillows just smiling. The mysterious woman had blonde, shoulder-length hair, tucked behind her ears, and was wearing a white shirt with ruffles down the front and on the sleeves, and blue polyester pants with her legs were crossed. As the witness turned away for a moment, trying to grasp what she was looking at, then looked back in the mirror, the strange woman began to dissolve into the bed.

A movie company visited the Amargosa Hotel in 1994. The location crew was looking for an out-of-the-way setting for its film, and it found one at the Amargosa. Director Gary Orona and Director of Photography, Roger Olkowski agreed, that the setting was out-right "creepy," with a "visceral feeling," especially the older section which seem to have an energy all its own. This was confirmed during the shooting of a scene with actress Monique Parent. During Take 1 of Scene 873, as Parent was walking down the darkened hallway holding a flashlight, she delivered her line, "Hello." The audio man quickly yelled out that he picked up another voice on tape.

Playing the brief scene back, a moaning or crying sound was plainly audible in the background. It's a sound that no one would ever forget. However, "the show must go on," and so it did. Another take with Parent uttering the words, "Is anybody there?" didn't produce an otherworldly sound, but rather a distinct shadow which followed her on film as she approached the camera. The eerie shade appeared over her shoulder as if watching her as she moved down the corridor. The crew was definitely "spooked" as they had somehow tapped into a restless hotel ghost.

Intent on finding out who or what was behind the strange occurrences experienced by the film crew, an impromptu séance was held by five crew members, along with someone taking notes and another person recording the events in one of the abandoned rooms near the filming location. With a makeshift Ouija board and candles, the crew summoned the spirit. The resulting session produced the

name "Hangman" and much more. Parent was suddenly seized by the energy of this spirit and began weeping uncontrollably. She was overcome by such sadness, the séance was quickly concluded. The next day, however, something even stranger happened to Parent. Somehow, in the middle of January, and while filming inside the entire time, her face and arms were burned, as if she had been out baking in the sun for hours. Was it her encounter with "Hangman?" This was too much to bear. In an attempt to find out what was happening to her and who was trying to frighten the crew, local medium and friend Alma Carey visited the Amargosa as part of the filming. Her immediate sense was that something evil in the older part of the building was channeling its energy toward Parent.

Carey walked through the building and immediately sensed a presence in area where filming was taking place, and went into the room where the spirit was contacted. She felt that in filming the séance, Parent's presence had triggered the paranormal events. She sensed that someone was hanged in one of the former, now abandoned, dorm rooms. The sense of something unsettling, something fear based had left an imprint there, and was very active. Reluctantly, Parent returned to the Amargosa with Carey and the two set out to find out more about "Hangman." They returned to the area and room where it all began.

The two-woman séance produced an almost instantaneous reaction from Carey that the person who was hanged did not commit suicide, but rather, was murdered in the room. Drawn by some otherworldly force, Carey and Parent followed a "psychic scent" to a patch of barren earth beyond the graveyard. It was here that Carey felt the boy who had been murdered in the dorm room, was buried in haste in unconsecrated ground. The fact that he had been murdered and buried outside the cemetery made for one angry ghost!

There was some measure of relief that at least the truth was now revealed; but did it send the restless spirit to a better place; perhaps. Or, maybe further research will be needed to reveal a name, and the circumstances behind the tragedy and a formal service can then be performed to right this injustice and truly allow "Hangman" to rest in peace.

One thing is certain; "Hangman" is not the only spirit who calls this building home. Two additional spirits are children who died during the 1918 influenza epidemic. Ghostly voices, disembodied footsteps, shadowy figures, and an occasional bump in the night still make the Amargosa a favorite for ghost hunters and adventuresome souls who like to visit this very spirited building

Diamond Springs
Diamond Springs Hotel

Particulars
545 Main Street,
P.O. Box 3273,
Diamond Springs, CA 95619
Phone: 530-621-1730
Fax: 530-642-0618

History

The town of Diamond Springs is California State Historic Landmark 487. Settled in 1848, Diamond Springs derived its name from its crystal clear springs and diamond deposits. During the late summer of 1850 a party of two hundred emigrants, led by a man named McPike, arrived from Missouri and settled the land. Among the richest spots in this vicinity, its diggings produced a 25-pound nugget, one of the largest ever found in El Dorado County.

The town thrived in 1851, and later became a contender for the county seat. Through its abundance of exploitable timber, lime production and agriculture, Diamond Springs retained its early importance. The growing town included a number of saloons, hotels, residences, general stores, a druggist, a carpenter, churches, stables, a temperance hall, and a post office.

The Diamond Springs Hotel was constructed near a Miwok Native American cemetery. The hotel also lays in the area where Sutter's original split shakes mill stood, and where miners and travelers spent the night. Originally built in 1916 by Antone Meyer, the business was continued by Antone's son, Carl, until it was sold to John Zannoni in 1932. The building has been used as a hotel upstairs, a bar, store, and restaurant on the bottom level. According to Nancy Bradley (1998), although the building brings in many ghosts, because of it's natural vortex, most of the apparitions have been there since before the hotel was constructed.

Hauntspitality

The Diamond Springs Hotel is noted for the numerous strange and unexplainable occurrences, which have been reported over the years. The spirits of the historic hotel are now a part of the ambiance and an integral fabric of the building. They are discussed as naturally as politics, weather and the food at the hotel. Spirits love to gather at this hotel for reasons yet unexplained, although there is a hint that it's proximity to a Native American cemetery may have something to do with the source of energy felt in and around the hotel.

The owners, locals, guests and staff have reported the presence of spirits on numerous occasions. People, who have spent time in the building, witnessed apparitions, heard unexplained sounds of people talking, and have listened as disembodied footsteps paced along the unoccupied upper floors. Besides the weird sounds that echo through the building, there are the musty odors, the feeling of being watched, cold drafts, and items that suddenly disappear. These are but a few of the anomalies attributed to the hotel spirits.

A number of individuals have reported seeing a misty figure of a man who enjoys a back booth in the restaurant. The phantom man is usually spotted with a dog in his lap before disappearing. The cantankerous- looking man is said to resemble a character right out of the Gold Rush days.

A psychic who visited the historic hotel, immediately sensed the energy of a man named Matthew, who reportedly died of cancer of the stomach on the spot where the hotel now stands. He had a dog-named Butch, and left two girls with relatives in Oregon. Matthew, according to the psychic, enjoys watching people eat and keeping an eye on the female restaurant staff.

A paranormal investigation produced other spirits including a woman who is often heard crying; and children playing in the kitchen area, and in the downstairs banquet room. The children love to play with the doors, water, dishes, and electricity in the building. A number of times, the lights in the building that were turned off the night before, have been found on the next morning.

A staff person who rented an upstairs apartment in the building with her husband and children often reported the sounds of children running upstairs in an area of the building where access was denied her children. Upon inspection, the door to the storage area where the sounds were coming from was still locked. No one could have gotten in, yet children were definitely running around inside---they had to be the ghost children.

There was another report of a spirit who jumped in the shower with a staff person, running it's fingers through the person's hair. The spirits are friendly, although the younger ones like to play games without discriminating between guests and staff. The Diamond Springs Hotel, after all these years and through so many transformations, is still active, and so are its spirits

Dorrington
Dorrington Hotel & Restaurant

Particulars
3431 Highway 4, P.O. Box 4307,
Dorrington, CA 95223
Phone: 209-795-5800 | Fax: 209-795-1926
E-mail: info@dorringtonhotel.com
Website: www.dorringtonhotel.com

History

Once called the Cold Spring Ranch, Clark and Benjamin Stockwell originally owned it in 1852. The Stockwells sold the 160-acre ranch to G.H. Woodruff for $600. In 1865, Woodruff expanded the ranch to 320 acres. The property passed through several owners until John Gardner, from Paisley, Scotland, bought the ranch from Minerva Hall for $1,300 in 1868. A declaration of homestead indicated that John Gardner homesteaded the property and gained clear title on February 12, 1880. He married Rebecca Dorrington, built a house known locally as the Gardner Mansion House, and had four children (John Jr. in 1854; Robert in 1857; George in 1865; and Elizabeth in 1861). A fire partially destroyed the house in 1881, and Gardner rebuilt the place into a hotel and general store for travelers a short time later. Gardner died of a stroke on October 13, 1897. Robert and Rebecca ran the business until 1910. A large pine tree fell on the mansion in 1950, leaving only two of the original rooms. The town of Dorrington was named after Gardner's wife, Rebecca.

Newspaper articles report that Rebecca met a tragic death, which is as mysterious as her ghost. Some people claim Rebecca froze to death during a severe snowstorm; some think Rebecca was killed by Indians; some tell a story of her falling down the stairs of the hotel and bleeding to death; while others say Rebecca died from pneumonia sometime late in the 1870's or 1880s. Some say the real truth is, Rebecca out-lived her husband, and died in Altaville on October 16, 1910 at the age of 83. The Calaveras newspaper stated she was a widely known person with a kind disposition. John Jr. died on December 29, 1880 at the age of 26 and is buried in Altaville. George fell to his death in a mine on January 20, 1902 in Angels Camp.

Robert (Rebecca's son) and his wife Julia E. (Farrar) gave Rebecca four grandchildren, Elizabeth, born October 1886, Rebecca, born October 1891, John Bryan, born May 1894, and Howard Lee, born July 1904. Robert died on January 28, 1920. Rebecca had one daughter, Elizabeth, who gave her a granddaughter, Reba, born in July 1877. Elizabeth married Harvey S. Blood in her parent's home on January 12, 1874. Reba Blood married Tilden Tognazzini and had one child, Harvey Blood Tognazzini who was born on January 6, 1909 and died on April 11, 1915. Reba's second husband was Dr. Alfred Grosse.

When you visit the Dorrington Hotel, ask about the legend of Rebecca's ghost, who is still known to haunt the restored hostelry. The Dorrington Inn is located along California's Scenic Route 4 in Calaveras County. At 5,000 feet in the Stanislaus National Forest, a shady village of cottages is a base for exploring the many nearby attractions. There are breathtaking views of the surrounding mountains. Among the famous persons who have visited the Dorrington Hotel over the years are Samuel Clemens, better known as Mark Twain, Roy Rogers and Dale Evans, and Robert Stack.

Hauntspitality

A number of guests, locals and staff have reported seeing and feeling the spirit of Rebecca Gardner. Rebecca has been sighted wearing a calico dress, and she has been known to move furniture, slam doors, lock visitors in their rooms, and some have seen fingerprints in places where no one else has been.

A lumberjack, staying in the hotel, saw a lady in a powder blue dress, and a white face looking at him when no one else in the room saw here. Rebecca oftentimes manifests in the attic window, always wearing a calico dress.

One woman reported about a time she was working in her office on the third floor of the hotel late at night, and she became locked inside. If not for the fact that someone passing by saw her frantically waving for help, she would have remained inside all night.

Rebecca's spirit has been heard crying in the middle of the night, a sobbing sound that is quite disturbing. The sound is said to begin softly, and then build to a mournful cry, and just as quickly, stops. No one has been able to identify the exact location of where the crying emanates---it just seems to come from everywhere. Add to that, the mysterious shadows that pass through the hallways preceded by an intense cold draft; doors which open and close by themselves; lights that go on and off in front of startled staff-persons and guests; unexplained footsteps who's source can never be traced, and; the eerie voices that seem to come from inside the walls of the hotel in the dead of night, and you have the haunted Dorrington.

Most definitely, the friendly spirit of Rebecca Dorrington lives on in the house her husband built, on the land she so loved. Ghost or no ghost, a visit to this historic gem will provide plenty of memories, even if some are of the after-life occupants.

Downieville

Durgan Flat Inn
(formerly Downieville River Inn & Resort)

Particulars
121 River Street, P.O. Box 412,
Downieville, CA 95936
Phone: 530-289-3308 | Fax: 530-289-0310 | Toll Free: 1-800-696-3308
E-mail: reservations@downievilleriverinn.com | Website: www.downievilleriverinn.com

History

Downieville, is the county seat of Sierra County, and is located on Highway 49 at the fork of the North Yuba River and the Downie River. Gold was discovered here in the summer of 1849 and John Potter built the first cabin here in December of 1849 on the north side of town. The town site was laid out in February of 1850 by James Vineyard. The town was known as The Forks when first settled, then became known as Downieville in 1850 after William Downie, a prominent miner in the area.

By May 1850, Downieville had 15 hotels and gambling houses, 4 bakeries, 4 butcher shops, and all the flat land was occupied. The south side of town was christened Washingtonville and the flat above the south side was called Murraysville. In 1850 James Durgan built a sawmill on the flat on the south side of town so the area became known as Durgan's Flat and Murraysville became known as Jersey Flat. Miners came to the area by the hundreds that spring. As the population of the area grew, Downieville served as a trading center for the Northern Mines. In 1851 the population of Downieville reached 5,000.

Era Gertrude Peckwith's husband built the central house as their residence while he mined for gold at his nearby claim.

Hauntspitality

The spirit of Era Gertrude Peckwith haunts the resort. According to the Coroner's record, Era died on August 28, 1958. She was 82 years old at the time of her death. Gertrude was 5'2" and weighed approximately 130 pounds with brown-graying hair and blue eyes. Era died from fractured ribs and sternum, and chest hemorrhage, when she accidentally fell down a steep bank while walking along a narrow trail at the Golden Eagle Mine in Downieville. She fell at about 11:00 a.m. on August 27th, and was taken back to her house by a friend. Her injuries were so severe, however, that she passed away at 5:00 p.m. on the 28th. As legends go, however, death would not stop Era from returning to the place she loved so much in life.

In Gertrude Peckwith's former room, Room 1, water spigots have been known to turn on by themselves, and guests have repeatedly complained of someone sitting on them or lying next to them on the bed. Staff has also encountered Era over the years. Her ghost has been known to make the doorknobs in the room red hot in the middle of winter, and freezing in the middle of summer.

Pets that come as visitors to the resort have also been spooked by Era. She has a way of keeping the animals on their toes, or paws. She is responsible for rapidly materializing cold spots, moving items from one place to another, phantom whispers, and disembodied footsteps that are heard throughout the house.

Era is often sighted floating around between her former bedroom, and the basement laundry room, chilling some guests to the bone, while scaring others by her sudden appearance and equally abrupt disappearing act. Shadows, cold spots, lights that turn on and off by themselves, noisy, unexplained footsteps, phantom impressions on the bed, and frightening animals seems to be Era's repertoire of paranormal playfulness. She has never harmed anyone; she just seems to want people to know that death can't keep a spirited woman down.

At the Durgan Flat Inn, the spirits are always with you as life and afterlife co-exist in peace and harmony.

OFFICE OF THE
Coroner of Sierra County
STATE OF CALIFORNIA

CORONER'S RECORD
PHILIP R. NEWBERG, Coroner

Downieville, California, August 28, 1958

Name of Deceased Era Gertrude Peckwith

Date of Death August 26, 1958 June 20, 1876 Place of Birth Beaver Dam, Kentucky

Place of Death Residence, River St. Downieville, Calif.

Body Found By August Pelletier

Address of Person Finding Body River St. Downieville, Calif.

Date of (Inquest) (Investigation) August 28, 1958

Place of (Inquest) (Investigation) Downieville, California

Sex Female Color or Race White Age 82 years

Single, Married, Widowed, Divorced

Occupation Homemaker

General Description:

Height 5' 2" Weight Approx 130 Pounds

Hair Brown-greying Eyes Blue

General Complexion Fair

Scars on Body

Property Turned Over None August Pelletier took charge

To Whom Given Address

Cause of Death multiple fracture of ribs and sternum, due to, fall down steep bank while walking along narrow trail at Golden Eagle Mine Downieville, Calif.

Autopsy Inspection by Dr. B. W. Hummeldt, M.D.

Disposition of Body Bergemann Funeral Chapel, Nevada City, Calif. Burial - Downieville Cemetery.

Remarks Niece - Marguerite Elledge, 1101 St. Louis Ave. Long Beach, C Injuries received at approximately 11 A. M. August the 27th, 1958, Fell down steep bank while walking along narrow trail at Golden Eagle Mine, Downieville, Calif. Medical care by Dr. C. C. Sutton, Downieville, Calif.

Signed Philip R. Newberg Coroner

Eureka
Abigail's 'Elegant Victorian Mansion'

Particulars

1406 "C" Street, 14th & "C" Streets,
Eureka, CA 95501-1765
Phone: 707-444-3144 | Fax: 707-442-3295
E-mail: info@eureka-california.com or
evm@humboldt1.com
Website: www.eureka-california.com or www.bbonline.com/ca/abigails

History

The Elegant Victorian Mansion is a National Historic Landmark featuring spectacular gingerbread exteriors, and opulent Victorian interiors. North Coast business magnate William Clark built in 1888. Clark's father, Jonathan, a physician for future General and President Ulysses S. Grant, co-founded Eureka in 1850.

When his father died in 1884, William, who had been running the family cattle ranch, moved back into town, took over the Clark banking, brewery, real estate, and mill operations, and erected the town's most opulent Victorian a few blocks away from his father's homestead. Later, as mayor and county commissioner, he entertained railroad baron A. Leland Stanford, California Senator A. W. Way and theatrical giant Lily Langtry at his residence. The Clark Estate remained in the family until 1942 continuing as a private residence until 1990, when Doug and Lily Vieyra opened it as an inn.

Hauntspitality

Doug and Lily Vieyra passed on this tale to us verbatim! "It was what we here at the inn call 'The Night of the Slamming Doors.' We have lived in the old house (build in 1888) for almost ten years now, and this event has happened only once. First of all, my wife and I do not necessarily believe in 'ghosts' or 'hauntings' -- per se. As educated world travelers, we think of ourselves as rational, and look for rational explanations behind unusual events and circumstances. One of our pleasures in this big old (sometimes empty, as it was on this particular night) mansion, is curling up in front of a fire, with only a few candles glowing for soft mood light and quietly listen to the gentle, soft music of the great classics - Mozart being our favorite, along with Vivaldi.

It was on one of these quiet evenings of quiet relaxation when a loud bang occurred upstairs. As we were alone in the house, our rational minds began building a scenario of what had caused the great noise - a door caught by a sudden gust of wind, slamming shut in all probability. As fresh air lovers, we often leave our windows and doors open; so this scenario seemed extremely plausible and greatly probable. With my wife left behind, curled up on the sofa, I climbed the stairs to the second of our two floors, to discover all of our doors still fully opened, but our windows had now all been shut. Well, I chalked off the discrepancy to my forgetful memory - I had probably closed all the windows earlier.

Satisfied that a solution to the mystery had been found, I returned down stairs and back to the Turkish Sitting Room and the warm fire. I had just sat down, when BANG!, once again - the loud sound again coming from upstairs. With a much greater anxiousness this time, I raced upstairs to find the cause of the mysterious sound. Perhaps a vase falling off a table, or a painting and frame slipping off the frieze molding - certainly a reasonable and rational explanation, I was sure. But there was nothing amiss; no fallen vase, no missing painting from the wall, in fact, nothing out of place - nothing out of the ordinary. But this time, while I was still on the second floor, I surveyed all the objects in each and every room to assess each item's probable sound, if leaving its appointed place of residence and abruptly landing in some new place. Only one thing could make the noise we had twice heard. The sound of a door being slammed shut. But all of our doors were still fully opened. Puzzled, I carefully and securely closed each and every door, to eliminate any future door banging. Finally satisfied, I returned once again downstairs to the warm glow of the fire and the beauty of Mozart, confident that this time the disturbances had come to an end.

When the third loud bang occurred, our rational composure began to weaken and crumble. With both of us now unnerved, I once again climbed the stairs to find the source of the mysterious noise. Looking high and low, I found nothing out of the ordinary; except the doors were all opened. Of course, doors don't generally bang when they open. I have long since stopped trying to figure out what happened that night - the night of the slamming doors. But I do know one thing - I am now less certain that there are rational, reasonable explanations for "things that go bump in the night."

According to the owners, some people speculate that the spirit of the house is a woman who has a taste for traditional jazz. One evening, a female guest told the owners she was a medium, and the rear parlor had a ghost who was trapped there.

Since then, a number of guests have reported strange events. Another guest in the Van Gogh Room complained that someone opened her door. Each time after the door was securely closed, the person would return to find it open. On another occasion, a house-sitting friend was awakened by music coming from downstairs. The Mansion is equipped with an electronic alarm system, so the sitter knew no one had broken in. She thought she left the radio or TV set on, she went down to check. The hand-cranked horn phonograph was playing by itself---for the second time. It has to be wound each time, and even stranger, the mysterious someone or something had selected a 1928 recording of the Duke Ellington band playing St. Louis Blues.

Doors in the house continue to open unassisted and personal things often disappear into thin air. So, when you visit, make sure you're up on your jazz, just ignore the occasional slamming doors and don't worry if you can't find your keys where you left them; they'll turn up somewhere. And, if you chance to meet the spirit of the house, know that she is friendly and enjoys the human guests!

Ferndale
The Gingerbread Mansion Inn

Particulars

400 Berding Street, P.O. Box 40,
Ferndale, CA 95536
Phone: 707-786-4000
Toll Free: 800-952-4136
E-mail: kenn@humboldt1.com
Website: www.gingerbread-mansion.com

History

The Gingerbread Mansion Inn is one of Northern California's most photographed inns. The home was built in 1899 as a residence for Dr. Hogan Ring, a Norwegian immigrant. Later, in the 1920's, Dr. Ring formed a corporation, added an annex, and converted the entire building into the Ferndale General Hospital. Bankrupt after three years, the building became a rest home for a short time, and was later used as doctor's offices, and then an American Legion Hall. In 1920, the people of Ferndale and of the surrounding valley faced a condition of inadequate hospital facilities and an arduous journey to Eureka for access to more modern and available medical attention. They decided to raise money through the selling of stock for a newer hospital. When $18,000 worth of stock had been sold, a meeting of the stockholders was called and after adopting an article of incorporation, they elected a board of directors who were empowered to secure a location and erect a structure suitable for such a hospital.

The home of Dr. Ring, together with adjoining lots, was purchased, and the work of enlarging and altering the property was pushed through quickly. The full cost of buying the property, renovating the building and equipping it was approximated $40,000. After three years of service, the hospital still struggled under $3,500 of debt. On July 7, 1924, the Board of Directors sent a letter of appeal to the stockholders, and the hospital was closed shortly thereafter. In the 1950's, it was changed to an apartment building. By the 1960's it was abandoned and dilapidated when purchased by two individuals who restored the building and converted the front (the original home) to their residence, and the back to improved apartments. As landscape designers, the owners created the existing formal English garden. Ken Torbert bought the mansion in 1981, and opened it as a bed and breakfast in 1983.

Hauntspitality

The Gingerbread Mansion Inn seems to cater not only to the living, but to the spirits of two children who reportedly run and play throughout the inn. Before being restored, the dilapidated old house had a history of being haunted, and was avoided by locals, particularly, young children. The fact that it was residence, hospital, rest home, doctors offices, an American Legion Hall and finally an inn, may help explain the paranormal activity that has been encountered inside the mansion. Over the years, odd things have been reported, including a picture that was hung in the front parlor, which mysteriously found its way into the lounge. On other occasion, guests reported walking up the main staircase and slipping on the slightly shortened thirteenth stair. Some people claim that they slipped not because of the shortened step, but because someone shoved them.

One guest spending his 20th birthday in a suite awoke in a state of panic because he was positive that someone was next to him in bed. On another occasion, two women guests who arrived from the Bay area just on the chance they might see the ghost children of the Gingerbread Mansion. They were not disappointed, as has been the case with a number of other guests who have witnessed the phantom children. Numerous guests have logged their encounters in the guest books, which are left in each room.

Cindi Rice provided the following story for our book: My husband and I spent one night at The Gingerbread last month, as part of a 10 day trip through Northern California. I had never heard about any hauntings there, so in no way was I on the lookout for anything unusual or even thinking about such a thing. We stayed in The Rose Suite, which is the suite on the second floor, facing into the street, with the circular porch in front of it. This particular room has an enormous bed and fireplace in the bedroom, and another fireplace in the bathroom, with a fainting couch in front of it.

When we returned from dinner my husband went up to bed, but I stayed downstairs in the front parlor, looking through the scrapbooks that were on one of the tables that held photos and the history of the inn. Finally I went upstairs, took a bath, and lay down on the fainting couch in front of the bathroom fireplace to read my book, with the door shut so the light wouldn't disturb my husband. After about 10 minutes I became aware that I wasn't alone in the bathroom. There definitely was a presence in there with me..... not sinister feeling, just.....there. I looked around, saw nothing, and tried to go back to my book, but the feeling of not being alone become stronger, and I decided being in the bathroom alone with the door shut was no longer such a good idea!

I turned off the light, shut down the fireplace, went into the bedroom, got into bed and fell asleep, with my right arm hanging wrist up over the side of the bed. Sometime later I was jolted awake by the very real feeling of someone dragging an ice cube very slowly across my right wrist. I was so startled that I actually slapped my left hand on my right wrist and firmly wiped it off, thinking that there was water there from the ice cube. Of course there was no water, just the still-very-cold sensation remaining on my skin. I was, at this point, very much awake, and laid there in the dark, assessing what this could possibly be.

The room became very cold, with a sort of pressure to the atmosphere. I tried to wake my husband up, but he was sound asleep, so I just continued to lay in the dark, observing. I was very startled, and somewhat crept out, but not really scared, because the energy in the room felt playful. It also had a lighter feel, as if it might be female, as opposed to the heavier feel of masculine energy.

After some thought I realized that what I had felt was someone dragging a freezing cold fingertip very slowly, and probably playfully, across my wrist. I accepted this explanation quietly, and continued to lay in the dark, waiting for anything else that might happen. That energy stayed in the room with me for about 15 minutes, and it felt as if it and I were just sort of observing one another. Finally the sensation began to slowly fading away, and I eventually went back to sleep.

When we got back home from our trip I sent an email to the owners, asking them if the house was haunted, and they replied that although they had never had anything happen to them, other guests had reported "things". I've never had a bona fide experience with a ghost before, but this certainly qualifies as one!

Reading the entries is worth a visit, alone, but there's is so much more to do at this magnificent inn. If you ever decide to visit the Mansion without your children, have no fear, because there are other children who would love your attention; however, be

Fillmore
Heritage Valley Inn

Particulars
691 North Main Street, Piru, California 93040
Phone: 805-521-0700
Fax: 805-521-0707
Website: www.heritagevalleyinn.com
E-mail: heritagevalleyinn@msn.com

History

The Piru Hotel was built as a second home for David C. Cook, Piru's founder, whose main residence is the town landmark, the Piru Mansion. Cook's first house, a three-story Queen Anne Victorian building, was located at the top of Park Street. It burned to the ground in 1981 and was completely rebuilt. Although the architect for the Piru Hotel is unknown, this Colonia Revival building dates to around 1888. At the turn of the century, the Piru Hotel was

the only stopover between Santa Paula and Castaic Junction. The hotel catered to cattle buyers, oilmen and the movie industry. While filming "Ramona" at nearby Rancho Camulos, Mary Pickford, Douglas Fairbanks and D.W. Griffith stayed at the hotel in 1911.

During its long and colorful history it has been known as the Piru Hotel, Mountain View Hotel, and the Round Rock. Later, the building appeared in the films, "The Five Heartbeats" and "The Silhouette."

According to their website, Harry Lechler was born in the hotel in 1912 when his parents owned it and spent his boyhood years there. The old Phone switchboard served not only the hotel but the whole town. When his parents bought the building in 1911, they changed its name from Mountain View Hotel to Round Rock Hotel for the huge boulder in the front lawn. In the 1950s, it was converted into a rest home and housed elderly residents until 1989. By that time, four more bathrooms had been added and the there were 15 bedrooms inside. The restored building has been renamed The Heritage Valley Inn, and it preserves the warmth and hospitality it has offered during the past 110 years. This historic hotel, a noted landmark, is also a place where the past reportedly comes to life when its friendly spirits get restless.

Hauntspitality

Our friend, renowned author and colleague, Richard Senate, has referenced this location as a haunted hot spot in the Santa Clarita Valley. Senate has been researching the building for an upcoming book that will feature haunted locations along Highway 126. There have been numerous reports in the past about the spirited population inside, including the suspected spirit of the first owner, David Caleb Cook.

Inside, there have been reports of odd noises, unexplained footsteps, rapidly materializing cold spots and occasional apparitions in the balconies and hallways. Certain rooms also have a spirited ambience as lights will sometimes turn on by themselves and faucets will be turned on by unseen hands. There is nothing frightening about the spirits, they are just enjoying themselves in this beautiful mansion, just as the living continue to relax in the slice of heaven.

Several psychics who have visited this building, immediately remarked that there are spirits from several periods who enjoy the building's hauntspitality. One psychic picked up on an actress and actor, another medium sensed David Cook and his wife, and yet another sensitive, came away with impressions of children and an elderly woman. There are few people who walk through the front doors, that don't express some kind of emotion that centers on the building's past. There is usually an instant connection to the history embodied in this structure; as if the walls are speaking to them.

Visiting paranormal investigators have also remarked about the playful yet highly charged environment. Meter readings are high in the lobby and second floor near some of the rooms. Numerous people have reported feeling as if someone unseen had walked right by them as their hair stood on end. No one has felt anything but "good vibes" inside this historic building.

One interesting story about the building involves someone's friend who along with her Mother drove up the place one day and spotted a man on the second floor balcony. As they got out of their car, the man called down to them and said "Hello!" Both women waved up at him, turned back to lock the car, and then made their way for the inn. When they looked up at the balcony, the man was gone. Both women remarked that the man looked kind of odd, dressed in black, wearing a shirt with what looked like a minister's collar around his neck. They couldn't make out many details.

Continuing to the front door, they noted that the place was closed for business. They knocked; figuring the man they just witnessed would help them. They waited for a response to their continued knocking, but no one came. Puzzled as to what just transpired the reluctantly headed back to their car. Just then, they heard a loud "Hello!" come from behind them. Turning once again to the second floor balcony where the voice was emanating from, they spotted the same man beckoning for them to come in. As they watched in disbelief, the man vanished into thin air. A little unnerved at this point, they two women headed for their car as quickly as their feet would carry them and left the inn.

The interesting thing is, David Caleb Cook came from Illinois and ended up turning Rancho Temescal into a profitable rancho with imported fruit trees and such... He was the founder of Piru... he was also a minister and loved having visitors.

Fort Bragg
The Lodge at Noyo River

Particulars
500 Casa del Noyo Drive,
Fort Bragg, CA 95437
Phone: 707-964-8045
Toll Free: 1-800-628-1126
Fax: 707-964-9366
E-mail: lodgekeeper@noyolodge.com
Website: www.noyolodge.com

History

A secluded riverside refuge is tucked into the edge of a beautiful forest near a colorful fishing village. Scotsman, Alexander Wentworth MacPherson, one of the first settlers in the Fort Bragg area and an important California lumber baron of the nineteenth century, constructed the original building in 1868. MacPherson was the first to build a logging mill in Noyo Flats. During the construction of the mill, he built a home on "Stony Point" and moved his family in. Some say he selected the spot so that he could count the logs from his window as they rushed down river. In 1908, Mr. Harry Holmes, another gentleman who made his living in the woods, purchased the property. Mr. Holmes was Superintendent of Woods for Charles R. Johnson's Union Lumber Company, and was very likely the highest paid salaried man in the area

The Union Lumber Company was in the process of purchasing all the smaller, independent mills for consolidation into one large mill. That mill was built where the Georgia Pacific Mill stands today on the Fort Bragg headlands. Mr. Holmes remodeled and added onto the Noyo River House. Today, a photo of the Holmes family enjoying the patio shortly after the completion of the renovation can be found in the lodge's second floor hallway. It was during the years from 1935 to 1950 that the Schlote's raised a family in the home. Mrs. Schlote is credited with creating the extensive gardens and ponds on the property and renaming the home Casa del Noyo. It was also Mrs. Schlote, who upon the death of her husband first began to rent rooms to fishermen and traveling visitors.

Privately owned until 1943, the lodge underwent a number of transformations for the next four decades. After that period, the Coast Guard took it over for a short time for lodging in World War II and for a brief period in the 1960s the Noyo Lodge became a youth counseling center. In the 1970s the lodge became rental property and in the 1980s it was an Italian restaurant with singing waiters. In 1992, two partners purchased the lodge and added the annex referred to as the Sunset Suites, overlooking the Noyo River Bridge and harbor entrance. Recent upgrades introduced by present ownership include the addition of fine period antiques, exquisite bedding with down pillows and comforters, and the service of a full country breakfast, served to order each morning.

Hauntspitality

According to a brochure distributed by the establishment, numerous "spiritual sightings" has earned the Lodge a reputation as one of America's "haunted hotels." The spirits of the Noyo River Lodge seem to be associated with a honeymoon couple who stayed in room 5 during the 1940s. During an evening excursion, they were both killed in a tragic automobile accident. The man was found wearing light-colored clothing, while the new bride wore a red dress. They have been frequently sighted in Room 5 by staff and guests wearing the exact same clothing.

On one occasion, a manager was showing Room 5 to potential guests, when a man in light-colored clothing and a woman in a red dress, both looking very pale, emerged from the room, walked passed everyone, and made their way down a flight of stairs. Outside of looking a little the worse for wear, the manager shrugged off the incident, as well as the strange-looking couple he had not previously seen checking in at the hotel. He continued showing rooms to the prospective guests, but when he was finished, he decided to ask the restaurant manager who was near the foot of the stairs at the time the mysterious couple passed him, where the pale- looking couple had gone. The restaurant manager never saw the couple come down the stairs. Furthermore, he checked the guest register thinking that someone else had checked the couple into room 5---the room was unoccupied!

Room 5 is not the only "strange" room at the Lodge. Rooms 1 and 3 are also said to have their share of unexplained events including:
- Doors mysteriously open and close;
- The imprint of a person often appears on a freshly made bed;
- A young girl dressed in white is often witnessed staring out of a window in Room 3 when no one else was checked into the room;
- Cold spots and unearthly draft seem to come and go within minutes;
- Water faucets have been known to turn on and off by themselves,
- Doors will sometimes open and close unassisted.
- Disembodied footsteps are heard in the hallways and some rooms.
- And, numerous other events are recorded by guests in the room journals.

In addition to the strange shadows seen darting across the walls of empty rooms and hallways, and the sighting of an occasional apparition, the Lodge is a great place to relax and get away from it all---all that is, except ghosts. However, no guests have ever complained about sharing their room or vacation with the otherworldly guests of The Lodge at Noyo River.

Fullerton
Angelo's and Vinci's Ristorante

Particulars
550 North Harbor Boulevard,
Fullerton, CA 92832
Phone: 714-879-4022
Website: www.angelosandvincis.com

History

Angelo's and Vinci's Ristorante (or as locals call it, A&V's) used to be known as "The Backstage," when it was located backstage of the Fox Fullerton Movie theater (located next door). The Fox Theater was once a vaudeville house and the former restaurant was the backstage. Bathrooms were down the stairs where the dressing rooms used to be. In those days, "Backstage pizza" was all they had and it was crowded. The ceilings were impossibly high and there were mirrors on the wall facing the Movie Theater. Today, there are more decorations including strings of colored lights, animatronic donkeys, posters and statuary.

Founder Steven Peck, renowned Hollywood dancer, choreographer and veteran actor of over 100 movies and television performances, has delightful photographs of over 40 years of famous stars, directors and dancers. Frank Sinatra, Dean Martin, Gary Cooper, Robert Taylor, Broderick Crawford, Kirk Douglas, Walter Winchell, Sam Wanamaker, Vincent Minnelli, Sylvester Stallone, Ted Danson, David Hasselhof, Ray Sharkey, Shirley MacLaine, Cyd Charisse, Dolly Parton, Joan Collins, Raquel Welch, Olympia Dukakis, Shelly Winters and so many more. Films from Paramount, Twentieth Century Fox, Warner Bros., MGM, Desilu, United Artists, Universal Studios, to name a few. Others who have been a part of the restaurant famiglia for over two decades include managers Virginia De Pasquale and Robert Ciccaglione, master pizza maker Frankie Mungia, Miguel Vaszuez, Maria Dadaruqa and owner, Cynthia Peck.

The current incarnation of "The Backstage" was built 35 years ago in an early L-shaped marketplace that dated to when Fullerton was an orchard and the local farmers would bring their produce in from the fields by horse and wagon to sell to the townspeople. The original wood trusses of the old roof system can still be seen in the Venetian Room. Roughly 20 years later, renovation of the building changed it from its original L-shape to a rectangle by adding the large wood barrel trusses, which can be seen in the Sicilian Room and the Piazza Fantasia. During the renovation in 1992, the old wood, terra cotta tiles and brick were salvaged and re-used to keep alive the feeling of bygone days.

At Angelo's and Vinci's Ristorante, there is a surprise in every corner! You will eat amidst the art of the great masters, in an Italian town square complete with the storefronts of old Italian butcher and cheese mongers, fruit and wine vendors, seamstresses showing their wares, and more. Fairy lights abound under cathedral ceilings as the family ancestors smile down at you from the Family Love Altar. You will be surrounded by colorful Sicilian puppets, the carnival masks and canals of Venice, and the romance of Romeo & Juliet. Don't forget King Kong, Dracula, Frankenstein, witches, ghosts and who-knows-what that awaits you in the Monster Wine Cellar!

Hauntspitality

Those who have visited the restaurant and are of the psychic persuasion have sensed the presence of at least four benign spirits. Various psychics who have come for a visit, primarily for the great dinner and spirited concoctions served at the bar, have inadvertently stumbled on a rather spirited population inside. Different psychics have picked up on a very outgoing, gray-haired man who seems to enjoy greeting people as well as stopping by various tables to see how the food is being appreciated by the guests.

Orb in the basement (Courtesy of the International Paranormal Research Organization)

Not often acknowledged, this friendly spirit doesn't seem to mind the rebuff and continues on his rounds, often caught out of the corner of people's eyes as he floats through the main room and the upstairs area. According to those of the psychic persuasion, this outgoing, personable phantom man always seems to be smiling at something.

The other spirits as described by mediums and sometimes sighted by staff and guests include an elderly woman, and young girl and a farmer-type; possibly from the days when the building served as a market. These energies have all been described as friendly phantoms. Sighted or felt, the ghostly contingent on the upper and main floors are described as being very busy but sometimes curious when the living see or acknowledge their presence. One waiter intimated that when he is downstairs he constantly sees things out of the corner of his eye and hears unexplained noises. Other people call the feeling creepy downstairs but not bad. Maybe it's all the unusual costumes and such that seem to play tricks on people's minds.

On one occasion a guest went downstairs to use the bathroom. As he reached the bottom of the stairs, he felt sure someone was watching him. He stopped in his tracks, looked around the room and then got a bad case of the chills. There was no one else in the area, so he simply brushed off the odd feelings and went into the bathroom. When he stepped out, he saw what looked like a man in period clothing staring at him from near the base of the stairs. Within seconds, the man just vanished into thin air. Not really frightened, and never a believer in spirits before this incident, he now believes and continues to come back the restaurant in hopes of having another encounter with the ghosts.

Then, there is the "spooky" basement area... This is an area where mediums sense a tie to the adjoining Fox Fullerton Theater, sensing actors and crew passing back and forth through the walls. Most do not venture upstairs but seem to enjoy the solitude and dim lights of this subterranean hideaway.

Several "gifted" individuals caught psychic glimpses of actors, actresses, stage hands, a maintenance man and a busboy or waiter. More often then not, those who do get impressions, sense that the energy is from 1900-1940.

Staff has reported seeing chairs move, or that place settings have been rearranged and that rapidly manifesting cold spots are common inside.

Another person said that a former owner is sighted in the main room greeting people and keeping an eye on the place. IPRO and the San Diego Ghost Hunters took several photographs in the basement and a few orbs were picked up along with some chills and anomalies on the EMF meters.

After a delicious meal, take a few moments to enjoy all the memorabilia and perhaps keep an eye out for friendly spirits. At Angelo's and Vinci's Ristorante the food attracts the living and the deceased and dinner and spirits takes on an entirely different meaning.

Orb on pole in the basement (Courtesy of the International Paranormal Research Organization)

California Hotel

Early views of the California Hotel (courtesy of the Launer Local History Room, Fullerton Public Library)

History

By 1900, a feed lot occupied the land, followed by the Fullerton Lumber Company, which appears, on Sanborn maps in 1917. The lumber company included a lumberyard and four buildings fronting Spadra (now Harbor). By the time Ira Gray and his seven-piece orchestra opened the California Hotel on January 15, 1923, nearly 200 Fullerton residents, under the auspices of The Fullerton Community Hotel Company headed by Charles C. Chapman, had donated $250,000 to erect the building.

Designed in a Spanish Colonial Revival style by local architects Frank Benchley and Eugene Durfee, it was intended to be a tourist hotel with 20 plush apartments and 55 guestrooms. Single rooms would go for $2 a day ($3 if you wanted a tub). R.E. Durbin, a hotel man from Long Beach put up $5,000 in exchange for being the first manager of the hotel. The 1933 earthquake damaged part of the building but did not deter its operation.

In back of the hotel, where the parking lot now exists, stood a city hall building which housed the Fire Department, city offices including the police station, and the city jail; all of these buildings were demolished in the mid-1950s. The U-shaped building had an open courtyard, which faced Harbor Boulevard. Commercial buildings occupied the bottom portion of the building as well as the lobby that provided access to the hotel located on the upper floors.

By the early 1930s Mutual Building and Loan Association of Fullerton, Dan O'Hanlon (Realtor), California Varsity Shop, C.H. Herron, C.W. McKenny (used cars), Lillian Yaeger (used cars), E.C. Wood (lunches), and The Brown Mug occupied the commercial space in the building. By 1945 the building had become a low-cost residential hotel with most of the ground floor taken up by small shops and storefront businesses. A 1955 sale recorded 38 double wooden beds, 15 single wooden beds, 11 iron beds, 22 double Murphy beds, 79 mattresses, an upright piano and stool, one rolltop desk, two gliders, one typewriter, two hotel signs, and numerous small liens as assets.

By 1964 the building was going to be demolished and replaced by a car wash. The building was eventually spared and there were designs to convert the building into small shops, restaurants and offices and the building was renamed Villa del Sol. Enclosing the patio for outside dining and events followed, and La Paz and the 5-star restaurant, The Cellar, anchored the new complex. Four of the current restaurants occupying portions of the former California Hotel are reportedly haunted (The Brownstone Café; Café Hidalgo; The Cellar; and The Stadium Tavern).

Brownstone Café

Particulars
North Harbor Boulevard, Suite 115-117,
Fullerton, CA 92832
Phone: 714-526-9123
Fax 714-526-9125

Hauntspitality
A possible murder or suicide victim refuses to move on, frequently visiting the Brownstone as well as a couple of other places in the Villa del Sol complex. One manager recalled a night when he received a call from the security company monitoring his establishment that his alarm had been tripped. It was almost midnight but he rushed over to inspect the place. A careful inspection revealed that all the doors were bolted shut and nothing was taken or amiss inside. As he was checking in with the security alarm company, they told him that while he was on the phone, something was triggering the motion sensor alarm and whoever or whatever it is was in there with him. Within seconds, a sensor in the kitchen was activated. The manager, still on the Phone and stationary, was then told by the security people that all the sensors were being tripped one after another as if someone was walking through the restaurant. The manager saw nothing, but felt as if someone was standing next to him. Hesitant, he turned around to where the perceived person would have been standing while at the same time planning a quick escape. When he turned, a cold gust of air hit him squarely in the face. Rushing out the door, he was hit by another blast of freezing air, followed by a crashing sound. Once outside, he looked through the door to see a heavy metal pot lying on the floor. All the pots are very heavy and stacked one on top of the other, so for the pot to end up on the floor meant that someone had to lift it up and toss it!

To this day, the motion detector sensors frequently trigger on their own, after hours. There are also objects that are moved, unexplained sounds, cold spots, disembodied footsteps, and what appears to be a phantom male presence occasionally manifesting. Sometimes, when 1930s-1940s music is played inside, the staff has heard the distinct humming sounds coming from someone invisible, trying to add their own otherworldly harmony to the old time tunes. This eerie humming usually causes the hair to stand on end of those hearing the sounds. Additionally, three people, including the owner, once held a séance using an Ouija board to contact the restless spirit or spirits of their establishment. Within a short time, the planchette flew off the board across the room causing the participants to abruptly halt their activity and immediately vacate the premises. On another occasion, two employees were standing behind the counter facing the entrance when the place was empty. They distinctly heard the sound of someone mumbling or talking in front of the counter but there was no one visible in the area of the sounds.

A paranormal investigation of the California Hotel, including the Brownstone Café was organized by the authors (International Paranormal Research Organization) with the aid of members from the Orange County Society for Psychic Research (OCSPR) took place in December, 2000. This investigation revealed that the entire building had a history of tragedy that has left an indelible imprint on most of the current establishments situated within the complex. The investigation produced the name of a young girl who is still waiting for her parents to come for her, at least two women, an angry man, and other spirits that seem to float between the connected Cafe Hidalgo and the adjacent Cellar Restaurant. In fact, the entire California Hotel building is psychically charged according to psychics and paranormal investigators.

The spirits seem to come from several time periods (1880s-1940s) when the area contained horses and stables, a lumber yard and followed by the hotel complex which contained a bank and car dealerships. During the course of the séance, the EMF meter spiked numerous times, an object flew off a counter, the digital thermometers registered cold anomalies, strange knocking sounds were heard when a tape was played back, and a candle repeatedly flickered then turned a bluish color when questions were addressed to the spirits.

Perhaps a 1930s murder victim, who died in this part of the building when it was leased commercially for some other purpose, still hangs around in a now unfamiliar restaurant setting. This would have been during Prohibition, and there is a chance that a portion of the California Hotel once housed a speakeasy or served as a place where something illegal was occurring when a murder took place. One suicide is known to have taken place at the California Hotel as evidenced by this February 10, 1958, article in the Fullerton Daily News Tribune. Perhaps this tragic event has left a psychic imprint at this historic site.

The other spirits may be residents of the hotel or prior structures on the property who never left. Who knows, since the police and coroner's records for that time have been destroyed, and most old-timers recall a murder, but the dates and names are hazy, like the invisible guests who still roam the establishment and the hotel!

LOCAL VICTIM

Police Rule Suicide in Hotel Leap

The death of a 79-year-old Fullerton man who jumped from the third floor of the California Hotel at 9:45 a.m. Saturday and landed on his head was listed as suicide, police reported today.

He was identified as Neri Hews Sipe, 112 E. Whiting Ave., a resident here of only two months. Taken by ambulance to St. Jude Hospital, he was given emergency treatment but was not admitted.

Transferred to Orange County Hospital, Sipes died at 10:45 a.m. The coroner's office reported cause of death was an extremely depressed skull fracture and numerous broken bones and abrasions. Police said Sipe has registered at the hotel five minutes before the death leap. He had taken a room on the second floor and had taken off his hat and coat in the room.

Funeral services were at McCormick Chapel Monday. The Rev. Walter R. Link, associate pastor of First Presbyterian Church, officiated. Burial followed at Loma Vista Memorial Park.

Survivors include the wife, Mary, of the home. A retired locomotive engineer, Sipe was born April 8, 1878 in Pennsylvania. He formerly lived in Arizona, and was a member of the Masonic Lodge in Winslow, Ariz.

Café Hidalgo

Particulars

305 N Harbor Boulevard, Suite #111,
Fullerton, CA 92832-1901
Phone: 714-447-3202
Fax: 714-447-9340

Hauntspitality

Perhaps the same murder victim described in the prior Brownstone Café story may haunt this building as well. This is not uncommon given that a physical barrier like a wall (which may not have existed during the 1930s when a murder reportedly took place in the building) rarely holds a spirit in check. The owner of the Café Hidalgo has had repeated contact with the unknown inside his establishment, relating events similar to those reported at the Brownstone Cafe.

One night, the owner was closing the kitchen with his chef. The two men were talking and playing a cassette tape which finally ran its course and stopped. For a moment the men ceased their conversation and there was total silence inside. Suddenly, and to the amazement of both men, another tape flew across the room and landed in front of the stereo. The tape, a Creedence Clearwater Revival classic, was thought to be a ghostly request. On another occasion, a manager opened the cafe in the morning and stepped inside. Within seconds after entering, the manager was met with an icy blast of air that felt like hitting a mass of energy. Uncertain as to what was taking place, the manager immediately heard his name whispered. This unnerving encounter didn't prevent the opening of the cafe that morning, but it did leave a lasting impression upon the frightened manager.

Other events that have taken place include shadowy figures moving down the hallway and along the walls, ghostly footsteps, flickering lights and mysterious sounds that come from unoccupied portions of the building.

A portion of the Cafe Hidalgo lies in the new part of the building, while the back portion lies within the originally constructed building where the kitchen is. Perhaps the spirit that frequents the Brownstone Cafe is the same spirit that calls the Cafe Hidalgo home, visiting each place when the mood strikes. Someday, psychic or paranormal investigators will hopefully discover the source of the hauntings in both places and perhaps find a way to release the troubled guest.

Research did turn up the names of two former establishments that existed in the 1930s; H.K. Smith's that served lunch, and The Brown Mug. This was the time of Prohibition, and there is a chance that the area the spirit inhabits once housed a speakeasy downstairs where a murder took place. Who knows, since the police and coroner's records for that time have been destroyed?

The Cellar

Particulars
305 N. Harbor Boulevard,
Fullerton, CA 92833
Phone: 714-525-5682
Fax: 714-525-3853

History
Opened in 1969 by Louis Schnelli, Swiss-trained restaurateur with meticulously high standards, The Cellar was sold in 1985 to Ernest Zingg. Zingg, a graduate of the Lausanne Hotel Management School in Switzerland, immigrated to Canada in 1960 where he opened the Ascona Restaurant. Located in Gravenhurst, Ontario, a local newspaper recently rated his restaurant "an oasis in a culinary desert." Offering gourmet dining in the classic tradition, Ascona is one of only 25 Travel Holiday award-winning restaurants in Canada. It was at a meeting of Travel Holiday award-winners that Zingg and Schnelli first met, leading later to Zingg's purchase of The Cellar.

Ernest Zingg not only maintained the excellence that has marked The Cellar during the past 28 years, but has added new amenities to further enhance the restaurant. Subtle changes have been made. Equipment changes have updated the kitchen. A wine cabinet that is thermostat controlled has been installed next to the bar. Other than that you will find the interior cozily furnished as it has always been. Current owner Ryan Dudley and his team have maintained the elegance of the Cellar for the bodied and disembodied alike.

The elegant surroundings include handsomely appointed tables, fine oil paintings, and antique china cabinets. Each table is set with monogrammed crystal, imported German china, and a crystal vase filled with a bouquet of fresh carnations. Velvet chairs and leather banquettes provide seating. An intimate and romantic setting is enhanced by crystal chandeliers and shimmering brass lanterns. The menu remains French in the classic tradition. There is an impressive selection of hors d'oeuvres which includes Sevruga or Beluga caviar, fresh seafood pasta tossed with cream and basil, and fresh salmon marinated in lemon, lime and tarragon sauce.

Hauntspitality
This restaurant seems to be the most haunted portion of the former California Hotel. There are so many stories of apparitions and anomalies, that it has achieved legendary status among local paranormal investigators and psychics. Unfortunately, very little information beyond hearsay exists about the paranormal population inside. Suffice it to say, that male and female apparitions are commonly sighted inside. Objects have been known to move on their own and staff is constantly confronted by cold spots or breezes, flickering lights, disembodied footsteps and other paranormal phenomena. The Cellar is not at the bottom of the most haunted list when it comes to Fullerton spirits.

The International Paranormal Research Organization (IPRO) with assistance from the San Diego Ghost Hunters conducted a paranormal investigation at the

Cellar on Monday, February 6, 2006 from 7:00pm–9:00pm. The investigative team consisted of Rob Wlodarski, Matt Wlodarski, Aimee Aul, Ruth Aul, Deann Burch, Robin Collier, Victoria Gross, Maritza Skandunas, Karen Ridens and Vinnie Skandunas. The following notes represent a summary presented by the investigators.

- DB, while in the main dining room near the far wall at the 2nd table from the wall adjacent to the wine barrel wall sensed that a man named Benjamin had a heart attack and was a family member of someone who works at the restaurant. He was 65+; over six feet tall and a distinguished looking man; who was proud of the accomplishments of others. The word "apple" came to mind to DB but she didn't know what the meaning is?

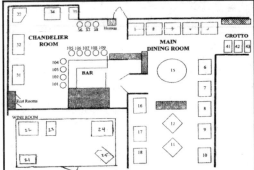

- Near the wine barrel wall, DB sensed a female energy.
- DB got chills every time she walked past the pillars near the center of the room. She sensed the energy of a divorce or separation in the room.
- Near the entrance to the kitchen DB go the distinct impression of misappropriation of funds and underhanded business dealings.

Floor Plan courtesy of The Cellar

- Near the right side of wine barrel wall - RC mentioned that she sensed a man standing there, observing the space like he was in charge (Maitre' D.?)
- Between Main Dining Room and Grotto DB felt uneasy as she entered. She picked up on a lot of tension, stressful female emotions and a sense of "Don't go there".
- DB watched RC enter this space for the first time like a drunken sailor. DB could see that the restaurant space unbalanced her. At the time, RC commented that the area was disorienting.
- DB and RC tried unsuccessfully to close the door to one of the wine racks. It seemed to coincide with the instability of the energies in this location.
- While in the grotto, at the first table DB obtained the name "Nancy" a female, a child-like energy that had a chemical imbalance. DB sensed the time period as the late 1940s or early 1950's.
- DB sensed a woman is in her 1930s by the name of Sara, who was brought here by an older man and a family member. The woman was abandoned in life and hasn't crossed over. She received some sort of medical treatment?
- At the second table, DB felt energy inside that wants the table pristine. DB also felt a tremendous amount of agitation of anything being out of place. The phantom woman took great pride in her service to others. While connecting with the female, several investigators heard two glasses clink together at table #3.
- MS, KR and RW also heard it glasses clinking at Table #3. Everyone checked to see if the glasses on the table had been bumped, but there were no glasses on the table or anywhere near this spot.
- At the back table, the furthest from entrance, DB felt that someone had horrible head trauma over left eye.

- DB heard a male voice singing in a deep, operatic voice, He was a heavyset man with dark hair and olive skin who was about 5'8" tall.
- DB witnessed Vinnie as he tapped into energies. Saw him physically change in stature and attitude.
- DB witnessed VS picking up on the owner at the table and could see him physically change. There was an overlay of energy of a man much bigger who carried himself in a more arrogant/powerful way than VS.

Karen Ridens and Vinnie Skandunas near Booth 38 (Courtesy of the International Paranormal Research Organization)

- DB felt three different personalities in the Grotto, Main Dining Room and Bar/Dining
- VG, while in the kitchen, sensed someone plotting some type of betrayal that has to do with money.
- In the back hallway near the wine cabinets VG sensed a woman from the 1940s-1950s. The woman was lonely and sad as if waiting for someone to return; only they never did.
- In the far back table VG got the impression of a Mafia meeting during Prohibition times.

Vinnie Skandunas sitting in haunted Booth 43 with a small orb next to him (Courtesy of the International Paranormal Research Organization)

- MS, KR and VS were drawn to the tunnel part of the restaurant where they felt a woman that was agitated. We felt like she could have had Alzheimer's.
- VS picked up a young woman in a long lace dress with long brown hair hanging down her back. She looped her arm through his like they were a couple. The spirit woman left and VS saw a phantom man go back toward the tunnel part of the restaurant. The man was wearing a white tuxedo with a white top hat and black hatband.
- The SDGH group encountered a young, high priced call girl that was trying to make the other man in the tuxedo jealous. VS got the name Margaret. RW said it was Maggie.
- VS sat in the back corner booth where he took on the persona of a very drunken man and couldn't stop laughing.
- MS heard the sound of paper crackling and KR and RW heard the sound of aluminum crinkling. Soon KR and DB heard a gurgling sound like wine being poured from a bottle.
- As VS began moving over one space in the booth, several investigators heard the clinking of fine crystal.
- While VS was sitting at a back booth, he took on the persona of a big man. VS felt like this man was the bodyguard of a boss or well-connected figure. Then VG took on the characteristic of a boss who was very angry. Several pictures taken by the SDGH group revealed orbs around VS.
- VS then picked up on a 40-year-old man who was wearing a tan suit. The man

used to sit in the back booth and watch the rest of the restaurant and may have been a manager here in the 1970s-1980s.

- While in the bar area and chandelier room RW sensed a male energy near booth 31; a female energy at the bar and a male energy near booth 35. The time frame RW was picking up on, was Prohibition era to circa 1945. These were individuals who continue to come back to this place. The woman may have been a high priced call girl or female escort in her 20s. She wore a tight red or pink dress, subtle perfume, had her hair in a bun and was actually quite classy. The two men were older and wearing suits. One appeared to be an owner or manager.
- RW got strong whiffs of steaks and alcohol including brandy and champagne.
- Near the Grotto, RW and several of the investigators sensed one or two women in the back booths as well as gangster-type people sitting in the back tables. Several members remarked that they heard a popping sound and something like foil being wadded up. There was also what sounded like glasses clinking.
- RW felt that the Grotto area of the restaurant was the most intense area of the restaurant. It seemed to have heavy energy as if a lot of underhanded deals went down here, and the men who sat in this area were high stakes individuals who were also powerful "money" people. This felt like their hideaway.
- RW sensed a forlorn woman in booth 43. She was distraught over some bad choices she made in life. There was a sense that the woman might have been pregnant when she was dumped by her boyfriend or lover.
- RW picked up strong meter readings near Booth 18 in the corner of the main dining room. KR's IR thermometer measured a five-degree drop in temperature in the same location.
- Several mediums picked up on a woman named Maggie or Margaret (Could this have been the Maggie from the Amerige Brothers Realty Office? If so, why did she follow us here? This seemed to be a very curious woman.

Several investigator standing in the Grotto area with an orb above them
(Courtesy of the International Paranormal Research Organization)

- RW sensed extensive imprinted and interactive energy from the 1930s-1940s inside. There was a feeling that this area might have first been used as a storage or laundry area when the hotel was functioning as well as a kind of hideaway during the Prohibition and Post-Prohibition Eras. Several of the personalities encountered inside seem to come from a time when there was a lot of alcohol consumed, private parties and social gatherings, clandestine business dealings, call-girl activity.

The Cellar may be at the bottom of the former California Hotel building but its tops with the spirited population that call this restaurant home.

The Continental Room

Particulars

115 West Santa Fe Avenue,
Fullerton, CA 92832
Phone: 714-526-4529

History

This rather non-descript building, painted yellow with red awnings, is located west of the Fullerton Train Depot and is accessed from Harbor Boulevard. It is now one of the hippest retro lounges in Orange County. However, it wasn't always that way. The plaque on the exterior of the building near the entrance reads: "Historical Site, Fullerton's Oldest Drinking Establishment, Est. 1925". The spacious but heavy on atmosphere bar was established by J. Leon circa 1925. Fullerton's first official bar, the building operated as a speakeasy during Prohibition. The bar was owned by Alex Lousar in the early 1940s and then by his son Mario Lousar. During this time, the area shifted to a more industrial land use and by the 1970s, became a hangout for a rougher element. Finally, in 1992, the bar was shut down by the local police. Too many brawls and complaints finally contributed to its closure.

During 2004, a revitalization movement that was aimed at creating a new feel and setting for the area, included this once famous bar. Along with new owners Carlo Terranova and Sean Francis who purchased this historic landmark, other establishments including Hero's, Steamers Jazz Café and Table Ten brought new life to this section of Fullerton. During renovation of the building, when the original floorboards were removed, old whiskey bottles were discovered under the flooring.

The Continental Room has no pool tables or dance floor; but it does have a small stage for musicians to perform, plenty of ambiance, great martinis and a very impressive jukebox filled to the brim with choice music selections. It also has several other surprises such as custom light fixtures, classic early photos of the area and past clientele, a small hideaway room adjacent to the entrance that can only be accessed by a special code, the original booths from the infamous Little Joe's Italian restaurant in Los Angeles (one booth is labeled as Frank Sinatra's booth) and plenty of ghosts to go around!

Hauntspitality

A preliminary paranormal investigation was conducted by the International Paranormal Research Organization (IPRO) after the building was reopened. The investigation revealed that the place had a very active spirited clientele. Gauss and EMF meters and IR thermometer readings produced electromagnetic spikes and drops in temperature throughout the building. The back portion of the building, including the rear hallway and bathroom areas registered the strongest measurements inside. There were constant anomalies recorded near the bar, juke box, two red booths to the left of the entrance across from the bar, the back area near the stage and the back hallway. One psychic described the building as railroad station where activity is going on constantly. The bar still draws people from all walks of life, including the afterlife.

Orb in near the bar (courtesy of the International Paranormal Research Organization – IPRO)

The psychic contingent also picked up on very strong energy from the 1930s, including two tough guys from the Prohibition era who were bodyguard types. There was a strong sense of excessive alcohol, clandestine meetings over money, prostitution and fighting. Several photographs picked up orbs and a misty form near the back portion of the building and stage area.

According to the investigators, this place was loaded with memories, imprints and active energy that continues to call the bar home. From the moment you step inside, it is as if a thousand invisible eyes are watching you, just checking you out. One investigator walking toward the bathroom had the distinct feeling of someone brushing passed them. There were rapidly materializing cold spots and strong feelings of being watched.

During a sitting in the private room off the entrance, several psychics picked up on two phantom women from the Prohibition Era, a manager, a man with connections to organized crime, a former waitress and a man who was murdered. The energy inside is dramatic and very active. Employees have felt, heard and seen things since the place reopened, and documented activity remains high.

At the Continental Room, martinis, music and spirits are served in equal portions, and the past is very much an active part of the present ambiance.

Spadra Ristorante

Particulars
136 E. Commonwealth Avenue,
Fullerton, CA 92833
Phone: 714-447-0775
Fax: 714-447-0644
Website: www.spadrarestaurant.com

History
The "Pacific Electric Depot" lies across the parking lot from the Santa Fe Depot. The building is "An austere, one-story Mission Revival structure, the Pacific Electric Depot on East Commonwealth provides an architectural transition from one age to another. While the basic style belongs to the first two decades of the twentieth century, the reduction of the format to the barest essentials hints at the functionalism of the 1920's. The Pacific Electric came to Fullerton in 1917, and established a line from La Habra at a cost of $425,000. Always a money loser, the Fullerton line ran from February 1, 1918 to January 1948. The citrus industry constituted the largest revenue source for the line. The depot, constructed between November and December, 1918, cost $10,000. The Spadra Ristorante (formerly Il Ghiotto), a fine Italian restaurant currently occupies the historic building.

Pacific Electric Depot Building date unknown (Courtesy of the Launer Local History Room, Fullerton Public Library)

Hauntspitality
There are rumors that the structure is spirited; and rightfully so. This was once the hub of pedestrian activity when it served as carrier for people and freight for over 30 years as the Pacific Electric Depot. Later, the building became a favorite local restaurant called Il Ghiotto. The structure is now home to the elegant Spadra Restaurant.

While the building was called Il Ghiotto, numerous staff reported experiencing unexplainable events occurring inside. There were times when staff would be cleaning up late at night and they would hear muffled conversations and the sounds of items being dragged across the floor. Every time they would check on the noises, no one living would be there and nothing would be out of place. There were also occasions when staff would report seeing people milling around just outside the building in Period clothing. They would do a double-take and the figures would be gone. The front door was prone to open or shut on its own, followed by phantom footsteps that could be heard for a coupled of seconds before stopping.

One employee remarked that working inside alone was never dull. It was like Halloween every night, since the place always seemed to have something mysterious and spooky going on. Another person remarked that while cleaning up at night, there were constant muffled voices, unexplained tapings, lights that would flicker, and sounds of things being moved or shuffled across the floor. It's as if the place took on its own persona when the crowds were gone. Perhaps the spirits were reclaiming their domain.

On one occasion, a waitress saw a man in a dark suit wearing a distinctive hat walk right by her and then through the wall, as if an invisible door had been there. Utensils would sometimes be moved from one table to the next, lights would flicker and chairs would end up being pushed back from the table as if a ghostly gathering had come to dine. No one was ever frightened by the occurrences, but rather amused or intrigued.

The paranormal activity seems to take place most frequently in the late evening when the customers have left and very few people are inside. There are reports of shadowy figures witnessed floating through the building; the muffled sound of people talking in unoccupied areas of the building; of lights going on and off on their own; of disembodied footsteps and numerous other events that the current staff will share with you if you ask.

Shannon LeClair and other staff at the Spadra Ristorante forwarded this information to us just before we went to press. Here are their stories unedited: The restaurant remains warm, friendly and comforting; until you find yourself standing alone inside. According to LeClair, "My first encounter occurred exactly like that. Before I had even realized, I looked up from counting the drawer to close up and found myself alone. I wasn't sure why I was left there alone, because we never leave anyone to lockup by them selves at night. So, from hearing many tales of the Il Ghiotto Ghost I was nervous and tried to finish up what I was doing so I could get out of there. Unfortunately, I was not that lucky. From the hall leading to the restrooms, which was next to where I heard two woman snickering at me, and they continued to chuckle and whisper as I ran out".

On other occasions employees have heard people setting the dining room tables, when no one else was there. Running water, doors opening and shutting on their own, and pictures falling in an impossible manner because of the way they are hanged are a few of the many unexplained things that have taken place inside over the years. Several times you'll swear that you'll see a person walk into the back pantry, and wait to see who comes out. After a few minutes when no one returns, you go in to the pantry to check it out and no one is there. Cold gusts of winds blow right through you on the calmest nights when there's no a breath of wind. Faucets turn on by themselves, wine glasses fall from the shelves, and lights will turn back on right after you have turned them off. There are always sensations of somebody standing next to you, although you are alone.

Most of the employees, including those that have been working there for over 16 years, still remain afraid of the restaurant. Ghosts and having spirited encounters is almost a daily routine at this popular Fullerton establishment. This is a fabulous place to visit without or without spirits, so we encourage you to try out the dinner and if you see any spirits, not the drinking kind, let us and management know.

Stadium Tavern

Particulars
305 North Harbor Boulevard, Suite 128
Fullerton, CA 92832
Phone: 714-447-4200
Fax: 714-278-0797

Hauntspitality
The spirit of who enjoys spending time at the Stadium Tavern may be a man affectionately called Chuck, who frequented the place daily in life. When he was found dead at home from a heart attack, his spirit apparently drifted over to the place he was so fond of when he had a body. One employee witnessed a spectral fog or mist floating up the stairs from the office (former hotel laundry area) while working downstairs alone. The fog just evaporated after floating up a few steps toward the restaurant.

Chuck doesn't seem to know or care that he no longer is on the earthly plane, and seems to prefer his former physical surroundings to a more ethereal plane of existence. There may also be a murder or suicide victim who haunts the place. A man wearing blue overalls or a blue shirt with jeans has been sighted several times standing against a wall or walking up the stairs from the basement, before vanishing. Objects are sometimes misplaced, the chairs occasionally creak as if someone invisible is sitting in it them and heavy, disembodied footsteps are often heard walking through the place or coming up the stairs when a lone employee or the owner is in side.

When the site was home to Heroes Bar & Grille, paranormal incidents were commonly reported. For instance, one evening in late 1997, night manager, Dave Dial was walking passed the stairs connecting the office and kitchen. Dial was startled to catch a glimpse of a shadowy figure standing at the bottom of the stairs. After doing a double-take the figure disappeared. There is no entrance or exit other than the stairwell, and no earthly visitor could have come and gone between Dial's first and second glance.

On another occasion, the manager was counting the cash from the register and closing up downstairs alone, while the rest of the staff was upstairs waiting for him to finish his job. Within seconds he felt that someone else was in the room with him. It that moment a person or thing came out of the liquor room and drifted out towards the startled mortal. Instead of disappearing suddenly, the haunting figure (between 20-40 years old, with dark hair and wearing something resembling a blue jumpsuit, or work shirts and pants of the same blue color) then floated back into the liquor room.

Another time, while in the liquor room, the manager was putting some things away when the door closed behind him; he had left the keys in the outside lock. As he walked over to the door, she heard the keys dangle in the lock and begin to turn as if someone was locking the deadbolt. As quickly as he could, he rushed the door and pushed it open before it could look. The strange thing was, there was no one anywhere around. The entire staff was upstairs in the dining area during the event. It would have been humanly impossible for someone to come down, shut the door, begin locking it then rush upstairs through the kitchen, and into the dining area in the time it took to push open the door. Everyone left the building quickly that night.

Then there was the singing novelty fish, "Billy Bass". The friendly fish occupies a place above the restaurant safe in the basement office by the liquor room. It wiggles and sings when a button is pushed. One night after closing, the manager locked the safe, turned out the lights and headed upstairs to go home. As he reached the top of the stairs, and was exiting the kitchen, the feisty fish burst into song. Even stranger, it was not the first song in the fishy medley, but the second song!

Even the police have encountered the spirits inside. Officer Gary Potts, a 17-year Fullerton Police Department veteran, related this frightful tale: "I was in Heroes after closing, so all of the doors were deadbolted and locked when I looked up and saw a man, 50 to 60 years old, standing by the carved wooden Indian at the end of the bar, which is near the door. I called over to Dave and said somebody was still inside, and then turned back and the man was gone. I searched all over, and, as I said, all of the doors were locked, but nobody was in the place." "Just recently, I was in the bathroom and noticed a shadow move across my arm as I was standing there. I looked up and nobody was in the bathroom but me. I didn't hear the door before or after the shadow appeared. I really don't believe in ghosts, but I can't say I disbelieve in them now!"

During the spring of 2006, a restaurant patron was with her preschool age son in the restroom, when she felt a sudden cool sensation engulf her. Her little boy quickly pointed toward the door and asked, "Mommy, who is that man?" The Mother, a little shaken, replied, "There's no one there, honey." The insistent boy while still pointing toward the door, blurted out, "Yes there is, right there!" Needless to say, the mother grabbed the boy by the hand and rushed out of the restroom. Visibly shaken, the mother returned to their table where she learned about the haunted history of the building.

The site is now home to the popular Stadium Tavern. Unexplained occurrences continue to take place at this busy corner of Fullerton history. It's a great place to hang out even though one of your drinking partners may actually be of a ghostly persuasion; and by the way, you'll have to pick up the tab!

Georgetown
Historic American River Inn

Particulars

P.O. Box 43, Main and Orleans Street,
Georgetown, CA 95634
Phone: 916-333-4499
Fax: 916-333-9253
Toll Free: 1-800-245-6566
E-mail: stay@americanriverinn.com
Website: www.americanriverinn.com

History

According to their Website, "The "Pride of the Mountains" was built in 1853, during the heat of the "gold fever" pandemic. It was the cry of "Gold!" that brought adventurers to Georgetown; it was the clear air, towering pines, and untamed beauty that kept them here. The mining camp, known in the mid-1800's as "Growlersburg" (perhaps because nuggets were so big they "growled" in the gold pans!), held riches beyond imagination. One famous nugget from the Woodside Mine, whose lode still runs under the American River Inn, weighed in at 126 ounces.

It is recorded that by spring of 1853, an estimated $2,000,000 in gold had been mined in Historic Georgetown. When the Woodside Mine collapsed, a number of miners were buried alive. This tragedy occurred behind the basement wall in the hotel. The Inn served as a stage coach stop and a boarding house for miners. Surviving many dreaded fires that were the terror of most mining camps, the original American Hotel (circa 1853) was damaged by fire in 1899. The building rose from the ashes to host travelers to this day, as the Historic American River Inn and Woodside Suites.

Hauntspitality

The spirit of a miner who survived the Woodside Mine disaster, but couldn't survive a bullet, haunts Room 5, his former domicile. Oscar, as he is fondly known, was murdered on the front steps of the hotel over an argument with a lady of the night. She in turn committed suicide a few days after Oscar's death, by leaping from the hotel balcony. Oscar has been known to turn on the lights in his room when guests are passionately involved. He has also been seen floating through the balcony door, walking across the room, and exiting through the door at the top of the stairs.

The tales about the spirit of Oscar have been handed down for over 50 years. Oscar is a part of the region's folklore. He was roughly five-feet-eight-inches tall and a miner who had come to the area to make his fortune. But it was never to be. Instead, he fell in love with a prostitute, and was killed over this love. The tragedy lingers on, as Oscar continues in spirit. The guest book at the Inn provides additional details about Oscar's nocturnal supernatural activities.

Room 5 has always had a air of mystery about it. During remodeling, workers and owners felt uneasy in the room. During sweltering days, the room stayed cold, and although everyone knew that a ghost was in the room, no one would actually admit it. Once the room was remodeled and guests began staying in it, the feelings about the room being haunted turned out to be accurate.

The apparition of a gruff-looking man was being sighted with frequency by a number of unsuspecting guests. One morning, at around 3:00 a.m., a newly married couple was awakened by a man dressed in old, tattered clothing who walked through the closed door from the outside balcony, and into the bedroom. The light switched on, the ghost smiled and walked through the bedroom door into the hallway. As he passed through the door, the light went off!

Guests are not the only individuals who have encountered Oscar's spirit. He has whispered the names of staff members and brushed by them when they were working; leaving them chilled to the bone. Oscar also opens and closes doors and loves to play with the lights when a room is being cleaned. Oscar may not be alone in haunting this establishment. Reports have also materialized about the presence of a young woman wearing a negligee and sipping on a drink. Perhaps the two are lovers and are wandering the same halls of the building they formerly inhabited unable to connect for some reason.

Georgetown Hotel & Saloon

Particulars
6260 Main Street,
Georgetown, CA 95634
Phone: 530-333-2848

History
The Georgetown Hotel is located in the Heart of the Gold Country. It was founded by George Phipps, and was formerly known as Gorges Town. The place emerged from a mining camp during the 1849 gold rush. It is California Historical Landmark No. 484. It was built in 1849 over the top of the Georgetown mine, one of the largest mines in California. The hotel was destroyed in a major fire on July 14, 1852. It was rebuilt in the same location only to catch fire again in 1856 and in 1896. Rebuilt once again, the hotel still stands much as it was in 1896, except for some modern up upgrades and repairs.

Hauntspitality
Sightings of the tall, dark man in his 50s, with salt and pepper colored hair, are not uncommon in the Georgetown Hotel. He may be the spirit of the former owner of the hotel who bothers employees in the kitchen, as well as keeps guests awake in Room 13. The Georgetown Hotel may be the only hotel in the United States that has a room 13. With this unlucky number comes a ghost. But, the spirit also haunts other parts of the hotel, including the kitchen.

Chefs and kitchen personnel have repeatedly mentioned witnessing the phantom intruder out of the corners of their eyes. Standing in the kitchen, the phantom figure silently stands motionless by a heater in the bar area with his hands securely planted on his hips. He has also been sighted with a pipe in his mouth walking through the building.

Sometimes staff enters the kitchen in the morning to find the pots and pans, spatulas and other utensils rearranged by unseen hands. Even those who close up at night have seen the phantom staring at them before they leave. He's there one minute, gone the next. The television set downstairs goes on by itself in the middle of the night, and lights will turn on and off for no apparent reason. The locked freezer door has been flung open by an unseen force, and locked doors upstairs have mysteriously opened even though nothing has been found missing. Strange knocks at the front door are sometimes greeted by an invisible guest. Even though it was snowing when it happened, there were no tracks leading up to the door!

Room 13 is the busiest place in the hotel for ghostly activity. Guests in the room have complained about everything from strange noises, bumps, and crashes to something, unseen sitting on their feet. The Georgetown Hotel, built over one of the largest mines in California, destroyed by several fires, is home to friendly spirits who seem to love partying with the living. Could the pesky spirit be the original owner George Phipps, or another lost soul awaiting an identity? Although considered unlucky, Room 13 may prove to be lucky for someone actually looking for a spirit.

Grass Valley
The Holbrook Hotel, Restaurant, Saloon

Particulars
212 West Main Street,
Grass Valley, CA 95945
Phone: 530-273-1353 | Fax: 530-273-0434
Toll Free: 1-800-933-7077
E-mail: holbrooke@holbrooke.com | Website: www.holbrooke.com

History

Listed as California Historical Landmark Number 914, the present hotel bar has been in continuous use since 1852, when it was known as the Golden Gate Saloon. The wooden building had a rear extension called the Exchange Hotel which offered food and lodging by 1853. The saloon was destroyed in the fire of 1855 and rebuilt out of fieldstone with a brick front. The Holbrooke, built in 1862 had the adjacent Golden Gate Saloon incorporated in the hotel building. The original Golden Gate Saloon built in 1852 is now enclosed by the Holbrooke Hotel built in 1862. It is the oldest continuously operating saloon in the Gold Country. Located in the scenic Sierra Nevada Motherlode, "the Heart of the Gold Country," the Hotel has hosted many luminaries from Ulysses S. Grant, Benjamin Harrison, James A. Garfield and Grover Cleveland, to boxers, Gentleman Jim Corbett and Bob Fitzsimmons. The Holbrooke also attracted writers Mark Twain and Bret Harte, dancer Lotta Crabtree, and internationally renowned actress-dancer Lola Montez. Of course, the history would not be complete without Black Bart.

The Holbrooke Hotel had its beginnings in 1852, when a wooden structure known as the Golden Gate Saloon was built. The Exchange Hotel which opened for business in January of 1853 was constructed as an annex behind the saloon. The Golden Gate was destroyed by the 1855 fire, but was hastily rebuilt out of local fieldstone and given a brick front. The Exchange Hotel suffered a similar fate in 1862, after which the present structure was built. The entire complex was purchased by D. P. Holbrooke in 1879, who transformed it into the Holbrooke Hotel which has been meticulously restored to it's Gold Rush days splendor.

This is the backdrop in which Stephen and Clara Smith built the Golden Gate Saloon and the Adams Express Office. Both of these wood structures would be devoured by the fire that consumed most of Grass Valley in the year 1855. The Smiths rebuilt the Saloon as a one-story fieldstone building, with a brick facade to protect from the next great fire. This is one of the longest continually operating saloons west of the Mississippi River and the back bar is the original dating to 1851. In 1862 Charles Smith, a relative, built the present structure next to the Saloon, calling it the Exchange Hotel. The hotel was noted for its convenience to the Gold Exchange (still in operation today). Like many other buildings of the time, the hotel was fortified against fire damage with heavy iron doors, brick and a foot wide layer of dirt and broken brick on the roof.

In 1879, the Hotel was purchased by Ellen and Daniel Holbrooke, retaining their name to this very day. Mr. Holbrooke died in 1884, and Mrs. Holbrooke continued to operate the Hotel until 1908. Elizabeth Johnson and her husband purchased the Hotel at public auction in 1908, and their daughters, Lily J. Cory and Sadie P. Finne, inherited the Hotel in 1922. After Sadie's death, the Hotel was sold to Emma and Harold Moneyhun in 1954.

By the 1970's the hotel was in decline. Mrs. Arletta Douglas, a long time resident of Nevada County "discovered" the Hotel in 1971 while working with the Grass Valley business community on a downtown beautification project. Mrs. Douglas finding the Holbrooke in disrepair led the efforts by concerned citizens to restore the Hotel. The restoration continued even after Mrs. Douglas sold the Hotel in 1980. In 1982, the refurbishment of the guest rooms was completed, and in 1983 the Holbrooke acquired the adjacent Purcell House for use as additional guest rooms. In 1989, ownership changed again.

Hauntspitality
A fire, dignitaries, a bar, and over 140 years of history provide the substance for the Holbrooke's ghosts which keep things lively. The upstairs hallway has been one of the areas of the hotel susceptible to apparitions, cold spots, and shadowy figures.

Staff and guests have frequently reported seeing a young woman, with blonde hair, attired in Period clothing, walking along the upstairs hallway, only to vanish in front of them, or disappear into an unoccupied room. She has been felt by many who describe their hair standing on end, and feeling as if they are being watched by someone standing off in the shadows. Of course, there is never anyone there that can bee seen.

Another invisible hotel guest belongs to a western gentleman who seems to favor the basement dining room, the Iron Door. On several occasions, this wraith has been spotted leaning against a post in the room, wearing a cowboy hat, stripped shirt, pant, boots, and spurs. He seems to like showing himself to guests and staff for a few seconds, then disappears without a trace.

Given the history of the hotel, the spirits could be any number of guests, travelers, or prior owners who have been so much a part of the Holbrooke's memorable history that they never want to leave. Many people have claimed to experience a strange uneasy feeling or a heavy air surrounding them while visiting this establishment; this is especially true at night downstairs near the Iron Door. Table 15 also continues to be a little odd, as the spirits seem to enjoy greeting the living as they pass between dimensions. At the Holbrooke, the unusual is the usual when you stop in for a visit.

Groveland
The Groveland Hotel

Particulars

18767 Main St., P.O. Box 289,
Groveland, CA 95321
Phone: 209-962-4000 | Fax: 209-962-6674
Toll Free: 1-800-273-3314
E-mail: peggy@groveland.com
Website: www.groveland.com

History

Groveland is located off of Highway 120, 23 miles from Yosemite. The Groveland Hotel is the largest adobe building in Groveland, and one of the oldest buildings in Tuolumne County. The building was one of the first permanent structures in Garrote (Groveland). The property was first used as a trading post, then a dwelling house until 1865. From 1866 until 1969, the property was dedicated exclusively to either the hostelry trade, or serving as a boarding house. In 1866, George Reed, conveyed title to Matthew Foot. The conveyance indicated that the Groveland Hotel property includes the trading post of Joshua D. Crippen & Co. which was purchased and occupied by George Reed in 1851. The Groveland Hotel (adobe building) was probably built for Crippen in 1850. Matthew Foot is the first owner of the subject property known to have operated a hostelry business at this location. Foot acquired the Reed property, and named the adobe building the "Garrote Hotel." In 1875 the town of Garrote (a name which translates to "hanging") was renamed "Groveland". The Garrote Hotel followed suit, and was renamed the Groveland Hotel.

Tourists to Yosemite became an important component of the Groveland Hotel's business trade. The next owner of the Grovel and Hotel was Thomas R. Reid, the son of Thomas C. Reid, who was born in Garrote in 1856. Thomas Reid acquired the Groveland Hotel, with James Tannahill holding a Deed of Trust, in 1883.. Reid sold his properties (including the Groveland Hotel) to Dedrick Meyer, the Estate of John Meyer, and Mrs. Mary A. Tannahill in 1887. Tannahill, whose husband James had passed away in 1884, sold her interest to the Meyers in 1890. The Meyer brothers, John Dedrick (Dick) and John Heinrich (Henry) ran the property. A single story, wood frame building was added along the west side of the Groveland Hotel by 1900. This building served as a bar. Two small outbuildings were also erected to the south of the adobe building. The Groveland Hotel was probably renovated as well.

In 1915 Timothy H. Carlon purchased the Meyer properties. In the spring of 1915 constructing began on the Annex building, and the adobe building was also renovated. Soon after the completion of the Hotel Annex, the first floor of the adobe building was converted to a restaurant. During the prosperous years of the teens and twenties, the Groveland Hotel became well known for it's parties and dances. In 1935 Carlon sold the Groveland Hotel, the hotel annex, and parlor. There followed a succession of owners after the Carlon era, struggling and sometimes failing to keep the business going. It was during these years that the hotel was also known as the Groveland Inn. In the 1940s, the Groveland Hotel Bar also served as a Greyhound Bus stop. The Groveland finally closed its doors in the late 1950's. Fortunately, the Groveland Hotel, Restaurant and Bar reopened in 1960. The enterprises lasted until 1969, at which time the property was sold through foreclosure to Western Lakes Properties Inc.

Boise Cascade remodeled and converted the Groveland Hotel and Hotel Annex into an office building complex for real estate agents and related professionals. The lumber company also terraced and landscaped the grounds and demolished the old bar room (built by Meyers). In 1973 Ray and Beulan Douglas and Bert and Josephine Pike acquired the Groveland Hotel. They leased the facilities to the Stanislaus National Forest USDA. During the government's stay, few changes were made to the buildings. The Forest Service moved back to the Buck Meadows area in 1986. The Groveland Hotel was sold shortly thereafter.

In 1986 the Groveland Hotel entered its darkest period in history. The new owners stripped both buildings of their interiors and then ran into financial disaster, ending in both foreclosure and bankruptcy. The Groveland Hotel and Annex buildings were left as empty shells and came perilously close to being condemned. In 1990 Peggy and Grover Mosley acquired the Groveland Hotel. By 1991 a major restoration effort began to return the buildings to their original splendor. By May 1992, the 1849 adobe hotel of Monterey Colonial Architectural Style and the 1914 Annex of Queen Anne ancestry were returned to their former glory.

Hauntspitality
According to a Groveland Hotel handout, Room 15 could be double booked when you stay at the hotel. Lyle, a loner and a kindly old gentleman is reportedly the permanent resident of Room 15. Lyle, whose last name is a mystery, is said to have come to the Groveland Hotel during the 1920's. He was a panner who prospected the Spring Gulch region, east of the hotel. A miner with exemplary taste, he chose nothing but the best when it came to his lodgings. Possibly a little eccentric, Lyle was said to have slept with a case of dynamite under his hotel bed. He liked the Groveland Hotel so well, that after his untimely demise in 1927, he opted for a permanent stay.

The management and staff are sure that the dynamite is gone from under the bed in the room Lyle formerly occupied, but as always, Lyle is finicky about his quarters and who comes to visit. Guests often complain that Lyle moves articles placed on the dresser top. In particular, Lyle seems to dislike women's cosmetics on "his" dresser top, and he's always fastidious about personal hygiene. Many people have noted that their faucet constantly turns on and off when there is no one in the bathroom. Lyle also seems to intensely dislike bright lights, and will often dim them when guests insist on having using too many lights at one time. Perhaps his days working in the mines made his eyes extremely sensitive to light.

A list of "Lyle" encounters include: Doors that open and close on their own; ladders moving from one position to another without human assistance; and lights being turned on and off, or dimmed by unseen hands. One winter when the hotel was devoid of guests, water was heard running. A check of the premises revealed a shower stall in one of the rooms still wet from someone taking a shower; an invisible someone. A woman staying in Room 15, put her sun tan lotion on the dresser, only to find it moved to the bathroom sink. No one else had been in the room after the lotion was placed on the dresser. Another guest occupying Room 15 reported a make-up case hopping off the dresser as she watched. A female staying in Room 15, placed her makeup on the dresser before going to sleep. She awoke the next morning to find all of her cosmetics on the floor in front of the bed. A couple spending a few nights in Room 15, reported that they tried unsuccessfully to open the door with the room key. After a master key was tried without luck, management called in a handyman who had to take a ladder around to the side of the hotel and climb in. As he was about to enter, the room key was tried one more time; it worked. Finally, the switchboard often receives late-night calls from an unoccupied Room 15.

Lyle's feisty spirit has also been known to dim or turn off lights when his name is mentioned. Weird light patterns will sometimes appear on the innkeeper's computer screen and no logical explanation can be found. Lyle is also blamed for hiding office items and personal items, opening or closing doors in fronts of startled guests and causing lights to flicker. On one occasion, an industrial washer door with its safety latch on suddenly flew open, spilling water everywhere. Numerous times, items are found broken or misplaced or candy left innocently in a guest's room, will be found devoured. Fire alarms are known to trigger by themselves and furniture is frequently found moved from their original location, even though no one came into a particular room after everything was initially in place for the night. There are numerous reports of a phantom man sighted in Room 15. The spirited gentleman is usually seen standing by the bathroom sink or chair. Guests will report witnessing an odd-looking man in there room one minute, who just mysteriously vanishes.

As you can see (or perhaps not), the benign, yet feisty spirit of Lyle still roams certain rooms and corridors of the history Groveland Hotel. This spirited miner continues to amuse guests and staff with his playful antics, as well as keeping an eye on things at the hotel from another dimension. The Groveland is one of the few places in the United States where you can enjoy a Murder Mystery Weekend in an actual haunted house. If your lucky, you can die while playing a character and possibly meet a dead character, "Lyle," in the same weekend. The Groveland is dying to entertain you; so drop in if you dare.

Hotel Charlotte

Particulars

18736 Main Street (Highway 120)
PO Box 787,
Groveland, CA 95321
Reservations: 209-962-6455
Fax: 209-962-6254
Toll Free: 800-962-6455
E-mail: hotelcharlotte@aol.com
Website: www.hotelcharlotte.com

History

Groveland, originally a Gold Rush town, became a sleepy farming community until the San Francisco Hetch Hetchy water project made it their headquarters and built a railroad yard and hospital for the work crews (both are now destroyed). From 1915 until 1935 Grovela nd was a boom town that supported seven hotels and 10,000 residents. When the work crews left, the town became a stop on the way to Yosemite. Then the Boise Cascade company built the Pine Mountain Lake community with a first class golf course, an airport and lake and staked out 5000 lots. This development has since grown from a summer home area to a retirement community to a thriving area with year round families, boosting the once sleepy Groveland to a travel and vacation destination in its own right In Charlotte's day, the hotel was a rooming house built to house middle management staff from the nearby Hetch Hetchy Dam building project. History tells us that proprietor Charlotte never married.

The 10 room bed & breakfast hotel is listed on the National Register of Historic Places, and is home to Café Charlotte, a full service restaurant & bar.

Hauntspitality

Local legend has it that Charlotte was in love with the man who regularly rented room 6, although he only saw her as a friend. It's said her ghost haunts room 6, and has been known to check in on the guests (particularly male guests) to make sure they are comfortable and tucked in at night. Charlotte is so popular; some repeat guests come back just to experience her again and again.

Ever since they took over the Hotel Charlotte in 2003, owners Lynn and Victor Upthagrove have grown accustomed to guests asking if their building is haunted. Two weeks after moving into the hotel, a parapsychologist came in off the street and asked Lynn if he could look around. She took him into room 6, and even though she'd never thought about ghosts before, his energy convinced her that the ghost of former owner Charlotte still inhabited the hotel. "He took photos into the mirror -- it was so interesting and he was so very convincing that he saw a ghost, it made me believe," says Lynn. While looking through the ghost hunter's camera, pointed towards the bathroom mirror in room 6, Lynn saw the room behind her, including a hanging lampshade, and the face of Charlotte floating in front of it! When she turned around, there was no one there. Lynn never heard from the investigator again and doesn't know if the photo ever came out, but she's been a believer ever since.

Guadalupe
The Far Western Tavern

Particulars
899 Guadalupe Street
(Highway 1 and 9th Street), P.O. Box 607,
Guadalupe, CA 93434
Phone: 805-343-2211
Fax: 805-343-6846
E-mail: info@farwesterntavern.com
Website: www.farwesterntavern.com

History

According to their Website, the story of the Far Western Tavern actually begins in 1912. There were rumors of ghosts floating around during its original incarnation as the Palace Hotel. The establishment served as a brothel with small cribs for additional guest services situated on the second floor. The Palace Hotel was built in Guadalupe by the late Carenini & Forni partnership, later sold to Elvezia & Angelo Ferrari, and finally bought by a third Swiss Italian duo, partners Clarence Minetti and Dick Maretti in 1958. Clarence and Dick were cousins, and the establishment owes much to the numerous family members who served as employees and advisors over the past four decades. Clarence and Rosalie Minetti and their family members now jointly own and operate the Far Western. For Clarence, the story of the Far Western has come full circle. Working as a kid in the nearby hayfields in the 1930s, Clarence remembers eating rib steak and spaghetti in the hotel dining room for under a dollar. Now his children serve local families in the same dining room.

The history of the Far Western Tavern is interwoven with the history of the Santa Maria Valley. The restaurant became a much-needed watering hole for the valley's hardworking farmers, ranchers and cowboys. In those days, the thick, hand-cut Far Western steaks still came from Minetti's Corralitos Ranch. Recipes for the establishment's now-famous "Susie Q's" Pinquito beans and salsa came straight from Rosalie Minetti's ranch-house kitchen. Today's Far Western steaks are still choice selections from trusted, local purveyors, hand-cut and hand-trimmed. As the valley prospered, the restaurant's regional cooking attracted VIPs from Vandenberg Air Force Base, who spread the Far Western reputation far and wide. Clarence Minetti and partner Dick Maretti were also early supporters of the Santa Maria Elks Rodeo. Under Minetti's 50-year leadership, the renowned Elks Rodeo has become one of the top 30 rodeos in the country. Cowboy clowns and rodeo champions have raved about the Far Western's popular Bull's Eye Steak at rodeos nationwide.

Accolades for the Far Western's mastery of Santa Maria style cooking has led to feature stories in Sunset and Gourmet Magazines, establishing the Far Western Tavern as a culinary landmark for Central Coast regional cooking. In 1996, the Far Western Tavern entered a new era. Co-owner Richard Maretti retired. Clarence and Rosalie Minetti and family – daughter Marie and son-in-law Steve Will, daughter Susan and son-in-law Paul Righetti, and son Tyke and daughter-in-law Sheryll Minetti – are new sole owners. Besides testing potential new entrees with Clarence and Rosalie, all family members are at work restoring the 85-year-old building to its original charm. As longtime landowners with strong ties to their Swiss Italian heritage and their Central Coast roots, the Minetti Family are pledging to carry on the "hospitality unlimited" which was first introduced in the Minetti ranch home.

Hauntspitality

The distinctive thumping of a peg-legged phantom sometimes interrupts conversation in this friendly steak house. A spirit can be heard walking noisily about in an upstairs room, just above the dining room. The unfortunate Mr. Franconeti who lost his leg in World War I, died in a fire-related death. Now there is an unexplainable cold spot in the corner where his ashes were found, and people still see, and hear Mr. Franconeti's ghost which still walks the upper floor. Former owners report a thumping sound frequently coming from the upstairs area.

Orbs on the left side of the stairs (Courtesy of the International Paranormal Research Organization – IPRO)

When the place was rebuilt and turned into a restaurant, a cold spot would still be present in the upstairs room--the spot where Franconeti reportedly burned to death.

One female employee heard someone coming down the stairs, and didn't wait to find out who it was since he was working alone. A former manager has seen an apparition. Objects have moved around unassisted by human hands. Once the steer head securely nailed to the wall was found turned upside down! A dark figure has been spotted moving in the back room, and one upstairs room is usually colder than the others.

Orbs upstairs and downstairs (Courtesy of the International Paranormal Research Organization – IPRO) Orbs upstairs and downstairs (Courtesy of the International Paranormal Research Organization – IPRO)

Other paranormal investigators have reported that a female spirit, possibly a prostitute, roams the upstairs area, with her apparition frequently spotted by people walking by late at night. Several employees have also come into contact with the phantom lady dressed in period clothing that will appear for a few seconds and just as quickly vanish through the upstairs walls. Some individuals have said that they have heard the rustle of a dress pass right by them when climbing the stairs. Other staff has heard their name called out when they were working alone.

135

A female psychic who visited the building said she was pinched on the arm, leaving a small bruise. She swore it was a phantom male, who didn't care for her or women in general.

Paranormal investigators and staff have had several encounters in the downstairs bar and bathroom area, and have felt as if they were being watched or followed. On another occasion, several guests reported seeing a spectral lady in Period clothing come up the stairs to the second floor, stand facing them for a second and then vanish. One woman went to the bathroom, and hen she came back, noticed a horseshoe-shaped bruise on the leg. It wasn't there before she went in, and she didn't hit her leg on anything before going in, or after coming out.

Phantom cold spots, uneasy feelings, disembodied footsteps and voices, apparitions and odd sounds are only part of hauntspitality that awaits guests. The Far Western Tavern may have a reputation for its bull's eyes steak, but it also has a spirited guest who doesn't seem to want to leave.

Visitors to the historic Far Western Tavern can always count on finding the restaurant's popular steak items and traditional favorites, but guests should always be on the lookout for more non-traditional fare: spirits! The Minetti tradition for sharing fine quality Central Coast cooking and regional recipes lives on as do their spirited clientele.

Guerneville
Santa Nella House

Particulars
12130 Highway 116,
Guerneville, CA 95446
Phone: 707-869-9488
Toll-free: 800-440-9031
E-mail: info@santanellahouse.com
Website: www.santanellahouse.com

History

The house was constructed around 1870, by Dr. Joseph Prosek, originally from Bohemia. The house was built from old-growth redwood from the local sawmills. It had four bedrooms, two with bathrooms. The house was heated until very recently by wood stoves. Water for the house is still supplied by a plentiful spring on the hill behind the house. Dr. Prosek died in 1920. His wife, Emma, survived him, and none of their children elected to keep the winery, so she sold everything but the olive press and a small two acre parcel of land on which the house sits, and lived out her remaining years alone in the big house. A few of the original olive trees can still be seen across the street.

At the urging of his friends, the Korbel Brothers, Dr. Joseph Prosek came to the Russian River area. At that time, the area was known for its logging and lumber mills, and Guerneville was then called Stumptown. Thousands of old-growth redwoods were cut down and milled, leaving tall stumps everywhere. In previously logged areas, the land was to be had for the taking if you were willing to clear it, which is exactly what Prosek did. He believed in the medical properties of olive oil and so planted 80 acres to olives, with 20 acres devoted to grapes. However, the area was not suited to olives and the olive oil was a losing proposition. Early frosts eventually claimed the entire orchard, and Prosek replaced them all with grapevines- probably also on the advice of the Korbels! His troubles were not over, as phylloxera claimed most of his grapes the first time around. However, he persevered, and bought phylloxera-resistant rootstock from the Korbels, which succeeded. During 1893, the Sonoma Viticulture Report announced that, "Dr. Prosek has a fine young vineyard just coming into bearing. He makes a choice wine, which commands a high price on the market." The Santa Nella Winery and olive press were across the street. The winery prospered until the 1950's, when it was absorbed by the Korbel property.

Hauntspitality

Owner, Kristina Tellefsen, believes that original owners Joseph and Emma Prosek still reside in the house, along with at least one other man who may have died in the house. According to Tellefsen, Emma has a good sense of humor. She helps out by supplying tools for household jobs, but she also likes to hide the tools just when people need them. One must politely ask for them to be returned and they usually do. A man

wearing a morning coat and top hat has been observed sitting in the upholstered chair in the Gold Room before disappearing. The owner thinks that this gentleman is none other than Dr. Prosek, who maybe waiting for his wife to get ready for church.

In the Prosek Room, guests have reported someone going into the bathroom in the middle of the night. Thinking it is their spouse, they are alarmed when they realize that the spouse is sleeping quietly next to them!

Many residents of the house have experienced someone knocking at the front door or ringing the doorbell, and upon answering, finding no one there. The house has a large veranda and many stairs which would make this an unlikely prank for local children as one would hear them running off.

Finally, there is a ghost cat in the Blue Room that loves to sit on the day bed. Tellefsen has never seen her, but she has seen small paw-like indentations on the bed and carpet in that room.

All of the spirited guests at the Santa Nella House are benign and do not frighten anyone. In fact, the spirits seem to enjoy the house as much as the living. Tellefsen says that she finds it comforting to know that the Proseks loved this house enough to continue to live here, even in the afterlife!

Half Moon Bay
Zaballa House

Particulars

324 Main St.,
Half Moon Bay, CA 94019
Phone: 650-726-9123
Fax: 650-726-3921
E-mail zaballahouse@earthlink.net
E-mail: info@zaballahouse.com
Website: www.zaballahouse.net

History

Half Moon Bay, a rural retreat is a small town with a very rich history. It was settled in 1840 by the Spanish and was once known as Spanishtown. The Zaballa House Bed & Breakfast occupies a home that was built by Estanislau Zaballa the husband of Dolores Miramontes in 1859, and is the oldest house still standing in Half Moon Bay. It has been fully restored as a bed and breakfast.

Hauntspitality

According to some guests, Room 6 is very haunted. Strange occurrences happen here with regularity including alarms that go off at all hours, phantom cold spots, keys that continually break, rattling windows, and disembodied footsteps and voices that come from unoccupied rooms.

Several guests have glimpsed shadowy figures along the hallway, darting and then vanishing in unoccupied rooms. Door knobs will turn as if someone is trying to get in. When people attempt to find out the cause of the commotion, there is never anyone there. On other occasions, the lights will flicker in certain rooms and beds that have just been made, will show imprints of people on them.

Psychics who visited the building are convinced that the spirit of Dolores Miramontes haunts the building as well as that of a young girl. At the Zaballa house, the only thing that is normal is the paranormal.

Hanford
Irwin Street Inn

Particulars

212 522 North Irwin Street,
Hanford, CA 93230
Phone: 559-583-8000
Fax: 559-583-8793
Website: www.irwinstreetinn.com

History

Built as a boarding house in 1890, the Irwin Street Inn is the first historic landmark in Hanford, preserving its original wooden detailing, 19th century artifacts and leaded stained-glass windows. The inn is comprised of four impeccably restored turn-of-the-century Victorian homes. The Inn offers 28 guestrooms, each featuring antique armoires, four-poster beds and clawfoot bathtubs. The hotel provides an outdoor heated swimming pool, tree-shaded lawns, two elegant banquet rooms and two meeting facilities. A complimentary hot breakfast is served each morning along with the complimentary spirits; the kind you can't drink and rarely see.

According to www.theshadowlands.net, "Now a restaurant, the Irwin Street Inn is home to at least 3 ghosts. There are occasional slamming of windows, moving of bed sheets, switching on and off lamps. Sometimes ghosts can be seen in the dining area and on the second "floor.

We're not sure if the haunted aspect is accurate, because we also came across this little ditty from a local; "I was born in Hanford, California 54 years ago.... as far as the Irwin Street Inn, my mother and father knew the family that owned that building and have NEVER heard a single story of a "haunting".

Having researched and investigated thousands of structures across the United States, one thing can be said with unwavering certainty, two people working in the same location for the same amount of time can have vastly different experiences, where one see and hears unexplained things and the other person reports nothing. So, we'll leave this for you to ponder when you visit. Keep an open mind when you enter and let us know what you sense. If you spend the night and have something unusual happen, keep us posted. If you take photographs, see if any orbs or other anomalies show up. We recommend that you talk to the current owners about all this before proceeding and see what they have to say. Be courteous as you try to sort out fact from fiction.

We've seen a lot of photographs over the years and can often pick out haunted locations or get a sense for potentially haunted environs from just looking at a visual. We also work with people who conduct remote sensing investigations for us to give us some insight into the possible haunted nature of a building. Psychic imaging, a pre-field psychic analysis of this particular location suggests that there is a high potential for a spirit or two. Several of the "sensitives" picked up on a woman and a child. We are anxious to get some more feedback on this establishment.

Healdsburg
The Camellia Inn

Particulars
Address: 211 North Street,
Healdsburg, CA 95448
Phone: 707-433-8182
Toll Free: 800-727-8182
E-mail: info@camelliainn.com
Website: www.camelliainn.com

History

The Camellia Inn, a charming 1869 Italianate Victorian Inn is located in the heart of Sonoma County's wine country. More than 50 varieties of camellias bloom on the inns landscaped grounds (Luther Burbank was a family friend and many of the camellias gracing the grounds are attributed to him). Interior architectural treasures include inlaid hardwood floors, beautiful double parlors and twin marble fireplaces. Each of the nine thoughtfully appointed guest rooms features a private bath.

The Camellia Inn was built as a home by contractor William H. Middleton for pioneer Ransome Powell in 1871. Powell, the son of a Tennessee farmer, was a tailor before fighting in the Mexican War. He came to California in 1849 with the Gold Rush. Failing to find gold he began to earn a living by hauling freight. Settling in Healdsburg in 1856, he began several ventures but it was real estate that made him his fortune. Powell's first four wives died, but he was married 23 years to his fifth wife, Louise Madeira, before his death in 1910. In 1892, Powell built a new home and sold the North Street residence to Dr. J. W. Seawell, who established the first Healdsburg hospital in the right wing of his home. It was called Healdsburg General then and a doctor's visit cost $2.00. Dr. Seawall and his partner, Dr. Frank E. Sohler, were hard-working physicians who insisted on the best equipment and the latest medical technology for their north county hospital. The Seawell family retained ownership until 1969.

From 1969 until Ray and Delmas (Del) Lewand purchased it in 1981, 211 North Street was a private residence. Looking for a small town atmosphere, the Lewands moved from Southern California and opened the Camellia Inn as the first licensed bed and breakfast inn in the area. Daughter Lucy Lewand joined them in running the inn after completing her Masters in Business Administration from University of California at Los Angeles. Ray and Del were involved in the daily running of the inn until Del's death in 2006. Although now mostly retired, Ray still helps out from time-to-time by delighting guests with his local knowledge of area wineries. Some evenings, Ray can be found pouring wines from Camellia Cellars, the winery he started. Lucy is proud to be part of the longest family-owned and operated inn in the Healdsburg area. She strives along with her innkeepers to combine modern business innovations with the charm and hospitality that made her parents as popular as innkeepers.

Hauntspitality

According to the current owners, the Camellia is no longer haunted. However, it did have a ghost attached to the property until recently; and who knows, another spirit may be waiting beyond the veil to make contact with the right person or paranormal persuasion.

The story goes that until 1988 the Camellia Inn had a large wooden water tower in the backyard, which was used primarily as a storage area by the inn. From time-to-time inn guests and staff would encounter a woman wearing a white cap, a jacket and an ankle-length dark blue skirt with a ribbon at her neck.

From the style of her attire it is assumed that she may have been a household servant or someone who worked in the building when it served as a hospital. The woman was always described as being about twenty years old, cheerful and fond of playing practical jokes on those she encountered.

On numerous occasions, the door to the water tower would open and close on its own, and people standing nearby would swear that the saw a young girl walk out of the door laughing, before she suddenly vanished. Apparently, after the water tower was torn down and replaced by the current swimming pool, the young woman was never seen again.

Could it be that the energy of the young girl was tied so strongly to the water tower (a place she may have occupied as servant's quarters or a hospital staff person or perhaps even died inside due to a prolonged illness), that her spirit moved on when the building was removed?

Some psychics believe that the removal of structural remains rarely releases the spirit; but rather, it is compassion, prayers, communication and forgiveness that offer closure to an unhappy situation. Water is often considered a way for spirits to move on, a kind of cleansing elemental force. With the replacement of the building with a pool, perhaps the young girl's spirit found eternal peace; we hope so.

If you ever make your way to Sonoma County's wine country, Healdsburg is a must see location. While you are there we suggest a stay at the historic 1869 Camellia Inn, where camellias bloom around this architectural treasure. A few nights of relaxation, and some wine and good food will surely lift your spirits in a house where the past and present for a brief time co-existed.

The Madrona Manor

Particulars

1001 Westside Road, P.O. Box 818,
Healdsburg, CA 95448
Phone: 707-433-4231
Fax: 707-433-0703
Toll Free: 1-800-258-4003
E-mail: info@madronamanor.com
Website: www.madronamanor.com

History

Located 65 miles north of San Francisco, The Madrona Manor is listed on the National Register of Historic Places. John Alexander Paxton, a very wealthy man, a State legislator from the Yuba County area, and engaged in mining, banking, and lumber, later helped promote the fledgling wine industry in Sonoma County. His home was built by Martin Hooten who had settled in the area in 1853. Paxton bought 240 acres from Hooten in 1879 for $10,500, and planned his new home, giving the contract to Ludwig and Guerne in 1880. The house would be constructed west of the town across the Dry Creek Bridge on a place known as Madrona Knoll Rancho.

Healdsburg workmen constructed the home containing 17 rooms, 3-1/2 baths, and 7 fireplaces. The Paxtons had two sons, Blitz and Charles, and a household consisting of Miss Ruth McClellan, Hannah's sister, a coachman, footman, groom, several maids, and at least one indentured servant. Paxton purchased the 40 acre Sterling Ranch in 1881 and five years later began a winery designed to use the grapes from Paxton's vineyards. In 1882, Paxton left New York for business, dying at sea just before his 69th birthday. Funeral services were held in Healdsburg on June 19 and his body was interred in a stone vault on the eastern slope of Madrona Manor under his favorite pine tree.

Hannah built a church at Matheson and East Street as a memorial in 1888. She passed away in 1902, at which time both Hannah and John Paxton's bodies were taken to San Francisco for final interment. Following the death of his father, Blitz took over the family home and presidency of the Bank of Santa Rosa. Blitz had two children by his first wife before their divorce in 1894. He remarried Jenny Bates. Charles Paxton took his own life after financial problems and the loss of his wife. Madrona Knoll Rancho was retained by Blitz and was used as a weekend retreat until he sold it in 1913.

Hauntspitality

John and Carol Muir purchased the Manor, and knew immediately it was haunted. During renovation, a crew of carpenters would work and camp in the house until the Muir's returned home on Friday evening. They would all talk about an eerie sense of being watched or followed, and tools would oftentimes disappear or be moved. After opening as an inn, guests would talk about personal items being moved to unexpected locations in the building. Room 201 is one of the more haunted rooms in the manor, and Room 101 is close behind in terms of paranormal phenomena. Once at breakfast a woman shrieked because a coffee cup revolved on its saucer right in front of her eyes.

SanDee and Bill Partridge from Buena Park, California wrote the Muir's about their stay at the Manor. After finishing their sumptuous meal, one of the French doors opened and in walked a little gray-haired lady who noticed SanDee looking at her. The elderly woman told SanDee that she was happy that someone could see her. The woman communicated the name Elsie, and wanted SanDee to follow her through the French doors. As soon as she walked through the doors,  the woman vanished. After dessert, she and her husband went into the music room where they found an article about someone else who had witnessed the lady in the manor, except for the fact that the description fit a young woman, while SanDee saw an elderly lady. The bond between the women was definitely psychic, and the elderly woman wanted SanDee to tell the owners how happy she was at the way it was renovated. SanDee had the good fortune to meet the ghost of the Madrona Manor.

One night a fire alarm went off in the major house, causing confusion among the guests. One guest left very early in the morning while the other guests stayed for breakfast and chatted. The spirits seem to like to play with the alarms and light switches. Carolyn Yarbrough wrote about her experience in the Manor in an LA Times article. As soon as she fell asleep downstairs in room 101, she was awakened by a woman standing at the foot of the bed. The woman was wearing a long black dress with a white "Peter Pan" collar fastened with a narrow black ribbon. Her features were that of a woman in her mid-30s. Yarbrough closed her eyes and forced herself to remain calm. After a moment, she looked toward the foot of the bed. The woman had now moved to a blue velvet chair by the window. As Yarbrough asked what the woman wanted, the slender, relaxed figure slowly dissolved. When Yarbrough talked about her experience the next day, she was told that the room 201, directly above her, was the haunted room, not hers; however Yarbrough was then told that ghosts are not imprisoned by walls, and they can go where they want.

At the Madrona Manor, the rooms are spectacular, the meals scrumptious and some of the guests are other-worldly.

Hollywood
All Star Theater Café & Speakeasy in the Vogue Theater

Particulars

6675 Hollywood Boulevard,
Hollywood, CA 90028
Phone: 323-962-8898 (AllStar Café)
Phone: 323-962-1599 (Vogue Theatre)
E-mail: dfisher10@earthlink.net
Website: www.allstarcafe.net

History

Once housed inside the historic Knickerbocker Hotel, the café has recently moved to the Vogue Theater which is located next to the very spirited Musso & Frank's and two blocks from Mann's Chinese Theater. Before the turn of the previous century, when Hollywood Boulevard was still Prospect Avenue, the Prospect Elementary School stood behind the site where now stands the Vogue Theatre auditorium. The school playground was located where the auditorium is today. The four room school house burned to the ground in 1901, killing 25 children and the teacher, Miss Elizabeth. Six children and Miss Elizabeth were found and identified in the theatre beginning in the Spring of 1997 (paranormal investigations were conducted by the ISPR), but in the winter of 1998, the ISPR had two of the children crossed over (by the clairvoyant members of the ISPR Investigative Team who are capable of such work).

Years later after the school house burned, a textile manufacturing plant was built on the site, which also burned to the ground within a few years. In 1934 - 1935, construction was in motion to build the Vogue Theatre, designed by the same architect (Lee) who designed the Million Dollar Theatre downtown L.A. This was one of his last architectural projects. Research into Sanborn Fire Insurance Maps for the area by IPRO was not able to establish a schoolhouse or textile plant on the property during the time period discussed by ISPR.

The Vogue Theatre opened as a movie theatre in 1936 and operated as such through the Spring of 1992, when the doors closed on the movie palace, leaving it empty (except for vagrants) until the Spring of 1997. At that time, the International Society for Psychic Research (ISPR) acquired the Vogue Theatre and implemented a three year research study of the property through ISPR Investigations and ISPR Ghost Expeditions.

Hauntspitality

ISPR provided the first opportunity worldwide for the public to participate in an actual scientific paranormal field investigation, combining both scientific and clairvoyant methodologies. The very haunted theater produced a gathering of ghost guests. In addition to a spirit named Miss Elizabeth and the several children, two 'resident male entities of the Vogue Theatre manifested. The first male was Fritz, was a German immigrant who worked as a projectionist for the Vogue for about 40 years. The other identified energy was Danny, was a maintenance engineer for

Mann Theatres. The theater was one of the Mann properties where he worked. Although both men died away from the theater in the 1980s, they returned to the place where the men spent a lot of time in life.

According to the Vogue/Allstar Café Website: "Paranormal experiences in the Vogue vary widely and include full form apparitions, partial apparitions, poltergeist activities (objects moved all over the property including the auditorium seats which up and down), odors (associated with one entity), some empathic episodes primarily with Miss Elizabeth and Fritz, residual hauntings (including that of fire smoke, audience  members seating in the seats), and at times, usually during Ghost Expeditions conducted inside the property - the Vogue has many visitors - other entities that have no tie or connection with the property, but are on-site temporarily."

According to Daena Smoller of ISPR, "The Vogue Theatre is the most actively haunted property in Hollywood, investigated, studied and documented since ISPR's founding in L.A. in 1972". ISPR claims to have documented over 4,000 individuals who have had paranormal experiences inside the theater since the summer of 1997. Smoller continued by saying, "We're not talking about a person who had a strange feeling - once, we're talking about thirty people out of 650, packed in an auditorium during a screening, who come out to complain about a little girl (a ghost) that's skipping up and down the auditorium aisle. We're talking about men attending a Film Fest over a month ago, who get pushed out of the way by a male ghost on the stairs. We're talking about a projectionist ghost that handled the projection changeover during a packed film fest screening, when the live projectionist fell asleep! That was in July of this year! And we're definitely not talking about a maid who thought she saw the reflection of a blonde woman in a Hollywood hotel mirror, so therefore it must be the ghost of Marilyn Monroe! We're talking about real Entities at the Vogue...and we've had the some of best try to expose this as fraud - from FOX Undercover, 20/20 to 48 Hours, and they usually end up walking out of the doors kind of freaked - experiencing the paranormal themselves! There's thousands of stories to tell on this property!"

The number people who have experienced the paranormal firsthand inside the Vogue includes celebrities to hundreds of producers, writers and executives from virtually every network and major studio including NBC, Dreamworks, MGM, MTV, FOX, Columbia TriStar Television and the list goes on. Currently, it is the opinion of the ISPR that the Vogue Theatre is truly one of the most actively haunted properties in L.A. due to the amount of actual documented paranormal activity that takes place within the theatre. The Vogue and ISPR has been featured on numerous network TV broadcasts, and it is claimed that most film crews have had paranormal experiences inside the Vogue. A cleansing was performed by ISPR, after four years of studying the energy inside. The intent was to release the seven resident entities from otherworldly bondage to the Vogue Theatre. After the crossing over of the Vogue Theatre entities, which is not open to the general public, the theater will once again close its doors.

All Star Theater Cafe & Speakeasy will open for business inside the theater, and the hauntings may be in Vogue once again.

Chateau Marmont

Particulars
8221 Sunset Boulevard,
Hollywood, CA 90046-2413
Phone: 323-656-1010
Fax: 323-655-5311
E-mail: chateaula@aol.com
Website: http://www.chateaumarmont.com

History
This castle-like hotel on the Sunset Strip, opened in 1929 and was renovated 1998. This legendary Hollywood hideaway is where Jim Morrison lived for a while. John Belushi died

in one of the bungalows away from the main building in 1982.

The hotel has played host to Errol Flynn, Humphrey Bogart, Bob Dylan, Clark Gable, Paul Newman, Roman Polanski and Sharon Tate, Billy Wilder, Julie Delpy, Christopher Walken, Dennis Hopper, John Lennon & Yoko Ono, Jim Morrison, Grace Kelly, Marilyn Monroe, Boris Karloff, Carole Lombard, Mick Jagger, Ringo Starr, Jean Harlow, Sidney Poitier, Dustin Hoffman, William Holden, Jessica Lange, Led Zepplin, the Jefferson Airplane, Spike Lee, Greta Garbo, Tim Burton, Michelle Pfeiffer, Robert De Niro, Leonardo DiCaprio, Keanu Reeves, Matt Dillon, Johnny Depp, Winona Ryder, Ellen DeGeneres, Courtney Love, and Sting.

James Dean and Natalie Wood first met at the Marmont, during a script rehearsal of "Rebel Without a Cause." When actor Montgomery Clift was almost killed in a 1956 auto accident near her home, Elizabeth Taylor brought him to the Chateau Marmont where she leased the penthouse for him to recuperate. The hotel is currently owned by Andre' Balazs.

Hauntspitality
According to several parapsychologists and ghost hunters, the Marmont, which has been home to almost every Hollywood legend, was also the site of John Belushi's death. Every kind of phenomena has been witnessed here. So creepy it's considered one of the top haunted hotels in USA. Whether John Belushi still visits Bungalow 3 where he passed away is conjecture.

This 1,500 sq. foot hillside bungalow has been visited by psychics, ghost hunters and friends holding séances trying to reach the gifted yet disturbed, deceased actor; a few have claimed success

Guests and staff have reported seeing unexplained shadows in the garden area and in the Marmont bar. There have been reports of ghostly conversations and parties coming from unoccupied rooms, and disembodied footsteps passing though the lobby late at night. Housekeeping have remarked that in some rooms, the furniture has a mind of its own, and after making a bed, sometimes the startled employee turns to find the impression of someone lying in the bed.

A screenwriter staying at the Chateau candidly remarked that several ghosts reside at the Chateau Marmont. This writer happened to working on a script in Suite 23 when at 3:33 in the morning he would be awakened by "something" which forced him out of bed, which is exactly what he needed in order to complete a script on time. This helpful phantom continued being the writer's alarm clock until the process was completed. The ghostly presence also manifested as a shadowy figure near the window a few times. Perhaps, as the writer suggested, it was a spirit who liked to harass writers, possibly hired by the agent or studio to ensure the script was completed on time.

Some say that a black performer who took a leap of faith out of an upstairs window roams the hallways at night, startling some staff and guests. The spirits may be restless but not harmful; they just love playing pranks where only a wink of an eye separates the past from the present, and illusion from reality.

The ambiance seems to lend instant credibility to the ghostly potential of the Marmont. If people don't like to talk about the spirits of the place, rest assured, or more appropriately rest uneasy that it's history and historical clientele have left something behind besides their Nome de plume on the guest register.

There are spirits who continue to call this moniker of Hollywood dreamers and dream makers, home. They may not always be heard or seen, but they are there waiting for an other-worldly audition or party to continue in death what they enjoyed so much in life, the marvelous ambiance of the Chateau Marmont. Here, they gladly cater to the living and spirited clientele.

El Compadre Restaurant

Particulars

7408 Sunset Boulevard,
Hollywood, CA 90046-3404
Phone: 323-874-7924

History

According to the current owners, the building was constructed sometime in the 1920s. It has served as a restaurant and bar since it opened and once housed Don Pepe's Restaurant. The original cash register is still in use, and traditional Mexican food and flaming margaritas await each visitor.

Hauntspitality

A tragedy during the 1950s may account for two of the three spirits reported

inside this building. There have been sightings of two shadowy figures of men walking near the piano after closing. They are there one minute, then they simply vanish. The phantom figures are believed to be two men who were gunned down and killed during a robbery that occurred in the 1950s when the building was called Don Pepe's. It seems as though this traumatic occurrence has left more than an imprint on the restaurant. It has also left behind two spirits who may not know they are dead and are stuck in the place that they meet their sudden and unfortunate demise. The two phantoms are usually witnessed as floating shadowy forms. They have been felt as rapidly materializing cold spots, and are blamed for turning lights on and off. The spectral guests have been known to move place settings, chairs and other objects, and are considered the cause of doors opening and shutting by themselves. On occasion and disembodied footsteps and voices are heard coming from unoccupied areas of the restaurant.

The bar area is also haunted by an unknown presence, believed to be a male, who remains close to the large mirror in the wall. There have been reports of a strange shadow suddenly appearing in the mirror, followed by a mist that forms around the edges of the mirror, and well as a strong sensation of being watched or followed inside. It's dark and a little eerie inside the restaurant, so it's easy to imagine that "something" is lurking just out of view, particularly if you've had a few margaritas or beers.

The current owners report that nothing unusual has occurred since they took over the place a few years ago; however, they did say that the prior owners constantly had strange and unexplainable events occur inside, and that the place was very haunted." Have the former ghosts left with the prior owners? Or, are the phantoms just waiting for the right time to reappear? No one knows for sure. Flaming margaritas and finicky phantoms are the bill of fare at this Hollywood hot spot.

Formosa Cafe

Particulars
7156 Santa Monica Boulevard,
West Hollywood, CA 90046
Phone: 323-850-9050
E-mail: vince@formosacafe.com
Website: www.formosacafe.com

History
According to some, the original brick building which was constructed around 1925 as a production office for United Artists. It was a perfect location for the likes of Mary Pickford and Douglas Fairbanks until they moved their office across the street (Warner Hollywood Studio is now its neighbor). Soon afterward, Jack's Steakhouse filled the space until 1939 when the Formosa Café began occupying the building. The building became a historic landmark in 1991 and to this day, it continues to operate as a renowned dining spot for anyone who wants good food, nostalgia and a chance to sight a celebrity. It's a dying breed of historic restaurants and café's that once hosted the who's who of Hollywood. When you step inside you swear that you have gone back in time to the Golden Age of Hollywood. The Formosa menu-makeover is guaranteed to draw new generations of deal-making clientele.

The walls of the Cafe are lined with over 250 black & white photos of the stars who dined here including: James Dean, Frank Sinatra, Paul Newman, Humphrey Bogart, Elvis Presley, Marilyn Monroe, Clark Gable, Marlon Brando, Jack Benny, Elizabeth Taylor, Jack Webb, Martin & Lewis, and Grace Kelly, etc.

Current celebrities who visit this establishment include Bono of U2, Michael Douglas, Nicolas Cage, Jodie Foster, Matthew Perry, Richard Dreyfus, Christian Slater, Robert Wagner and Britney Spears. All of the photographs were autographed by the celebrities themselves. Frank Sinatra enjoyed chicken chow mein the day following his Oscar wining role in "From Here to Eternity." Marilyn Monroe dined here while making "Some Like it Hot," and Elvis dropped by while making "Kid Galahad."

This was Bogart's favorite bar and Gable and Monroe dined here while making "The Misfits." The Formosa was also a favorite hang-out for Elizabeth Short, the victim of the famous "Black Dahlia" murder case. The restaurant is also home to several spirits.

Hauntspitality

If walls could talk, then this place would have never ending stories to tell the living. There are many rumors of spirits in this café that the living and dead appear evenly matched inside. Staff and guests have been confronting the ghost guests for years. Cold drafts will suddenly manifest out of nowhere, engulfing the unsuspecting person. Several people have felt someone unseen brush right by them as they were walking back to their station.

Several guests have reported seeing "things" out of the corner of their eyes. These "things" include figures of people in Period clothing who are there one minute and then gone the next. Several times, individuals have reported seeing a person wearing 1930s clothing, looking just like you or I, standing and staring at them, and the next second, they are gone. On numerous occasions, staff has reported hearing conversations taking place after hours when the place is devoid of guests. The party-like exchanges are sometimes animated followed by laughter, glasses clinking and then total silence. It gets a little eerie and spooky after dark; most staff says or thinks out loud. The late night employees are usually the ones with the unexplained experiences since, the business hours tend to be noisy and distracting for both the living and dead.

The stories of hauntings in this landmark restaurant are as fascinating as the clientele who visited the building. Some say the ghosts of Elizabeth Short and Humphrey Bogart are frequent guests, still partying, or looking for someone as they pass through the building. There have been reports of misty forms, of a former owner who is still seen in his favorite booth, as if waiting to greet the clients he cared for so much in life.

The rumors of objects being moved, disembodied voices, cold drafts, the feeling of unseen people passing by and electrical anomalies are as common as a celebrity visit. The history of this building and the emotional imprints spanning over 80 years are sure to contribute to its haunted reputation. The ambiance, food, service and memories evoked by the celebrity photographs lining the wall, are part of the very best in Hollywood hauntspitality served up at the Formosa.

Knickerbocker Hotel

Particulars

1714 North Ivar Avenue,
Hollywood, CA 90028

History

The Glen-Holly Hotel built in 1890, the first hotel in Hollywood, was originally located at the corner of what is now Yucca St. and Ivar Avenue where the Knickerbocker Hotel now stands. The Knickerbocker Hotel is now a security apartment building with a huge crystal chandelier in the lobby. E.M. Frasier was the architect who designed the building in 1923, in the Renaissance Revival/ Beaux Arts style as a luxury apartment building. The Knickerbocker Hotel was in its youth a mainstay in the life of Hollywood's beautiful people. Valentino made regular appearances at the bar. Marilyn Monroe

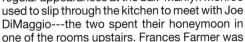

used to slip through the kitchen to meet with Joe DiMaggio---the two spent their honeymoon in one of the rooms upstairs. Frances Farmer was dragged with only a shower curtain draped around her through the lobby of the Knickerbocker.

Elvis once lived in the Knickerbocker and loved the hotel so much that he is said to have named a song for it: Heartbreak Hotel. D.W. Griffith made it into the lobby from his 10th floor suite before collapsing underneath the chandelier. He died at the Temple Hospital in Hollywood on 24 July 1948, of a cerebral hemorrhage.

For a time, William Frawley (Fred Mertz in I Love Lucy), lived in the Knickerbocker Hotel. He would come down every night to have a cracked walnut put in his drink. One day, he went out in front of the hotel and dropped dead on the sidewalk of a heart attack.

In 1962, a celebrity dress designer named Irene Gibbons jumped out the window of one of the hotel's bathrooms. Her suicide note blamed money and marital problems, but others speculate that it was because of an affair gone badly with Gary Cooper. Irene's body landed on the hotel canopy, where she remained unnoticed for days.

Beginning on Halloween night of 1926, the first year anniversary of her husband's death, Harriet Houdini held a séance on the roof of the Knickerbocker Hotel every year, hoping to receive a message from him.

The séances continued until Halloween of 1936, where it is said that she received the message "Rosalee," which, though not the secret code word, was a personal name of hers that had been etched into her wedding band.

The Knickerbocker housed Elvis Presley and the Jordanaires during the summer of 1956, when Presley was here recording the Elvis album, and filming Love Me Tender. Jerry Lee Lewis also had a suite early in 1958. Its Lido Room was host to many parties for Hollywood stars. The Knickerbocker was closed and the rooms converted to apartments in 1971 and the hotel bar was sealed up because of an overactive poltergeist population.

Hauntspitality

It has been said that a number of ghosts lurk the corridors of the Knickerbocker and come down from time to time for a cup of coffee in the comfort of the familiar hotel bar. As one of the three oldest hotels in Hollywood, it's only appropriate that it should be one of the most haunted. The former bar area located on the left side of the main entrance, was nestled privately against a wall where the original bar entrance used to be located. The corner of the former bar is where Valentino's spirit has been sighted from time to time. Another spirit is an unidentified male ghost who appeared at the former All-Star Café serving counter, dressed all in black, and imposing enough to send a startled spectator running.

Many have claimed to see Marilyn Monroe wandering through the place, and the girl's bathroom is apparently notorious for sending squeamish young ladies running. They complain of hearing knocks on the door. The mirror also produces the reflection of a short-haired woman. Doors have opened and closed unexpectedly, metal and other items have been heard rattling, and several apparitions have been reported over the years.

Richard Senate during an investigation of the Knickerbocker with his wife, and psychic, Debbie, for the Sightings program, produced some interesting results. Senate began with his dowsing rods, and they went crazy. As Senate was discovering at least three paranormal hot spots, the employees who work at the cafe told of the ceiling fans breaking a blade in a bizarre way; lights going on and off by themselves; and phantom forms appearing and disappearing. All of the evidence confirmed what Senate found while dowsing. One intense location was under the lobby chandelier (he later learned it was the spot that D. W. Griffith, collapsed in 1948). A séance in the former All-Star Cafe yielded even more information. Debbie Senate contacted a former Bell Captain who still wandered through the place he had worked for so long. Another spirit came through---it was Frances Farmer. She was stuck in the hotel, but didn't seem to mind the place she had grown fond of in life. Finally, the spirit of David, perhaps D.W. Griffith was contacted. He was on his way to meet a man named Roach (Hal Roach?).

The cafe has been featured numerous times on the History Channel, Discovery Channel, Sightings, E! Mysteries and Scandals, on World's Scariest Vacation Spots, and High Class Haunts for the Travel Channel, as well as written up in local newspapers and magazines.

Although the famous Knickerbocker now provides the Russian community with apartments, converting the former rooms into living spaces, its spirit population is reportedly quite active. A visit to the historic building may produce more than a few memories, since the afterlife clientele are doing quite well inside.

The Magic Castle

Particulars
7001 Franklin Avenue,
Hollywood, CA 90028-8600
Phone: 323-851-3313
Fax: 323-851-4899
Website: www.magiccastle.com

History
    The Magic Castle was the private home of banker and real estate magnate Rolland B. Lane who constructed the house in 1908. Lane owned much of what is now Hollywood, and dreamt of turning the land into orange groves, farms and ranches. However, a severe drought ended his dreams for a citrus empire. Forced to sell, the Lane family moved away in the 1940s. The mansion was the converted into a home for the elderly, and after that, into small apartments. By 1960, the mansion was being considered for demolition. It was during this time that Milt Larsen, a writer on the NBC TV show Truth or Consequences, met the owner, Thomas O. Glover. Larsen's office was fortuitously situated on the ninth floor of an office building that overlooked the Lane Mansion. Larson's late father, William W. Larsen, Sr., was

a renowned magician and always wanted to have an elegant private club devoted entirely to magicians.

    During September of 1961, Milt Larsen along with friends and volunteers restored the former Victorian mansion to its original elegance. Today, the Castle has become the world-famous "home" to the Academy of Magical Arts, Inc., and their invited guests. The Magic Castle is split into three floors and a basement. Spirits (the kind you drink) are found in the five bars tucked away inside: the Grand Salon; the Palace of Mystery; the WC Fields; the Hat & Hare, and the Owl Bar. Famous magicians and celebrity hobbyists who have played here include, Jay Ose, Johnny Platt, Kuda Bux, Billy McComb, Cary Grant, Steve Martin, Johnny Carson, and Jason Alexander.

Hauntspitality
    The biggest problem in defining the spirit population at this establishment involves discerning the illusion from the real thing. There are quite a few effects that look so real that it's hard to tell if you're looking a phantom or the results of prestidigitation. There have been numerous reports of no-magic related paranormal activity inside. Psychic and investigators are quick to point out that although the building is designed to feature magic and magic-related effects, there is much more going on inside that can be attributed to the unknown. Unexplained phenomena are constantly pitted against possible magic-related events. The discerning individual is usually able to sense the ghost from the illusion.

    Psychics in particular point to the history of the building as the battery for the spirits in the building. First it was a house, then a home for the elderly and finally apartments. Some of the energy from prior incarnations is still imprinted in it's walls and there is a certain amount of paranormally charged activity inside that dates back to the early 1900s and a time when elderly guests lived and died inside. Several 'gifted" individuals has picked up on a man who lost everything and was forced to leave his home (probably Roland Lane?) and an elderly woman who limps around the building looking for help (a rest home retiree?). Measurable cold spots, unusual spikes on EMF meters; dowsing rods that jerk to point out haunted areas inside the mansion; ghostly voices and disembodied footsteps, are but a few of the trademarks of a haunted location found in the Magic Castle.

One of the Castle's most famous members, master magician, Dai Vernon, often sat in the bar area entertaining and teaching guests as the Magician-in-Residence at the "Castle". Vernon died in 1992 and many say that he never left the building, continuing to perform feats of magic from beyond the veil. The may be another spirit in the building as well. Some say that a magician once died on stage, and he is still seen in the theatre where he last performed.

Famed ghost hunter, and friend, Richard Senate once visited the Magic Castle. In his book, Hollywood Ghosts, he states, "My journey to this place wasn't only to enjoy the magic shows and dining, but to quietly investigate the ghosts that might lurk within the mansion. My first goal was the "haunted" pub, located in the lower part of the house. There was something more there than tricks installed by the Magic Castle to entertain guests. There are real ghost visits from time to time."

Senate asked about their ghost, and a bartender told him that Lawrence was a popular bartender back in the late 1970s. Lawrence died suddenly at a relatively young age and regulars claim they still see his spirit. The affable ghost moves items, and floats around, as if checking up on the clientele. Another spirit who is fondly called Irma, is also part of the spirit population inside the club.

Fox TV presented a two-hour special in 1989 about the Magic Castle. The Search for Haunted Hollywood special focused on several haunted Hollywood hot spots. During the segment, Milt Larsen, the founder of the Magic Castle, said he encountered the spirit of Irma during a rain storm on Friday, January 13th, 1988. According to the segment, Milt Larsen was sleeping in his tower office when he was awakened by a loud clap of thunder. A subsequent power outage threw the Magic Castle into pitch blackness. Milt stumbled around the room until he found his flashlight. As he was inspecting the place, he hear music coming from the piano in the room below. Although the power was off, the mansion was securely locked down for the evening. Flashlight in hand and a little apprehensive, he went in search of the eerie music. Reaching the room where the music was coming from, he opened the door and the music ceased. The piano in the room is a trick piano, but it has to have power to work. On this night the power came from Irma the ghost.

Our good friend and natural born psychic and medium, Alma Carey who appeared in numerous national television specials on the paranormal and is currently working on several books (818-972-2953 for psychic readings or special events; Website: www.almacarey.com) has worked at Magic Castle and knows about its "real" spirits up close and personal. According to Carey, about 15 years ago, she was seated alone and in costume in the downstairs ballroom area on a Saturday afternoon. While on-call at the Castle for private readings, she was waiting for her private party to be escorted downstairs after their luncheon. Carey was situated a few feet directly in front of the back stairs leading up to the second floor. There was television and newspaper coverage of the event that day. A contingent from Japan, was given VIP treatment as the Magic Castle which is generally closed on a Saturday afternoon.

While waiting downstairs, Carey witnessed a 30-40 year-old male enter the back door. He was Caucasian, about 5'7", medium build, with short, light brown hair, and wearing tan trousers, a light green shirt, brown-green jacket with a tie, and brown shoes. He was very "ordinary-looking" and she had never seen the man in the building before. The man walked straight up to Carey, looking down at the floor the entire time as he approached in a slow deliberate pace. His eyes were gazing at the ground rather than at Carey. As the man closed in, and was roughly two feet away from Carey, he walked past her and went up the stairs. About 30 seconds later, two men from the Magic Castle maintenance crew came into the ballroom from upstairs to change some light bulbs, bringing ladders with them. Carey told them that she had just witnessed a man enter the room, walk right by her and go upstairs as though he belonged in the building. The men said there wasn't supposed to be anyone else there, and asked what he looked like.

After giving the maintenance men a description of the unusual intruder, one of the men blurted out that the same man had been sighted before by others, but no one had ever been able to find him. One maintenance man said that he had once been on a ladder, when the same man walked in and proceeded to go upstairs. He had called out, but the man kept walking and disappeared upstairs. He'd hurried down from the ladder and chased after the man, but the guest was nowhere to be found. It happened to several people who worked inside over the years. Everyone who saw this person described him the same way; looking down toward the floor and walking passed everyone. To this day, no one knows the identity of this Magic Castle spirit.

According to Carey, the séance room is another haunted spot. There have been a couple of deaths reported in that room over the years while conducting the Houdini Séance. They have been considered natural causes, since the people who died were all elderly. However, during the séances, people have been seeing shadowy figures moving around in the darkness.

Master magician Jules Lenier, a friend of Carey's recently died in a nearby hospita. After his passing, house staff, valets, bartenders and waiters began reporting strange occurrences and sightings taking place in a few specific spots Jules used to sit. The spot at the bar, where Jules sat while in the "Irma's Room" bar, had the light go out under the bar. They have been unable to correct it by merely changing the bulb. The light went out on the hour of Jules's death. So far, the electrical issues have not been satisfactorily corrected. Jules also had a seat outdoors, in front of the Castle, where guests, while waiting for their cars would sit to smoke. Jules was a chain smoker, and he was there almost every night. There was a plaque put up on the wall years ago, labeling the area the "Jules Lenier Lounge". On the night of his death, the lights went out in front of the Castle, and they couldn't correct the problem right away. Then the lights began to go off and on in a strange manner, without a common sense solution. In addition, the fountain turned itself on and the staff couldn't turn it off. The valets said this went on for a week, and then finally ceased.

According to Carey, there was another, secret spot within the Magic Castle, where one could go "outside" while still being "in" the Castle, if one wanted to smoke. It was an especially good private location when it rained. Jules used to buy a carton of cigarettes called "New York" brand. A day or two after his death, a new, unopened pack appeared on the wooden bench back in the "private" area. Jules wouldn't have left it, and everyone questioned had no knowledge about the cigarettes being placed there. Jules was a member of Carey's Paranormal Studies and Investigations group, a gathering of magicians from the Magic Castle who had psychic abilities and a keen interest in the paranormal. Jules appeared on television with Carey on several of her televised psychic investigations on national television. Jules and Carey made a pact: whoever died first, the other was to look for them, make an effort to contact the other, and remember to pay attention to the one who'd just crossed over. Carey went to the Magic Castle to take some photographs, and captured an orb immediately above his seat in the "Jules Lenier Lounge", and also above the other areas where he enjoyed sitting. Carey will present her findings in a book she is currently working on.

At the Magic Castle, there is the always a sense that one isn't alone and there is a feeling that many spirits still roam the halls and rooms. Here, the show must always go on and no one really seems to care if the spirits are a slight of hand illusion or the real thing. This is one place where hauntspitality is ongoing all the time and is included in the price of admission.

Oban Hotel

Particulars
6364 Yucca Street,
Hollywood, CA 90028
Phone: 213-466-0524

History
Constructed during the 1930s to provide affordable housing for the hundreds of Hollywood wannabe's who flooded into the area seeking employment and stardom. By the 1940s, stars such as Glenn Miller, Harry James, Clark Gable, Marilyn Monroe, James Dean and Orson Welles spent time at the Oban on their way to fame and fortune.

Hauntspitality
The Oban seems to be haunted by a stuntman named Charles Love, who doubled for actor Harry Langdon, who committed suicide in February of 1933.

There is also a female ghost, several male entities and a very mean-spirited phantom who appears in the basement. Writer's, Laurie Jacobson and Marc Wanamaker, visited the Oban while working on their Hollywood Haunted book. They wandered through the building and felt cold spots, a pervasive feeling of being watched, a measurable energy force, and through information provided by a psychic, that Charles Love may have been murdered, and that is why his spirit still roams the building. Their hair stood on end, and they were told by the owner, that apparitions have been sighted over the years.

Additional psychic investigations were conducted inside; one involved noted paranormal investigator Barry Taff, which yielded additional spirits in the Oban. The group encountered an angry energy in the basement which produced a smell so foul; it drove several of the team members away.

Yes, the Oban is still haunted. Given its history and association with Hollywood, the movies, the big bands, as well as those who came with a dream of making it in the industry and perhaps never made it home, it is no wonder that residual energy remains at this Hollywood Hotel. Here, a little Love goes a long way.

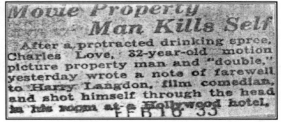

Movie Property Man Kills Self

After a protracted drinking spree, Charles Love, 32-year-old motion picture property man and "double," yesterday wrote a note of farewell to Harry Langdon, film comedian, and shot himself through the head in his room at a Hollywood hotel.

FEB 16 33

The Radisson Hollywood Roosevelt Hotel

Particulars

7000 Hollywood Boulevard,
Hollywood, CA 90028
Phone: 323-466-7000
Fax: 323-462-8056
Reservations: 1-800-695-8284
Toll-Free: 1-800-950-7667
Website: www.hollywoodroosevelt.com

History

The stylish hotel, named after Theodore Roosevelt, lies in the heart of Hollywood. The hotel was designed to be the focal point for the film world. In fact, the first Academy Awards ceremony was held in the Blossom Ballroom in 1929. The Roosevelt has continually hosted movie premieres, opening night galas, and various parties. The building was constructed in 1927. Douglas Fairbanks and Mary Pickford helped make the Hollywood Roosevelt a reality, and the grand opening drew John Gilbert, Gloria Swanson, Greta Garbo, Will Rogers, and Clara Bow.

It wasn't until 1983, that the Roosevelt underwent a multi-million dollar restoration project. The hotel was reopened in March 1986---a gala ceremony attended by fifteen hundred celebrities and well-known personalities.

Hauntspitality

Employees of the Roosevelt Hotel report seeing the reflections of deceased guests in hallway mirrors. The ghostly reflection of Marilyn Monroe is seen in a mirror that used to belong to the star, on display in the lower elevator foyer. The ghost of Montgomery Clift has been seen pacing the ninth-floor hall and sometimes

he can be heard practicing his trumpet. Carole Lombard's apparition has been spotted in the top floor suite she shared with Clark Gable.

There are a number of spirits at the Radisson Hollywood Roosevelt Hotel including Marilyn Monroe and Montgomery Clift. According to a number of psychic investigators who have joined in the phantom search, there area a number of lesser known spirits who roam the Roosevelt. The Blossom Ballroom is the scene of a mysterious cold spot identified in 1985 by a personal assistant to the general manager;

it has been investigated and confirmed scientifically as a circle of cold energy approximately thirty inches in diameter. The temperature in the circle is about ten degrees cooler than the rest of the room. Although there is no explanation for why the area continues to exist, the spot dissipates when the room is crowded and returns again when the activity has subsided.

Psychics picked up on a man in black who is partly or solely responsible for this energy vortex, and that he is filled with anxiety. Perhaps he was a nominee during the first Academy Awards presentation, and is still awaiting the results--or worse, he can't believe he lost.

A cleaning lady was dusting the tall, dark-framed mirror in the general manager's office when she caught a glimpse of a blonde girl staring at her in the glass. Quickly turning around to say something to someone she thought was a curious guest; she found no one there. She reported the incident only to find out that the mirror once belonged to actress Marilyn Monroe. The mirror was originally situated in her poolside suite. After she died, it was moved several times, ultimately ending up near the lower level elevator landing. People come from around the world to gaze into the mirror hoping to catch a glimpse of Marilyn.

Psychics who have come to investigate the mirror have all sensed an aura of sadness and tragedy associated with the object. No one has yet successfully obtained a photograph of Monroe when she appears in the mirror; she seems adamant about avoiding further publicity.

Montgomery Clift is another spirit who toys with guests and staff. He spent three months in Room 928 while filming From Here to Eternity, and has been known to brush by guests and staff in the corridor outside the room where he once paced for hours, rehearsing his lines. He is also known to be difficult on those spending the night in "his" room. His spirit oftentimes creates a ruckus by moving objects, and in general being downright inhospitable.

There is also a spirited writer in the personnel office, who types incessantly after the office is locked up for the night; an electrician who turns the lights on and off in the Star Suite (Rooms 1101/1102); a soundman who calls the switchboard from empty hotel rooms; and complaints from guests about noisy parties taking place in unoccupied rooms adjacent to where they are staying.

The television show Sightings sent renowned psychic investigator Peter James to the hotel during the spring of 1992. He confirmed the presence of Carmen Miranda in a hallway on the third floor; Humphrey Bogart near the elevator; Errol Flynn, Edward Arnold, and Betty Grable in the Blossom Room; and Montgomery Clift in Room 928. While checking out the Tropicana Bar, he sensed Marilyn Monroe's ghost still maintaining a bond with the hotel. The hotel now puts out an eight page press release detailing its phantom film stars and their latest appearances.

During a celebration at the hotel for the office of Los Angeles District Attorney, there was an uninvited guest. Lasting well into the night, the party was winding down when a man and his wife were walking around the mezzanine area admiring the collection of vintage pictures on the walls. They were startled to see a man with white hair sitting at the piano near the door to the balcony of the main ballroom. The couple watched in silence as the elderly got up, strolled toward them, and then suddenly vanished in thin air. They quickly reported this to the front desk.

The very next day, a maintenance engineer, completing a project on the third floor, saw a man wearing a white suite standing in the hall, looking from side to side as if confused. Seeing the man's confusion, the engineer approached the man and asked if he could be of assistance. Without saying a word, the strange-looking man walked down the hallway toward the fire escape door, and then proceeded to walk through it. The stunned engineer, frozen in his tracks for several seconds, pulled himself together and ran to report the incident.

Renowned paranormal investigator and author, Richard Senate and his ghost-hunting team selected the Blossom Room as their first monitoring target. They were attempting to further document the cold spot that had been reported in the ballroom since 1985. The team spread, and with arms outstretched, searched for the cold spot. It didn't take long for them to hone in on the circle of ice. It was a distinct column of cold, and a search for hidden vents or air-conditioning elements to explain the anomaly proved futile. The column of cold was measured as being almost three feet in diameter and at least six feet high. Psychic Debbie Christenson Senate felt the presence of a young man within the cold spot, but was unable to solve the riddle of why he remained, and what caused the cold spot to remain stationary in the ballroom. In fact, it appears that the mysterious spot has become colder over the years, dropping a few degrees in temperature.

The next target was the mirror which seemed to contain the remnant energy of Marilyn Monroe. A number of strange events occurred when a documentary team attempted to reenact an event for a Halloween special in 1989. The crew was unable to film the mirror because they were sprayed by nearby fire extinguishing equipment. A psychic confirmed that Monroe did not like the cross-dressing actor who was portraying her. After several failed attempts to film the mirror for the special, they decided to use a similar mirror one flight up---Marilyn would not cooperate, at least while using "her" mirror.

Proceeding to the ninth floor, the team began their investigation of Montgomery Clift. For years, guests have complained of nightly trumpet practice sessions, but all attempts to stop the spirited music have failed. Staff has reported seeing his apparition in the hall leading to his room, while others have heard blasts from a trumpet late in the night, as well as cold spots, and being softly pushed around. The team brought a trumpet into the room in the hope of eliciting a reaction. During a séance conducted by Debbie Senate the room became cold as Debbie went into a trance. She contacted a spirit who would not give its name, but did say that there were children who were not taken care of; that were fathered but not recognized; then the spirit left. Each member of the team felt a presence in the room. The next morning the trumpet was found on the carpet several feet from where it had been placed.

Guests continue to report the sounds of loud parties and children playing in adjacent rooms that turn out to be vacant. Phones have been lifted from receivers in empty suites, and a lobby maid was pushed into a supply closet by unseen hands. Other employees have reported strange shadows, the intense feeling of being watched, cold spots, and mysterious pacing in the hallway on the ninth floor, and refuse to work Room 928. Others hear discarnate voices calling out for them. People still clamor to spend the night in Clift's Room and are not disappointed. One woman was awakened while spending a night with her husband in Room 928 by a hand patting her shoulder as she was reading in bed. Thinking it was her husband, she turned to find him asleep. In 1989, a television crew planned a shoot at the hotel, but the filming outside of Clift's room was continually disrupted by failing equipment.

The Roosevelt Hotel still caters to Hollywood's celebrities, although some are dead. Visit this historic hotel for a memorable dining experience, or spend the night in a fabulous and sometimes haunted room. Your stay will instantly transport back in time, where you may even spot a deceased celebrity or two. Even those from another world know a good thing, and remain behind to continue enjoying memories of their bygone glory days.

The Viper Room

Particulars
8852 Sunset Boulevard,
West Hollywood, California 90069
Phone: 310-358-1880
E-mail: viperinfo@viperroom.com
Website: www.viperroom.com

History
The Viper Room is located just west of Spago on the Sunset Strip. The building has a long and colorful history that includes mobsters Bugsy Siegel and Mickey Cohen who visited here during the Prohibition when a jazz bar was known as "The Melody Room." During the 1970s, Jim Morrison and "The Doors" played here. The Viper Room opened in 1993 and was partially owned by actor Johnny Depp who named the club "after a group of musicians who called themselves Vipers."

Courtney Love, Drew Barrymore, Sean Penn, Joan Osbourne, Tom Petty, Cameron Diaz, Christina Aguilera, Alicia Silverstone, Juliette Lewis, Christina Applegate, Bruce Springsteen, the Stone Temple Pilots, Smashing Pumpkins, Billy Idol, Sheryl Crow, The Knack, the Red Hot Chili Peppers, Iggy Pop, Mick Jagger, Uma Thurman, Nicole Eggert, Tom Hanks, Michael Keaton, Bruce Springsteen and many more celebrities have visited or played this famous landmark.

The Viper Room became a young celebrity club hot spot before River Phoenix died here of a drug overdose. The young actor's death made headlines when he collapsed on the sidewalk outside the purple awning of this Sunset Strip nightclub on Halloween night of 1993. River Jude Phoenix was born on August 23, 1970 in Madras, Oregon. His Father, John Lee Bottom and Mother, Arlyn Sharon Dunetz gave birth to River Jude, Rain Joan of Arc, Joaquin Raphael, Liberty Butterfly, and Summer Joy. River starred in Joe Dante's Explorers, Rob Reiner's Stand By Me, The Mosquito Coast, Indiana Jones and the Last Crusade, I Love You to Death, Dogfight, My Own Private Idaho and Running on Empty. River was also

an accomplished guitarist. River also sang and played guitar in The Thing Called Love. Phoenix was set to play the interviewer in Neil Jordan's adaptation of Anne Rice's Interview with the Vampire, and nearly completed the independent thriller Dark Blood, with Judy Davis before his untimely death.

Phoenix died from an accidental drug overdose of heroin and cocaine outside the Viper Room. On the night of his death, he became ill while on stage. Red Hot Chili Peppers bassist Michael Balzary and John Frusciante were present along with Johnny Depp. Phoenix staggered out of the night club followed by Balzary and Depp. After leaving The Viper Room, River collapsed on the sidewalk and went into seizures. His brother, Joaquin Phoenix, was present, along with River's girlfriend Samantha Mathis. River had stopped breathing and was rushed to the Cedars-Sinai Medical Center. He was pronounced dead at 1:51 AM PST on the morning of October 31, 1993.

Hauntspitality

As one might suspect, the sudden and unexpected death of River, left a lasting imprint on the Viper Club as well as River's distressed energy. Not that his was the only spirit associated with the club, but his stature in the acting community and his close circle of caring friends, made this tragedy the most memorable. According to psychics, there are at least two other spirits who frequent the establishment. Both are considered males and seem to date to the 1930s with connections to the mod. Their names remain hidden in the fabric of the building, and although they are not permanent ghost guests, they have been sighted as misty forms or shadowy figures and as cold spots that suddenly materialize. People have reported hearing coughing sounds, hearing their names called out and hearing disembodied voices and smelling cigar or cigarette smoke in the bathroom area.

Then there is the spirit of River Phoenix. Our friends and fellow researchers, Richard and Debbie Senate visited the Viper Room after River's death. In his book, Hollywood Ghosts, Senate states, "We finally stopped. There was a sign that read: "The Viper Room." I assumed it was a night club. Debbie was quiet now.... her mood had changed dramatically. He died here, she said.... All of the sudden, Debbie seemed to suffer some sort of attack. Her hand went to her temple. I remember she stumbled back onto a parking meter. I rushed in to hold her up.... He's here, she mumbled, as passers by stared at us. She could see him.... He's saying he wasn't a drug addict. He was so young. He had his whole life before him... [He] died from an allergic reaction to it.... His last words were prophetic, I'm gonna die!".

Does the restless spirit of River Phoenix still haunt the establishment where he took his last breath? Is he alone, or as others in the psychic community suggest, that there are several prior deaths associated with this building and that River is part of this spirited entourage. We all hope he finds peace and is able to continue his journey without being stuck, or confused. Try saying a lilttle prayer for him when you visit the club; it will be music to his ears.

Yamashiro Restaurant

Particulars

1999 N. Sycamore Ave.
Hollywood, CA 90068
Phone: 323-466 5125
Toll Free: 3234624523
Fax: 323-462-4523
E-mail: info@yamashirorestaurant.com
Website: www.yamashirorestaurant.com

History

Since 1914, Yamashiro has witnessed the birth and glamour of Hollywood's "Golden Age", the war years, and the current period of interest in Eastern cultures. Yamashiro, which means "Mountain Palace" in Japanese, began as a dream for the Bernheimer brothers in 1911. They decided to construct a hilltop mansion above Hollywood Boulevard to house their Asian treasures. Hundreds of skilled craftsmen were brought from the Orient to recreate

an exact replica of a palace located in the "Yamashiro" mountains near Kyoto, Japan. Their dream became a reality in 1914. When the building was completed, Yamashiro had 300 steps that led up the hillside through superbly landscaped Japanese gardens to the 10-room teak and cedar mansion, where carved rafters were lacquered in gold and tipped with bronze dragons. A Sacred Inner Court formed a lovely garden in the center of the building and was filled with sculptured plants, stone hewn pools and rare fish. This Inner Court provided light and air to the surrounding rooms where the walls were covered with lustrous silks and hung with antique tapestries.

Landscaping was a $2 million effort and resulted in California's foremost Japanese gardens. Hillside terraces were filled with 30,000 varieties of trees and shrubs, waterfalls, hundreds of goldfish, and even a private zoo of exotic birds and monkeys. Miniature bronze houseboats floated along a maze of tiny canals through a miniature Japanese village. A 600-year-old pagoda was brought from Japan and set beside a lake which once housed rare black Australian swans and is now converted into a modern swimming pool. When one of the Bernheimer brothers died in 1922, their extensive Asian collection was auctioned off. During the late 1920's Yamashiro served as headquarters for the ultra-exclusive "400 Club". Created for the elite of Hollywood's motion picture industry during its Golden Age celebrities included Bebe Daniels, Frank Elliott, Lilian Gish, Ramon Navarro, and a veritable Who's Who of actors, writers, directors and celebrities in Hollywood at the time. During the Great Depression, Yamashiro remained open. Rumor has it that during those tragic years, beautiful (though starving) actresses were available at Yamashiro for hire for the evening to those who could still afford such pleasures.

Hauntspitality

The restaurant and grounds have long been known to be a favorite haunt for the living as well as afterlife guests. It may just be that one of the Bernheimer brothers, as well as a few former patrons and staff remain behind to service the living, or at the very least, co-mingle as they do their thing. The stories from staff persons include shadowy figures that are seen out of the corner of their eyes while cleaning up at night; an occasional apparition of a man in a brown suit and a lady in white who enjoys dropping in on guests; place settings that are mysteriously moved, flickering lights; rapidly manifesting cold spots; unexplained voices that will call to unsuspecting waiters; and, disembodied footsteps that are occasionally heard coming from unoccupied parts of the building.

There have been times after closing when staff will hear what sounds like a party going on in a closed part of the building. When they rush to see who is still hanging around, there is no one there. Other times, faint music can be heard late at night when no music is being piped in via recordings. The chills are so common that one psychic who visited the building said that there are more people partying from the other dimension inside than the living. This historic "Mountain Palace" is one place you don't want to miss, where dinner and spirits go hand-in-hand.

Independencee
Winnedumah Hotel

Particulars
P.O. Box 147, Independence, CA 93526
Phone: 760-878-2040
Fax: 760-878-2833
E-mail: info@winnedumah.com
Website: www.winnedumah.com

History
The hotel was built for Hollywood crews to film westerns. Early movie crews filled the lobby and guest rooms including Roy Rogers, Gary Cooper, Norma Talmadge, Gabby Hayes, Bing Crosby, and Iron-Eyes Cody.

Built in the 1927 by Walter Dow of Burbank, California, the Winnedumah Hotel offers the charm of old-fashioned hospitality with today's conveniences. Enjoy the Winnedumah's special feeling in a lobby filled with overstuffed chairs and a field-stone fireplace in a dining room sunlit by French windows.

Hauntspitality
Winnedumah is a Paiute Indian name which means "stand where you are," although the spirits of the hotel never seem to stand in one place for too long before disappearing. A sacred place to Native Americans, the land seems to possess a unique energy which may contribute to the constant sightings of spirits within the hotel.

One ghostly image that is often sighted in the hotel is that of a woman who appears in 1930s attire. She has been seen standing next to one of the guest beds, peering out the window. Her pattern is to appear in a grayish dress, stare out of a bedroom window, and vanish as guests watch in awe.

Another guest was relaxing in the lobby, when a woman, this time wearing a blue dress and a round hat that was en vogue in the 1920s, walked toward him, looked around as if lost, then vanished. The wraith didn't seem to notice the guest, but he certainly was aware of her. He remarked later, that she seemed to be an actress, or someone associated with the movies or theater, the way she walked and looked.

Another phantom female has been often sighted in room 134 and many believe that she is responsible for doors opening and closing by themselves; electrical problems; cold spots; the strange shadows that are often observed on the walls, disembodied voices and footsteps; and the feeling of being watched or followed. Some individuals sense a mystical quality about the place, one that may come from the fact that the local Native Americans believed the ground on which the Winnedumah stands to have been sacred.

Ione
The Heirloom Inn

Particulars
214 Shakeley Lane,
Ione, CA 95640
Phone: 209-274-4468
Fax: 209-274-6716
Toll Free: 1-888-628-7896
E-mail: sherry@theheirloominn.com
Website: www.theheirloominn.com

History

The discovery of gold in 1848 enticed gold seekers from around the world to this area. Nestled in the foothills of the Sierra Nevada range lie small villages where the 49ers courageous settled. Ione was a supply center to the gold camps in Jackson, Sutter Creek, and Amador City. Today it is still "small town, U.S.A." with the friendliness, the character and the charm of another era. According to information provided by the inn, it was originally built for J.H. Stevens circa 1863. Stevens was one member of a seven-man committee that selected the site and secured plans for the Ione Methodist Church.

In 1873 Stevens sold the home to John Browning. Browning's wife was the daughter of Patrick Scully, an early Irish settler in California's Gold Country. The Scully descendants continue to live in Ione. In 1923 the house passed to the Lane family then back to a member of the Scully family, Clarence Scully, in 1931. In 1980 Patricia Cross and Melisande Hubbs purchased the home and established The Heirloom Inn bed and breakfast there. Stevens was from Virginia, so he had the architecture of the home reflect the stately Southern mansions from where he hailed. The home is architecturally unique in California and the Gold Country, with a fan transom over the front door, deep set windows (with much of the original glass), balconies, and pillars.

The paneling and staircase are not original but were added in the early 20th century. The kitchen replaced the original cookhouse in the early 20th century as well, but the outdoor fireplace is possibly a part of the cookhouse. The horse stall has been remodeled into the Carriage House that accommodates two sleeping rooms.

The newest structure on the Inn property is a two-room rammed earth building constructed by David Easton, an ecology-concerned contractor. Easton made the 16-inch-thick walls of earth from the site and completed the building with pine, cedar, and redwood lumber from Amador County.

Hauntspitality

The spirit of the Heirloom is rumored to be a causality of the Civil War; unfortunately, no one is quite sure if he belongs to the Union or Confederacy. He has been frequently sighted standing silently on an upstairs balcony looking out at the horizon with a hand over his heart. There have been reports of this spectral guardian soldier rolling tobacco leaves into cigars, perhaps a testimony to his days in the south where tobacco was a major crop---that would tend to indicate a Confederate soldier. However, when sighted, witnesses have also described the phantom as wearing a dark-colored uniform---perhaps indicating a Union soldier.

Guests and staff have reported that they have seen the soldier sitting down in one of the rooms putting on his boots and shining them. Witnesses also report the subtle detail of epaulets ensconced on his shoulders. The other-worldly soldier prefers going about his own business and in following his own routine, almost oblivious to the guests who have watched him in fascination and apprehension.

A psychic once confronted the specter on the second story of the inn. The uncommunicative man ignored the psychic while she watched him stand on the balcony for a beat, enter on of the rooms of the inn, take off his jacket, remove his saber, hang it on the wall, grab a book, and sit down. The psychic also picked up on the spirit of a young girl, a woman of Spanish descent, and a man of African-American ancestry has also been sighted at the bed and breakfast. The pretty, young girl seems to be dressed for a party; the phantom woman has been seen cleaning and washing; and the man has been spotted working with metal tools---perhaps a handyman or former blacksmith.

The Heirloom seems filled with nostalgic reminders of bygone days, as well as a few spirits who seem content to remain behind in familiar surroundings.

Ione Hotel and Golden Star Restaurant & Saloon

Particulars
25 West Main Street, P.O. Box 757, Ione,
California 95640
Phone: 209-274-6082
Fax: 209-264-0750
Toll Free: 1-800-298-7782
Website: www.ionehotel.com

History

The hotel, restaurant, and saloon were destroyed in a fire in 1988. After a year-and-a-half of extensive renovations, it reopened again, still retaining the ambiance of the 1800s. The Ione Hotel sits comfortably along Sutter Creek, in the heart of the Gold Rush country, lying to the south of Sacramento. The small town of Ione was first established as a trading post and flour mill, and was branded with the unpleasant name of "Bedbug." When the Ione hotel was first built in 1850, the name of the town was changed from Bedbug to Freezout. Freezout welcomed a number of weary travelers until the name Ione, became permanently attached to the town. The present hotel was constructed in 1910 after a terrible fire destroyed the original building. Rumors have it, that the ghosts that haunt the hotel were responsible.

Hauntspitality

Three spirits are rumored to haunt the historic Ione Hotel. One incident involved two burly bikers who were arguing over a woman in the hotel. Other guests were complaining, and the owner had to tell them to quiet down. As she was talking to the bikers, and icy cold breeze entered the room, and blew right passed her--- she felt this same cold before. The temperature change was felt by the two men, because they sensed something and began looking around the room. They had no idea that they were standing in a haunted room, and noise upsets the resident ghost named "George." Within seconds, a force seized both men and pushed them together in a rather curt manner, causing their heads to collide.

According to Tom and Dorothy Shone, the ghost of George is still alive and kicking in his former room, now Room 13. Many people have felt his presence over the years in the hotel, many actually picking up on the haunted nature of the place as soon as they have entered the hotel. George was said to be a miner of Polish decent who loved to play cards, drink, and spend time with his friends in, that's right, Room 13. An occasional guest will feel the gentle tug of George while they are sleeping, as if he is trying to wake them. George has done this to a number of visitors over the years. Preferring to disturb single people, George rarely, if ever, bothers couples.

While George keeps the staff and guests busy upstairs, the spirit of Mary Phelps and her young child keep everyone on their toes downstairs and in the restaurant. The restless spirit of Mary Phelps has been seen in the lobby, and hotel dining room. Legend has it, that Mary's child Ian, lost his life in a major fire at the hotel, and her spirit is still searching for her son. The two spirits can sometimes be heard calling out to each other, yet never connecting. Guests and staff have seen a small boy running around the hotel, as well as stopping near Room 9. Mary was once encountered in the dining room by a former owner. Her apparition was more like a pillar of smoke rising in the shape of a woman, and wearing an old style dress. The young boy has been spotted running though the dining room and saloon before vanishing. A cook once spotted the young boy, dressed in late 1800s attire as he ran within a few feet of him in the kitchen, then vanished.

Management says that Mary has helped put stacks of dishes away several times---its one thing the staff never complains about! The Bridal Suite may have its own wraith, although most people feel the energy belongs to Mary Phelps. A female figure will often appear in front of a guest's bed, stand there staring at the occupant, and then vanish.

Other accounts of the spirits include a time when a kitchen employees and the owner witnessed a hazy, apparition float through the dining room. The smoke-like form was almost pyramidal in shape with a rounded top like a person's head. The hovering mass began to vibrate as the owner literally attempted to blow the vapor away, which only succeeded temporarily. The mass returned a few minutes later. In the dining room, all of the candles have relit themselves except for one table in the right corner of the room. After the candles are finally be extinguished, the doors would be locked, and windows tightly closed. After a few minutes passed, all the candles relight, except for the one table, where an apparition has been sighted on a number of occasions. Finally, all the candles were removed, and this provoked a horrible stench in the room, until an aromatic candle was hurriedly added to the decor. This stopped the smell, and the dinner crowd was able to dine without the nauseating smell. When everyone had left, the place was locked. The next morning, a sickeningly sweet smell filled the dining room, and all the candles that had not been moved, were found burned to the nub.

The spirits of George, Mary, and Ian continue their other-worldly rounds at the historic Ione Hotel, and entertain guests and staff in a place they call home.

Jackson
The National Hotel

Particulars
2 Water Street,
Jackson, CA 95642
Phone: 209-223-0500

History
The historic hotel is located in Jackson, California, a town of less than 4,000 inhabitants. Jackson is located southeast of Sacramento, and north of Sonora. Every governor of California since the 1860s has spent a night in this famous hotel. John Wayne, and John Ford stayed at the hotel. The National Hotel was built circa 1849, near springs used by Native Americans, as well as those journeying through California in search of gold. The building which housed miners and travelers, and may have also served as a bordello, burned down in 1862. The hotel was rebuilt on a more solid, brick basement, and has been restored to its gold rush era elegance.

Hauntspitality
Although paranormal investigators and psychics agree that a number of spirits inhabit the building, just how many is anyone's guess. One spirited guests is named Jeffrey, a young boy around eight-years-old who is usually accompanied by his three-year-old sister who is sighted wearing a pinafore type dress and black button up shoes. The two youthful specters playfully romp through the hotel without concern for the living. Another spirit belongs to a beautiful woman wearing 1800s attire indicative of a woman of wealth and stature. She is often seen wearing a full-length, lavender dress, long white gloves, ornate hat, and sports a hand fan. From all accounts, the ghostly female is completely unaware of the children as she strolls down the hallway, descends the stairs, and disappears. According to a renowned, local psychic, the female spirits both young and old are believed to be named Sarah, and Milly, although no one knows which name belongs to which spirit. A fourth spirit is that of a Terrier/ Cocker spaniel who also frequents the hotel. Consensus has it, that the dog belongs to the children, and if you see them, you are likely to find the dog close behind.

The spirit list continues, according to Bradley (1998), and includes a cat, several miners, and an 18-year -old boy from New England. Staff has had numerous encounters with the spirits of the hotel. People will suddenly feel out of breath, as if they have picked up on the energy of someone who is sick, and having trouble breathing. Others hear footsteps that never seem to belong to anyone human. Strange lights will emerge under doorways, waking guests, who upon inspection never find a source for the radiant light.

Guests have reported that the water faucets in sinks and tubs will suddenly turn on by themselves, or that someone will join them in bed. Loud crashing noises in various parts of the hotel late at night are always quickly inspected. Nothing broken or turned over has ever been found associated with the sounds. Then, there is the annoying fact that personal items are sometimes taken by unseen hands and moved to another part of a room, or the hotel, or the mysterious voices which are often heard, yet the source never found. Occasionally people have reported smelling lilac, a scent that belongs to a bygone day, and is attributed to the spirits of the place. All the antics ascribed to the friendly spirits of the National Hotel merely add to the ambiance. It's truly a place where the past comes to life---literally, and ghosts are a national pastime!

Jamestown
1859 Historic National Hotel

Particulars
18183 Main Street , P.O. Box 502,
Jamestown, CA 95327-0502
Phone: 209-984-3446
Fax: 209-984-5620
Toll Free: 800-894-3446
E-mail: info@national-hotel.com
Website: www.national-hotel.com

History

The historic hotel lies is in the heart of the Gold Country, between Yosemite National Park and Lake Tahoe. The authentically restored National Hotel in Jamestown is one of the 10 oldest continuously operating hotels in America (operating since 1859). During 1859, Heinrich and Hannah Neilson established a hotel, bar and restaurant, that was to become known as the National Hotel. The two wooden buildings were among the first permanent structures in this early (1848) gold-rush town of Jamestown. Earlier establishments were mostly tent and non-permanent wooden structures. The National Hotel has been in continuous operation from this date having survived two damaging fires in 1901 and 1927 which severely damaged the National Hotel, which had to then be remodeled

The fire of 1901 destroyed several blocks of Jamestown, but only damaged the National Hotel. Fire in 1927 destroyed the Forester Hall, located next door, and severely damaged the National Hotel, which had to then be remodeled. Today's restoration work was begun in 1974 by present owners and has been ongoing some 32 years later. During Prohibition, the National Hotel was raided several times. as read in The Union Democrat of January 5, 1927, which stated that government agents were looking for liquor. Agents seized; 9-50 gallon barrels of wine, 1-100 gallon barrel of wine, 1-demijohn of wine, 2-10 gallon kegs of brandy and corn whiskey. Owner, Joe Graziano was fined $500. Legalized prostitution was conducted here until the late 1930's and gambling including slot machines until 1949.

The original back bar is still utilized today and a working cash register dating to 1881 is also in view, although it is handicapped by the fact that a maximum of $6.95 can be rung at any one time. Much of the wood wainscoting which is visible throughout the building is original, although it was originally built as floor to ceiling wall paneling.

A story provided by the hotel (researched by a local writer) follows: In 1897, the railroad arrived in Jamestown. John Davies came west from Massachusetts to work on that railroad in 1895. Back in Quincy, John's parents had died and he had money troubles and couldn't find work. This was why he responded to a poster in Boston about working on the railroad. Leaving his fiancé, he promised to send for her as soon as enough money had been saved. He arrived in San Francisco in 1895 anxious to begin work and headed towards the Sierra Nevada foothills where it was said he could find work on a railroad headed for the foothills. He soon worked his way up to being a track-laying foreman and wrote his fiancé back in Quincy and said that when the train reached its ending in Jamestown he would send for her and they would have a small house as he had been promised an engineer's position at the terminus. About a year later, the train reached Jamestown, but Davies was not present.

Railroad records only mention that Davies didn't show up for work one day. He was never seen again. Journal entries show that one of the people to which Davies owed money was a criminal in Boston. It isn't known if Davies ever sent the gangster money or not. However, it was reported that two tough-looking men had arrived on a ship in San Francisco and were asking questions about the railroad and, in particular, John Davies. It was just a short time later that Davies disappeared. Some believe he had gone into hiding while others thought that he must have left the country. Those who knew of his love for a girl in Quincy felt that they had gone away together.

Once the track was laid into Jamestown, a young woman arrived in town and took a room at Jamestown's National Hotel on Main Street. Her name is unknown as a later fire in the early 1900s destroyed all records. However, people remembered that the woman went to the Sierra Railway station every day asking the railroad workers about John Davies. She could be heard during the night sobbing in her room.

She never discovered any information about Davies' whereabouts and her visits to the train station grew further and further apart until she almost never left her room. At night, she was often seen walking through the halls. No purpose was ever discovered as to why she did this. About four weeks after her arrival, the innkeeper found her body laying on the bed. A piece of paper lay on the small nightstand that read, "John Dearest, I love you so much and will never give up searching for you." She didn't sign the note and her death was a mystery. The local doctor just said that her heart stopped and that there was nothing else wrong with her. Could it be she died of a broken heart as some claim? Was Davies missing or dead? Does this mystery woman still roam the hallways of the National Hotel searching for her lost love? Is she the ghost which hotel employees endearingly call 'Flo'?

Hauntspitality
Their Website states "Flo generally stays upstairs in the hotel, seemingly favoring the rooms in the front of the building although she has, on occasion, been seen early in the morning downstairs, floating through the dining room and right through the walls. Each of our guest rooms has a notebook which welcomes guests to share their experiences and comments. There are numerous accounts of doors slamming, lights going on and off, clothing being dumped from suitcases onto the floor, and a woman's sobbing coming from the hallway in the middle of the night. Whoever she is, she adds a little extra spice to all our lives. Many a non-believer has left here with a whole new attitude. Our housekeepers say they have gone into rooms only to be greeted by icy cold air within the room even though the heater was working."

"Flo," is considered a friendly ghost. She is known for perpetrating harmless pranks and responsible for myriad unexplained events. No one is quite sure of Flo's origin, nor how long or why she is there, but the current owner has been hearing stories of the ghost for over 24 years. Flo generally stays upstairs in the Hotel, although she has occasionally been sighted early in the morning downstairs by the employees, floating through the dining room and right through the walls.

The housekeeping staff has probably had the most experience with Flo. Both staff persons are very superstitious and their eyes get as big as saucers when the guests tell them of their strange experiences. One of the housekeepers told the owner that she has gone into various rooms in the winter, when the door and window was closed, and the heater on, only to be greeted by icy cold air within the room.

Each of the guest rooms has a notebook which encourages guests to share their experiences and provide comments about their stay. Several of these books have numerous accounts of doors slamming, lights going on and off, clothing being dumped from suitcases onto the floor, and loud women's laughter coming from the hallway in the middle of the night.

According to management, Flo seems to enjoy living at the National Hotel, and she adds a little extra spice to everyone's life. Many a non-believer has left the hotel with a new attitude and respect for the mysterious female phantom. Recent events seem to indicate that Flo is expanding her horizons. She has been held responsible for moving tables and chairs in the restaurant area, toying with the lights, and opening and closing doors, as well as other unexplained occurrences.

While she is still sighted on a regular basis in the upstairs portion of the hotel, she has also been playing her little tricks on the chefs, downstairs. According to those who work in the kitchen, pans have fallen off of the shelves; spoons and ladles have been observed swinging freely; the coffee filter dispenser has flown out of coffee maker; and cabinet doors will open and shut unassisted; and the list goes on.

It is reported that this hotel is frequented by other female apparitions as well. One woman reported that while having dinner at the restaurant, she was constantly kicked in the leg, though no one was at the table with her. She also reported a loud crash just a few minutes later coming from the kitchen. After the crash, she felt a breeze rush past her as the doors swung open behind her and closed again. When asked, numerous employees will confirm many of the strange occurrences without hesitation.

A recent update from the hotel suggests that the spirited Flo has expanded her paranormal horizons. Visit the hotel and take a peek at the information on file about the spirits and perhaps you will add a paragraph of two, yourself. One thing is for certain; this is one hotel where you have to learn quickly to "Go with the Flo".

The Jamestown Hotel

Particulars
18183 Main Street,
Jamestown, CA 95327
Phone: 209-984-3902
Fax: 209-984-4149
Toll Free: 800-205-4901
E-mail: Info@JamestownHotel.com
Website: www.jamestownhotel.com

History

The Jamestown Hotel is centrally located in California's Gold Country near Yosemite National Park, Columbia State Historic Park, Railtown 1897 and the Dodge Ridge Ski Area. The hotel features a saloon with old-time oak bar and 11 antique-filled guest rooms with private bathrooms. It was first built in 1858 as a wood-frame boarding house. At various times, it operated as a bordello and a bus depot. At one time, it was the Motherlode Hospital and a few recent hotel guests were born there. The Hotel burned down twice along with much of Jamestown. During the 1970s, San Francisco brick was used to remodel the hotel exterior. Purchased from the Crocker family in the 1980s, the hotel underwent a major restoration and is now an 8-room bed and breakfast hotel with a fine restaurant and old-time bar.

Hauntspitality

According to their website, "The hotel's downstairs houses a fine dining restaurant and old-time bar open to the public as well as hotel guests. The Jamestown Hotel also comes with a ghost story that has all the elements of a pulp romance novel. It seems that Mary Rose, granddaughter of Frank Sullivan -- a Jamestown prospector who struck it rich in the 1850's -- fell in love with a handsome British soldier. They wished to marry, but both families were adamantly against it, and Mary's lover's influential parents arranged to have him shipped off to India. Unfortunately, while there he was captured during a Hindu-Muslim uprising, chained, tortured and killed. Naturally Mary Rose took the news hard, especially since she was carrying her lover's child. One spring morning, she arrived in Jamestown and checked into the then Mother Lode Hospital's room number 7. The melancholy woman didn't speak much to anyone, preferring to spend her days forlornly gazing out the window. When the time came to give birth, something went terribly wrong and neither mother nor child survived. They were interred in the nearby cemetery, overlooking the town of Jamestown.

Mary Rose and her British Lieutenant are the hotel's oldest and most constant tenants. Guests have heard moans from room 7, as well as seen misty apparitions, one that is wrapped in chains. There have been materializing cold spots, unexplained footsteps pacing along the hallway, and disembodied voices heard coming from various parts of the buildings. We suggest paying this place a visit and seeing how the other side lives.

The Willow
Steakhouse & Saloon

Particulars
18723 Main Street,
Jamestown, CA 95327
Phone: 209-984-4338
Fax 209-984-1684

History

Sally Hamilton in her book entitled, Hotel Willow, provides the incredible history of the Hotel Willow, and is the basis for much of the information that follows. In 1849, Portuguese emigrant John Pereira came to California from Louisiana. By 1855, he built the Jamestown Hotel, which was later changed to the Hotel Willow. By 1863, the building burned to the ground. By 1896, with the railroad on its way, Pereira rebuilt the Hotel Willow, and Pereira leased the building to C.C. Stone. By October, the 20 room hotel was completed, furnished, and ready for guests. Within a short time, additions were made to accommodate more guests. The new addition was in the area of the present dining/banquet room. By 1897, the hotel was once again enlarged. In 1879, C.C. Stone sold his interest in the hotel to W.T. White of Coulterville. Soon, A.E. Smith became a partner. Al Boyd performed the duties of chef, and Charles Hummeltenberg was the bartender. Hummeltenberg was forced to leave, and committed suicide shortly thereafter.

As time passed, A.E. Smith sold his interest to Frank Mayer of Nevada, who brought his wife Pauline, and four daughters Amelia, Bertha, May, and Lillian to the Willow. Mayer bought a bar from San Francisco in 1898, and it is still in use today. In 1898, Herbert, the four-month old child of Mr. and Mrs. W.T. White died. By the turn of the century, the hotel added electricity, a new standing bar, offices, new paint, and wallpaper. The dining room was leased to an R.L. Harris. In 1899, Frank Mayer bought out W.T. White. During the same year, Mayer's daughter May married William Young, while Bertha married William Leland. In August of 1899, Mayer bought out John Pereira. Two weeks after becoming sole owner of the Willow, Frank Mayer and his daughter Lillian were killed while visiting San Francisco.

Mrs. Robert E. Lee, President McKinley, Archie Stevenot, and Bat Masterson have all reportedly stayed at the hotel. In 1902 Amelia Mayer became Mrs. Charles Calkins. After two months of marriage, her husband died from typhoid-pneumonia. In 1903, S.C. Jensen was shot in the foot while standing in the bar room. Other shootings have occurred over the years. Louis Rosenthal attempted suicide in  his room, followed by Frank Cameron's suicide. Bertha died from blood poisoning. Pauline Mayer died from an unknown cause in 1917. Amelia managed to hold onto the hotel through all the family catastrophes. By 1926, Amelia remarried Andy Froehlich, and they had four daughters, Catherine, Eugenia, Virginia, and Joan, and a son, Robert. The family took up residence at the Willow Hotel.

In 1928, the Froehlich's leased the bar to Gus Ratto. A short time later, Ratto climbed the stairs to the second story, called for his wife Rena, who was shot dead, and then he turned the gun on himself in a double tragedy. Amelia Froehlich died on January 27, 1933, and in the same year, Frank Paff took over as owner. In 1934, Ruby East opened a grocery store in the Willow in an area which today contains the bar. In 1939, Frank Paff sold the Willow to Clay and Ellen Neff's who turned the decor into a Polynesian motif. In 1948, F.N. and Betty Ledger, and H.S. Kirkbride bought the Willow from the Neffs, who soon gained it back through default. In 1959, the Neffs sold the Willow to George Maul, Geoffery Hughes, and Rexford and Elsie Starks. In 1961, Hughes & Starks sold the hotel to John and Mary Stevenson. In 1971, Dan and Mary Lou Brunner took over the Willow. In 1972, the Willow was purchased by Sean Mooney, Kent Grunewald, Jim Leixvold, Michel Willey, and Mike Cusentino. On July 21, 1975 a fire devastated the building. It was finally reopened, and Kevin Mooney came from San Francisco to manage the bar. Another fire hit in October, 1978, and again in 1981. Kevin Mooney and Shannon Whittle finally owned the Willow outright in 1984. Shannon left in 1992, and her interest was purchase by Matt Ward. On October 1992, the Willow celebrated its 130th anniversary. In 1994, the Hotel Willow became the Willow Steakhouse and Saloon. The late 1950 was the last time the building actually functioned as a hotel.

Hauntspitality

A number of spirits are said to haunt the Hotel Willow. This belief was given additional credence by a team of parapsychologists, who conducted several séances in the hotel in October, 1978. Led by well-known Bay area psychic, Frank Nocerino, the group reported considerable contact with "energy activity" (ghosts) during their sessions. At least nine different ghosts were identified, and Nocerino claimed that the motive in all the fires was revenge.

Two spirits may have worked the gold mine that once ran beneath the Hotel Willow and collapsed in the late 1800's, trapping 27 miners and crushing them to death. Another is the ghost of a loud, foul mouthed woman who stayed at the hotel more than twenty years ago. A third spirit may be Frances Davis, a former employee who felt he was wrongly accused of theft and sentenced to San Quentin. A couple killed in a murder/suicide in 1928, along with others who perished in the great Jamestown fire of the 1890's, may account for a number of other ghosts who roam the building. There have been numerous articles and a book published about the history of Hotel Willow.

Customers and employees have reported seeing the spirit of a short man roaming through the halls, as well a man dressed like a gambler, wearing a black suit. This wraith has been spotted several times at the bar. Additionally, the figure of red-headed figure of a woman murdered by her husband in the 1890s has also been spotted. A room where a former tenant hanged himself was the focal point of a fire that erupted in 1975. Some startled witnesses claimed to have seen dark "figures" dancing around in the flames.

A regular customer sitting at the bar one Sunday morning felt someone nudge her. She turned around to face a nice looking gentleman, about 5'8", slim, with dark hair and a mustache. He was wearing a three-piece suit, white shirt, black string tie, and a black hat with a medium wide, flat crown. In the time it took her to blink, the man had disappeared without a trace. She didn't hear any footsteps or the door opening or closing.

One late winter night around closing time, the owner had a strange looking man sitting at the bar wearing sunglasses who kept asking questions about the ghost. When the man finally left, Kevin went into the kitchen to lock up. As he stood there, he noticed two red eyes staring in through the door window. Kevin tried opening the door to investigate, but the door wouldn't budge. Pushing with all his might, the door opened; but no one was anywhere around.

A woman was lying in her sleeping bag in front of the round table looking out into the dining room at booth #2 when she witnessed a very short, older man wearing baggy pants, and a Levi-type shirt. He was looking at the booth and the lamp when he disappeared around the corner. Vicki started screaming, everyone ran back there to see what was wrong when she asked who else was there, and she went on to explain what she had seen. There was no one else in the building at the time. Before she left, she took pictures of the booth. When she got the pictures back there were two faces in the picture of the booth.

A list of other unexplained events provided by management includes:
- A former bartender, while sleeping upstairs, was awakened in the middle of the night by a man in his 60's wearing pajamas and a bathrobe, who angrily stared at him before vanishing.
- Staff has heard laughter coming from the dishwashing room when is was vacant;
- The toilet flushes in the men's room, when it is unoccupied;
- Invisible children have been heard chanting in the back dining room;
- A staff person was tapped on the shoulder, then pushed while vacuuming the back dining room late at night, when the person turned around, there was no one was there;
- A phantom baby was heard crying twice in the same night;
- A lone staff person was pushed near the ice machine;
- Spices flew off the shelf, landing about 10 to 12 feet away;
- Staff have heard tapping on the mirror in the front dining room;
- Lights in the kitchen go off and on by themselves;
- The television in the bar turns on by itself;
- After a fire, scratching sounds, and loud moaning sounds are heard coming from inside the building;
- The large picture in the back dining room fell to the floor early one morning landing on a table---nothing broke. No one would put the picture back up, and reported a bad energy emanated in the dining room that day;
- Waitresses don't like going in to the back dining room late at night by themselves; they felt extremely uneasy.

The Willow Steak House is considered one of the most haunted restaurants in the United States, and a visit may provide an encounter with the paranormal that you can write us about---happy haunting!

Jenner

Jenner Inn

Particulars
Coast Route 1, Box 69,
Jenner, CA 95450
Phone: 707-865-2377
Fax: 707-865-0829
Toll Free: 1-800-732-2377
E-mail: innkeeper@jennerinn.com
Website: www.jennerinn.com

History
The Jenner Inn has been operating continuously, in a quiet, sleepy little way, since Mr. A.B. Davis erected a lumber mill in 1904. The tiny hamlet was christened "Jenner by the Sea", and a hotel/post office was built to accommodate the anticipated bustle of a booming town. The mill thrived for ten years, supplying lumber to rebuild Santa Rosa and the San Francisco Bay Area following the great earthquake of 1906.In 1914 Mr. Davis died and his son and heir closed the mill. During this time the hamlet developed into a village, with the building of a school house and perhaps 50 dwellings.

Five of those dwellings are now part of the Jenner Inn. Three large homes became suites with both fireplaces and kitchenettes, plus several additional private rooms. Four smaller cottages are individual romantic, little hideaways. Lovingly and comfortably decorated with antiques, wicker, house plants, and unique touches, each has a distinct character and personality.

Hauntspitality
One focal point for the Jenner Inn hauntings is the old Victorian cottage built at the turn of the century. For the owners, sharing the place of their dreams with ghosts was not spelled out in the escrow documents, but they accepted it. The first clue about the house ghosts was found in a scrapbook of old newspaper clippings and notes left by prior owners and guests. The data details past visitor comments regarding hearing footsteps when they were alone; a guest told of hearing children laughing and playing, but upon inspection, no one was anywhere to be found; another guest reported witnessing an older woman with grey hair and knit cap standing in the doorway of the cottage. The woman stood in the doorway for a few seconds, then vanished.

A male guest watched as a man wearing a grey shirt with suspenders, and "mutton chop" whiskers suddenly appeared out of thin air. The pensive apparition stood for a few minutes as if contemplating something, then vanished. The guest remarked that the phantom was so life-like, that he mistook the gentleman for a handyman.

A housekeeper was cleaning the rustic cottage, when she stopped dead in her tracks. Standing before her were two people dancing up a storm. She had never seen this couple before, and she knew that they weren't guests. As she was about to ask them who they were, the two ghostly characters vanished.

One time, two people checked into the Inn wearing 1920s costumes. They were Roaring Twenties re-enactors who came to the Jenner every month. The man was dressed as a "gangster," and his wife as a "gun moll." That night, a number of unexplainable events took place at Mill Cottage, including the fact that the cottage will fill with an overpowering odor, and no one was successful in locating the source. The irony about the guest's outfits was that during Prohibition, liquor was illegally smuggled into small coves, and areas similar to the one surrounding the Jenner Inn. Perhaps the smell was associated with the days when cheap liquor was enjoyed by many who had access to it for wild nights of partying. Just maybe, the people wearing the 20s outfits stirred up a few spirits who had something to do with the transportation of illegal spirits.

This haunted hideaway is Jennerous to a fault in providing a relaxing atmosphere and friendly spirits.

Joshua Tree
Joshua Tree Inn
Bed & Breakfast

Particulars
61259 29 Palms Highway,
P.O. Box 340,
Joshua Tree, CA 92252
Phone: 760-366-1188
Toll Free: 1-800-366-1444
E-mail:inn@joshuatree.com
Website: www.joshuatreeinn.com

History

Located in the Beautiful Little Village of Joshua Tree adjacent to the "Joshua Tree National Park" the inn is constructed in the hacienda style or architecture with its U-shaped design. It has the old mission-style clay roof, and is adobe-like in construction. They have a large pool in the courtyard, heated by Mother Nature.

Hauntspitality

The Yucca Valley, east of San Bernardino, is one of the most exotic areas in California. Gnarled and twisted Joshua Trees grow beside dramatically colored piles of rock in the desert, creating a strangely beautiful and decidedly unusual landscape. Perhaps this extraordinary vista has somehow contributed to urologists' long-cherished theory that there is a secret base for spaceships hidden in the area. Another group believes that the location is a prime spot from which to observe "elementals"--tiny beings whose work supports the natural surroundings. Members of a conference on spiritual development that was held in the Valley some years ago reported both hearing and seeing the diminutive supernatural creatures.

Then there is another group of people who believe that a certain hostelry in the Yucca Valley is haunted by the ghost of legendary musician Gram Parsons. Parsons, who almost single-handedly invented the country-rock genre in the '60s and '70s during his tenure with the Byrds and the Flying Burrito Brothers Band and who is credited with discovering Emmylou Harris. She was only 26-years-old when Parsons died of an overdose of morphine and tequila at the Joshua Tree Inn on September 19, 1973. Since his death, the inn has become an important destination for many fledgling musicians who feel that Gram's spirit lingers there--especially in Rooms 8 and 9.

Evelyn Shirbroun is one of the true believers, which is fortunate because she owns the Joshua Tree Inn. "Yes, I believe,"' the personable innkeeper began. She went on to explain, "Since we've had it [the Joshua Tree Inn] as a bed and breakfast, the most consistent conversation relates to the moving mirror--the mirror in the bedroom of Room 8 moves for no apparent reason. There was a structural engineer who stayed in there, and he kept saying, '"There's no reason for that mirror to move like that." Shirbroun remarked that the engineer was beside himself when he came to breakfast in the morning. He had tried everything conceivable to explain the mirror's movement; but could not.

Despite his scientific leanings, that engineer was never able to solve the mystery. Perhaps if he'd known that the mirror was the only piece of furniture remaining in the room from the time Gram Parsons had died there, it might have helped to ease the engineer's confusion. "Most of the guests feel that the moving mirror is caused by Gram" Shirbroun explained. The only time an apparition has actually been seen was by a guest in another room. "The guest was a fellow musician and a pretty straight kid," Shirbroun said. Nonetheless, the musician reported a presence in his room and swore it was Gram Parsons.

Shirbroun's most personal proof of the specter came in the days before she opened the inn to the public. She originally bought the place to use it as a retreat for abused children. At that time, she knew nothing about Gram Parsons, much less his ghost. She did, however, know that the kids in her care used to complain about seeing something or someone in the closet. Shirbroun didn't know the stories about the ghost of Gram Parsons at all, so she began rotating the kids in the rooms. However, no matter which children she assigned to which rooms, it was only those children in Rooms 8 and 9 who were ever bothered by the presence of a ghost.

It was not long before Shirbroun met Ben Fong-Torres, a former editor at Rolling Stone magazine and author of the book Hickory Wind: The Life and Times of Gram Parsons, who told her the whole story. This was knowledge that Shirbroun kept to herself. "I could not tell anyone about a ghost being around the grounds, this being a therapeutic milieu for kids" she explained. Not much later, Shirbroun changed the focus of the business to that of a bed and breakfast. From that point on, both the musical disciples and the ghost stories began to flood in.

Although Parsons was a brilliantly talented and creative musician who virtually dedicated his life to his craft, his trailblazing contributions were not widely recognized during his lifetime. Ironically, it was a series of events immediately after his death--and unconnected to the music industry--that introduced the name Gram Parsons to mainstream America.

By 1969, Parsons had ended his tenure with the Byrds and become close friends with Rolling Stone Keith Richards. That unfortunate association started Parsons on a long, sad descent into drug and alcohol abuse. The end began in the third week of September, 1973. Parsons arrived at the Joshua Tree Inn with some friends to begin another of their drug-fueled retreats. What happened from the time of their arrival at the inn until the last few moments of September 18th, when one of his companions noticed Parsons' labored breathing and phoned for an ambulance is unknown. Ail that is known for sure is that Gram Parsons was declared dead of an overdose less than an hour later.

Immediately following Parsons' death, a veritable circus ensued; more than enough commotion to cause any spirit to become restless. Parsons' stepfather claimed the young man's body and arranged to have it shipped east for the funeral. Gram's friends, however, felt that the musician would not have wanted this and, in as bizarre a heist as has ever been executed, they stole the casket containing Parsons' corpse and took it back to the desert. There, in an attempt at cremation, they set fire to their friend's body. Not surprisingly, the ill-conceived and illegal, impromptu cremation was soon discovered and charges were laid against Gram's friends. What was left of the musician's charred remains was sent back east to his family.

Evidence of the influence of Gram Parsons as a ghost was probably first seen during the trial against Gram's would-be cremators. The case came to court on November 5, 1973; the date that would have been Gram's 27th birthday. Despite the seriousness of the charges brought against the deceased man's friends, they had only received fines and suspended sentences.

Since that time, the site where the men tried to dispose of Parsons' body has become something of a cult shrine for young musicians who wish to honor Gram's memory and his contributions to the world of music; and the Joshua Tree Inn has become a central meeting place for those who hope to commune with Grams spirit. Psychics who have visited the haunted Rooms 8 and 9 have come away with the definite impression of a spirit. The ghost, presumably Gram himself, creates what the sensitives have described as "heaviness" in these rooms. It has also been noted that the ghost likes to "borrow" guests' personal possessions such as toiletries and keys. Despite this, or perhaps because of it, the faithful return again and again, year after year, to the Joshua Tree; Gram's old haunt.

Julian
Julian Gold Rush Hotel

Particulars
P.O. Box 1856, 2032 Main Street,
Julian, CA 92036
Phone: 760-765-0201 | Fax: 760-765-0327
Toll Free: 1-800-734-5854
E-mail: b&b@julianhotel.com
Website: www.julianhotel.com

History

This authentic 100-year-old Victorian is listed on the National Register of Historic Places, and is a California State Landmark and Point of Historic Interest. The town of Julian had prospered for a brief time during the gold rush boom of 1876-77, but by the 1890s, the town returned to its rural lifestyle centered on farming and ranching. Albert Robinson was a freed slave who came to the town of Julian which was still ensconced in a racial mentality. Thinking that the west would not have the prejudice that his home state Missouri held, he proceeded to establish a two-story Victorian Hotel facing the main street of Julian. It was aptly called, the Hotel Robinson.

The hotel had previously served as a bakery and tavern. Robinson served the community providing accommodations for weary travelers.

However, his death on June 10, 1905 revealed the true character of the town, still racially motivated into the 20th century. His remains were not allowed to be buried with the other "white" citizens of Julian in the community cemetery. The Robinson family was told to have Albert's remains sent 45 miles west of Julian.

Hauntspitality

The body of Albert Robinson was driven out of town by bigoted locals, but not his pioneering spirit which seems to remain in Room 10 of the hotel. Reported events include: Unattended windows which open and close by themselves; strange noises coming from unoccupied rooms, including Room 10; cold spots that can be felt even on the warmest days; doors slamming shut on their own; the imprint of a person materializing on the edge of a bed, as if someone just sat down; and objects constantly being moved in the kitchen; phantom footsteps that are heard descending the stairs leading from the second floor, although no

one is ever seen walking down; a shadow that is frequently seen through a stain-glass window that separates the stairs from the dining area; and someone can often be heard opening and closing doors on the unoccupied second floor.

On more than one

occasion, Albert has manifested in front of a startled guest for a brief period of time, before vanishing. Most witnesses think the amorphous shape they see is Albert. Housekeepers have reported the smell of smoke in Room 10, freshly made beds will be founding disarray, doors will open and shut by themselves, furniture will be moved by unseen hands, people will hear their names called out by someone unseen, and foggy shapes will appear in the mirrors as housekeeping are performing their duties. While downstairs, staff has heard footsteps on the second floor coming from unoccupied areas. Disembodied footsteps are often heard descending the stairs, and some witnesses have seen the apparition of Albert Robinson passing by the stained glass window adjacent to the stairway. One staff person reported seeing a menu floating through the hotel.

Some people say that a less friendly spirit also inhabits the hotel, and has been known to cause quite a stir. The playful phantom had shattered mirrors; made furniture fly across empty rooms, and objects, including balls of light were frequently seen throughout the hotel; that is until an exorcism was reportedly performed, ridding the hotel of a malevolent spirit and leaving behind the friendly ghost of Albert to cater to the hotel's guests. A stay at the Julian Gold Rush Hotel is like striking it rich in hauntspitality and the very best in local hospitality; oh, and be sure to say hi to the spirit of Albert Robinson if you get the chance.

Klamath
Historic Requa Inn

Particulars
451 Requa Road,
Klamath, CA 95548
Phone: 707-482-1425
Toll Free: 866-800-8777
E-mail: innkeeper@requainn.com
Website: www.requainn.com

History

A hotel has been operating on this site almost continuously since the 1880s. This incarnation was constructed in 1914 as a 22-room hotel. The building is plain, almost utilitarian, built for rustic comfort rather than Victorian stylishness. The Requa Inn is the ideal accommodation in Redwood National Park offering a spectacular view, 11 comfortable rooms, delicious home-cooked food, and camaraderie with other guests, and a real sense of serenity. The inn is surrounded by the stunning scenery of the north California coast, in the center of Redwood National Park, on the Klamath River, just one mile from the ocean. The inn's dining room, which overlooks the Klamath River, is called Bailey's in honor of W. T. Bailey, the man who built the Requa Inn in 1914. W. T. Bailey was known for his enthusiasm and hospitality; both traits still much alive at the Inn to this day.

Hauntspitality

Those who occupy this historic treasure as well as a few lucky guests have been privileged to have paranormal encounters with the spirit or spirits of the inn. Some people think that the primary ghost is that of Captain William Crone, the one time owner of the Inn. According to the current owners, Captain Crone, was a Danish seaman who became famous for his knowledge of salmon fishing on the Klamath River. Crone was also reportedly the first to successfully navigate sea-going ships in and out of the mouth of the Klamath River. His sea going ships hauled goods and lumber along the California coast until trucks took over the freight business. His worldwide adventures as a seaman provided plenty of fodder for grand and colorful stories of adventures in far away places. He was a colorful local character, a good story teller and a fair businessman. He was apparently a very popular person in the area. Captain William Crone died at a hospital in Eureka California in 1952. This is the person many think frequents the rooms closest to the ocean at the inn. He is certainly one of the "friendly" ghosts at the inn.

A local newspaper, *The Daily Triplicate* of Crescent City, California in a story dated October 31, 2006 by reporter, Cornelia de Bruin discussed the fact that during the five years the owners have managed the Requa Inn, David and Barbara Gross have heard six unrelated reports from guests who claim to have noticed a chill in the air or seen a shadowy figure moving inside the building. Most of

Haunted Room 10

the reports about the paranormal come from people who occupy Rooms 7, 10 and 22.

One guest, who reassured the owners of her strong psychic abilities, asked the spirit if it needed anything. The psychically connected woman quietly suggested that the spirit to guide her to the scrap books in the house and show everyone who he or she was. The place the scrap book fell open to, was the only photograph of Captain Crone that is in the book. On another occasion two

"sensitive women" also ended up in a strikingly similar scenario. They were also led to the picture of Captain Crone.

The question is, does Captain Crone haunt the building alone? Some gifted people say that there are at least two other friendly spirits inside; one a female, possibly the wife of a former owner and one child. Their identities are still cloaked in darkness, but their energy is felt

Haunted Room 22

by those who stay here. Other guests have described feeling cold spots in one area of the building or feeling someone unseen brush right passed them.

The occasional disembodied footsteps in the upstairs hallway, shadowy figures, unexplained sounds, and rapidly manifesting cold drafts of air, are all part of the ambiance of this haunted historic hideaway in the center of Redwood National Park, on the Klamath River.

Knight's Landing
Snowball Mansion Inn

Particulars
42485 Front Street,
Knights Landing, CA 95645
Phone: 530-735-1122
Fax: 530-735-1122
E-mail: cherylfuhring@yahoo.com
Website: www.bbonline.com/ca/snowball/index.html

History
This historic building was constructed in 1872 by John Wells Snowball for his bride Lucy Knight, the daughter of William Knight, founder of Knights Landing and Knights Ferry. The inn is located only 30 minutes from Sacramento, 60 minutes from Napa, just 2 hours from Bay Area. The property contains 7 1/2 acres of gardens, gazebos, a private lake stocked with fish and Sacramento River frontage for jogging and bird watching.

Hauntspitality
This Italianate brick mansion is reportedly haunted by Lucy Snowball, wife of John Wells Snowball who built the mansion. After the birth subsequent untimely death of her daughter, Lucy became inconsolable, blaming herself for the child's death. The remorseful and reclusive Lucy outlived her husband and remained in the house until her death. Her restless spirit is still searching for forgiveness, or perhaps her daughter in the afterlife. Today the mansion is known for its plethora of paranormal phenomena including:
- Windows that rattle on their own in a calculated pattern throughout the entire home.
- Guests have been awakened by rattling doors and doors that will open and close without human assistance.
- Lucy is blamed for setting off smoke detectors.
- Sometimes the front doorbell rings. When people check to see who is there, the porch is deserted.
- A former owner said he moved because he grew tired of seeing the apparition of the young mother floating throughout the house.
- Guests have reportedly witnessed Lucy's spirit caring for a phantom child in various rooms before vanishing.
- Staff and guests have reported hearing phantom music drift from the upstairs ballroom when the room is unoccupied.
- Rapidly materializing cold spots are reported in the hallways and in certain rooms.
- Disembodied footsteps are heard in unoccupied rooms.
- Phantom voices call out in the middle of night.
- A baby is sometimes heard crying in one of the bedrooms.

The Travel Channel featured the Snowball Mansion on its series "Haunted Bed and Breakfast Inns". When you book a room here, you may end up sharing it with Lucy Snowball, the matron of the manor who still roams "her" house attempting to put to rest her guilt and remorse.

La Canada
Newcomb's Ranch Inn

Particulars
Angeles Crest Highway 2,
La Canada Flintridge, CA 91011
Phone: 626-440-1001
Fax: 626-440-1025
Website: www.newcombsranch.com

History
During 1888, a master trail blazer and cabin builder named Louie Newcomb visited the area. Newcomb built his first cabin about a quarter of a mile northeast of the present day Newcomb's Ranch. From this small but cozy cabin, a steady stream of hunters, hikers and friends visited Louis. A frequent guest and friend of Newcomb's was William "Sturde's" Sturtevant. A plan was hatched between the two to create a toll trail to charge users 25 cents. Louis spent years developing a trail from Sturde's Camp in the upper Santa Anita Canyon leading into Chilao high country and beyond. The toll trail never really worked as there was no way to patrol and collect fees from the many miles of trail.

Newcomb soon found an alternative occupation as one of the first Forest Rangers in the newly created "San Gabriel Timber Reserve". Louis served in this capacity for many years, building numerous cabins and trails still used today. Eventually Newcomb settled down, got married and bought a home in Sierra Madre. He sold most of his land to his cousin Lynn Newcomb Sr. in 1929, leaving the high country for good in 1940 feeling that the newly created Angeles Crest Highway had "ruined the place". Newcomb's Ranch Inn was built in 1939. The Ranch has changed many times over the last several decades, serving as a restaurant, hotel, general store and gas station. Much of the original two-story structure was destroyed in a fire in 1976. The building was rebuilt and opened as a restaurant run for many years by Lynn Newcomb Jr. Today, Newcomb's Ranch is owned by Dr. Frederick H. Rundall, a lover of nature with a passion for the mountains.

Hauntspitality
Although it has been rebuilt after a disastrous fire in 1976, there are several spirits in this rustic looking bar/restaurant. It is the only restaurant and bar in Angeles Forest, and a favorite stop and meeting place for hikers, bicyclists, motorcyclists, skiers, campers and day-trippers of all ages. It is also a favorite hangout for its spirited clientele. People sensitive to ghosts and paranormally inclined individuals have been able to come up with five resident spirits, although they are pretty certain that more phantoms reside in the building.

The spirit count includes a female, over fifty, who keeps a stern eye on the place. She is described variously as rough looking, wearing a bib or apron and looking older than she really is. She seems to patrol the entry, hallway leading to the rooms, the kitchen area, and the ladies bathroom. A second spirit is described as an outdoorsy-type male in his 50s, who wears jeans and a brown shirt. The man is sighted outside in the parking area, in the dining room and bar. One person thought he had a beard or moustache.

A third spirit likes to hang out around the bar and bathroom area. He has been described as kind of creepy looking, heavyset, in his late-30s and he likes drinking, partying and playing pool. One psychic felt that he died in a motorcycle accident and returns to his favorite haunt to continue with his routines.

A fourth spirit is rumored to be a male who the psychics associate with dying in a fire. He patrols the hallway and upper level rooms. He is responsible for moving items and opening and closing doors.

A final spirit is a female who may have worked in the building or lived there. She is sighted as a misty form near the bar and bathroom areas, and has called out people names.

More investigative work has to be done here to help sort out the spirited clientele, appropriately identify who they are, and why they are still here. In the meantime, this is an oasis on the Angeles Crest Highway and good food, music, drinks and spirits await every guest who visits this very special historic hideaway.

Lafayette
Lafayette Park Hotel & Spa

Particulars

3287 Mount Diablo Boulevard,
Lafayette, CA 94549
Phone: 925-283-3700
Toll Free: 866-925-0222
E-mail: reservations@lafayetteparkhotel.com
Website: www.lafayetteparkhotel.com

History

Elam Brown served as wagon train master for fourteen families who left St. Joseph, Missouri on May 1, 1846. Elam's party crossed the Sierra Nevada Mountains days before the Donner party became stranded. Elam's party entered Sutter's Fort on August 10, 1846. In 1847, Brown purchased a 3,329 acre Mexican Land Grant named Rancho Acalanes. In February 1848 he built his first home on the Rancho along with two other families, thereby creating the first community in central Contra Costa County.

During the 1850s, redwood lumber harvested in the Canyon/Moraga area was hauled to Martinez for shipment to San Francisco and the Lafayette area became a resting spot for travelers to refresh themselves on their journey. Because the name Acalanes was not accepted for the town name, the founding fathers tried the name Centerville. Unfortunately, this name was already taken. Finally, the name Lafayette was selected. Lafayette remained a quiet farming town until the late 1940s when a building boom occurred.

The Lafayette Park Hotel & Spa is nestled in the hills of Lafayette, and offers the only Five Star Diamond experience in the East Bay. The French Chateau-style property is centrally located near the business centers of Walnut Creek, Concord, San Ramon and Oakland, and only 30 minutes from the San Francisco. Experiencing this jewel of the San Francisco East Bay where the accommodations, food and spa are exceptional is a must for travelers. Experiencing the paranormal is an added bonus.

Hauntspitality

The spirited activity reported in this exceptional hotel seems to center on young girl and a spectral man. No one is quite sure what happened to these to souls, which would account for the hauntings, but perhaps the spirits are tied to events in the distant past; a time the preceded the construction of the hotel. As with many ghost stories, the names, dates and events that may have contributed to the hauntings are lost in the mists of time. One thing is certain, these benevolent spirits occasionally make themselves known to selected staff and guests. There's nothing harmful or frightening about these energies, since all of the reports are of friendly phantom occurrences.

The unexplained events seem to occur most frequently on the first, second and fourth floors and in the kitchen. There have been occasional reports from housekeeping and guests of a young girl jumping on certain guest beds before suddenly vanishing. The child has also been known to call for her Mother, and her footsteps and laughter are reported in unoccupied hallways and rooms. According to one psychic who visited the hotel, a young child died on the spot of the current hotel when the area was still used for agricultural purposes. Another "sensitve" person said that the young girl may have died on a wagon train that was passing through and was buried nearby. The playful child seems to still be looking for her family, as her energy roams the current hotel.

Other paranormal events that have been reported inside include soda machines that seem to have a mind of their own, dispensing cans when they feel like it; as if a specter has deposited money and left without retrieving the reward. On other occasions, paintings will mysteriously fall off the walls, as if lifted by unseen hands. Rapidly materializing cold spots, disembodied voices and footsteps and lights turning on and off on their own, are a few of the unexplained events that take place inside.

The kitchen also seems to be a focal point for paranormal activity. Some of the staff who work the kitchen area have reported hearing ghostly conversations come from unoccupied areas, and will hear the sounds of crashing implements when the area is unoccupied. Upon checking, nothing will be out of place. Electrical malfunctions are occasionally reported in the kitchen, and shadowy figures have been noted by staff that see the apparitions out of the corner their eyes while working late. Several people have reported hearing their names called out by an unseen presence and have been touched on the shoulder or felt a tug at their clothing by an invisible, yet benign force. One person said it felt like a child tugging at her clothing, as if seeking attention.

This five star hotel is also a five star haunt where guests get first class treatment with an added bonus of possibly meeting their friendly spectral guests.

Laguna Beach
The Beach House Restaurant

Particulars

619 Sleepy Hollow Lane, Laguna Beach,
California 92651
Phone: 949-494-9707
Fax: 949-494-7597
Website: www.thebeachhouse.com/Laguna.htm

History

The Pike Family have owned and operated this local business for over 30 years. The restaurant has served Laguna Beach patrons as well as guests from around the United States in the very best hospitality and romantic dining. Here, you can enjoy breathtaking views of the Pacific Ocean and award-winning coastal cuisine. Established in 1968, the timeless ambience of the former home of Hollywood film star Slim Summerville is a treasured Laguna landmark. It is also rumored to be haunted by at least two friendly spirits.

In the 1920's, the lanky, New Mexico native and Hollywood film star, Slim Summerville, built a get-away beach house on the sand at Sleepy Hollow in Laguna Beach. His was the only residence on the beach side of the Lane. Slim joined the Mack Sennett troupe in 1913, becoming a member of the Keystone Kops and part-time gag writer. Moving on to the Sunshine Comedy studios at Fox, he became a director of comedy shorts in the early 1920's. In the 20's , he switched back to acting and made a series of feature comedies with Zazu Pitts.

Hauntspitality

According to their website, "Depending on how you regard the supernatural, these stories may be a little difficult to buy into but it's too good a piece of Laguna folklore to pass up! On such story began about 9 o'clock in the morning in 1973, the unforgettable superb chef, Tommy Sims, was at the grill when a little "chill" ran down his spine. He says he then saw a tall, slim man in a white shirt and dark slacks about to descend the nearby steps to the storage basement. Tommy's first thought was that he was a salesman checking the stock for reorders, a common occurrence." "Then I saw his face," Tommy says, matter-of-factly, "I had seen his picture many times. It was Slim Summerville, the old movie star. But I knew he had died in this house many years before". For some unexplainable reason, Tommy says the visitor didn't alarm him. There was nothing ghoulish in the experience. Instead, he felt a "friendly" presence, not spooky. "So, I kept watching the top of the steps, just a few feet away. They were the only way in or out. But he didn't come back. I finally went down there and looked around-even into where the mops and things are stored...but he had vanished. The place was empty".

Another Beach House employee said she had several experiences and "he seemed to be a pleasant man, sort of looking things over". "I saw him again one morning in his bathroom. It's where I always changed my clothes when I came to work. As I walked in, he came walking out, wearing a bathrobe". Unfortunately, no one checked the shower walls for moisture, too busy watching Slim turn down the hall and disappear!

And still another occurrence was reported by Joseph Covino and a second staffer. One evening, while both people were taking a break in the upstairs employee lounge, they suddenly encountered a very strong gust of wind that blew a window open. Additionally, a wall-mounted paper-towel dispenser which ordinarily had to be hand operated began spinning towels off at a terrific clip. Both men immediately left the room! All this mystery in a prime location that is very popular for parties is an added bonus.

Several guests, including the authors, have witnessed shadowy figures and felt cold spots suddenly materialize in the bar and kitchen areas of the restaurant. On one occasion, someone reported seeing a female in her 30s staring at them for about three seconds before vanishing. On another occasion, a man in his 40s, thin and wearing jeans and boots was observed staring out at the ocean in the dining area before suddenly vanishing. There are also reports of disembodied footsteps and what sounds like a conversation or party going

on, when the restaurant is quite. Could the spirits be Slim, his wife and a few Hollywood friends still enjoying the ambience?

At this beautiful restaurant, you get more than a great dinner for your money. You also get an unforgettable view and some real Laguna Beach hauntspitality.

Royal Hawaiian Restaurant

Particulars

331 Pacific Coast Highway,
Laguna Beach, CA 92651
Phone: 949-494-8001
Fax: 949-497-3696

History

The building dates back to around 1918 when it was originally constructed as a residence. There is an unsubstantiated claim that the house originally belonged to Slim Pickens. The building also served as an art gallery and real estate office before being converted by Frances Cabang into the Royal Hawaiian Restaurant in 1947.

Hauntspitality

Management has reportedly witnessed a white figure on the stairs leading to the restrooms. There have also been smells of strong odors of flowers in the building when all of the guests have left for the night and only staff remains.

One ghost story centers on a woman who was supposedly killed while crossing the road in front of the restaurant in the 1960s. There are also indications that a former worker named Virginia, who committed suicide in 1996 in a nearby apartment separated from the restaurant by an alley, haunts the building. Perhaps two female phantoms call this restaurant home providing differing stories for the female phantoms.

According to several witnesses, one of the spectral tenants is that of a woman in her 60s, perhaps the suicide victim. The elderly phantom figure has always been spotted in 1940s Period clothing including "granny" glasses, black platform shoes and donning a 40s-type hat. She is usually accompanied by cold spots or drafts of chilly air and a strong wisp of lavender or gardenia perfume. The lady in white seen climbing up the stairs leading to the bathroom maybe the female who died tragically in front of the restaurant years ago, her spirit remaining near the spot of her untimely demise. Are there two spirits who haunt this building? Well, we suggest you make a point of visiting this local dining spot in the artsy Laguna Beach community where the line between reality and illusion is fragile to non-existent. Here, the living receive the royal Hawaiian treatment, where all guests are no more than step away from the afterlife.

The White House
Restaurant & Nightclub

Particulars
340 South Coast Highway,
Laguna Beach, CA 92651
Phone: 949-494-8088
Fax: 949-494-0986
E-mail: info@lagunabeachwhitehouse.com
Website: www.whitehouserestaurant.com

History

By the late 1800s, visitors were making an annual pilgrimage on rutted trails through the canyons to camp at Laguna Beach each summer. By the time painter Norman St. Claire visited from San Francisco in 1903, Laguna already had become a popular tourist destination with a hotel: the Hotel Laguna. Like tourists of any era, St. Claire returned home with glowing reports and landscape paintings that led his artist friends to follow him south. It wasn't long before artists like William Wendt and California marine artist Frank Cuprien moved to Laguna Beach. Within a few years, Laguna Beach had a permanent population of about 300 people—half of whom were artists.

Because Laguna Beach was building hotels for tourists while other landowners were building bunkhouses for vaqueros, the flow of celebrities continued. Famed actress Mary Pickford cut the ribbon opening a new stretch of Pacific Coast Highway in 1926. Errol Flynn filmed Captain Blood near Three Arch Bay. Many of Harold Lloyd's comedies were shot on Forest Avenue. And John Steinbeck wrote Tortilla Flats while staying in Laguna Beach. Hollywood stars who maintained homes here included Pickford, Judy Garland, Rudolph Valentino, Charlie Chaplin, Mickey Rooney, Victor Mature, Bette Davis, Slim Sommerville, and Ozzie and Harriet Nelson. Possibly the oldest restaurant in Orange County, it was established in 1918. Totally renovated and remodeled, it now serves innovative casual California cuisine.

Hauntspitality

There are spirits aplenty at this historic establishment. Long been considered a local hot spot for food and music, the building has been equally touted in the paranormal field as one of Orange County's top haunted restaurants. The legends and facts mix together like a fine salad, to give you an exquisite taste in the spirited selections available at this landmark property. There are the normal spirits that most people who are not sensitve to such things enjoy, and then there are the three plus energies that inhabit the building. The friendly phantoms are into playing pranks or simply checking out the assortment of humans that come to sample the cuisine or music here.

Two psychics who visited the building immediately sensed a woman and a child who enjoyed watching people as they entered. A male energy reportedly made the kitchen area his domain and was responsible for numerous unexplained events that occurred in the kitchen such as dishes being arranged, pots and pans suddenly shaking or falling to the ground and of staff being pushed or shoved while working.

Staff have reported that people's names will be called out by an unseen presence; music will come from unoccupied areas of the building; phantom footsteps will be heard throughout the building; cold gusts of air will pass right through guests and staff; people will smell perfume or tobacco for a few seconds before it disappears; shadowy figures are seen gliding down hallways before disappearing; items will move on their own or simply vanish only to reappear somewhere else in the building; ghostly parties are often heard; a young boy can be heard running and giggling in the building although no one can see him; and lights will turn on or off unassisted. Finally, several individuals have seen a woman in Period clothing float passed them out of the corner of their eye. When they turn to look, no one is there. At the White House, the spirits come with the fare; at no extra charge.

Lake Arrowhead
Bracken Fern Manor
Bed & Breakfast Inn

Particulars
815 Arrowhead Villas Road, P.O. Box 1006,
Lake Arrowhead, CA 92352
Phone: 909-337-8557
Fax: 909-337-3323
Toll-free: 1-888-244-5612
E-mail: brackenfer nmanor@earthlink.net
Website: www.brackenfernmanor.com

History

According to their website, Chicago "Bosses" raised an eyebrow in 1925 when Bugsy Siegel concocted the idea of a 1.3 million dollar private gambling resort in the mountains east of L.A. Club Arrowhead of the Pines was hugely popular with the rich and famous of Hollywood and opened July 4, 1929. The posh new club included many state of the art conveniences such as electricity wired from Redlands. In the elegant Clubhouse, gin was distilled from Artesian well water, dice rolled, and starlets tangoed.

The building that is now Bracken Fern Manor housed a market on the first floor with a soda fountain and butcher shop. Upstairs was home to the "girls" who were aspiring actresses and fancy ladies who provided entertainment for the club members. Below the market was an ice house with a discreet access/egress to the underground tunnel that connected the speakeasy to the girls' living quarters.

The Bathhouse was complete with a snack bar and an Olympic-size swimming pool fed from a natural mineral spring. Further amenities included a ski tow, BBQ, tennis courts, horseback riding, an administration building, gas station, barber shop, and 80 timeshare cabins in the woods.

During these Prohibition times, Model T's came to the resort equipped with extra gas tanks to fill with gin for resale on the black market below. So successful was this little resort in the mountains, that it helped convince the Bosses to front the money for another little gambling spot in the middle of nowhere -- Las Vegas. Bugsy's over-budget excess of a million dollars and delays in completion ultimately cost him his credibility with Chicago. The story goes that a "punk kid," Mickey Cohen, came to the Club and sought to take over control. He ambushed

Bugsy and had him thrown, bound and gagged, over a cliff in the high desert. Left for dead, an old miner found Bugsy and nursed him back to health. For this the miner was handsomely rewarded. When Bugsy returned to the Club, he tried to have Mickey "taken out." Instead, it was Bugsy who ultimately

met his demise at Virginia Hill's home one evening after dinner.

The bordello, known as "The Crib", was active through World War II. The first-floor market continued to run for several years after the Bosses lost control due to private property buy-outs.

Thelma Blanchard, the last storekeeper, is alive and well in Simi Valley, California with lots of vivid memories of the place. The "old brothel" completed restoration in 1993 and is now Bracken Fern Manor Country Inn, a House of Fine Repute and Certified Historic Landmark in the State of California. The former ice house is now Bracken Fern's wine cellar. Though the underground tunnel has long been closed, the old door and steps coming out of the ground can still be seen from the street as well as from the wine cellar.

Gambling continued in the speakeasy up to so recent a time as 1955. The speakeasy is now a private residence but has been home to churches and restaurants. The original 80 cabins were eventually sold as private property. The bathhouse became an apartment building but without the pool (due to cracking.) Mickey Cohen, last heard, was in a Chicago nursing home, ailing from Alzheimer's.

Hauntspitality
Old steps that come up from the secret tunnel that was once used by gangsters evading the Sheriff are still visible along with at least one ghost from the past. Legend has it that a young woman (named Violet by management) waited here for her lover who never returned. She is still frequently seen or heard walking the halls and visiting some of the rooms in search of her lost love. She is seen wearing a long white gown before suddenly vanishing.

During renovation, a construction crew member, alone in the building while two other members of the crew were out getting additional supplies, heard laughter and sounds of people having a good time on the second floor landing. Thinking his friends had returned by way of another entrance, he began ascending the stairs while calling out to his co-workers. There was no response, although the merriment continued until he reached the second floor landing. Calling out again to his friends without a response, the laughter and playfulness relocated to the third floor. As he stood in the darkened hallway, he heard footsteps coming quickly toward him, yet he saw no one. Within seconds, the footsteps and some invisible, icy force passed right through him. With that, the worker rushed downstairs and narrowly avoided knocking over his returning co-workers.

Several staff and guests have reported seeing a woman in a long, flowing white dress walk down the hallway on the second floor and suddenly disappear. She has also been sighted in the guest rooms, briefly turning toward the person who intrudes on her private moments, then suddenly vanishes. There are numerous reports of doors opening on their own, people seeing a specter in Violet's Room and Jasmine's Room on the third floor, lamps swaying back and forth, furniture or personal items being moved by an unseen force, and an invisible someone who

Courtesy of Alma Carey of PSI

occasionally joins people in bed.

Our friend, gifted psychic and fellow researcher Alma Carey, the Director of Paranormal Studies and Investigations, conducted a paranormal investigation with her group at this historic hideaway during November, 2005. The overall feeling of the inn, according to Carey, was warm and inviting. We all felt the presences of delicate beautiful women. The group took a number of photographs that produced orbs in the second floor hallway on fifth step up. Here, two group members felt a cold spot on this step. Orbs, temperature anomalies, unusual noises and other unexplained phenomena were reported during PSI's stay. The conclusion was that the building was definitely haunted.

The Bracken Fern Inn is home to more than just a friendly spirit named Violet. It is a place with a spectacular setting, historical ambiance, mountain serenity, fine food, and a wine tasting cellar.

La Jolla
The Grand Colonia Hotel La Jolla

Particulars
910 Prospect Street,
La Jolla, CA 92037
Phone: 888-530-5766
E-mail: info@thegrandecolonial.com | Website: www.thegrandecolonial.com

History

The Grande Colonial Hotel (originally known as The Colonial Apartments and Hotel), is La Jolla's oldest original hotel constructed in 1913. Designed by Richard Requa, it was described as, "a perfectly appointed apartment hotel, with the finest sun parlor and lobby overlooking the ocean on the Pacific coast." George Bane, who became sole owner of the Colonial in 1920, commissioned architect Frank Stevenson to upgrade the hotel. The existing building was moved to the rear of the property and a new, four-story, concrete, mixed-use building was erected in its place. Completed in 1926 the new hotel boasted 28 apartments and 25 single hotel rooms, the first sprinkler system west of the Mississippi; solid, unsupported, reinforced cement stairways and fire doors that still exist.

After the opening the new Colonial, Bane leased the property to W. S. Beard (from Hollywood). Unhappy with the way Beard ran things, Bane reorganized the business in 1931, and R.C. Bugler was brought in as the manager. The La Jolla Drugstore, next door to the Colonial was purchased in 1926 by Kansas native Silas O. Putnam, and the drugstore was moved inside the Colonial. Later the Colonial was a temporary home to some of Hollywood stars Charlton Heston, Dorothy McGuire, Groucho Marx, Jane Wyatt, Eve Arden, Pat O'Brien, David Niven and more, well into the late 1950s. During World War II, the hotel became home to soldiers from Camp Callan. Over time, the once grand hotel fell into a state of disrepair.

In 1976, three local partners purchased the Colonial and changed the name to the Colonial Inn. The restoration process took over four years to complete. The 75-room property was returned to its original grandeur. No expense was spared - from mahogany trim and wood moldings to stylish leaded glass chandeliers and crystal doorknobs. The restoration process received the "People in Preservation" award from the Save Our Heritage Organization. In 1980, the space once occupied by Putnam's drugstore became Putnam's Grille. During 1988 the building was sold to a Japanese-based investment firm, Tokyo Masuiwaya California. In July of 1998, Franklin Croft LLC and Fargo Hotel investors LLC joined forces to create Fargo Colonial LLC and purchased the hotel. Putnam's Grille closed in February 2001 and reopened as the NINE-TEN Restaurant, one of the most prestigious eateries in San Diego County.

Hauntspitality

Portions of the original hotel have long been rumored to be haunted. Given its illustrious past, the hotel's spirited clientele don't seem to want to leave any time soon. According to Charlyn Keating Chisolm in her Hotel, Resorts and Inns internet guide (http://hotels.about.com/cs/hauntedhotels/p/hau_grandecol.htm), "The rooms below the North Annex of the Grande Colonial Hotel were once apartments, occupied by two men in one apartment, two women in another. The foursome would often throw loud, raucous parties. Apparently, long after their deaths, the group continues the party, as guests hear loud sounds coming from below the lowest guest rooms in the middle of the night. The rooms now house a bakery, and every time the hotel employees investigate the guests' complaints, they always find the bakery empty and locked up tight."

The Legends of America website (www.legendsofamerica.com/CA-HauntedHotels3.html), states, "Near a meeting room called the Sun Room, heavy footsteps are often heard on a staircase. It sounds as though several men are running up and down the stairs and culminates in slamming doors. Some sixty years ago, this room was used as a temporary barracks for single servicemen during World War II."

According to www.hotel-online.com, "At 3:00 a.m. on June 6, 2004, the 60th anniversary of D-Day, a guest in room 144 at The Grande Colonial Hotel in La Jolla, Calif., awoke feeling a bit odd. Suddenly, she heard heavy footsteps on the staircase outside of her room. Up and down, several people ran stomping on each step and a door was repeatedly slammed. This continued for a while. At last, the frightened guest opened the door and peered out but there was no one to be seen. She was certain she heard multiple heavy footsteps of men running up and down the uncarpeted stairs. She discovered the slamming door was not from a guest room but rather from a meeting room. She notified hotel staff and was assured no late-night meeting was taking place in the room. At her request, the guest was moved to another room so she could sleep a bit easier. The meeting room in question was the Sun Room. Sixty years ago, the room was used as a temporary barracks for single servicemen during World War II. The area did not have carpet at the time. Hardwood floors still exist under the carpet today. The historic battle known as "D-Day" occurred on June 6, 1944. Perhaps what the guest heard was the spirit of those soldiers who were reliving the events of the 60th anniversary of the Normandy Invasion. "

Finally, Glen Haussmann in his 2003 article about Historically Haunted Hotels, states, "Guests in the North Annex of The Grande Colonial Hotel in La Jolla, Calif., sometimes complain of noises in the wee hours of the night from the guests below. Loud voices, doors slamming and heavy footsteps have been heard. However, below these rooms is the bakery, not guest rooms. Once upon a time this area housed apartments where neighbors-two men lived in one apartment and two women in the other-often got together for parties. Apparently, they enjoyed it so much that they still continue their party to this day. The hotel staff investigates every complaint and the outcome is always the same. The bakery is empty and locked tight for the night.

A stay at this historic hotel is hospitality and hauntspitality at its best. Here, current staff and past clientele serve up an unforgettable experience that will take your breath away.

Lincoln
Beermann's Beerworks

Particulars
645 5th Street,
Lincoln, CA 95648
Phone 916.645.2377
Website: www.beermanns.com

History
Lincoln's early industries included railroad, ranching and farming. A fast-growing city with more than 27,000 residents, Lincoln still retains a small town feeling with broad, tree-lined streets and a downtown plaza. The city's heritage can be seen in the renovated Beermann's Beerworks building in the historic section of Lincoln. The Independent Order of Odd Fellows (IOOF) and the Masons built this edifice in 1864.

Beermann's faithfully restored this historic hall to its Victorian splendor. Beermann's Lodge Hall, on the second floor, remains much as it was in 1864, with its early Victorian Italianate arches and tin ceiling. And it was just that, a Lodge Hall, the place to meet and greet, just as it is today. A panorama of historic, painted scenes graces the walls while imposing, nostalgic antler chandeliers shed a glow on guests enjoying the Lodge Hall's Cowboy Cuisine, a creative menu with an abundant selection of steaks.

Hauntspitality
When walls talk, there are affirming echoes of wealth made and fortunes lost, of love and betrayal, of scandals and of everyday life. The colorful history of this building is clearly etched in its walls. As with many historic buildings that undergo renovation, spirits usually become restless. Such was the case with Beerman's Beerworks. Although more paranormal research has to be conducted, the stories of apparitions, voices coming from unoccupied areas of the building, rapidly materializing colds spots and disembodied footsteps are common occurrences inside the building. A place with so much history is bound to have its share of ghost stories. As time goes on, we hope that this section continues to expand as readers begin sharing their experiences.

At Beerman's, a cold draught takes on a whole new meaning. Keep your senses peeled and your camera ready when visiting. You really never know what kind of spirits they'll be brewing inside.

Long Beach
The Hotel Queen Mary

Particulars
1126 Queens Highway,
Long Beach, CA 90802-6390
Phone: 562-435-3511
Fax: 562-437-4531
Toll Free: 800-437-2934
Website: www.queenmary.com

History

The *Queen Mary* is permanently docked at Pier J at the south end of the Long Beach Freeway. It is not only a world class tourist attraction, but contains a 365-room floating hotel with restored original first class staterooms; several restaurants (Sir Winston's, the Verandah Grill, and Promenade Cafe); the breathtaking Observation Bar; and offers an unforgettable Sunday brunch---it is a magical place that takes you back to another time, where you can dine and imbibe in the company of spirits.

The lure and magic of the *Queen Mary* is as strong today as it was when Job 534 was completed. On September 26, 1934, an estimated crowd of 200,000 people braved the cold winds and intermittent rains at the John Brown & Company shipyard on the Clyde River in Scotland to hear His Majesty, King George V, and Her Majesty, *Queen Mary*, usher the largest ship in the world into history. The Royal Mail Ship R.M.S. *Queen Mary* had a long and illustrious career. Her early years began with her maiden voyage on May 27, 1936, as the prize of the Cunard Line. She carried 1,742 passengers (708 in First Class, 631 in Second Class and 403 in Third Class, a crew of 1,186 men and women, 100 reporters, and 6,124 sacks of mail.

Life on board the ship for First Class passengers was a slice of heaven, as they were afforded every conceivable luxury and convenience. The crew and staff were highly trained to cater to the needs of everyone on board. The chefs were experts in their field, hired from some of the finest restaurants in the world. The dining salon had the largest floor space and seating capacity, and by square feet, was the largest room ever built within a ship---by historical standards, the three ships Christopher Columbus used to discover the New World could have been placed inside the dining room, along with the Cunard's first steamship. Stood end to end, the *Queen Mary* was less than 229 feet shorter than the Empire State Building, taller than the Eiffel Tower, and Washington Monument, and over twice as tall as the Pyramid of Cheops. Her height, from the keel to forward funnel, is greater than Niagara Falls.

Recreation space aboard the ship is equivalent to a large football stadium. The main engines could generate a total of 160,000 horse power, which would equal the pulling- power of forty large locomotives. The refrigeration needs of the ship would be equivalent to that of 15,000 tract homes. Her anchors equal the weight of twenty automobiles. She contains ten miles of carpeting, 700 clocks, and 600 phones. Over 500,000 pieces of glassware, china and table silver were used on board, along with 21,000 table cloths, 30,000 bedsheets, and 210,000 towels. Over 15,000 bottles of wine and spirits were stored in the wine cellar; and the interior decor was fashioned out of fifty-six of the world's finest and rarest woods. No wonder it was dubbed the "stateliest ship afloat."

A number of celebrities sailed aboard the *Queen Mary*, including: Fred Astaire, Greta Garbo, Bob Hope, Gloria Swanson, Elizabeth Taylor, Clark Gable, David Niven, Loretta Young, Marion Davies, Buster Keaton, Mary Pickford, Laurel and Hardy and many more. Prominent figures also included the Baron and Baroness de Rothschild, the Duke and Duchess of Windsor and the Vanderbilt's.

During her war years, she transported over 800,000 troops as well as passengers and refugees. She used her superior speed and maneuvering tactics as well as night-time black-outs on board to elude German U-Boats. She was well-equipped for fending off potential air strikes, carrying: anti-aircraft guns on the bow, stern and above the bridge; machine guns which were located in strategic positions on the ship's upper decks; six three-inch guns; and electrically fired anti-aircraft rocket launchers, which were adapted for high-angle and low-angle targets. The *Queen Mary* was a "marked" ship by Adolf Hitler who offered $250,000, as well as instant hero status, to the U-Boat commander who would sink her. Her destination points included India, Australia, South America and Africa.

Although the ship was fortunate enough to escape the enemy during the war, it was not exempt from tragedy. On October 2, 1942, while sailing off the coast of Ireland, the *Queen Mary* accidentally struck her escort cruiser the HMS Curacoa, literally slicing it in half. Three hundred thirty-eight sailors died at sea as a result of the tragic incident. On June 20th, 1945, she arrived in New York with 14,777 American soldiers. Her tour of duty was not complete until she served for nine months as a transport carrier for American servicemen during 1946, carrying 18,900 wives and children to New York.

After being converted back to passenger service, she began her true post-war service on July 31, 1947. Gradually, with the advent of other, more improved and time-saving modes of transportation including jet aircraft travel, she was sold. After 1,001 transatlantic crossings; three million miles at sea; transporting over two million passengers including 800,000 troops during World War II; and surviving being a "marked" ship by Adolf Hitler, the *Queen Mary* arrived in Long Beach on December 9, 1967, after her final transatlantic voyage. At exactly 12:07 p.m., John Treasure Jones, the *Queen Mary*'s last captain, announced the end of one career for the Queen of the Seas, and ushered in another... a tourist attraction. The ship is currently docked at Pier J at the south end of the Long Beach Freeway, and is listed on the National Register of Historic Places, attesting to its unrivaled past and expert craftsmanship.

Hauntspitality

The *Queen Mary* is arguably the most haunted ship in the world. There are daily sightings of ghosts and eventful encounters dutifully recorded by the ship and the authors. A book entitled The Haunted *Queen Mary* (available aboard the *Queen Mary* or from G-Host Publishing) documents numerous reported encounters as well as providing a summary of the ship's history. Gifted psychic, Peter James, the resident authority regarding ghosts aboard the *Queen Mary*, said as many as 600 ghosts roam the stately ship, making a pretty crowded ghost ship. And who would blame the spirits for congregating aboard this magnificent luxury liner--- apparently one still need reservations, even after death.

The spirit of 18-year-old John Pedder is one of the most frequently sighted spirits on board the ship. He died after being crushed to death in water-tight door number 13 during a routine drill on Sunday, July 10, 1966. Pedder has been given the nickname, "The Shaft Alley Specter," and his restless spirit is often seen or felt near the door that took his life.

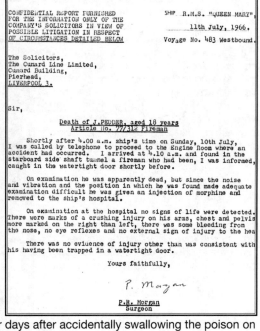

The apparition of Senior Second Officer W.E. Stark has been spotted in his quarters, as well as on deck on a number of occasions. Like John Pedder, Stark represents another victim of a senseless tragedy. Stark accidentally drank tetrachloride and lime juice, mistaking it for gin, and died several days later. No one took it seriously because Stark down-played the incident. By the time he was taken to the hospital, it was too late. He died less than four days after accidentally swallowing the poison on Thursday, September 22, 1949.

There are numerous sightings of men in overalls, and boiler suits dating from the 1930s and 1940s observed, and heard in the engine room, alleys, and boiler room below decks. Many visitors report hearing voices calling out for equipment or barking orders, as well as catching a glimpse of workers who simply vanish into thin air.

The first class pool area has been a paranormal hot-spot. Some psychics claim that the dressing room hallway is actually a gateway to another dimension, where spiritual energy flows to and from the ship using the water as a conductor.

Guest drawings of three pool spirits and an early picture of the 1st class swimming pool

A young, attractive, woman in a miniskirt, is sometimes viewed walking down the stairs leading to the pool, and then vanishing behind a pillar. Security personnel and workers often report "party" sounds coming from the pool area after dark. When they check on the commotion, there is no one around. Water marks have been observed coming from the pool area, even though the pool has been drained for years. Other spirits observed in the pool area include an elderly woman in a period bathing suit, two women wearing bathing suits, and a young child looking for her mother. The pool area also served as a place for soldiers to bunk during World War II. The conditions there were said to be bleak, and it has been suggested that several men suffocated in their bunks due to the oppressive conditions below deck.

The presence of a cook has been felt and observed in the main kitchen area of the ship. There are unconfirmed rumors that during the war, irate soldiers cooked him in the oven. His spirit appears to haunt the kitchen area, possibly still upset that the crew turned on him so viciously. His antics can be heard, seen and felt according to many witnesses.

During a séance performed by our friends, gifted psychic Debbie Senate and her husband, author, lecturer and paranormal investigator Richard Senate, a former Italian POW interrupted the convocation. His troubled spirit related stories of many POWs who were kept below deck and treated as less than human while the ship served as a troop transport. The Italian phantom said he witnessed many men die while he was a prisoner. The POW's were not given a proper burial and disposed of at sea. Security personnel, guides, and workers have repeatedly heard the moans, and disembodied voices well below deck, possibly representing those unfortunate men who died away from home and loved ones, and without proper burial rights.

Some of the spirits of 338 men who died when the *Queen Mary* accidentally

Curacoa before colliding with the Queen Mary

struck the *HMS Curacoa*, literally slicing it in half, linger below deck near the bow of the ship, and on certain nights have been heard crying out in the darkness.

A former switchboard operator and a woman in charge of the stewardesses and bellboys during the voyages have been contacted through a séance, and they both materialize in front of unsuspecting visitors and staff throughout the ship---they are still performing their duties in the afterlife.

The spirit of a woman dressed in 1940s clothes has been observed sitting at a coffee table in the Promenade Cafe before vanishing in front of several witnesses. The main ballroom is another area where ghostly parties occur on a regular basis. Here, apparitions are frequently observed dancing the night away. Glasses are know to clink, bottles are raised in toast, period music filters through the room and laughter emanates from another dimension as though fond remembrances of a bygone era are re-enacted for those lucky enough to partake.

A Lady in White has been frequently sighted in the main dining area aboard ship, as well as waltzing into the First Class lounge wearing a backless, white evening gown. She sometimes strolls over the grand piano (now in Winston Churchill's Restaurant) as if listening to a ghostly rendition on the keys, or dances by herself for a few moments before vanishing into thin air in front of startled witness.

Guest drawing of the spirited Lady in White

The exhibit rooms on the sun deck, and the officer's quarters on the sports deck have numerous stories of ghostly soldiers, phantom first class patrons enjoying dinner, shadowy workman tending to their chores, a phantasm of a 1930s woman standing near the piano and disappearing, a spectral officer making his rounds, and various unidentified luminous shapes floating down the hallways, as well as disembodied voices calling out to people. Guests have also reported unexplained events in rooms on the "M", "A", and "B" decks such as A-110, A-138, A-162, A-170, B-123, A-181, B-304, B-401, B-409, B-421, B-423,

B-462, B-512, M-029, M127, M-140, M-147, M-202 and M-220.

Ghostly voices of children playing and running are heard in the first class nursery exhibit area, the sports deck, sun deck, promenade deck, main deck, and corridors. Often, guests report their clothes being tugged by playful ghostly children, as well as the sounds of children sliding down banisters on the stairwells connecting decks.

Other incidents of paranormal activity have been reported over the years by security guards, staff, crew and paranormal investigators. For unknown reasons, doors that are locked one minute, mysteriously become unlocked the next, triggering alarm lights in the security office. This occurs most frequently with the doors near the swimming pool. Inspections have been unable to turn up any culprits. Someone or something appears to be playing tricks on them. Numerous other accounts of strange phenomena, including unexplainable noises, such as the sound of footsteps when no one is there; banging and hammering, as if someone is working on long-since removed equipment; voices; enigmatic cold spots and winds in air-tight areas; lights going on and off of their own accord; and objects disappearing, or being moved---and the list continues to grow. During Halloween 2001, the ship and its spirited restaurants were featured on a Food Network special entitled Haunted Restaurants.

Since being launched in 1936, historical sources place the death toll aboard the *Queen Mary* at 55 (not including prisoners-of-war who reportedly died aboard ship). Of the 55 documented cases, 39 were passengers and 16 were crew. The ages range from a child who died at birth, to a 77-year-old woman who died of a heart attack. The causes for most deaths include: Heart attacks; people jumping overboard; accidental falls during rough seas; drug overdose; accidental poisoning; and being crushed to death. However, psychics and investigators believe that the spirits aboard the ship actually number in the hundreds.

For those who really want an incredible and unforgettable adventure into the mysterious depths of the *Queen Mary* in search of the spirited population on board, then look no further than our friend and world renowned psychic investigator Peter James. James is the foremost authority on the spirited clientele of the ghost ship and enjoys a world-wide reputation for his knowledge of the paranormal history of this ship. We highly recommend that you check out his Website: www.peterjamesinvestigations.com. James also delights audiences during his extremely popular ghost tours. On this exclusive tour, the spirits often interacts with the charismatic James and his guests as he takes the dinner and spirits tour to an otherworldly level. You can also purchase his best-selling DVD (Ghost Encounters on the *Queen Mary*) by going to his website. We heartily recommend his book, tour and DVD as a way of better acquainting yourself with this ship of spirits.

Prior to going to press, we learned that Peter James had died. His earthly presence will be greatly missed. We're sure he will begin manifesting about his favorite haunt, the *Queen Mary.* Thanks for the memories Peter.

The Turret House

Particulars

556 Chestnut Avenue,
Long Beach, CA 90802
Phone: 562-624-1991 | Fax: 562-432-8204
Toll-free: 888-488-7738
E-mail: innkeepers @ turrethouse.com
Website: www.turrethouse.com

History

This meticulously restored Victorian home located in a historic residential district of downtown Long Beach was built in 1906 by, Kansas carpenter, Horace Dominy. He was married to his child bride Calla-Mae Jones and bought the lot for $1000 to construct the building as their new home. The house remained in the same family until 1991 when it was purchased by the previous owners who painstakingly restored the home to its original Victorian beauty. Under the ownership of Brian Pforr and Jeff Wilkins, the partners added their own personal touches and design to create a unique traveling experience. Each of the five guest rooms features its own theme and offers a private bath with claw-foot tub and shower. Jensen "Real Flame" fireplaces are located in each room to allow our guests to enjoy a romantic bedside fire on those cool evenings. The Turret House is a pet friendly inn and our own mascots, Alli, Waldo, Winston and Dayton would love to have other pet friends visit them.

Hauntspitality

Ancestors of the original owners, who came to stay at the Turret House, wrote the current owners as follows, "Bonnie and I [Marc & Bonnie Jones of Olympia, Washington] had such a great time at the Turret House. It was amazing to be back in my former family home for the first time in 30 years. It felt really good to see it restored and cared for. The ghost stories were interesting, especially since we twice experienced the wall light in the Provincetown Room bathroom turning itself on after Bonnie turned it off. Was it great-grandma Calla May, or my young niece Jacquelyn, or just a faulty florescent bulb? Regarding this, I have an additional piece of information to pass on to you. Thursday I talked to my mother (Calla- Mae's granddaughter Laura May). She told me Calla actually did die in the house. In 1927, when my mother was about 1 year old, Calla suffered a heart attack at home and was dead before help arrived. I hadn't known that. As far as Mom knows, Calla and my sister's infant daughter Jacquelyn Ward are the only family members to die at the house. My great-grandfather Horace Dominy, my grandparents John Connor and Rosalind (Dominy) Connor, and the elderly women who rented rooms at the house over the years all passed away in hospitals or rest homes."

Two psychics who visited the house claimed that the spirits of an elderly woman and a confused young child were present in the house. Since no historical information was available to the psychically inclined people, they were unaware that Calla May died in the house and an infant named Jacquelyn also passed away inside. When the current owners, Jeff and Brian bought the house, Jeff fell of the roof and swears he was pushed. Guests have reported seeing apparitions, hearing disembodied footsteps coming from unoccupied rooms, and feeling cold spots in different locations. In addition, when the current owners moved in, they couldn't keep the mirrors from fogging, and their pets just kept staring at one particular wall, seeing something that humans couldn't.

At the historical Turret House in Long Beach, the spirits of Calla May and Jacquelyn seem to still have the run of the house. A visit here will guarantee a hauntingly good time, where ghosts and guests often cross paths and the veil that separates the living and dead is ever so thin at this fabulous Long Beach inn.

Los Angeles
Alexandria Hotel

Particulars

501 South Spring Street,
Los Angeles, CA 90013
Phone: 213-626-7484

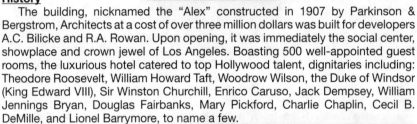

History

The building, nicknamed the "Alex" constructed in 1907 by Parkinson & Bergstrom, Architects at a cost of over three million dollars was built for developers A.C. Bilicke and R.A. Rowan. Upon opening, it was immediately the social center, showplace and crown jewel of Los Angeles. Boasting 500 well-appointed guest rooms, the luxurious hotel catered to top Hollywood talent, dignitaries including: Theodore Roosevelt, William Howard Taft, Woodrow Wilson, the Duke of Windsor (King Edward VIII), Sir Winston Churchill, Enrico Caruso, Jack Dempsey, William Jennings Bryan, Douglas Fairbanks, Mary Pickford, Charlie Chaplin, Cecil B. DeMille, and Lionel Barrymore, to name a few.

The opening of the nearby Biltmore Hotel in 1922, three blocks to the west, followed by the Great Depression, sent the Alexandria into a decline. In the early 1950's the Parkinson firm altered the distinctive parapet and made other changes on the interior. In April of 1970, the Alexandria reopened after extensive remodeling by the S. Jon Freedman Company. Today the Alexandria caters to low-income tenants. The Palm Court (originally called the Franco-Italian Dining Room) is a Historic-Cultural Monument of the City of Los Angeles.

Hauntspitality

The question is not if the hotel is haunted, but just how haunted it is. The most frequent sighting is that of the mysterious "lady in black" who has been spotted throughout the building. There are those who believe that the spectral lady was a former resident who died of a broken heart. According to the book "Hollywood Haunted" by Laurie Jacobson and Marc Wanamaker, the hotel is haunted by a ghost dressed in black, wearing a large hat with a veil. Witnesses have reported spotting this manifestation on numerous occasions. Those who are sensitve to such things describe the energy as very sad and soulful; a woman in mourning.

Psychics who have had a chance to walk

213

through portions of the building describe it an extremely active place. They point to those in the film industry who visited the building as well as numerous dignitaries, as having left an indelible imprint on the landscape; if only walls could talk!

People report hearing phantom arguments taking place, disembodied laughter, ghostly business meetings, spectral dancing and ethereal music coming from unoccupied areas of the building. Some say that when Nancy Malone and Lisa Mitchell brought back old Hollywood to the hotel, naming rooms after famous former residents and decorated the interior with portraits of stars and photographs of early Hollywood that the ghosts returned, or came out of the woodwork so to speak.

When author Laurie Jacobson interviewed Nancy Malone, who sighted the "lady in black", Malone said that while she was hanging pictures on a hallway wall early one morning, she witnessed an unusual looking woman dressed in black and wearing a large black hat standing at the far end of the hallway. The woman turned and just walked away; right into another dimension.

Jacobson believes that the phantom lady might be a former resident who died after losing a loved one and continues to grieve as if it was yesterday. There are so many stories and so many impressions revolving around the spirit population in the lobby and various floors that it's like a hotel filled to the brim with afterlife guests. Disembodied footstep often follow people for a few feet then stop when people turn around to find that there is no one else there. Others have heard their names called out or felt a cold breeze rush by as if someone unseen passed right through them. There are plenty of unexplained noises and events to write a book about.

At the Alex, the old and the new are part of the complete package. It's difficult to separate the living from those who are still doing their thing on the other side of the veil; a mere chilly breath away from the land of the living.

The Comedy Store

Particulars
8433 Sunset Boulevard,
Los Angeles, CA 90069
Phone: 323-650-6268
Fax: 323-656-6225
Website: www.thecomedystore.com

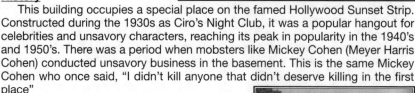

History
This building occupies a special place on the famed Hollywood Sunset Strip. Constructed during the 1930s as Ciro's Night Club, it was a popular hangout for celebrities and unsavory characters, reaching its peak in popularity in the 1940's and 1950's. There was a period when mobsters like Mickey Cohen (Meyer Harris Cohen) conducted unsavory business in the basement. This is the same Mickey Cohen who once said, "I didn't kill anyone that didn't deserve killing in the first place"

After the 1950s rock and roll replaced clandestine mob activities and celebrity dinners. By the mid-1970's, the building became home to the Comedy Store. The three story building has a main stage, backstage dressing rooms, a basement storage area below the stage, the original showroom and the main showroom, a kitchen, an annex off the kitchen. Offices are located in the second and third floors of the building. Stories are told of gangster Mickey Cohen conducting personal business in the basement of the club, which included murder.

Comics, Arsenio Hall, Roseanne Barr, Damon & Kennan Ivory Wayons, Jim Carey, Garry Shandling, Paul Rodriguez, Pauly Shore, Yakov Smirnoff, Andrew Dice Clay, Robin Williams, Whoopi Goldberg, Sandra Bernhard, Michael Keaton, Jay Leno, and David Letterman, are among but a few of the hundreds of successful comedians who have played the club.

Hauntspitality
The famous Comedy Store, located on Sunset Boulevard in Los Angeles, has been the site of hundreds of unexplained events. Owner Mitzi Shore, comedians, and staff have had repeated contact with the paranormal. Dr. Barry Taff, a renowned parapsychologist as well as other ghosthunters have visited the club, all coming away with one conclusion---the building is haunted, and there are plenty of ghosts to go around.

The International Society for Paranormal Research (ISPR) under the direction of Dr. Larry Montz investigated the establishment. Once inside, the group proceeded down the long, dark hallways until they reached the main stage room.

There, the atmosphere became almost unbearable. One member had difficulty breathing. Similar sensations were felt in the Green Room. As the group stood in the middle of the room, a shadowy figure was seen standing next to the left of the stage. It lingered a moment, then vanished. While sitting in a booth in the back of the main section next to the stage, there was an eight degree drop in temperature. The magnetometer needle was oscillating in the middle of the scale. Several of the team members could feel their arms and necks being touched, and one member had his hair played with by an unseen force, while another had her collar moved. Finally, a male energy entered the trance-medium. While the magnetometer was moving back and forth, and the temperature dropped two more degrees, a man's voice said his name was Gus, and that the place he was in right now, was Ciro's. Then a shadow moved behind one of the group members, but was quickly told to leave by Gus. As several comedians entered the room, the spirit left. A change in locations produced a presence of someone who had broken their back or neck upstairs in one of the offices---he committed suicide. The ISPR team was immediately informed that a comedian had jumped off the hotel roof next store to the Club. In the Belly Room the energy shifted from agitation, to anger. Another spirit entered one of the women in the group, and the rest of the members said that her face took on an incredibly mean expression with her eyes outlined in thick, black circles. The woman began spewing forth grunting and growling sounds.

According to the Haunted Houses Website (www.hauntedhouses.com/states/ca/house16.htm) "There are least five ghosts that hang around the building, all that originate from the 1940's and 1950's, probably as a result of Mob activities. They become most active when the place is quiet, especially in the early morning hours. Though, they have been known to be active during different times of the day as well." Other reported paranormal phenomena witnessed inside include:

- A chair gliding across the stage in the main showroom in its own.
- The ghost of a man in a brown leather bomber jacket has been frequently sighted;
- A guttural snarl was heard coming from the basement area beneath the stage, followed by an immense force which began pushing the metal gate across the entrance, causing it to bulge out and groan. This was followed by a shadowy figure materializing in front of the gate, and radiating deep malevolence;
- A piece of black cardboard falling and hitting the hand of a staff member, where he found his name written on the other side.
- When Sam Kinison performed at the Comedy Store, the spirits would always act. People would hear disembodied voices angrily chanting, "It's him. It's him. It's him." whenever Sam would go into his "yelling mode". The ghosts toyed with the lights, and interfered with the sound system. One night, Sam boldly challenged the ghosts to show themselves and all the lights all went out.
- One afternoon, Blake, a security guard was playing a video game in a room near the kitchen. He suddenly felt a presence behind him. Out of the corner of his eye, he saw a man dressed in a WW 2 brown leather bomber jacket. Turning to say something, the man dematerialized in front of him. The same afternoon, the same man in the brown

leather bomber jacket, appeared in a third floor office. He was crouching in a corner, terrified. He faded away before her eyes. Could this be a man who was murdered by Mickey Cohen's gang?

- The basement is reported to be the heart of the building, because that is where the Mob supposedly tortured and /or killed those who got in their way.
- Dr. Barry Taft and the UCLA parapsychology team investigated The Comedy Club in 1982. When they got to the backstage area by the dressing rooms, two coins fell from the ceiling. When they got to the basement, Taft picked up the horrible pain in his legs, possibly from an unfortunate person who may have had their legs broken by the mob.
- Security person, Blake, was inside at 3:00a.m., when he heard a loud growling sound coming from the basement. When he went down to investigate the padlocked gate in front of the basement was bending out, as if something was pushing it and trying to get out. The gate suddenly snapped back into place and before his eyes was a huge black form standing in front of the gate that radiated evil and malevolence. Blake flew up the stairs and out of the building as fast as his legs would carry him.
- Another time Blake and a friend were in the basement when a piece of black cardboard fell from seemingly nowhere, hitting Blake's hand. When he turned the cardboard over, his name was scrawled on the back.
- In 1994, a "Haunted Hollywood," television segment was filmed in the main room. In the back of the room, a psychic witnessed three men; all dressed in 1940's style suits, sitting at a back table for a few seconds before vanishing.

There's nothing funny about the spirits of the Comedy Store. Formerly Ciro's, a notorious nightclub, there is quite a bit of energy still calling the building home. It's a place where comedy and tragedy go hand in hand. From tears to laughter, the once legendary Ciro's is now the Comedy Club, a place where, if the comedians don't knock you dead, perhaps a ghost or two will. It's still the in-spirit place to be.

Figueroa Hotel

Particulars
939 South Figueroa Street,
Los Angeles, CA 90015
Phone: 213-627-8971
Fax: 213-689-0305
Toll Free: 1-800-421-9092
E-mail: info@hotelfigueroa.com
Website: www.figueroahotel.com

History
This building was constructed circa 1925. Also serving as a YWCA, it has been transformed today into a popular hotel. This vintage and enchanting 12-story property with a large, spacious lobby exudes a romantic Spanish Colonial/Gothic architectural style with beamed ceilings and soaring columns, tile flooring, ceiling fans, Moroccan chandeliers, and medievalist furnishings such as big floor pillows made of Kurdish grain sacks, Persian kilims, and exotic fabrics draped from the ceiling. Elevators lead to equally artistic and comfortable guest rooms. Each guest rooms comes with a bed with a wrought-iron headboard or canopy, a Mexican-tiled bathroom, and Indian fabrics that double as blackout drapes. In the back of the building is a splendid garden deck with a mosaic-tiled pool and Jacuzzi, and the Verandah Bar.

Hauntspitality
This building contains a number of spirits according to those with psychic gifts. Several people have witnessed shadowy figures disappear through walls in the lobby. Guests have heard the sounds of children playing in some of the corridors when there are no children anywhere around. Guests have had unseen visitors knock on their doors late at night. When they peer out their door, there is no one there. They then call down to the lobby to see if housekeeping was responsible, but are told no one from the staff came to their room. There are icy chills that engulf staff and guests, sending shivers up their spine. Disembodied footsteps, phantom voices, flickering lights, bathroom faucets or toilets that activate by themselves and other anomalies are commonly reported inside.

Although there are no specific names given to the spirited population in the building, several "gifted" individuals suggest that former staff and guests, including a few children, still call the building home. So many strange things occur here the paranormal becomes normal. Eerie sounds are said to emanate throughout the hallways and the rooms, televisions turn on by themselves at night and will not shut off, and the elevator moves to a certain floor on its own accord, stopping, and then opening an invisible ghost guest.

Remodeled and open for business, this historic Los Angeles gem is just the place to unwind and get away from all your troubles. It's a building where the past truly comes to life.

Four Oaks Restaurant

Particulars

2181 N. Beverly Glen Boulevard,
Los Angeles, CA 90077
Phone: 310-470-2265
Fax: 310-475-5492
Kitchen: 310-475-9260

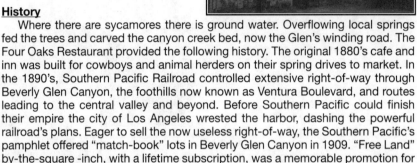

History

Where there are sycamores there is ground water. Overflowing local springs fed the trees and carved the canyon creek bed, now the Glen's winding road. The Four Oaks Restaurant provided the following history. The original 1880's cafe and inn was built for cowboys and animal herders on their spring drives to market. In the 1890's, Southern Pacific Railroad controlled extensive right-of-way through Beverly Glen Canyon, the foothills now known as Ventura Boulevard, and routes leading to the central valley and beyond. Before Southern Pacific could finish their empire the city of Los Angeles wrested the harbor, dashing the powerful railroad's plans. Eager to sell the now useless right-of-way, the Southern Pacific's pamphlet offered "match-book" lots in Beverly Glen Canyon in 1909. "Free Land" by-the-square -inch, with a lifetime subscription, was a memorable promotion for what would later become Sunset Magazine.

In 1910, the recorded lot owners were a Mrs. Curry and her mother. It is unknown whether they merely collected the rents, or monitored profits from the other businesses that gravitated to the often flooded roadside cafe. During the Carey Nation years, illegal whiskey and associated diversions flourished. The last owner uncovered some of this history in the sixties. There was a secret compartment downstairs, built with false shelves. Once removed, he found all the workings of a still, complete with tunnel to the adjoining house. Extraordinary things were found in the walls during that renovation. Beautiful little metal boxes of dried, disintegrating rouge pots were stuffed next to old wine and whiskey bottles, purses, and other forgotten evidence of the occasional police raid.

During prohibition the "hooch" no doubt attracted a crowd. People would dine downstairs in what was then the bar and main dining room. After dinner, they'd climb the stairs to visit the working women who lived at Cafe Four Oaks. The windows of the interior dining room (facing the patio) had been painted opaque, when the room apparently served as the best whore's boudoir. The central dining room contained a long narrow corridor, joining four small bedrooms. Two more bedrooms were in use where a coffee station and restrooms are now located, and another upstairs.

A faded building permit dated 1927, legitimized the bedrooms as a single dining room. The great four-branch oak in front, weathered all this change, the turning of the century, the shepherds and settlers, the railroad, prohibition, automobiles, and the growth of Los Angeles through the world wars. But it wasn't to last. In the late 1940's, the stately, generous four oaks were foolishly cut down to make way for a parking lot. Yet, the sycamores, fine evenings of elegant dining, and the long- standing restaurant remain intact. Steve McQueen, Vincent Prince, Elke Sommer and Joe Hyams frequented the restaurant.

Hauntspitality

With such a history, identifying the phantom figure that is often seen in the restaurant, both upstairs and down, may be next to impossible. Prohibition may be the most likely source of the haunting, given the fact that as a bordello, and semi-speakeasy, violence was sure to have left some paranormal imprint on the landscape.

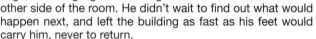

One night, a busboy who was safe-guarding the place after renovations had been completed, saw something that scared him into quitting. As the story goes, the busboy was alone and sleeping by the fireplace when a light coming from that area jolted him awake. Startled, he jumped to his feet in time to witness a large, radiating figure hovering near the other side of the room. He didn't wait to find out what would happen next, and left the building as fast as his feet would carry him, never to return.

A former owner, who never believed in the ghosts of the Four Oaks Restaurant, finally had an convincing encounter. Having often stayed in an apartment at the restaurant, he was awakened by a loud noise coming from outside his bedroom. As he leapt out of bed, the door to his room blew open, and a glowing featureless phantom entered. The terrified man screamed at the ghost to go away and the spirit didn't belong in his place. After several seconds, the mysterious figure vanished.

Busboys, waiters, and other staff members usually feel a presence in the restaurant. They also report people carrying on conversations, smelling smoke and perfume, and witnessing items move by themselves when they are about to close for the night. No one seems to enjoy working alone in this building and more often than not, you'll find staff staying in two's until the building is shut tight for the night.

Haunted dining room (Courtesy of the International Paranormal Research Organization – IPRO)

One story goes that a woman was murdered upstairs during the 1940s, and since that time, it is her restless spirit that haunts the building. Recent interviews confirm that paranormal events continue inside. Footsteps are sometimes heard on the floor above the restaurant where the office is. The soft steps indicate a female, yet no one is ever found in the flesh when an

Haunted stairs leading to the kitchen (Courtesy of the International Paranormal Research Organization – IPRO)

Haunted upstairs area (Courtesy of the International Paranormal Research Organization – IPRO)

inspection of the area is made.

Busboys in the kitchen area report mysterious voices which can be heard sometimes, yet, after a thorough inspection, no one can ever find the source. The phones act up late at night, and begin ringing in succession, even though no one is ever on the line. Doors open and close by themselves as if a phantom is coming in and out at will. There are the cold spots that suddenly manifest, chilling people to the bone. There is also the occasional feeling of being watched from an unoccupied part of the restaurant. Although the strange games that are often played with the lights are attributed to wiring problems, some staff persons blame it on the spirits of the restaurant, spirits who still linger from the Four Oaks spirited past.

Whether you come for the spirits, the great brunch, or for the ambiance, this place is sure to provide a lasting memory. There may actually be a spirit for each oak at this historic building.

LA Golndrina Restaurant

Particulars
17 West Olvera Street,
Los Angeles, CA 90012
Phone: 213-628-4349
Fax: 213-687-0800
Website: www.lagolondrina.com

History

The La Golondrina occupies the former Pelanconi House, a one-story building with an exposed basement which houses the restaurant (the street level was lowered by three feet in the late 1920s by Christine Sterling). The balcony over the street has always existed, and the building was remodeled and extended to North Main Street in the late 1920s. Originally, the Pelanconi house was a small, square house fronting Olvera Street.

The former Pelanconi House was built as a residence by Giuseppi Covaccichi circa 1855-1857. It is one of the earliest existing buildings in Los Angeles constructed of fired brick. Jose Covaccichi was born in 1824 in Italy, and married Joaquina Elibarria of Sonora, Mexico. Covaccichi bought the lot in 1855 from Loretta Valencia, and changed hands four times between 1858-1871 (Garcia, Gazzo, Mascarel, and Revera). In 1871, Antonio Pelanconi bought the lot after arriving in Los Angeles in the late 1850s or early 1860s.

Pelanconi married Isabel Ramirez and after Pelanconi's death in the late 1870s-early 1880s, Isabel remarried Giaccomo Tononi. In 1917, the property was turned over to Antonio and Isabels' children, Petra, Lorenzo, Honorina, and Isabel. Tononi owned a winery across Olvera Street, and according to one of the children, her father stored the better wine at the Pelanconi House. Some of the wine bottles were discovered in the 1920s when Olvera Street was being graded.

The restaurant was established by Consuelo Castillo de Bonzo in 1924. It was acquired by the State of California as part of the El Pueblo de Los Angeles State Historic Park in the 1950s. The restaurant occupies two levels, while there is office space on the third floor which is where the Pelanconi family used to live.

Hauntspitality

There are at last count, three spirits who reportedly roam the restaurant and the third floor office area. One of the spirits has been dubbed the lady in white. She makes herself known throughout the building, keeping an eye on staff and guests. Workers have frequently had run-ins with the specter. During seismic retrofitting to the building in 1994, 1995, workers reported that their tools were being moved on the job, and that when a worker was alone, the bathroom door would open and shut by itself. Needless to say, some workers wouldn't return alone, and brought friends or family members to keep them company while they worked in the building late at night. Most of the work was performed after the restaurant closed.

Sometimes there are cold drafts which blow through certain areas of the building when all the doors are closed, and there is no way for the air to come inside. Upstairs, where the Flamenco Dancers prepare for their presentation, a number of times they have reported a chilling cold sweep through the room, actually cause the costumes to blow, and yet no doors or windows are open to allow a draft inside. Noises like thumping or walking sounds occur frequently on the third floor, when no one is using the upstairs area. In addition to the thumping sounds, there have been loud crashes which have caused the owner and staff concern. Thinking that something heavy has fallen, they race upstairs and find nothing out of place, and no sign of life.

A number of staff have caught sight of the lady, as a kind of peripheral visual experience--there one minute, gone the next. The lady in white has been sighted floating up the stairs to the third floor, and disappears in front of startled witnesses. A phantom man enjoys materializing on the lower floor near the bathroom area, and he has been heard coughing as if to get attention, as well as materializing, then walking through a wall. A restless female child has also been seen and heard playing near the kitchen and bathroom areas of the building. She is not shy, and will soemtimes tug at your clothing. You may also catch sight of her out of the corner of your eye.

The La Golondrina is a wonderful restaurant that caters to the living as well as the possible spirit of one of the Pelanconi's who chose to remain behind to watch over the place. The occasional cold spot will only temporarily replace the warm and friendly atmosphere in the restaurant. On a warm day, you can also sit outside and watch the tourists pass by. If you get the slightest bit frightened, have a shot of tequila--it will surely brace you for anything out of the ordinary that may happen.

223

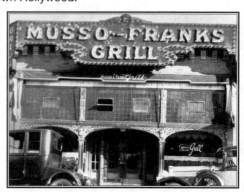

Musso & Frank Grill

Particulars
6667 Hollywood Boulevard,
Los Angeles, CA 90028-6220
Phone: 323-467-7788

History
Musso & Frank Grill, a legendary local landmark was established in 1919 by John Musso and Frank Toulet. This historic haunt lays claim to being "the oldest restaurant in Hollywood". Virtually all of the other legendary Hollywood restaurants like The Brown Derby, the original Chasen's, Ciro's, Romanoff's, and the Trocadero have vanished; but Musso & Frank has survived and prospered in downtown Hollywood.

Musso & Frank's has long been a hangout for screenwriters and assorted celebrities. Since the Writer's Guild was located nearby on Cherokee, it became a favorite watering hole of writers such as F. Scott Fitzgerald, William Faulkner (who mixed his own mint juleps here), John O'Hara, Dorothy Parker, Dashiell Hammett and Raymond Chandler; even Ernest Hemingway.

Sadly, because most of these legendary authors were lured to Hollywood by studio money, and out of their element, many of them ended up drinking their lives away at the bar here. Actors from the nearby studios also dropped by, starting as far back as the 1930's. Mary Pickford often had funnel cakes here and used the booth to conduct business as the queen of early Hollywood. Silent-movie star Tom Mix used to dine next to a window here, so his fans could see him. Charlie Chaplin liked their martinis; he and Paulette Goddard were regulars. Humphrey Bogart, the Warner brothers, Jack Webb and Peter Lawford also frequented the restaurant.

Even today, famous faces are standard at Musso & Frank including Tom Selleck, Al Pacino, The Rolling Stones, Henry Winkler, Sean Penn, Brad Pitt, Nicolas Cage, film-maker David Lynch, and Ben Kingsley. In August of 2001, Woody Allen threw a party there for the opening of his film "Curse of the Jade Scorpion". Guests included Helen Hunt, Charlize Theron, David Ogden Stiers, DreamWorks' Jeffrey Katzenberg and Elizabeth Berkley.

Even today, famous faces are standard at Musso & Frank including Tom

Selleck, Al Pacino, The Rolling Stones, Henry Winkler, Sean Penn, Brad Pitt, Nicolas Cage, film-maker David Lynch, and Ben Kingsley. In August of 2001, Woody Allen threw a party there for the opening of his film "Curse of the Jade Scorpion". Guests included Helen Hunt, Charlize Theron, David Ogden Stiers, DreamWorks' Jeffrey Katzenberg and Elizabeth Berkley.

Some customers have been coming in this establishment for over 50 years. The restaurant offers a rare sense of continuity and stability on the ever-changing Hollywood Boulevard. The Musso & Frank Grill looks like the dimly-lit place where Humphrey Bogart and Raymond Chandler would have spent time dining or drinking during their illustrious careers. It has a unique film noir setting and a club atmosphere, replete with wood-paneled walls and mahogany booths. This is a place that is staffed by career waiters who wear bright red jackets that match the red leather inside the high-sided mahogany booths. The waiters aren't the only aspect of this place that seems to span time; it's also rumored to be haunted by spirits from bygone eras who love this historic place.

Hauntspitality

Musso & Frank serves old-fashioned American/Continental food as well as old fashion hauntings. Do patrons from the past still call the restaurant home? We'll, if the paranormal stories of rapidly manifesting cold spots, phantom parties, misty and shadowy specters in Period clothing, a speakeasy female apparition, music from the past, disembodied footsteps, flickering lights, place settings being moved by unseen hands, and staff being followed or touched by invisible ghost guests, are true, then this landmark restaurant is truly one of the most haunted Hollywood venues around. There have been several reports of the ghost of silent movie heart throb Rudolph Valentino being sighted inside over the years. Valentino's spirit must be extremely restless considering all the places he reportedly visits in the afterlife; He is one busy spirit!

Adjacent to the legendary and very haunted Vogue Theater, there are numerous stories of ghosts in the Musso & Frank establishment. There is supposed to be a secret area accessible only from inside the restaurant that was used as a private club and speakeasy during Prohibition days that also contains a spirit or two.

The building reportedly had an underground access tunnel for politicians, crime figures and celebrities, to enter and leave the building without being seen by fans or police. How much is legend and how much is fact is difficult to separate; and to some extent "Who cares"! Everyone loves a good mystery. Legends intrigue people and sometimes the facts are simply not the end all for those who love to reach their own conclusions about legendary Hollywood characters.

According to one source, the wood-lined walls and red-leather banquettes in Musso and Frank are every bit as teeming with ghosts as the footprints outside of nearby Graumans Chinese Theater. There is no end to the potential list of spirits who come for a visit.

Years ago, the Travel Channel did an interesting segment on Haunted Hollywood and focused on select haunted hot spots frequented by famous Hollywood personalities. Musso and Frank was one of the featured establishments and our friend and fellow investigator/author appeared on camera in search of the ghost of Rudolph Valentino! There was a booth inside that was known to be Valentino's favorite. According to staff, Valentino and his leading lady Pola Negri would dine here before partying at the Ambassador Hotel and the famous Coconut Grove. Senate, in his book, Hollywood Ghosts, stated, "I told of the stories I had collected on the sighting of Rudolph Valentino several years ago. A woman was visiting the place and went to use the restroom in the back of the restaurant. It was evening and as she went back, she saw a smiling young man. He was rearing a white shirt, tan slacks and a simple tie. His shirt sleeves were rolled on his tan arms. He smiled at the woman. She knew almost instantly that he was a movie star, but she couldn't place him. She looked back toward her friend at the table for a second, did they see her with this celebrity? She glanced back, her movement took less than a second or two, but he was gone. It wasn't until later that she identified the apparition as that of Valentino."

There are few things that have changed over the years for this Hollywood icon. It still caters to celebrities and continues to produce quality food for people from all walks of life. There is a certain ambience that hits you when you walk in. It's like being instantly transported back to the Golden era of Hollywood.

The building is like a repository of memories and some of those memories actually materialize when you least expect it as paranormal phenomena. Here, the past and present collide, and on any given night you might just as easily run into someone from the 1930s as you would from the 21st Century.

Like a fine wine, Musso and Frank just gets better and better.

Philippe's

Particulars

1001 North Alameda Street,
Los Angeles, CA 90012
Telephone: 213-628-3781
Fax: 213-628-1812
Website: www.philippes.com

History

Philippe's is one of the oldest and best known restaurants in Southern California. The eatery was established in 1908 by Philippe Mathieu, who claimed the distinction of having created the "French Dipped Sandwich." According to legend, one day in 1918, while making a sandwich, Mathieu inadvertently dropped the sliced French roll into the roasting pan filled with juice still hot from the oven. The patron, a policeman, said he would take the sandwich anyway and returned the next day with some friends asking for more dipped sandwiches. And so was born the "French Dipped Sandwich."

Harry, Dave and Frank Martin purchased Philippe's from Mathieu in 1927. They operated the restaurant 24 hours a day, 7 days a week until World War II. The business grew steadily through the depression of 1929 and World War II mainly by virtue of the dedication and perseverance to duty of these hardy Kansans. Philippe's was forced to move to make way for the then new Hollywood-Santa Ana 101 freeway, and in 1951 relocated to the present location, which was a machine shop with a hotel on the second floor. Change does not come rapidly at Philippe's, so most of what we are today is very much what we were and did years ago. We like to say that only the prices have changed. The food is great, the ambiance memorable, and the price of a cup of coffee (a nickel until 1977) is now a dime. If you haven't visited this establishment you are missing out on the long display counter with 10 servers,

called carvers who take care of preparing your entire meal. Sawdust floors, hot mustard, paper plates, neon signs, wooden tables and you can weigh yourself on the same scale that was used by Norman Rockwell for the Saturday Evening Post.

MacDonald Harris of the New York Times ("Real food in L.A.," March 1990) wrote, "There is an air of camaraderie among the customers, a kind of unspoken friendliness and consideration that's rare in a big city . . . The customers are people of all kinds: shoppers, residents of nearby Chinatown, businessmen, Amtrak workers from the station, people who have been coming here for years and are now bringing their children. More than any other place I can think of,

Philippe's typifies the democratic spirit of Los Angeles . . ."

Philippe's is located one block north of the Union Depot Train Station, Metro Rail Station, and Olvera Street. It is located on the fringe of Chinatown, within one mile of Dodger Stadium at the intersection of North Main, Alameda and Ord Streets. There is also an added bonus when you come here for a bite to eat... spirits from a bygone era.

Hauntspitality

The spirited population inside, may actually be a combination of energy from the early years of the building when it operated as a hotel, and it's later incarnation as Philippe's. There are numerous instances of a woman in her 30s ascending the steps to the second floor simply vanishing as she reaches the second floor landing. Wearing either a maid's outfit or someone who might be considered part of a cleaning staff, she rarely interacts with the living, rather, she goes about her chores that seemed to be focused on the second floor. Could this woman be related to the hotel that once occupied the second floor of the building?

Another phantom is that of a young boy who enjoys running through the building, giggling and smiling, as if playing after-life hide and seek. He is rarely sighted, but has been heard over the years when the place is quite, usually after hours. Psychics have suggested that the young boy is between 7-9 years old, and that he may have died in the building or while playing outside.

Another ghost guest is reportedly a former employee who died, and yet remains attached to the building. Perhaps after years of faithfully serving the owners and visitors, death was only a minor stumbling block to returning to the restaurant. Occasionally sighted cleaning tables, or floating through the kitchen, this 60-something prized former phantom employee can't seem to get enough of the friendly family-like atmosphere. Once an employee, always an employee.

Sensitive individuals who visit the building can often tune out the hectic goings on and focus on the energy that still calls this building home. There are at least three spirits that "gifted" psychics have tuned into, with other energy from the past adding to the psychically charged atmosphere. Most people would be unaware of anything unusual, because of all the commotion usually taking place inside. The quiet hours would be the most revealing, and it would be fun one day to bring a group of psychics in for a full investigation to try and better document the hauntings.

Until then, occasional cold spots, unexplained footsteps, a child's laughter, a vanishing woman and possible former employee are the order of the day and will simply co-mingle with a plethora of satisfied customers who frequent this landmark eatery in Los Angeles. At Philippe's spirits come at no extra charge.

Sunset Tower Hotel

Particulars

8358 Sunset Boulevard,
West Hollywood, CA 90069
Phone: 323-654-7100
Fax: 323-654-9287
Toll Free: 1-800-225-2637
Website: www.sunsettowerhotel.com

History

"I am living in a very posh establishment, the Sunset Tower, which, or so the local gentry tell me, is where every scandal that ever happened, happened..." - Truman Capote in a letter to Leo Lerman dated December 8, 1947. Formerly, The Argyle, after an extensive renovation by esteemed decorator Paul Fortune, hotelier and restaurateur Jeff Klein reopened the building as the Sunset Tower Hotel. Designed in 1929 by prominent Los Angeles architect Leland A. Bryant, the building was a landmark from its opening and a favorite of Hollywood stars for decades. It was also the first high-rise building on the Sunset Strip.

This historic building has been restored to its status as a crown jewel of Hollywood's Sunset Strip and as Hollywood's finest surviving example of Art Deco architecture. With 74 elegant rooms, most with views of Beverly Hills, the Hollywood Hills and downtown Los Angeles, it is considered once again, the prime hotel destination on the Sunset Strip. The Sunset Tower embodies the glamorous history and distinctive style of Los Angeles with a long and fascinating history.

It was also known as The Argyle Hotel and before that, the St. James's Club & Hotel. As the St. James, it housed a private club, hotel and restaurant, with members such as Liza Minnelli, Elizabeth Taylor and David Bowie. It was also the locale for memorable poolside scenes from the movie 1992 "The Player," and has also appeared in the "The Italian Job", "Get Shorty" and "Strange Days".

Hauntspitality

According to staff and psychics who have visited this impressive historic building, it is loaded with guests from a former time. There is an array of spirits representing several periods of this building's storied life. Some people have witnessed phantoms dressed in 1930s attire, while others have reported mob-types and movie stars such as Jean Harlow and Marilyn Monroe.

Although apparitions are hard to come by, there are shadowy figures gliding down hallways and between rooms. There are regular ghost parties that go on all night in unoccupied rooms. People report hearing voices that seem to come out of nowhere and footsteps that follow people. When they turn around, no one is there.

In its heyday, the hotel hosted the likes of Errol Flynn, Clark Gable, Jean Harlow, Marilyn Monroe, Frank Sinatra, Elizabeth Taylor and Howard Hughes.

Mobster Bugsy Siegel lived in a sprawling first-floor apartment during the 1930s and 1940s, while John Wayne, lived in what is now the Argyle Spa

The colorful past is most likely responsible for the spirited clientele who continue to visit this building. By all accounts, the unusual is the usual at this hotel. The hotel is still packed with today's legendary stars as well as a few stragglers from the past who still enjoy the biz.

The legends that haunt this hotel still seem to enjoy the ambiance that made this one of the finest hotels in its day; a fact that has not diminished one iota through the years, the name changes and renovations. When you come for a visit you are sure to be greeted by more than just the living clientele.

Los Olivos
Mattei's Tavern

Particulars
2350, Railway Avenue
Los Olivos, CA 93441
Phone: 805-688-4820
Fax: 805-688-7083
E-mail: brothers@matteistavern.com
Website: www.matteistavern.com

History

This historic stagecoach stop is located roughly five miles north of Solvang. It was built by Swiss immigrant Felix Mattei in 1866, and was also known as the Central Hotel and Hotel Los Olivos. According to their brochure, in 1886, there was a gap in the coast railroad from Port Harford, now Avila Beach, to Santa Barbara. If you were traveling along the coast, you would have had to get off the train at Avila, take the Pacific Coast narrow gauge train to Los Olivos, then take the stagecoach to Santa Barbara. If you did this, you came to Mattei's Tavern and spent the night. Felix Mattei, an Italian-Swiss, opened the tavern in 1886, just as the town of Los Olivos was being formed. You can see a painting of Mr. Mattei, painted by Clarence, one of his sons, centered over the fireplace in the lobby. To the right is a self-portrait of Clarence and to the left is a painting of Felix's wife, Lucy.

Mrs. Mattei was a member of the Women's Christian Temperance Union, the same organization that provided Carrie Nation with her axe---they did not condone drinking of the demon rum. When the tavern first opened, the bar was in the room to the left of the lobby entrance, but it only lasted a year. In 1887, Lucy pronounced that there was to be no bar attached to Mattei's, and Felix built a new, separate building, where the bar is today. About four years later, Lucy again threw the rascals out, extended the building from the fireplace to the bar wall, and turned the bar into a bedroom. It was to stay a bedroom until 1962. During this time, spirituous distillates were sneaked into the restaurant by devious means, and consumed on the sly.

Currently, the bar, with its original first floor, serves openly and without fear. The back bar, built in 1914, came to the tavern from the now defunct "Yellow Jacket Saloon" in Buellton. To the right of the bar fireplace is a frosted glass window that says 'Mattei's Bodega." The original window met an untimely, but colorful end in the winter of 1977, when a bar chair sailed through it. To the left of the fireplace, hangs an original Budweiser poster of "Custer's Last Stand" from the turn-of-the-century. In the lobby, Clarence Mattei's palette rests over the clock, and his charcoal sketches of his wife Merle, and Gus Berg, Felix Mattei's best friend and card partner are also visible. The Chinese man in the Lyle Lovett suit is Gin Lung Gin, cook at the tavern until the early 1940's. Gin was famous for making dove pies out of birds shot by guests during hunting season. He was most known for not being too particular about picking all the shot from the birds, giving his pies a noticeable crunchiness.

In the hall leading to the cooking area, there is an article written in 1932 about Mattei's. The building looks the same, the road out front is sort of paved, and the trees are a bit bigger, but that's about all. The current cooking area and dining room were added on the site of the old kitchen, in 1974. From the broiler, to the right and around the comer, is the water tower. Built in 1886, it once served as water supply for the restaurant. Later, when piped water came in, the tower became a chicken-plucking room, a cannery, and a laundry room. Today, its original walls intact, it is a favorite dining room. The sun porch, with its white wicker furniture, is the most popular room. This was the public dining room since its addition in the early 1900's.

These cottages, once used as hotel rooms, are now in private rental. During the 1920's and 30's they were favorite getaways for Hollywood stars. The first cottage was rented yearly, for John Barrymore, who used to come to the area to hunt doves, enjoy the quiet and, drink lots of whiskey. The center dining room, with the red wallpaper and big chandelier, was the family dining room. In the early 1930's, the family dining room was filled with chauffeurs, while, in the wicker

room, ate Clark Gable, Gary Cooper, Carole Lombard, and all of the Hollywood stars of the day. They had come to Mattei's on their way to a party at Hearst's San Simeon.

In the front room, to the left of the lobby entrance, you can see a picture of the Mattei family taken in the early 1900's. This room, once the barroom, then the stagecoach office, was also a card room. Fred Mattei, one of the sons, and proprietor of the tavern until his death in 1962, used to keep a big round table set up in the room for games of poker. From this room, money changed hands, and rumor has it that ownership of automobiles, livestock and even real estate did, too. Notice the lettering over the door on the front of the room. This is the original lettering for the stagecoach office, painted there in 1886. The tavern stopped being a hotel in the mid-1960s, and the upstairs rooms, once used as art galleries, have been closed since 1977. Today, they are offices for the restaurant that await renovation.

Hauntspitality
A psychic investigated the tavern years ago, and ran into the ghost of a man with white whiskers. The encounter was brief, but there was no mistaking the whiskered gentleman as a part of the ghostly clientele. The kindly man seemed to be from the late 1800s and somehow tied to the place. Perhaps it was Swiss immigrant Felix Mattei who constructed the building.

There have also been accounts of visitors seeing a woman wearing a white dress who was poisoned before the turn of the century in the tavern. Sensitive people have picked up on a Victorian-Period woman who seems unhappy, and leaves a trail of perfume as she passes by.

Things in the tavern have been known to move around with the help of the spirits. Mysterious cold spots; strange, moving shadows on the walls, and apparitions have been noted with some regularity in the tavern. Guests have reported seeing individuals pass by out of the corner of their eye only to turn and find no one there. There are accounts of disembodied footsteps and voices that call out to staff from another world. There has been one report of a phantom boy who was sighted running through the dining area and vanishing just before he reached a wall. Sometimes there's a strong sense of being watched or followed by unseen eyes.

Some people believe that after Felix Mattei died in 1930, his spirit settled in the tavern and remains to this day. Certainly, the colorful history, and age of the building add to the spirited ambiance. A visit may produce more than a good meal, or a thirst quenching drink--you may see a ghost.

Malibu

Duke's Malibu

Particulars
21150 Pacific Coast Hwy.,
Malibu, CA 90265-5219
Phone: 310-317-0777
Fax: 310-317-0677
Website: www.dukesmalibu.com

History

The Las Flores Inn was built around 1915 to serve tourists driving up the coast from Santa Monica at the turn around where the coastal dirt road leading to Malibu ended and the Rindge Ranch property fence restricted further travel. The Las Flores Inn later became the Malibu Sea Lion Restaurant, which featured a tank of live sea lions in the parking lot. The restaurant attracted visitors from all around the southland who came to view the sea lions, gaze at the Pacific Ocean and grab a bite to eat on their journey along the famed Pacific Coast Highway.

The sea lions were eventually removed and the ownership changed hands. The Malibu Sea Lion Restaurant later became known as Charley Brown's Malibu Sea Lion or simply Charley Brown's. The restaurant served as a makeshift dormitory for fire crews who narrowly escaped flames that engulfed a neighboring building after gusting winds carried cinders across the Pacific Coast Highway. Charley Brown's lasted until the mid-1990s before giving way to Duke's Malibu.

This popular spot, which opened in 1996, has 300 feet of windows that provide unforgettable sunset views and occasional glimpses of dolph ins and other sea life that pass by. The walls are lined with surfing history paying homage to Duke Kahanamoku (the restaurant's namesake) and other memorable surfers.

Although surfing was first introduced to California at Redondo Beach by George Freeth of Hawaii in 1907, it was another Hawaiian, Duke Kahanamoku, who taught the sport to early Malibu surfers beginning in 1927. The Duke was a great friend of actor Ronald Colman who built #16 Malibu Colony in 1926-1927 as one of the first "Colony" beach cottages. Coleman also loved to surf. It was at the Santa Monica Swim Club that aspiring surfers such as Bob Butt, Wally Burton, Pete Peterson, Johnny McMahon, and Chauncey Granstrom, learned the sport from The Duke and his co-worker, Tony Guerrero. The group went up the coast when Rancho Malibu opened to the public and made their way to Malibu Point through a hole in the fence at the Malibu Potteries. The "Point" began one of the three most notable surfing spots in the United States. Duke's is a reminder of the days when surfing was king and the king was the Duke. The memorabilia inside is not the only reminder of bygone days; there are also a few ghosts that call the building home.

Hauntspitality

Like the Malibu Inn, Moonshadows and the Paradise Cove Beach Café, Duke's is also reportedly haunted. It seems that spirits like Malibu and love being close to the water. Add to the mix the currently closed Pierview Inn, Neptune's Net, and Alice's on the pier and there doesn't seem to be an eating establishment that doesn't have a spirit or two hanging around. Psychics who have visited the

building retort, why not haunt this place, it's like heaven.

Those sensitive to the paranormal have no doubt a young woman and middle-age man frequent the bar, entry area and seating area to the right of the entryway. Some say the restrooms are also haunted. Most of the actual ghost stories date back to when the building was occupied by the Malibu Sea Lion and Charley Brown's. One psychic even stated that there may be a spirit dating to the Las Flores Inn days. No one knows for sure who the spirits are, but former staff swear that they used to see apparitions and occasional shadows float down the walkway heading in both directions after entering the building. After closing, people would report hearing their names called out by unseen guests, and would occasionally be touched or pinched.

One psychic while walking toward the bathroom got the distinct impression of a young woman from the 1930s who used to frequent the building, as a worker or guest, and who died on the Pacific Coast Highway. She apparently was fond of the place in life and continued to visit the building, occasionally showing herself to a select few people. A phantom man, possibly a former owner or manager is also rumored to hang out near the bar, where staff has reported hearing a gruff cough or seeing an apparition for a split second before the man vanishes.

There are reports of cold spots and the uneasy feeling of being watched or followed in the restroom or in the western portion of the building. Some people have smelled perfume, or felt as if someone unseen brushed by them as they were walking toward the bathroom. Late at night, the building does seem to take on a different persona; one where unseen guests begin to make their presence felt.

There is nothing harmful or disturbing about the spirits inside; they are simply guests who seem to love hanging around the building. Before the building became Duke's a waitress remarked that she saw a 10-year-old child suddenly appear before her, smile and then walk right through a wall. That would make three spirits residing in the building. It does have a lot of history, and if walls could talk, we are sure they would have a lot to say about the phantom clientele who occasionally co-mingle with the living. At Duke's the food is great and the atmosphere, with or without the spirits, is simply heavenly.

Malibu Inn

Particulars
22969 Pacific Coast Highway,
Malibu, CA 90265
Phone: 310-456-6060
Fax: 310-446-2104
E-mail: info@malibu-inn.com
Website: www.malibu-inn.com

History

The Malibu Inn has been at its current location for more than 83 years. Built in the 1920s as a multi-purpose building after the Roosevelt Highway opened, the building served as a café, real estate office, trading post, bar and liquor store. The original building was demolished in the 1950s and a new building constructed in its place.

The current Malibu Inn has undergone several architectural modifications since the 1950s. Its history and services have changed with every owner. The current owners, Nurit Mitchell and her husband Stuart, said the new establishment's bold, golden yellow signifies its return to its golden age of yesteryear, providing the community with superior quality one would expect from a Malibu establishment. The ambiance has shifted from a bar and beef bungalow to a family-oriented, high quality eatery while retaining its base audience of locals, students and tourists. The walls are filled with reminders of those who frequented this place when Malibu Colony was in full swing as a haven for movie stars, and there are also photographs of the building before demolition in the 1950s. The new inn provides a more unrestricted flow of energy from the bar to the performance stage, and

the food is to die for. The only thing that hasn't changed over the years, are the ghosts.

Hauntspitality

After years of interviews with current and past staff, as well as information obtained from psychics who have visited this place, there is ample evidence to suggest that at least seven distinct energies remain inside. Psychics suggest that there is a man and a woman from the 1940s (they refer to as Sam and Christine) who had something to do with the building (possibly having owned it or worked there) and remain behind because this is "their" haven or heaven. The energy surrounding the bar is another matter. There is a strong male energy who may have been murdered in the parking area that stays close to the bar. The man is described as being tall, sporting a moustache and have salt and pepper hair. They also sensed a female actress from the 1930s and a chef who still remain inside. The actress loves to sit by the front window booth to the right upon entering. She seems forlorn as if waiting for someone to return. The chef calls the kitchen his, and still seems to be cooking afterlife dishes for his unseen guests. Finally, teo psychics sensed a woman in her 20s-30s with long, dark brown hair, possibly from the 1950s-1960s who frequents the main dining area. The overall impression of the place was favorable, with impressions of prior fights, rowdy behavior, dancing and drinking having been a strong imprint on the building. The back bathroom area also had some heavy energy associated with drugs, fighting and excessive drinking.

A staff person recalled that while working in the food preparation area with two other workers, that she suddenly experienced a cold draft of air on her neck. It was as if someone were standing behind her blowing on her shoulders and neck trying to get her attention. She knew it wasn't the air conditioning because it was off. Also there was no vent where she was standing. She turned around quickly, thinking that it might be an employee joking around. After all, they were familiar with the ghost stories. When she turned, there was no one there. The other two employees were standing ten feet away busily preparing food. She went back to work and had the same thing happen again. She changed positions, muttered for whoever it was to stop and the blowing stopped.

On another occasion, an employee was closing up for the night when he heard what sounded like someone preparing food in the kitchen. It was long after that kitchen was closed, but he heard pots and pans being moved around, and the sound of a plate hitting the floor. Thinking someone was still in the building, he grabbed a bottle and headed back to the kitchen area. There was no one there. Nothing was out of place and nothing being prepared. Suddenly, he was engulfed in an icy cold draft. Feeling that there was someone behind him, he quickly raised the bottle, turned and was ready to hit someone. As he turned around he glimpsed a man in a white uniform wearing a chef's hat dart from the kitchen toward the bar. He gave chase, but to no avail; he was alone in the building. He quickly grabbed his things and left.

On another occasion, two employees closing down the bar said that a tall man walked right past them toward the bathroom. They yelled out that the bar was closed and wanted to know how he got in; the doors had been locked. One of the men gave chase and ended up in the men's bathroom where, the strange looking man was last sighted. There was no one there. The two employees searched the entire building to no avail. They were alone.

There have been constant reports of the smell of freshly prepared food coming from the kitchen when it has been closed for the night. Staff have heard voices of people arguing coming from the bar area and bathroom, yet there is never anyone there. Some staff has witnessed an attractive young woman standing in the front window after closing down for the night. When they go back in to check, there is never anyone there. There are repots of rapidly materializing cold spots, shadowy figures, items being moved by unseen hands and disembodied footsteps at this historic restaurant.

With its illustrious history and visits by Hollywood celebrities, bikers, and visitors wanting to soak up the local color, it's no wonder that this restored building has so many spirits floating around. Who wouldn't want to hang around this place, with its great food and view of the Pacific Ocean? It's got ambience to die for, or to live on for in the case of its spirited clientele.

Moonshadows

Particulars

20356 Pacific Coast Highway,
Malibu, CA 90265
Phone: 310-456-3010
Website: www.moonshadowsmalibu.com

History

The once popular surfer hangout back in the 70s transformed itself into a beachside romantic dining location with an awesome sunset that alone, is worth the visit. Those lucky enough to nab the view window tables can watch the surf and sea life. It is romantic and they have plenty of seafood options on the menu. Here, you can enjoy a glass of wine while looking out over the vast expanse of Pacific Ocean that occasionally provides a view of Santa Catalina Island. The restaurant, which has been there since 1971, has recently undergone a complete makeover. On weekends, Moonshadows doubles as one of Malibu's hottest nightspots, where locals and visitors share the facility.

Moonshadows also has a treat that few know about; it's haunted! Although no one is sure who the phantom ghost guest is, almost everyone agrees that someone unseen occupies the building. Occasionally felt and sighted as a misty form, this benign spirit, believed to be a male, is reportedly responsible for the ice cold drafts and feelings of being watched or followed one feels inside the building.

Paranormal investigator and writer, Jeff Dwyer in is latest book entitled *Ghost Hunter's Guide to Los Angeles*, adds "The foggy image of a ghost appears in the mirror in the men's restroom." The Shadowlands webpage, an online site dedicated to the paranormal, states, "In the women's restroom, the water faucets have been known to turn on by themselves."

Paranormal investigators and psychics alike have felt a male energy inside the building; possibly a prior owner or someone who died in or nearby, haunts the establishment. Although some "sensitives" feel that the spirit belongs to an elderly man, others have felt a woman and a young man, who may be related. Some staff persons have felt an unseen energy brush by them, leaving them a

little shaken. Other has actually seen a floating form in the bathroom area. The shadowy image eventually glides right through the wall.

There is something for everyone at Moonshadows. You can have a great view, a wonderful dining experience, or have a brush with the unknown. Here, sun, sand, surf and spirits are all part of the bill of fare.

Paradise Cove Beach Cafe

Particulars

28128 West Pacific Coast Highway,
Malibu, CA 90265
Phone: 310-457-2503
Fax: 310-457-3273

History

The restaurant is located in stunning Paradise Cove adjacent to the Pacific Ocean. Famous as a location for numerous film and television shoots over the years. Back in the 1970s, the Morris family bought 30 acres adjoining Paradise Cove from Fred Roberts and subsequently purchased an additional 40 acres adjacent to the Cove, creating the configuration that is seen today. During the 50s and 60s, the small community beach was host to movies and television shows such as Beach Blanket Bingo, Gidget and Sea Hunt.

While fishermen and locals were busy with the rigors of hauling in the daily catch, others simply enjoyed the crystal clear waters and warm summer days. When the Kissel family bought Paradise Cove, the restaurant ambiance was maintained with a laid back atmosphere, good food, and a beach a few steps away. Today, the tiny shack that once primarily served locals and movie stars has been transformed into the Paradise Cove Beach Cafe, with a stunning view of the Pacific Ocean to die for.

Hauntspitality

Long known to be a favorite hang-out for the living, it also has the reputation for catering to other-worldly clientele; and why not hang around a place that has so much action, features a stunning view of the Pacific Ocean and caters to people from all walks of life? It's not heaven, but it'll do. Oh, there's one other fact that might account for it's paranormal reputation; the cafe lies adjacent to a Native American village where burials were unearthed by archaeologists in the past. So, who are the spirits and what do they do, exactly?

It took some snooping around and several visits to come up with a potential ghostly guest list, as follows: One spirit is believed to be a former female employee who loves to rearrange place settings and move objects to her after-life liking. This benevolent phantom, although choosing to remain invisible so far, can sometimes be heard late at night opening doors and inspecting the cafe to ensure that customers are well-taken care of.

According to one staff member, the phantom female worked at the cafe before it became a well-known restaurant. She happily went about her routine for over thirty years, making numerous friends along the way. When she finally retired, she still came back to the restaurant to continue her relationship with the former employees she befriended over the years. After her death, the former employee apparently decided that instead of moving on, she would remain behind to continue taking care of her favorite place on earth; the restaurant at Paradise Cove.

A second spirit is believed to be a man. Perhaps a former staff member, owner or patron, this pesky spirit likes the kitchen and dining areas, and may work hand-in-hand with the deceased waitress to ensure that the cafe continues to run smoothly. A mysterious voice sometimes calls out the names of employees, opens doors, turns lights on and off, may also be responsible for the disembodied footsteps that sometimes follow the clean-up crew in the early morning hours. There are also pesky cold spots that will suddenly manifest in the kitchen and main dining area.

Working alone late one night, a restaurant employee heard the door to the kitchen open and close, followed by footsteps that moved in his direction. Frozen in his tracks for a few seconds and thinking it was an intruder, the sound of the footsteps passed right by him followed by a cold gust of air; no flesh-and-blood person, no shadowy figure---nothing. After the cold gust of air brushed by him, the footsteps stopped. It took the stunned employee less than a minute to grab his coat and keys, lock up and leave. From that night on, he refused to work in the restaurant alone.

The Paradise Cove area is unique, not only because of its natural beauty and the fact that Native Americans found the area to be an excellent location for a village, but for it's stunning location right on the Pacific Ocean. The spirited occupants only wish that you enjoy the ambiance as much as they do. After all, they enjoyed it so much while they were alive, that they continue to call the Paradise Cove Beach Cafe, home in the after-life!

Mendocino
The MacCallum House
Inn & Restaurant

Particulars

45020 Albion Street, P.O. Box 206,
Mendocino, CA 95460
Phone: 707-937-0289
Fax: 707- 937-2243
Toll Free: 1-800-609-0492
E-mail: machouse@mcn.org
Website: www.maccallumhouse.com

History

The hotel/restaurant is positioned atop rugged coastal cli ffs overlooking the Pacific Ocean against a backdrop of redwood and cypress forests, in the small town of Mendocino, which was once a lumber mill town. The Gray Whale Bar offers seasonal views of gray whales. They migrate twice annually, passing close to the shore. The following information was provided by management, and was written and researched by Owen Scarborough. Born Emma Shirley Kelly in 1859, "Daisy" MacCallum was a nickname which matched her sunny disposition. It is said that Daisy was responsible for adding another "e" to her family name because in adolescence she thought the shorter spelling too "Irish" - the Irish weren't highly esteemed then. So, she was "Daisy" Kelley

until she married Alexander MacCallum, her father's bookkeeper, at age 20. Daisy's parents, William and Eliza, were from Prince Edward Island on Canada's East Coast. They crossed Panama and arrived here in August 1855. William and his brother, James, first came in search of gold, however, James died of cholera, and William very nearly died. Fortunately, when he and Eliza later came that way, there was a railroad to accommodate the bride. Daisy was a devout and determined lady with a will of iron, and though she was never "called to ministry" as her mother was, a hands-on Baptist preacher, she built a church in back of MacCallum House---now a health food store.

The house was a wedding present from her parents. The architect and builder was John D. Johnson, who did many of Mendocino's long lasting redwood, New England style Victorian homes. Before the house was ready for occupancy Alex, Daisy and their first child, Donald, lived there with her parents. The Kelley House stands across the street; now a museum. The completed MacCallum house got a rave review from The Mendocino Beacon. The family only lived in the house for three years. Daisy's love of change and travel partially explains it. She was also a voracious reader, reading everything from potting plants to tomes on Sanskrit. Having been toted around by doting Pomo Indians as an infant on their cradle boards, and raised in a Mendocino when every third person was Chinese, she had an early exposure to other cultures.

In 1885, Daisy and the family moved to Glen Blair, East of Fort Bragg, and rented the house to the Henry Brown family. Her daughter, Jean, was born at Glen

Blair, and Daisy started her lifelong interest in horticulture---her roses still bloom around MacCallum House. In 1908 Daisy's son Alex died. Donald her firstborn, accompanied his mother back to Mendocino where the house had been impacted by the 1906 earthquake. They began to repair the damages. Daisy had the house moved to its present location - a little lower on the lot and to the West. She added the back part at that time because she needed the extra room, for a growing "army" of nieces and nephews, and the constant flow of interesting professional people. Artists, writers, musicians visited---as they still do in her absence - to enjoy the ambiance of her questing spirit.

Daisy got around! But she always returned to Mendocino, "The most beautiful spot on God's green earth". She was wiry and petite, scarcely 5-feet tall---but a giant in spirit who never let her troubles get her down. As a friend once said of her, "When in doubt, she dug...;" and in her garden, many roses remain. She died at age 94 in 1953. The house chronology reads:

- 1850-William Kasten, first Caucasian settler, shipwrecked German seaman, built the first cabin on the headlands and filed claim on the area.
- Daisy's father purchased 5-acre tract bordered by Main and Lansing for $2650;
- 1852 - Henry Meiggs built the first mill, and Daisy's father was in the crew---he was probably the best railroad builder of that period;
- 1855-William Kelley brings his bride, Eliza Ford, to Mendocino;
- 1859-Daisy is born;
- 1879-Daisy marries Alexander MacCallum;
- 1880-Daisy's first child, Donald, is born (died 1960);
- 1882-MacCallum House built;
- 1885- the MacCallums move to Glen Blair;
- Jean is born (died 1970);
- 1896-MacCallums move to San Francisco;
- 1908-Alexander dies (Daisy moves back to Mendocino);
- 1909-MacCallum House moved to its present location on the lot (addition is built);
- 1953-Daisy dies, age 94;
- 1953-1974 -MacCallum House maintained by family;
- 1974-William and Susan Norris bought the house and it became a Bed and Breakfast Inn;
- 1976-Tim Cannon leased the first floor to open the MacCallum House Restaurant and Gray Whale Bar;
- 1986-Rob Ferrero purchased the restaurant and bar operation from Tim Cannon;
- 1985-Joe and Melanie Reding purchased the Inn and have maintained the original atmosphere of the house while updating and enhancing the home;
- 1996-Alan Kantor assumed the restaurant and bar operation.

Hauntspitality

According to management and gifted psychics, The MacCallum House spirits are Donald MacCallum, the repressed son of Daisy and Alexander, and Daisy who had a fondness for the home. Donald's former bedroom is now Room 6 at the inn, where women staying in the room, frequently become the focus of Donald's attention. Unfortunately for the phantom boy, his mother doesn't let him get away with much hanky-panky.

Dirty Donald, as he has become known, was caught one time by his mother fooling around in what is now the Greenhouse Suite. She never forgave his hormonal transgressions, and from that time on, she made sure he remained a bachelor, acting as his sexual guardian the rest of his life.

Sometimes, women guests in Room 6 report having erotic dreams, as well as having the feeling that they are sharing the room with a strange man. The stories are so numerous, that no one doubts their veracity. A psychic confirmed the presence of Donald, and a staff member once went into Donald's former room. His hair immediately stood on end, and the temperature in the room was freezing. The staff person left immediately. That fact that a man had entered his domain produced a rather cold response.

Late-night partygoers, who returned to the hotel, reported seeing an elderly woman sitting in reception area. The woman bid a polite welcome, and quickly walked into what used to be Daisy's room. The curious guests followed the mysterious woman, and upon entering Room 5, found no one there. It was as if the woman just vanished. The guests quickly checked out.

A number of Daisy's favorite possessions are still in the hotel, along with Donald's rock and shell collections, which are kept in an attic. When the staff tried to move Donald's collection into the lobby as part of a proposed display, they were commanded by a ghostly voice to put them back in the attic, because Donald wanted them there---they complied immediately.

A couple, who visited The MacCallum House, won't soon forget their encounter with its spirits. As a surprise birthday present for her husband, the couple decided on the spur of moment, to look for a room in Mendocino. There wasn't much available, but they were finally directed to The MacCallum House. Upon reaching the house, they checked in to the attic suite. An omen of things to come occurred when a large black bird landed on the roof, and perched over their window. After dinner, the couple went upstairs to their room. As they prepared for bed, the wife became uneasy, and couldn't go to sleep without closing the door to the adjoining room, and leaving the bathroom light on---it was out of character for her.

The couple finally went to sleep, that is until 1:30 a.m., when a loud sound woke the wife up out of pleasant slumber. She found herself sitting upright in bed in a pitch black room. The light in the bathroom was turned off. She shook her husband awake, and asked him if he turned the light off. He said he hadn't. They both got up and turned the light back on. Back in bed, the wife's husband drifted back to sleep, while she apprehensively laid in bed. Within a short time, the woman began to hear the door to the other bedroom creaking open, and since the windows were tightly closed, it wasn't the wind making the sounds. This was followed by footsteps outside the bedroom door. The floorboards creaked from the weight of someone moving about. The events unnerved the wife, who instead of investigating alone, chose to cover her head with the blanket and pray for morning to arrive, which it did without further incident. The next morning, the woman found out that her experience was not unusual.

The lights, noises, and footsteps were said to be a common occurrence in the house, and that the couple were the latest to experience the spirits. According to the innkeeper, certain guests in Donald's former room have been driven out from noxious odors that seem to have no detectable source. One afternoon a man asked if he and his wife could change rooms because of the foul smell that seemed to envelope the room. The strange part was, the husband couldn't smell a thing, it was only his wife who detected the odor. And so it seems, the spirited mother and son combination still keep things pretty lively for those who manage and visit The MacCallum House Inn, especially women. The good news for females spending the night is that Donald's spirit, though sometimes curious, is kept in check by his ever watchful mother.

Mendocino Hotel & Garden Suite

Particulars

45080 Main Street, P.O. Box 587,
Mendocino, CA 95460
Phone: 707-937-0511
Fax: 707-937-0513
Toll Free: 1-800-548-0513
E-mail: reservations@mendocinohotel.com
Website: www.mendocinohotel.com

History

The Hotel is located on Main Street, in the heart of Mendocino Village. Mendocino is situated on California's rugged North Coast in historic Mendocino, 200 miles north of San Francisco. Also nearby are towering redwoods and pines, as well as rustic beaches and parks. Art and culture thrive in Mendocino. The Mendocino Hotel represents the only hotel in town still in existence from when it was a booming port of the logging trade. The original portion of hotel dating to 1878, encompasses the lobby, lobby bar, dining room, kitchen, and upstairs guest bedrooms. The establishment originally opened as The Temperance House when the town had a population of around 20,000 inhabitants. At the time the town of Mendocino boasted 19 saloons, several pool halls and a few houses of ill-repute. Early settlers from Maine, Connecticut and Nova Scotia sailed around Cape Horn to find the western coastal wilderness already populated with Indians, Chinese and the rough loggers, but built homes and eventually brought their wives to the region. Thanks to these early settlers from the East Coast, many of the buildings in Mendocino bear striking architectural resemblance to houses, shops and church steeples of small New England towns.

In 1975, R.O. Peterson purchased the run-down hotel and retained a cadre of designers and local artisans and craftsmen to authentically restore it. Mr. Peterson gave the designers carte blanch to purchase as many period antiques as they felt were necessary to give the hotel the right atmosphere. Approximately 90% of all the pieces date to the late 19th century. Most of the remaining 10% represent items commissioned specifically for the hotel. When the dining room was designed, many special items were added to give it a warm, welcoming, relaxing space: period wallpaper by Schumacher, a rug custom designed and woven to simulate an authentic piece from the era, period mirrors, ceramics, original oil paintings, an enormous sideboard purchased in England, and a 1920s coffee machine. Of special note are the glass screen room dividers. The crests of the British towns were placed in walls dividing first and second class passengers in British railway stations in the late 19th century. Mr. Peterson purchased the crests, had them shipped to Mendocino and the wooden frames were built locally to house the beautiful glass pieces. Other screens in the room that have decorative glass in them are also original pieces, although older than the crests. The Mendocino Hotel is the only remaining hotel from a time when Mendocino was a booming port for the logging trade. The original structure of the hotel, dating to 1878, remains today and encompasses the lobby, the lobby bar, the dining room, the kitchen and upstairs rooms.

Hauntspitality

A number of mysterious phantom-like figures appear both in and around the hotel, although no one has been able to determine their identity. Considering the conditions that fisherman and loggers faced while the town was active in the late 1800s, there is little wonder that ghosts inhabit the hotel. No doubt, a number of fishermen and loggers lost their lives while in their line of work, and choose to remain in the peaceful setting rather than move

on. However, one beautiful young woman, who appeared in the lounge and spent a few moments gazing out the window before mysteriously disappearing, was neither a logger nor a fisherman. Nor is another Victorian-looking woman who haunts Tables 6 and 8 in the restaurant---she has been sighted staring at guests and staff from a mirror, and then vanishing.

A front desk clerk witnessed the woman in the mirror late at night after stepping into the back office. The female clerk got the urge to look through the office window into the lounge area. To her wonderment, she saw a beautiful, well-dressed woman, with long blonde hair standing in the lounge window gazing out toward the bay. The night clerk remembered how real the girl looked, although her clothing was from a different time period---Edwardian style, almost "Gibson-girl" fashion. The night clerk also recalled hearing her name called out, even though it was a childhood nickname no one in the hotel could have known about. As the night clerk took her eyes off the woman for a second or two, the woman disappeared.

Maids have reported making up the twin beds in Room 10, then leaving for a minute to get fresh towels, and coming back to find a body-shaped indentation in the bed. No one could have come in or left without being seen by the maids. The front desk clerk confirmed that many people have felt a benign presence in the room that had a somewhat oppressive feel to it---not harmful, just a heavy feeling.

Another guest felt as if he were pushed by an unseen presence while walking down the deserted wooden staircase. Room 307 is another room where a young boy and his mother claim to have watched in awe as a mist formed in the mirror and a man's face appear---the face remained in the mirror a good five minutes before fading away.

A hotel flyer states that a series of mysterious figures have been frequently sighted in the hotel, including a Victorian woman who haunts Tables 6 and 8 in the restaurant, and a beautiful young woman who appears in the lounge. There are also the whispered names of staff members when they are alone, as well as unexplained footsteps, and mysterious cold spots. The Mendocino Hotel is a wonderful place to get away from it all; well, almost everything!

Mokelumne Hill
The Hotel Leger
Bed & Breakfast

Particulars
8304 South Main Street,
Mokelumne Hill, CA 95245
Phone: 209-286-1401
Fax: 209-286-2105
E-mail: hotelleger@aol.com
Website: www.hotelleger.com

History

The Leger Hotel is listed as California State Historic Landmark #663, and a portion of the building served as the Calaveras County courthouse from 1852 to 1866, when the county seat was removed to San Andreas. George W. Leger then acquired the court building and made it a part of his adjoining hotel, which has been operated since early gold mining days. It was first known as the Hotel de France. It sits on a small hill which overlooks the Mokelumne River and is one of the most elegant inns of the Gold Country. George Leger, an immigrant from Hesse Kassel, Prussia, purchased the hotel on May 31 of 1853 from Alexis Yacht.

It was destroyed by the fire of 1854. Leger rebuilt that same year, a one-story structure of brick and rhyolite blocks, and reopened for business. An adjoining building once served as the Calaveras County Courthouse, while Mokelumne Hill held the county seat. Leger acquired the building after the seat was lost and made it a part of his hotel. The building was damaged in the fire of 1874, after which Leger added a second story and the building restored in 1879. The hotel's lobby was the first place in town to have electric lights. The lights were strung out in front of the hotel when they were first illuminated, an event which most of the town turned out

to see. The Hotel Leger has been known by several different names over its long history, such as the Hotel de Europa, the Union Hotel, the Grand Hotel, and the Hexter House.

Hauntspitality

Several ghosts have been spotted in this legendary two-story hotel. Staff has been grabbed from behind by an invisible force in the kitchen. This area of the hotel seems to be a focal point for strange events including the feeling of being watched, items moving on their own, footsteps, and cold spots. The transparent image of a man has been frequently sighted walking through the back dining area from the bar. The spirited gentleman has been described as being dark-haired, rather tall, and usually wearing a pin-striped shirt. He is most

Haunted Room #8

Haunted Room #7

frequently seen during warm summer days, when the air is still. He seems to glide across the floor in a slow and deliberate manner. This phantom has also been seen upstairs in the hotel, in room 8, leaning against the wall. When the strange man isn't showing himself, his footsteps can oftentimes be heard slowly making their way down the hallway corridor. Perhaps it is the spirit of George Leger, who bought the hotel in 1853.

Rumor has it, that Leger was killed near Room 8. A couple of more ghosts haunt the Leger including a lady in white who paces back and forth in front of the window in Room 2. A woman was apparently burned to death in a tragic fire that struck the hotel in the 1870's. The room has had its share of strange events including the windows opening and closing by themselves, and the smell of smoke, when there is no one smoking and no fire in the hotel. The staff decided to name the lady in white, "Elizabeth." In Room 3, a rocking chair moves back and forth by itself. The room is also the favorite haunt of a little boy who has appeared in the antique rocker only to suddenly vanish as suddenly as he appeared. One time, a staff person was working in Room 7, when she removed a photograph of George Leger from the wall. Within seconds, the woman was drenched to the bone by an invisible source. Finally, barely audible sounds of a woman crying can be heard in a part of the building that has been remodeled into a small community theater.

Current owner Mark Jennings says that although the spirits have not manifested for him, unexplained events continue to occur with regularity at the hotel. Room 7 and the bathroom across the hall are areas which guests often report activity. The very heavy door to the bathroom will sometimes open or slam shut in front of startled witnesses. There is no way according to Jennings, which any kind of draft can move that door, or slam it shut with such force. Inside Room 7, guests often report the windows opening by themselves no matter how many times they are securely locked. Then there are the frequent footsteps heard in the unoccupied corridors and the repetitious pacing and movement which bring staff and guests into the hallway; yet there is never anyone in the corridors at the time.

There are still reports by housekeeping that a few minutes after making a bed military style, with the sheets securely tucked, they later return from performing other chores to find the bed rumpled as if someone invisible jumped into bed and took a quick nap. In the lobby, candles are occasionally knocked out of the candelabrum on the piano by an unseen force. A prostitute called Edith, so-named by a psychic, is often sighted floating around the parlor. There is also a sad, red-faced farmer from the 1940s who is occasionally witnessed inside the building. According to information sent by the hotel the following events have been documented:

- "George walks the town," says Ron Miller, the Leger's former owner. "I've seen him. He looks exactly like his picture on the stairs." Miller's wife, Joyce, remembers the time she showed a prospective guest through the hotel. Suddenly the woman turned pale and ran outside, later explaining that a spectral man had stood behind Joyce, nodding his head approvingly as she recounted the building's history. Shortly afterward, the Millers' son, Ronnie, asked them who was staying in "George's room." "No one right now," his mother replied. "Oh, yes there is," the boy answered. "A man just came out and asked me to be quiet."

- In Room 2, guests report seeing a Victorian woman -- maybe one of George's girlfriends.
- In Room 3, people see a little boy.
- Maids make the beds in rooms 10 and 11, returning later to find them torn up. The wildest story is the midnight cattle drive down Main Street -- sounds of mooing, hoof beats and cowbells. Guests have rushed to the window only to see a dark, deserted street.
- A staff person cleaned the dining room after a party, using three keys to lock three doors before leaving late at night. Upon returning the next morning, the doors were all unlocked and the room was found in disarray. Tables were shoved together. Dishes, glasses and silver used.
- On one occasion, the hotel manager leaned against the ice machine in the former dungeon chatting with a plumber who asked if the place was haunted. The hotel manger shrugged and the next thing she knew, she was shoved hard enough to knock her forward, leaving red marks on her shoulder for two days.
- The manager of the hotel coffeehouse, has had trouble with her truck, which unlocks itself; but only when it is parked in front of the hotel. She has actually witnessed the lock opening by itself as she stood in front of the truck.
- On another occasion, she was actually locked inside the truck and to get out, had to roll down the window and unlock it with a key from the outside.
- Late one evening while working alone, the hotel bookkeeper, gathered her papers and opened the door leading to the basement/dungeon. To her amazement, the stairwell was filled with colored balloons. She pushed them aside and descended the stairs. After placing the books in the safe, she turned to find the stairwell completely empty; the balloons had simply vanished into thin air.
- Mark Boccuzzi who heads Bay Area Paranormal Investigators, assisted by Scott Mossbaugh, co-founder, and five field technicians, Nancy Benson, Stacey Ellis, Ryan Morris and Lori and Jamie Fike performed a paranormal investigation of the building. The team "medium," felt numerous spirits in the building. She witnessed drunken men in the basement speculating about their fate. In the lobby she saw George Leger who is still keeping tabs on the hotel.. Finally, she witnessed a shy, thirties woman wearing Victorian clothing who asked if everything was all right. Boccuzzi recorded a column of energy on his tri field meter as the team performed an investigation.

The past is so imbedded within the walls of this historic hotel that it is no wonder the spirits find the place to their suiting; and so will you when you select the Leger as your next haunted vacation stop.

Monrovia
Aztec Hotel

Particulars
: 311 West Foothill Boulevard,
Monrovia, CA 91016
Phone: 626-358-3231
Fax: 626-359-9356
E-mail: info@aztechotel.com
Website: www.aztechotel.com

History

The bewitching Aztec Hotel is a National Register site situated along historic Route 66. The distinctive landmark building was constructed in 1924 by architect Robert Stacy-Judd who was inspired by Mayan and Aztec structures. This was his Stacy-Judd's first commission in America. He would later design the Masonic Temple in Tujunga, the First Baptist Church in Ventura, and the Atwater Bungalows in Elysian Park. The hotel has served as a hotel, speakeasy and bordello. During the 1930s, numerous stage and screen personalities spent time here, including: Fred Astaire, Errol Flynn, Clark Gable, Ava Gardner, Judy Garland, Katherine Hepburn, Gene Kelly, Janet Leigh, Peter Lawford, Frank Sinatra, Ginger Rogers, Red Skelton, Spencer Tracy and Esther Williams to name but a few.

Hauntspitality

According to Rob Wlodarski & Anne Wlodarski in their book, California Hauntspitality (2002), at least one female spirit haunts this historic hotel. Legend has it that a woman occupying Room 120 died while making love, accidentally hitting her head on the room heater. Since then, all of the rooms situated to the west of Room 120, have problems with the heating. Although the heaters in certain rooms are inspected and found to be in working order, guests have often complain of being chilled to the bone.

Recent conversations with long time employee, Wanda Lee Johnson, provide a different spin to the hotel's tragedy. Johnson said that after careful research, a woman named Jerry Lynn (also known as "Kitty") committed suicide in Room 120 in 1929 after a romance soured. This was during the time of Prohibition when the cellar of the building served as a speakeasy. Since Jerry's death, her specter has been frequently sighted or felt in the downstairs women's bathroom, at the foot of the stairs on the second floor, and walking or floating along the corridor near Room 120. Johnson said that by all accounts, the spirited female is not mean or angry; she is simply "stuck" in the building and occasionally appears to some of the guests and staff.

What is interesting is that the frequently sighted spirit of Jerry is always described in the same manner. She is witnessed as being quite beautiful, tall, around 25 years-old with light colored hair, and wearing a broad-rimmed hat, a long, tan-colored dress with pearl buttons, matching gloves and high heels. She is frequently seen walking near Room 120 before disappearing as well as standing at the top of the stairs leading to the room where her tragedy occurred prior to fading away in front of startled witnesses. There are also reports that come from guests frequenting the women's bathroom. There were some days when the air-conditioning was not working and it was in the hundreds outside, and every part of the hotel was sweltering, yet the woman's bathroom was so cold, people said it felt like being in a freezer.

There was another time when Wanda Johnson's husband was standing near the bathroom waiting for his wife that he suddenly was engulfed in a freezing circle of cold air followed by a tap on his shoulder. He turned around and there was no one there. Other times, the doors to the lobby will inexplicably open and close and there won't be a living soul in sight. There have also been reports of alarms being triggered in parts of the building that are unoccupied, and occasionally, lights will turn on or off unassisted. One recently interviewed resident claimed to see a shadowy female figure walk passed her bathroom door as she was about to step into the shower. When she went to see who had entered her locked room, it was empty (her room was 121, directly across from the "ghost" room).

An investigation conducted by the International Paranormal Research Organization (IPRO) in conjunction with San the Gabriel Valley Paranormal Researchers (SGVPR) on Saturday, November 15, 2003, produced numerous interesting anomalies. The group consisted of Rob Wlodarski, Matthew Wlodarski; Ginnie McGovern; Victoria Gross; Deann Burch; Christi Flowers, Alma Carey Robin Collier, Dan Larson; JoJo Wright; Neal Nisperos, Charles A. Coulombe, Gary V. Coulombe, Diane Melvin, Adrian Calderon, Dee Rivas, Jacob Strunk, David Betz, Richard Stouvenel and Laurie Fernandez. Using dowsing rods, Tri-field meters, gauss meters, tape recorders, EVP equipment, IR thermometers, digital and 35mm cameras and two VHS camcorders, the following results were obtained:

- The second floor seemed like a funnel for energy, and the basement had a strong feeling of death and secrets. There was a smell of alcohol and a sense that the area was used as a speakeasy and for gambling purposes.
- The ballroom energy was lighter, as if people were celebrating.
- The women's bathroom in the downstairs lobby was also a place of heavy, very active energy. Several people got the chills standing in the doorway. There was a definite sense of at least one female presence there.
- In room 120, there was a feeling of sadness, a senseless tragedy and personal drama.
- There were layers of drug abuse, prostitution, gambling, a flophouse, movie stars, Mafia, bikers, and homeless throughout the building.
- According to several psychics, the most intense areas were the rooms to the right, just off the lobby, just before entering the bar area. Kind of a waiting or sitting room, there were at least two spirits, an elderly male and younger female who were actually sitting down in two chairs. One of the psychics was conversing with the couple as high meter readings were observed and the dowsing rods pointed in the direction of the chairs. The spirits were aware of us, but not that concerned about us, except that we seemed to be disrupting their conversation, and repeatedly stepping in their energy fields. This annoyed them to no end.

- The bar area was also filled with a tremendous amount of energy.

Bright orb in the cellar courtesy of the International Paranormal Research Organization–IPRO)

- Several group members heard muffled conversations and felt male and female energy wandering throughout the bar area, passing from the kitchen, through the bar and into the lobby. It was as if an entire dimension filled with people co-existed along side. It was kinetic, frenetic and extremely draining.
- The second floor hallway seemed very active. Several investigators and psychics felt like they were walking right through unseen guests.

Psychics Ginnie McGovern, Christi Flowers and Deann Burch with orb above them (Courtesy of the International Paranormal Research Organization–IPRO)

- The current office, adjacent room and women's bathroom all had spikes on the meters and the dowsing rods verified that there was quite a bit of activity taking places. There is a lot of imprinted energy from past events, somewhat like a stream of energy that flows from the entrance in a path and then diverts toward the front desk, upstairs, toward the ballroom and toward the bar.
- The laundry room had a very low energy associated with it; what might be called "seedy." This area seemed to house a homeless or derelict energy. There was a sense of one or more deaths here or very near this area.
- A walk-through of the red room (Room 124) produced a sense of unhappiness and someone stuck here. It felt like a male energy that was not too happy with us being in there. He was very possessive of his space.
- The next room was a mustard-colored room (Room 122). This room instantly felt like a young woman was present inside. She did not seem confined to this room, and could easily pass from here to the adjoining rooms, indicating that she was not trapped but remained out of choice. One of the psychics sensed a prostitute.
- Room 120 was one of the strongest sensory rooms in the building. One investigator sensed that a woman died in the room and gave her the name "Kitty" because he heard several purring sounds, like a cat. This young woman had a sad life and was betrayed and possibly murdered. The meter readings on the bed were active as were the dowsing rods. She does not trust or like

Rope-like form on the bottom right of the photograph (Courtesy of the International Paranormal Research Organization–IPRO)

men. She seems to be benign and non-threatening, and is not a physically manipulating spirit. Several of the female psychics who entered the room became emotionally distraught. There was a noticeable electrical energy in the room, and several times people felt cold, tingly or warm.
- Across the hall in room 121, the green room, there was a sense of pain and anger. There was also conflicting feelings of love and happiness, perhaps indicating bleed-through from several occupation levels.
- Upon entering Suite A-7, the room seemed alive. It was electrically charged and several groupmembers sensed a female on the sofa and a male energy pacing near the bed. We did get some high meter readings near the sofa, bed

and closet area. Several times people reported getting orbs with their digital camera and feeling a tingling sensation in their arms and backs. The energy inside the room felt very friendly energy. The woman seemed to enjoy the room and liked looking out the window near the sofa, but she also seemed lonely. This was not an easy life, nor a life she envisioned for herself, but gave the impression that she was a trooper and stood by her husband's side. There was a sense of one or two children in the room, but this was not very strong energy. Only afterward, did we find out that the architect, who built the place and his wife, occupied the room while the building was being constructed.

- In the ballroom area, several psychics remarked that they sensed people dancing, bottles of champagne being popped, food being served, and people having a great time. This room emanated a strong party-like atmosphere. Several times, investigators remarked that they felt as if people were bumping into them, or they got an electrical charge or zap while standing in the room.

- The basement area was like walking into another world. The energy was unlike any other part of the building. There were reported smells of whiskey. There was a lot of activity here, but it was secretive and very controlled.

Strange rope-like anomaly in Robert Stacy-Judd's room (Courtesy of the International Paranormal Research Organization–IPRO)

Psychics sensed several layers of occupation down here, where ordinary people, celebrities and political people came from different time periods for different purposes. There was also a feeling that one or two people died in the basement. Once again, there were areas of high meter readings and several orbs were captured on tape. Several people felt as if they were being watched in the basement area. There were also periodic feelings of being chilled to the bone and of electrical energy passing through certain locations.

A dark mist in front of psychic Deann Burch at a 2nd floor room (Courtesy of the International Paranormal Research Organization-IPRO)

In conclusion, much more investigative work needs to be done here to isolate the various energies and dimensions that exist. There are several layers of occupation and energy that need addressing and energies that have to be moved out to create a better flow in the building. The imprinted energy is always there, making certain areas alive to people whom are the least bit sensitive to the paranormal. These areas where trauma or negativity has taken place will continue to affect the living, causing physical and emotional reactions to past events recorded or etched in the physical landscape. The active energy inside is equally strong and impressionable. Some of this energy is not positive; although at no point did anyone feel threatened. The Aztec is like a train station of souls; some souls are just passing through, while other forms are stuck in their trauma or negative past.

Electronic Voice Phenomena (EVP)

The playback of tape recorders yielded some interesting EVP as follows:

- In the ladies sitting room off the lobby you can hear a faint yet audible sound of a baby crying?
- In suite A-7 there is voice on tape saying: What!
- In the basement you could hear music being played, like from a jukebox, but there was no radio or any music playing anywhere nearby at the time.
- In the sitting room area next to the bar, several psychics sensed a phantom elderly man an woman sitting with the group. An investigator then asks the spirit to say its name, and as Ginnie asks Esther if we can take her picture before we leave, there is a discernable male voice on tape coughing or saying something in response.
- In room 120 the psychics sensed a female from the 1920s-1930s in the room who may have had an abortion. They get the name Violet. On the tape at counter #417, there is a sound like, yes or Hi? This is followed by a loud Ohhhh, can be heard on tape at counter number #421].

Digital and 35mm photographs

IPRO developed over 120 photographs inside the hotel. There were at least 15 photographs with large and small orbs, funnel-shaped forms, and transparent, large, orange blobs in the photographs:

Thanks to current owner Kathie Reece, The Aztec is undergoing a facelift that will lighten up the place and bring it back to a semblance of its glory days. As reports continue to manifest, it seems that Jerry is not the only spirit who calls the Aztec home. There are at least two other male energies and several females. Some say a few spirited children are also present. The ballroom, Room 120, the basement that used to be a speakeasy and several rooms on the 2nd floor are discernable paranormal hot spots. This is certainly one of the most haunted places in southern California.

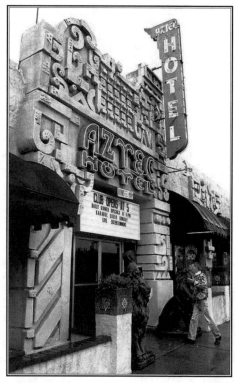

Montara

Goose & Turrets B&B

Particulars
835 George Street (mail: POB 370937)
Montara, CA 94037-0937
Phone: 1-650-728-5451
Fax: 1-650-782-0141
E-mail: rhmgt@montara.com
Website: http://goose.montara.com

History

The original building now housing the Goose & Turrets B&B, opened for business on April 15, 1908 as the Town Hall, post office, and general merchandise store operated by Lawrence J. Kent, the first postmaster. The building was designed by Will Sparks and built by M. A. Guynn. During August 6, 1927, the Spanish War veterans dedicated the Nelson A. Miles (General of the Army during the Spanish American War) Camp No. 10. A carefully preserved flag from those days still hangs in the house as does a photograph of the old boys.

The mortars flanking the main entrance were used on shipboard in that 1898 war and were donated by the Benicia Arsenal on Admission Day 1929. It was a well known fact that Montara Beach and Half Moon Bay were prime operating areas for rum runners during Prohibition, and nearby Devil's Slide was the favored dumping ground for bodies of those who got caught between dueling factions.

Also shoot-outs on the beach added to the gory count. During World War II, the captain of the artillery school on Montara Beach and his family and junior officers lived in what is now the Goose & Turrets. Grace Trimingham (Jepsen), a teacher at the Montara Grammar School and the only available single woman, remembers coming to parties here during that period.

After the war, a realtor named Mrs. Berger acquired the place, and local lore says she sold and resold it several times without ever divesting herself of the property. By 1965, Carl and Vivian Hess owned the property and lived here with their children, horses, and assorted pets. It was probably under this regime that the well planned gardens were established. Daughter Carla Hess remembers that her father rented the upstairs hall, which is now the Hoche-Mong's 2,200 plus square feet of living space (in the 1940s, the hall was host to illegal prize fights, and then was transformed into a church).

During the 1970s, the Hesses used much of the building as a nursing home. There is another cloudy period, when the building might have served as a nudist colony. In 1979, Marc Marcus, a local jazz musician, bought the place to use as residence, studio, and performance space. There were Sunday afternoon jazz concerts; art shows in the parking lot; and ballet lessons were given upstairs. A food co-op functioned in one of the six garages. Exercise classes were held in the large open spaces upstairs. Raymond and Emily Hoche-Mong purchased the 14-room house in 1983 and made it, first, their comfortable and spacious residence,

and, second, a friendly bed and breakfast.

Hauntspitality

According to the current owners, "They do not know the name of the ghost but they have a photograph of him in a group of war veterans found at the house taken on some special occasion with flags and decorations." According to management, the ghost is rather mousy looking, and guests who converse with spirits have told us that he is here because he has no other place to be and he was quite happy when he partied here.

The friendly spirit opens doors for one of the owners when she has her arms full of groceries, but, personally, she thinks he could do a little yard work too, in order to pay for his room and board.

One guest, who saw poorly, walked the wrong way from her room to her bathroom and happened upon our ghost and some other friends in the common area discussing the whereabouts of a missing friend. Excited, I asked if she could tell if the other ghosts were other men in the photo - she couldn't see well enough to know.

Over the years we are convinced that our ghost plays tricks. We will all, individually, search for a missing item - absolutely thoroughly. A couple of days later it will reappear in plain sight where we know we had already looked. I'm so grateful to have found whatever it is, that I'm not upset with our ghost. We have never named him.

We do know that he guards the house. No matter what is left open, unlocked, unclosed, etc., nothing ever disappears. Although he does not do yard work, he does move around the property making sure all is in order. We've been here 23 years, and for the first time we have marauding deer (there have always been lots up the road) - I certainly hope this does not mean our ghost has left.

Montara Beach and Half Moon Bay were prime operating areas for rum runners during Prohibition, and nearby Devil's Slide was the favored dumping ground for bodies of those who got caught between dueling factions. Also shoot-outs on the beach added to the gory count.

Monterey
Monterey Hotel

Particulars
406 Alvarado Street,
Monterey, CA 93940
Phone: 831-375-3184
Fax: 831-373-2899
Toll Free: 1-800-727-0960
E-mail: info@montereyhotel.com
Website: www.montereyhotel.com

History
Harry Ashland Green was an enthusiastic promoter of the Monterey Peninsula as a travel destination. Realizing that few could afford to stay at the elegant Del Monte Hotel, he envisioned a "European" style hotel convenient to the trolley cars, and in 1904 completed the Monterey Hotel. The hotel had gas and electric power, a cage elevator with gilt edging, the lobby had carved redwood ceilings and the staircase was of solid oak. There were twin dining rooms and a male only bar.

Originally, there were around 70 guestrooms, about one third of them with private baths. As late as 1924 a single room with a private bath ran for $2.50 a night. By the early 1960's the run-down building was converted into a residential hotel. In late 1982, Carl Johnson, the CEO of vintage Hotels stumbled on the inconspicuous doorway of the hotel and immediately saw the inherent beauty of the property. His painstaking reconstruction took almost three years and two million dollars to complete. In 1995 the building was once again sold. The current owner envisioned restoring the hotel to its original "European" splendor and in 1996 began renovation and complete interior redecoration. What you see now, is the former splendor of this vintage hotel brought to light; a restoration project that would have certainly pleased Harry Ashland Greens.

The architect, William Henry Weeks studied at the Brinker Institute in Denver, Colorado. In 1894, he settled his family in Watsonville. Weeks was appointed architect for the Spreckels Sugar factory, plus its manager's cottages, schoolhouse, and barns in 1897. By 1910, the architectural firm had grown to include his brother Hammond and Ralph Wyckff, and offices in Watsonville, San Francisco, Oakland and San Jose. Some of his buildings, such as the Speckles Sugar factory have been demolished, but others are still standing including: Goldstine Drygoods Store (now Plumes Coffee Shop); H.A. Greene Victorian (now Consuelo's Restaurant); Ordway Pharmacy Building (now Alvarado Mart Variety Store); Elks Lodge Building (now Regency Theater); A.R. Underwood Building (now J.C. Penny's); and the Carnegie Library (now MIIS Administration Office).

Hauntspitality
Is the Monterey Hotel haunted? Based on the following stories provided by General Manager, Maureen Doran, we're sure it's the only logical conclusion you can come to.
- Guests staying in Room 303 stated that their lights came on at 3:30 a.m. for no apparent reason.
- On or near Room 209, it has been reported that the privacy sign moves from

door to door. It is not witnessed first-hand, however, the guests in the room will swear they put out their sign, yet the next morning the sign will be on an unoccupied room door, nearby.

- Several housekeepers have reported crying coming from Room 315, although it is unoccupied.
- A front desk clerk, Vanessa Cavasotto, who was a non-believer until this incident, saw a man in the courtyard wearing a trench coat. She went to ask if he needed help, but no one was there.
- The General Manager, Maureen Doran, once spent the night in Room 402. While lying in bed trying to sleep, she felt a "presence" in the room. At one point she felt as if there was something right above her, almost close enough to touch. The feeling wasn't frightening, just very real. She was new at the hotel and was spending the night for the first time, trying to get a feel for the place; it was as if the spirits were checking out the new manager.
- A woman called Doran to ask if there had been any new sightings of ghosts at the hotel. Apparently, the woman had stayed there in 1998, at which time she witnessed a large female figure in pioneer clothing standing in front of her in the middle of the night. The woman told Doran that she closed her eyes for a second and then opened them and the figure was gone.
- Several front desk employees have occasionally witnessed apparitions out of the corner of their eyes while working the front desk. Whenever they turn to look in the direction of the spectral forms, they always disappear!
- One night, front desk employee, Charles Stagner, was cleaning up from the nightly milk and cookies, and saw a man wearing a blue mechanic-like uniform, dark blue pants and a red cap, walk towards the kitchen. Curious, Stagner followed the man into the valet area, but by then, the uniformed man had vanished. This is the most prevalent ghost at the hotel; a janitor named Fred.
- Lisa Cameron, a guest and an employee of Moonstone Hotels reported unusual activity when she stayed at the Monterey Hotel. Both experiences began with strange dreams, which made her awaken out of a deep sleep or feel like she was awake. The first experience occurred when she had a sleepless night in Room 309. At 3:30 a.m., she woke up and thought there was someone in the room; she could feel something moving around her. She then fell back to sleep again and the dream began again. Also, the ceiling light went on by itself in the middle of the night and woke her up.
- Guests have often reported strange sightings, feelings of being watched or followed and unexplained happenings, such as lights, ceiling fans and televisions turning on by themselves in the middle of the night on all floors of the hotel.

See for yourself if the stories about this historic hotel being haunted are true. Spend a night or two if you dare, and let us or management know what happened. It's a safe bet, even if you don't encounter a hotel spirit first hand, you won't leave disappointed

Stokes Restaurant & Bar

Particulars

500 Hartnell St, (Polk & Madison Sts),
Monterey, CA 93940-2802
Phone: 831-373-1110
E-mail: info@stokesrestaurant.com
Website: www.stokesrestaurant.com

History

With over 171 years of vibrant history, Stokes, is an adobe landmark in Old Monterey, that is the ideal backdrop for Chef Brandon's rustic food. The interior layout of booths and banquettes brings a subtle intimacy to the dining space. The stencil design and decorative painting by artist Daniel Peterson add an ethereal dimension to the building. His "distressed renaissance style of ornamental painting" bathes the building in the gold, sun-drenched warmth of an aged European villa. The following is a historical time line provided on their website:

1833 A single-room tile roofed adobe is built by Hoge and Benjamin Day;

1834 English sailor, James Stokes, arrives in Monterey. Stokes turns druggist and doctor and becomes consulting physician to Governor Figueroa;

1837 Bachelor Dr. James Stokes buys the property from Ambrose Tomlinson;

1840 James Stokes marries Josefa Soto de Cano, a widow with four children. They soon have two children of their own;

1844-1848 To accommodate his growing family, Stokes, enlarges the adobe into a handsome two-story house with seven rooms and a wing for the kitchen and store room. Although it was one of the more formal homes of the period, it still retained its architectural simplicity. Many of the town's social functions, such as Cascaron balls, were held in its sala. A stone wall is built to surround the house as well as several sheds, one of which is used to house the press producing California's first newspaper, The Californian. Besides his physician and druggist practice, Stokes serves as Mayor of Monterey and runs a general store in his home called Gran Barata. He acquires large land holdings in San Jose as well as around Monterey;

1855 Josefa Soto de Cano, Stokes' beloved wife, dies;

1856 Executors of the Stokes estate sell the adobe for $2,000 in gold to Honore Escolle, a Frenchman who came to Monterey when he was 21 years of age;

1856-1886 Escolle brings the oven from his unsuccessful bakery in the fashionable Washington Hotel onto the property and converts it into the first kiln in California, where he bakes his bread and other items for his bakery, as well as turkeys for his neighbors at Christmas time. Escolle imports a French artisan, Pierre Lambere, to assist him in making experimental pottery, which he sells at the Corner Store (now part of the Cooper-Molera Adobe);

1886-1890 The home is conveyed to Escolle's son-in-law, A.A. Manuel. James "Dick" Sargent purchases the Stokes adobe from Manuel;

1890-1948 Sargent's brother-in-law, Mortimer Gragg, purchases the home. Mortimer & Martha Harriet (Hattie) make the Stokes adobe the center of the social life of Monterey, until Hattie's death in 1948;

1950-1980 Mr. and Mrs. Gallatin Powers open Gallatin's Restaurant in Stokes Adobe quickly earning a reputation for warm hospitality and gourmet dining. The restaurant becomes one of the most popular destinations on the West Coast. Employees vow that the adobe is haunted by a man in the dress of the 1800s (Dr.

Stokes?). A persistent apparition of a beautiful woman in an upstairs room (Dona Josefa?) is also seen by employees;

1980-1984 Stokes Adobe remains vacant;

1984-1995 Various restaurants occupy Stokes Adobe. Stories of ghostly apparitions continue with the overall consensus that Hattie now haunts the Adobe;

1996 Kirk and Dorothea Probasco with Chef Brandon Miller open **Stokes Adobe Restaurant** on June 12, 1996;

2001 After extensive remodeling, painting and the addition of a wood-burning pizza oven, Kirk, Dorothea & Brandon reopen Stokes Adobe as **Stokes Restaurant & Bar.**

Hauntspitality

One thing is for certain, this restored 1840s adobe is haunted. The question is, how many spirits actually call the place their afterlife home. Since the death of Martha Harriet Gragg (Hattie), as she was affectionately called, in 1948, strange things have been reported inside. Although Hattie is considered one resident phantom, at least two others haunt the establishment. Some people say that the other spirits are James Stokes and Josefa Soto de Cano Stokes, the original owners, and other suggests that a child or two still remains in this historic home. Some of the stories provided by the establishment include:

- Employees during the 1950s-1980s swear that the adobe is haunted by a man in turn-of-the-century attire. Many people think it is the spirit of Dr. James Stokes
- Another apparition of a beautiful woman is frequently sighted by staff in an upstairs room. The resemblance fits the description of Dona Josefa Soto de Cano Stokes. She may be tending to her spirited children.
- During the 1980s-1990s, Staff begins reporting a phantom woman floating through the building that some believe to be prior owner, Martha Harriet (Hattie) Gragg. Hattie died while trying to save her house from foreclosure. Going through very hard financial times, Hattie committed suicide, her heirs sold her home and she felt betrayed; hence her restless spirit roams the building frustrated at any new owner who tries to make her home theirs.
- During the 1950s, a Monterey newspaper article described an event that took place inside late one night after the conclusion of a social gathering. According to the article, the restaurant had already closed when the owners stopped by for some champagne. As they were sipping the bubbly, they began hearing what sounded like several women talking upstairs. As the wife went to investigate, she heard women clearly talking in the apparently vacant room. Not dismissing the possibility of ghosts, she called out to the phantom females in Spanish, telling them that they were welcome to stay as long as they allowed the owners to have the restaurant back in the morning. As the story goes, she told her skeptical husband what had happened. Before leaving the building, she affectionately called out to one woman she called Carmencita asking for a sign if the woman could hear her. At that moment every crystal in every chandelier in the restaurant tinkled in unison. The husband never doubted the existence of ghosts after that.

- The music system inside had turned itself on in the early morning hours when the building was vacant.
- The figure of a woman climbing the main staircase has been witnessed by guests and staff alike.
- Disembodied footsteps have been heard upstairs when the space is unoccupied.
- Employees who reportedly took a nip or two during working hours said they were tapped, pushed or otherwise harassed by an unseen force.
- While workers were cleaning up after the restaurant had closed, they spotted a man in period clothing standing at the head of the stairs for a second or two before vanishing.
- On other occasions, staff has reported hearing babies crying upstairs, even though no one human was up there.

- Attendees of a social function witness a wine glass suddenly lift from a guest's hand and fly across the room. The glass landed without breaking.
- In the bar section of the restaurant, a candelabra slid across the piano in front of startled witnesses.
- Cold spots and sudden gust of cold air have been felt throughout the building.
- An obnoxious bartender didn't last long in the restaurant. Apparently, he treated customers without respect and received quite a few complaints. The spirits took care of the rest. After having glasses fly off the shelves, a large mahogany begin moving ominously on its own and crystals on a chandelier begin moving by themselves, the bartender quit on the spot.
- Some nights the windows will open by themselves and all the lights turn on inside even though there is no master switch. On one occasion, the police came when they thought someone had broken into the place. They called the owner who met the police outside. An officer with a key opened the door and went inside. He heard someone climb the stairs and went up after the culprit. The policeman chased the man through the banquet room and reached a smaller room. He stood outside the opened door and demanded that the individual surrender. At that moment the door slammed shut knocking the gun out of his hand. Reinforcements came, they forced open the door and no one was inside.
- When the place was called Bindel's restaurant, a staff person, while polishing some tableware in the banquet room, heard a woman crying. As he looked up, a woman in a long white dress appeared, actually spoke to the person, telling hem she was sad, and then vanished. The former owner believed that the spirit belonged to Evangeline Estrada. Evangeline's boyfriend, Juan, went of to war for statehood tand never returned. Her inconsolable spirit continues to reach out for him beyond the grave
- A lady wearing a long black gown has been sighting walking up the stair before disappearing.

As you can see (or often feel), this place contains a mother lode of spirits. Here, you can eat, drink and party with the spirited energy that makes this one of the most haunted historical eateries in California. In addition, you might try the Ghost Walk of Old Monterey. The tour concludes at the very haunted Stokes Adobe restaurant (www.montereyghostwalk.com).

Moss Beach
The Moss Beach Distillery

Particulars
Beach Way and Ocean Boulevard,
Moss Beach, CA 94038
Phone: 650-728-5595
Fax: 650-728-0220
Toll Free: 800-675-MOSS
Website: www.mossbeachdistillery.com

History

The restaurant is located at Moss Beach, south of San Francisco, on Highway 1, a few blocks west of Highway 1 on the corner of Ocean and Beach Streets. Since 1927 when it first opened its doors, the Distillery has been known by several names: Frank's Roadhouse; The Galloway Bay Inn; and finally, the Moss Beach Distillery. The Marine View Beach Hotel (now demolished) occupied a piece of land next to the Distillery. The Moss Beach Distillery, originally a hotel/house of ill-repute, was constructed on a steep cliff overlooking the Pacific Ocean during an era when Half Moon Bay was noted for being San Francisco's biggest supplier of contraband from Canada. The endless isolated coves and beaches provided perfect cover for clandestine activities which included bootlegging, hijacking, trysts, and even murder. Numerous movie stars, socialites, musicians, politicians, and underworld types frequented the Roadhouse during its heyday.

Hauntspitality

Hundreds of sightings have been reported at the restaurant and nearby beach, bluffs, and highway. Love and tragedy appear to have left a lasting imprint on the physical environment. The most talked about apparition is that of the mysterious "Blue Lady" who returns to haunt the cliffside restaurant. According to a newsletter put out by the Distillery, Bay area psychic Sylvia Brown conducted a séance at the Distillery for NBC TV's Unsolved Mysteries. During the evening, Brown contacted many spirits: Mary Ellen Morley (thought to be the "Blue Lady"), a victim of a car crash which occurred close to the area; her lover John Contina who was murdered on the beach below; another woman named Anna Philbrick who was involved in the love triangle with the Morley and Contina; and an elderly woman (possibly a Mennonite from the 1800s) named Hanna Elder who ran a house of ill-repute on the site of the Distillery and buried her still-borne child under the restaurant.

Historian June Morrall, however, thought the ghost may have been a regular customer back in the 1920s, when Moss Beach was a secret drop-off point for illegal whiskey. According to customers who frequented the Distillery during Prohibition, there was one mysterious woman who came every night wearing blue chiffon to hear the handsome young piano player. The woman was married, and as the story goes, their affair ended when the husband caught the two alone on the beach. The woman in blue was accidentally stabbed to death. Neither man stayed for questioning. Could this be the spirit of Anna Philbrick? Could the piano player who was subsequently murdered, be John Contina?

Former director of marketing, Jan Mucklestone, checked official records, and verified that Mary Ellen Morley was killed while driving an automobile along old Bayshore Highway on November 3, 1919 (she although earlier reports said her husband was driving). Before she died in her husbands arms, she asked him to take care of their young child, "Little Jack." Is she the "Blue Lady" everyone sees? Some believe that the ghost of the "Blue Lady" may instead, be Anna Philbrick. John Contina's spirit communicates through Morley, who related to Browne graphically how he died, and who killed him. Did a jilted Philbrick kill herself in the waters below the restaurant out of despair when she found out Contina loved Morley? Is all the activity at the Distillery related to Morley, Contina, Philbrick, and Hanna, or is more, as yet unidentified spiritual energy attached to this now famous restaurant for the living? There are other stories associated with the ghosts of the Moss Beach Distillery.

Over the years chefs, waitresses, managers, and patrons of the Distillery have heard the ghost of the "Blue Lady," and have witnessed her on a number of occasions. They have seen the young woman's phantom standing near the piano, outside the ladies' room, and dancing alone in deserted rooms. They occasionally hear their names whispered by some unseen presence when they are alone in the dining room or kitchen. Some employees feel a light tap on the shoulder or back, only to turn and be confronted by emptiness. A boy once ran screaming from the restroom, insisting that he was touched by a bluish lady covered in blood.

Managers working late at night would hear all the faucets suddenly come on, and they'd have to go to shut them off, when they returned to their office the door would be locked from the inside. Lights will frequently turn themselves on and off, frustrating managers and staff.

Neighborhood children have told stories of a woman in blue that chased them away from the nearby cliff, saying it was too dangerous to play there. A small boy while resting in a church pew in the Distillery hallway saw the Blue Lady in the dining area. Other young boys come out of the men's room asking their fathers why a woman dressed in blue is allowed into the men's bathroom---if she is Mary Ellen Morley, perhaps since she was separated from her child in a car crash, her spirit continues to protect the children in the area from coming to harm.

In 1978, two sheriff's deputies attended a séance along with several employees at the restaurant. Although there was an inexplicable cold spot, and a candle that suddenly ignited, no apparition was observed. The deputies left the restaurant at 3:30 a. m. and headed north on Highway 92, a notoriously dangerous road which wound through a twisting canyon. On a hairpin turn, the driver lost control, and flipped the car. Paramedics arrived and found both men not seriously injured. The next day, one of the deputies got a call from the tow-truck driver who picked up the car the previous evening. The driver asked one of the deputies how the pretty girl in the short blue dress fared. He saw her standing in the road crying and bleeding. The deputies swore they saw no one after their accident. Needless to say, the deputies never came back to the Distillery.

Pat and Dave Andrews, who owned the restaurant from 1972 to 1990, had a number of stories. One night Pat was doing the payroll, when her checkbook levitated off the desk and sailed around the office! Knowing the history of the building, she told the prankster to put the checkbook back, and the ghost complied. On a number of occasions, they closed the restaurant and returned to their rooms below the restaurant only to find them bolted from the inside. They had to crawl through the bathroom to get back in. Also, they heard strange and unexplainable noises drifting down the staircases from the floor above, including: The sounds of high heels walking along the restaurant floor; chairs and table being moved; and the sounds of a piano playing even though there is no longer a piano there. Every time they investigated they found nothing moved, and no doors or windows opened. Another ghostly prank included the bathroom shower which would turn on unassisted; obviously a clean spirit.

The spirit or spirits also love to play with the coffeepots, make the lights flickers, and generally make a ruckus upstairs. Candles would blow out, and then mysteriously relight hours later, and when a computer was installed to electronically track drink orders, orders for wine no one had typed in would appear on the screen; A long-time husband and wife cleaning crew were working downstairs late at night when everyone else had departed. They both heard what sounded like chairs being thrown around directly above them. Together they

crept slowly up the stairs to see what was causing the commotion---they found nothing out of place, and not a soul around. As they were going back downstairs, the sounds of boxes being moved could be heard in the rooms below. They cautiously checked the rooms downstairs, again, finding nothing out of place, and no one around. Another time, as the husband passed the ice cream cooler in the kitchen, the containers were spinning around by themselves. The husband also witnessed a table knife turning by itself on one of the dining room tables.

A waitress named Ruth recalled taking a drink order at table #3, was continually being tapped on her shoulder by an unseen hand. The third time she turned, again greeted by empty space, she noticed a local dog named Skip whose tail was caught in the back door. As she released the whimpering dog from its predicament, she realized that perhaps the taps from an invisible hand were meant to help her focus on Skip's situation.

After closing one evening, Dave Andrews ventured into the wine cellar to put some bottles of wine away. The room was neat and well organized. To prevent anyone from accidentally being locked in the chilly room, the wine cellar could only be locked from the inside. The following day, he returned to the cellar to stock the bar for the night but could not open the door---not even when help was summoned. Finally, Dave went around to the tiny window in the side of the cellar to see what was wrong. In stunned silence, he saw every bottle of wine in the cellar piled against the door, unbroken. The cellar window was too small for anyone to crawl through; except, perhaps a ghost!

The annual Thanksgiving dinner at the restaurant often included employees who didn't have a place to go; of course they always set a place for the Blue Lady. At one of the dinners a new waitress brought her four-year-old son. The boy ran into the bar area from the dining room after dinner, claiming a very pretty lady dressed in blue was standing in the room; of course she was gone by the time the adults went to check.

In February 1992, two waitresses saw a stool tip over and do a somersault! In August 1992, all the settings in the rest aurant's automatic thermostat system were mysteriously changed. The complicated reprogramming would have taken most people three or four hours to perform. The owner called the heating company, and they reported that the thermostat could not be changed manually; furthermore, the owner had the only access key. In 1993 and assistant manager had closed the restaurant down tightly. Locking all the doors, windows, double checking for good measure, he proceeded downstairs to do his book work--- it was after midnight, and he was positively alone. The restaurant's phone system includes an intercom, connecting the offices, and can only be used from a phone within the adjoining offices. For three nights in a row, the intercom to his office beeped. Each time the intercom rang after midnight, and each time the fearful assistant manager refused to find out who was on the other end of the call.

During another Thanksgiving celebration, waiter Sam Atwood stood alone next to the salad bar when he heard his name called out three times. Quickly looking in the direction of the voice, there was no one anywhere around who could have been playing a practical joke on him. On another occasion, when the waiter was putting up Christmas decorations, every bow and ornament fell down---nothing would stay in place. Deciding the effort was futile that day, he chose to try again the next day. Everything went up without a hitch---he surmised that the forces that be were not in the spirit the prior day;

After the restaurant entered the computer age, all point-of-sales-print-outs for transactions displayed the date and time. Once inputted, it is next to impossible to change. One night however, a frightened staff person reported that the computer date on the sales transactions were all dated "1927," the year the Blue Lady allegedly died. The owner calmed the employee and because no one could input the correct date, the computer company had to be called out the next day to repair the machine; no one could explain how it happened, except the spirits!

Jennifer Towner has been a waitress at the Moss Beach Distillery since 1988, believes that the Blue Lady is most active when skeptics challenge her existence. According to Towner, a waitress was rather flippantly telling a new hostess about the Blue lady when a chair by the hostess station flipped over all by itself---the Blue Lady apparently wanted to be taken seriously. Another time Towner remembers a waitress getting swatted in the behind with a spatula when she was in the kitchen, alone.

Another story involved a couple who were regular customers for a number of years. Although they never saw the ghost, they have come to believe in some strange force. The woman said she has lost four expensive earrings over the years, but only one from each pair. A few times, the couple would look around immediately after the woman noticed the earring was missing, while other times the staffed helped in the search. The end result was, the earrings were never found. Now, she wears only inexpensive jewelry when visiting.

After remodeling, and reopening in February, 1997, a number of events took place: One kitchen phone repeatedly had problems and had to be repaired four times within a two-week period; the back bar counter contains three bottled beer coolers, and only the day barkeep has a set of keys to open the coolers. She proceeded to unlock all three coolers, then left for a few minutes. Upon returning, two of the coolers had been locked. It took keys to open and lock the coolers, and she still had the keys in her possession; the rapid ringing of the seven phone lines (including the pay phone) one line at a time, occurred frequently, usually between 10:00 and 11:00 on weekends. When the phones were answered there was an immediate hang-up. After the first line hangs up, the second line goes through the same routine until all the lines have gone through the process. Now when this happens, each line is successively placed on hold which stops the ringing of all but the pay phone. When each line is taken off hold, the sound on the other end of the line is like an open extension, and occasionally a soft, unintelligible whisper is said to be heard on each line---the lines are not dead, only the person on the other end is.

On Sunday, April 13, 1997, Mike Cohen and Bill Gillespie were reinstalling a new Oasis machine in the downstairs bar set up area. Cohen removed the clear plastic top from the heavy unit to keep it from falling off as Gillespie lifted it into place. He placed the top of the bar sink counter immediately to his right, next to his right leg. Leaving the bar for about 15 minutes, both men returned to find that the plastic top was missing. The entire area was thoroughly searched by three people to no avail. Finally, a carpenter spotted the top wedged tightly in a corner below the front bar, between a compressor and the wall. It was impossible to have rolled there, and the place was very difficult to get to. Additionally the location had already been checked once before; it is as if the lid vanished, then materialized!

During May, 1997, Stephen Skogerson, a waiter, was standing at the waiters' station in the Torres Room (the Main Dining Room) at around 5:00 p.m. when a wine glass flew from the bar area, nearly missing his head. The glass, which came from a wooden nearby hanging rack, landed on the carpeted floor without breaking. There was no way given the way the glasses are stored (upside down and far back in the rack) that it could have accidentally fallen out and flown by Skogerson's head. Another waiter observed the phenomenon. In June of 1997, an employee, while closing up at 12:30 am, shut off the television and went downstairs to finish locking up. He returned upstairs to find the TV on again. Turning the TV off once again, he had left something downstairs and had to retrieve it. Once again he came back to find the TV turned on. This time, he heard a childish giggle. Making one final inspection of the place and satisfied that no one else was in the restaurant, he went home.

On June 5, 1997, Manager Ellen King was in the adjacent Cabaret Room with Bill Gillespie when she noticed a strange movement in the main entry foyer at around 7:00 p.m. A large Tiffany lamp above the host desk began swinging rapidly, while another, smaller Tiffany lamp situated a few feet away remained motionless. A paranormal investigator and psychic happened to be investigating the restaurant and filming for a ghost hunting segment of a television program called "The New Edge" when the event took place. Both individuals, with special equipment on hand, picked up on a presence situated directly beneath the lamp. The entire event lasted for approximately 30 minutes before gradually subsiding. The "swinging" Tiffany lamp is said to be an original dating to the early days of the restaurant, while the other Tiffany lamp is a reproduction.

On June 9th, King closed and locked the restaurant for the night. When King left, all the lights were off, but because she forgot to clock out, she had to return. After closing up once again, King was about to get into her car. She then noticed that the antique Tiffany lamp in the main foyer had been turned on. She did not go back in to turn it off.

A visit to the Moss Beach Distillery will not only provide you with an incredible view of the ocean, and a sense of history, but an opportunity to use your sixth sense and see of the spirits of this historic hot spot.

Moss Landing
Captain's Inn at Moss Landing

Particulars
P.O. Box 570,
Moss Landing, CA 95039
Phone: 831-633-5550
E-mail: res@captainsinn.com
Website: www.captainsinn.com

History

The Pacific Coast Steamship Company building was constructed in 1906 following the San Francisco earthquake. The Castro family received the property in a land grant. Later in 1868, the property was owned by Charles Moss, the town's namesake, and Donald Beadle (both in shipping). The Pacific Coast Steamship Company purchased the property in 1881 and built the two story structure. The Pacific Coast Steamship Company was sold in 1917 to the Pacific Steamship Company run by John Scudder. The Capurro Family owned the property in the mid-1900s and used it as a family residence. The York family established the Moss Landing Harbor Chapel here and regularly held church services in the building. In more recent years, the building has been home to countless Moss Landing Marine Laboratories students.

The building was originally constructed as an office building with six individual offices and a parlor. In later years one office became a kitchen, with a dining/laundry nook added later, along with a narrow bathroom. The simple colonial revival style is in vernacular pyramid cottage form used just after the turn of the century in "company towns". The porch front is simple Tuscan order. The two downstairs front windows are Queen Anne cottage style. The simple fireplaces include bricks salvaged from damaged buildings in the 1906 earthquake made by the Santa Fe masonry. This building has been fully renovated and recently opened as a bed and breakfast in by Captain Yohn and Melanie Gideon. The effort to save this building has been awarded a historic preservation award from the Moss Landing Chamber of Commerce. In the back, a boathouse with guestrooms has been added. This building takes advantage of views of wildlife and the marshlands.

Some interesting tid-bits about the house include: Much of the lumber had the Pacific Coast Steamship Company Stamp on it. Nearly all the lumber is old growth redwood and the original floors are Douglass fir. A piece of the original wall can be viewed in the Inn's upstairs Chart room. Many of the original 1906 carpenters autographed the back of the lumber and trim boards. The owners have preserved their signatures and returned them to their locations in the building. Many, many

couples have been married here. Weddings were held when there were families, when it was a church, and now as an Inn. Some of these couples have come to the Inn for anniversaries and tell us of their stories. There used to be a harbor seal in residence here. It used the redwood staircase to go to its favorite room, the bath tub upstairs. Finally, the owners found many interesting items in the walls and cubbies when we renovated. The "finds" include a handwritten love letter, children's black and white school photos, 1912 business journal, 1940 Easter candies, milk bottle caps, a silver spoon, 1908 Christmas card, and more; some are on display in the dining room.

Hauntspitality

When we solicited the owners about whether their inn was haunted, we received this kind reply, While we do not much believe in ghosts ourselves nor ever experienced one while here, we had a visit to our inn by a medium who located a spirit with a sense of humor. She said his name was "Wallace" and that he had been an accountant for the company who first occupied the building (originally the Pacific Coast Steamship Company building built over 100 years ago). In his life he had been very serious, always working, and saving for fun in the future... someday. Unfortunately the someday had never come for him, and he had died while hard at work late one night of a heart attack. She said he was now having the fun he had missed during his life, she claimed she could hear his giggles, and that he was always in the North West corner of the building where he was assigned an office when working."

Continuing, the owners said, "The unnerving part was some of the stories she told about the pranks this spirit bragged about pulling on us. She said he laughed about a cookie fire and the magic wall by the attic stairs, and the coke spill. While taken on their own these little comments may seem empty, but this medium had never been here nor met us before. We immediately thought of three events:

- During our very first inspection from a rating guidebook, the batch of cookies we were baking burned terribly, although they had only been in the oven for five minutes. I was panicked. This could have been a disaster for our inspection, but the vent fan handled it. Was this Wallace giggling as we rushed around to contain these blackened cookies?
- During construction renovation of the inn we installed a spiral staircase to the attic. The medium never saw nor knew of these stairs. This required putting in a new wall. The poor contractor would measure and measure and then put in the wall. He would then try to install the stairs, but the space was too small. He would tear out the wall and moved it after re-measuring; yet again the stairs would not fit. He was miserable because the wall had plumbing pipes that had to be redone too. In all it took four tries!
- There is a spot in our library room on the carpet that appeared before we ever had guests, it cleans easily, but is always reappearing, so we clean it again. Oddly enough all these events happen in the same corner of the house, and I can almost imagine this "Wallace" giggling at his practical ghost jokes.

The owners have since blamed Wallace for the little mistakes that occur in the building that seem to have bad timing, like the breakfast that slid onto the floor while all the guests gawked; the wine glass that spilled during the wedding toast, or the salt shaker that goes missing as soon as someone asks for it. When things go awry, the owners can conveniently blame the humor filled spirit, Wallace. As the owners humorously concluded, "Luckily, his house corner does not include any guest rooms."

The Captain's Inn at Moss Landing earns 3 Diamond Distinction in hospitality and one platinum star for hauntspitality. The primary goal at Captain's Inn is to provide visitors with a charming seaside retreat that showcases the warmth and hospitality of Moss Landing. They also provide the additional amenity of a spirit with a sense of humor.

Murphys
Murphy's Historic Hotel & Lodge

Particulars
457 Main Street,
Murphys, CA 95247-9628
Phone: 209-728-3444
Fax: 209-728-1590
Toll Free: 800-532-7684
E-mail: reservations@murphyshotel.com
Website: www.murphyshotel.com

History

The Murphys Hotel was first opened in the summer of 1856 by James Sperry and John Perry, and was known for many years as the Sperry & Perry Hotel. The hotel thrived as the natural stopover for Matteson's Stage en route from the railhead at Milton to the Calaveras Big Trees, which had just been discovered by A.T. Gus Dowd in 1852. The grove of giant sequoias was one of the greatest natural wonders of the nineteenth century, attracting people from all over the world. Mercer Caverns, discovered in 1885 by Walter J. Mercer one mile away from the hotel, also enticed many visitors to the area, as did the rich gold diggings.

Notable guests who stayed at the Murphys Hotel during its early years include Mark Twain, Horatio Algiers Jr., John Jacob Astor, Thomas J. Lipton, J.P. Morgan, and former President Ulysses S. Grant. Copies of the original registration signatures of these notables may be viewed today in the hotel's lobby. The original register now resides at the Calaveras County Museum in San Andreas.

Fire destroyed most of downtown Murphys and damaged the hotel in 1859. The hotel was protected because of it's stone construction and iron shutters, and was restored and reopened in 1860. The hotel was operated by a succession of owners over the next 100 years, undergoing two name changes, first to the Mitchler Hotel and then, in 1945, to the Murphys Hotel. In 1963, a group of 35 investors purchased the hotel. Former University of the Pacific students, they had been coming to the hotel since 1942 as members of the informal Murphys Ale and Quail Club, and called their investment group the "Murphys Ale and Quail Corporation." Numerous improvements were made to the facility over the years, including the addition of the two motel wings just west of the original structure.

In 1978, several original members as well as two new investors formed a new corporation called MAQ, Inc. The group achieved a listing for the hotel on the National Register of Historic Places. In 2003, long-time Calaveras county resident Dorian Faught became only the sixth owner of the Murphys Hotel. Under Faught's careful guidance, additional enhancements and improvements to the hotel are being made, with close attention to preserving the character and feel of this very historic facility.

Almost 150 years after it first opened, the Murphys Hotel still hosts travelers touring the central Mother Lode region, while also functioning as the true center piece for the downtown Murphys business community. Local fraternal, service, and professional organizations use the hotel for their monthly meetings, and the hotel regularly hosts seminars, retreats and board meetings for a number of state associations, cities and other organizations from outside the area. The Murphys Hotel is not simply a preserved relic of the nineteenth century. Rather, it proudly continues its long-standing tradition of serving the needs of its community and travelers from around the world.

Hauntspitality

Since the hotel is the second oldest, continuously operating hotel in the United States, there is little wonder that the spirits of former occupants have often been sighted. According to management and staff, the second floor of this establishment seems to be the most intense as far as paranormal activity goes.

Those who have spent time on the second floor have reported witnessing misty apparitions, unexplained footsteps, doors opening and shutting, lights which seem to have a mind of their own, and cold spots that seem to materialize within seconds, engulfing staff and guests alike.

Based on several eyewitness accounts, the image of Black Bart has been sighted numerous times, floating along the second floor hallway, always eluding those who follow in hot pursuit. Black Bart appears as elusive in death as he was in life.

Other unidentifiable noises and shadowy figures that have been described as both male and female, greet guests visiting Murphys, although none are harmful. According to Murphy's Law, if there are such things as spirits, you'll find them at the hotel when you least expect it.

Napa

Napa River Inn

Particulars

500 Main Street,
Napa, CA 94559
Phone: 707-251-8500
Toll Free: 1-877-251-8500
Fax: 707-251-8504
Website: www.napariverinn.com

History

The Napa River Inn built in 1884, is situated within the Historic Napa Mill, and is listed on the National Register of Historic Places. This area of Napa entertained commercial activities prior to the 1847 founding of the town. The Mill contains restaurants, cafés, an art gallery, jazz club, chocolate shop, spa, and many outdoor dining areas. The Hatt/ Napa Mill Buildings are the last vestiges of the once thriving Main Street industrial and commercial center of the late 1800's and early 1900's Napa City. The lives and times of owners, workers and community are imprinted within their walls. By 1879 the first warehouse built by Captain Albert Hatt was located on Fourth, Main and Brown Streets. Hatt gradually outgrew that warehouse.

During 1884, Captain A. Hatt built a large brick warehouse at the foot of Main Street. The building was two-stories high with and asphaltum floor. The brick for the building was made on-site with materials from the Napa River. Within the building was a skating rink which became the scene of frequent social events. The rink was also used as a basketball court and gym by the Napa Lookout Athletic Club. By 1887, Hatt added another two-story building to his warehouse. The first floor was a warehouse with corrugated iron covering the roof. The second floor was eventually named Hatt Hall, intended for secret societies, including the Unity Lodge, No. 3 and Royal Argosy. In later years, the hall served as the armory. It contained a dining room, library and an anteroom. During 1893, Hatt added another section to his warehouses creating a complex, which extended to the western bank of the Napa River.

Captain Hatt's wife Alma (Hogan Hatt) died in January 1898, after which, Hatt incorporated his business as The A. Hatt Warehouse and Lumber Company. The daily operation of the business became the responsibility of Albert Hatt, Jr. The A. Hatt Company business continued to supply coal and other commodities to Napa County agencies, businesses and residents for several more years. Then, following Albert, Jr.'s suicide, Captain Hatt sold the business to the Robert Edward Keig.

Albert Hatt (top), and Albert Hatt Jr. who committed suicide

273

On June 9, 2000 at 4:00pm the Napa River Inn, welcomed the first guests of the hotel, Mr. & Mrs. Gary Bennett of Napa. The Embarcadero Building located on Brown Street, which replaced one of the old warehouses across from the Napa Library on Brown Street and on the riverfront of Captain Hatt's steamship dock. Containing 26 rooms designed with an elegant yacht in mind, featuring a cheery theme of yellow in the wall coverings and furnishings with cherry wood wainscoting, coffered paneling and brass bathroom fixtures.

Hauntspitality

A Travel Channel special that aired during October 2002 entitled Haunted Hotels, brought to light the haunted nature of this beautiful, historic place. According to rumors that were circulating after renovation, the spirits of Albert Hatt Jr. was believed to be the primary phantom.

According to history, the new century at first appeared to be a time holding promise and happiness for Albert Junior's family. Sadly, that promise was unfulfilled when Margaret Riley Hatt developed a serious medical condition in late 1905. Around October of that year she underwent surgery to remove a tumor at St. Winifred Hospital in San Francisco. Margaret seemed to be on the mend by early 1906. Then while visiting her step-mother, Mrs. John Riley, in San Francisco on March 21 Margaret became critically ill and had to be rushed to St. Winifred's. For about a week, the doctors attempted numerous medical procedures, including another surgery, to save her. But it was all for naught as Margaret died on Thursday, March 29, 1906 at 8:30 p.m.

Courtesy of Matt

According to her obituary in the Napa Weekly Journal dated April 6, 1906, Margaret was survived by more than one child. They were: Madie, Muriel, Bert, William and of course Cyril. Margaret was buried within the Hatt family plot at Tulocay Cemetery. Also according to the obituary, Margaret was 40 years and 2 months old at the time of her death.

Now a widower with five young children to care for, Albert Jr. did his best to continue living his life, provide for his family and live up to his father's expectations. Sadly, however, issues of failing health continued to plague Albert Hatt Jr. Faced with declining health and business troubles, Albert, Jr. took his own life. On April 1, 1912, at the age of 46, he committed suicide by hanging himself from the beam within the family's warehouse. He too was buried within the Hatt family plot at Tulocay Cemetery in Napa. As for his orphaned children, they were taken in and cared for by his sisters. And from all indications, they went on to live normal lives.

Captain Albert Hatt, Jr. who hanged himself in what is now a bakery is reportedly the primary spirit in the building. His wife Margaret is also rumored to haunt the inn. Staff and guests have spotted the couple wandering the hallways before vanishing. Those two spirits are not the only ones who greet guests. Apparently Robert Keig, who died in 1975, is also a spirited suspect.

Two of the paranormal hotspots in the establishment are Room #208, above Sweetie Pie's Bakery, and Room #207. One woman said she heard the doors to both the rooms open and slam shut, even though the hotel staff confirmed that those rooms were unoccupied at the time.

Newspaper correspondent Kathleen Dressen wrote an article on March 21, 2004 about the ghosts of the inn. When Dressen asked the General Manager about the ghost who haunts the building, the reply was a nonchalant, "Which ghost?" Reliable witnesses have come forward over the years with numerous tales about two male spirits, a female phantom and possibly a child ghost or two. One of the more spectacular sightings is that of Albert Hatt Jr. who hanged himself from a beam in the warehouse on April 1, 1912 in the area now occupied by Sweetie Pies Bakery. People have witnessed his body swaying from the rafter one minute, then gone the next.

Strangely, the paranormal sightings in the building were not of Hatt, but of a Lady in White. The stories always seemed to be the same. People claimed to see a young woman in a white dress wandering the hallways in search of something or someone before vanishing. Could it be Margaret, who loved her husband, but died of a tumor, leaving her distraught husband with a broken heart and five children to manage? There are plenty of other unusual events that occur in the building including:

- One guest complained that someone continually turned off the fireplace in her room, making it freezing cold.
- Another guest from University of California Davis got so cold in the room that it became unbearable.
- The hotel's maintenance engineer set up pictures for a celebration for the Napa River Inn being named in the National Trust of Historic Hotels. While in the storeroom, cleaning his painting supplies in a deep sink, plastic glassware bins near where he was standing suddenly flew off the shelves.
- Otis added that he felt no malevolent force.
- A security guard and night auditor would be in the building by himself when the elevator kept going up and down. The elevators can not go up by themselves. He has also walked down the hallways and had the hair on the back of his neck stand on end.
- A guest put her clothes in a drawer, closed it and turned away. When she turned back around, the drawer was wide open.
- Another guest who kept coming back said she heard a dress swish down the hallway. Then a door opened right across the hall in #208 (Room 208 is directly above Sweetie Pies, where Capt. Hatt reportedly hanged himself) and shut by itself. This was followed by the sound of heavy footsteps make their way down the hall toward room #208, yet no one could be seen. A door to room #207 at the end of the hall opened and closed with a lot of force.
- During November 2003, the Napa Valley Register published John Ingram's Letter to the Editor. Ingram, a Napa resident, related an experience his friends have while visiting the hotel for the first time. According to Ingram, The couple encountered a man coming down the stairway and asked him the location of the restaurant. The man said, "This is no dining establishment, this is Napa

Milling and I'm the owner, Robert Keig." After they walked past him, they noted a "distinct smell of hay and grain." When they turned around, he had vanished. Later, they saw a photograph of Robert Keig, who purchased the Mill from Captain Hatt in 1912. "They went ballistic," reported Ingram. "The man in the photo was the man they encountered on the stairs that night."

- A reporter who stayed at the inn started to explore the building, just to get a feel for the place. As she walked into the Hatt Hall, a large ballroom, she heard a heavy dress sway down the hall. She was sure that someone unseen was with her in the Hatt hall. A very cold breeze passed right by her more than once during her time in there.

- Another guest stated, "My husband and I, along with our good friends stayed one night at the Napa River Inn.. The room was great. We retired very early and that is when we had a slight problem. Someone in the room above us paced all night long [even though the room was vacant]!

- People continue to report loud disembodied footsteps, invisible people banging on the walls, a elevator goes up and down by itself, unexplained voices and smells, rapidly materializing cold spots, photos with orbs, apparitions, and an uneasy sense of being watched or followed.

At the Napa River Inn, you have to take your Hatt off to the spirited clientele. This is one visit you'll never forget; one where the spirits try and keep you on your toes and a very thin veil separates the past from the present.

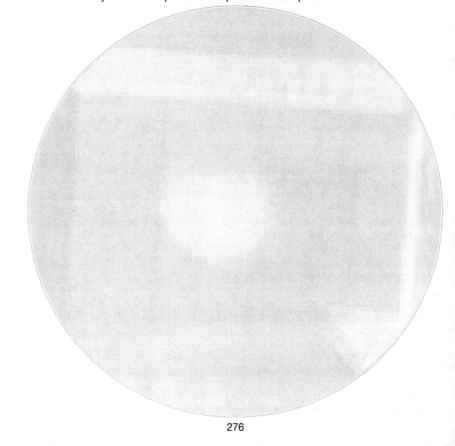

Villa Romano Restaurant of Napa Valley

Particulars

1011 Soscol Ferry Road,
Napa, CA, 94558
Phone: 707-252-4533
E-mail: romano@napanet.net
Website: http://www.villaromanorestaurant.com
E-mail: romano@napanet.net

History

Businessman Elijah True built the Soscol House in 1855. He located the inn on the north side of the junction of the county road (today's Highway 29) and the Old Ferry Road (now named Soscol Ferry Road). The inn was a two-story "L" shaped structure with wood lath siding and contained eleven bedrooms upstairs. Downstairs, there was a dining room, gambling room, and a bar. It was an inn typical of its time, with the wife and children helping in the daily operations.

By 1872 the Soscol House was a "liquor saloon" that was run by Elijah True. In July 1905, the "Vallejo, Benicia and Napa Valley Railroad Company" opened an electric line, which ran from Benicia through Napa to Lake County. A 1913 timetable notes the Soscol stop, next to the Soscol House, as a "flag" stop. The Soscol House continued to serve the traveler as a "saloon" in the early 1900s, as a "roadhouse" in the 1940s, and as a "dining room" in the 1950s, and then later as an antique shop.

The building has been altered several times by successive owners, having had some parts removed and other parts added, but it has retained some of its original character and appearance. The Soscol House was finally moved to its current location on the old Patwin Village site. Today the restored building serves as the Villa Romano Restaurant of Napa Valley.

Hauntspitality

This County Landmark and National Register building has a storied history.

When an archaeological investigation in 1978 uncovered, stage coach tokens, bullets imbeddved in the floor boards, signs of gambling and prostitution, the group also got a glimpse of the past through it's spirited residents. During the excavation, the building was temporarily moved down the road from its original location, awaiting a new home. While the intermittent rains played havoc with the investigation, it also provided an opportunity for several of the archaeologists to explore the house. Although it was basically gutted, it was

still a formidable building, with creaky stairs, numerous sectioned rooms, bullet holes in the floor and rusty square nails protruding from the beamed floors, walls and rafters. It was a spooky building, and there were many times when you could feel that you were being watched by unseen eyes. There were times when you could hear people talking upstairs when it was unoccupied.

On one occasion we heard a woman's voice cry out from the downstairs area when several of us were upstairs. Running down the rickety stairs, thinking someone was in need of help, we were astonished to find the place deserted. It wasn't the wind playing tricks on us, because there the air was deathly still. The voice however, seemed a little unearthly as we reflected on the cry. Only people who have heard a voice from beyond can understand that the intonation is not quite like you and I talking.

On another occasion, someone saw a tall, thin, middle-age man walk through one of the downstairs walls, as if there might have been a door there at one time. It was a fleeting glimpse out of the corner of the person's eye. It was a little unnerving but by now we were getting used to paranormal events taking place. While excavating the area where the Soscol House once stood, we stayed in a very haunted building adjacent to the site of the former house. Things would happen inside all the time. So, visiting the old house, and having paranormal events take place got to be normal. Still the sight of someone walking by, who looked real, and then just walked through a wall was a little creepy. One person said he was grabbed from behind, while another person heard footsteps go up the stairs. Following right behind the heavy, pounding clomping sound, there was no one in sight.

Even after the restoration process was completed, people still felt that the place is haunted. There were the disembodied footsteps, an occasional glimpse of a shadowy figure, unexplained voices and cold spots and the feeling of being watched or followed. The spirits in the establishment are friendly and the food is to die for. It's a great place to visit and experience Napa spirits firsthand.

Nevada City
The Red Castle Inn
Historic Lodging

Particulars
109 Prospect Street,
Nevada City, CA 95959-2831
Phone: 530-265-5135
Toll Free: 1-800-761-4766
E-mail: stay@redcastleinn.com
Website: www.redcastleinn.com

History

One of California's premier bed and breakfast Inns, the 1857 landmark brick mansion was built by an Illinois businessman John Williams (who became a lawyer) and his son Loring Wallace, for his wife Abigail. John and Abigail Williams with their son Loring Wallace crossed the Great Plains by wagon in 1849 to stay with relatives in Napa. Abigail taught school there while John and Wallace came to Nevada County in search of gold. The men located claims at Caldwell's Upper Store, later named Nevada City. Mining the nearby streams at Deer Creek and Gold Run brought enough of the precious metal to enable them to purchase property and build two ranches on Gold Flat where

Abigail joined them and Wallace married a neighbor named Caroline Humes. John developed Nevada City's first water company. Loring became District Attorney, Squire Williams a town governor, the family prospered and eventually their business and mining ventures kept the men in town more and more. The time had come to fulfill John's long held back dream and in 1857 he began to build the tall brick mansion on the crest of Prospect Hill that would be their town house. It stands today as a monument to those who came to California lured by the promise of easy riches, but unlike most emigrants who returned to their homes "back in the states", stayed to civilize and build a new state, leaving a tangible legacy in the state landmark known today as The Red Castle Inn.

Abigail, who loved children (she had two, Loring, and a baby girl who died in childbirth), later in life, adopted several of them. The house is the only authentically preserved Gothic Revival building in Nevada City's Historic District. The 4,000 square feet mansion had four stories, sixteen rooms, two master bed rooms (for John and Abigail, Loring and Cornelia Elizabeth Humes), a formal parlor, and verandah. A governess and staff were also an integral part of the daily functioning of the mansion. Williams was 68, when he passed away on February 8, 1871. Loring followed John Williams to the grave in 1874, leaving two widows behind. The funeral services for both father and son were held at the same time and day of the week, three years apart, in the mansion. The death of both men signaled the demise of the property. Cornelia Elizabeth died unexpectedly on June 18, 1883. Abigail could not afford the house, and sold it. Before it sold, however, the governess died in the house. The home was purchased by Jim Schaar in 1963, who set about to restore the building.

Hauntspitality

The benevolent "Woman in gray," possibly the Williams' nanny, is rumored to wander the building, frequently seen or felt by staff and guests, particularly in what used to be the former children's quarters. The red brick house that dates back to 1860 is known for ghostly activities. Lady in Gray, looks just as real as you and I; until she floats right through a solid door before your eyes. When the atmosphere is right at the Red Castle Inn, people say that the ghost of a young governess might watch over you at night. The phantom lady reportedly smoothes the hair off your face, like you would to a sleeping child, tucks you in, pulls the sheets around your shoulders. At the inn, misplaced objects and a heavy drawer that won't stay closed are blamed on the ghost.

Several spirits make the Red Castle Inn their home. One of the frequently sighted apparitions is believed to be John Williams, his wife, Abigail, and their governess who is referred to generically as, the "Lady in Grey." Workman who assisted in the renovation of the mansion constantly remarked of the uneasy feeling that someone was watching them. It turned out, that one day, the invisible people had felt for a long time, materialized. The workman described an elderly spirit wearing a black frock coat, similar to what a judge would wear, watching him as he was working, as if inspecting the progress. The spirits of the Red Castle also play tricks on just about everyone. No one seems immune from the pranks of the ghosts, which include objects frequently being moved from one part of the house to another. A strange man was sometimes sighted outside the house in period clothing by guests, only to vanish as they called for help. In fact, the unearthly man was spotted on a snowy evening, standing outside. When the guest went to investigate, they no only didn't find the man, but there were no footprints left in the snow. The "judge-like" man has been spotted by guests, just passing through before disappearing.

On one occasion, a guest was rudely awakened from a peaceful slumber by the feeling of pressure on his legs. As he lifted himself to a sitting position, the weight seemed unbearable. Suddenly he caught a glimpse of a youthful woman standing in the room. The woman yelled out for "David," and instantly, the pressure was lifted. It was as if a child was sitting on the man's legs one minute, and then after being scolded, jumped off. Another guest after a New Year's party retired to her bed. She was not alone. As she was about to nod off, she watched as her door opened, and a woman wearing an 1800s Victorian gown entered the room holding a dog. The female guest described the woman as looking grey. As the guest sat up, the spectral woman sat on the edge of the woman's bed petting the dog, and carrying on a one-person conversation for a minute, then said a few more kind words before leaving the room. The following morning the guest asked about the strange woman in Victorian dress, and was told that she had been visited by the Gray Lady; a ghost.

The Gray Lady is oftentimes sighted on the fourth floor, when she tended to the children in life. However, she has also been sighted in other rooms, and on other floors along with the spirit of John Williams. A spectral, Civil War soldier has also been spotted, although less frequently than the other ghost guests. The spirits have played with the lights; visited guests in their rooms; been responsible for unexplainable footsteps throughout the house; materialization's; moving objects; opening and closing doors; inexplicable voices echoing through the mansion; and a variety of other paranormal activity. All these playful spirits seem to have one goal, to make your stay at the Red Castle Inn, an unforgettable one; after all, to most of them, it's still their home, and you are their guest.

Newport Beach
Anthony's Riverboat Restaurant / Ruben E. Lee

Particulars

151 East Coast Highway,
Newport Beach, CA 92660
Telephone: 949-673-3425

History

The building was constructed in 1963/1964 as a combination of Ruben's Restaurant and the Robert E. Lee ship on the Mississippi. The building was supposedly constructed by a man who owned Rubens restaurant, loved the Robert E. Lee and attempted to replicate the ship as a home for his three new restaurants (San Diego, Cincinnati and here in New Port Beach). Essentially, he combined Rubens with the Robert E. Lee and came up with the Ruben E. Lee. The Ruben E. Lee Restaurant closed down in 1983, and was eventually turned into a Nautical Museum/restaurant/shops/ convention space. Over the years the restaurant has changed names many times. Its latest incarnation is Anthony's.

Hauntspitality

Members of the International Paranormal Research organization (IRRO) were invited to conduct an investigation of Anthony's as well as other areas aboard the Ruben E. Lee docked in Newport Beach. The investigation took place on Friday, September 5, 2003 and involved Robert J. Wlodarski, Matthew Wlodarski, Ginnie McGovern, Victoria Gross, Deann Burch, Dan Smith and Robin Collier. The paranormal summary follows;

- Upon entering the building to the south of the restaurant occupied by the nautical museum, there was an immediate sense of a man in his 40s-50s who was attached to the ship because of the current exhibit. The dowsing rods confirmed that man was Duncan Gleason, whose exhibit was on board at the time of the investigation.
- A query using the dowsing rod, also confirmed that there was a man in his 30s-40s who considered the entire

Haunted Hallway (Courtesy of the International Paranormal Research Organization – IPRO)

building his, although he particularly enjoyed the restaurant area and third floor of the ship. He was extremely curious and may have worked on board during the 1960s and lived nearby. The sense was, that this man died off the ship, but came back because he spent so much time on board in life. He appeared to be a former cook/chef, or waiter. He is constantly moving around, as if in a hurry and rarely seems to stay put. He was about 5-6" to 5-8" but quite a proud man with dark receding, hair. He hated when things were not being the way "he" liked them, and would move items around all the time. He enjoyed the music, but didn't have time to stand around, as he had things to do. This man is constantly on the go.

- There was another spirit or energy on board. He seemed disoriented, scattered

Although the ship is of recent origin, it has plenty of spirits to keep visitors occupied. By our count, there were at least 3-4 active spirits who were primarily male. The restaurant had its share of energy, but the spirits were not confined to this are of the ship and moved around as they pleased. The next time you have dinner at Anthony's, keep an eye out for a former chef, a frustrated male singer and while touring the ship, for other specters that are floating about with the tide.

Haunted stairs (Courtesy of the International Paranormal Research Organization – IPRO)

Oakhurst
Sierra Sky Ranch

Particulars
50552 Road 632,
Oakhurst, CA 93644
Country Lodge Reservations: 559-683-8040
Steakhouse & Saloon, 559-658-2644
Fax: 559-658-7484
E-mail: skyranch@sierratel.com
Website: www.sierratel.com/skyranch

History

During 1876, the ranch property was essentially a camp owned by a man named Caster, but by 1898 it was the largest cattle ranch in California. The main ranch house, built before the turn-of-the-century, still stands today. The ranch was a major supplier of fruit, vegetables and meat to the region containing more than 7,000 acres with 4,000 head of cattle and roughly 200 employed ranch hands. The Caster's home was a mansion, but hard times during the late 1920s forced the family to sell off most of their land. By 1934 the ranch had dwindled in size to only a few hundred acres. It was ultimately sold to the state and converted into a tuberculosis sanitarium. Most of the patients were extremely ill and many perished inside. During 1942 the Army bought the property and used the facilities for WWII soldiers to rest and relaxation. Some men were amputees and wounded veterans. The Army constructed a large mess hall which is now the restaurant. The current owners have worked feverishly to restore the ranch to its former grandeur and it now provides comfort for those seeking to get away from a hectic lifestyle with 27 guest rooms.

Hauntspitality

When the owners bought the place and began restoration, there were already numerous rumors about spirits. It all began when there were no guests staying in the renovated rooms, and the lights were off and doors to the rooms kept open. First, there was the strong perfume smell that filtered through the library. The scent was reminiscent of an elderly woman's perfume, one from a much earlier time period called Lilies of the Valley. There was also the mysterious sound of a note being played on the piano when no one was anywhere near it. The lone note was sustained for many seconds before fading back into the past; the note turned out to be a middle C. The practical phantom joker has also caused the Halloween decorations to fall from their perch onto the piano bench. Sometimes, the toilets are flushed by some invisible force, items will suddenly vanish and reappear in another location and lights have been known to suddenly turn on or off without human assistance.

Some guests have witnessed a white light or mist; suddenly materialize in front of them. Once a female bartender felt some moisture on her cheek and said it was "just like a wet kiss." When Phil related his story, he was able to fill in a little of the history of Sierra Sky Ranch as had been told to him. The owner of the 100-year-old ranch is his daughter-in-law Kim Coles. Her parents are Terry and Louise Bishop of Carmel Valley. Mr. Coles began talking about the folklore, history and then his own experiences with the supernatural. Mr. Coles prefaced his information by saying the he was reared Catholic and that he is a Christian

man and is very level-headed. He lives on the property in a downstairs room. What he has witnessed he considers strange and unexplainable; something that his Christian upbringing didn't prepare him for.

According to one of Coles' stories, a ranch hand named Elmer worked on the ranch during the 1930s. He became so distressed at the sale of the place he had come to call home, that he committed suicide. Elmer reportedly bled to death within the ranch confines.

Many believe that since that fateful day, Elmer's spirit remains trapped at the ranch. Another phantom named Sarah, was a nurse who worked in the tuberculosis sanitarium. Roughly in her fifties, she worked with terminal patients including two children who ultimately died downstairs in the room she occupied. Shortly after their deaths, Sarah contracted tuberculosis and passed on.

During the 1980s a television crew came to the ranch to follow-up on the story of Elmer, the nurse and the two ghostly children who roam the buildings as spirits. They found evidence which supported the stories about the ghostly clientele.

Perhaps these other-worldly guest of long ago remain because they have unfinished business, are trapped, or simply like the area. Elmer, Sarah and the two spectral children may only be the tip of the paranormal iceberg at this fabulous country ranch that serves up great country cooking, views to die for and a friendly spirits to keep things lively!

Oakland
Heinhold's First & Last Chance Saloon

Particulars

48 Webster Street in Jack London Square,
Oakland, CA 94607
Telephone: 510-839-6761
E-mail: info@heinoldsfirstandlastchance.com
Website: www.heinoldsfirstandlastchance.com

History

Jack London Square is where Captain Thomas Gray, grandfather of the famous dancer Isadora Duncan, began the first ferry service to San Francisco in 1850. The building was initially used as a bunkhouse for those working in the area and actually opened for business as a bar in 1883 by John Heinhold. It is where Jack London borrowed the entrance fee for the University of California from the owner. Heinold's First and Last Chance Saloon was originally called J.M. Heinold's Saloon and was constructed from the timbers of old whaling ships. The bar's current name dates to the 1920s and derives from the fact that it is at the Port of Oakland, so it was the last bar a ferry passenger, and

later a serviceman, could drink in before boarding ship, and the first one to greet him upon his return. As a good-luck talisman, servicemen would leave money on the walls, ensuring they would be able to buy a drink when they landed back on shore.

Jack London would frequent the bar and listen to sailors' tales, and many of the tales and the tellers later appeared in his books. Other former patrons of the saloon include President William Howard Taft and writers Robert Louis Stevenson, Robert Service, Ambrose Bierce and Erskine Caldwell. The smallish bar had been in business for 23 years when the 1906 earthquake destroyed San Francisco, leaving everything inside the building severely slanted. It also caused an old clock to stop, and it still registers the time the quake struck.

Hauntspitality

Jack London's motto was, "I would rather be ashes than dust! I would rather that my spark should burn out in a brilliant blaze than it should be stifled by dryrot. I would rather be a superb meteor, every atom of me in magnificent glow, than a sleepy and permanent planet. The proper function of man is to live, not to exist. I shall not waste my days in trying to prolong them. I shall use my time."

Heinold's is filled with old foreign currency, newspapers, business cards, license plates and photos. Many of the furnishings are original, including the bar.

The original gaslights still illuminate the saloon and the walls are creosote stained from the smoke that built up over the years. These are not the only things old and unusual associated with the building; it is also home to numerous spirits.

Psychics or those "sensitve" to the spirit world need only pass by or walk in to see or feel the energy inside. One psychic told us that the place was "loaded" with former occupants who still come to visit and relive old times at their former haunt. When the building is unoccupied, people swear they see things going on inside, as well as hear ghostly voices coming from behind closed front doors. It's as if spirited celebrations are occurring on a regular basis. These non-paying customers have the run of the building and no hassles from the building when they pick their visiting days to coincide with the building being closed to the public.

There are other stories that have circulated about phantom forms that glide effortlessly right through the walls in front of startled patrons. Muffled whispers from unoccupied, unearthly sounds of things being dragged across the floor, objects that will occasionally move on their own, doors that will suddenly open unassisted and those pesky cold spots that will surround guests for a few seconds before departing, disembodied footsteps, and a smell of long ago tobacco are but a few of the many phenomena that have been reported inside.

A visit here is a must, since it may be your last chance to get a glimpse of the unknown while visiting this unique venue in Oakland.

Oceanside
Hunter Steakhouse

Particulars
Address: 1221 Vista Way,
Oceanside, CA 92054
Phone: 760 433-2633
Fax: 760 721 9585
Website: www.paragonsteak.com

History

Reportedly, the site of the restaurant lies on reinterred remains of the old Buena Vista Cemetery above the Buena Vista Lagoon. This area was an extremely important area to the Native Americans who had numerous villages in the area several thousand years ago. As the Native Americans were assimilated into the mission system, these outlying areas became home to settlers and homesteaders. By 1884, this location supported the Buena Vista Cemetery, and the remains of early inhabitants of Oceanside and Carlsbad were interred here. Estimates vary as to how many people were actually buried in the pioneer cemetery, but the upward end of speculation scale places the dead at around 50 people. The cemetery was one of the oldest in San Diego County.

Numerous factors contributed to the demise of the cemetery, but the word "progress" seems to encompass all of the contributing elements. Post World War II expansion throughout southern California was the first step in local change. The need for housing created a need to upgrade transportation, and real estate became a very valuable commodity. Since freeway expansion was necessary to accommodate the growing population, developers recognized the opportunity to buy real estate that could take full advantage of the vital access links to the region. By 1970, as the new freeway expansion neared completion, the old cemetery became prime real estate with immense development potential. A deal was brokered for the land and the last obstacle to build, was relocating the cemetery.

Official accounts of the removal process provide no clear resolution to the burial issue. Some reports claim all the bodies were removed, while other accounts suggest that some or all of the bodies may not have been removed. There is no official record as to where the bodies were removed to, if they were removed at all. This smacks of the movie, "Poltergeist"! Were all the graves actually located and every body removed? Since little time or money appeared to be set aside for this unpleasant task, the assumption today is that only a cursory removal of readily accessed graves took place. Most of the graves may have been actually avoided during initial grading; or worse yet, simply desecrated. As time went by, another gruesome story surfaced. A former employee in charge of the grading process told of the haphazard removal of grave markers that were simply broken up and became fill for the freeway and that some of the bodies were shoveled up into bags and reburied downslope under fill. Some say that several bodies still remain in the area of the former Buena Vista cemetery, while the other disinterred remains were reburied under or near the current Hunter Steakhouse, formerly, the Hungry Hunter. With the desecration came the potential for a haunted environment. Today, the restaurant is surrounded by lush landscaping and the only hint of what might lie beneath surfaces inside the restaurant in the form of restless spirits.

Hauntspitality

The restaurant, reportedly constructed on the site of desecrated human remains, is haunted. John Lamb in his book San Diego Specters, details some of the more haunted accounts that have taken place inside the building. John, a former patrol officer working the graveyard shift with the Oceanside Police Department in 1982, was constantly being called to investigate break-ins at the establishment. The security alarms would go off and the police would arrive and find nothing. Finally, as Lamb states, "Fifteen years passed before I finally began

Orbs in the back parking area where burials still remain, and the front of the restaurant
(Courtesy of the International Paranormal Research Organization - IPRO)

to solicit information on the haunting. Luckily during that intervening period, the unearthly phenomena were ongoing".

The energy is thick inside, yet few patrons are aware of anything unusual. Only those sensitive enough to pick up on the "vibes" or those who have had encounters inside are aware of the paranormal side of this beautiful and well-respected eatery in Oceanside. Employees bear the brunt of the encounters and the ghost stories are so common they are shrugged off as normal occurrences. Here is a condensed list of hundreds of reported phenomena:

- A former waitress was working late one evening when she witnessed something unusual in the dining room. The "thing" was a misty human-like form that was floating through the air for a few seconds before disappearing. The amazing thing was, the form was between floors, gliding along a physical dimension from the past where the actual ground surface was much lower than it is today.
- There have been numerous occasions when employees reported hearing disembodied voices echo throughout the building where the source could not be located.
- On another occasion, an employee was touched on the shoulder. When the person turned around, there was no one, human that is, anywhere around.
- A spirit from the late 1800s once manifested in front of a startled staff person and just as quickly, disappeared.
- A chandelier in the dining room began to sway back and forth.
- One evening just after closing, a loud crashing sound was heard coming from near the reception desk. The manager ran to see what the problem was and found that a large wooden window frame had suddenly dislodged from its setting and fell to the floor. The frame had been nailed in place, but somehow, it was dislodged.

Orbs seen from second floor landing (Courtesy of the International Paranormal Research Organization - IPRO)

- A Native American contingent once came for dinner. After a few minutes, they left saying that they felt that their ancestors were here; meaning that they thought the building had been constructed on an archaeological site.
- A waitress had her hair toyed with by someone invisible in a small service alcove in the northwest corner of the first floor dining room.
- A bartender had a brush with the paranormal when he was closing the bar. After neatly arranging the wine bottles on a back shelf, he left for a few minutes. Upon returning, the bottles had all been moved forward to the very edge of the platform without falling off.
- A female apparition was sighted near the stairs to the bar area.
- Several employees working in the kitchen and dining area often hear their names called out by someone with a soft, feminine voice. This disembodied spirit repeatedly calls out to employees from beyond the grave.
- The doors inside the building will mysteriously close by themselves, even though they are wedged open.
- An employee working on the second floor, felt someone walk right passed him. When he turned, there was no one there.
- Lights in the kitchen that were shut off after closing, would be found on the next morning when the establishment was opened.
- On one occasion, a staff person carrying a tray full of glasses and dishes, accidentally hit the wall with the tray and all the items were about to fall to the ground when an unearthly had seemingly pushed the falling end of the tray to a balanced position.
- Guests have felt someone unseen gently nudge them, particularly on the second floor

- Unexplained pounding sounds have emanated from the floor above the bathroom when people have been inside.
- Lights will often flicker on their own and disembodied footsteps and sounds come from unoccupied areas of the building.
- An employee, who was washing his hands in the bathroom, saw a misty form in the mirror floating behind him that disappeared into the wall.
- Unexplained power surges and electrical anomalies frequently occur.

Orbs during closing time (courtesy of the International Paranormal Research Organization - IPRO)

- A bartender witnessed the wine bottle being shaken by an unseen force and a bottle of beer just fall off a shelf.
- A staff person who was working in the storeroom, watched in disbelief as a full, heavy wine box flew off the shelf and narrowly missed his head.
- The credit card machine suddenly began spewing out paper on its own. Normally this could only happen by manual operation.
- An elderly man in period attire has been sighted standing near the dining room window for a few seconds before vanishing. This apparition has been sighted on several occasions staring solemnly toward the hills.
- Numerous times there have been sudden and quite noticeable drops in temperature.
- Our friend and co-investigator Maritza Skandunas of the San Diego Ghost Hunters, was able to obtain some updated stories from informant Tom Foster who interviews current staff as follows:
- People get touched on the shoulder a lot
- People that work there hear their names being called all the time.
- An apparition has been spotted in the men's bathroom
- The liquor cabinet is a focal point for numerous unexplained paranormal events.
- Glasses, bottles and other items have been rearranged on the bar counter.
- The main stairway has been a paranormal hot spot of late.
- A window inside the restaurant just fell out and broke on the floor. The window was tightly secured and there was no way it could of fallen out.
- A patron driving a new car came in for dinner. The lights shut off automatically. When he went back to his car after eating, the battery had been completely drained.
- Numerous reports of apparitions and strange occurrences have been referenced in the parking lot.

This Oceanside establishment is always bustling with activity. It's a great place to dine with your friends as well as have a potential encounter with one of their many spirited clientele. Steak your claim to this haunted locale where dinner and spirits are always on the menu.

Orbs near investigator Karen Hovland (courtesy of the International Paranormal Research Organization - IPRO)

Jolly Roger

Particulars

1900 Harbor Drive North,
Oceanside, CA 92054
Phone: 760-722-1831
Fax: 760-722-5364
E-mail: oceanside@jollyrogerrestaurants.com
Website: www.aloharestaurants.com

History

Although this impressive harborside restaurant didn't open until the 1970s, it is haunted. There is no evidence to suggest that a Native American village or cemetery once occupied this location, or that a tragedy took place on this spot, but we do know that the area once contained several establishments on or near the spot of the Jolly Roger Restaurant as seen by the photograph below.

Hauntspitality

There has been an unsubstantiated rumor that a band of gypsies frequented the area and a tragedy befell several members of the troupe. If this is true, then the haunted nature of the building is tied to time in Oceanside's history when the area was dominated by motor courts, markets, malt shops and more transient element dominated the cultural landscape.

The area prior to when the restaurant was constructed (courtesy of the Jolly Roger Restaurant)

There is another possibility as to why the building may be haunted. The spirit may be tied to the former interior décor. As our friend and fellow author Ed Okonowicz states in his book, Possessed Possessions: Haunted Antiques, Furniture and Collectibles, "Mysterious movement. Unexplained happenings... Caused by What? Perhaps by ... haunted objects." " ... Objects may miss the former owners who thought of them differently, and the items may be trying to send out calls for help, or gain the current owners attention." Many believe that objects contain energy and therefore can vibrate and impact our dimension. Old furniture, jewelry, dolls and such have been known to affect those who purchased the item, not really knowing the history. The effect is sometimes called a haunted possession that has a significant impact on the new environment it is placed in.

With the Jolly Roger, the spirits in the restaurant may be attached to the antiques and relics originally brought into the building by a former owner to grace the building's interior and provide a pirate-type ambiance. Years ago, the antiques and relics originally brought into the building were taken down and stored in a closet. Eventually they were discarded. When this occurred, at least one spirit became restless. But this is not the only ghost who calls the restaurant home.

A KMB Channel 8 news special documented entitled, "Menu Offers Food, Wine & Spirits... Real Spirits!" aired in 2005 and discussed the spirited side of this local restaurant. According to the broadcast, employees at the Jolly Roger say the restaurant has become the favorite haunt of several ghosts. Some of the spirited stories include:

- A general feeling by staff that they are constantly being watched or followed.
- Staff hear scratching sounds and disembodied footsteps coming from unoccupied areas of the building.
- Some people have been tapped on the shoulder or have felt as if someone has brushed right by them.
- Employees frequently hear footsteps going up and down the stairs when no one human is anywhere around.
- There are numerous reports of employees seeing lights dim, or go on and off on their own on the second floor.
- The wine and spirits area of the building has had a lot of reported activity and unexplained events take place.
- Bottles of alcohol will suddenly begin vibrating on their own, especially the expensive bottles.
- People who have glanced in the mirrors located inside have sometimes witnessed a pirate looking back at them.
- A longtime employee, who spent the night at the bottom of the stairs waiting for an opportunity to see a ghost, looked up at the top of the stairs an saw a handsome pirate staring down at her.
- A ghost hunting team from Orange County investigated the building and noted five distinct spirits inside: from an older gentleman to an eight-year-old child. The young boy is said to favor the downstairs dining room.
- People report seeing shadowy figures dart by out of the corner of their eyes.

A recent investigation by the International Paranormal Research Organization (IPRO) and the San Diego Ghost Hunters (SDGH) confirmed that the Jolly Roger is a very haunted local establishment. The authors along with psychic Ginnie McGovern and SDGH founder Maritza Skandunas conducted a preliminary investigation of the establishment. Before the group entered the building, a couple members sensed a tragedy on the spot and that someone had met a violent death in the area occupied by the current building.

Upon entering, the group was immediately drawn to the stairwell area leading to the second floor. Here, McGovern sensed a spectral woman with unusual clothing watching the group from the stairs. As soon as McGovern acknowledged the woman, she vanished.

There were numerous impressions, strong EMF meter and orbs in the room

Orbs in the wall at the entryway to the building
(courtesy of the International Paranormal Research
Organization - IPRO)

to the right after entering the building was thick with energy. McGovern immediately sensed a gypsy woman, a boy under ten years of age, a sailor-type male energy and a young girl. The other two investigators then began recording large, bright orbs on their digital cameras and several times while taking photographs, their hair stood on end. The longer they stayed and tapped into the energy, the more they were convinced that the restaurant acted as a vortex or portal for energies to pass through. It wasn't so much a feeling of tragedy inside, but more of a sense that the place acted as a focal point where energies gathered.

The closer it came to sunset the more the energy shifted and seemed to intensify; the group all became aware that they were not alone. It was as if the energies inside were coming to inspect the group and see what we were up to. The manager and a staff person told us a little bit about the spirited nature of the building after we related what we had sensed during the walkthrough.

The investigative group concluded that the building had more than a four spirits inside and that future investigations were warranted to gather more data on the nature and extent of hauntings.

At the Jolly Roger, your dinner may not be on the house, by the spirits certainly are. These benign energies keep the staff on their toes and keep the customers coming back for another chance at catching a glimpse of the ghostly contingent.

Orbs in a dining area (courtesy of the International Paranormal Research Organization - IPRO)

Ojai
The Moon's Nest Inn

Particulars
210 East Matilija,
Ojai, CA 93023
Phone: 805-646-6635
Fax: 805-646-4995
E-mail: katja@moonsnestinn.com
Website: moonsnestinn.com

History

The 1874 building represents a converted schoolhouse. The Moon's Nest Inn was also known as the Ojai Manor Hotel, which is one of the oldest structures in Ojai. In 1874, an oblong, brick schoolhouse was constructed in Ojai. The building consisted of one classroom, and two anterooms, a sixteen-foot high ceiling, and four windows on each side to allow sunlight in. The bricks were supplied by Abram Blu mberg, and the first teacher was Mrs. Joseph Steepleton. Jerome Caldwell, F.S.S. Buckman, Agnes Howe, Clara Smith, and Anna Seward, taught at the brick schoolhouse. Howe claimed the schoolhouse had more bats than students. By 1893, the little brickhouse school had grown too small to meet the needs of a growing community. The building had also served as a church, meeting place, and social hall from 1874-1894. Finally, the schoolhouse was abandoned.

After abandonment as a school, Ezra Taylor, who ran the local machine shop, used the place as his residence. In 1910 it became the home for the A.E. Freeman family. It was during this time, that the brick exterior was covered over by wood. G.L. Chrisman bought the Freeman home in 1916, and Alton Downs lived there into the 1930s. In 1946, the building was once again used as a school by Major Richard Cannon. In 1947, the school closed and Mr. and Mrs. Joseph Cataldo converted the school into the Ojai Manor Hotel, remodeling the place to accommodate seven rooms for rent. In 1998, the Ojai Manor Hotel was once again remodeled and the named changed to the Moon's Nest Inn.

Hauntspitality

Ghosthunter, Richard Senate and his wife, Debbie Christenson Senate, a gifted psychic, ventured through the Ojai Manor Hotel several years ago (prior to its present incarnation) to discover if the building was haunted. Brian Black was the sound expert, Pat Fry was the historian, and Kay Rolfe headed the video crew. Stories had circulated for quite some time that strange and unexplainable things were occurring inside. Staff and guests reported experience a feeling of being watched, hearing voices and footsteps coming from empty rooms and corridors, and noticing shadowy figures appear in the hallways and guest rooms. The paranormal events were quite harmless as the investigator tried to prove, once and for all if the inn was haunted; and is so, who might be responsible for the paranormal activity.

Debbie Senate was told nothing about the history of the building or of the recorded paranormal events that took place over the years. She toured all the guest rooms and tried to get an impression of the energies were locked inside. Debbie immediately detected depression in one room, and a choking feeling in one of the closets. As she walked the hallway, she heard the faint sounds of children laughing and playing. Debbie concluded that a man who was very upset, committed suicide in the closet of one of the rooms and remained behind.

The Senates also picked up on a very stern woman, who seemed to be a former teacher that believed rules must be adhered too, and that everything had a proper place; even in the after-life. Debbie Senate sensed that the children were more like memory imprints, than ghosts, and their school memories were feelings of laughing, playing and yes, even doing their assignments.

The Moon's Nest Inn, though a former schoolhouse, now has only one major rule; to come and relax and "nest with the spirits of bygone days."

Ojai Valley Inn & Spa

Particulars
905 Country Club Road,
Ojai, CA 93023
Phone: 805.646.5511
Toll free: 1-800-422-6524
Fax: 805.646.7696
Website: www.ojairesort.com

History
This luxurious resort was the dream of wealthy Ohio glass manufacturer and philanthropist, Edward Drummond Libbey. During 1922, Libbey began building a country club and golf course. He commissioned famed architect Wallace Neff to design the clubhouse in the traditional Spanish Colonial style. Renowned golf course architect George C. Thomas, Jr. was commissioned to design a course from the natural terrain that was immediately hailed as "the cream of Southern California courses."

During 2004 the resort underwent a complete renovation. The resort has long been a favorite with celebrities such as Clark Gable, Walt Disney, Judy Garland, and Nancy and Ronald Reagan.

The hotel has consistently been recognized as one of the top resorts in the United States. This historic landmark is a member of Historic Hotels of America and according to staff and guests, a part of its storied past still manifests in Room 5.

Hauntspitality
Those who have visited the building, who might be considered sensitive to the paranormal, suggest that Edward Libbey is still walking the halls of his beloved creation. Others say the spirit or spirits belong to the earliest inhabitants of Ojai, the Chumash. Their villages and campsites are known to have existed through the valley, and what attracted them to this area, continues to bring guests from around the world here; the healthy climate and almost mystical surroundings. Of the over 300 spacious rooms and suites, most rooms have fireplaces and terraces with spectacular mountain and golf course views. One room in particular is reportedly spirited.

According to paranormal investigators, Room 5 seems to be a focal point for many odd and unexplained events that have been reported in the "haunted" room. Visitors have reported feeling quickly manifesting cold spots, a sense of being watched or followed by an unseen presence, an occasional unexplained sound that will emanate from the bathroom, disembodied footsteps and flickering lights.

One psychic who visited the resort sensed a Native American energy surrounding the place. She even suggested that the resort may have been built on a former campsite or village. Others say that the energy of a male presence is not the only spirit to frequent this resort location. Occasionally, sensitive individuals have reported the sounds of ghostly children playing in the hallways and a spectral lady who has been spotted in the lobby.

This is one location that needs additional investigation. We have provided the basic information with the hope that someone can add to our knowledge about the haunted nature of this historic hideaway.

Take a trip to this fabulous resort in a very special environment, and even if your visit doesn't turn up a spirit, it is sure to revive yours.

Orange
Rutabegorz

Particulars
264 North Glassell Street,
Orange, CA 92866
Phone/Fax: 714-633-3260
Website: www.rutabegorz.com

History

Rutabegorz situated in Old Town Orange, was built in 1915. It was once home of early citrus ranchers Daniel and Annie Crawford and their children. The spacious dining room and patio offers a place to relax and catch one's breath while "antiquing" in Old Towne Orange. The place took its name from a spin on the word for the unloved turnip — the rutabaga. Over time Rutabegorz has evolved through numerous menu additions and changing consumer tastes over the years into today's full service health conscious restaurant. The house has served as Tony's Mexican Restaurant and the Golden Maize, a South American restaurant prior to Rutabegorz.

Hauntspitality

This one-story building with a cellar is a very haunted location. The restaurant seems to cater as much to the spirited clientele as it does to the living. The owner and staff have had so many unexplained events take place over the years that they told us to "take our pick" as far as which ones we want to use for our book; so we did just that. Besides the spirits affectionately called Danny and Annie (after the original owners, the Crawfords), there is also a little boy and young girl who also make this restaurant their home.

Comeau remarked that when she opened for business in 2000, things immediately began to happen and the resulting events proved to be a pleasant welcome. According to Comeau, the first day they opened, nothing seemed to work and numerous things began falling off the wall. The Coke machine suddenly malfunctioned and then blew up; the cash register wouldn't open; several doors refused to stay shut; the electricity in the house stopped working; and, there were other small events that led them to conclude that they were not alone within the confines of their new establishment. The immediate collective sense was that for the restaurant concept to work, the living and the dead would have to find a way to co-exist. In time, the spirits seemed to accept their new owner and everyone now occupies the former home in peace and harmony; that is, most of the time.

A prior owner had two children who constantly reported seeing a little boy walk out of the kitchen toward them. This occurred at the same time each day. The owners were never frightened; just curious. Over time both children just got used to their phantom playmate as did their parents who basically adopted the phantom boy.

Numerous staff and guests have reportedly witnessed the spirits named Danny and Annie walk through the corridors and rooms in the house. The specters are usually dressed in Period clothing and although mindful of those watching them, pay little attention to the living and go about their other-worldly duties as if the house still belonged to their family.

There have been reports of muffled sounds and unusual noises coming from unoccupied areas of the house; strong feelings of being watched by invisible eyes throughout the establishment; and, an occasional glimpse of the phantom inhabitants taking a stroll through their former residence.

An employee reported walking down a corridor when she suddenly stopped in her tracks. In front of her was a man working on a ladder. He didn't seem to fit the period, and no one was scheduled to do odd jobs that day. Unsure of what to do, the woman turned away for a second, then looked back and the man had vanished into thin air, with his ladder and equipment.

Another frequently reported spirit belongs to a lady that most feel is Annie Crawford, the original owner of the house. She is sighted and felt upon entering, as if she is inspecting those who come into her home. Some "sensitive: individuals pick up on the spectral lady the moment they enter the house, even catching a brief glimpse of a woman staring at them for a moment before fading away. hose who have been lucky enough to see the phantom guests seem to feel that the spirited occupants are watching over the place and keeping an eye on the food and service.

One psychic who recently visited the restaurant immediately sensed a strong female presence in the house upon entering. This sturdy-framed woman, as she was described, may have been Annie Crawford.

Add to the list a couple a children and a male energy; place settings that manage to rearrange themselves; voices that are not discernible coming from unoccupied areas of the house; and an occasional cold gust of wind that sends a shiver up your spine, and you have haunted Rutabegorz!

We heartily recommend that you drop in and have some delicious food and ask about their unseen visitors. The owner wants us to qualify the phantom aspect of the restaurant by stating emphatically that the spirits are always around but are never malicious; just a playful group of wandering souls who call Rutabegorz their home.

Victorian Manor Tea Room

Particulars
204 N Olive,
Orange, CA 92866
Phone: 714-771-4044
Fax: 714-771-3667
Website: www.victorianmanor.com

History

The boundaries of the Rancho Santiago de Santa Ana were validated in 1857 and the Yorba and Peralta families continued to use the land currently occupied by the Victorian Manor Tea Room. In the early 1860's, Leonardo Cota borrowed money from Abel Stearns, and put up his share of the rancho as collateral. When Cota defaulted in 1866, Stearns filed a lawsuit to demand a partition of the land, so that Stearns could claim Cota's section. After two years of litigation, the rancho was divided into 1,000 units parceled out to the heirs and to the claimants. Two Los Angeles lawyers involved in the lawsuit were Alfred Beck Chapman and Andrew Glassell, took some of their fees in land. They had already began buying other sections of the rancho as early as 1864. By 1870, they owned about 5,400 acres in what is now downtown Orange. It seemed like a good location for a town; the nearby Santa Ana River provided water, the soil was rich and a stage road ran nearby. Chapman hired a surveyor to divide the land into tracts of 40, 80 and 120 acres. He called the area Richland and began selling the lots.

Although Chapman later called himself the "father of Orange," the development of the city was guided by Captain William T. Glassell, Andrew Glassell's brother. He laid out the downtown area, bounded by Maple, Grand, Almond, and Lemon Streets, with Chapman and Glassell Streets meeting in a central "Public Plaza." Captain Glassell's home and office, on the west side of the Plaza Square, was the first building in Richland. The captain also supervised the construction of the A.B. Chapman Canal from the river to provide irrigation for the farm sites. (a portion of the canal's path may be traced along Canal Street, behind the Mall of Orange). By the end of 1871, there were a dozen houses in and around Richland. The first school was opened on March 26, 1872, meeting at first in a private home. By August, a one-room schoolhouse was opened at the corner of Sycamore and Lemon. During 1873, the first local store opened for business (Fisher Brothers, on the north side of the Plaza), the first civic organization was formed (the Orange Grange), and the first church congregation met (the Methodist Episcopal). In 1873, Richland's application for a post office was refused because there was already a Richland in Sacramento County. The townspeople selected the name Orange instead.

The town of Orange began as a farming community, although it took several years of trial and error for the settlers to discover the most successful crops. The first crops were grains such as barley, oats, wheat corn and rye. Many of the farmers then planted grape vines, primarily for raisins. Grapes were a major product until the 1886 blight that killed thousands of vines in Orange and surrounding communities. The settlers also tried growing tropical fruits such as bananas, pineapples and guavas, but without much success. In 1873, the farmers began planting orange groves.

The City of Orange was incorporated in 1888. However, Orange dates back to

1869 when Alfred Chapman and Andrew Glassell, both lawyers, accepted 1,385 acres of land from the Rancho Santiago de Santa Ana as legal fees. Soon thereafter, the men laid out a one square mile town with ten-acre farm lots surrounding a forty acre central town site. The center of the town site became known as the Plaza, which has become the symbol of the community. Today, the Plaza and the original town site contain numerous historic buildings.

This Queen Anne Victorian home was built by William D. Granger and his wife Ella P. around 1904. To date, we know that the Grangers had at least one child, a daughter named Grace who was listed as being a student in 1907. Granger helped open the First National Bank of Orange in the town plaza, becoming its first president from 1905-1924; the bank that is still operating today. The former residence and boarding house, currently operates as a locally renowned tearoom. Carol Cox, the president of Old Town, Orange, purchased the home with her husband Jim and after months of renovation, opened for business. The five tea rooms service clientele from Orange County

Hauntspitality

You get more than high tea in this beautifully restored Victorian; you get high spirits. According to owners Jim and Carol Cox and Peggy Stahler, vice-president of the Orange County Society for Paranormal Research (OCSPR), there are spirits a plenty in this Victorian house. Paige Austin in her recent article about the Victorian Manor Tea Room states, "Rumors of ghosts and hauntings have long circulated in Old Towne, but now members of the Orange County Society for Psychic Research [OCSPR] have set out in search of proof." In March of 2001, Stahler led about 30 members on a fact finding investigation of the old house. Each individual was responsible for recording their impressions of the spirited clientele. The preliminary findings produced the following results:

- Thirteen people reported the presence of children's spirits. Several individuals sensed a young girl with curly, blonde hair and a little boy who enjoys relocating silverware to get attention.
- Eight people reported sensing an elderly woman with dark, graying hair, as well as a younger woman wearing her wedding dress who enjoys following people around and making sure nothing is out of place.
- A couple of members reported witnessing a young girl who enjoys visiting the house with her Aunt Cora.
- A few individuals reportedly contacted a young boy named Erin.
- The sad presence of a spirit named Emilie, who reportedly committed suicide after the loss of her child, was detected.
- A Maryann Thomas associated with the date 1926, was perceived.
- A Confederate Civil War veteran named either Lou, Gregory, or Gerald, who came to Orange and fell in love with a woman named Wanda Olberg,

The haunted Blue Room where a phantom female is often spotted standing in front of the window (Courtesy of the International Paranormal Research Organization – IPRO)

also roams the building.

- Two women name Hedda and Amber was also sensed by some members.
- Two members reported encountering a specter of a man who accidentally fell to his death down the stairs.
- According to Carol Cox, there have been far too many events that have taken place since she and her husband bought the place to recount them all. However, some of recorded events include:
- A tug-of-war with the front door where the owners continually lock it and the spirited guests repeatedly undo their efforts;
- New light bulbs in the chandeliers often get untwisted from their sockets or go out after being replace, as if a mystery guest is playing with them;
- Cold drafts have been reported by numerous individuals including the owners, as if someone unseen has walked right through them;
- Some of the rooms in the house have a definite paranormal atmosphere inside where people feel chilled to the bone or feel as if they are being watched;
- A visiting psychic who dropped by for a spot of tea, remarked matter-of-factly that there were numerous spirits residing in the house;
- A guest who came for tea ended up talking to one of the spirits, not knowing that the person was a ghost. Only afterward when she described the woman in period clothing did everyone come to realize that the "other" person, who came for tea, was from the other side.

During the evening of Friday, September 28, 2001, The International Paranormal Research Organization (IPRO) conducted a paranormal investigation at the former Granger home. With the help of the OCSPR including four psychics (Pat Bryan, Ginnie McGovern, Michael Kouri and Peggy Stahler), the communication circle (as its called by the society), spent four hours in contact with numerous entities including a former Granger Nanny named "Rosalie," an elderly lady named "Donna," a child named "Matthew," another child, a woman named "Aunt Cora" who frequents the building as a "guest ghost," a woman named Emilie who fell from the second story balcony while pregnant, a man who called himself "Earl;" W.D. Granger; W.D. Granger's son; .D.C. Pixley, a friend of the Granger's; a banker friend of W.D. Granger who gave his name as "Mr. Utt," and several other spirits unrelated to the house including a woman who said she died during the September 11th bombing of the World Trade Center and two boys who died in a recent car crash.

The activity in the house was filmed and a tape recorder monitored the entire event. IPRO conducted several more investigations in 2003-2005, and each time, more paranormal investigative data was obtained.

This is truly a meeting place of mind and souls! Whether you come for a spot of tea or to spot a spirit, you will not be disappointed with your visit to this historic Victorian house, which is truly a house of spirits!

Orb on the shoulder of the male séance participant (Courtesy of the International Paranormal Research Organization – IPRO)

Palm Springs
Korakia Pensione

Particulars
257 South Patendio Road,
Palm Springs, CA 92262
Phone: 760-864-6411
Fax: 760-864-4147

History

Nestled in the heart of the southern California desert at the base of the San Jacinto Mountains, this Moroccan style inn was built in 1924. The Moroccan villa was originally named Dar Marroc and was the former hideaway of Scottish painter Gordon Coutts. The villa served as the venue for Coutts to re-create his earlier life in Tangier by employing a wide variety of architectural features that promoted a Moroccan décor. The flamboyant Coutts would often be found regaling tales in his studio, demonstrating his artistic and intellectual breadth with such visiting artists as John Lavery, Agnes Pelton, Nicolai Fenshin and Grant Wood. Dar Marroc quickly became the hot spot for the art community. It is rumored that even Winston Churchill has painted in the villa's Artist Studio, which today still retains its original pine floors and turret windows. Korakia means "crows" in Greek.

A story goes that the artists' wife, a model named Gertrude, was widowed shortly after the couple moved to the home. Shortly thereafter, Gertrude fell in love with her dead husband's good friend. The couple threw grand parties, and one night at one of the grand soirée's, Gertrude walked in front of an oncoming car near Korakia, and met her death. The breakfast inn today actually consists of two historically renowned villas.

Fashion photographers often use the interestingly designed resort to shoot their models. Korakia remains a popular rendezvous for an eclectic crowd, including renowned actors, writers, producers and photographers. Notable celebrity sightings that have occurred around the mosaic tiled pool reveal an impressive lineup of the art community's biggest "movers and shakers." Such sightings include Laura Dern, Mary Steenburgen, Dwight Yokum, Andy Garcia, Peter Coyote and New York Times publisher Arthur Sulzberger Jr.

There have been sightings of the hottest young stars such as Chris O'Donnell, Jennifer Jason-Leigh, Elizabeth Shue and Alicia Silverstone

Hauntspitality

Allegedly the resort it is haunted by the Gertrude Coutts, who has been seen walking along the road on the anniversary of her death. Numerous other strange occurrences have been also recorded at the resort including:

- Cold chills are frequently felt by guests and staff on extremely hot days inside the resort.
- Guests have reported that their clothes have been neatly rearranged while they left their rooms to enjoy the resort grounds.
- Unexplained ripples of water have been seen on the surface of the pool that blows against the wind. One person reportedly said that it was as if someone unseen was swimming.
- When photographers have had their models pose here, the costume people have remarked that when they leave for a moment, they will return to find the model's clothes removed or replaced by another article of clothing.
- Some people have claimed to have seen the figure of a woman walking along the road on the anniversary of her death, only to vanish within moments of being sighted.
- A psychic remarked that a strong male energy also dominates the grounds and enjoys mixing with the current clientele as a gracious host; possibly Gordon Coutts!
- Several guests have reported hearing what sounded like parties going on in a nearby area of the hotel. When the go to check on the source of the noise, there is no one there and the area they heard music and laughter coming from, is deathly silent.
- The Travel Channel aired a special called "Haunted Hotels" that featured Korakia. During the segment, numerous paranormal events that have taken place at the resort were discussed including sightings of Gertrude, the rapidly manifesting cold spots on the hottest of days, disembodied footsteps, sounds of phantom parties and that fact that on any given day, you could just as easily see a specter as a celebrity.

Korakia Pensione is a place to die for and a must visit resort when you come to Palm Springs. Here, there is a very fine line between the past and present, where ghosts and guests share equal billing.

Pasadena
Holly Street Bar & Grill

Particulars
175 E. Holly Street, Pasadena, California
91103
Phone: 626-440-1421
Fax: 626-440-1426
E-mail: hollystreetbarngrill@earthlink.net
Website: www.hollystreetstreetbarandgrill.com

History

Pasadena, California got its start in the Midwest during the winter of 1873. An Indiana resident, Dr. Thomas Balch Elliott, assembled together a group of more than 100 families that had grown tired of the bleak Indiana winters and desired a more moderate climate throughout the year. They called themselves, The California Colony of Indiana. The railway connecting Pasadena to Los Angeles was completed in 1886, contributing to the growth of the community, which became incorporated the same year. The next 10 years brought advances such as electric street lighting, paved streets, and a sewer system. The Rose Parade and Rose Bowl have provided Pasadena with worldwide recognition and the city's recent renovations of buildings and businesses along the old commercial district area of Colorado Boulevard between Orange Grove and Arroyo Parkway

have rejuvenated the economy, history and nightlife of Old Pasadena.

Ambitious entrepreneurs L.H. Turner and A.B. Stevens began a mortuary in 1895 on the corner of Raymond and Holly Street joined forces to help the bereaved of Pasadena. The current building which houses the Holly Street Bar and Grill and offices at 95 North Marengo Avenue was built by renowned architect Sylvanus Marston in 1922. According to literature on the building, this historic landmark combines an old world charm and elegance with a contemporary flair. The Courtyard has the feel of something found in a small European village and the interior contains contemporary art and lavish seating arrangements. Jazz music often soothes those relaxing in the lounge and the restaurant caters to business luncheons, breakfast meetings and other events. The building's unique history includes being constructed in 1922 and containing the Turner and Stevens Mortuary from 1922 until the mid-1980s. The conversion of the building into commercial space drastically transformed the original setting. The Holly Street restaurant occupies a part of the mortuary that was used as the carriage house or

Turner and Stevens, Mortuary owners

garage, carpenter's shop and embalming rooms.

Hauntspitality

Yes, a portion of the former mortuary, now a restaurant is haunted; at least that's what owner Alexis Nassif and several psychics claim. You wouldn't suspect a thing if you didn't know the colorful past of this stone facade structure. However, given the fact that it was a mortuary operating as far back as 1895, and that the restaurant occupies a portion of the building where the recently deceased were brought prior to the final disposition of their mortal remains, the place certainly lends itself to hauntings. Even when you walk inside, there are few if any thoughts that the restaurant is spirited; unless you are a psychic and are sensitive to such energy or have worked in the restaurant for a time. It's not that anything negative or bad happens to those who come to visit, or those who work inside; but something does happen. There have been numerous reports of shadowy figures appearing and floating down the hallway, bottles occasionally flying off the top shelf of the bar; unexplained cold spots that will suddenly engulf individuals; an frequent scent that people will pick up on in certain portions of the restaurant and a sadness that overcomes some in the storage area and back offices of the restaurant (they were used as the embalming rooms).

Psychics and paranormal investigators from the International Paranormal Research organization (IPRO) investigated the Holly Street Bar and Grill and came away with the following observations:
- Popping and loud, hollow sounds were perceived in the upstairs office.
- A little girl's voice saying "Daddy, Daddy", can be heard on tape.
- A confused and restless male spirit was sensed in the computer room where physical changes to the building seemed to have angered him.
- Extreme sadness was felt in certain areas of the restaurant.
- Giggling and playful children were sensed in the bathroom area and main staircase of the adjoining office building.
- Investigators felt that the results of an influenza epidemic were imprinted on this location. Some of those participating believed numerous bodies from a widespread epidemic were brought to the mortuary.
- A dark figure dressed in black was discerned lurking in the office and kitchen areas.
- A scent related to the time the place served as a mortuary was picked up on.
- A male presence was sighted in the bar mirror.
- The spirits of a small boy and girl were noted in the third story window and main staircase.
- Several members felt as if they were being watched in certain areas of the restaurant.
- A member witnessed and heard horses' hooves between the garage and chapel.

- There were strong feelings that the place once served as a bordello and a speakeasy
- Most investigators experienced the overwhelming sensation of death in the basement. This is where the bodies were stored in vaults.
- People witnessed a man walking by them in the back dining room area while they were peering into the mirror. When then turned around toward the restaurant, there was no one there. This mirror seems to act like a portal to another dimension.
- Pots and pans will sometimes move back and forth on their own in the kitchen.
- Disembodied footsteps are often heard in the back hallway of the kitchen leading to the office and wine storage room.

Additional research into the adjoining offices that are blocked from the restaurant by drywall partitions, tell even more strange and unexplainable tales. Those who occupy the first and second floor offices can rattle off a litany of events. There are repeated stories of a young girl in white who peers in the entrance to the building, only to have a startled receptionist turn pale when the child vanishes in front of her. There is also a young girl dressed in green who is sighted at the bottom of the staircase leading to the second story, as well as little boy who seems content to play in the upstairs hallways.

Other events reported by occupants include: Strong odors that materialize in the chapel and other downstairs offices; a spirit who whistles the same four notes over and over; computer keyboards that begin typing; monitors that go blank or produce strange images; doors that open and shut on their own; loud rattling and banging sounds that emanate from unoccupied upstairs rooms; papers that shuffle on their own or are suddenly tossed across an office floor by someone unseen; stools or chairs that levitate or move unassisted; and, voices that filter through areas of the building that are devoid of human inhabitants.

Apparitions have been sighted on every floor, particularly where the embalming and viewing rooms used to be. Repeated encounters have occurred in the basement, stairwells and first and second floor hallways and in the chapel area. Several individuals have sensed an angry minister in the chapel who doesn't appear happy with the fact that the former chapel is now being used as offices.

A building manager was once in the basement with his wife when they confronted an apparition on the stairwell leading to the second floor. The non-descript image stood above the two people for a few seconds, then floated away, leaving the two with only one thought: Get out!

A recent visit by a psychic investigator accompanied by the authors, yielded evidence of a uniformed man and several children waiting for their parents to come for them in a storage area that would have served as a viewing room when the mortuary was functioning.

At the Holly Street Bar and Grill and adjacent offices, the past collides with the present where dining and working with spirits occurs on a regular basis. Try this unique adventure in dining and you'll be dying to come back for more.

Paso Robles

Paso Robles Inn

Particulars
175 E. Holly Street,
Pasadena, CA 91103
Phone: 626-440-1421
Fax: 626-440-1426
E-mail: hollystreetbarngrill@earthlink.net
Website: www.hollystreetstreetbarandgrill.com

History

The founders of Paso Robles, and later the hotel, were brothers Daniel and James Blackburn, who bought the El Paso de Robles land grant in May 12, 1844. The hot springs discovered by the Franciscan priests of nearby Mission San Miguel in 1797, represented the main area attraction. The railroad came to Paso Robles in 1886 and the city was incorporated on February 25, 1889. The El Paso de Robles Hotel Company, Inc. was formed in November, 1889 and work began on the hotel designed by famed architect Jacob Lenzen. The hotel was completed at a cost of $160.000. This showpiece had all the amenities to rival other hotels in California.

The building burned to the ground the night of December 12, 1940. The fire was discovered on the second floor at 9:00 p.m. by the night clerk J.E. Emsley, 55, who ran downstairs, sounded the alarm, and dropped dead of a heart attack. The hotel manager E.W. Santelman routed the 200 guests and got them out safely before the building was destroyed. Only the wing containing the ballroom was saved, and exists today at the northwest corner of the present property.

The Paso Robles Inn was begun shortly after the hotel burned to the ground, and opened in February of 1942. Presently, the Inn offers 88 rooms, a full restaurant, coffee shop, wedding and banquet facilities, and a lounge that features live entertainment on weekends. Restoration of the Grand Ballroom is currently underway, along with the addition of 12 more Hot Spring Spa rooms. Future plans also include the addition of a full-service health spa, salon and conference center by the end of 2001.

Hauntspitality

When the calls come, it's usually after dark, and always from room 1007. The phone at the front desk of the Paso Robles Inn rings, and when the clerk picks it up, there's no one at the other end. The phantom calls have happened several times over the past few weeks, according to hotel management. Each time staff members have gone to investigate; there's been no one in the room. At least, that's how the story goes as employees of the Paso Robles Inn relate what they say are the shenanigans of a ghost they think might be haunting their hotel.

At first, inn management wrote the calls off to a phone system glitch. Then,

308

they started joking that it might be a ghost doing the calling, with front desk clerks making log entries to that effect -- "The ghost in [Room] 1007 called me again." But the tale really took off on February 1, when 1007 called 911. When police arrived that night, the room, which requires an electronic key to open, was again found empty. To dial 911 from the inn's rooms, callers have to hit 8 and 0 before 911, said general manager Paul Wallace. "That's not a glitch," Wallace said. "That's not someone (just) dialing (zero)." but who? After rereading a newspaper article about a 1940 fire that destroyed the original hotel, Wallace began to theorize about who the ghostly caller might be. According to the article, night clerk J.H. Emsley discovered the fire on the second floor of the hotel on Dec. 19, 1940. He rushed downstairs to the first floor, sounded the alarm, and then died from a heart attack on the spot.

Wallace said the 911 call went out in close to 9:05 p.m., the time Emsley sounded the alarm the night of the fire. Police records show the 911 call came in closer to 9:30, but Wallace stands by his theory. Thanks to Emsley, all of the hotel's guests were evacuated safely, But. Wallace said he thinks the ghostly clerk doesn't know that. Police are skeptical about the ghost theory. Paso Robles Police Officer Terry Johnson said the police department receives a number of mysterious 911 calls, some even from addresses that don't have a phone in operation, "That is not the only place we've gotten an inexplicable 911 call," Johnson said: The number of phantom calls picks up during stormy weather Johnson said. However, the weather was clear the night of the call from the inn. Wallace called Pacific Bell that day, but the company found nothing wrong with the hotel's phone line. A contractor inspected the inside phone system, but also found no glitches, Wallace said. Pacific Bell spokeswoman Heather Alexander said the phone calls seem to be out of the ordinary. "We really have no indication that what s being described is what's actually occurred; although it certainly sounds unusual.

Mike Childs, head of maintenance, isn't sure what to make of the phone mystery. Childs went to room 1007 to inspect the phone line the evening of the 911 call. The phone had called the front desk several times that day, and Childs went to see if there was a mechanical reason for the malfunction. While standing in the room, Childs witnessed the phone light up and call the front desk. When he tried calling the desk himself, the phone, which has two lines, cut him off and called the front desk on the second line. When the clerk picked up the call, all she heard, was a squelching sound on the other end, Childs said. The phone spirit isn't the first ghost story to haunt the inn. A cook is rumored to have quit two days into his job after encountering a woman wandering the courtyard. When the cook approached her, the woman reportedly vanished before his eyes. Ghosts or no ghost, there has been no shortage of lore attached to it. The inn is also rumored to be a favorite haunt of legendary outlaw Jesse James.

The most common sighting at the hotel is the "Lady in White." There have been numerous stories about this female specter for over 50 years. She has been most frequently sighted early in the morning standing on the bridge in the garden area. Her apparition has reportedly greeted numerous staff and guests, wearing what has been universally described as a whitish nightgown or robe; hence the moniker, "Lady in White." She seems to be aware of those watching her before she disturbingly vanishes in front of her startled witnesses. There is some speculation that the friendly female phantom is in fact a former housekeeper named Blanche who worked at the inn for over 40 years before passing away. Instead of choosing another plane of existence, it seems that Blanche decided to remain behind in what may be considered her earthly home, keeping an eye on the staff and guests, just as she did in life.

Another unusual story centers on the black cats that have recently turned up at the inn while the Ballroom was being remodeled. The Ballroom is the only remaining portion of the original building not totally destroyed by the 1940 fire. The current cats seem to have a tie to the original building. According to a newspaper article, on December 17, 1940, a bellman reported seeing a black cat appear in the lobby. The employee was convinced that the cat was an omen of something bad. Two days later, on December 19, 1940, a devastating fire engulfed all but the ballroom, and claimed the life of J.H. Emsley the night clerk who died in the lobby where the cat was sighted.

Why are black cats showing up now? Perhaps it's another omen, although not of devastation, but of impending change. You see, the ballroom is being renovated and 12 new rooms and a spa are being added to the inn, bringing life at the hotel full circle. With a visit to this landmark inn, you'll be tended to by a courteous and friendly staff and possibly be visited by the Lady in White, Mr. Emsley and even the infamous Jesse James.

Petaluma
Cavanagh Inn

Particulars

10 Keller Street,
Petaluma, CA 94952-2939
Phone: 707-765-4657 | Fax: 707-769-0466
Toll Free: 1-888-765-4658
E-mail: info@cavanaghinn.com
Website: www.cavanaghinn.com

History

The City of Petaluma, California, was settled in 1850. It is believed the name of the town means 'flat back hills' in the language of the Miwok Indians. The town was incorporated in 1858, making it the oldest city between San Francisco and Eureka. The Victorian house was constructed in 1902 as a family residence with the cottage added 10 years later. The two buildings share a lawn, a large magnolia tree and are bordered by a white picket fence. Redwood floors and octagonal redwood landing reached by a beautiful staircase add to the beauty of the house which contains a library, parlor, fireplace, back porch and garden area.

The U.S. Census for 1880 shows that justice of the peace; John Cavanagh and his wife Adelaide (Delia Carrigan) and their seven children lived in this beautiful house. The Cavanaghs were born in Dublin, Ireland, sailed for San Francisco in August 1850, and arrived in Petaluma in 1857. The Cavanagh Lumber Company was founded in 1867 and this family business thrived until 1971. The Cavanagh lumber company was noted for some of the finest rare redwood, and the warehouse was one of the original river trading posts, which are older than the city of Petaluma. In 1861 Cavanagh helped found Emmitt Rifles, a militia composed of citizens of Irish birth. During the early, 1860s he was elected marshal of Petaluma and in 1866 became justice of the peace.

Their fourth child, John Edward, took over the business when his father died in 1899. John was a colorful character who married Nellie Ingram in 1891 when he was 24. The Georgian Revival home was built by John for Nellie. John and Nellie had two children, John "Jack" W. Cavanagh and Agatha. John and his son, "Jack" continued running the family business. In 1912, Jack built a Craftsman Cottage on the property and after marrying his childhood sweetheart, Viola Sartori in 1913. Sisters Ella and Emma Cavanagh lived their later years in the house.

Hauntspitality

An article in www.metroactive.com under the heading "Best Local Haunted House", states "There Is Something Mysterious afoot at the Cavanaugh Inn. Formerly the home of a soft-spoken, well-mannered woman named Adelaide Cavanaugh, the charming old Victorian is now beautifully restored, comfortably charming . . . and haunted. Late at night, according to numerous guests, footsteps can be heard and felt, creaking against the floorboards as someone paces back and forth in the Magnolia Room. At such times, the bedroom closet--which is permanently locked--can be heard opening and closing. The innkeepers' best guess is that the ghost is the spirit of Adelaide herself, who, it is reported, was

always a bit of a flirt around menfolk. According to reports, she still is, somewhat preferring the company of men to that of women. Having a ghost in the inn hasn't hurt business in the least, by the way. Most guests find Adelaide to be as charming now as she apparently was when she was alive."

The friendly, spirited occupant of the establishment is rumored to be Adelaide Cavanagh, one of the first residents of the historic inn. Adelaide is said to frequent the Magnolia Room and also pays visits to other rooms in the house. She still considers this home and her footsteps are often heard climbing the stairs or making their way down the hallway. Adelaide enjoys moving things around; it seems if something doesn't meet with her approval, she'll do some rearranging.

Guests and staff have reported that doors in the house will sometimes open on their own; an occasional cold spot will suddenly manifest; a smell of perfume used long ago that will permeate an area one second and then be gone the next; and a few unexplained noises can be heard coming from unoccupied parts of the. The unexplained events that take place here are usually attributed to the spirited Adelaide. Everything that has been reported to date is friendly and no one has been frightened of Adelaide's spirited pranks.

Numerous guests have been reported feeling a non-threatening presence, or have actually seen a specter in their room. The Magnolia Room is one place in the house that you are most apt to run into the feminine phantom. There is some speculation that Adelaide prefers men, because she is most often sighted by men, and seems to focus most of her attention on males.

One guest had quite an encounter with the spirit or spirits of the house. While fast asleep, he was suddenly awakened by a cat jumping on his bed in the middle of the night. In the morning he told the owners about the incident, but was puzzled when they said their cat slept in their room all night behind a locked door. He went on to say that he also heard two women having a conversation in his room. He heard the women talking above a whisper but couldn't quite make out the details.

The owners have also made contact with Adelaide. While with a housekeeper in the Magnolia Room, both were hit by a sudden gust of freezing air that literally froze them in their tracks. There are the occasionally strange noises that are heard by guests and owners, but most are attributed to the age of the house. Adelaide, the gentle spirit of the Cavanagh Inn, is always eager to lend an invisible hand to guests.

The Farris family has catered to numerous guests since they bought the house. All come and go, relaxed from their pleasant stay at the inn, except one, Adelaide Cavanagh who refuses to leave her former home; and who can blame her.

Placerville
Albert Shafsky House

Particulars
2942 Coloma Street,
Placerville, CA 95667
Phone: 530-642-2776
E-mail: stay@shafsky.com
Website: www.shafsky.com

History

This 1902 Queen Anne Victorian bed and breakfast in the Placerville Historic District provides a wonderful taste of rich heritage, both inside and out. The bed and breakfast is situated in El Dorado County, just an hour from Lake Tahoe or Sacramento, California. On May 24, 1873, Aaron Yara Shafsky was born in Kishinev, Moldavia, near Odessa above the Black Sea. He arrived in California in 1889 with his brothers and changed his name to Albert Shafsky. Together, they started a dry goods business in Fort Bragg, California, first selling their merchandise to the men at the nearby lumber camps, and then establishing their first store in Fort Bragg in 1892.

While brothers Harry and Samuel Shafsky operated the store, Albert with horses and wagon traveled all over the coast, taking orders, selling goods and establishing the name of the Shafsky Brothers. In 1898, Albert was naturalized as a citizen of the United States in the Superior Court of the City and County of San Francisco and married ("Kitty") Dora May Smith. They had five children, with three being born here in Placerville. Albert Shafsky left Fort Bragg in 1901 and settled in Placerville, where he opened a department store downtown, first in the Douglas Building, then moving in 1909 to a new building on the old Kunkler lot on the Plaza.

The store was known for having the first glass show windows and a milliner who made ladies' hats. Albert was a Placerville City Council Member from 1906-1910 and Mayor of Placerville from 1906-1908. A copy of the Shafsky genealogy was kindly donated to the Inn by the Shafsky family, and guests are welcome to read more about this fascinating family while staying at the bed and breakfast. These as well as many other interesting books are available in our ever-expanding book collection.

Hauntspitality

Current owners Rita Timewell and Stephanie Carlson have provided the following information about their spirited house, when they took over the inn in June of 2002:

- Music could be heard when no guests or radios where on in the house.
- Disembodied footsteps could be heard coming from the upstairs area when no one else was staying with them.
- Lights would flicker on and off on their own.
- One morning, while trying to make breakfast, the stove was turned off. The owners turned it back on, and off it went again. This went on about six times until they finally said out loud "Albert stop it, we need to get breakfast ready" and that was the last time the stove ever acted like that again.
- The owners have found pennies on the fresh cleaned floor.

- Light bulbs that were on one minute will go out; upon further checking, they are found to have been unscrewed.
- Guests who once stayed at the inn were told the owners that they could leave their door open if they wanted to, since they were the only ones staying that night. The guests responded, "We are the only paying guests you mean". When the owners asked what they meant, they stated that the house had other residents besides them, and that was without the owners mentioning Albert's ghost.

At the Albert Shafsky House B&B you don't have to always remember to lock your door, sometimes Albert will do it for you! We have had guests report a number of times that they have left their room for a moment and the door is locked when they return—often when no one else is home.

Albert is a fun loving spirit who seems to think it is fun to play little tricks like this with us and our guests. He is also fond of standing at the foot of beds in the middle of the night and watching over you while you sleep. We have had several guests who mentioned they thought some one was in their room while they slept. On one occasion a guest reported that her shoes were neatly arranged under the bed when she woke up from a nap. It seems that Albert has quiet a sense of humor.

One afternoon the guests had all checked in and were either outside or in their rooms resting. Suddenly there was a loud crash from the living room and as I ran out to see if the guest in the adjoining room was alright, she poked her head out of her room. That was when I realized that an entire shelf of books had cascaded to the floor—for no apparent reason, other than our resident apparition!

Albert Shafsky still seems to live at our B&B and as long as he wants to stay with us, he is welcome. Voted "Best B&B" by the readers of the Mountain Democrat 2005, 2006 this historic house is a delight for the living and provides a permanent haunted holiday for those in the spirit.

Carey House Hotel

Particulars
300 Main Street,
Placerville, CA 95667
Phone: 530-622-9100
Toll Free: 1-800-854-9100

History

The Carey House was originally established in 1857. When it was constructed, there was hot and cold running water, and grand staircase and an elegant lobby crafted out cherry wood and mahogany. The Carey House was situated along the stage line that ran through Placerville from San Francisco. Horace Greeley spoke from the balcony and rich and poor used the hotel during feast and famine.

Hauntspitality

The Carey House ghosts were brought to light during a Travel Channel segment that aired during 2002. Renowned author and gifted psychic, Nancy Bradley has also illuminated the spirited side of this historic landmark. Some of the stories that have circulated over the years include:

- Bradley discovered the spirit of Arnold Wiedman, a horse and wagon operator in the late 1800s, along with his wife, Margaret and a baby, lived in Room 212 at the Cary House Hotel. Arnold died because of influenza and his wife and child had to live here until her parents sent her money to bring the two of them home.
- Cold spots are often felt in various parts of the hotel, materializing in an instant and then vanishing.
- Guest and staff report hearing laughter and feminine voices coming from unoccupied portions of the building.
- During a stay in Room 212 a couple from Richmond experienced an apparition of a man in the room. He was at the foot of the bed one minute and then gone the next.
- Shadowy figures have been sighted floating down the hallway corridors before disappearing into unoccupied rooms or right through the walls.
- Guests have reported that the knobs to their doors will sometimes jiggle or turn. They will usually jump out of bed and try and confront the individual. There is never anyone on the other side when the door is opened.
- One story goes that a miner was wrongly executed for a crime he didn't commit. He was hanged on the front steps of the Carey House and his spirit has resided in the building ever since. Psychics say that the poor miner hides in the lobby, cowering in fear that he will be sighted, caught and tried again.
- Another sprit is said to belong to Stan a former employee and desk clerk who loved flirting with the women guests and enjoyed drinking brandy every chance he could. The legend goes that Stan didn't have much luck with the ladies and the little he did have ended when he tried to pick up on another man's wife. In anger, the jealous husband reportedly stabbed Stan to death. Stan is said to be responsible for rattling doors, appearing in the elevators, following female guests and harassing other staff.

There are few places inside the hotel to hide from the spirits. This is one of most haunted places in Placerville where you don't have a ghost of a chance to escape the paranormal. It's easy at this haunted hot spot to be Carey[d] away by the spirited clientele.

Hangman's Tree Tavern

Particulars

305 Main Street,
Placerville, CA 95667
Phone: 916-622-3878

History

The town, originally known as Dry Diggins, grew and prospered with regular stage stops, a temperance league, churches, and a new, more peaceful attitude toward life and fellow man. This is reflected in a final change in the town name from Hangtown to Placerville. The town with its narrow, winding streets took center stage during the gold rush days. It was the first large gold rush camp after the discovery of gold at Coloma. Like many gold rush towns which sprung up quickly during the late 1840s, the town contained a mixture of log cabins, tents, wood-frame stores, stables, brothels, and saloons. Where men, moonshine, merriment, money, and Mother Nature are thrown together for even short periods of time, trouble is not far behind, and Dry Diggins was a focal point for trouble.

During the winter of 1849, several men were accused of robbery and attempted murder. A jury of miners returned a verdict of "death by hanging"--- lynch law was in force. The men (including Irishman Dick Crone) were hanged on the spot now occupied by Hangman's Tree, and Dry Diggins became the location of the first recorded lynching along the Mother Lode --- its name aptly changed to Hangtown. The name had an immediate effect on the population, taming the miners; for fear that if they misbehaved they too would end up swinging from the end of a rope. The hangings took place from 1849 to 1853, and although only four hangings can be authenticated, speculation has it that the number was probably much higher.

Today, Placerville contains an abundance of refurbished store fronts, behind which stand many buildings dating to the roaring 1840s-1850s. In 1849, when the city was called Hangtown, vigilantes executed men for various crimes. This was the site of Elstner's Hay Yard, on which stood the "Hangman's Tree." The stump of the tree is under the building on which the plaque is placed (California Historical Landmarks (1979, rev. 1982). A mural of the old oak is displayed over the back wall of the lounge bar, although the stump of the real "hangman's oak" lies several feet below the existing structure. Authentic relics of the tree are preserved by the owners. Outside, hangs "George," a lone 49er, and reminder of Hangtown's more violent days. The Hangman's Tree has been a bar since 1933.

Hauntspitality

Hangman's Tree has a certificate of authenticity, which reads, "This is to inform that The Hangman's Tree Lounge #103 has been certified to be haunted." This certification was provided by members of Gold Rush Ghosts of Diamond Springs, California. The business is also a State of California Historical Landmark.

The ghosts of claim jumpers and outlaws, many sentenced to hang from an old oak tree here, are said to occasionally intrude on patrons and employees of this small cafe/tavern/restaurant.

Several people have reported seeing apparitions while passing by the establishment in their automobiles late at night. One local, whose father built his home on the American River, and resided in Placerville for over 50 years, claims to have heard the desperate cries of criminals dangling from the end of a rope, as the life was slowly squeezed out of them. She said that after coming to town for supplies, and as the sun began to set while she stood near the hanging tree, she could hear blood-curdling screams that made her shudder in fear.

Another local whose grandfather sentenced many of the criminals to their eternal doom, has witnessed a greenish light emanating from the basement of Hangman's Tree, and rise up to surround the building--- especially on a full moon. There have been times that the eerie green glow cast the shadow of the hanging tree on the building.

Several locals recall seeing the mysterious shapes of what appear to be desperadoes, walking the street in front of the cafe. Other residents of the town confirm seeing the ghostly shapes of long deceased gunfighters roaming the s treet near the spot where the old hanging tree once stood. A bartender working late, long after the last customer departed, reported seeing a male specter walk right through a wall. A psychic later confirmed the sighting, identifying the spirit as that of the former caretaker of the old oak who had the responsibility in life, to tend to the bodies of those hung from its branches---a responsibility that he seems to perpetuate from another dimension.

One longtime resident, while imbibing at the bar, had to use the restroom. As she approached the door to the ladies' room, she saw a man exit. He had an odd look about him, as if he came from another time period, wearing black, and dressed in a period top hat. Thinking that the men's restroom was out of order, or that the man might be participating in a play or parade, she dismissed the incident until returning to the bar. She asked about the strange man, but no one had seen him, nor was there a special event that day which would have accounted for his strange attire. A waitress recalled that while talking to customers about ghosts during Christmas, the lights suddenly dimmed for a few moments, then returned to their normal level of brightness.

Inside the Hangman's Tree, a number of unexplainable things continue to happen, including:
- An ever-present feeling of being watched or followed;
- The jukebox, which begins playing music unassisted;
- Restroom doors that are opened and closed by an unseen force;
- Shot glasses that are resting on the shelf one minute, then mysteriously make their way to where the ice is kept when the bartender turns his back;
- Conversations with fellow customers who simply vanish in front of startled guests and staff;
- A specter that appears wearing a top hat and walks through walls; and much, much more.

The old west days continue in full swing from another dimension at this haunted saloon, where the dead are still hanging around.

Placerville Coffee House

Particulars

594 Main Street,
Placerville, CA 95667
Phone: 530-295-1481

History

One of the most unique Java houses and entertainment venues in the region,

the Placerville Coffee House is three stories of art, music, spooky caves, private nooks, good company, food and great coffee. The Pearson's Soda Works building is a California Gold Rush landmark. Its stone walls house a mining shaft which hides behind creaky rusty metal doors. A walk into "The Cave" reveals hidden rooms and a tunnel that goes back into the hillside of "Old Hangtown." Originally a brewery and restaurant, this watering hole has seen the likes of Pony Express Riders, outlaws and law men who helped define the cowboy and miner life-style.

According to their brochure, the building located at 594 Main Street was once the home of Pearson's Soda Works, which was established in 1852 by John McFarland Pearson. Mr. Pearson was an early Placerville businessman who had emigrated from Scotland and had his start in the area as an ice merchant. Mr. Pearson had established an ale and syrup factory west of the Old Fountain Hotel, at the approximate location of the current building. In July of 1856, however, a devastating fire, the second of three that year in Placerville, consumed most of the downtown buildings, including the structure in which Mr. Pearson conducted his ale and syrup business.

During this time, John McFarland Pearson maintained his ice business in a building near Carey Alley, while storing the ice in a building on Bedford Avenue. In 1859, he advertised both of these buildings for sale. This same year, a new building was constructed, which Mr. Pearson soon occupied This new structure, which is now the front section of the bottom floor of the current building, was constructed of Mariposa slate, with a facade of rough-dressed local rhyolite, suitable to withstand another fire. John McFarland Pearson's Soda Works thrived on Main Street. In the new building, Mr. Pearson expanded his business to include his own soda water which he manufactured on the premises. A 135-foot abandoned mining tunnel carved into the hill behind the building served as a cooler in which Mr. Pearson stored ice and other perishables. Pearson originally supplied ice to the people of Placerville by retrieving it from a location north of Riverton. This area is still known as Ice House, named after the building he constructed there to store ice. By 1890, however, Pearson was purchasing this commodity from the Union Ice Company, who shipped it via rail from Sacramento. He offered many items for sale, besides ice and the soda that he made on the premises, which included syrups, beer and ale, butter, and eggs.

Many of the names on the accounts of Pearson's business read like a who's who of early Placerville. These names include James Blakeley, John Rafetto, Fleming Jones, Nicola Avansino, Frank Phelps, Nicola Fossati, G. Myers, George

Skinner, DeBernardi, S.J. Alder, and Robert, James and John Blair.

On August 7, 1891, after having been ill for some time, John McFarland Pearson passed his home, which was located at the northwest corner of Pacific Street and Cedar Ravine. Earlier that day, he drafted his will with the aid of his friend James Blair, and his son-in-law, Robert Blair, According to Pearson's will, the building and soda business were passed to his sons, John and William. After seeing to the matters of their father's death, the two brothers set forth to expand their father's business. They added wine and liquors to their sale list; they began syrups and ciders, and became fire insurance agents.

In 1897, the two brothers added the second story to the building, constructed of 150,000 bricks from George Morton's Kiln in Placerville. A hydraulic lift was installed to save the cost of 200 hand carriers. This new addition to the building served as the bottling room; and the hydraulic lift was used to move bottles between the two floors. A photo of the building during this period shows that the large sign on the front of the building which now reads "Placerville Soda Works" once read "Wholesale Wines and Liquors".

William Pearson eventually moved to Concord, in Contra Costa County, with his wife, Sadie, and their daughter, Georgia, where he ranched and became a merchant. In April of 1917, William sadly committed suicide by shooting himself for reasons unknown. Four months later, his brother John died as a result of a heart attack. During John's funeral procession through town, all of the businesses closed in respect. When John died, his wife Clara inherited the Pearson building. By 1920 the soda business had been sold to the Scherrer Brothers, thereafter becoming the first Coca Cola franchise in Placerville. The building, however, stayed in Clara's ownership until it was passed to two of her relatives after her death in 1971. From 1920 through 1973, the building had several tenants and underwent changes to its original condition.

In 1974, Roger and Antoinette Douvres purchased the building and rehabilitated it by adding structural support, lights, a new stairway, and recreating a soda fountain reminiscent of the turn of the century. The Douvres also restored the facade to its original material with rough-dressed rhyolite blocks, in 1980 title transferred to the Douvres' daughter, Suzanne Bickel. Ms. Bickel effectively preserved the integrity of this historic building by having it placed on the National Register of Historic Places in 1985. This status discourages any actions that would diminish the historic qualities of the building. Thanks to Suzanne Bickel and her parents, a remnant of the early history of Placerville has been restored to its original appearance and has been preserved for the benefit of current and future generations. Now a locally famous coffee house, the former John McFarland Pearson Soda Works building, no doubt, because of its long, and illustrious history, is rumored to be a very haunted location.

Hauntspitality
When the Placerville Coffee House was opened in 1996 by Mike and Pat Rideout, there were already plenty of local rumors about spirits occupying the building. Ghostly voices, particularly heavy breathing sounds were said to come from inside the old mine shaft. Renowned psychic Rosemary Dean visited the old building and encountered a phantom shape that identified himself as a 27-year-old miner named Virgil, who was killed in the mine during a cave-in. This restless spirit refuses to believe he is dead and still feels that life treated him unfairly. He

chooses to remain behind, to protect his domain.

Female staff have often reported seeing spirits, or at the very least, hearing disembodied voices coming from inside the mine area. Sometimes the voices sound like several people are engaged in an argument, and the angry exchange grows louder until a brave soul enters the mine. There is a phantom dog that also makes the old soda works building his home, continuing to wait for his owner to return. The upper portion of the building is said to contain the ghost of a stocky man who sports a mustache, and wears a straw hat. This spirit is very playful, enjoys people, and has fun playing tricks on the staff and visitors. The portly man seems to have died from a heart attack while working in the building, and he likes where he is---on the other side of the veil.

Other apparitions include a thin, elderly woman who appears to be from the Late-1800s, called Alice. She tends to the bathrooms, and other areas of the building that frequently need cleaning. Death does not seem to diminish her desire to keep the place neat and tidy, and she doesn't seem to like messy people.

Another story involves security guards who happened to drop in on the place while making their rounds. As they looked inside the building, they watched in amazement as silverware was being picked-up by unseen hands, and thrown across the room. Needless to say, they didn't bother to apprehend the unseen intruder. Employees have had doors shut as they were about to enter a room, or there will be times, when perfectly functioning doors will not open at all. Staff has felt as if they were being watched, and have reported being pushed by invisible hands.

There are wonderful musicians and storytellers who visit the establishment to entertain both the living and the dead.

The Seasons Bed & Breakfast

Particulars
2934 Bedford Avenue,
Placerville, CA 95667
Phone: 530-626-4420
E-mail: stay@theseasons.net
Website: www.theseasons.net

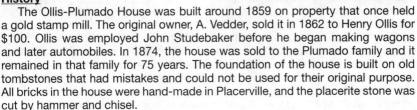

History

The Ollis-Plumado House was built around 1859 on property that once held a gold stamp mill. The original owner, A. Vedder, sold it in 1862 to Henry Ollis for $100. Ollis was employed John Studebaker before he began making wagons and later automobiles. In 1874, the house was sold to the Plumado family and it remained in that family for 75 years. The foundation of the house is built on old tombstones that had mistakes and could not be used for their original purpose. All bricks in the house were hand-made in Placerville, and the placerite stone was cut by hammer and chisel.

The Cottage, one of two extra buildings on the grounds, was originally a chicken coop and was later rebuilt as a home for a seamstress, known to everyone as Miss Jo. Before Bedford Avenue was paved, it was lined with poplars and was lower than the current street level. What is now the main floor of the house with the parlor, dining room and kitchen, was once the second floor with two bedrooms. Later owners replaced the marble fireplace in the parlor with one built of stones that they had hand-picked in travels to various places. The Seasons is named for a series of paintings by artist and former owner Ann Gladwill, which depict life in El Dorado County California at different times of the year.

Hauntspitality

Several psychics have had the good fortune to step into this historic home and soak up the local color, as well as the spirits. There is a psychic consensus that at least three spirits reside inside. According to gifted psychic and renowned author Nancy Bradley, and the owners of the inn, a male spirit named Buck and female phantoms named Catherine and Margaret grace the historic hallways and rooms.

The congenial spirits blend flawlessly with their surroundings, and outside of a few disembodied footsteps, some chilly breezes, a door or two that opens on its own, and an occasional apparition who is peeking in from time to time, all is well at this enchanting and other-worldly inn where ghosts and guest commune together.

Pleasanton
Gay Nineties Pizza Company

Particulars

288 Main Street,
Pleasanton, CA 94566
Phone: 925-846-2520
Fax: 925-846-0565
Website: www.gayninetiespizza.com

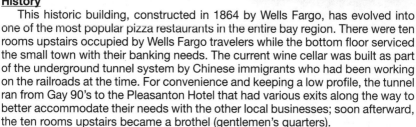

History

This historic building, constructed in 1864 by Wells Fargo, has evolved into one of the most popular pizza restaurants in the entire bay region. There were ten rooms upstairs occupied by Wells Fargo travelers while the bottom floor serviced the small town with their banking needs. The current wine cellar was built as part of the underground tunnel system by Chinese immigrants who had been working on the railroads at the time. For convenience and keeping a low profile, the tunnel ran from Gay 90's to the Pleasanton Hotel that had various exits along the way to better accommodate their needs with the other local businesses; soon afterward, the ten rooms upstairs became a brothel (gentlemen's quarters).

During 1950, the building became a local sprits establishment called "The Blue Goose." In 1959, a small Pizza oven was purchased to keep up with the demands for Pizza. Business begins to Boom and The Blue Goose Bar becomes "Gay 90's Pizza." The first and only Pizza parlor in Pleasanton or it's surrounding areas. Long before Robert and Suzanne Earnest purchased the restaurant in 1984, the phenomenon has assisted many ladies with their delinquent pregnancies. The restaurant is frequently visited by pregnant women who are overdue. Often these Ladies will begin labor the very next day or even as they're walking out the door.

Hauntspitality

Current owner Robert Earnest, who has owned the building since 1984, has experienced numerous unexplained incidents inside. While in the basement, Chinese voices have been heard along with strange banging sounds, groans, coughing and footsteps. On the main floor, the owner's dog used to run into the room, abruptly stop at the cashier's station, and bark at something unseen. The dog, with its hair standing on end, refused to budge while continuing to bark. As the owner looked toward the mirror, he saw the letters "BOO" being spelled out with a small heart drawn underneath. It was as if a ghost was standing in front of the mirror writing the letters with a spirited finger. To this day, the letters cannot be rubbed off or cleaned away.

When Earnest bought the building and was living in the apartment above the pizza parlor, he invited his son and parents over to celebrate Christmas. The young boy suddenly blurted out, 'Daddy, who's that lady?' " When Earnest and the parents turned toward the corner of the room where the boy was looking they saw a woman standing at the window looking down on Main Street. As they looked on the woman turned to face everyone. She looked to be in her forties as she smiled at the stunned group. Her outfit was that of a saloon dance hall girl with a lot of cleavage showing. As quickly as she materialized, she just as abruptly vanished.

According to staff and guests, the second story of the building is the most active. In the 1880s, this portion of the building contained ten rooms for exhausted travelers when Wells Fargo owned it. Subsequently the area was converted into a two-bedroom apartment, then an office for the owner. Numerous locals, and people just passing by have reported a lady in a Victorian blue dress, peering out the window from the upstairs two-bedroom apartment that now consists of office space. This spectral lady has also been sighted by people standing outside the building when the bar is closed. Several witnesses have looked up toward the second floor window which faces Main and Abbie Streets, and watched as a woman vanished in front of their eyes.

Motorists passing by during off-business hours have also remarked that a strange-looking woman was standing in the upstairs window one minute, then dematerializes the next. Described as someone who looks "human," the phantom lady will suddenly manifest or disappear in front of startled witnesses. Cold chills felt by those standing in the room are also attributed to the Lady in Blue and plants will not grow near the window where the woman is frequently seen. There is also a refrigerator in the room whose door will suddenly open or close when no one is near it, as if someone is inspecting the contents. Descriptions of the female suggest a woman who worked in bar or saloon, since she is short in stature, rather plumpish, and likes to wear heavy makeup. Perhaps she was around when the building served as a speakeasy and bordello.

Besides the frequent sightings of a female apparition upstairs, there are unexplained footsteps, cold spots, occasional odd noises that occur downstairs, doors that open and close by themselves and lights that turn on unassisted.

If you are a pizza lover and you're looking for a different topping, try spirits. The Gay Nineties is the only place around that offers this unique combination.

Pleasanton Hotel

Particulars
855 Main Street,
Pleasanton, CA 94566
Phone: 925-846-8106
Fax: 925-846-0531
Website: www.pleasantonhotel.com

History

Formerly known as the Farmer's Hotel, the building was constructed around 1865 by an early settler named John W. Kottinger who came here in search of gold. Kottinger named the town after Civil War hero General Alfred Pleasanton. Educated in law, Kottinger was appointed county judge, and presided over the town of Pleasanton which had become known as the "most desperate town in the west."

Bandits and desperadoes like Joaquin Murietta would prey upon those striking it rich in the area. In an attempt to keep order, Kottinger converted his own barn into a jail which is still located near the Pleasanton hotel on Ray Street. Prisoners were led via tunnels from the Court House to the jail to prevent daylight escapes or rescues. Kottinger also built a tunnel which connected his hotel (The Farmer's) to the local saloon. The Pleasanton Hotel burned down in 1889 and had minor fire damage in 1915. It has been faithfully restored and is a full-service restaurant, lounge and banquet facility.

Hauntspitality

The top floor of the Pleasanton Hotel, now strictly a restaurant, maintains a strong spiritual energy due to a murder of a woman which reportedly occurred in 1870. The maze of corridors on the second floor seems to contain a presence or two from the era when the place catered to gamblers and gunmen. There is no mistaking the fact that the restaurant still caters to other-worldly guests as evidenced by numerous occasions when footsteps can be heard coming from unoccupied parts of the building, or when doors will suddenly open or shut without human assistance. The lights have been known to inexplicably flicker, turn off or suddenly come on. It has been determined not to be faulty wiring that leads most to suspect a paranormal clientele.

On a number of occasions, staff has reportedly witnessing shadowy figures or misty forms out of the corner of their eyes. After the brave individuals give chase, they invariably find themselves alone in the area where the phantom figure disappeared. Then, there are the unmistakable cold spots that seem to come out of nowhere to chill people to the bone; and it's not the air conditioning nor drafts that cause these seemingly random events.

A local psychic once visited the building; upon entering, she immediately remarked that she felt the energy of a man in uniform still occupying the premises. Others, however, have felt a female presence as well as heard faint voices of people conversing; perhaps a poker game still being played on the other side, or a heated argument involving unresolved issues. This locally renowned restaurant caters to those looking for a great meal, and those who remain behind from another era still enjoying the ambiance and who have no problem sharing the Pleasanton with the living clientele.

Portola Valley
Alpine Inn

Particulars

3915 Alpine Road,
Portola Valley, CA 94028
Phone: 650-854-4004

History

    The Casa de Tableta also known as Alpine Inn Beer Garden was listed on the National Register of Historic Places in 1973 (Building - #73000447). The history was gleaned through an article by Steve Staiger, the City of Palo Alto historian and a staff member at the main library. The Alpine Inn is one of the oldest businesses on the Peninsula. During the 1850s, Felix Buelna, a former mayor of San Jose, opened a gambling house, where his friends could play cards, socialize and have a drink. Buelna's roadhouse was established along the Old Spanish Trail. Buelna's sold the roadhouse to William Stanton, a Menlo Park coachman, reputedly to cover his losses in a poker game. During 1870, Englishman, William Tate Philpott, leased the roadhouse for five years before William Stanton resumed management, when it became known as Stanton's Saloon. When Stanton died in a railroad accident, his family leased the business to F. Rodriguez Crovello, known to his customers as "Black Chapete."

    When Stanford opened in 1891, the students congregated at Black Chapete's and University officials pressured San Mateo County officials to close the drinking establishment. But county officials did nothing, as saloon keepers dominated San Mateo County politics. Charlie Wright, one of the former Mayfield saloon owners, began a partnership with Crovello at the Alpine roadhouse. Charles Schenkel then took over management of the roadhouse and renamed it the "Wunder." In 1907, Portola Valley farmer Walter Jelich bought Schenkel's lease and continued the saloon's operation. In 1909 the State of California passed a law prohibiting the sale of liquor within 1 _ miles of schools and universities, including Stanford; however, the Alpine Inn was just outside the new limit. During World War I, the U.S. Army's Camp Fremont in Menlo Park created a dry zone surrounding the camp; Once again the roadhouse was outside the "dry zone." Soldiers joined the locals and students in alcoholic consumption.

    By 1911 all interests in the saloon had passed to Julius Schenkel, the brother of Charles. The Volstead Act of 1919 forced the closure of saloons around the country. All this meant was that rum runners and speakeasies became sources of alcoholic beverages until the repeal of Prohibition in 1933. Illegal liquor activity in San Mateo County was notorious and shipments of illegal liquor were smuggled into the county along the coastline. During this time, the establishment was "Schenkel's Picnic Park" and non-alcoholic beverages were sold, with more potent beverages available to those in the know.

    At the end of Prohibition, Schenkel retired, and Enrico Rossotti and his wife took over, eventually purchasing the property from the Stanton family. He ran the business a saloon with grilled food until 1956. Don Horther and John Alexander took over the roadhouse in 1956 and renamed it the "Alpine Inn Beer Garden"; however, patrons today still call it "Rossotti's" or "Zott's." Now, students and Silicon Valley workers make up a bulk of the business clientele. On weekends, bicyclists, motorcyclists and horse riders enjoy the Inn.

Hauntspitality

Does a spirit from the days when the building served as a roadhouse run by Felix Buelna still haunt the Alpine Inn? Some people who work there and others who come for a visit are convinced that "something" haunts the building, whether it be a "Gold Rush-type", or a former cowboy.

On more than one occasion people have spotted a salty old gentleman wearing a cowboy hat, bandana, dark boots and wearing chaps standing in front of the building, only to mysteriously vanish. Others have smelled tobacco inside when no one was smoking, and felt chills that run up their spine while inside. Muffled conversations coming from unoccupied areas, glasses moving on their own, rapidly manifesting cold spots, and shadowy figures are reported when the place is in "quiet" mode.

This establishment is filled with over 150 years of history and in that time quite a few people left their imprint on the landscape. At least one person who visited the building seems to enjoy hanging around. Perhaps the man died a violent death during a gun fight, or maybe this is where he visited frequently when he was alive and had a lot of fond memories. Then again, if psychics are right, there is more than one spirit who finds the Alpine Inn an afterlife sanctuary.

We suggest you visit this hauntingly historic building and put your psychic senses to the test and see what you feel inside.

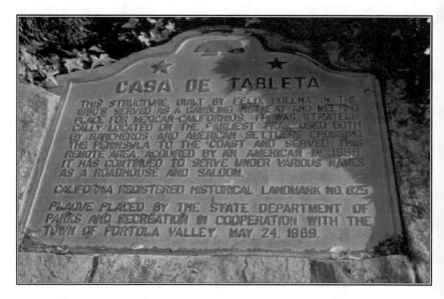

Redlands
Morey Mansion
Bed & Breakfast Inn

Particulars

190 Terracina Boulevard,
Redlands, CA 92375
Phone: 909-793-7970
Fax: 909-793-7870

History

We recommend that you call first before visiting. As we were going to press, the establishment was closed. However, we were told that after some changes, the place would reopen as a bed and breakfast. According to a planning commission line item in April 2006, "earlier this month, the Planning Commission approved Janet Cosgrove's application for a permit to use three of the Morey Mansion's five bedrooms for the venture. "

David and Sarah Morey were early pioneers in Redlands. David Morey was born in Pennsylvania, October 7, 1824. He came to California around 1850 and worked as a miner, shipbuilder, and agriculturist, until he came to Redlands in 1882. Sarah J. DeForrest was born in Cayuga County, N. Y., and, wed David Morey in May, 1870.

Mr. Morey initially built a cabin, twenty feet square, on the twenty-acre ranch which he had purchased before coming here, located on Brookside Avenue, and here they lived for ten years. The ranch was set to orange trees in 1883, and Mrs. Morey looked after the property while her husband earned their daily bread by following his trade. In 1884 Mrs. Morey planted a small seed bed, putting about two thousand orange seeds in to the ground. Encouraged by her success, she planted about 25,000 seed, and sold the little trees to Judson & Brown for ten acres of land on the opposite side of the street from their ranch and ten shares of water. Once again she planted about the same amount of trees and in 1889 sold the bulk to Matthew Gage (who just completed the Gage Canal system), for $20,000 and more land. The Moreys finally moved to Terracina and built their mansion. The house had four fireplaces and was a showplace for the community.

Mr. Morey was the third president of the Redlands Water Company and he helped lay the foundations of the Bear Valley dam. Mrs. Morey assisted in the circulation of subscription paper. After Sarah's death in 1901, David contemplated moving to San Diego. After signing papers to sell to an investor, David calmly walked upstairs, went into the Tower Room, scribbled a note that said he could not live without his Sarah, and then committed suicide. Additionally, Clark Gable and Carole Lombard are said to have spent the first night of their honeymoon at the mansion.

Hauntspitality

Several séances that have been conducted inside, revealed that Sarah Morey and her husband David have never left the building they so loved. They are not alone. A third spirit belongs to a young girl who is frequently sighted wearing turn-of-the-century clothing. A fourth ghost has been described as a thin, elderly man with white hair, wearing a tweed jacket and black hat, similar

to something a servant might wear. The elderly gentleman is always sighted as a faceless apparition.

A HGTV special entitled "Haunted Houses" previewed the Morey Mansion as a premiere Bed and Breakfast Inn. The special episode concluded with a statement that at certain time, the house had more spirits than living persons occupying the mansion. This was considered one of the most haunted houses in San Bernardino County.

The friendly spirits have made life very interesting for former owners, occupants, and guests. The spirited foursome will not only appear in front of startled witnesses, but they have been felt as quickly materializing cold spots, and their disembodied footsteps are frequently heard using the stairs or walking down the upstairs hallway. Occasionally a door will open or close by itself, and the lights have been know to flicker on and off when the spirits are around. The Tower room is also one of the haunted hot spots in the house, and footsteps are sometimes heard pacing back and forth in the unoccupied room. Whenever someone goes to inspect, no one human is sighted, and the curious are left to experience a cold blast of air, or the feeling of being watched.

According to a recent article (10/27/2006) by Staff Writer Matt Wrye, "Morey Mansion is said to contain the spirits of its owners", the presence of David and his wife, Sarah, can still be felt, and even seen, in their old home on Terracina Boulevard. Lights have been known to suddenly flicker for no logical reason in the Blue Room (The Morey's bedroom when they were alive). Current owner, Janet Cosgrove, although never experiencing anything paranormal herself, she has heard quite a few of the ghost stories. On one occasion a staircase light began flickering when she played the piano, and her dogs wouldn't venture into one of the hallways. The closet in the Blue Room has a doorknob that has been know to move as if someone unseen was attempting to open it. Other guests have heard what they describe as the sound of a pocket watching ticking although they were alone in the room. There are reports of shadowy figures being seen by guests out of the corner of their eyes late at night and of a man wearing a top hat and pin-stripe suit gliding down the hallway only to vanish. Staff who have spent time in the Blue Room always remark that they feel as if someone is watching them as they cleanup.

The Morey Mansion and its ghost stories will remain a legacy for years to come. This architectural marvel is a must-visit for those who love to be pampered, even if the attention is delivered by a spirit or two, or three or more!

Riverside
Mission Inn

Particulars
3649 Mission Inn Avenue,
Riverside, CA 92501
Phone: 909-784-0300
Fax: 909-683-1342
Toll Free: 800- 843-7755
E-mail: sales@missioninn.com
Website: www.missioninn.com/home.htm

History
According to their website: The Mission Inn is California State Historic landmark #761. Frank A. Miller (1857-1935) made adobe bricks for a small 12 room guest house which opened in 1876. By adding to the building, Miller fulfilled his dream by recreating this early California mission style setting of a hotel. The Mission Inn was built from 1903-33 in the middle of Downtown Riverside. Its eclectic architecture and unusual art and artifact collections make the Inn a favorite tourist spot.

During 1902 Miller built a four story U-shaped hotel enclosing a large central courtyard. Over the next thirty years Miller added three more wings to the structure. The Cloister Wing, built in 1910, added more guest rooms the large Music Room, an art and gift shop, and the St. Cecilia Chapel. The Spanish Wing came next in 1913-1914, designed by Myron Hunt. The Spanish Patio offered guests an outdoor dining experience. Two floors of additional guest rooms, including the Author's Row suites and Miller's own private suite, were added in the late 1920's. The International Rotunda Wing, completed in 1931, featured an open-air, five-story spiral staircase, another art gallery, the Famous Fliers' Wall, the St. Francis Chapel, and the Court of the Orient.

Miller's guests included President Theodore Roosevelt, Maude Adams, Sarah Bernhardt, Madame Modjeska, Hamlin Garland, Pulitzer Prize winner, Charles Fletcher Lummis and visiting members of the royal houses of Sweden, Russia, and Japan were honored at banquets. After Frank Miller died in 1935, the Mission Inn began a slow decline. The family sold the Inn in 1956, and numerous owners occupied the hotel until 1976 when the Riverside Redevelopment Agency purchased the Inn.

From 1985-1988 extensive renovation took place. Before opening again, owner/developer Carley Capital of Madison, Wisconsin, filed for bankruptcy. It wasn't until 1992 that long time Riverside resident Duane R. Roberts formed a new corporation, the Historic Mission Inn Corporation, which purchased the inn on December 30, 1992, exactly seven and a half years after it was closed. A Gala opening was celebrated in May 1993.

Hauntspitality

Staff and guests have reported phantom figures, and strange events occurring throughout the building. Perhaps some of the many guests who spent time at the Mission Inn over the last 90 years have returned to enjoy the good old days. One staff member stood looking toward the fireplace where he observed a number of people sitting and talking. A quick glance away, and then back to the scene, and the group had vanished. The staff person recalled that all the people, particularly the men were dressed in period clothing and wearing hats and coats. The men sported mustaches, while the women wore gorgeous dresses. On another occasion, a staff person was passing through the lobby when she saw several phantom figures standing in the lobby near the stairs. As she stopped to get a better look and the strangely dressed clientele, they vanished.

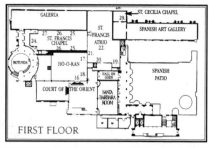

FIRST FLOOR

GROUND FLOOR

The spirits of the Mission Inn have also been heard by the pool. On one occasion, the sound of exotic birds was distinctly heard, although there were no such animals around at the time. After doing a little research, a staff person mentioned that the original owner, Frank Miller, had once decorated the pool area with ornate bird cages filled with exotic birds.

Another phantom has been sighted standing at the top of the stairs, gazing down at guests before vanishing. The ghostly presence was described as wearing clothing from the early 1900s. Other ghostly visitors include an elderly gentleman wearing a cut-away coat and black tie. As the man stood on the stairs looking at two guests ascending the steps, he vanished. Loud noises, as if people were having a party, occasionally come from several unoccupied rooms in the hotel. After complaints and inspections, there is never anyone in the unoccupied room.

The same "party room," has also received complaints from guests occupying the room who say their lights go off and on at odd hours of the day and night. Additionally, the television set seems to have a mind of its own; turning itself on, and frequently changing channels.

Finally, the restaurant has had its share of cold spots and ghostly figures floating and vanishing in front of startled witnesses. Glasses have been lifted from trays while customers have watched in disbelief. One unoccupied table suddenly materialized four guests dressed in 1920s attire; the women were wearing dark blue dresses, and the men wore pinstriped coats. Thinking a group of actors had made their way in and seated themselves, a waitress went to take their order. As she approached the festive group who were animatedly talking and laughing, they suddenly vanished. There are also reports of a phantom white dog that patrols portions of the building. Additional stories follow:

- People staying in Room 215 report lights the size of a bowling ball floating inside.
- In Alice Miller's former room on the 4th floor in the southeast corner of the building, staff and guests report unseen hands touching them, rapidly manifesting cold spots and apparitions of Alice.
- In the Bridal/Honeymoon Suite directly across from Alice Miller's room, there have been numerous reports of people being shoved while on the spiral staircase of this two-level room.
- The catacombs, an area closed to the public since 1992 has been the site of many unexplained phenomena including a ghostly figure, cold spots, disembodied footsteps and ghostly voices.
- In Frank Miller's Room on the 4th floor in the northeast corner of the building, people have reported a strong male presence inside.
- There have been quite a few reports of misty and shadowy forms along hallways throughout the hotel, particularly along Author's Row and near Alice Miller's room. The 2nd and 4th floor hallways that run along the pool have frequently produced sightings and unusual paranormal occurrences.
- The dining room has also had its share of unexplained encounters with apparitions and orbs.
- The rotunda area has been known to produce instant chills and an occasional misty form.
- Several ghostly figures have been sighted in the Spanish patio area, and people report unearthly laughter, unexplained voices and occasional sounds of children playing.
- The St. Francis Chapel Courtyard is a known location for paranormal events including disembodied voices.
- The storage building behind the hotel has had multiple reports of a male spirit and unexplained noises. One story suggests that a construction worker lost his life during the remodeling of the hotel and remains in this area.

The Mission Inn is a spirited rendezvous for past and present visitors alike. It's a historic place where the living and departed always seem to have a good time; a place where the Mission for its spirited population is to entertain the guests!

331

Sacramento

Hartley House Inn

Particulars

700 22nd Street,
Sacramento, CA 95816-4012
Phone: 916-447-7829
Fax: 916-448-4689
E-mail: randy#hartleyhouse.com
Website: www.hartleyhouse.com

History

The Boulevard Park Subdivision was Sacramento's first subdivision that was built between 1905 and 1915, on land that had been the popular Union Racetrack 1800 to 1848 and from 1849 to 1899 the California State Fair Grounds. Two requirements to build were that the home must cost at least $3,950.00 to construct and that there could be no livestock. Many of the first residents were politicians, judges and other professionals who wanted to live close to the Governors Mansion located at 16th and H Streets. The Craftsman Bungalows and Colonial Revival construction in this area contrast with the Victorian, Delta Type, Queen Anne and Italianate houses built before the turn of the century in adjacent areas. In addition to the boulevards on the 21st and 22nd Streets, a unique feature of this area is the private parks in the center of the two blocks bounded by those streets and by F and H Streets. Hartley House is located in one of these blocks.

Hartley House, a Cube-Type Craftsman/Colonial type structure was built in 1910 for Carter Blair Hartley, from Wales, who worked for the Southern Pacific Railroad. The Hartley family lived in the house until it was sold to Faith Murphy, who converted it into a gentlemen's boarding house in 1953. In 1987, the present owner, Randall Hartley purchased the home back into the original family for the operation of Hartley House Bed and Breakfast Inn. The impeccably restored exterior looks newly finished on this large example of mainstream eclectic taste, circa 1905. The angled bay is design holdover from Victorian house types. Wide Craftsman-style eves shelter formal Colonial Revival trim on a dignified symmetrical facade. The stately character of the interior is preserved in original inlaid hardwood floors, stained woodwork, leaded and stained glass windows and original brass light fixtures converted from gas.

Hauntspitality

This is all the information we could obtain from owner Randy Hartley. So, we know it haunted in a friendly way, and you'll have to visit to find out more about the spirits of the house. Hartley states, "When I purchased the property about

20 years ago, there were supposed to be two ghosts (male & female) residing in my bed & breakfast. I heard stories, but I have only two incidents where the gentleman spirit said hello during the day in the parlor and one evening said thank you to me one evening while I was setting the table for breakfast. These incidents were about 19 years ago and often guests and friends will say that they feel the presence of happy spirits but I have not. I do know that they are a happy and playful pair; especially the woman."

According to local lore, a woman died in the house and the spirited gentleman lived across the street. Apparently, a Romeo and Juliette story theme as she supposedly took her own life. There have been numerous reports of lights being turned on by themselves, of the piano playing when the room is unoccupied, and a female guest waking up to have her hair in curls. There was also a guest who took a photo in parlor and the image of a male ghost wearing clothes from the early 1900's appeared on celluloid. The phantom gentleman was not dressed casually, but rather dressed in a suit, shirt and tie and looking very dapper.

Do former members of the Carter Blair Hartley family still love the house so much that even in death, they remain behind to welcome guests from around the world? Or, did a secret affair take place inside resulting in the woman taking her life out of remorse? You'll have to find the answers to these questions when you come for an extended stay at this historic home turn bed and breakfast.

San Andreas
The Robin's Nest
Bed & Breakfast

Particulars
247 W. St. Charles Street,
San Andreas, CA 95249-1090
Phone: 209-754-1076
Fax: 209-754-3975
Toll free: 1-888-214-9202
E-mail Address: info@robinest.com
Website: www.robinest.com

History

During 1895, John Snyder, County District Attorney, built this magnificent home for his bride, Elizabeth O'Connell. Local newspapers referred to it as a mansion and one of the finest residences in the mountains. Rowena, the Snyder's daughter was born here and Mayme, Elizabeth's sister, resided here as well. The house was for the most part unoccupied from about 1939 to 1979. During that time it became known as the "Haunted House" of San Andreas and often used as a model for high school art class. One of the resultant pictures, a water color, currently hangs in the front parlor.

The house was sold in 1979. During 1982 the start of a careful restoration to the home's original Queen Ann Victorian style began. The original dirt basement was converted into owner's quarters plus a gift shop (subsequently converted into a guest room). The huge unfinished attic was converted into five guest rooms. It subsequently received an award for Architectural Excellence by the Calaveras County Historical Society. In 1984, Robin Brooks officially opened her doors to the public as a Bed & Breakfast Inn. Her first guest was Rowena Snyder. The current owners are William & Karen Konietzny.

Hauntspitality

Here's the spirited scoop from the owners, William & Karen Konietzny who reported the following experiences:
- We were visited in 1998 by the publisher of Dark Regions Press, and Joe Morey and his wife who is apparently a spiritualist. The visit was prompted by comments made from a previous guest who claimed to have heard ghosts. They advised us that the spirit or spirits inhabiting our old mansion are benevolent. Our guests have told us numerous stories since then.
- A man was heard singing in the shower in an unoccupied room.
- Guests in one room reported hearing people checking in very late in an adjacent room. In the morning they found out that the room next to theirs was actually unoccupied.
- A guest overheard two women talking and laughing in an adjacent room. Later she found out that the room was unoccupied at the time.
- A lower level occupant heard furniture being moved in the parlor above him late in the evening. He assumed it was the innkeepers rearranging furniture

from a conference that was held earlier. Unfortunately the explanation was of an unearthly nature; the Inn was empty at the time.

- On a fairly regular basis, the main entrance door (located one level above the basement level quarters) opens and closes on its own and footsteps are then heard proceeding across the parlor; however no one human can be found to account for these disturbances.
- Often, loud crashing noises emanate from the dining room, although it is unoccupied. On one occasion, William Konietzny was in these quarters below and his wife was on the upper level.
- On three separate occasions over a three year period, a loud "whomp!" was heard throughout the house. In one case it occurred three times in five minute intervals. It was as if the house had minor single vibration earthquake-like tremors. Despite the name of our town, we aren't on or near any known faults and no one else experienced the strange rumblings.

At the Robin's Nest you can snuggle up and relax with a friend, loved one of their friendly ghost. This is one place where you'll never really be alone.

San Diego
The Cosmopolitan Restaurant & Hotel

Particulars
2660 Calhoun Street,
San Diego, CA 92110
Phone: 619-209-3525

Delaware North Companies
DNC Parks & Resorts at San Diego LLC
Plaza del Pasado
2707 Congress Street, Suite 2-G
San Diego, CA 92110
Website: http://www.cosmopolitanrestaurant.signonsandiego.com/

History

Juan Bandini was the son of Jose Bandini, who was a native of Andalusia and was born at Lima in 1800. Bandini married Dolores Estudillo, the daughter of Jose Maria Estudillo in 1822. He built La Casa de Bandini across Calhoun Street from La Casa de Estudillo, completing the structure in 1829. Although born and educated in Lima, Peru Bandini became a Mexican citizen after traveling to California in 1819 with his father who was the master of a trading vessel. The gracious Bandini home with its grand ballroom became the social center of Old Town San Diego. Bandini held various offices under the Mexican Regime, but eventually supported the American cause with supplies and horses. A charming public speaker, fluent writer, excellent dancer, fair musician and fine horseman, Bandini was also involved in early San Diego and California politics.

His first wife was Dolores, daughter of Captain Jose M. Estudillo, and their children were: Arcadia, who married Abel Stearns and afterward Colonel Robert L. Baker; Ysidora, who was born September 23, 1829, married to Cave J. Couts, and died May 24, 1897; Josefa, who was married to Pedro C. Carillo an alcalde and a member of California's first legislature in 1847; Jose Maria, who married Teresa, daughter of Santiago Arguello; and Juanito. His second wife was Refugia, daughter of Santiago Arguello (a sister of his son Jose Maria's wife) and their children were: Juan de la Cruz, Alfredo, Arturo, and two daughters, one of whom, Dolores, was married to Charles R. Johnson, and the other, Victoria, (Chata), to Dr. James B. Winston. Juan Bandini's daughters were famous for their beauty.

Bandini sold his home to Frenchman Adolph Savin for $600, and a portion of the house became a dry goods store. He died at Los Angeles in November 1859. After the Civil War, the house was bought by Albert Seeley sometime around 1869, who operated a postal service and stagecoach line between San Diego and points north. A second story was added and the Casa

The Cosmopolitan Hotel circa 1870s (Courtesy of the San Diego Historical Society)

became the Cosmopolitan Hotel around 1870.

In July of 1928, the Casa de Bandini was again in the hands of a Bandini family member, Cave J. Couts Jr., who restored the building and leased it for use as a restaurant, and the Miramar Hotel until 1936. In 1945, the last private owners were the Caldwells and the facade was modified. The house was finally acquired as part of Old Town San Diego State Historic Park.

The current owners are Delaware North Companies (DNC Parks & Resorts at San Diego LLC) who have initiated a tiered restoration plan designed to achieve the look and feel of the late 1860s when it served as the Cosmopolitan Hotel. Current restoration plans are for the building to serve not only as a fine restaurant, but also by 2007, to open nine guest rooms to the public. The revival of the 1870 hotel image will not require you to take a stagecoach to reach building hotel as guests did in 1870s to enjoy a great meal and memorable stay, but you may very well be required to visit with former guests and owners who reportedly roam the building; you see this is one of the most haunted historical structures in San Diego. Once completed, guests and ghost will have a unique opportunity to co-mingle in this unique setting.

Hauntspitality
With such a colorful history dating back to 1829, it is no surprise that the spirits of Casa de Bandini are also flamboyant characters. To date, no formal paranormal investigation has taken place in the house, yet staff was kind enough to provide some information about the paranormal activity that has taken place since the restaurant has been in operation. A recent change in ownership and preliminary changes to the interior and exterior have not diminished the sightings of former occupants; Current staff continues to report friendly apparitions and unexplained phenomena throughout the building.

There is some contention among employees and prior owners as to the identities of the two most prominent spirits in the building. Those who have encountered the apparitions can only say that one is a female and the other a man of average height but a little overweight. Could the spectral duo be the earliest owners of the building, Juan Bandini and his first wife Dolores? Several investigators and psychic who have spent time in the building are only sure of one thing; that there are more than two

Soaring orb inside the restaurant (Courtesy of Alex Sill, International Paranormal Research Organization – IPRO)

spirits who call the former Bandini House and later the Cosmopolitan Hotel, home. The stories told about the phantom population inside seem to confirm that besides the original owners, there may be a cadre of prior hotel guests and former staff members haunting the building.

Frequently before opening, or after closing, staff has reported seeing the ghost of the Lady in White floating through the building. She has been sighted in the dining area and patio, as well as slowly climbing the stairs to the second floor. Several people have followed the specter only to have it vanish in front of their eyes or simply walk through the walls. She has been described as wearing a long, flowing, white dress and her dark hair tied in a bun. That's not the only female presence in the building. A younger, beautiful girl (perhaps one of the beautiful Bandini daughters) has also been sighted downstairs in the bar area and main dining room. She has floated through the area and even glanced or smiled at startled employees before vanishing. Some people have glimpsed the young girl and Mrs. Bandini while also catching a quick whiff of perfume that vanishes as quickly as the sweet fragrance materializes.

Orbs on wall and ceiling inside the restaurant (Courtesy of the International Paranormal Research Organization – IPRO)

Another frequently spotted figure is that of an elderly man, who roams the ground floor of the building and is occasionally witnessed on the second floor balcony overlooking the Casa de Estudillo. The male is described as a military-type man, short and stocky, and he frequently appears in the main dining area, floats around for a few seconds, and then dematerializes. Sometimes his misty form is preceded or followed by the smell of tobacco. Other times, a gruff cough or throat-clearing sound is heard when he decides to appear.

The strange appearances of a man and a woman are not the only anomalies in this place. Unexplained events are part of the daily occurrences reported throughout the building, especially on the more secluded second floor. A former security guard refused to patrol the second floor alone, because of the chilly reception he would receive. The man swore that doors would open and close in front of him, or that misty forms would pass in front of him. On one occasion, he even heard a voice that told him to leave.

Security has also reported hearing disembodied footsteps making their way up the stairs or slowly shuffling along the second floor hallway. There have been reports of several voices in ghostly conversation that can be heard echoing throughout the building late at night. Doors that have suddenly slammed shut, or gingerly open, and lights that have turned on and off by themselves. Frequently after business hours, people have heard glasses clinking and what sounds like a full-fledged party, taking place, yet upon checking the area was deserted.

Some people report that as they walk through the building, they often feel as if someone is watching or following them. There have been times when staff has felt someone unseen breathing down their necks. Then, there are the unexplained cold spots that can be felt in the building, even when the area surrounding the icy spot is ten or more degrees warmer. Mysterious lights can be seen in the windows late at night, as if someone is walking through the building holding a candle. Several passers-by have reportedly witnessed a woman holding a candle standing on the balcony overlooking the Casa de Estudillo for a few seconds before vanishing.

Perhaps the Bandini family is watching over their former home. On the other hand, as one person suggested, given the long and varied history of the building, the two spirits sighted so far may be only the tip of a paranormal iceberg. The former Casa de Bandini/Cosmopolitan Hotel is a wonderful place to visit even when you're not hunting ghosts. Here, you can sample delicious Mexican cuisine and even spend the night... if you dare.

El Fandango Restaurant

Particulars

2734 Calhoun Street,
San Diego, CA 92110
Phone: 619-298-2860
Fax: 619-298-0120

History

Located in Old Town Historic State Park, the restaurant was built on top of a home constructed by Jose Nicasio Silva between 1830 and 1843. Silva lived here for many years with his wife, Maria Antonia Machado de Silva and their children. Their home stayed in the family for over 100 years, and subsequently became a boarding house, saloon, restaurant, art studio, souvenir shop, museum, and church. It is now home to the El Fandango Restaurant. It is said

that during the American capture of Old Town in 1846, Maria Antonia rushed from her adobe home to the flag pole in the center of the plaza and saved the Mexican flag from capture. Well-known author and paranormal investigator, Richard Senate suggests, that it may be the patriotic spirit of Maria Antonia who haunts the El Fandango.

Hauntspitality

According to a plaque on the wall of the El Fandango restaurant, an employee arrived at the r estaurant a little after 4:00 a.m. to being preparing for the 8:00 a.m. opening breakfast. It was a dark and somewhat damp morning, as the employee let himself into the restaurant. As he had done many times before, he walked by the main, inside dining room to turn on the lights. As he proceeded by the dining area, he glanced in and saw a woman in white sitting at the table in the far corner of the room. After a careful, more focused look, he noticed that the woman had a hazy, cloud-like appearance. The employee realized that he could be confronting an apparition, so he ran to turn on the light. Once the light was on, he cautiously re-inspected the dining room and found no one. He was reluctant to tell his friends about his experience with the ghost, but he was certain about what he had witnessed at the dining room table. The employee decided to discuss his experience with his wife who encouraged him to mention it to some of his friends.

The story spread and a couple who were very active in documenting the history of San Diego concluded that the sighting was valid and not unusual for Old Town, considering similar sightings had been reported at the Whaley House and the Casa de Estudillo. Further research indicated that the restaurant was constructed directly over the original Machado family home. In the mid-1800s many of the Machado family members lived and worked on the exact spot that the employee observed the phantom woman.

An orb is visible on the back wall (Courtesy of the International Paranormal Research Organization – IPRO)

Renowned Ghosthunter Richard Senate and his psychic wife, Debbie Christenson Senate, visited the El Fandango. Once inside, Debbie began sensing on a woman standing in the doorway, and proceeded to get the name, Maria Antonia Silva. In response to a question by Richard, Debbie said that the woman's spirit remains because she likes it here, and likes to come back every once in awhile to visit. A year later, according to Richard, he saw an article on El Fandango's ghosts by John J. Lamb in the Ghost Trackers Newsletter (June 1997 issue (Vol. 16, Number 2), discussing El Fandango's ghost as an archetypal White Lady, who is customarily seen seated at a corner table.

Other investigators who have studied the restaurant have come away convinced that one or several energies inhabit this building. Most agree that the strongest presence in the building is that of a woman, and it is her spirit that seems responsible for all the unexplainable things that happen inside.

Numerous psychics, who have visited the restaurant over the years, have sensed other energies belonging to family members and former employees. Staff and visitors continue to feel cold spots and sense someone unseen watching them in various parts of the restaurant.

When the place is devoid of most visitors, there is an unnerving feeling of an unseen presence carefully watching your every move. Phantom footsteps, unexplained voices and occasional doors shutting on their own, have been reported by staff. There's nothing negative about the spirited population inside… they're, just keeping an eye on things.

The El Fandango Restaurant is a place where you can have a delicious lunch or dinner, a drink at the bar, or a relaxing snack on the outdoor patio; and the spirits are included at no charge!

Horton Grand Hotel

Particulars
311 Island Avenue,
San Diego, CA 92101
Phone: 619-544-1886
Fax: 619-239-3823
Toll Free: 1-800-542-1886
E-mail: horton@connectnet.com
Website: www.hortongrand.com

History

The brick facade, bay windows, and main stairway of the hotel were taken from the Grand and the Kale Saddlery hotels, built in 1886. The Kale Saddlery is most famous for its association with Wyatt Earp. The Ida Bailey Restaurant (named after a famous San Diego madam and hostess) and the Palace Bar provide dinner and a festive atmosphere for guests and locals. President Benjamin Harrison and Wyatt Earp visited the hotel which acquired its name in 1907 in honor of the New Town San Diego's founder, Alonzo Horton.

Before it was known as the Horton Grand it was also called the Brooklyn, and Kale Saddlery, two hotels constructed in 1886. Instead of destroying both hotels to make way for progress, Dan Pearson, a developer, used portions of both hotels to create the Horton Grand which opened in 1986. The four-story hotel lies at the heart of the historic Gaslamp Quarter, and consists of two "wings" connected at street level by a glass atrium that encloses the lobby. One wing is Victorian in construction while the other is more ornate with a touch of gingerbread styling.

From 1912, the bottom floor of the Horton was home to the Kale saddle shop, the largest maker of saddles in the west which attracted Roy Rogers, Leo Carrillo, Tom Mix, and Jackie Coogan. While the Saddlery was a fine example of what was called 'cowboy Victorian" architecture, it was the Grand Hotel that stood out as the Victorian jewel of downtown San Diego. The hotel's most glamorous period occurred in the mid-1930s when a lively vaudevillian named Bob Johnson operated the hotel. He ran the theater next door and became well known for his burlesque reviews and colorful song and dance routines. Besides his association with the entertainment industry, he also had many contacts with the world of horse racing and boxing. The Palace sports bar at the Horton Grand became the center of action for the elite set. Professional sports people and entertainers often frequented the place for talk and imbibing. George Jessel, comedian Lou Costello, and boxer Joe Louis were all regulars.

By the mid-1960s, the area was in decay, and the Horton Grand became just another rundown building. In 1981 downtown San Diego was cleared to make way for a shopping mall called Horton Plaza. Both of the old hotels were to be destroyed. When word got out, the public was outraged. A group stepped in to try to save the hotels, and felt that relocation was the only answer. Both buildings were painstakingly taken apart piece by piece and stored in a warehouse until a proper site could be chosen for them. The hotels were relocated in the newly revamped Gaslight District. The Horton Grand would come to rest on the site of Ida Bailey's brothel. It seemed appropriate to relocate these historic buildings to an area whose history so well represented a young rowdy frontier town. The hotels were pieced together brick by brick, and all usable artifacts were salvaged to guarantee the buildings were as authentic as possible. Craftsmen from Europe were brought in to restore the split oak staircase.

Hauntspitality

Roger A. Whittaker used the Gaslamp district as a hangout in the mid-1800s. The brash, hard drinking gambling man who had no respect for the law, was also a reportedly a pimp. One night, Roger's gambling debts finally caught up with him, and there was a search party out for blood. His getting caught cheating didn't help matters. He had already been shot once that fateful night, but he was able to make it back to his hotel. He hid out in an armoire in his room, fighting for his life. He felt safe, thinking the men wouldn't look for him in a piece of furniture. He was wrong. Just as he thought he was out of danger, the armoire door swung open and an adversary shot him dead. Whittaker was finally free from his huge gambling debts, and his physical body.

The Horton Grand is haunted by the spirit of Roger Whittaker, who resides in Room 309; the place of his sudden demise. Whittaker's specter has appeared too many employees and guests. One time, a female guest asked the very real-looking apparition where the ice machine was, only to watch him vanish before her eyes. Psychic Shelly Deegan, once saw a group of twenty ghosts dressed in 1890s clothing while walking up the spiral staircase to the third-floor ballroom. The phantom group was having their own party! Another psychic, Jacqueline Williams, said the spirit of Whittaker enjoys his permanent stay at the Horton, along with other friendly spirits that management has named, Gus and Henry.

In Room 309 numerous paranormal events have taken place, including: Lights mysteriously going on and off; the bed will shake when no one is in or near it; pictures move from one part of the unoccupied room to another; the closet door flies open in front of startled witnesses; guests see apparitions; and children are known to have talked to "special playmates" only they can see. Ghosthunters, psychics and reporters who have spent the night in Room 309, have emerged with accounts of being pushed and pulled by an invisible entity. A diary in room 309, at the Horton Grand is filled with accounts of encounters with Roger.

The few members of housekeeping, who aren't afraid to enter the room alone, sometimes can't get in because the room is deadbolted from the inside, although the room was unoccupied at the time. When housekeeping finally got inside the room, the soap was misplaced, lamps are on the bed, curtains are tied in knots and sometimes the distinct outline of a man's body is visible as an indentation on the bed!

The diary in Room #309 suggests that although not everyone has an encounter with Roger, the people that do sometimes have physical contact, such as being awakened by an icy hand on their shoulder, or having their arm gently tugged on, then awakening to see a strange mist floating at the foot of the bed. One lady wrote of feeling something brush against her back for at least two minutes while she was sitting on the bed. Another startled woman felt two cold hands suddenly go about her shoulders almost like a ghostly hug. A number of guests reported a good night's sleep having been interrupted by stifling heat in the room. When they tried to get the air conditioner on quickly, it was already set at 65 degrees. Even opening the windows doesn't seem to beat the heat. One woman stated that she didn't mind the heat since her husband always kept the bedroom too cold.

Roger also kept one couple up most of the night with the sounds of a ghostly poker game. They could hear the cards being shuffled and dealt as well as silver coins being dropped on the table. Another couple was playing cards when they decided to take a break and go out to dinner. They left the cards stacked in a neat pile on the bed. When they returned there were two hands of cards laid out; one was a full house! Another couple, except for a lone King of Hearts, lost an entire deck of cards. On another occasion, married guests left the room and saved some champagne for Roger, who obliged by polishing off the glass. His spirit also messed up their beds, turned a picture around, placed a vase of flowers between the beds and put the man's sunglasses atop the only lamp left on; now that's a lively spirit.

Other ghosts as well, make the historic hotel their home. Heavy footsteps are often heard in other rooms. Guests spending the night in Room 309 have complained of excessive noise in the room above them. When checking out, they are usually told the room above them was vacant all night. One spirit is that of a man walking around on the third floor dressed in western garb, until he disappears. Spend a day at the Horton and enjoy the ambiance, or spend the night and have a grand time partying with the ghosts.

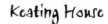
Keating House

Particulars

2331 Second Avenue,
San Diego, CA 92101-1505
Phone: 619-239-8585
Fax: 619-239-5774
Toll Free: 1-800-995-8644
E-mail: inn@keatinghouse.com
Website: www.keatinghouse.com

History

The Keating House is a fine example of the Queen Anne Victorian residences built in San Diego during the boom years of the 1880's. The original owner of the house, George James Keating was one of eighteen children. He was born in Halifax, Nova Scotia in 1840. At the age of eighteen, he had completed a liberal college education and having a strong desire to enter business for himself he came to the U.S. in 1866 settling in Kansas City. Keating was a successful business man, who in the span of less than 20 years, created one of the largest agricultural implements businesses in the world, amassing more than two million dollars.

In 1886 he and his wife Fannie, for reasons of health, moved to San Diego where they made substantial investments in the city's booming real estate market. One of these purchases was their residence at 2331 2nd Avenue (now known as the Keating House) which was intended as temporary lodging until he could arrange to have a larger mansion constructed a few blocks away. This mansion covered an entire city block, but was torn down years ago. Keating died unexpectedly in the "temporary" house on the morning of June 22, 1888. His benevolent spirit is said to still haunt the house. The house remained in the Keating family until the death of Mrs. Keating in 1909. In 1975, the house underwent extensive restoration and in 1984, Keating House was opened to the public as a Bed & Breakfast.

Hauntspitality

Owner, Ben Baltic, confided that Mr. Keating is the prominent spirit of this historic Victorian home. Baltic also wrote us regarding his experiences at the Keating House as follows: I must start by saying that I do not believe in ghosts; I am a rational man. On my bookshelf you'll find books by Hume, Voltaire, Plato, Locke and Rousseau, to name just a few. In my world there is no room for Bigfoot, leprechauns or Astrology; logic rules supreme. As far as I'm concerned, ghosts rank about even with those little green space aliens that make a business of abducting earthlings for weekends of sex in distant galaxies: they simply don't exist.

Two years ago I bought Keating House, a Queen Anne Victorian home built in San Diego during a land boom in the late 1880's. The house had been converted to a Bed and Breakfast Inn twenty years ago and I, in the midst of a mid-life crisis, traded my corporate job, with corner office and fireplace, for a new one as an innkeeper. Little did I realize the train wreck my cozy little belief system was headed for when I did this? I can now trace its ruination to one man, a man by the name of George Keating. It was Mr. Keating, a 19th century industrial magnate who first occupied the house, died suddenly in it, and, as near as I can tell, never left.

While in escrow the prior owner, perhaps motivated by the Real Estate doctrine of full disclosure, related to me many stories of encounters between Mr. Keating and his guests. This included a celebrated incident involving a middle-age man with a beard dressed in a Victorian nightshirt seen entering a bathroom one morning. The man later emerged from the bathroom dressed in a Victorian suit and hat. One guest swore that the man had entered the bathroom with out any bag or change of clothes. Another guest waiting in the hall swore he heard the shower running and noticed steam emerging from under the bathroom door. Both were startled to see the man emerge fully dressed. His unusual dress was thought to be that of an eccentric or a man dressed for a theater production. When they entered the bathroom immediately after this man left, they were surprised to find the shower, sink and towels dry and cold. Two other guests encountered the "phantom" as he left the house that morning. All were intrigued by his dress. The man never spoke but tipped his hat to the guests as he departed the house. Of course, no gentleman fitting this description bearded or otherwise, was staying in the house. His entry and exit from the bath could not be explained. Needless to say, this specter was the topic of much discussion at breakfast. A day later, the guests were shown a picture of Mr. Keating borrowed from local archives. All of them swore it was the man they'd seen and after the event, the house was in a commotion for weeks.

I listened to this and other stories about Mr. Keating as any attentive skeptic would. The owner impressed me as a bit of a braggart. The businessman in me appreciated the value a ghost might have in the marketing plan of a struggling Bed and Breakfast. I found the stories amusing, but as far as I was concerned they were the products of an overactive imagination or outright fabrications of the owner. I was still in escrow when I attended a Christmas party hosted by the local association of bed and breakfast owners. It was at this party that, quite by accident, I met the man who'd converted the house from an apartment building into an inn some 20 years prior. The first words out of his mouth were, "So, have you met Mr. Keating yet?" We did not have much time to talk. At the time my only interest was on restoring the house. I had a million questions for him about plumbing, floor plans and windows. He answered as best his memory served, but always turned the conversation back to Mr. Keating. Upon leaving, his parting words were, "Good luck with the house and Mr. Keating." I laughed and thanked him. I am not laughing anymore.

Encounters with Mr. Keating began as soon as work began on the house. I began receiving reports of an oddly dressed bearded gentleman making brief appearances where work was being performed. Sometimes he was seen peering in a window or standing briefly in a door. On one occasion, a man hired to refinish the floors engaged him in several one sided conversations. The contractor and I had never met. He naturally assumed that the oddly dressed bearded gentleman that regularly appeared in the doorway of the room he was working on was the owner. He thought it rude that the man always vanished while his back was turned and never responded to any of his questions; therefore, the contractor was quite startled when I showed up for an inspection one afternoon and introduced myself. Over the course of the renovation I received similar reports from roofers, plumbers and carpenters. Even the maid, a Hispanic woman of deep religious beliefs, began reporting strange noises and passing shadows in the empty upstairs bedrooms. Afraid for her job, she did not speak directly to me about any of this but confided in the Chef instead. At one point she refused to go upstairs unless he accompanied her and checked all the rooms first (To this day she still blesses herself before heading up the stairs to clean.)

Of course I dismissed all this as "ridiculous". I was still working my day job at this time and the reports came second hand. I hadn't seen or heard anything myself so logically there couldn't be anything to these stories. It was easy to dismiss it all as some sort of mass hysteria or someone pulling my leg. The worst I could imagine was that someone off the street had gained unauthorized entry to the house. Perhaps it was one of the many "characters" the previous owner had encouraged to hang around. I resolved to change all the locks when the renovations were finished. It was only when I began to have my own experiences with the strange male apparition that my attitude began to change.

The first time was shortly after reopening when I was checking in a guest. Unbeknownst to her, we were the only people in the house when I was showing her a room. She paced the room while I stood in the doorway explaining the features to her. My back was to the hall and she was facing me. Suddenly, while looking at me, she got the oddest look on her face. Her eyes opened wide as eggs. Being a professional, I made a conscious effort to ignore her odd expression and kept talking. The next morning when she came down to breakfast and abruptly asked me to explain who the bearded gentleman with the hat was, that came up the stairs and stood behind me while I'd been showing her the room the day before. It was all I could do to remain calm. No one could have come up those stairs and stood behind me without my knowing it.

When I began sleeping in the house, more strange occurrences followed. As far as I was concerned all the strange noises emanating from the attic late at night could be explained away as deferred maintenance. Just because it sounded like someone was walking back and forth up there didn't mean it wasn't old pipes or the furnace. The strange thing was that every time I went up into the attic I'd find the light turned on. I know I didn't leave it on. I was very careful about turning it off and locking the door behind me when I came down. What made it stranger still was the fact that I was the only one with a key to the attic. No one else could get up there. I assumed it was a crossed circuit or a quirk in the old wiring. I told myself that eventually I'd put the electrician on it.

My trouble with the lights did not end there. One night I found myself alone in the house. Before turning in I made my rounds of the house and out buildings turning on nightlights, checking the doors and windows. When I was satisfied that all was secure I turned in upstairs in one of the bedrooms. I fell asleep reading. Around midnight I awoke. The first thing I noticed was that the reading light was still on. Still half-asleep I reached over and turned it off. Then I realized that the overhead light was on too. That was strange. I hadn't remembered turning it on at all. I woke myself up and sat up. That's when I realized that all the lights in the room were on; even the ones in the bathroom. I got up and turned them all off wondering how I could be so absent-minded. As I was climbing back into bed I noticed a light coming from under the hall door. I opened it and discovered that all the lights in the hall were on too. I certainly hadn't left any of them on. As I began turning them all off, I noticed light coming from under every door in the hall; in fact, every single light in the house was on as well as in the out-buildings! I was sure that a call to my partner would explain the practical joke, since he had the only other key to the house. His groggy protest at my early morning call convinced me that it wasn't him. I briefly considered calling the police, but I told myself that

I needed my sleep more than I needed the police and returned to bed.

That's when I remembered the attic light. I'd recently had it rewired and placed on a separate circuit. I hadn't had any trouble with it since it had been rewired. I had been up in the attic that afternoon and the light was off. I had no doubt about that. If someone was playing a joke on me they couldn't possibly have gotten to that light and switched it on. The only key was in my wallet. No one knew that but me. I took the key out of my wallet and headed upstairs. The attic light was on! In addition, the emergency flashlight, stuck to the side of the furnace with a magnet, had been turned on too! How was it possible? I did not fall asleep for many hours. When I finally did, it was from the fatigue of mental calculation. My twin pillars of logic and reason were beginning to fail me. Hindsight has taught me that denial is very powerful. I continued to dismiss reports of Mr. Keating's antics until about six months ago, when I had my own encounter with Mr. Keating. It was the proverbial straw that broke the camel's back.

Baltic has plenty of other stories he can share over breakfast. To check up on the latest antics of George James Keating, all you have to do is pack your bags and come visit this historic haunted hideaway for a few days. Here, the spirit of the former owner has the run of the house; no Keating!

Old Town Mexican Cafe

Particulars
2489 San Diego Avenue,
Old Town San Diego, CA 92110
Phone: 619-297-4330
Fax: 619-297-8002
Website: www.oldtownmexicancafe.com

History

The Old Town Café lies across the street from the most haunted house in America; the Whaley House. Visitors to this wonderful café can enjoy homemade tortillas and great margaritas, as well as the spirited side of the building. Although the current restaurant dates to 1977, when the current owner bought the building, it had also been a Safeway store and meat packing plant. The owner told us that the original building might date back to the 1920s. It's multiple uses and early date of construction, lends itself to a haunted history.

Hauntspitality

The past seems to linger inside this fabulous Mexican restaurant. When you step through the front door and look to the right, homemade tortillas are continuously churned out the old fashion way; by hand. On the left is the bar area that provides memorable spirits (the drinking kind) to accompany the tantalizing food and tasty chips and salsa. Continuing left, passed the bar, is the large dining area that appears to represent the older portion of the building. It is in this portion of the restaurant that the paranormal activity seems to be most prevalent. According to psychics and investigators, three spirits have been identified to date. From this portion of the restaurant toward the back, inclusive of the restrooms, kitchen and far back room, sightings are frequent and the energy is palpable.

On one occasion, a young Hispanic male was sighted near the door leading out the east side of the building. The apparition stood there a few seconds stared at a staff person, then vanished through the door. Other people have sensed his presence mid-way through the eastern portion of the building where orbs have been captured on film. Other people have reportedly walked by the area and immediately became chilled to the bone; as if they just walked right through someone unseen. Psychics, who recently visited the restaurant, immediately sensed a young boy's spirit. They felt that he might have been a dishwasher or kitchen helper, and may have died in the building or nearby. They said that his spirit seemed drawn to the place, perhaps returning to the location where he once worked.

Others have sensed an elderly male in his 60s and younger female in her 20s or 30s, who occupy the back portion of the restaurant. They have been frequently sighted in the kitchen and bathroom areas, and in the eastern and southern portions of the building. According to researchers, the two spirits appear to be from different periods, yet are aware of each other as they both maintain a watchful eye on the restaurant. A tape recorder was left on in the back portion of the restaurant while investigators had lunch. When it was replayed later in the day, there were numerous unusual clicking sounds, a tapping sound and a gruff male voice audible on tape. At one point, a child's laughter can be heard over the voices of several people talking. Perhaps it's the playful energy of this child that

Orb on second ceiling beam near the fan and white oblong mist on left portion of ceiling
(Courtesy of Alex Sill, International Paranormal Research Organization – IPRO)

is responsible for moving objects such as glasses, napkins and utensils.

Several photos taken inside have exhibited orbs, but only in the southern and eastern sections of the restaurant. More paranormal research has to be conducted in this restaurant after hours, when it is quiet, to get a better idea of who the spirits might be. Could they be remnant energy from the period when the building served as a grocery store or meat packing plant... or do they go back farther in time?

Only time and cooperation from the spirits will tell. In the meantime, the very best in Old Town hauntspitality will greet you as you visit this local eatery.

If you don't see a friendly spirit in here, try walking across the street to America's most haunted dwelling: the Whaley House and you're sure to have a spirited visit to one of California's oldest communities.

Theater in Old Town

Particulars
4040 Twiggs Street,
San Diego, CA 92110
Tickets: 619-688-2494
Phone: 619-688-0960
Website: www.theaterinoldtown.com

History

Although the current occupants told us that the building has been cleansed of their "pesky" spirits, a recent visit suggests otherwise. Since the building dates to circa 1970, it's hard to imagine how it can be, or could have been so haunted. It's the ground, the soil, and the history of the area that may contain the answers to some of the building's haunted history. Given that the haunted and historic Seeley Stables are adjacent to the theater and the old stage route ran by the current theater building and stopped at the Cosmopolitan Hotel (formerly the Casa de Bandini Restaurant and now returning to its original incarnation as the Cosmopolitan Restaurant and Hotel), there is every reason to believe that the use of the area from the 1830s-1970s may contribute in some fashion to the hauntings.

Hauntspitality

Reports of a ghostly old codger, nicknamed "George" by the staff, may be someone related to the nearby Seeley Stables or perhaps an individual connected to a time when the stagecoach passed through the area. However, he is not the only spirit who takes center stage at this Old Town venue.

Other investigators who have visited the theater, came away impressed with the amount of paranormal activity that has taken place inside. Investigators who have been allowed inside have felt the presence of several energies. They have also captured numerous orbs and mists and have documented cold spots throughout the building. In order to evaluate the claims that the theater is no longer haunted, the current owner allowed the International Paranormal Research Organization (IPRO) and San Diego Ghost Hunters to jointly investigate, to confirm the absence of spirits after the reported cleansing. What we found upon entering was anything but a "cleansed" environment. It turned out to be one of the most active establishments within Old Town State Historic Park. The final report from the investigators follows:

- Numerous orbs were captured on 35mm film and digital cameras in the lobby and main theater area.
- Psychic, Ginnie McGovern, sensed a strong male energy in the lobby. While being immediately pulled to the northeast portion of the lobby, McGovern encountered a gruff male presence that was chewing tobacco and spitting. She sensed a trapper/prospector-type person, wearing an old rumpled hat, buckskins and a vest. He wore a long sleeve, pale yellow cotton shirt and McGovern picked up the name, Jeremiah. He was "pushing" McGovern toward the north-northeast and trying to show her an outbuilding (Livery Stable) and he told her psychically that he was a blacksmith.
- In the theater, McGovern sensed a woman named "Mary." She had a cold feeling on her right shoulder when confronting this spirit. Mary was in the fourth row center left, and she related how she was a schoolteacher in the area who loved the new theater, including all the action and drama. She was

not original to the theater, but loved to attend rehearsals and plays. McGovern stated that others have witnessed the woman as a misty form inside and she wears a long dress, which people can hear swishing by. She comes from a much later period than the prospector/ blacksmith. We were later told that a former schoolteacher named Mary Chase Walker had a play done about her in the theater with children in attendance.

- When the group was discussing the schoolteacher, audible banging, clicking and tapping noises were heard coming from behind the curtains on the left had side of the stage. A quick look around by group members indicated that no one else was in the area where the sounds were emanating.
- The camera Maritza Skandunas was using suddenly turned off on its own while she was taking photographs on stage.
- Several of the investigators remarked that their batteries were repeatedly going dead.
- McGovern contacted a man who was angry and who displayed a physical deformity. He is responsible for moving things around backstage. The man had a five-year-old son (named Tom, according to McGovern) that he can see but is unable to contact. Based on psychic communication, the father died in a fire near the theatre and the boy died from a disease. There was a sense of confusion going the entire time and that the child is still grieving over the death of his father. The investigative group formed a circle and gently helped guide the son to his father and then into the light. The two energies were told they could come back to the theater anytime they wished. Letting a spirit go does not mean banishment from the place it resides. It's an process of making the spirit aware of its surroundings and letting them know that they can go other places, yet still return anytime they wish without the longing, anger, confusion or uncertainty.

- On stage, a strong male energy was responsible for a lot of the paranormal activity that has been reported. He is trapped and confused. The group heard an unsettling sound like a hammer hitting something.
- Paranormal Investigator/Psychic, Karen Ridens had an eerie feeling while standing backstage, center. She sensed that there was an angry spirit who had consumed too much alcohol when he was alive. This man is responsible for moving things according to Ridens, and is often seen as a dark shadowy figure around the stage.

- In the downstairs dressing room, several investigators sensed a strong male energy with a mental handicap.
- Karen Ridens developed heart palpitations, while others experienced headaches, nausea, and depression.
- Ginnie McGovern sensed that a man was misdiagnosed with a medical

Orbs on stage and an unusual light in the upstairs area (courtesy of the International Paranormal Research Organization – IPRO)

Orbs and mists (courtesy of the International Paranormal Research Organization – IPRO)

condition and given the wrong medication. The side effects caused him intense suffering and he hid in the downstairs area. He may have been an actor with stomach cancer.

- Maritza Skandunas felt as if she was stabbed in the stomach while standing in the dressing room.
- Upstairs in the production booth, almost everyone in the group felt a heavy pressure as they walked through the area. The feeling was that a strong male energy was dominating this area and he liked to control things. The group picked up male voices on the digital tape, confirming that this area had a great deal of energy.
- While standing on the top of the landing where the stairs lead to the second floor, one investigator heard someone coming up the stairs and then felt a sudden chill engulf him.
- Preliminary analysis of EVP from this investigation confirms that a male energy, spirit child and phantom woman responded on tape with simple answers to questions that were asked. More in depth recording is sure to reveal additional data on the spirit population inside the building.

The Theater in Old Town is anything but spirit free. In fact, as time goes on, it seems to draw more and more energies. The minute you enter, it's like stepping back in time, partly because of the wood paneling and western flavor. We highly recommend taking in a play here, where the building is a stage and some of the people inside are actors playing parts from another dimension. Otherworldly performances continue to be staged inside the building along side modern-day thespian performances. It's hard to tell who the real show stoppers are the spirited performers or the performing spirits.

U.S. Grant Hotel

Particulars

325 Broadway,
San Diego, CA 92101
Phone: 619-232-3121
Fax: 619-239-9517
Toll Free: 800-237-5029
E-mail: usgranthotel@usgrant.net
Website: www.usgrant.net

History

U.S. Grant Jr. and his wife Fannie were married in New York in 1880, and moved to San Diego in 1884, in part because Fannie was having health problems. They prospered as Grant became an assistant district attorney while his wealthy wife, bought the Horton House in 1895. In 1905 the old Horton House was demolished to make way for the U. S. Grant Hotel, which Grant planned as homage to his late father. But in 1909, before the new hotel was opened, Fannie died.

San Diego decided to honor Civil War hero Ulysses S. Grant by dedicating a hotel in his name. Citizens were awed by the elegance of the hotel which included colonnades of travertine marble, crystal chandeliers, detailed plasterwork, paneling of the finest mahogany, and contained 220 guest rooms.

Over the years, the Grant hosted Charles Lindbergh, Albert Einstein, Henry Ford, Franklin D. Roosevelt, and scores of Hollywood stars. The hotel has been exquisitely restored, and is listed on the National Historic of Historic Places.

Hauntspitality

The U. S. Grant Hotel claims to have Fannie Josephine Chaffee Grant, the first wife of Ulysses S. Grant Jr., as its resident ghost. She prefers the Crystal Room as her favorite haunt. Her spirit has been seen by employees, guests, and even by Secret Service personnel stationed at the hotel during the 1992 presidential election campaign. Why the Crystal Room, since it wasn't completed at the time of her passing, no one really knows.

A hotel spokesperson confirmed that there are many sightings of Fannie wearing turn of-the-century clothing, or strolling in or near the Crystal Room. She has also been sighted in the Crystal Room puffing a cigarette or causing the crystal chandeliers to rattle or move. Other employees reported that sometimes on a hot day, portions of the room will be icy cold, and they will hear a barely audible voice. Fannie is however, not a mischievous spirit, just a relaxed soul enjoying the comforts of a first class hotel.

You can take everything for Granted here, except, Fannie!

San Francisco
Four Seasons Clift Hotel

Particulars
495 Geary Street,
San Francisco, CA 94102
Phone: 415-775-4700
Fax: 415-441-4621
Toll Free: 1-800-65CLIFT
E-mail: res@clifthotel.com
Website: www.clifthotel.com

History

The Clift Hotel was constructed from a single, two thousand-year-old redwood tree harvested from northern California. The wood has been restored to its original luster. Standing majestically in the heart of San Francisco near Union Square, The 17-story hotel opened in 1915, and is still considered one of the top hotels in San Francisco. The hotel takes its name from lawyer Frederick Clift, whose father owned land at the corner of Geary and Taylor Streets at the time of the 1906 San Francisco earthquake.

Clift inherited the land from his father when the city was rebuilding, and decided to construct an elegant, earthquake-proof hotel in the heart of the city. George Applegarth, an ambitious young architect, was hired to design Clift's dream place. Applegarth used steel-reinforced concrete, to construct a building which profoundly impacted the future of San Francisco architecture. When the original twelve-story hotel opened in 1915, Clift took up residence in the rooftop stone bungalow, which is the Spanish Suite today (Room 1509).

Sixteen years after it opened, Clift died, leaving the family business to 36-year-old Robert Odell who promptly renovated the hotel, which was reopened in 1936. Odell moved into the Spanish Suite with his wife, Helen. Robert Odell was six-foot-six with piercing eyes, and was strong-willed. Many employees feared him. Odell committed suicide in the Spanish Suite in June, 1973.

Hauntspitality

Odell's spirit reportedly roams the hotel, but employees claim that his suite is where most of the activity takes place. One guest, who often uses the Spanish Suite, and housekeeping personnel who maintain the room, state that the glass sliding door which leads out to the balcony, oftentimes opens slowly, and then closes by itself. Additionally, items have been known to regularly disappear from a display table even when the suite is unoccupied, and securely locked.

The ghostly activity, though not confined to Room 1509, is most intense in that area of the hotel. Cold spots, voices, and unexplained footsteps are also part of the benign spirited history of the hotel. Another guest awoke in the Odell suite to witness trash cans flying through the air! On several occasions, staff and guests have watched as the huge, double wooden doors opened by themselves and then slammed shut with such force that the wood molding has cracked. Staff have seen strange shadows float through the room, and the lights turn on and off by themselves. Odell was strong-willed in life and also it seems, in the after-life.

Mansions Hotel & Restaurant

Particulars

2220 Sacramento Street,
San Francisco, CA 94115
Phone: 415-929-9444
Fax: 415-567-9391
Toll Free: 1-800-826-9398
Website: www.themansions.com

History

The Mansions Hotel and Restaurant is located between Laguna and Buchanan Streets. The neighborhood includes some of San Francisco's most prestigious homes. The Hotel is a short walk to fashionable boutiques, clubs and restaurants. Richard Craig Chambers built the mansion in 1887. He had become one of the richest and most politically powerful men of his time. At eighteen he left his home in Richland County, Ohio and journeyed across plains and mountains, reaching Sacramento at the height of the gold rush. By 1851, he left for the Mormon diggings on the American River, moved to the Upper Feather River Mines in Plumas County, finally pushing on to Nevada. Chambers explored the entire west traveling as far north as Helena, Montana, before settling in the Utah Territory where he became superintendent of Senator George Hearst's Webster and Bully Boy mines. In 1872, the chance discovery of a rich vein of silver changed his life. After more than 20 years of struggle, Chambers assembled backers that included Senator Hearst, and with a deal in hand, he became part owner and superintendent of the mine. Although the official name was the Ontario, many called it the "Plumas Asylum".

Chambers founded a newspaper, becoming one of the most powerful political voices in the inter-mountain region. He moved San Francisco beckoned, and the Sacramento Street showplace he built was a statement. Next came his admittance to the Pacific Union Club in 1892. By 1894, he was listed in Our Society Blue Book. Chambers married, built his mansion, and died in 1901, just after his wife had passed away. Since Chambers and his wife had no children, his two nieces inherited the mansion. They soon turned the classic revival structure into two houses by moving the original building to the east side of the lot and adding a second half with its own entrance and address. Perhaps the women didn't get along, or maybe the hobby of Claudia Chambers, had something to do with it. Claudia adored pigs and raised them as pets. Then Claudia was killed in a freak accident where legend has it that she was sawed in half. Today, no one can agree how the accident occurred.

A series of people lived in the double house after that, but no one stayed long. The building, once the pride of Pacific Heights, had deteriorated into a run down rooming house. During 1997, Bob Pritikin bought the structure in 1977 and transformed the dilapidated relic into an elegant hotel and restaurant. Rooms were decorated in crushed velvet, brocade, crystal and pigs---ceramic pigs, wooden pigs, metal pigs and painted pigs. The new owner was determined to keep Claudia happy. Though one can only wonder at her reaction to the dinner show, which included renditions of "Moonlight Sawnata" and "The Last Time I Sawed Paris", performed by Pritikin on his saw, or to the tune of magic tricks involving a floating head--said to be a likeness of Claudia. Is it any surprise the two Mansions are said to be haunted?

Hauntspitality

Actor Vincent Schiavelli, who portrayed the disturbed subway spirit in the movie, Ghost (1990), encountered a female ghost as he entered his room at the hotel late one night. In 1991, an apparition materialized in front of several witnesses during a séance in a third-floor suite. That ghost's photograph is now part of the hotel's haunted gallery. In July 1992, a scientific study conducted by the JFK University, Office of Paranormal Investigation, discovered powerful electromagnetic forces in the old section of the hotel. The results confirmed the impressions of eminent psychic Sylvia Brown, who sensed numerous spirits in the hotel.

In August 1992, a man and his wife checked into a room in the old mansion. Ten minutes later, the man returned to the front desk in a state of shock. His face was ashen. His whole body was shaking. Something had frightened him badly, but he refused to talk about it. Since he had already checked in, the clerk was forced to charge him. "I don't care," the guest said. "I just can't be here anymore!" Owner Bob Pritikin commented, "The man just didn't know there were ghosts in the hotel. We get all kinds of weird things happening in this place."

One resident ghost is said to be Claudia Chambers, Senator Chambers' niece who in 1887, built one of the houses that now comprise the hotel; many guests claim to encounter her. Famous psychics Lorraine and Ed Warren told the owner that in their opinion, his magic shows were making the hauntings in the hotel, worse. The appearance of "Claudia" as a disembodied, talking head during the magic show's dramatic finale is certainly gruesome. The Warrens also felt a heavy concentration of energy in the Josephine Room. They found the spirits responsive to very personal questions. One entity identified itself as Julia, and asked the group to help her son, Henry Ross, by sending him to the light. Henry, she explained had committed suicide in the house when he was only 21.

Paranormal investigators and psychics have reported mysterious activities on the third floor; an area where most guests have reported encounters with the unknown. Psychic Sylvia Brown went into a trance in the hotel in 1991, and spoke about the house having once been a brothel and described a girl in a turn-of-the-century maid's uniform whose presence could still be felt. Her name was Rachel, and she died a traumatic death at nineteen---she planned to be married but contracted tuberculosis. She wonders why so many people are invading her world.

During another trance in the hotel's Empress Josephine Suite in 1992, a Ouija board went wild. Two wine glasses fifteen feet away, shattered and dissolved into lumps of molten glass. The remains of the glasses are still on display in the Billiard room. An unruly guest was decked once by a heavy door that suddenly came loose from its hinges and fell on him, and, a toilet seat lid ripped itself loose from steel hinges, a crystal wine glass exploded in the presence of several guests, and the diaphanous form of a lady has been seen frequently on the grand staircase.

Jessica Lee, owner of LA Productions, wrote to Bob Pritikin about her experience in the Mansions on February 5, 1998. Lee spent the night during a storm in the luxurious Four Poster Suite. She dressed for bed at 1:30 a.m. As she turned the lights out and closed her eyes, a bright force of light burst into the room. From under the covers, she could see that the lights had been turned on. As she got up to look around, she noticed that the light was not coming from

356

the light bulbs, but rather a floating, three-dimensional, luminous form undulating near the ceiling. There was a bright red light flashing through the smoke alarm. The entire spectacle was throwing off enough light to read by! For several hours, she watched the beautiful formation, female in essence. Its opalescent light would intensify as the tendrils floated toward her, and diminished as they receded. After the event, she thoroughly inspected the room, and found that the light had its own source, and was not caused by the storm or natural causes. She simply enjoyed the ethereal light show, and never did find out whom or what caused it. Perhaps Claudia's spirit is just reaching out to a sympathetic soul.

The Queen Anne Hotel

Particulars
1590 Sutter Street,
San Francisco, CA 94109
Phone: 415-441-2828
Fax: 415-775-5212
Toll Free: 1-800-227-3970
E-mail: stay@queenanne.com
Website: www.queenanne.com

History

This Victorian jewel was built in 1890 on the corner of Sutter and Octavia Streets in the lower Pacific Heights neighborhood of downtown San Francisco by prominent Senator James G. Fair. Fair was one of the Comstock Load Silver Kings, and he also constructed the Fairmont Hotel atop Nob Hill as a reminder of his penchant for architecture and his unlimited finances. The structure originally housed Miss Mary Lake's School for Girls which was essentially a grooming school for wealthy, young wannabe socialites in San Francisco. Officially opening on February 15, 1890, the building somehow managed to escape total destruction during the 1906 earthquake due to its location three blocks from the firewall.

The first floor, now containing the lobby and salon, were originally the "infants' classroom" which held 65 students. The parlor was once the students' gymnasium, the board room was initially the pantry, and the library, kitchen and employees areas once served as the school's dining room and kitchen. An apartment building now rests on the site of the original playground at the corner of Octavia and Bush Streets. The second floor originally contained three connecting drawing rooms, and a music room, library, history, art, mathematics and three general classrooms. The third and fourth were designed as dormitories for the 65-75 boarders. Each sleeping area was uniquely designed with fireplaces, toilets, closets, storage areas that could hold up to five large Saratoga trunks and spectacular views of the city. The third floor contained the infirmary and a large medicine closet, while the attic served as another trunk storage area which was illuminated by a skylight.

In 1899, the building was sold to the Cosmos, an exclusive gentlemen's club which operated until around 1911. Eventually, the building was sold to the Episcopal Diocese who founded the Girls Friendly Society Lodge, a haven for young, working women. The Diocese Lodge existed until around 1936. From that point, the building had several owners until it was abandoned and boarded up. In 1980, the K.R.V. Company bought the property and restored it to its former grandeur, converting it into its current incarnation, the Queen Anne Hotel. The Queen Anne opened for business on April 15, 1981 as a luxury guest house. In 1983, the building was awarded the Five Star Award for excellence, the smallest property in San Francisco to achieve this honor. The Queen Anne is a forty-eight room full service boutique hotel with Bed and Breakfast ambiance and warm European character. Last revitalized in 1995, the property combines modern conveniences with old world charm.

Hauntspitality

This former school for girls offers old world charm, a unique historical backdrop, modern conveniences and a few spirits to be sure. Given its past, there is little wonder that a few spirits lurk inside. From all accounts given by psychics, staff and guests, the overwhelming contention is, that female phantoms rule the roost in this hotel. They may be energy from the young ladies of the former Miss Mary Lake's School for Girls or from the time when the building served as the Girls Friendly Society Lodge. Certain rooms like #311 and #410 reportedly have more activity than most, although the attic, stairs, lobby and other rooms have their share of stories.

There have been reports over the years of closet doors in a few of the rooms suddenly opening or closing as if some unseen occupants are busy packing or unpacking. Lights in some parts of the hotel have been known to suddenly turn on or off unassisted. There are the proverbial cold gusts of air that seem to come from nowhere and engulf guests and staff; the occasional sounds of children or young girls giggling and laughing; and muted conversations of women coming from unoccupied areas of the hotel. The former attic is one place where ghostly voices and sounds of girls playing have frequently been heard late at night. Whenever anyone went to inspect the source of the noises, they were greeted by silence and the feeling of being watched or followed by unseen eyes.

There are also reports, primarily from men staying in one of the guest rooms, of being pushed or held down, especially when making love. The feeling as described by the participants, it that some kind of energy seems to press or hold them down, or push them off the bed. Perhaps one or two of lady-like girls from Miss Mary Lake's School for Girls will only tolerate so many shenanigans in their former rooms? There are other incidents of disembodied footsteps in the hallways and attic and the continual complaints of being watched in certain areas of the building.

Room #410, formerly Mary Lake's office, has its own unique stories which seem to happen only to single men staying in the room. On several occasions, single males have reportedly felt loose covers pulled up to their neck as if someone was gently tucking them in. During an episode of Haunted San Francisco by Indigo Films for the Travel Channel, a recent guest, single and male of course, was so exhausted when he went to sleep in Room 410, that he didn't have time to crawl under the covers. When he woke up, he was startled to find that a blanket had not only been draped over his body, but that the blanket had been neatly tucked in around him! Perhaps Mary Lake is still caretaking at the inn; although this time her attention is turned to eligible, single men, rather than adolescent girls.

There is definitely an additional perk to staying at the Queen Anne that is not listed in the brochure. The friendly spirits of this building, primarily female, are always eager to please their guests, or at the very least, make life a little more interesting for those looking for an other-worldly adventure for those choosing to stay in one of San Francisco's most beautiful Victorian hotels. It's truly a match made in heaven!

San Remo Hotel

Particulars
2237 Mason Street,
San Francisco, CA 94133
Phone: 415-776-8688
Fax: 415- 776-2811
Toll Free: 1-800-352-REMO
E-mail: info@sanremohotel.com
Website: www.sanremohotel.com

History
The three-story Victorian structure was originally built by A.P. Giannini, the founder of Bank of America. The building served as a boarding house for the local dock workers who could not find lodging after the great earthquake. In 1970, Tom and Robert Field took over the ownership of the San Remo Hotel, and performed extensive restoration.

Hauntspitality
An employee named Gary shared some of his experiences with us regarding the San Remo spirits.
- One of the ghosts came late at night to the room I was sleeping in. The spirit started to rub my back. At first I thought that I was imagining what was happening, but it was real and disturbing. Suddenly, the part of my back that was being rubbed began to get really cold until I finally told whatever it was to just leave me alone because I was trying to go to sleep. After that, the rubbing stopped.
- While I was working in the office late one night, I saw an elderly man sitting on top of a desk rocking himself back and forth. The man just looked right at me, and then he disappeared.
- Some times I felt someone standing behind me and other times I heard footsteps following me through the hotel. Whenever I turned around, there is no one there.
- On one occasion, a guest came to the front desk and said that he was locked out of his room and that he left the keys inside (there is no way to lock the room without the key). When I went with him to open the room with the master key, we found his keys bent into a "V" shape and sitting on top of his dresser!
- Numerous times people have complained of misplacing things in their room. They swear that they put something somewhere, then go crazy trying to find it. They tell me that the item suddenly and mysteriously ends up somewhere else. Even stranger, the items will appear in another guest room and the guests return the item saying it's not theirs. They have no idea how it got in their room.
- The spirits have been known to take keys and other personal items, always returning it to another location.

Some people believe that former guests still haunt the San Remo. Toward the end of the 1960's a Madame in San Francisco's red-light district was a long-term tenant at the hotel. She died in the south portion of the building around 1980 and her body was not found for several days. Her spirit has been reported roaming the building ever since. The is also an elderly gentleman who enjoys playing pranks on the staff and guests.

A front desk manager, who worked alone numerous times, reported that the lights go on and off by themselves and doors inexplicably open and shut unassisted. Although no apparitions have actually been seen to date, witnesses frequently report strange shadows, colds spots that suddenly manifest, unexplained footsteps, and the strong feeling of being watched. At the San Remo, the past truly comes to life; or *afterlife!*

York Hotel

Particulars

940 Sutter Street,
San Francisco, CA 94109
Phone: 414-885-6800
Fax: 415-885-6990
Toll Free: 800-808-9675
E-mail: yorkhotel@worldnet.att.net
Website: www.yorkhotel.com

History

From the early days when part of the building served as a hidden speakeasy, until today, the York Hotel fills a chapter in the history of San Francisco. If the walls could talk, they would surely have plenty to say; and sing. Italian immigrants Caroline and William Haus built the hotel in 1922 naming it the Glen Royal. William died shortly after its opening, yet Caroline managed to keep the hotel running until 1926 when she sold it. The new owners, William Stout and Norton Cowden ran the hotel under the name, Empire Hotel. On a misty night during the height of The Prohibition, the York Hotel illegally opened its now renowned Plush Room Cabaret. Merrymakers found their way through a maze of subterranean passageways to reach the secret cabaret. There, San Francisco socialites gathered to hear the top entertainers of the era. As prohibition faded into history, the Plush Room became one of the area's hottest nightspots. In 1956, The York Hotel, formally known to San Franciscans as the Empire Hotel, was used as a film site for Alfred Hitchcock's "Vertigo". Extensive restoration began when new owners took over in 1994.

Hauntspitality

As the story goes, during Prohibition, the Plush Room Cabaret operated illegally within the hotel for the social elite of San Francisco. One night, as the stage lights dimmed, a tall, slender man wearing a top hat and tails entered the cabaret, walked confidently across the stage and sat down at the grand piano. He played tune after tune, request after request for the enthralled audience. As the night wore on, the playing suddenly ceased as the handsome stranger suddenly slummed over the piano, dead! Since that time, the phantom stranger has been witnessed floating down the halls and in the basement of the hotel. The playful and friendly spirit is called, Lester, and he is said to be that young piano player who died suddenly during a Prohibition performance many never forgot.

Staff and guests have reported seeing a young man fitting the description of the piano player appear out of thin air or suddenly vanish as they look on. The wandering phantom enjoys playing with the living rather than for them. Stories of lights turning on by themselves or doors opening and closing without human assistance, are but a few of the other-worldly tricks that continue to keep the legend of Lester going strong over 60 years after his untimely demise. Even if you are not fortunate enough to encounter Lester during your visit here, you will not be disappointed with the other "visible" delights that this beautiful hotel has to offer.

San Jose
Hyatt Hotel St. Claire

Particulars
302 S Market Street,
San Jose, CA 95113
Phone: 408-295-2000
Fax: 408-977-0403
Toll free: 800-441-0776
E-mail: info@thesainteclaire.com
Website: www.thesainteclaire.com

History

The Sainte Claire Hotel was constructed on the spot where a brick building housing the Eagle Brewing Company stood. When developer Thomas S. Montgomery purchased the land in 1923, the Eagle Brewing Company had been closed since Prohibition. After finding several investors he demolished the brewery and began construction in his hotel in 1925. The Hotel Sainte Claire opened in October 16, 1926 at a cost of around one million dollars. Some of its celebrity clientele included: Clark Gable, Carole Lombard, Eleanor Roosevelt, Judy Garland, Joe DiMaggio, Bob Hope and John F. Kennedy. By the 1970s the Sainte Claire was a declining hotel that catered to low income individuals and families including senior citizens. During the 1980s, the hotel was part of a much needed restoration project. This was short-lived and the Sainte Claire closed from 1988-1991. A final chapter in the hotel's history began in 1991 when Manou Mobedshahi restored the hotel to its former elegance.

Hauntspitality

When the historic hotel was brought back to life after intensive restoration, complaints began surfacing that other "things' were also brought back from the dead; it's spirits. People working or staying on the third and sixth floors in particular reported cold spots, unexplained voices, disembodied footsteps and apparitions roaming the corridors. The past refused to die in this establishment. The longer the restored building catered to new clientele, the more stories about haunted hallways and room surfaced. Visitors claimed that they definitely felt things while walking along the sixth floor hallways. People would report seeing figures out of the corner of their eye, wearing Period clothing dart down a hallway and just vanish. There was a report that a rollaway bed with a pillow mysteriously made its way to the roof without human assistance. Housekeeping would often feel as if they were being watched or followed or their name would be called out while working in an unoccupied room. Sometimes a door would slam shut or lights would turn on while they were busy tidying up a room where the guests had just checked out.

Some staff reported hearing parties and piano music come from the second floor where a lounge had once stood after Prohibition was repealed. The bar was eventually moved to the ground floor, but that didn't stop the spirits from partying on in their former haven. The lobby and lounge areas are where paranormal activity has been frequently reported over the years. A staff person had been shoved by someone unseen in the lobby and others had spotted phantom forms that simply vanished into thin air. The shoving experience has since been reported by others working in the lobby late at night. A housekeeper claims that she and a colleague saw a young boy sitting on the steps between the third and fourth levels. As they were about to ask the boy a question, he vanished in front of them. On other occasions, staff have reported seeing shadowy forms dressed in wedding garb float into Room 215; the honeymoon suite. Finally, a guest who stayed in the hotel reported smelling tobacco in a non-smoking room. This event occurred twice where the distinct tobacco smell filled the room, only to dissipate in a matter of seconds. It's as if a phantom spirit dropped by to enjoy a smoke and then depart. At the historic Sainte Claire, the past and present co-exist on a daily basis and the paranormal is the norm.

Wyndham Hotel

Particulars
1350 North First Street,
San Jose, CA 95112-4789
Phone: 408-453-6200
Fax: 408-437-9693
Toll Free: 1-800-WYNDHAM
Website: http://www.wyndham.com/
hotels/SJCAP/main.wnt

History

Formerly known as the Le Baron Hotel, the new Wyndham hotel is situated in the heart of Silicon Valley, in San Jose, California.

Hauntspitality

According to local legend, a salesman was believed to have committed suicide in one of the hotel rooms. A number of accounts by staff and guests suggest that his restless spirit remains in the hotel wandering down certain corridors, and occasionally manifesting in front of employees and guests.

The phantom male is often seen wearing a dark suit and slowly walking down a hallway and disappearing before anyone can talk to him. No one has been able to come up with a name for this elusive spirit and although he isn't harmful, suddenly manifesting cold spots, doors opening and shutting by themselves, and lights that seem to have a mind of their own, are all blamed on the phantom male.

At the famous Wyndham Hotel, you never know who you might run into when you turn a corner: a member of the staff, a fellow guest, or perhaps a gentleman from the past who refuses to leave.

San Juan Bautista
The Cutting Horse

Particulars
307 Third Street,
San Juan Bautista, CA 95045-0322
Phone: 831-623-4549
Fax: 831-623-1769
E-mail: ezehna@hotmail.com

History

Preliminary research information that was gathered by Ellen Zehna indicated that prior to European occupation; a Native American village existed around Third and Mariposa streets. Situated on the site of the current Cutting Horse site was The St. John's Hotel, a two-story adobe building constructed around 1840. By 1856 the town had four general merchandise stores and Third Street was lined with saloons and businesses, including a blacksmith and wheelwright, gunsmith, livery stable, bakery, jewelry store, horseshoer and the Sebastopol Hotel (present site of Daisy's). The St. John's was a popular place during the 1850's and 1860's as the Concord stagecoaches running between San Francisco and Los Angeles would always stop there. Isaac Mylar, author of the book "Early Days at Mission San Juan Bautista" did not remember the first man that ran this place, but stated that later on, it was operated by Luis Raggio, Sr. The building was two-stories, and had two steps leading down to the first floor which contained a saloon with a billiard table. There was also a restaurant in the rear of the first floor. The upper story contained a hall that was used for dancing.

It was in the saloon in this building that Bart Taylor was shot in the shoulder by Pablo German. There was also a crazed Mexican who came into town and shot Manuel Butron through the center of the breast; he was presumed dead. Swift justice prevailed and the perpetrator was hanged; however, Butron eventually recovered from the wound. The fire of 1867 destroyed most of the buildings on Third Street forcing Giacomo Ramoni (AKA "Giacoma") the owner of the property, to build a row of fireproof stone buildings. The first to be completed was the building in which the "Old Relay Station" was later situated. Shortly after this a baker named John Murphy built a small building (now the Cutting Horse's third dining room). Murphy then leased the building from Giacoma for five years. The building became San Juan's first bank in 1919. The present main Cutting Horse building constructed of sandstone was finished in 1871 and was considered the finest and most durable stone building ever erected in San Juan. In the 1870's this building was operated by a Frenchman named Quern, called the French Hotel. In the 1880's a Spaniard by the name of Ambrosio Rozas ran the barroom there. After that, there were several different owners including Art Baldwin and Charlie Kessling.

During the late 1800's the entrance to the bar was at the left-hand corner of the building. The bar itself ran along the wall that adjoins the Cutting Horse third dining room; the old bank building. In the 1880's an argument that was started in this bar was settled just outside the barroom door. The argument ended when one of the men fell to the wooden sidewalk with a bullet in his heart. Antoine Taix acquired the building in the early 1890's. For a long time, the present-day Cutting Horse building was commonly called the "Taix Building". Present day local historians still refer to it as the old Taix Building. Antoine Taix had left France for the United States in February 1871; finally arriving in San Juan Bautista in 1893 and operated a meat market in the Taix Building for many years. He died in January 1939 at the age of 86.

The small "Murphy" building (the Cutting Horse third dining room; now locally known as the "Bank of America Building") housed the First National Bank of San Juan in 1919. The Bank of America building had numerous tenants after John Murphy moved his bakery to Hollister in 1874. During the quake of 1906 Joe Bravea, Sr. was operating a shoe shop there. Then it became a drug store and later a hardware store; until the First National Bank occupied the building in 1919. This bank later became the Bank of Italy, the TransBank, and then the Bank of America.

An 1894 photo from the San Juan Bautista Historical Society depicts the present-day main two-story Cutting Horse building as the front of a brothel. During 1906-07, the six-mile San Juan Pacific Railway that joined the Southern Pacific Coast Line at Chittenden with a depot near town was constructed. During that time about 200 Chinese laborers were housed in the upstairs portion of the building. Around 1910 Ed Spitz had a barbershop in the present Cutting Horse building. The barber pole in front of this shop was a classic sign of old San Juan, beautifully carved and painted bright red, white, and blue. An article in the San Juan Mission News dated August 31, 1928 states: "Mr. William Alton, proprietor of the barber shop next to the Vincente Restaurant (now Daisy's) has purchased the Ellis barber shop in the Giacomazzi (or Giacoma) Building. Mr. Alton will run both shops." An April 4, 1928 article in the same newspaper states: "Ed Pearce will open a real estate office in the Taix Building just above the Bank of Italy."

In 1959, the block bounded by Third, Fourth, Mariposa and Polk Streets was purchased by Larry and Paulina Lushbaugh. They restored the building and Mrs. Rose opened the Cutting Horse restaurant & Bar at the location of the previous Brass Lantern Restaurant and Bar. In the 1960's, Larry Lushbaugh put back the balcony and painted the entire building. Lushbaugh sold the building to Paul Porter. Al Maida named "The Cutting Horse", and Ralph Lopez bought the property from Paul Porter. The Cutting Horse was owned and operated for a time by Chuck and Linda Taylor who sold the business to their daughter Elizabeth "Liz" Killian, all leasing the property from Mr. Lopez. In 1999, The Lopez's opened a doorway from the first Cutting Horse dining room into the old Bank of America building, creating the existing third dining room. In late 2001, Frank and Ellen Zehna acquired the Cutting Horse from Liz Killian. Drinks have been sold at the present Cutting Horse bar almost continuously for the past 148 years.

Hauntspitality
San Juan Bautista boasts another haunted local besides the Mariposa House. In fact, some say that this local haunt has had more events go on inside than the Mariposa. Owned by Rafael and Mary Lopez, and run by the Zehnas, the history of the property dates back to the late 1700s. Once a popular hotel, the building has several ghostly guests who not only frequent the restaurant portion of the building, but other areas as well.

As one legend goes, around 1900, a rich cattleman sold all of his cattle and bought a wife. The woman he would marry was the daughter of the upstairs brothel owner. As the ebullient young woman finished packing her belongings to join her husband, in haste, the bride-to-be was carrying her suitcase down the stairs when she accidentally tripped and fell. In one horrific moment, her body tumbled down the wooden steps and ended up in a crumpled heap at the base of the stairway; her honeymoon was cut short by her cruel fate. The distraught groom reportedly never left, dying of loneliness where his bride had her tragic fall.

Although the spirited stories are still trickling in, at least two female phantoms are known to materialize to staff and guests. A back stairway in the restaurant that leads to the conference room is one paranormal hot spot where a phantom lady (most likely the tragic bride) whose portrait used to hang on the stairway wall, is said to frequently make her presence known. Those who take the climb up the stairs often report a feeling of being watched, touched by something unseen, or feeling something unearthly brush by them.

The Cutting Horse was once operated by Chuck and Linda Taylor, who then sold the business to their daughter Elizabeth "Liz" Killian, (they all leased the building from Mr. Lopez). Early on during their ownership, the Taylors were greeted by the resident ghost when they entered the kitchen late at night. To their indignation, a rinsing hose from one of the sinks suddenly detached itself and sprayed all of them before mysteriously reattaching itself to the sink! This mischievous greeting was a spirited way for the deceased to acquaint themselves with the living.

Present-day long-time Cutting Horse customers confirm that a portion of the building once served as a brothel and they remember three "ladies of the night" living upstairs with a Madam. The Madam is believed to be one of the resident spirits who still loves entertaining the living. One waitress has witnessed men in cowboy outfits walk down the staircase, and then disappear as they reach the front door.

Many strange events involving electrical devices continue on a daily basis. Lights that were turned off the night before are frequently on the next morning. Exhaust fans that were disengaged upon closing the kitchen at night are mysteriously activated the next day. The staff constantly has to bring in ladders to screw back in light bulbs in the high chandeliers; after they were working fine the night before. There are pesky footsteps that make their way through unoccupied areas of the building and mumbled conversations often echo from parts of the restaurant that are not in use; at least by the living.

The next door Posada de San Juan Hotel was built over the site of the town's "hanging tree" where many unjust hangings took place. Numerous ghosts are witnessed walking the hallways as well as visiting the main lounge. One phantom who frequents the hotel is a lady who comes down the hallway and sits in the lounge. This spectral female has been spotted standing at the top of the stairs and also walking up and down the staircase at various times. On several occasions, a staff person will see the spectral lady looking like a regular person come down the stairs and sit in the lounge, as if waiting for service.

When a staff person went over to see if a woman needed help; she vanished. There are other strange occurrences inside the recently constructed hotel, but you'll have to visit to hear those stories. While visiting San Juan Bautista and the adjacent Posada hotel, see if you can spot their spirited clientele. If the ambiance doesn't conjure up a misty form or shadow right off the bat, then saddle up to a table, rest your weary bones and enjoy the food and spirits; either kind will do!

Mariposa House Restaurant

Particulars

37 Mariposa Street, P.O. Box 322,
San Juan Bautista, CA 95045-0322
Phone: 831-623-4666
Fax: 831-623-2858
E-mail: dining@mariposahouse.com
Website: www.mariposahouse.com

History

The Mariposa House Restaurant is located in the only true Victorian in San Juan Bautista. The home was built in 1892 by John Anderson. The original site of the home was on the corner of Third Street and Mariposa Street in San Juan. In 1972 the home was moved to Fourth Street and Mariposa Street to make room for the current South Valley National Bank (was Bank of America when the home was moved). The home was a private residence until 1975 when it was converted into the Mariposa House Restaurant.

Hauntspitality

Perhaps the most intriguing part of the house is the resident ghost named Rachel. She has been witnessed by numerous individuals, including staff and Ripbenburg. Rachel reportedly died from peritonitis shortly after giving birth. She is described as Hispanic, in her late 20's with long dark hair. Ask about her when you come by.

Ripbenburg's business partner, Barbara, who lives upstairs from the restaurant, has never seen Rachel,, but has felt her presence numerous times. A friend of Barbara's, who was spending a couple of nights, seemed to set Rachel's spirit free. The first night her guest reported feeling a cool breeze on different parts of her head as she lay in bed. On another occasion, and once again very late at night, both the guest and Barbara were awakened by the sound of someone walking up and down the stairs several times. Barbara thought it might be her daughter who often stays with her, coming in late. Curious after several rounds of loud footsteps, tromping back and forth, she finally got up to check the situation out; there was no one anywhere to be seen in that part of the building.

One Sunday afternoon, after closing for brunch, Barbara and Dennis decided to take a walk up town. As they were about ready to leave, they were both standing in the wait staff area. As Barbara turned to walk away from the area she briefly saw a red dress disappear around the corner. Quickly giving chase, she never found the owner of the red dress anywhere inside.

Numerous individuals, who have witnessed Rachel, see her wearing a red dress. One weekend night, around midnight, Dennis was putting things away in the refrigerator. He was alone in the restaurant when he felt a gentle tap on the shoulder. He turned around quickly, but there was no one there!

When Barbara and Dennis decided to reopen the Mariposa House, Dennis was carrying a few items into what used to be an old bedroom. He was in the house by himself. Suddenly there was a very sweet, citrus fragrance all around him, almost like a palmate that many women wore in their hair during the turn of the century. He sat on the window sill and said, "It's was nice to be with you

369

(Rachel) again!"

Several years ago, prior to Dennis having an interest in the restaurant, he was having lunch towards the end of the lunch hour. At the time there were only two patrons in the restaurant, including himself. As he had finished his lunch Barbara came up to talk to him. There was no conversation of Rachel or spirits; in fact, spirits didn't even enter his mind. As he got up to leave and turned towards the door, he saw out of the corner of his eye a young woman, possibly in her mid 20's, standing at the entrance of the kitchen area. She was opaque with long dark hair and a light colored robe. Stopping in his tracks, he turned to Barbara and said, "There's someone else here." Barbara said, "I know. She's been very active lately." It seems Rachel goes through times when she's very active and periods when there's no sign of her presence.

The greatest activity seems to have occurred several years ago: Silverware was moved to odd places after being set up the night before; flowers that were on the tables, would be found upright in the middle of the floor; a dishwasher (Ofelia) working for Barbara was pregnant and Barbara would tell her to go upstairs and lay down to rest. After a few minutes, a frightened Ofelia came running downstairs very frightened. She said that she felt cold fingers rubbing her stomach and there was no one else in the room with her. From that time on, she never went upstairs alone; and a young boy would occasionally get up to go to the kitchen at night for something to eat. That's when he'd report seeing a strange lady cooking at the stove who would vanish in front of him.

This place has it all: delicious food and friendly spirits. Enjoy!

San Juan Capistrano
El Adobe Restaurant

Particulars
31891 Camino Capistrano,
San Juan Capistrano, CA 92675
Phone: 949-493-1163
Fax: 949-493-4565
Website: www.eladobedecapistrano.com

History

The building that now houses the El Adobe de Capistrano Restaurant was originally two separate structures. The Miguel Yorba Adobe (the north half) was built in 1778 as a private residence, and the south half of the current building was built in 1812.

This second half was called the juzgado and used as a justice court and jail. In 1912 the Vanderleck family connected the Miguel Yorba adobe and the courthouse to form one home. Later the building was turned into the restaurant. The adobe, besides being a jail, also served as a store, a stage depot and a hotel. According to the Landmark Plaque in front of the restaurant, entitled the Miguel Yorba Adobe, The adobe was originally built in 1840 as two separate structures: The northern building was a residence, while the southern building served several functions including a stage depot, courtroom and jail. The two structures were connected around 1911 and renovated to serve as two homes. In 1948, the structures were combined into a restaurant.

Early photographs of the El Adobe provided by the El Adobe Restaurant

Hauntspitality

According to several paranormal researchers, when the jail portion of the restaurant was converted into a wine cellar, staff and guests began reporting a feeling of being watched or followed. In addition to the spooky confines of the former jail, the spirit of a headless monk has been seen wandering the area outside of the restaurant. A paragraph on the www.ghosts.org Website states, "The jail portion has been converted into a wine cellar for the restaurant, and it's here that waiters and others report a feeling of being watched. In addition to the creepy jail, the ghost of a headless monk has been seen wandering the street outside of the restaurant." Psychics and paranormal investigators alike are familiar with the spirits of the El Adobe. Although you might expect Richard Nixon's ghost to be one of the phantom contingent (he loved the place while he was President and living in San Clemente), his spirit seems to prefer his birthplace/museum in Yorba Linda to the confines of this fine, Mexican restaurant. However, inside and around the garden of this historic adobe, are ample spirits to satisfy everyone's taste for the afterlife.

After talking to staff persons, one fact reverberates through the entire restaurant; It's very haunted and by more than one spirit. The overwhelming feeling of those working in the restaurant, is that the basement spirit belongs to a young girl. This was later confirmed by a "sensitive" waitress who worked at the El Adobe for over ten years. The woman witnessed a Native American or Hispanic girl about 16-18 years old. She noticed that the girl had long, black hair, was very thin and gaunt looking, was crying and shackled to the wall. She was uncertain why she remained trapped in the basement area (former jail). Frequently sighted in the basement, the young phantom girl doesn't seem to understand what she did to cause the punishment that was inflicted upon her. She is forlorn and her pain is felt by those who happen to intrude on her space at the wrong time.

A waitress, who was once confronted by the anxious spirit, reportedly had a mini-conversation with the girl. The young girl was adamant that this was not her world and she wondered why she was here; she sorrowfully asked the waitress where her child was, and then asked the waitress to pray for her soul. The waitress stated that the basement, now a storage area for wine and other things, is a place that no one will visit alone. She said that even the men are reluctant to visit the area without support.

The spirit of the young girl is not the only phantom who inhabits El Adobe. The stories are plentiful of other specters that enjoy the after-life ambiance inside the abode; in fact; there is hardly a nook or cranny that does not have some spirit associated with it. It has been called a vortex or portal by some. One frequent comment by those visiting is that no one has ever felt threatened; it's just spooky sometimes.

Psychic Ginnie McGovern and orb over lamp on the left (Courtesy of the International Paranormal Research Organization – IPRO)

As for the other ghost guests, reports of a smiling, blonde woman from the turn-of-the-century, wearing a white dress (or night gown) has been spotted standing behind unsuspecting patrons or staff in the upper balcony mirror. According to the numerous reports, the female phantom is there one minute, but when people see her and turn around; she simply vanishes.

Some of the other reported events include: shadowy figures that are sighted upstairs and down, floating through the various rooms; unexplained voices and conversations which come from unoccupied rooms; footsteps that do not belong to the living; noticeable smells of cigars and strong body odors; cold spots or icy breezes that materialize from nowhere; a headless man who some say looks like a monk; and, items that are in place one minute, are found moved to another location the next.

A recent visit by the authors to the El Adobe resulted in the identification of

Orb in center of the wine rack (Courtesy of the International Paranormal Research Orgainzation – IPRO)

at least six major energies in the building. Downstairs in the cellar, dowsing rods and psychic impressions seemed to point to the presence of a male who was incarcerated in the current wine cellar area. This man may have died of starvation or disease while imprisoned. There was also a sense of a young, dark-haired woman who frequents that area, perhaps visiting her lover who was placed in the holding cell by her parents for attempting to marry their daughter without consent.

Upstairs in the main area we encountered a fair-complected woman in her 20s-30s who may have occupied the building and who now guards her domain. Her countenance has been occasionally sighted inside, gliding through the main dining area and through the walls. In the outside bar area, we picked up on a strong male presence who is very territorial. This spirit is somehow connected to the back courtyard and may have died there. His restless energy has caused items to move; contributes to quickly manifesting cold spots, he has been sighted as an apparition; and a gruff cough or growl can sometimes be heard near the bar area.

A fifth energy belongs to an elderly woman, perhaps the family matriarch who with her stern look and veil, may be in mourning. She is a dominant energy near the entrance and kitchen areas of the establishment, we sensed two young children playing throughout the building.

The El Adobe is like a way station for spirits, where the people who work there and come to visit, never know what awaits them, as far as the spirits go. As one friend stated, "The only things you can always count on there are the spirits and having a great meal."

So, take a journey to San Juan Capistrano for the swallows, to view the Mission and then relax at the El Adobe for your dinner and spirits.

San Luis Obispo
The Sanitarium Spa

Particulars

1717 Osos Street,
San Luis Obispo, CA 93401
Phone: 805-544-4124
E-mail: info@thesanitariumspa.com
Website: http://www.thesanitariumspa.com

History

The Hageman Sanitarium was built in the 1880s as one of the area's first private hospitals and served as a retreat for patients with non-contagious diseases or recovering from minor operations. A local machinist named J.C. Waterbury supplied the $5,000 construction cost and his wife, a nurse, was one of the sanitarium's first employees. In 1912, Mrs. Kenyon bought the building and turned it into a boarding house for railroad workers and then it became a women's boarding house. In those days, the neighboring establishment served as a bordello, so there's reason to speculate that "women's boarding house" may have been a polite euphemism. Over the years, the home's original 13 rooms were not enough to meet the demand for housing and Mrs. Kenyon added a kitchen to the back of the building. She also boarded up the second story veranda and turned it into a closet for the upstairs bedrooms. By the start of the World War II, the boarding house's clients were exclusively women.

During the mid-1980s, the Kyle family purchased the aging building and rented it out as a sorority house. During the 1990s the building served as a fraternity house. After extensive renovation, the Sanitarium opened June 2005 and features a garden, in-room soaking tubs and fireplaces, and the quiet that comes with little intrusion from the outside world. The Sanitarium offers five rooms in the Main House and two suites in the Outpatient Ward which is a private detached house. As operators of the bed & breakfast, the four women act as midwives in the rebirth of the sanitarium. By converting the historic manse into a comforting retreat, the ladies are doing with the building just what they intend to do for their guests: restore them in both body and spirit. Originally a site for mental and physical recovery, the Sanitarium's steam baths, yoga classes and creative workshops uphold the facility's curative character.

Hauntspitality

There have been numerous reported paranormal events that have taken place inside this historic building. With an exceptional history as a functioning sanitarium, boarding house for railroad workers, a women's boarding house, a sorority house, a fraternity house and finally as a retreat for mental and physical recovery, the former sanitarium lives on. It's historic background has also contributed to many spirited events since it latest incarnation.

Staff and guests, though never frightened, have reported seeing and feeling things that are not of this dimension. The cold spots in certain portions of the building are a normal occurrence as are items that will disappear and then reappear somewhere else; lights that have a mind of their own; doors that will be opened by unseen hands; disembodied footsteps that come from unoccupied rooms; occasional muffled voices, and frequent conversations that do not belong

to the living; and the sightings of a man and several women in Period clothing inside the building.

This is a must visit place, where relaxation, meditation and healing bring people from all walks of life to enjoy the atmosphere. During your stay, you will be pampered by the living as well as paid an occasional visit by former occupants of this historic home that simply refuse to leave. Maybe they are benefiting from the therapeutic ambiance in the building that seems to bond the living to the former occupants. Be sure to ask about the latest paranormal experiences when you come for a stay.

Santa Cruz
Cliff Crest Bed & Breakfast Inn

Particulars
407 Cliff Street,
Santa Cruz, CA 95060
Phone: 831-427-2609
Fax: 831-427-2710
E-mail: innkpr@cliffcrestinn.com
Website: www.cliffcrestInn.com

History

The following family information is based on the family history submitted by C. Victor Jeter on August 10, 1999: The third son and the eighth child of William Griffin Jeter and Elizabeth McCutchen Berry, William Thomas "Will" Jeter was born on September 19, 1850 on the family farm in Illinois. Will remained on the farm until the age of six when his father headed to California in 1857. After stopping in Livingston County near Chillicothe, Missouri, William's father decided to buy land and run a farm until his death in 1867. Will remained in Missouri until 1876, the year after the death of his mother. In the intervening years he worked on the farm, was educated in the public schools, and then later started to read the law and engage in business activities.

Deciding to take a vacation from his business activities and budding law practice, Will headed west to see the sights and to visit with his uncle, Thomas Horatio Jeter, who had arrived in California from Illinois just prior to the Civil War. Will stopped briefly in Virginia City, Nevada and finally reached California in 1877. Planning to stay for only a short time before returning to Missouri, Will ultimately settled in California and attended Hastings Law College in San Francisco. After completing his studies, Will began his practice in Santa Cruz, California. It is thought that his sister, Harriet and her attorney-husband, Zack Goldsby were also living in Santa Cruz at the time and that Will entered into practice with his brother-in-law.

Will married Jennie Fuller Bliss on March 2, 1885 at the First Methodist Church in Santa Cruz. The couple had no children and during the ensuing years, Will became a well-known member of the Santa Cruz Bar Association and was admitted to practice before the Supreme Court of California. During 1884, Will was elected chairman of the Democratic Central Committee of Santa Cruz County. He was twice re-elected district attorney in a heavily Republican county, and served as a member of the Santa Cruz City Council and as the Mayor of Santa Cruz. Will also accepted the position of president of the Santa Cruz County Bank in 1893, a position he would hold for the next 37 years. William and Jennie purchased their Queen Anne-style home on Beach Hill in the 1890s. It was designed by D. A. Damkroeger in 1887 and underwent several changes during the Governor's ownership including the addition of Jennie's room, the circular solarium and a belvedere. John McLaren, the landscape architect of Golden Gate Park in San Francisco and a personal friend of the Governor, designed the gardens for the Jeter home. After the death of the incumbent Lt. Governor, Will was named Lt. Governor of California on October 25, 1895. He served most of his term as "de-facto" governor because of the ill-health of Governor Budd and was admitted to practice before the Supreme Court of the United States at Washington, D.C. on

October 20, 1908.

Will Jeter battled to purchase the "Big Basin" area north of Santa Cruz for public use and later procured the Felton big trees for Santa Cruz County as a public park. He learned on his deathbed that coast redwood grove passed into public ownership. On 12 May 1934, a flag-draped bronze tablet attached to one of the giant redwoods was unveiled as memorial to "William T. Jeter, 1850-1930, whose unselfish efforts made possible the ownership of the Santa Cruz County Big Trees Park." The "Jeter Tree" is still standing at the end of the second millennium, as it was at the end of the first and will forever be a source of inspiration and pride to all in the family who visit. The Governor passed away on May 15, 1930. His beloved wife, Jennie, outlived him by almost twenty-nine years and passed away 10 months shy of her 100th birthday in 1959 driving her buggy to town almost to the last. They both rest in the mausoleum, corridor "B", crypt #54, of the Santa Cruz Memorial (IOOF) cemetery. Cliff Crest remained in family ownership until 1968. Since then it has been completely restored and is currently operated as a "bed-and-breakfast" by owners who have knowledge of and a great deal of respect for its history.

Hauntspitality

Marsha Gibbs has worked as the gardener/landscaper at the Cliff Crest through three owners and for 20 years. She provided the following information about the resident spirits: Formerly referred to as the Gray Room (now "Jennie's Room"), on numerous occasions when Gibbs was alone in the house waiting for guests to arrive, she often heard footsteps in the room because the office was right below it (the office was subsequently moved and is now another guest room). The footsteps were often accompanied by the distinct sounds of furniture being moved. When Gibbs would check, there would be no one in the room, or entire house for that matter.

There were other times when Gibbs would help clean the rooms during the week. She placed the pillows in a certain position on the bed in Jennie's Room. It was a simple routine that was performed for each room; however, when Gibbs left the room and came back with the newly arrived guests, the pillows had managed to find a new position on the bed!

According to local lore, the room was once occupied by the original owner, Jennie (Bliss) Jeter. She reportedly died in the room; which may help explain the unusual activity associated with it. Jennie loved the house and lived a long and happy life there, and there's no reason to assume that she ever left. Jennie's benign and happy spirit has been felt by numerous people since the house became an inn. In fact, several individuals who visited over the years always requested Jennie's room because they said that they would arrive from the city stressed out and on edge, but after a few days, would feel completely rejuvenated. It was as if that room has some kind of healing or relaxing ability. Many guests said that the room had a miraculous quality to it. Could it be Jennie's calming spirit?

The following story (a historical tid-bit rather than a true ghost story) was provided by Constantin and Adriana. In November 17, 1907 William Jeter received a telephone call from Major Frank McLaughlin. Frank McLaughlin had built the Golden Gate Villa, a glowing Queen Anne Mansion that crowns Beach Hill in Santa Cruz. It was 1 year after the devastating San Francisco earthquake and exactly two years after Major McLaughlin's wife's death. McLaughlin was a

powerful, flamboyant and controversial man of the Gold Rush Era. He was a friend of Thomas Edison and came to the West around 1887 to find a dependable source of platinum for filaments of the electric light bulb. When tungsten subsequently proved more practical as a filament material, McLaughlin turned his interests to the surrounding gold fields. He raised $12 million in the 1890's in order to divert the Feather River from its bed so that placer gold could be mined from the bottom. He did this with a 2-mile wall that resembled the Great Wall of China and McLaughlin became known as the "King of the Feather".

With the $12 million of other people's money invested he expected a return of at least $12 million. All he found at the end were rusted picks and buckets instead of gold nuggets because the forty-niners had worked the riverbed with hand tools and what they left behind was not worth mining. McLaughlin departed from the mining adventures and devoted his time to politics. He told Jeter on the telephone: "Come to my house immediately". Jeter replied that he was busy and could not come at once, but would be there as soon as he was at liberty. Then McLaughlin spoke in a changed tone: "You must come at once. I have just killed my Bob (his pet name for his step daughter Agnes) and I am going to kill myself." True to his word, McLaughlin swallowed a fatal dose of potassium cyanide, and drew his last breath as his friends arrived. Incredibly, Agnes was found alive. He had shot her at 11 a.m. the same day and doctors could do nothing for her wound in her head. Priests attended her until she died at 6:30 that evening. McLaughlin left many farewell letters and instructions before his death. This is evidence that he had long and painstakingly planned his desperate act. In an explanation to Jeter he wrote of financial reverses he had hidden from the world, his dread of poverty and horror of leaving Agnes unprovided for. "To leave my darling child helpless and penniless would be unnatural and so I take her with me to our loved one (wife). She is the very last one who could face this world alone," he wrote in his last words to Jeter. There is a 12 by 9 foot jeweled glass window in the Golden Gate Villa that is thought to represent Agnes McLaughlin. The tragedy left the Golden Gate Villa empty for a long time because, like many sites of mysterious death, the mansion was widely thought to be haunted.

When you stay at this fabulous inn and you are feeling anxious and stressed, try spending a night or two in the room of former owner Jennie Fuller Bliss.

Santa Maria
Santa Maria Inn

Particulars
801 South Broadway,
Santa Maria, CA 93454-6699
Phone: 805-928-7777
Fax: 805-928-5690
Toll Free: 1-800-462-4276
E-mail: innkeeper@santamariainn.com
Website: www.santamariainn.com

History

The Inn is nestled in the picturesque hills of the Central Coast wine region. The Inn originally opened is doors in 1917, and quickly became a favorite place to relax for the Hollywood in-crowd such as Rudolph Valentino. This historic California Inn is a short drive to Solvang and Santa Barbara. According to the Santa Maria Inn, the old palm and magnolia trees directly in front of the Entrance are reminders of the Inn's floral heritage. Frank J. McCoy, who came to the Valley in 1904 to work for the new Union Sugar plant, saw that a comfortable hotel was needed, and proceeded to build the Santa Maria Inn. His love of flowers can still be seen throughout the Inn such as the award-winning Rose Garden, which to this day contains some of his original plantings and has become the favored backdrop for weddings. The Patio, which hosted McCoy's first flower gardens, is now a quiet retreat with its antique water fountain and brick courtyard. Presidents, ambassadors, actors and actresses, and corporate magnates stopped here while making their way along California's historic El Camino Real between San Francisco and Los Angeles.

Hauntspitality

Guests staying in Room #210, Rudolph Valentino's former suite, have reported feeling a phantom presence in the room, particularly near the bed. On several occasions, guests have reported seeing a misty shape of a male standing in front of their bed as fixated on them. Within seconds, the figure just vanishes. There have also been reports of strange knocking sounds coming from inside the walls of his former room along with quickly manifesting cold spots and the lights that will sometimes flicker. A number of guests and staff have sighted a phantom they have affectionately named "Captain," roaming the corridors of the hotel. Room 103 is another haunted locale, where guests have reported the doors opening and closing in the early hours of the morning, followed by the sound of people walking down the hallway; every time the noises are checked out, no one, human that is, can be found responsible.

A gardener once reported seeing the image of a man he thought was a guest, standing on one of the landings of an outside stairway, until the man vanished into thin air. The curtains in room 216 sometimes move by themselves, even though all the windows are tightly sealed. Room 144 also had a distinct chill associated with it. One member of the ghost hunting team had a bar of soap float across the room while he took a shower. A couple reported hearing footsteps and several mysterious rapping's come from their room late at night.

During September 3, 1989, a group of ghost hunters led by Richard Senate and his wife, psychic, Debbie Christenson Senate, checked into the Santa Maria Inn to investigate the reported hauntings. The investigating group gathered in one room

where most of the strange events are said to have taken place. Debbie was able to reach a female spirit called "Peppy," either a nick-name or given the affectionate name because of her boundless energy. Instead of contacting Valentino, or the often-sighted, Captain, the spirit of a lost soul called Peppy from the 1930s, came through. The names mentioned by Peppy in the séance corresponded to follow-up research conducted by Senate regarding the spirit's mention of the Hearst and Marion Davies families.

The Santa Maria Inn offers a romantic retreat from the hurried life, with a chance to enjoy good food, pleasant scenery and a few friendly spirits.

Santa Monica
The Georgian Hotel

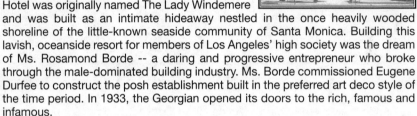

Particulars

1415 Ocean Avenue,
Santa Monica, CA 90401
Phone: 310-395-9945
Fax: 310-451-3374
Toll-Free: 1-800-538-8147
Website: www.georgianhotel.com

History

According to their Website, The Georgian Hotel was originally named The Lady Windemere and was built as an intimate hideaway nestled in the once heavily wooded shoreline of the little-known seaside community of Santa Monica. Building this lavish, oceanside resort for members of Los Angeles' high society was the dream of Ms. Rosamond Borde -- a daring and progressive entrepreneur who broke through the male-dominated building industry. Ms. Borde commissioned Eugene Durfee to construct the posh establishment built in the preferred art deco style of the time period. In 1933, the Georgian opened its doors to the rich, famous and infamous.

During prohibition, the hotel was home to one of Los Angeles' first speakeasies and soon became the rendezvous for many up-and-coming Hollywood studio executives and celebrities including Clark Gable and Carole Lombard, who sought secluded weekends away from the cameras. The oceanfront verandah provided a stage for martinis, jazz and notorious figures including Bugsy Siegel and Fatty Arbuckle.

The primary reasons for the hotel's popularity and success were the exclusive, secluded location and the discriminating manner of Ms. Borde and her staff. The Georgian accommodated out-of-town guests, especially those coming in from the desert, who were seeking a cool seaside refuge from the hot summer months. It was considered to be one of the most modern facilities of the time and featured a beauty parlor, barber shop, playground and dining room. Yet, the end of prohibition and expansion in the 1950s marked the end of a free-spirited era; Los Angeles began to develop into a major metropolitan city and people began to settle permanently. During this time, The Lady Windemere was sold, renovated and renamed the Georgian. The property remained a favorite vacation spot for jet setting Americans and Europeans.

During the 60s, the Georgian became a popular retreat for active seniors who wanted to enjoy the ocean views and Pacific sunsets while affording the opportunity to stay as long as they wished. For more than 25 years, the hotel was the envy of passerby's longing to live in the elaborate, old-fashioned building with the spectacular ocean view. In the Spring of 2000, a two million dollar renovation was completed. This project included the addition of numerous elegant amenities to the Georgian's guest rooms such as magnificent furnishings, elegant draperies, and black and white photographs, which grace the art deco hotel lobby. Additionally, there were changes to the hallways leading to the meeting facilities, the addition of a newly-constructed workout facility and suites.

Today, the Georgian has a reputation as the hotel of choice for entertainment industry executives, celebrities and couples in search of a romantic getaway. Just as the Georgian's oceanfront verandah was once home to a racy speakeasy for Hollywood's golden age elite, it has recently become an intimate retreat for prominent entertainment figures including director Oliver Stone, Robert DeNiro and Arnold Schwarzenegger.

The Georgian Hotel is a member of the Historic Hotels of America under the National Trust for Historic Preservation and is officially recognized by the City of Santa Monica as a historical landmark.

Hauntspitality

As the hotel website states, "According to legend, [the hotel] continues to play host to a number of other unearthly guests, whether they be famous or infamous. In the hotel's Speakeasy Restaurant, both staff and guests have reported a number of strange phenomena over the years. At many times when the restaurant is completely empty, employees have heard loud sighs, gasp and have been startled by a disembodied voice that greets them with, "Good Morning." At other times the sounds of running footsteps are heard throughout the restaurant when no one is there and a number of transparent apparitions have been seen. So, perhaps if you stop to have a libation at the Speakeasy you'll bump into none other than Robert DeNiro if you're lucky, and if you're not, you might "bump" into an unearthly presence for which you cannot see

Staff and guests at the Georgian frequently report spectral activity inside the historic building. The hotel attracted celebrities from Hollywood upon opening, and with a backdrop as a speakeasy, there are tales of late night escapades and unpleasant partings at this place. At least one spirit refuses to leave the hotel and continues to manifest to this day. A number of people have heard unexplained voices come from unoccupied areas of the building as well as strange footsteps, cold spots, and an occasional door that will open and shut on its own. More paranormal activities have been reported in the early morning hours than at any other time of the day.

There have been reports of hearing someone in high-heeled shoes walking across a wooden floor. Upon inspection, no one human is ever found to be responsible; and even more amazing, the distinct sound of shoes hitting a hardwood floor is hard to explain since the floors are carpeted! Near the entrance to the hotel, a security beam connected to a bell designed to alert the front desk when an impending guest enters, will often go off by itself. Those who work in the kitchen have witnessed glasses and dishes rattling, and heard the door to the kitchen open, only to find themselves alone. There are also numerous reports of mysterious voices that greet employees as well as the unsettling feeling of being watched or followed along empty corridors or unoccupied areas of the building.

Staff has also reported that items sometimes appear out of thin air in the corridors as well as in the restaurant. On several occasions, people wearing clothes from the 1930s have been spotted dining or dancing in the restaurant, only to vanish or slowly disappear as onlookers stare in disbelief. Sounds of period music also filter through the restaurant late at night after hours. Several female phantoms have also been witnessed walking down the corridors before disappearing into a room that is later found to be unoccupied.

Thanks to the fact that the Georgian has recently been featured on several paranormal televisions shows, it's reputation as a top-notch hotel has been extended to include a prominent group of after-life clientele. It seems that the living and those from beyond the veil seem to co-exist in harmony, occasionally meeting in the dining area or other rooms and corridors of the hotel. You never know if you'll run into a real-life celebrity or one from the distant past when you step through the hotel's front door.

Although a stroll through the building is likely to titillate your senses because of the decor and stunning ambiance; you might also get a response from your sixth sense when you see a shadowy figure dart out of nowhere, an object moves by itself, a door opens on its own, music from the past echoes through a darkened room, or a smell from a bygone era wafts passed you where there should be no such smell.

Today, the Georgian serves up luxury rooms with a view, dining in style and spirited companionship for those who don't mind sharing their good times with those still partying in the afterlife.

Patrick's Roadhouse

Particulars

106 Entrada Drive,
Santa Monica, CA 90402-1249
Phone: 310-459-4544
Website: http://patricksroadhouse.info

History

The landmark establishment lies across from the north end of Santa Monica State Beach and south of Will Rogers State Beach at the foot of Pacific Palisades. This spot has an amazing history that dates back several thousand years. According to archaeologists, the general area may have supported a Gabrielino village that was subsequently destroyed by the construction of the Pacific Coast Highway and the development of the immediate area. Sometime in the late 1800s, a railroad ran close to the current establishment, but was subsequently disbanded. During its railroad days, a small building, possibly a depot was situated on the site of Patrick's. As the story goes, when the railroad folded, the building was either torn down or remodeled and enlarged sometime during the late 1920s. The remodeled building was then converted into a hotel/bordello/speakeasy. The rear portion of the building was supposed to have contained several cribs to service the clientele and was operating during the 1930s.

By the 1970s, the building was called Roy's, a hot dog stand that catered to locals. In 1974, the history of the building and its name changed forever, and a legend was born. That year, Bill Fischler reportedly stopped in with his youngest son, Patrick and ordered the dog de jour. The hot dog was bad; Bill complained and the owner told him if he didn't like the food to buy him out, which Bill did the next day; The name was changed to Patrick's Roadhouse; business picked up; and Arnold Schwarzenegger helped make it famous (there's a huge chair with a sign on it that says "Reserved for Arnold Schwarzenegger, and no one else sits there). Patrick's Roadhouse attracts tourists, regulars and locals. Stevie Nick's orders breakfast from the pick up window outside; Kate Hudson has been coming here since she was a kid; and Charlize Theron comes with her mom for the Chili Fries. Other regulars include Sean Penn, Michael Keaton, Sylvester Stallone, Julia Roberts, Linda Hamilton, Ted Danson, Ali MacGraw, Cindy Crawford, Roseanne Barr, Tom Cruise and Nicole Kidman. Bill ran the restaurant for 26 years, before passing away. His daughter Tracie now carries on the family tradition. To stay close to his favorite place on earth, Bill Fischler's cremated remains were sprinkled on the Palisades across the street from where Patrick's Road house stands.

Hauntspitality

Some people say that Bill Fischler's spirit has never left his restaurant where he caters to clients from a different vantage point. Others who are sensitive say that Bill is joined by at least two other spirits; a woman in her 20s and a feisty, older woman. No one agrees on just how many spirited clientele call the establishment home, but that it is haunted is not disputed.

Several psychics who visited the building have remarked upon entering of a young woman in the back who tried to please men until her heart was broken.

She was in love and her suitor left her one day and was never heard from again. She is occasionally seen as a misty apparition in the back portion of the building, and has been heard crying. The same young woman has been described as a forlorn actress who died without getting her big break. Another energy who some believe is a feisty female who loved to cook, is said to be responsible for rearranging silverware or moving pots and pans around. She is noisy and cantankerous, and makes no bones about who she likes and dislikes. A third spirit is said to be a kind, gentle male who is simply watching over the place he loved. He is felt more than sighted, and his benevolent energy is said to permeate an area when he is present. Cold spots, feelings of being watched by unseen eyes, electrical anomalies and shadowy figures add to the ambience of this landmark establishment.

Here, the ghosts and guests are constantly fighting for a good table and great food. Once you come for a visit, "You'll be back"!

Santa Paula
Familia Diaz

Particulars
245 South 10th Street,
Santa Paula, CA 93060
Phone: 805-525-2813
Toll Free: 1-888-658-8868

History

The building was constructed in 1929 as a bakery, and then it became the Las Quince Letras saloon. In 1936, Jose and Josepha Diaz with their family of six lived in a 20-by-20 foot room, with only a thin wall separating the house from the noisy saloon where music would blare until 2:00 a.m. In 1936, the capacity was 23; today the restaurant holds 150. The wine came in barrels from Ojai. The "ice box" was stocked when the ice man made his rounds. Sodas cost five cents and beer just a dime. Josepha Diaz did all the cooking, and there were no refrigerators, cheese graters, blenders, or electric wires. Everything was fresh and made from scratch. The Diaz tradition lives on and expands, as a bar was added around 1983. With the new bar came more room for patrons waiting to sample the excellent food and spirits.

Hauntspitality

Dan Diaz has reported witnessing a ghost in the bar area after closing. The male spirit seems to appear only in the new addition of the restaurant. On one occasion, Diaz saw something move out of the corner of his eye while working late at night. As he turned toward the bar area, he saw the apparition of an elderly man wearing a Mexican hat with a tassel hanging down. As the stunned Diaz stood in amazement, the elderly man, moved away from the bar, walked toward a back door in the bar area, and then disappeared through a narrow corridor connecting the bar with the kitchen. Diaz gave chase, but was unable to find another living soul in the building. The ghostly man simply disappeared.

On another occasion, a pot fell in front of Diaz, as he was standing in the area between the front door and the bar. The pot had been secured, and could not have fallen by itself. It had to be lifted and dropped by someone, in this case, the pesky ghost. Other times, the ghost has played with the phone lines late a t night, causing the lights in the phone to light up as if several calls were coming in at the same time. Each time the receiver was picked up, the line was dead on the other end. Perhaps it is the elderly neighbor who lived in a house approximately where the bar now stands. The man apparently wore a hat similar to the one Diaz saw, and died in the house, just before it was demolished. The elderly gentleman may continue to perform some task that he repeatedly acted out in life, a task that carried him right through the present bar area and into another world. Visit the distinctive and friendly Familia Diaz restaurant for great Mexican food, and a chance to see if you can spot the invisible customer who enjoys the ambiance and the new bar, but never has to pay for a thing.

Glen Tavern Inn & The Grove Restaurant

Particulars
134 North Mill Street,
Santa Paula, CA 93060
Phone: 805-933-5550
Fax: 805-933-5559
Website: www.glentavern.com
E-mail: rooms@glentaverninn.com

History

The Inn was built in 1911 when Santa Paula was a booming oil town. Its stately design is the work of architects Burns and Hunt, a firm renowned for their monumental properties throughout coastal California. Now a Federal landmark the Inn has lived to tell of the colorful eras and antics spanned by its near 100 year history. True to its Wild West beginnings, the hotel's 3rd floor once operated as a gambling parlor and house of ill-repute. During Prohibition, a speakeasy was added to these dubious diversions. In Hollywood's early hey-day the town was a favorite big studio filming location. Stars including John Wayne, Carol Lombard, Harry Houdini and Steve McQueen enjoyed the gracious accommodations – and the bar.

An early Santa Paula Chronicle headline read, "A Hotel (The Glen Tavern), known as 'The Little Potter' which is the admiration of the traveling public, where the visitor will find first-class accommodations, good food, properly prepared, and courteous treatment". Additional historical footnotes for the Glen Tavern Inn follow: The Bungalow/ Craftsman, Tudor Revival structure was built in 1910 and completed in 1911, the architect/builder was Crookshank & Summers, Hunt and Burns; The hotel has 41 suites (one brochure reads 44) on three stories, a dining room, bar, pool & a few rooms with spas; J.N Crane owned the Glen Tavern Inn during 1917 and perhaps before; As a salute to WWI draftees in Ventura County, a special banquet and dance was held at the Glen Tavern Inn. Dancing took place in the spacious lobby, which was decorated in flags and flowers (August or September 1917?); October 1918, and influenza hit the region and all restaurants and hotels were closed; During 1919, The Glen Tavern Inn was purchased by Mr. & Mrs. Charles D. Estep; Ignace Jan Pederewski, composer, pianist checked into the Glen Tavern Inn (Aug-Sept 1921?); Ted Loy Fugua and Beatrice Fugua owned the Glen Tavern Inn from 1971-1977; During July 1981 the building became Ventura

County Landmark #65; During September 1984, the building was listed on the National Register of Historic Places (#84001225); as of January 2004, the current owners are Tom and Rosanna Jennett, and their daughter Monica De La Torre manages the building. The fabulous Grove Restaurant

opened in December, 2006 after a recent fire. This is dinner and spirits at its best.

Hauntspitality

Based on the Glen Tavern website, "Rumored the most haunted structure in Ventura County, the Tudor-style hotel was built in 1911. A number of guests have reported odd manifestations in their rooms late at night, and at least 75% of the hotel staff has encountered one of the several phantoms that wander the inn. According to perhaps the most well-known Glen Tavern Inn ghost tale, a crooked card dealer was shot to death in the 1920s during one of the infamous 3rd floor poker games, and haunts the hallways to this day."

Based on numerous investigations conducted at the Glen Tavern after it reopened, orbs are abundant, as are numerous apparitions. The EVP at this location is spectacular, with children, several women and a male recorded on tape. This is a quality paranormal research laboratory where anything can and usually does happen to investigators. EMF spikes and cold spots are commonplace, as are the sightings of shadowy figures and odd occurrences.

According to our friend and renowned author and paranormal investigator, Richard Senate in his book, The Haunted Southland: Ghosts of Southern California, Perhaps the most haunted structure in Ventura County is Santa Paula's Glen Tavern Inn. The Tudor-style hotel was built in 1911, and almost from its beginning, rumors of ghosts have swirled around the place. The former manager, Mrs. Dolores Diehl, confirmed that a number of guests have reported odd manifestations in their rooms late at night, and at least 75% of the hotel staff has encountered one of several phantoms that wander the inn. Many of the reports center on room 307, where she claimed to have spoken to the phantom presence and learned that his name is "Calvin." She described the apparition as middle aged, with long hair and a pointed beard. One theory surrounding "Calvin" is that he was murdered in that room after an illegal poker game in which he may or may not have been cheating. Another theory holds that "Calvin may have been part of the motion picture industry. In the early 1920s, dozens of western films were made in and around Santa Paula. Perhaps the persistent phantom was a member of the cast or crew of one of those films.

Rope/funnel-like anomalies inside (Courtesy of the International Paranormal Research Organization – IPRO)

Orbs galore during renovation in 2003 (Courtesy of the International Paranormal Research Organization – IPRO)

The Glen Tavern Inn was the most elegant establishment in the era, and played host to many movie stars and companies. In 1986, a group of students, investigating the reports of ghosts visited the inn. One student, using infrared film, photographed all of the rooms and places where ghosts have been sighted. When the film was developed, a strange image appeared in the photograph taken in room 307. The faint apparition seemed to be a man with long hair and a beard! Yet, when the student took the picture, she had been alone in the room. Although most of the ghost sightings have revolved around 307, other ghosts have been encountered throughout the historic inn. Visitors have witnessed a spoon fly across the dining area by itself, and one waitress reported seeing chairs move by themselves in the restaurant late at night.

Senate continues by stating that skeptics derided the accounts, saving they were the creation of the former management in an attempt to secure publicity and attract visitors. Though some of the reported ghosts may well have been glamorized, the vast majority seems to be real events witnessed by ordinary people. Hallucination and overactive imagination could account for some of these sightings, but not all. Debbie Christenson Senate spent several nights in the lobby of the old hotel. Once, at three a.m. she heard footsteps running down the stairs! She looked up, thinking it was one of the guests coming down for something. She heard the footfalls grow louder but she saw nothing there. The sounds went right by her but there was no one there! She paused, and said to herself. "I must be imagining things," then, the sounds came again! Now they were going up the stairs. As the invisible thing passed her on the foot of the stairs she felt a distinct chill sweep up the stairs. Checking with the hotel staff, she learned that this wasn't the first time the footsteps were encountered late at night.

According to Senate, by far, the most impressive sightings were those personally witnessed during the one-year investigation of the Glen Tavern Inn. Rumor holds that room 308 of the hotel was used by the late magician Harry Houdini. The story is that Houdini was forced to spend the night at the place in the mid 1920's when the railroad line north was damaged in a rain storm. At that time the third floor was mostly attic space. Houdini wanted a place to store his magic props where he could watch over them so no one would discover his secrets. I was never able to confirm that the great magician ever stopped in Santa Paula -- but, the legend continued that he once slept in room 308 at some point in the inn's past. On the nights of November 8th and 9th, 1987, my wife and I spent the weekend in the "Houdini Room" of the old inn. Debbie and I didn't want

Funnel-like energy in the hallway (Courtesy of the International Paranormal Research Organization – IPRO)

389

to sleep in the room. She claimed the room gave her the "creeps." That morning a strange thing did happen that I am at a loss to explain even after all these years. At about 8:40 AM, the bathroom door moved back and forth several times. At first I thought it was caused by me walking around in the bathroom after taking a shower. Debbie pointed out the motion of the door. I stopped walking around and sat on the bed -- the door continued to move. It started moving again after a short pause. In a minute or two it stopped. I attempted to restart the movements of the door by walking up and down, but there was no movement. I even tried stomping on the floor, but the door remained still.

Debbie went to bed early and she said she felt someone sit on the edge of bed while she had been alone. She had consumed a tall glass of wine with dinner and I put the odd feeling on the effects of the wine. I went to bed about midnight, sleeping on the side of the bed that faced the door of the narrow room. I was very, tired from a long day. I found myself unable to sleep in the strange bed. I glanced up toward the door and, in the dim light that filtered into the third floor room, I saw a jet-black form. It appeared in the doorway. It just stood for moment, its arms hanging down at its sides; I couldn't see a face on the form. It seemed almost like a shadow. After several seconds it moved to the left and vanished. It seemed to be a man. Debbie, who was exhausted, was fast asleep. There was no sound. Could it have been the ghost of Harts' Houdini? I don't think so, but it was something out of the ordinary. Do I feel that the Glen Tavern Inn is haunted? Yes! I have seen something there that I can't explain that confirms the idea that the old hotel does have phantom residents/

Dolores Riccio and Joan Bingham in their book, Haunted Houses USA state that the Glen Tavern Inn is one of the most haunted places... ever investigated. The events just keep on happening! Last week, guests saw a spoon float across a room. Apparitions, sounds, strange aports, all sorts of events are happening now." Among the "strange aports," or levitating objects, is an ice scoop that flies across the room, as repeatedly witnessed by the staff---just a taste of the strange energy that permeates this haunted hideaway in Santa Paula. The inn, a National Historic Landmark, has been visited by many of the rich and famous, including such diverse personalities as Clark Gable and Carole Lombard, Harry Houdini, and Rin-TinTin. Possibly, it is also host to the ghost who resembles Buffalo Bill Cody. It's the so-called "Rin-TinTin Room," Room 307--which boasts a Jacuzzi---that is the most haunted and has been the focus of several psychic investigations. The famous canine star really did stay in that room, because one of his movies was filmed right on the premises.

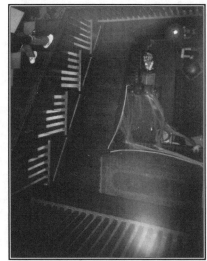

An unusual light in the stairwell (Courtesy of the International Paranormal Research Organization – IPRO)

Cheryl King, another California psychic, doesn't usually deal in spiritualism, but one day when she went to the Glen Tavern Inn for lunch, she felt guided to go up to Room 307. Ms. King saw an image that looked like Buffalo Bill, with a string tie, long hair, and a beard, while she meditated in the Pin-Tin-Tin Room. This event was reported by Thia Bell in the Ojai Valley News, January 28, 1987. It wasn't too long afterward that the image Ms. King saw was actually photographed!

Richard Senate's investigating team, culled from his Ventura College class on ghost hunting, gathered at the inn in October of 1986 to conduct a séance. The medium was Debra Christenson Senate, Richard's wife. During the séance, Debra received a message from a spirit who identified herself as "Jennifer." According to her communication with Debra, Jennifer had died while staying at the inn in the 1930s--in Room 306. That same evening, the investigation team found plenty of witnesses among the staff to previous supernatural events--unexplained footsteps, the flying ice scoop; or waitress Para Decker, who often had heard her name called down an empty corridor or felt something give her a push.

Before they left, one of Senate's students, Catherine Dickerson, took thirty-six photos with infrared film while she was alone in Room 307. She reported that she felt chilly while she was in there; nevertheless, she bravely persisted, taking shots of all four corners of the room. When the film was developed, all the frames were green with no images on them, except one--and that one flame held an ectoplasmic being that looked like Buffalo Bill Cody. When she saw the mysterious photograph, the inn's owner and manager, Dolores Diehl, sought out documentation verifying that Dickerson was alone in Room 307 at the time, and that the film had not been altered by the photo lab that developed it. There were no light leaks or other problems with the camera. With affidavits from the developer and those who observed Dickerson alone in the room with her camera, Diehl called a press conference, her first, to tell the story and exhibit the photo. The conference was reported by Thia Bell in the Ojai Valley News, January 28, 1987, and by Stephen Craig in the Fillmore Herald, February 5, 1987; much of my information comes from those two articles and from Richard Senate. The photo itself is now on display at the inn for all to see.

Informed about the Dickerson photograph, Cheryl King went back to the inn on January 17 and had another go at Room 307. This time she received the names "Cal" and "Elaine" and the date "August 1917." (The inn was built in 1911). She also noticed a distinct chill that filled the room, and again she saw, over her head, the image of the same Buffalo Bill character. (Senate comments that many of the old silent-film Westerns were filmed in that area and what may be coming through is an actor in Buffalo Bill costume.) Ms. King then got the urge to do some automatic writing, although this is not usually her field. Three words appeared on the paper under her hand, "very scrolly," as she described them. The words were: "murder," "gold," "attic." Ms. King added that she perceived a green bag

A mist in the hallway (courtesy of the International Paranormal Research Organization – IPRO)

391

hidden in the rafters and heard a cry for help. It happens that there is a story about an illegal card game that took place at the inn years ago. There was a fight, a gun was drawn, and a man was killed. Senate says there are subtle messages that the murdered man had hidden a treasure 'somewhere in the inn. He adds that there was a lot of strange looking movie people who came to Glen Tavern during its early days.

Grace Coveney. a psychic who has a radio show, also received an image of the Bill Cody character while she was walking down the hall on the third floor of the inn. He was laughing when she saw him, happy with changes that have taken place in his old hangout. But Coveney says there are actually three ghosts: a child who plays on the first floor, a woman in Room 218, and Bill.

Susie Kantell, a Los Angeles psychic, confirms this and adds that the child knows the man, but neither of them knows the woman. The child is eight years old and is not allowed to go upstairs,

Kenny Kingston, who bills himself as "Psychic to the Stars," also visited the inn, and his impressions were reported in the Santa Paula Chronicle, October 2, 1987, by Marianne Ratcliff. Kingston detected the spirits of Clark Gable, Carole Lombard and Charles Laughton--along with his regular spirit guides (they travel with him), who are his mother, Clifton Webb, and Chief Running Bull. Ratcliff reported that Kingston found the inn to be a happy place with pleasant vibrations---and, definitely, one or two spirits in the closet of Room 307. Later Richard Senate confirmed this to me and added, "In Room 307, Kenny stated that the room had many stories to tell "You ought to rent this room to a mystery writer," he said; "They could write fantastic mysteries in this room. The stories would write themselves." He felt there were several spirits in the place."

Senate took another team back to the inn; about the time we were finishing this book, "to conduct a ghostly census." (This was a new term to me, but I think it's an outstanding idea in haunted places that seem crowded with different impressions. The Whaley House in California comes to mind, and The Myrtles in Louisiana.) "From the information we collected," Richard said, "no less than six phantoms call the place home."

Large orb in the hallway (courtesy of the International Paranormal Research Organization – IPRO)

The International Paranormal Research Team (IPRO) conducted several investigations inside the Glen Tavern after it reopened. With the help the San Diego Ghost Hunters, The California Society for Ghost Research and the San Gabriel Valley Paranormal Researchers, the following observations were made by various investigators and psychics:
- I walked in the front door and was immediately hit by a different time period... My immediate sense was the 1920s. I whiffed alcohol and pipe tobacco, although historically this was probably Prohibition time and alcohol would have been outlawed. As I entered the foyer, I felt as if I was walking through several people from the 1920s-1930s, although I would venture to guess that many of the people I sensed came from early and later periods... It was like mix of time and energies here.

- I sensed anger and betrayal as well as gambling and some secret meetings taking place. I also sensed dancing and events in the bar area/dining room, with people celebrating and having drinks, like a social mixer. Within seconds, I felt that I was at a wake or funeral ceremony. I thought I heard someone say that he was a good man?
- There was a sense of several deaths in this building because the casket scene gave way to different emergency scenes involving police and medical personnel from different time periods. The uniforms were different in each case. My sense was murder, a drowning, a knifing, a beating and overdose.
- A brief interview with a few people involved with remodeling the place produced several interesting stories: Jesse and Bobby said that they have had things happen to them while staying in the building. Bobby related that while he was staying on the 2nd floor, he always had trouble going to sleep. While trying to doze off in his room, he would hear heavy footsteps by his bed that would ultimately come to a stop… and there would never be anyone there.
- There were stories about doors opening or slamming shut, and of various rooms that seemed to have a life of their own. Guests would occasionally report their shower turning on by itself in the middle of the night, or lights turning on or off for no apparent reason. There were strange sounds like children playing or people walking when no one was anywhere around to account for the noises. There were times when staff would not like walking the corridors alone at night. The feeling of being watched or followed was very intense.
- Stan said that while they were varnishing the second floor landing, that little imprints of feet would appear without a beginning or ending… they would just be there. To add to the mystery, it was only the left foot that would be imprinted on the varnish after it was painted. After several coats of varnish were laid down, and with the imprints continuing after each coat, the crew decided to just leave the imprints in the varnish and let it dry. You can see several of the imprints as you pass from the first floor to the second.
- One psychic witnessed a Victorian looking woman standing next to Bobby. She was formally dressed and smiling. I felt like this woman was looking after Bobby in a kind of surrogate mother fashion and I told him about her. She was protecting him from some of the not-so-nice male energy here. I took several photos that had a couple of orbs on them, one with an orb on Bobby's face.
- There were at least three spirits in the dining/bar/kitchen area: A cook, a bartender and a Victorian lady. The two men looked like they were dressed from the 1920s. The sense in here was 1920s-1930s. There was also a sense that something bad happening in the kitchen, perhaps someone died?
- On the stairwell leading to the second floor, there was a strong sense of two or three children playing. They were running back and forth and knew that they shouldn't be. Two were boys and a young girl and they seemed to be between 7-10 years old. They were aware of each other in their dimension. There was a sense that the children were fine with the first and second floors but would not venture on the third floor because someone did not want them to go up there.
- Most of the rooms on the second and third floors were active. Psychics sensed a prostitute, gambler, poker games, heavy drinking and an actor on the second floor. There were military personnel in some of the rooms, and possibly soldiers stayed at the hotel or were part of a USO-group?
- There was a strong male and female presence on the 2nd floor, and a murder may have occurred on the south side of the building; possible strangulation involving a lover's quarrel, suicide or prostitution.
- Psychics sensed a shift in energy on the third floor. There were no children

on this level. Several people felt as if something was buried or hidden in the walls on this floor; like a secret compartment. This floor had a sense of drugs, alcohol, sex and some violence. This was like a den of iniquity. There is some transient energy here as well as a room or two where people stayed for long periods of time, as if renting rooms for months on end.

On October 25, 2006 as part of an annual KIIS FM Halloween special hosted by JoJo Wright, a small KIIS FM crew, including the author who served as the paranormal expert, spent eight hours inside the building as part of a live broadcast. During the evening, the team had several unexplained encounters on the second floor. There were the usual manifesting cold spots, the EMF meter spikes, countless orbs and shadows that seemed to dart quickly down the hallway before simply disappearing. Then we had two very unusual encounters. The first took place on the second floor in front of a fire door near rooms 210 on the east and 221-222 on the west. This is also the same area where, during a Halloween event a year before, the door knob in front of Room 222 began rattling on its own (the room was unoccupied at the time). While facing the closed fire door, I could clearly see the distinct shadow of two feet under the door, backlit by the hall light on the other side. I knew there was no one on the other side (living that is) because the hotel had been cleared by the owners and staff for this event. I yelled back at one of the other KIIS personnel standing near Room 210 and the landing that someone was standing on the other side of the door. As the outline of the feet pulled back, I ran toward the door and pushed it open. There was no one anywhere around. I tried all the room doors but they were locked. After looking around for about 10 seconds, the hallway became icy cold and I left immediately. The second unusual event took place near Rooms 219-220. As JoJo, Chad and Daniel from KIIS FM were setting up in the rooms, we all heard a loud and extremely frightening scream come from the end of the hallway (behind a repair wall from a recent fire (Rooms 201-208). Everyone jumped up, gathered in the hallway and said, "Did you hear that?" It was truly a bloodcurdling scream; something I had never heard in all my years of investigating. We began checking out all the rooms to make sure no human was responsible or playing a prank on us. As soon as we began looking in the rooms the temperature in the hallway dropped from an ambient 70 degrees to between 49-52 degrees. This was followed in short order by a strong smell of coffee near room 222 and 223. Three unexplainable events occurring in succession are highly unusual. We never found the source of the scream, cold spots or coffee, although we surmised it was the spirits of the inn having fun with us.

At the extremely haunted and historic Glen Tavern Inn, you will certainly get to meet the spirited clientele up close and very personal. Whether dining at the delightful Grove Restaurant, having a drink at the bar, spending a night in one of their remodeled rooms, or simply lounging in the lobby, you can bet your life (or afterlife) that the other-worldly occupants residing at the Glen Tavern Inn, are still in charge.

Saratoga

Bella Saratoga

Particulars
14503 Big Basin Way,
Saratoga, CA 95070-6011
Phone: 408-741-5115
Website: www.bellasaratoga.com

History

Formerly known as former Bella Mia, which was owned by Fred Maddalena, current owners Ellen and Bill Cooper have created an incredible fare of California Italian cuisine such as salmon ravioli in tomato dill sauce or hearty meat lasagna with pepperoni, ground beef, cheese and eggs. Samuel H. Cloud built the Victorian for his family in 1895, right next door to his general store, the Farmers Union; now called Harmonie Day Spa. A derailed streetcar mortally injured Cloud in front of the house, where he was taken and soon died. After Cloud's death, the house was occupied by his descendants, and then became a teahouse, a space for an antique dealer and home to the Saratoga News. The 108-year-old Victorian home harbors mouth-watering aromas from the kitchen, candlelit dining, and porches on two sides with brightly painted architectural details.

Hauntspitality

The Cloud family seems to be the focal point to many of the ghost stories associated with the building. So many people have witnessed spirits and unexplained phenomena that the paranormal has become the normal. The cause for most of the disturbances may be untimely death of Samuel, who was struck by a streetcar in front of the house and died inside; the suspected imprisonment of a mentally disabled child in a closet; and the death of a grandchild in the home while her mother was away. According to their website, many people, including former employees say that they have seen a ghost walking the premises, opening and shutting doors.

In a cover story by reported Shari Kaplan in the Los Gatos Weekly Times entitled Ghosts 'go bump in the night', The Bella Saratoga restaurant is home to spirits. According to the owner, numerous former employees would feel something unearthly brush by them when they were working, or would hear doors opening or shutting on their own. The employees are not the only one's who sense or see the unexplained. Several guests have also encountered the unknown while visiting this historic establishment. Other people sense that the spectral visitors inside are usually gentle, but can sometimes act up. The owners says that the building's spirited past draws in numerous patrons who are curious about the ghosts. The former owner when the building was called the Bella Mia used to sleep upstairs in his office. Quite a few times he would report being awakened by the upstairs doors slamming on their own. When the building was home to the Saratoga News, former columnist Willys Peck said that employees use to constantly report seeing or feeling the presence of a ghost in the building.

Other individuals associated with the house have reported seeing a woman and two little girls in the house, who subsequently vanished. There have been reports of electrical anomalies, items being moved or relocated by unseen hands, the feelings of being watched or followed, unexplained rapping on the doors or walls; phantom shadows that would disappear through walls; faces peering out of various windows when the building was unoccupied; unexplained footsteps and muffled sounds of people talking coming from unoccupied rooms; an apparition climbing the stairs to the second floor only to vanish into thin air; a little girl has been frequently sighted upstairs, as if looking for someone; and there are cold spots that will rapidly materialize and the water in the restroom has been known to turn on by itself felt.

There is no Cloud hanging over this restaurant. The spirits may be plentiful, but they are benign. At this legendary establishment, you are treated to only the very best in dinner and spirits.

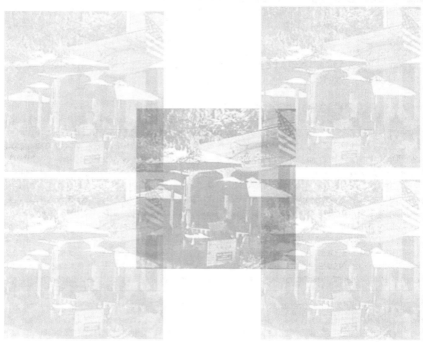

Scotia

Scotia Inn

Particulars
100 Main Street, Scotia, P.O. Box 248,
Scotia, CA 95565
Phone: 707-764-5683
Fax: 707-764-1707
Toll Free: 1-888764-2248
E-mail: stay@scotiainn.com
Website: www.scotiainn.com

History

The Inn is 3.5 miles north of the scenic Avenue of the Giants Redwood Forest and 23 miles south of Eureka on the scenic Eel River. The town of Scotia was established in the early 1880's and was originally named "Forestville." Scotia is company owned by Pacific Lumber, which was established in 1869 and is the largest redwood lumber mill in the world. The original Scotia Inn was constructed in 1886 as a home for officials of the company. In 1888 the need for logging Scotia became very apparent, so the building was enlarged to accommodate travelers from the south and the many lumberjacks of the area.

The town of Scotia was originally founded in the early 1860's as "Forestville," and was the original home of the Pacific Lumber Company. The Scotia Inn was constructed in 1886, and used as a home for officials of the Pacific Lumber Company. In 1888, the building was enlarged to accommodate travelers arriving by stagecoach from the south and lumberjacks employed by Pacific Lumber. It was in this same year that the name of the town was changed to "Scotia", a name chosen because many of the early loggers were from Eastern Canada. 1890 saw the first electric lights in Scotia, as well as running water. The town was, by this time, connected by rail to Eureka. A round trip ticket cost $1.60. In June of 1895, a fire which began in the mill, blazed out of control and destroyed the mill, planning office, cookhouse and much of the town of Scotia. In 1923, the old hotel was torn down and the Mowatoc Hotel was begun. This year also saw the construction of the Eureka Inn to the north and the Benbow Inn to the south.

These three hotels were built in anticipation of increased travel through the area attributed to the new Redwood Highway, which ran past the Scotia Inn's front door. The name of Mowatoc Hotel was chosen because of the Modoc Indians. The diamond in Scotia Inn's logo can also be found in the architecture of the building itself and is an old Modoc symbol. In 1924, a second unit of the Mowatoc Hotel was completed, giving the inn 135 rooms. The name Mowatoc was to last until the late 1940's when it was changed to Scotia Inn. In 1964, the Eel River Valley experienced a severe flood which destroyed some neighboring towns and affected a large part of Scotia itself. The inn closed its guest rooms in 1975, and continued operation without them until 1985 when many were completely renovated.

Hauntspitality

The spirit of the Scotia Inn is fondly called Frank by the staff. He is a very mischievous but harmless spirit who slams doors, loves to turn lights off and on, and in general, enjoys throwing a little scare into guests and staff. Frank may represent the spirit of a man who committed suicide at the inn back in the 1950s. Frank has been known to follow women into the bathroom, and then abruptly disappear when he has sufficiently frightened them. He also likes to show himself, and then get guests and staff to follow him after in hot pursuit.

Another congenial spirit is said to be that of a little girl who has been heard running and laughing down the corridors of the hotel. A number of people have heard the child playing games, giggling and playfully darting down corridors, most of the time, oblivious to the occupants.

Legend has is that before the freeway was built; a road bridge fronted the inn. One day, a speeding car struck and killed a little girl as she was playing on the bridge. If true, this tragedy would account for one of the spirited clientele at the inn.

The numerous accounts of a child playing and pulling pranks inside, would lead one to believe that the tragedy in front of the inn might have a basis in fact. Add to this spectral mix, Frank, and it's hard to tell who is responsible for all the shenanigans inside.

You can take your pick on who to blame for the odd things that sometimes happen at the inn, but you'll only have yourself to blame if you don't pay a visit to this gorgeous, but haunted inn.

Sonoma
Bartholomew Park Winery

Particulars
1000 Vineyard Lane,
Sonoma, CA 95476-4845
Phone: 707-935-9511
Fax: 707-935-0549
Website: www.bartholomewparkwinery.com

History

Bartholomew Park Winery was founded in 1994 by the Bundschu family, whose vision was to produce handcrafted, vineyard-designated wines. The first recorded planting of wine grapes on the Bartholomew Park property was in the early 1830s. Hungarian nobleman Agoston Haraszthy purchased the land in 1857 and christened it "Buena Vista." Many consider his first vintage the birth of the California wine industry. When Count Haraszthy was forced from the property for financial reasons in 1867, the land was acquired as a country estate by the Johnson family. Upon her death, Kate Johnson willed the mansion and a large portion of the property to the Catholic archdiocese, who in turn sold it to the State of California. In 1920, the property was transformed into a State Farm for Delinquent Women that housed prostitutes and drug addicts. The house burned to the ground under mysterious circumstances some years later.

The current winery building became an annex for the local "Home for the Feeble Minded" and later the Sonoma Valley Hospital. At the onset of World War II, the property was sold to Frank Bartholomew, president of United Press International. It wasn't until Frank's wife Antonia discovered old grapevines on the property, that they learned the viticultural significance of their land and resurrected the Buena Vista label. In 1968, they sold the brand name and the original 15-acre winery site, keeping more than 400 acres and the vineyards for themselves. The Bartholomew's devoted their later years to the creation of an exact replica of Count Haraszthy's villa. With the Bundschu family's involvement, the historic winery building and surrounding gardens have been fully renovated. Bartholomew Park Winery has embarked upon a mission to produce vineyard-specific wines among the finest in world. The age of the winery and its storied past seem to be the cause for their ghost population.

Hauntspitalty

Numerous people have heard the ghost stories at this historic winery. It's literally spirits guarding the spirits; the ethereal watching over their liquid counterparts. According to Carolyn Tillie's Ultimate California Wine Blog featuring the Bartholomew Park Winery, "Behind the tasting bar, where the wine is stored, is an elevator lift to the second floor, a sort of hospital ward, the skeleton of which is still visible. Right as you enter the tasting room, immediately on your right, is a large wooden door with an elaborate lock and key. Behind that door is a hidden stairwell which leads to what was the morgue. If you are lucky enough to visit the winery on a day when one of the pouring staff are available to show you around (as it is not part of the regular tour), there are a number of amazing stories of ghosts... It seems back when the building was the home for fallen women, one particular woman named Madeleine kept trying to escape. I was told she would sneak out at night, be found by troopers the next day, and was brought back. This apparently occurred on a number of occasions until it was thought that Madeleine finally made her great escape. However, years later when the building was being retrofitted for earthquake compliance, a skeleton was discovered - Madeleine's skeleton. Many people who have worked there over the years have stories of things they have heard or experienced. When I have brought friends to visit the winery, they get spooked out by the hallway and framework of the individual rooms upstairs. I get the willies downstairs, looking at the door which leads to the morgue, which is now used as a break room and wine storage..."

Author Jeff Dwyer in his Ghost Hunter's Guide to the San Francisco Bay Area (2005) says that, "During the time when the winery served as a woman's prison, a hospital and a morgue, lives were lost under horrifying circumstances and some of the deceased continue to make the old building their home. A short time after the winery opened, employees heard voices singing in the cellar that once housed prisoners. The choir is heard in the afternoon and again late at night.

Columnist Daedalus Howell in his article, Wine Tasting Room of the Week: Bartholomew Park Winery in the June 7-13, 2006 MetroActive Website states, "The kid sister of wine juggernaut Gundlach Bundschu, stately Bartholomew Park Winery is nestled in the Sonoma hills on the site of a former women's prison--an odd but scenic locale for something that sounds like it belongs in a Henry James novel. The warden and guards are long gone, and I was warmly greeted inside by a sage trio of wine women perched behind the counter. Kathy and Connie are veteran staffers recently joined by Mychal, to whom bits of their wisdom seem to drift, effortlessly, like the filaments of a dandelion. When I mentioned the local lore about a prison ghost at the winery, wide-eyed Mychal confessed to having just heard of it, Connie reiterated my query neutrally to Kathy, who effectively exorcised the ghost by nonchalantly saying, "She's gone." Public-relations lesson learned: there is no ghost. No worries, Bartholomew Park makes up for its lack of the supernatural with a bevy of preternatural wines. "

Staff has reported feeling uneasy while walking through portions of the old winery. Gifted psychics who have walked through the winery remarked that the place is alive with spirits who once worked at the winery as well as several females who call the place home. There are sorrowful cries and pleading moans that have been heard in the former women's prison area; disembodied footsteps come from unoccupied areas, the feeling of being watched or followed is common in the building, and an occasional apparitions are sighted. This all adds to the ambiance of this historic vineyard.

Staff and guests have also reported that the spirits are very picky about the music that is played at the winery. Apparently, if certain music is not appreciated by the spirits, they will make sure it doesn't stay on long. Lights have been known to flicker and doors shut on their own. Sensitve people immediately pick up on the ghostly nature of the winery and the abundant energy that remains behind, imprinted on the winery landscape.

We definitely recommend a visit to this historic haunted winery on a trip through the wine country. Taste a few wines or buy a few to take home and enjoy. However, while you're visiting, catch up on the latest tales of the paranormal and keep your eyes open for the spirits guarding the spirits.

Buena Vista Winery

Particulars
18000 Old Winery Road,
Sonoma, CA
Phone: 707/938-1266
Toll Free: 800-926-1266
Website: www.buenavistawinery.com

History
Buena Vista Winery is the oldest continually operating winery in California. It is listed on the National Register of Historic Places and is a Sonoma County Historic Landmark. The winery was built in 1857 by Count Agoston Haraszthy de Mokcsa who laid the basis for modern California wine making. Haraszthy de Mokcsa was convinced that you did not have to plant vines on well-watered ground, so he planted on well-drained hillsides. Chinese laborers dug tunnels 100 feet into the hillside, and the limestone they extracted was used to build the main house.

Frank Bartholomew, a well known journalist in his day and former head of AP (Associated Press), purchased 500 acres of Sonoma land a few years after Repeal of Prohibition without knowing an abandoned winery came with the property. Bartholomew revitalized the vineyards, caves and winery, and actually made a profit where Haraszthy never had. The winery was purchased next by the Racke family who are major wine producers in Germany. Young Marcus Moller-Racke was, and is, the driving force behind the project, even though he was called home to Germany to take over all the family businesses. The winery, which is surrounded by redwood and eucalyptus trees, has a specialty-foods shop, an art gallery, and picnic areas. The guided tour, which includes a tasting of premium wines, is $15, but the self-guided tour is free.

Before there were vineyards in every valley north of San Francisco, before Napa and Sonoma were household names, before there was a California wine industry at all, there was Buena Vista. Founded in 1857, Buena Vista is California's oldest premium winery, and its history is as colorful as it is proud. Just outside the town of Sonoma, the original winery is now a California Historic Landmark, and home to our Tasting Room & Visitor's Center.

Buena Vista's founder, Count Agoston Haraszthy, arrived in Sonoma County as a Representative to the State Legislature from San Diego (nearby Vallejo was the capital at that time). Previous to this post, he had been Sheriff of San Diego, founder of a city in Wisconsin, ferryboat owner and member of the Hungarian Royal Guard. But chief among the Count's many interests was growing grapes. Upon arriving in Sonoma, he planted some of the state's first European varietals and laid the foundation for Buena Vista's winery buildings.

As California's wine industry grew, so did the Count's role in its leadership. He brought back thousands of vine cuttings from Europe and published an account of his journey, which helped to bring California's wine industry into the world spotlight. Unfortunately, he met an untimely demise not long after. While exploring rum interests in Nicaragua, legend has it that Count Haraszthy perished crossing a crocodile–infested river; a dramatic ending for a vibrant and important figure in California wine history.

Buena Vista lived on, however, and became a prominent name in California winemaking until the great earthquake of 1906 destroyed its underground cellars. It was not until 1940 that the winery drew new breath under the direction of journalist Frank Bartholomew. With the help of famed winemaker Andre Tchelistcheff, Bartholomew restored Buena Vista to its original grandeur.

Hauntspitality

According to paranormal investigators and psychics, the winery has a tragic side that is responsible for the "other" spirits found at the winery. There are numerous reports of unseen people screaming for help, shadowy figures darting throughout the building, rapidly materializing cold spots, and disembodied footsteps. One psychic said that the imprint of the mining tragedy where the owners were more concerned with saving their spirits buried in the cave in rather than the buried miners, has left an indelible imprint on the local landscape. Could the dead miners still be reaching out from beyond the grave for help?

You can also ask paranormal tour guide Carla Heine who takes tourists on her tour that blends the paranormal with local history. According to Heine, "Over at the Buena Vista Winery, the chill in the wine cellars is more than a function of geology -- the ghosts of 19 Chinese workers killed in the collapse of a cave still haunt the place."

If you want to know more about the "other" spirits at the winery, we suggest you take Carla Heine Twilight Tours, featuring two-hour tours of 13 sites of Sonoma's haunted sites and buildings. She lectures on Sonoma history and the pre-historic culture of the Native Americans who used the valley for religious rituals. Her tour includes this very haunted winery.

The Sonoma Hotel

Particulars
110 West Spain Street,
Sonoma, CA 95476
Phone: 707-996-2996
Fax: 707-996-7014
Toll Free: 1-800-468-6016
Heirloom Restaurant: 707-939-6955
E-mail: sonomahotel@aol.com
Website: www.sonomahotel.com

History
Sonoma has enjoyed a colorful and rich past and is considered the "cradle of California History." The Miwok Indians first chose it as a sacred meeting ground. Soon after The Sonoma Mission was the last site of the 21 missions founded by Fr. Junipero Serra, and later, General Vallejo established his home and Mexican Military Outpost here. In June of 1846, General Vallejo's reign ended when a group of semi-military Americanos raised California's Bear Flag on the Sonoma Plaza, proclaiming California an American Republic. In 1862, Count Agoston Haraszthy, a Hungarian Nobleman, planted 500 acres of the finest cuttings from Europe and built a winery east of the pueblo. Here the first growth of California's world class wine production began and still flourishes today.

The Sonoma Hotel building was built in 1880 by German immigrant Henry Weyl. Weyl opened a dry goods store and a butcher shop on the street level and a community/social hall on the second floor. In the 1920's the Sebastiani family opened the Plaza Hotel and began its long and wonderful career as a charming local inn.

Hauntspitality
At least one friendly spirit roams this historic building. Some say that the phantom is Chinese and enjoys frequenting the bar area. Staff and guests have reported seeing a man of Chinese descent appear, and then suddenly vanish in front of them. Perhaps this apparition is from the time when a Chinese laundry occupied the back patio area. Others believe that more than one benign spirit calls the Sonoma Hotel home in the afterlife.

The following information is provided by the hotel: "The frequency and commonalty of completely unsolicited and spontaneous psychic awareness on the part of hotel and restaurant guests is so routine, it is now taken for granted." Those frequent comments range from "There's a ghost in the building," "Has anyone ever told your there is a psychic presence here," to "Did you know you had a haunted building," and "Have you ever seen a ghost here."

A Native American who once visited the Sonoma Hotel said that he was the son of a medicine man and that he definitely sensed the presence of spirits inside. The friendly spirit, a unanimous consensus for their benign other-worldly guest, is affectionately called Fred. Fred is prone to playing tricks on staff and guests and throwing a tantrum or two.

A maintenance man while repairing a second floor guest room left for lunch. Upon returning, the room had mysteriously filled with steam which caused extensive damage to the walls, ceiling and furniture. The maintenance man, blamed for the fact that the steam release valve had not been properly closed and the thermostat turned off so no steam could accidentally escape before he went to lunch. The man swore on a stack of bibles, besides being a man of integrity and very responsible, that before he left, everything had been turned off. Guess who finally got the blame. Yes, it was mischievous Fred! Later, while assessing the damage, the maintenance man and hotel manager watched in amazement as a can of paint flew across the room, spilling on the floor and causing even more damage.

During renovation, another maintenance man routinely drove by to inspect the building during off-hours. On one occasion, around midnight and in the company of a passenger, he drove by and glanced at the place. A few blocks beyond the hotel, the maintenance man asked if the passenger observed anything unusual. The passenger quickly chimed in that he witnessed a Chinese man in "Coolie-style" clothing sweeping the sidewalk. With that, the maintenance man stopped the car and told his friend that he had seen the same thing but was reluctant to say anything at the time.

There have been reports of swiftly manifesting cold spots, disembodied footsteps, shadowy figures gliding down the hallways then vanishing through walls, voices that cannot be traced to anyone human, and a feeling of being watched or followed by unseen eyes. Who was this phantom man? Well, history suggests that sometime between 1872-1884 a Chinese laundry operated on site, and one of the workers died a violent death. A visit to this historic and haunted building could produce Fred or a Chinese gentleman still performing tasks in the afterlife. If you don't encounter the Sonoma Hotel's friendly spirits on your visit, you won't have any trouble enjoying the atmosphere and hospitality.

Valley Of the Moon Saloon

Particulars
17154 Sonoma Highway,
Sonoma, CA 95476
Phone: 707-996-4003

History
The bar is over 100 years old, and some say it was built on top of a Native American village.

Hauntspitality
The ghost of this saloon likes the pantry doors closed, because anytime they are left open, they are mysteriously closed a short time later. Sometimes the furniture in the bar is rearranged when no one else is present. Lights have been known to go on and off without assistance. Certain records will pop out of their slots in the jukebox. A tenant reported that a bar of soap just floated into his hand while he was taking a shower. So much happens in the saloon that it becomes part of the everyday atmosphere. Some people just ignore the events and continue drinking or talking.

Owner Carolina Ceelen has seen it all over the years she has run the place. The sound of pool balls hitting one another has been heard when no one is playing pool. Money from the cash register that has been counted and bound has been found tossed around---no money has ever been found missing. Bicycles stored in the back room have suddenly begun swaying back and forth, then stop abruptly. Ceelen was alone in the pub one afternoon when the spirit touched her arm. Another time she was gently patted on the rear. Additionally there are: The rapidly materializing cold spots; doors that open or close unassisted; lights that have a mind of their own; occasional shadowy figures that manifest; furniture or place settings that are rearranged by unseen hands; burglar alarms that are inexplicably triggered, unexplained noises, and other unusual events to last an after-lifetime.

The playful spirit occasionally touches people, knocks the records out of their slots in the jukebox and mixes the bills in the cash register. The spirit also makes himself at home in the upstairs apartment. There is one story about a prior owner taking a shower. As he was reaching for some soap, it was handed to him by the ghost. Some of the people, who visited the building, took the spirit-thing to another level by setting a place at the table for the wandering wraith. Other people who have spent time in the building as owners or caretakers have reportedly had someone unseen spend the night with them in their bed. Paranormal investigators have captured orbs and mists on film and a guest even captured a smoky-white manifestation hovering over one of the tables at a party. The man who took the photograph did not smoke

At the Valley of the Moon, every hour is party time for the playful spirits; so if you're suddenly spooked, just order another drink and try to convince yourself that it's all in your mind; Good luck!

Sonora

Gunn House Hotel

Particulars
286 S. Washington Street,
Sonora, CA 95370
Phone: 209-532-3421
Fax: 209-533-3835
E-mail: info@gunnhousehotel.com
Website: www.gunnhousehotel.com

History

The hotel is named for Dr. Lewis C. Gunn, a native Philadelphian who was lured to the area to seek his fortune in the California gold mines. Recognizing the vast beauty of the terrain, he settled in Sonora, where using local labor he built the area's first two-story adobe building as his home and subsequently as his place of business after failing as a gold prospector. In the early 1850's Dr. Gunn started the Mother Lode's first newspaper. It was called the Sonora Herald. During his tenure as owner and publisher Dr. Gunn's presence and editorials persistently created controversy among the towns-people. The unflattering controversy culminated with an angry crowd burning the paper's printing press

During the late 1800s the building served as a county hospital. For the next half-century a local Matriarch named Josephine Bisordi attracted gold miners, tourists and local residents to the newly renovated and renamed "Italia Hotel." The magnet for staying at the "Italia Hotel" was the unique sleeping rooms, as well as the famous home-cooked meals that Josephine personally prepared. In 1960 the hotel was again extensively renovated. It was at that time that the new owner, Margaret Dienelt appropriately named it "The Gunn House." During the early Television Western Series era, many of which were filmed in the Sonora area, the hotel became a favorite staying place for the actors and crews

Hauntspitality

According to the owner, numerous unexplainable little things happen around the hotel all the time, including:
- Things will fall off kitchen shelves for no reason.
- Housekeepers report that the lights frequently go off and on at random.
- Sometimes staff have trouble opening doors to certain rooms, as if someone's pulling on the other side; however the room is always vacant.
- A husband staying with his wife in one of the guest rooms was thrown out of bed by an unseen person; they plan on returning.
- Other guests have reported seeing the image of a person standing at the foot of the bed in Room 12.
- A team of parapsychologists evaluated most of the rooms with electronic meters and concluded that Room 3 produced the highest anomalies yet.
- Disembodied footsteps are heard in the second floor hallways.
- Shadowy figures are sometimes seen darting between rooms or through walls.
- Unexplained voices are sometimes heard coming from vacant room.
- At the Gunn House, the perfect vacation and getaway often includes a visit by one of their other-worldly clientele. The only thing normal at this historic stopover is the "Para"normal.

Snowshoe Brewing Company

Particulars

19040 Standard Road,
Sonora, CA 95370
Phone: 209-536-1445
Website: www.snowshoebrewing.com

History

The building that now houses this casual restaurant, began as the Pickering Lumber Co. The structure was built around 1920, and the office building that houses the Snowshoe Brewing Co. is one of three original buildings left from the mill town of Standard. The building was designed by architect William Wilson Wurster who had also designed Ghirardelli Square in San Francisco. High ceilings and big windows give the restaurant and pub an airy feel.

When you visit, pay attention to the large door of the storage area behind the bar. It's the original safe used during the Roaring '20s by the first inhabitants of the building. A walk through the restaurant and brewery reveals many artifacts from the building's past, including photos, old lumber company tokens (used in lieu of cash), townsite maps, and old business documents. When the current owners began renovating the building they found all kinds of old office equipment, records, survey maps and some baseball memorabilia from the company baseball teams of the early 1900's. They even found spots where carpenters had signed boards and dated them under plaster walls 100 years ago."

Hauntspitality

An old building holds many secrets and some walls talk to certain people. The owner of the brewing company as well as staff and guests have heard and felt things that can't be readily explained away or summarily dismissed, even by the most hardened skeptic. The basement area is a paranormal hot spot where people have sensed and even experienced a phantom man in a bowler hat and black suit who walked in front of the brewery to the former President's office -- now a banquet room. The spirited gentlemen vanished as quickly as he manifested.

Some people have heard disembodied voices and footsteps in the basement and other parts of the building, while others have sighted shadowy figures or felt cold spots suddenly engulf them. At the Snowshoe, where the past and present go hand-in-hand, you never know what kind of spirits they'll be brewing. This is a great place to sample both kinds of spirits!

Sterling Garden Bed & Breakfast

Particulars
18047 Lime Kiln Road,
Sonora, CA 95370
Phone: 888-533-9301 or 209-533-9300
Fax: 209-532-0498
E-mail: ctucker@mlode.com
Website: www.sterlinggardens.com

History
During 1848 the Sonoran Camp (now Sonora) was one of the first of the western mining towns of the 1849 Gold Rush. In 1892 the Kincaid Flat

Mining Company ran a 3,000 ft. tunnel starting at Sullivan's Bar under Kincaid Flat. Over the years millions of dollars in gold was recovered in the Sonora area. Sterling Gardens Bed & Breakfast is located on Kincaid Flat, on the site of the former Kincaid Gold Mine. This beautiful Bed & Breakfast has an outdoor garden for weddings and special events, and is a great place to get away from it all and relax.

Hauntspitality
Most of the sightings associated with the historic area where the Sterling Gardens B&B is now situated, have occurred in the area surrounding the inn. A phantom male, possible from the Gold Rush era, has been seen along the road leading to the structure. This is also the area where one of the entrances to the old Kinkaid Gold Mine was situated. Although the entrances have been permanently sealed, it doesn't seem to stop those who worked in the mines from coming up for a breath of fresh air.

The next time you come for a restful stay, keep an eye out for a restless miner who may know the way to hidden fortunes buried below the inn. Our suggestion is, don't follow him or you may end up as the next apparition.

South Pasadena
The Bissell House
Bed & Breakfast

Particulars

201 Orange Grove Avenue,
South Pasadena, CA 91030
Phone: 626-441-3535
Fax: 626-441-3671
Toll Free: 800-441-3530
E-mail: info@bissellhouse.com
Website: www.bissellhouse.com

History

The Bissell House is designated as South Pasadena's Cultural Landmark No. 36. During the late 19th Century, Pasadena's Orange Grove was lined with beautiful mansions, some of which still stand. Built in 1887, The Bissell House has been the southern anchor of this famous street, which was traditionally referred to as "Millionaire's Row." This three-story Victorian mansion was constructed one year before South Pasadena's

incorporation as a city. It was first owned by Miren S. Daniels, a businessman who came to California from Massachusetts. After his death, the house was acquired by Thaddeus Updegraff, a well-known Pasadena physician.

The house was then acquired by William Southerland McCay, a prominent architect of Southern California. McCay and his wife, Anna Bissell McCay, lived in the house from about 1903 and into the 1950's. Mrs. McCay was the daughter of magnate Melville Bissell of Michigan, who made his fortune designing and manufacturing carpet sweepers. Mrs. McCay was one of Pasadena's most beloved philanthropists. She was a founding member of the Pasadena Chapter of the American Red Cross, which became her life's work. Mrs. McCay once hosted a dinner party for guest of honor, Albert Einstein. Professor Einstein reportedly caused a stir when he preferred the company of McCay's 7-year old niece to that of the adults. After spending an hour visiting with the youngster, he escorted her to dinner in the dining room and a place at the table was quickly set for her. In an era when children were seldom seated for dinner with the adults, this caused quite a stir. Years later when visiting the house, this niece shared how that evening was a highlight of her life and Einstein made an impression on her she never forgot.

Hauntspitality

The following information was provided by the current owners. According to Juli Hoyman, whose family owns the inn, the stories represent their own experiences as well as those told to them by guests and prior owners. According to Hoyman, the owners of the property in 1972 purchased the building when it was in disrepair. When they performed a walk-through of the house with a realtor they were armed with a flashlight. The wife told us that the house had a well-known local reputation as being a very haunted building and she felt on more than one occasion, a cold presence sweeping past her on the stairwells. There were numerous other occasions when she was at home, alone, where there was a sense of a presence in the house with her. The rumors of benevolent ghosts in the house persisted through this ownership. No one was ever afraid of the spirited population although run-ins with ghosts were a frequent occurrence.

The next owners of the house told the current owners the same thing; that the spirits were restless, but very friendly. By this time, the paranormal events were commonplace. There were times when they would catch a glimpse of a woman wearing a red dress from a mirror. The couple lived on the second floor and often felt a presence and heard disembodied footsteps on the stairs.

On one occasion the owners actually saw a woman they believed to be Anna Bissell McCay. They constantly saw lights turn on and off by themselves and

the television seemed to have a mind of its own, turning itself on when the area was unoccupied. Their mother, while living on the first floor insisted that she had a ghost enter her room late one night, turn on the television, sit down and watch for a few minutes before departing. She also witnessed a tall man in a top hat and tails dressed in Victorian style standing out in the front yard for a moment before vanishing into thin air.

Other reported events include:
- The head housekeeper, who worked in the house for 10 years, often heard a woman's voice calling her name while she was upstairs vacuuming. There was no one else in the building at the time, when the disembodied voice called out for her.
- The current owner's sister has also heard voices coming from unoccupied portions of the house.
- On another occasion the friend of a guest who was staying in one of the rooms, insists she saw a ghost on the third floor, wearing a red dress, which was exactly like the one a prior owner had seen.
- A manager working for the current owners witnessed woman in a white lace dress with hair in a Gibson bun peering out of the Garden Room on the third floor when no one was in the house at the time.
- The current owner's daughter-in-law, having just arrived for the first time, was hoping to have a "ghost" encounter based on all the stories that she had been told; she got her wish. While standing near the elevator and discussing the paranormal aspect of the house, a distinct knocking came from inside the elevator. They quickly opened the door but found no one inside. The spirit must have heard the talk about ghosts and decided to leave a calling card.
- A couple who stayed during the summer was in the Garden Room talking about ghosts when the glass in their bathroom cracked in half for no apparent reason.

- The innkeeper & her sister decided to sleep in the Garden Room to try it out. It was about 1:00am, and the whole house was quiet. All of the guests were asleep on the second floor and no other guests were on the third floor. As they got in bed and were quietly talking about ghosts, they both heard footsteps right outside the door. They know no one could be out there, but the sound had "weight" to it, like a person. One sister had been hearing things all week in the house and the other was dismissing her stories as fantasy. As they tried to rest, she commented that their pillows were uncomfortable and suggested the sister get some from the Rose Room. Her sister immediately froze, recalling the footstep sound. They agreed it would be safe to open the door as they knew there can't possibly be anyone out there. As one sister left the room, the other became strangely groggy and rolled over on her stomach. She heard the bedroom door open and loudly shut three times in succession. The sister came running in from the Rose Room and both women shared what had just happened. They both realized that instead trying to scare one another; they had been privy to the strange and unusual universe of ghosts. After checking both rooms and the hallway area and finding nothing out of place or moved, and that no one had been awakened by the slamming sound from downstairs, they knew it wasn't their imaginations playing tricks on them.
- A week after this very odd experience the innkeeper was in the basement getting supplies for the inn. Working in the half lit room, she wished to herself that she had turned on all lights, and immediately the lights snapped on! The innkeeper's sister had the same thing happen to her while she was in the dark earlier that week.

Many guests who have stayed at the inn have remarked that they definitely feel a presence in the house. Some people say its feminine, others a male and a few suggest that the house may hold more than one spirit inside. Could the spirit or spirits be the original owner Miren S. Daniels; the second owner Thaddeus Updegraff, a well-known Pasadena physician; or even William Southerland McCay, a prominent architect of Southern California and his wife, Anna Bissell McCay?

The only way you'll know for sure if the house is spirited, is by visiting this beautiful 1887 South Pasadena Cultural Landmark. When coming to view an amazing Greene and Greene home, or taking in a play at the Pasadena Playhouse or even having lunch or dinner at the Holly Street Bar and Grill, just add The Bissell House Bed and Breakfast to your list of "must see" places, where millionaires were as plentiful in the past as spirits are today. During your stay, you may be one of the very lucky guests to experience the afterlife in this life.

Springfield
Springfield Inn

Particulars
PO Box 123
Springville, CA 93265
Phone: 559-539-7501
Fax: 559-539-7502
Toll Free: 1-800-484-3466
E-mail: info@springville.com
Website: www.springvilleinn.com

History

Springville has witnessed Indian wars, the Spanish, loggers and settlers. Prior to the first settlers reaching the Springville area, the region was home to Native Americans who lived off the land and in harmony with it. The first pioneers to reach Springville arrived in 1849. Avon Coburn laid out the town in 1885. It is not surprising that the explorers & pioneers recognized the value of living in this area with its bounty and excellent climate. John McKiearnan was possibly the earliest to settle in the Springville area in about 1849, although John Crabtree is said to be first to settle in Springville proper. McKiearnan registered a land patent for 160 acres in 1856 and his land extended from near the present-day rodeo grounds to Sequoia Dawn. With the Native American being placed on a reservation in the Alto Vista district in 1856, settlers made their way to the Tule River watershed to file for land.

William C. Daunt settled in Springville around 1860 on a site he purchased from Crabtree for a store, home and post office. The first home in downtown Springville was that of John Crabtree which was located where the service station is today. Later the home became a health sanitarium & in 1885, was tom down and replaced by the Springville Hotel. When Avon Coburn laid out the town in 1885, he built a planning mill near the river East of Soda Spring. This became a recreation spot for visitors to Springville who came to swim, dance & get away. This attracted other business-minded families and soon Springville had a general merchandise store, drugstore and other service stores. The Springville Hotel, built in 1885, was the hub of the social life of the town for many years. It was always a welcome site to visitors coming to Springville or who were on their way to other areas such as Mountain Home, Camp Nelson and Camp Wishon. By 1900 Springville was beginning to look like a town.

The Porterville Northeastern Railroad came to Springville in 1911 and during the same year, the Wilkinson Building, was constructed. The next year, Charles Elster built the Elster Building, the brick building across the street from the inn. These were the first permanent buildings in Springville and the only remaining original buildings left today. With the coming of the railroad, Springville became a resort town on the weekends. Dancing occurred in either the dance hall on Main Street or at the swimming hole at Soda Springs. The Springville Inn (formerly the Wilkinson Hotel) still stands as a reminder of bygone days. It is also a stopover point for those visiting the Giant Sequoia National Monument. The Kemmerling family has tirelessly and lovingly maintained the building's tie to the past.

Hauntspitality

According to their website, "The Springville Inn caters to four very special and unique guests. They are residents who have watched over the Inn for almost 100 years. They are not demanding or critical, they never offer their opinion on how to run a country inn, they are not malevolent, they do not disturb the quiet of night and their enjoyment is not derived from scaring people. But, there is a definite presence about them. These bodiless, ethereal and lustrous creatures are The Ghosts of The Springville Inn."

Their ghosts chiefly inhabit the original part of the building (formerly the Wilkinson Hotel). Local historian, Jeff Edwards, told the owners that there was no coroner or morgue in Springville, so when a person died, their bodies were placed on ice in the upstairs rooms of the hotel to await transport by stagecoach or train to Porterville.

Management can only speculate as to the true identity of their ghosts as historical records are vague; however, they are referred to lovingly as: The "Young Man," a handsome logger in his twenties was likely working in one of the numerous mills of Mountain Home; the "Little Girl" who is around eight-years-of-age and is appropriately clothed in a turn-of-the-century dress; the "Woman", beautiful and elegant with flowing blonde hair, wearing a long dress. She is often seen floating on the Penthouse balcony or wandering the second floor hallways in the main building; and the "Old Man" who enjoys keeping a watchful eye on the kitchen area and has frequent contact with the staff. He generally only appears in the main kitchen of the inn or the upstairs service kitchen. He is usually seen staring into the dumbwaiter joining the two kitchens. He is not shy as he frequently manifests to the chefs and kitchen staff.

The most frequent sightings involve a young man who moves fluidly around the bar area and up what was the original grand staircase which brought guests from the lobby straight upstairs. This phantom man is a flirt, habitually brushing up against women to make his presence known. He is said to be a logger who was shot outside the Inn, in the streets of Springville. According to legend, guests carried him into the Hotel where he bled to death. Occasionally he has been seen walking hand-in-hand with the "Little Girl", but not recently or by any current staff members.

Numerous employees and guests have experienced the friendly ghosts at this inn. A former employee washing dishes in the kitchen, quit after witnessing the "Little Girl" watching her in the mirror which hung in the dishwashing area. The owners quickly removed the mirror and the "Little Girl" has not been seen since.

At this establishment, the ghosts Spring[ville] into action when guests arrive; an amenity that most hotels can't offer.

413

Summerland
The Big Yellow House Restaurant

Particulars

108 Pierpont Avenue, P.O. Box 779,
Summerland, CA 93067
Phone: 805-969-4140
Fax: 805-565-4889
E-mail: info@bigyellowhouse.com
Website: www.bigyellowhouse.com

History

The restaurant is located in the town of Summerland along Highway 101, east of Santa Barbara, and north of Ventura. The resident ghost, nicknamed "Hector," has been written up in books and magazines. Current ownership downplays the paranormal, preferring to concentrate on dinner rather than the spirits. The ghost stories reflect events which in no way reflect the views of current management toward the spirits reported in their establishment.

The current restaurant was formerly a home that was built in 1884. In 1883 the town of Ortega was visited and purchased by Henry L. Williams, an Easterner and a Spiritualist, who was attracted to this "land of sun and enchantment" by the even year-round climate, beautiful views of the Pacific and coastal ranges, and for the feeling of peace and serenity. He renamed this town "Summerland" and built a house his new wife overlooking the ocean and began organizing a center for spiritualistic community living. But Williams died in 1899 by falling down an oil well on his own property. Consequently, his dream of a spiritualistic community passed on as well, because the oil business was booming in Summerland. The house was remodeled soon after by the widow of Henry Williams. She adopted the "San Francisco Victorian Style" familiar to her new husband, George F. Becker.

In 1925, a man of means, Becker purchased a controlling interest in the H.L. Williams oil properties, forming the Summerland Oil Company. It was at this time that our "Big Yellow House" would receive its new face and more closely resemble what we see today. A second floor was added and all the rooms were enlarged. The new structure had concrete on the outside instead of bare wood. In fact, the walls of the house, inside and out, are eight to ten inches thick concrete. Mr. Becker required a new nickname during this remodel - "Cement Becker". The mansion was the talk of Summerland and everyone was anxious to see it completed.

Mr. Becker wanted nothing but the best; his elegant and elaborate taste can be clearly seen in the imported Australian gum wood used for all pillars, staircases and paneling. The wood was hand carved by two Frenchmen in Summerland and considered works of art. The same wood was also used to create the elegant built-in buffet that lined one wall and now surrounds the bay window in the Dining Room. The tile used on the sun porch and fire place was shipped from the East Coast. The downstairs fireplace tile was hand crafted to depict the Santa Barbara Channel Islands. The upstairs had two additional features unheard of at this time in Summerland: A secret door and a mysterious fireplace. The secret door was at the end of a long cedar fir closet in the bedroom. Few people knew the door existed and no one knew where it led to. The "Mysterious Fireplace" was built in the Master Bedroom. A storage compartment for the family valuables was designed into the fireplace. When the right panel was moved, the mantel would rise, revealing a small strongbox. The furnishings were equally as elaborate and opulent: Satin wall-paper with twenty four carat gold trim, heavy oak furniture and green velvet upholstery. When the house was completed in 1912, it became the center of the Summerland social circle. The Beckers were extremely proud of their home. After the passing of Mr. Becker on Christmas Day, 1932, Mrs. Becker maintained the house for just less than two years. The house stayed in the original family until 1974. This was the year that the mansion became The Big Yellow House, receiving its first coat of the bright memorable color, readily seen from a distance.

The building was originally part of a spiritual center established by H. L. Williams in 1883. Williams believed that through "mediums," the living can communicate with the dead, and that there were seven levels of heaven. The nearest physical domain, was earth, which was also called "Summerland," hence the name of the town. The building was used for elaborate séances, and well-known spiritualists of the day attended lectures and meetings. The desire to use the facility as a retirement home for those who were practicing spiritualists soon changed when oil was discovered in the area, and capitalism replaced spiritualism. The large, yellow house was converted into a restaurant in 1973.

Hauntspitality
One of the spirits occupying The Big Yellow House Restaurant is named Hector, a mischievous prankster who smashes dishes, rattles doorknobs, makes windows open and close, turns lights on and off, and tugs at waitresses' skirts. Richard Senate (1993) reported that Hector has played numerous tricks to surprise staff and guests. Two other spirits are also said to reside within the confines of the structure.

On one occasion, a prior manager locked all the windows, and was about to leave when he felt a cold breeze filter through the place. He went back to the part of the house where the breeze was strongest, and noticed that the windows he had just locked were now open! The manager locked everything up tightly once again and left. Returning the next morning before any of the other staff had arrived, he was surprised to see the same windows open wide once again. Another time, a manager entered the restaurant one morning to find all of the tables stacked on top of one another to the ceiling; each table had the silverware, napkins and table cloth in place. One waitress came into the library room to find all the dishes smashed, while another felt her dress being tugged at by an unseen hand as she walked on the second floor late one night.

Ghosthunter and author, Richard Senate, brought in a paranormal investigating team years ago to determine if the Big Yellow House was haunted. A medium in Senate's group entered a trance- state and her voice literally changed; becoming raspy and the room became deathly cold. The strange voice complained of chest pains before the medium fell forward in a deep sleep. Other psychics have picked up on several entities who remain nameless, wandering spirits, who seem to still enjoy the confines of the restaurant. Other investigators had visited the site over the years including a team from UCLA's parapsychology laboratory who recorded enough anomalies to deem the house "very" haunted.

Author Rod Lathim (1995) in his book about the Big Yellow House, discusses at length the history of the house, and his many paranormal encounters while working there. Lathim cautions that since he wrote the first book back in 1975, some ghost stories, "have been stretched and twisted beyond recognition," including Hector, the ghost Lathim himself named in 1973. Pick up Laithim's book at the Big Yellow House when you visit and find out the truth about the spirits as you enjoy an incredible view, delicious food and a good selection of spirits; both kinds!

Sutter Creek
Sutter Creek Inn

Particulars
75 Main Street, P.O. Box 385,
Sutter Creek, CA
Phone 209-267-5606
Fax: 209-267-9287
E-mail: info@suttercreekinn.com
Website: www.suttercreekinn.com

History

The Sutter Creek Inn is the oldest Bed & Breakfast west of the Mississippi, dating back to 1859. Situated in Gold Rush Country along Highway 49, you pass through the town of Placerville to reach Sutter Creek. State Senator Edward Voorhies lived in the house with his wife and family in the 1880s. The graceful white mansion was built in 1859 by John Keyes for his young bride, Clara McIntyre. Keyes designed the house in the popular New England style to help his wife, who came from the east, acclimate to the new territory.

The couple lost their only child to diphtheria, which devastated Clara. Keyes died, leaving 34-year-old Clara a widow then. Two years later she met and married State Senator Edward Convers Voorhies on March 29, 1880, in the rose garden behind her house. They had two children, Earl who died in World War II, and Gertrude who lived to the ripe old age of 90. As the house passed through a succession of owners, the only constant was the ghosts.

Hauntspitality

The ghosts of Senator Voorhies, and his daughter Gertrude, a phantom flasher, and elderly lady are frequent ghost guests at the Inn. Gertrude has materialized in front of several guests who were relaxing in the lounge. After performing a polite curtsey, she abruptly vanished. A phantom flasher has also been known to sneak up on unsuspecting female guests and drop his attire, then disappear. A pet cat, once entered the kitchen, hissed and arched its back at some unseen force, then was picked up and tossed harmlessly across the room. After that incident, the cat and ghost seemed to get along, as the cat never again entered the kitchen. The spirits of the inn have been discussed by authors Antoinette May, Mike Marinacci, Dennis Hauck, and Nancy Bradley & Vincent Gaddis.

The current owner said she was actually guided to the inn during 1996 after a spiritualist told her that she would find a new home in the mountains and be happy there. She found the Sutter Creek Inn, and after adjusting to the climate and spirits, she loved her surroundings. Over the years, Way and others have seen a tall man wearing old-fashioned clothing standing in the doorway. One time, the man appeared when other guests were in costume. He apparently liked the company, because he was seen smiling before he disappeared in front of the owner. If you don't mind an occasional friendly spirits, then the Sutter Creek Inn is one of the in places to stay when visiting the gold country.

According to the owner, "Occasionally we feel the presence of a spirit, believed to be the previous owner. In thirty- five-years that our family has owned the house it has become less frequent. We attribute this to the feeling that they are pleased with the love and care given to their home. They were very sociable people and we think they enjoy the fact that we have opened the house to guests who seem to love and respect the atmosphere created here."

Vallejo
Starr Mansion Bed & Breakfast

Particulars
503 Mclane Street,
Vallejo, CA 94590
Phone: 707-645-8164
E-mail: starrmansion@gmail.com
Website: www.starrmansion.com

History

Abraham Dubois Starr built the Starr Mansion in 1869; an aristocrat, local politician and friends with the social elite the San Francisco Bay area. Starr was a close friend of Leland Stanford. Active in politics, he traveled in 1873 to Philadelphia as a delegate to the Republican convention, which nominated Ulysses S. Grant for reelection. Starr was born in Ohio on October 14, 1830. He crossed the plains to California in pursuit of riches during the California gold rush in 1850. Good Diggings were found and, when he had accumulated sufficient capital in 1851, he tried hi luck running supplies to the gold miners and settlers. In 1854 he opened a general produce business in Sacramento.

Through his businesses, he found that flour was very much in demand and became the proprietor of the Buckeye Grain Mill at Marysville in 1857. In 1868 Starr moved to Vallejo, was elected a supervisor of Solano County, served as a director for the California Pacific Railroad and started building his first grain mill in South Vallejo. The South Vallejo Mill (later became General Mills in 1925) was completed in 1869 and was producing 2200 barrels of flour a day. Because of Starr, Vallejo became the largest employer, producer and exporter of grain in California. In 1884, he expanded and started building another grain mill in Crockett California, which later became the C&H Sugar plant. By 1891 the Crockett mill was completed and produced 8000 barrels a day, and was to become the largest producing mill in the world. The Starr Mills exports were feeding Asia, Europe and Central America and were well renowned throughout the world until well after the First World War.

A.D. Starr first met his future wife, Mary Anna Teegarden, in 1850 during the migration across the plains. He moved to Marysville and married Mary in 1856. A.D. and Mary had one child born in 1861, named Ada Deborah Starr. During the 1880's Mrs. Starr and Ada traveled often to Europe and Egypt. Ada met and married Judge Bachgrevinck, Danish minister to Alexandria, Egypt. She never returned to America. In 1889 during a trip to England, Mrs. Starr fell over a balustrade onto a marble floor and severely injured her head. She soon died while in the hospital. Ada's concert grand piano remains in the home. In 1893 A.D Starr lost his fortune from a bank panic. Relatives were able to save this house while A.D. went to live with his brother at his Oakland home. From there A.D. faded into obscurity and died in 1894. Many of the Starr Family photos remain in the house.

The Starr Mansion stayed with the Starr Family until 1933; it was sold in a state of disrepair to Mr. and Mrs. Clarence Rothschild. Mr. Rothschild was a Jewish immigrant from Germany. He worked at Mare Island as a pipe fitter. Clarence (The Great Rothschild) was also a popular ventriloquist, magician and amateur plane

pilot. Mr. Rothschild had many performances booked throughout California and the surrounding states. In the 1960s and 1970s, the mansion received numerous renovations and received many locally and nationally renowned rewards for architecture and interior design. Clarence died in 1978 and his surviving wife, Helen, lived in the home until 2003 when it was sold. Helen passed away in October of 2005. Many Rothschild Family photos remain in the house, including some of 'The Great Rothschild'.

In 2003, the Scharz family purchased the dilapidated Starr Mansion. The house was neglected for over 25 years. The Scharz family owned the mansion for approximately 18 months. They put a new roof on the home and auctioned off 98% of the original antique furnishings, art and accessories (some of which are known to have come across the Atlantic on the Mayflower). On April 15, 2005 real estate investors, Evelyn Kaeser and Dennis DeLancey, purchased the Starr Mansion. By this time the house has withstood three major earthquakes with the first occurring in the 1880's (which destroyed all the brick mansions on Mare island and some throughout Vallejo), 1906 (which leveled most of San Francisco) and 1989 Loma Prieta (which caused substantial damage to buildings and other structures throughout the San Francisco Bay Area). The Starr Mansion survived all those natural disasters with minor damages. The mansion had not been maintained since the late 1970's. A major exterior and interior restoration (including repairs from the 1989 Loma Prieta earthquake damage) was needed to take the house back to its original Victorian era splendor.

The Starr Mansion architecture is of the very rare Second Empire Italianate Victorian era with Mansard roof and eyebrows over the Italianate arched windows. During restoration of the exterior, it was discovered that the home was only painted twice over the last 140 years. The Mansion is completely constructed with redwood (even the interior moldings). The exterior siding is almost two-inch thick redwood. The Interior has many unique features: including the two original Italian marble fireplace mantels with the original coal burning iron inserts. Large crown molding and corbels throughout the first floor were hand molded in place from plaster. The first floor has the original red oak floors and curved walls. After the mansion construction was completed in 1869, A.D. Starr hired five Italian artists to paint murals on every ceiling in the home. Two of those murals still exist on the upper floors. Numerous original gold leaf gas lighting fixtures are still in use today (electrified). In 1869 the Starr Mansion was also ahead of its time technologically with central heating. The original coal boiler is still heating the mansion today. As of December 2005, the mansion is now Vallejo's first Bed & Breakfast and boasts seven guest rooms.

Hauntspitality

The current owners lived in the house about two weeks before unusual things began happening. One night they went to bed as usual. It began like any other night, then the ambiance suddenly changed. While lying in bed awake on his side with the owner facing his wife, he felt something at the side of the bed, poking him. The jabs were very solid and directed at the upper half of his back. It was a constant poke similar to someone jabbing a finger in ones back. The husband did not move, as he felt a chill over his body and his hair stand up on the back of his neck. They were the only two people in the house at the time and the bedroom door was locked. He knew because of the circumstances that it had to be a ghost, but par for the course with sprits, when he turned around, there was no one there.

When the current owners purchased the mansion on April 15, 2005, the building was a very dilapidated and already had a reputation in the neighborhood as being haunted. No one would approach it or step foot on the grounds because it really did look scary and unsound. After purchasing the house, restoration took six months to complete, which made the house livable. After moving in and although the house felt warm and comfortable, some unexplained things would occasionally happen. The doorbell was the most frequent occurrence. According to the owners, it began as early as the first week of purchase. Most of the time one of the owners would be alone in the mansion when the bell would ring. The usual scenario would be that the door bell would ring, the owner would go to the door, open it and no one would be there. Thinking it was a prank and instead of answering the door right away, the owner would look out the front bay window to see if someone was at the door and no one in the flesh would be standing by the front door. Although the doorbell has been changed to a new system, it still rings randomly on its own.

The current owners and staff encounter the mysterious doorbell about two or three times a month. However, there are periods when the ringing is much more frequent than others. Another eerie incident occurred when a man in his seventies stopped by and informed the current owners that he worked on the house as a painter back in the 1950s. He used to talk with the second owner of the house and was told that one of the wives killed herself in the closet under the stairs by the entry way. Six months later, the current owners first manager immediately asked if the house was haunted and we she was told no. The female manager continued to feel a presence in the entryway by the closet. The owners asked her for more details and the manager said that she saw a woman with dark hair standing by the closet who was very sad, but not angry. Over the following three months, the first

manager reported a cold area by the entry closet and the intermittent presence of the woman.

Another story involves a dog. Guests who have stayed in the house have reported hearing children running up and down the corridors, laughing and giggling on the third floor. There have also been reports of a dog sniffing and scratching at bedroom doors. The reports are generally the same. As the guest get ready for bed, they will begin hearing what sound like a dog outside their door. They will sit up in bed as the scratching and sniffing sounds that can only come from a dog grew louder and louder. Finally, one of the individuals jumps out of bed and slowly opens the door to see what is responsible for all the clatter. When the door is flung open, there is nothing there. A peak down the hallway always reveals an empty corridor, with no dog in sight. As an interesting historic tid-bit, the previous owner's daughter contacted the current owners about some belongings in the house. Because of some unusual events related to the ghost dog, they asked the daughter about her mother who had lived alone in the home for over 25 years. One question in particular was, did she have any dogs. The daughter informed the owners that her mother passed away in October and that she did have four German Shepard's.

As a final note, the owners reportedly heard from the previous owner that a boy had drowned in a well located on the property. This may account for the sounds of children running through the house as well as the laughter. Perhaps the child had a dog and both are united in the afterlife, playing benign pranks on the living.

There is little doubt that this historic gem is haunted by either Abraham Dubois Starr, Mary Anna Teegarden Starr, Ada Deborah Starr, a boy who may have drowned in the yard and a spirited dog. This house is a five Star(r) establishment in our books when it comes to spirits.

Ventura
Bella Maggiore Inn

Particulars
67 South California Street,
Ventura, CA 93001
Phone: 805-652-0277
Fax: 805-648-5670
Toll Free: 1-800-523-8479

History
The Bella Maggiore Inn is a beautifully restored Italianate building in downtown Ventura that was built in 1927 by renowned architect Albert C. Martin. Martin (1879-1960), the older brother of Los Angeles architect Emmett G. Martin, completed his formal education in architecture and engineering at the University of Illinois in 1902. In January of 1904, Martin moved to Los Angeles to accept a position as a superintendent of construction for Carl Leonardt & Company, a major building contractor on the West Coast.

In 1908, Martin established his own office in Los Angeles. Among Martin's significant commissions were the Ventura County Courthouse in Ventura (1911-1912), the Chapel of Mary Magdalen in Camarillo (1913), St. Alphonsus Catholic Church in Fresno (1914), the Million Dollar Theater in Los Angeles with William L. Woolett (1918), the New Calvary Cemetery entrance gates in Boyle Heights (1923), St. Vincent de Paul Catholic Church in Los Angeles (1923-1925), St. Monica's Catholic Church in Santa Monica (1925), the Boulevard Theater in Los Angeles (1925), the Los Angeles City Hall, with John C. Austin, John Parkinson and Austin Whittlesey (1926-1928), the Bella Maggiore (1927) and the May Company in Los Angeles with S. A. Marx (1940). Albert C. Martin died in Los Angeles on April 9, 1960. The firm bearing his name, AC Martin Partners, continues to play an influential role in Southern California architecture.

Hauntspitality
The well-known phantom of the Bella Maggiore Inn is the restless spirit of a suicide victim named Sylvia. A team of ghosthunters under the direction of Richard Senate set out to examine the numerous reports of hauntings to learn if the stories about poor Sylvia were true. The investigation involved fourteen members including a psychic who performed several experiments, including a midnight séance. During the ghost hunt, one of the researchers had her toothbrush and tube of toothpaste fly from the sink and leap into the shower stall with her. She also claimed to have heard a woman sobbing near one of the rooms. At around 2:00 a.m. a male in the group went downstairs in the lobby when he heard footsteps, like someone was dancing, coming down the stairs. When he looked, there was no one there. Within seconds, he smelled rose-scented perfume in the area. Another ghost hunter saw the closet door in her room open by itself, followed at 3:47 a.m. by an apparition in long, white light hovering in the closet door. Yet another ghosthunters room became very cold, and the woman claimed to see a figure standing at the corner of her bed.

During a séance, several of the group recalled seeing odd lights; feeling electric charges pass through the room; hearing buzzing in their ears; and noting a definite chill pervading the room. The séance produced four distinct personalities: Mark who apparently died at the hotel from an drug overdose in the sixties; Elizabeth, the spirit of a little girl who was murdered a long time ago; an unnamed, unpleasant entity that growled, and laughed; and Sylvia Michaels from Atlantic City who hanged herself in a closet in Room 17 around 1947. Sylvia was sad but not harmful, and likes to show herself primarily to men.

Recently, during a two-day taping of a segment of Haunted Hotels by Authentic Entertainment for the Travel Channel, two incidents worth mentioning occurred.

- A producer, while on the second floor of the building, close to Room 17, heard distinct, low-range notes being played on a piano downstairs. The same few notes were repeated for a few seconds followed shortly by a woman's voice calling out for "someone" to cut that out. It was a scenario one might expect from a mother scolding a child. Curious, the production person, knowing the piano was downstairs, rushed down to see the individual who was playing the piano. There was no one in sight, and the piano keyboard was closed. Confused, the woman ran upstairs to see if she could locate the source of the strange voice she heard. After searching empty Room 17 and checking out the hallway with no luck, she ran into an assistant on the shoot. She explained what just happened, and to her surprise, the stunned assistant related her story.

- It seems not more than 45 minutes earlier, the assistant had been standing in the same hallway by herself when she heard the piano play a few notes followed shortly by a woman's voice curtly say "Would you stop that." The assistant's search for the mysterious piano player and the woman who called out from seemingly nowhere proved futile.

Could it be that a spirited mother and child also occupy the building? Or, could this be Sylvia who hanged herself in Room 17 calling out to child she left behind?

At the Bella Maggiore in Ventura you can spend a quiet evening relaxing in style, savor the delicious food and be entertained by their other-worldly guests!

Landmark No.78

Particulars
211 East Santa Clara Street,
Ventura, CA 93001
Phone: 805-643-3264
Fax: 805-643-3267
Website: www.landmark78.com

History

Legend has it that in the late 1800s, an Italian family moved to Ventura with their beautiful daughter, Rosa. She was forced into a loveless marriage to a much older husband who was frequently out of town for long periods of time. Rosa became despondent until a young Italian caught her fancy. They became lovers, and Rosa became pregnant. Her husband was humiliated, and her lover left for San Francisco, never to return. A despondent Rosa hanged herself in her room (now the upstairs bathroom). The present-day restaurant was originally, the Carlo Hahn residence, a two-story Victorian house constructed in 1912.

The early residence may in fact have been constructed to compliment an elaborate house built next door (since demolished) which was owned by Giovanni Ferro, Hahn's business partner. The house was converted into a fine local restaurant in the 1970s by Ed Warren. When he first converted the historic structure into a place of fine dining, it was called The Big Green House and later changed to the Santa Clara House named after the frontage street. The new owners, Jorge Ramirez and Darleen Ramirez have lightened up the atmosphere and changed the name to Landmark No. 78 which fits the plaque on the front lawn to the left of the entrance which reads: Historic Landmark No. 78 (Carlo Hahn House).

Hauntspitality

A phantom female named Rosa, is said to wander through the upstairs area, and the downstairs dining/bar area, playing pranks on staff, and customers. Several staff persons have reported an unseen presence on the upper floor, terming the feeling unnerving, claustrophobic, and just plain, creepy---in fact, many of the staff only go upstairs in pairs. Management also seemed reluctant to use the upper room for dining when the lower dining areas were filled. They preferred to use the area for special banquets. The old staircase leading to the

HISTORIC LANDMARK
No. 78

CARLO HAHN HOUSE

This house, built in 1912 for prominent Ventura businessman Carlo Hahn, was designed in a late Victorian Style to complement the grand and elaborate Schiappapietra Mansion that was once on the adjoining parcel. The round gable windows, low pitched roof and heavy eave brackets reflect Italianate detailing.

City of San Buenaventura Historic Preservation Commission

upper floor which was once the sleeping area for several family members is one focal point for the hauntings of a spectral lady described as wearing either a long, red, green, or blue dress.

Richard Senate once took his Ghost and Hauntings class to the Santa Clara Restaurant. A woman in the class brought her child to the haunted house. Once inside, they proceeded toward the staircase. As the child began ascending the stairs he called to his mother, pointing toward the landing, and asking who the beautiful lady was. The mother quickly looked in the direction the child was pointing, but saw no one there. On another occasion, a young waiter mounted the staircase. As he looked into a mirror, he saw not his reflection but the face of a young woman wearing a turn-of-the-century dress, and with a slightly elongated neck. The frightened waiter left the scene as quickly as his legs could carry him down the stairs. Relating the story to the owner and staff, he refused to go up again, alone.

During another ghosthunting foray by Richard Senate, the entire class confirmed that the women's bathroom on the second floor seemed to be filled with some kind of energy. The class also felt chills on the stairs and was unanimous in their opinion that the area was dominated by a very strong energy source. Then, there is the strange feeling one gets in the red room, which is located just off the staircase. Many have felt a strange presence lurking inside, including one psychic woman who reported seeing a sad image drifting through the room.

A current waiter confirmed the ghostly stories, adding, that sometimes he is left alone to close up. Per his routine, he begins in the upstairs area, locking the windows and doors, then proceeds down the staircase into the dining room and bar areas. He dislikes closing the upstairs area, saying that the feeling is sometimes oppressive, and more often than not he senses that he's being watched. It may be his job, but he doesn't have to like it.

Gifted psychic, Lisa Williams in her show, Life Among the Dead for Lifetime TV, visited the restaurant during one of her episodes and came face to face with the spirit of Rosa. She identified the forlorn female phantom and assisted her in crossing over. She also identified energy, a male, associated with the property.

The stories continue to be told of cold spots, mysterious shadows followed by gusts of air on the upper floor, phantom footsteps, an occasional slamming door, and electrical problems. Perhaps all of the paranormal events that have taken place over the years are attributable to the spirit of Rosa; or perhaps there is more than one energy who haunts the building. Come visit this Ventura landmark, for a meal or a drink; but make sure your clear as to the kind of spirits you're ordering!

Haunted bathroom and stairs where Rosa is sighted (Courtesy of the International Paranormal Research Organization – IPRO)

426

Pierpont Inn

Particulars

550 Sanjon Road,
Ventura, CA 93001
Phone: 805-643-6144
Fax 805/641-1501
Toll Free: 1-800-285-4667
E-mail: info@pierpontinn.com
Website: www.pierpontinn.com

History

For over 70 years the Pierpont Inn has been owned and operated by descendants of the same family. Present day general partners Spencer and Scott Garrett are fourth generation Venturans, descendants of the Snodgrass and Vickers families. The Snodgrass family came to California in the 1840s and settled in Ventura in 1868. The Vickers family settled in Ventura County in the 1880s. In 1909, Fred Snodgrass married Josephine Vickers, merging two Ventura County pioneer families. Spencer and Scott Garrett acquired the Inn in 1999 from the family of Mattie Vickers Gleichmann - the sister of the Garretts' grandmother, Josephine Vickers Snodgrass. Today, Spencer and Scott Garrett maintain the tradition of family hospitality that is the foundation of the Pierpont Inn.

The history of the Pierpont Inn dates to 1891 when Dr. Ernest Pierpont left his medical practice in Illinois and brought his wife and two sons to Ojai, California. After Dr. Pierpont died in 1905, his wife, Josephine, in 1908, enlisted the designing skills of Hunt, Eager & Burns to build an inn in Ventura for her younger son, Austen. The inn was given the family name, Pierpont, which also soon became the name for the rapidly developing Ventura bay area. Austen Pierpont managed the Pierpont Inn for only a few years before pursuing his first love - architecture. The Inn in Ventura was finally sold in 1915 and it changed owners several times in the next thirteen years. In 1928, Gus and Mattie Vickers Gleichmann purchased the run-down Pierpont Inn for $80,000.

The young entrepreneurs met in Ventura County at the Vickers Home Ranch on old Ditch Road. Mattie's oldest sister, Josephine, had married baseball ball player, Fred Snodgrass. One winter, Fred, who was playing winter ball, brought home another ball player, Gus Gleichmann, and introduced him to his wife's sister, Mattie. Gus saw one career end when he suffered a serious injury and another begins as he married Mattie in 1921; on crutches. The two left Ventura to accept hotel management positions at Chowchilla. They returned seven years later with their children, Ted, age five, and Nancy who was three, purchasing the Inn. Mattie, Gus, Josephine and Fred labored long and hard to make ends meet and the hard work finally paid off.

Gus' mother, lovingly known as "Mother Gleichmann", lived with the couple when they were restoring the Inn. "Nanna" as she was called by her grandchildren, cared for Ted and Nancy and occasionally tended the front desk though often she could be found sitting with her yarn and crochet needles at one of the little tables that Gus had made for each side of the entrance door, crocheting afghans for different members of the family. Gus' sister, Minna, and her husband, Fred Pfiffer, lived in Ventura and Fred was a great help to Gus. Together they built three private cottages on the property.

When the Inn was purchased, the property included the five and a half acres of the present-day Pierpont Racquet Club and many years before the tennis club was built by Spencer and Scott Garrett, one of the previous owners of the hotel had envisioned a swimming club and had built a large pool and a bathhouse with many changing rooms. Gus and Fred converted the bath-house into sleeping quarters for the Inn employees; the pool was never filled with water. Gus passionately pursued his dreams until a winter night in 1938 when he was killed in an automobile accident on his way home from Ojai; Mother Gleichmann, who was with him, survived. Mattie chose to remain at the Inn in order to complete what Gus had left unfinished. From 1939 to 1942 Mattie's dedication to offering comfortable accommodations and good food paid off by a gradual accumulation of "regulars". During World War II the military established fortifications at the bluff and along Vista del Mar Drive. Guns, cannons and search lights were placed on the Inn property and naval officers and enlisted personnel were billeted at the Inn.

Ted Gleichmann left Ventura during high school to attend New Mexico Military Academy and from there he joined the Army Air Corps. After he was honorably discharged he relieved his mother of her managerial burden, and he also began to improve and expand the Inn. In l947, the Inn finally began selling alcohol at an attractive bar next to the dining room. Ted expanded the dining room and the main building by adding the Anacapa Room.

The small cottages built by Ted's father and Uncle Fred Pfiffer gave way to the present East Wing and the Bluff House now stands where the honeymoon cottages once were. The Santa Rosa Room was once the family living room with bedrooms for Gus and Mattie, Nancy, Ted, and Mother Gleichmann located behind the doors of the corridor leading to the Santa Rosa Room. Earlier changes occurred with the construction of the Ventura Freeway, completed in 1962. The three larger cottages and the stairway that led down the bluff to the beach disappeared. The cottages were replaced by a new West Wing. The two cottages that remain today were part of the original property - the larger one built by Austen Pierpont. In 1975, Spencer and Scott Garrett, grandsons of Mattie's sister, Josephine, approached Ted to lease the adjacent property for the development of a multi-sport recreational facility. Tragically, as plans for the Pierpont Racquet Club were being finalized, Ted was diagnosed with a brain tumor that claimed his life in November of 1976 a year and a month before the racquet club opened.

Surviving Ted were his wife, Vondra, and his two children by a previous marriage, Theodore Vickers, Jr. (Vic) and Sally. At age 27, Vic led the way as the third generation of the Gleichmann family to manage the Inn. Vic served the Inn until 1990 when he and his wife, Judy, retired. Nancy Henson, Ted's sister, who had been employed by the Inn, also retired that same year. It was in 1990 that The Gleichmanns decided to radically transform the county landmark.

Nancy's son-in-law, Rod Houck, became president of the family corporation and led the family as they began to make the first major renovations in over thirty years. With the financial help of San Luis Obispo's Sterling Hotels, they made internal changes and began redefining the Inn's future. The family's primary goal was to preserve the integrity of the original building commissioned by Josephine Pierpont. In so doing, the two remaining cottages on the property were rebuilt in the same style as in the early 1930s; the seventy rooms, eight of which were suites, were returned to a lighter color scheme and a more traditional decor. Overstuffed sofas and chairs furnished the new lobby and a pictorial history of the Pierpont Inn was mounted on one of its walls. The work of local artists was added throughout the dining and lobby areas, perhaps as Ted might have envisioned.

On Easter Sunday, 1992, the family celebrated Mattie's birthday with the grand opening of The New Pierpont Inn. Three years later in March, extended family and nearly 500 friends and patrons surprised Mattie with a party in honor of her 100th birthday. Mattie died in 1997 a month short of being 101. The next year, 1998, the Gleichmanns turned the Inn over to another owner who had the capital to make needed improvements and the Inn was advertised for sale. In August of that year the family received an offer from a Santa Barbara based company. The offer was accepted by the Inn; however, Spencer and Scott Garrett, as general partners of the Pierpont Racquet Club, chose to exercise their right of first refusal; met the purchase terms; and acquired the Inn. Escrow eventually closed in January of 1999. The Inn's new owners are yet another generation of the Vickers' family. It was Spencer and Scott's grandfather, Fred Snodgrass, who had introduced Gus to Mattie. Fred's wife, Josephine Vickers Snodgrass, their grandmother, was Mattie's sister. Hence the Pierpont Inn, after seventy years in the Gleichmann family remains in family hands - in the hands of descendants of the Vickers, one of Ventura County's earliest families. In early 2000, the Garretts began an extensive remodeling of the Inn with an emphasis on maintaining the architectural and historical integrity of the Inn. By the end of the year 2000, all of the rooms had been completely remodeled. On November 24, 2000, the Austen Pierpont Suite was unveiled. In January 2001, Ted Gleichmann's old house built in the mid-1930s was converted into an executive retreat and conference center, and in April 2001, the Rose Garden Cottage re-opened after renovation.

Hauntspitality

The following information involving staff and guests at the Pierpont was provided by the Pierpont Inn: Most of our "visitors" from another time seem to be friendly. It appears they have had such a good time here at the Pierpont; they simply don't want to leave. They seem to be happy "guests from the past." We hope that all of our guests will enjoy their stay here so much that they will want to return time and again. A majority of our paranormal experiences have been reported since the start of restoration. Some spirits seem to be of former owners. It is reassuring to know that, if that is the case, they are still watching over the Pierpont and very much interested in her future. The inn has had a long history of caring and involved owners. Scott and Spencer Garrett follow that tradition.

Jeannie Poff/Hostess (two experiences in 2000): On one occasion, Jeannie went to seat guests coming for dinner and after being seated the guests complained that the table was leaning. Thinking it was a maintenance problem, she went to inspect another table that she planned on moving the guests to. The second table (in what is called the Crow's Nest) was also leaning. Feeling that no one would believe her, she went and called Manny (who is a busser) to examine the table as well. Manny confirmed that the table was, indeed, leaning. Jeannie found a table that was not leaning and re-seated the guests. However, the next morning, neither table was leaning. Another time, late at night, after the restaurant had closed, Jeannie went to get a cup of coffee in the kitchen alley. The entrance to the alley is through two swinging doors. After she had passed through the doors and gone to the end of the alley to retrieve her coffee, she looked back at the doors because they were making noise and they were still swinging, very strongly. No one else had gone through those doors except Jeannie; no one she could see, that is!

Bruce Barrios/DJ - not an employee (March 200]): It was a Monday or a Tuesday around 10 p.m., just before the bar was about to close. Bruce Barrios (who works for George Schlatter on the American Comedy Awards) and his friend Patrick (who works for Embassy Suites) came in for a last call after a long day's work. Jeannie Poff had just finished dinner in the alcove of the bar and had bid them good-night. Shortly after she left, and while Bruce was seated at the bar near the television, he saw in the corner of his eye on the left side of the alcove something that moved. He looked hard and saw a vapor-like mist that was formed by three ribbon shapes gently floating above the table in the middle of the alcove. Bruce turned to tell his friend about the sight he was seeing and when he turned back, the "mist" had disappeared. The bartender said Bruce's face was ashen white. Bruce felt maybe he was just tired since neither his friend Patrick nor the bartender had seen the "spirit"; however, when he and Patrick went to the car and opened the door, the car emitted the powerful odor of flowers like those at a funeral, sweet and sad. The odor was only in the car, not outside. No watering of the surrounding gardens had taken place and the car was brand new; so this was not the residue of a former car owner. Bruce and Patrick both experienced this odor at the same time.

Alexis Rachel/Graphic designer - not an employee (November, 1999): While working on the graphic layout for our menus, Alexis was using the computer station located in the old stair landing (now directly above the Front Desk and closed off to the general public.) This was late at night and no one else was upstairs. She said she distinctly heard a ruffling sound pass in back of her that sounded like stiff taffeta of a woman's petticoat. At the same time a cold breeze passed over the area. There were no windows open at the time as it was in November.

Rafael/busser (early 2001): Rafael was alone, closing down the kitchen late at night. The glasses used to serve water were stacked above the dishwashing area on a rack that is tilted backward on a diagonal in order to prevent them from falling. The glasses were stacked in large square and sectioned plastic boxes to keep them from touching each other and from possible breakage. As Rafael stood to the side of the racks, he saw one of the boxes filled with glasses lunge forward on their own and fall to the floor, shattering all the glasses inside the box.

Sean/server (October/November, 2000): Sean was in the alley of the kitchen where the coffee was served (same area as Jeannie Poff's experience). From that area as you stand by the swinging doors you have a clear view into the back bar. He looked toward the back bar to see if guests had been seated, since that was his assigned area for the evening. The area was completely vacant. He looked up again to review the area (this took a second) and he clearly saw a woman dressed in costume from the Edwardian period (1901-1910). She was elegantly attired in a satin dress, with long white gloves, her dark hair in a high chignon and a feathered hat, the final accent being an umbrella. Sean rubbed his eyes to make sure of what he was seeing and upon opening them, the lady was gone; however, a couple (modern day) were sitting in the very chairs the "phantom lady" had occupied. This experience took place shortly after the Ventura County History Fair.

Kirk Benitz/Banquet Captain (worked at the Pierpont for 11 years. These experiences have happened over the last few years): Kirk had gone upstairs to use the copy machine and as he was coming back down the hallway he noticed someone looking back at him. At the end of the hallway upstairs is a door with glass panels. Normally, Kirk would always see his own reflection in the glass. But this night he realized it was not his reflection but that of a man wearing period clothing, with a hat, that was staring back at him. He looked up again to confirm what he felt and the man was gone. Kirk is frequently responsible for closing down the San Miguel/Santa Rosa banquet area at night after events have ended. Over the years he has worked in the area, the lights down the long hallway frequently turned on or turn off by themselves; even after someone has deliberately flipped the switch to "counteract" the existing light.

Patty Torres/Bar Manager (worked here for eight years). A few years ago she was upstairs when she felt a presence behind her. When she turned around, she thought she saw a woman quickly hurrying down the hallway behind the copy machine. Patty went around the corner to check out who it was and found no one there. That hallway leads to the roof and not to a guestroom. Recently, she and Kirk Benitiz were cleaning up the Anacapa-Marine room after an event. Just as they happened to be talking about all the recent "ghost experiences" that have occurred since construction began in 1999, the microphone in the room which had been turned off suddenly began making loud crackling noises. Patty accused Kirk of playing a trick on her; however, Kirk was equally disturbed by the sudden noise because both of them knew the microphone was off. They both got up to check the mike and it was, indeed in the off position.

Larry/houseman (fall of 2000): Larry's responsibility as houseman is to come in late at night after banquet guests have left and clean the banquet rooms. He and his assistant went into the Anacapa/Marine room to begin vacuuming. Larry had to leave to get supplies and told his assistant to stay put. The assistant was sitting at a table when he saw a transparent man and woman approach him. When they began to approach his table, he quickly left the room, quite shaken. When Larry returned, he told him the story. Larry felt the young man was just tired. He told him to go into the San Miguel room and begin vacuuming there instead. When the assistant entered the room, he said he saw the room was filled with people having a banquet and the tables were filled with food. The couple he had seen earlier was in the room and they motioned for him to come in, as if inviting him to the party. Within seconds the people, the food and the couple vanished. The assistant immediately left the room and told Larry what happened and that he was leaving for the night.

Kathy Farrell/Catering manager (early 2001): Kathy was at the copy machine upstairs in the early morning. She saw the Special Projects Manager walk behind her and head toward the General Manager's office. She also saw a little girl about three-years-old holding his hands and giggling loudly. She saw Joey, the Manager, followed by the little girl as he went into the office; Kathy called out to the manager and asked who the little girl that was with him. The manager stepped out of the office and said he didn't know what she was talking about; there was no child with him!

Martine/dishwasher (Two experiences happened in the fall of 2000 and early 2001): Martine was leaving to go home late at night after finishing the final washing of all the dishes after a major banquet evening. When he approached his car in the lower parking area (designated for employees) he saw a young woman he could see right through dancing in the area by the trash bins. She was waving her arms and jumping into the air and seemed completely unaware of his presence. As he went to get into his car, she disappeared. On another night, he was washing the dishes and turned around to see a presence of a man in the dishwashing area. He thought the chef had gotten him some help, but when he went to explain to the person what his job would be the man disappeared.

Miguel/Sous - Chef (summer 2000 - Miguel has worked here for several years): The extra plates and serving pieces used to be stored in an old guestroom of the Inn upstairs. One has to walk down a darkened hallway to get to this guestroom. He went into the room to retrieve what he needed in supplies and had trouble turning on the light. The light fixture in the room was the last remaining original light fixture in the entire hotel from the time that the inn opened in 1910. The only way to turn on the light was to pull on a very long string. Miguel pulled and pulled several times but the light would not turn on. Then, he said in frustration, "Come on, help me, I'm trying to help your family (meaning the family that owns the inn." At that moment, the light turned on.

Juan Busser (fall, 2000): Juan was asked to check out a disturbance in the ice machine in the East Wing. As he approached the machine, he heard loud banging sounds. When he reached the machine, the door where the ice comes out, was moving wildly up and down on its own. Juan left immediately without attempting to repair the machine. However, the next day, the machine was inspected and found to be in perfect working order.

Guests of the East Wing (summer, 2000): Guests had checked into an East Wing room with a fireplace. It was a perfect summer day. As they went to unpack, the drapes began swaying, as if a strong wind had entered the room. All the doors were closed, the flue to the fireplace was closed and the thermostat was not on. The swaying continued for some time before the drapes abruptly stopped and went back into position. The guests went to the bar to ask what the disturbance might be. They were told about spirits who enjoy visiting their "special room" from time to time; they probably just wanted to say "hello". The guests seemed a little shaken, but reassured, returned to their room. The incident did not happen again during their stay.

Night Auditor (A former employee told this story to Ventura ghosthunter, Richard Senate on March 24, 1986): The Night Auditor was working on the books late at night. At that time, the bookkeeping office was on the second floor of the old Inn in what used to be Guestroom 6 (now Cynthia Thompson's office). She was joined by a Front Desk clerk who had come up to check on some receipts. As they discussed the daily totals of tile receipts, a well-dressed gentleman in a dark suit entered the room and sat down comfortably and nonchalantly in a chair. The women turned to look at their visitor and ask him what he needed and the man disappeared before their eyes. The auditor gasped as the man disappeared and realized she recognized the gentleman.

"Oh my god, that's Ted!" she said. The man named Ted she referred to was Ted Gleichmann, owner and manager of the Pierpont Inn from the early 1950's to 1975 when he died at the age of 52 from a brain tumor. She told Mr. Senate that the man had entered the room in a very natural and familiar way and seemed very interested in how the business of the Inn was progressing, something Ted Gleichmann had done on a daily basis all of the years he ran the Inn.

The Noisy Party (This was related to Ventura ghosthunter, Richard Senate around 1995): A lady and her traveling companion had just checked into their room as part of a planned family reunion. She was a former schoolteacher and very particular. She said this was during the middle of the week on a Tuesday night. As the evening progressed, she and her friends began hearing loud noises coming from the room next door. She said they were noises one would associate with a New Year's Eve party: The blowing horns, noisemakers and dancing music. They also heard the voices of many people loudly having a "good ole time". She complained to the front desk and asked to be moved to another room. The front deck obliged, but when the management went to the room next door to ask the guests who were making the noise to keep quiet, no one answered the door. Upon entering the room, management discovered that it was in perfect check-in condition; there any evidence of a party. When they checked their books, they saw that no one had recently checked into that room. Other guests had also called the front desk to complain about the noise apparently caused by other-worldly guests.

Time Warp (The author, who frequented the Pierpont during mid-1970s): On three separate occasions, unexplained things punctuated his staff. The first time, while in the large, cottage in the back of the hotel, a shadowy figure wearing a broad-brimmed hat floated down the hallway, passed the bedroom and out the back door. Thinking it was an intruder, the author began giving chase only to find that the back door was deadbolted. During that same stay, sounds came from the living room as if people were rearranging the furniture. There were sounds of a sofa being moved and other adjustments to the furniture taking place. Jumping up from the bed, and thinking it might be housekeeping, the author ran into the living room to see who was responsible for the commotion. Much to his surprise, there was nothing out of place and no intruder. On another occasion, while finishing a drink at the bar, the author's attention was diverted for a few seconds toward the dining room where a strange-looking man in a rumpled, brown suit, wearing horn-rimmed glasses, walked into the dining room and right through a closed door. Never has a Jack Daniels been consumed so quickly, and never has bartender's ear been so needed. The description according to the bartender sounded like good ole Gus Gleichmann who it seems, worked late and always liked to give the place a once over before heading to bed. A third incident was recently conveyed to Cynthia Thompson. It's a strange time-warp tale by the pool that you'll have to ask Cynthia about when you visit the hotel.

The authors along with friend and well-known author and ghosthunter Richard Senate, taped a segment for **Mysterious Journeys**, A Matthews/Zimmerman production for the Travel Channel recounting a few paranormal events which took place at the Pierpont Inn. The thin line between this world and the next is definitely crossed often at this grand inn overlooking the ocean. But, even if you don't witness something unusual, the food and view are extraordinary and enough to keep **you** coming back again and again; along with the spirits!

Victorian Rose Bed & Breakfast

Particulars
896 E. Main Street,
Ventura, CA 93001
Phone: 805-641-1888
Fax: 805-643-1335
E-mail: victrose@pacbell.net
Website: www.victorian-rose.com

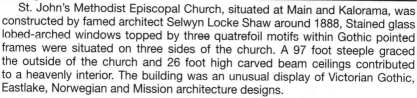

History

St. John's Methodist Episcopal Church, situated at Main and Kalorama, was constructed by famed architect Selwyn Locke Shaw around 1888, Stained glass lobed-arched windows topped by three quatrefoil motifs within Gothic pointed frames were situated on three sides of the church. A 97 foot steeple graced the outside of the church and 26 foot high carved beam ceilings contributed to a heavenly interior. The building was an unusual display of Victorian Gothic, Eastlake, Norwegian and Mission architecture designs.

The original floor plan provided for two vestibules, a balcony, sanctuary, altar, reception room, and office space. At least 35 known ministers lead the congregation at this church from 1888 until 1957. The church became a wedding chapel and is now a wonderful and enchanting inn. Cherubs guard the sanctuary that has been thoughtfully designed to accommodate several cozy sitting areas. Added tranquility is provided by an indoor fountain. It took over two years for the Bogatch family to restore the 1880s church.

Hauntspitality

Although no longer a church, the place is still blessed with a bevy of spirited clientele. There is never a dull moment inside this antique adorned building. There are five guest rooms, all it seems with stories of spectral visitors. While visiting this truly unique inn, one is just as likely to encounter a phantom guest, as a paying one.

This is a famous stopover for renowned local paranormal researcher and author, Richard Senate on his Ventura ghost hunting expeditions. Featured on several travel shows featuring haunted locations, this structure is considered one of the most haunted locations in Ventura. Although no longer a functioning church, it is still blessed with a bevy of spirited clientele. There is never a dull moment inside this unique, antique-adorned building. The fact that almost every nook and cranny contains some relic of the past only adds to its eccentric, homey feel. You can't help but feel blessed inside this sanctuary from the hustle and bustle of Main Street. Cherubs guard the sanctuary that has been thoughtfully restored by the Bogatch family to accommodate several cozy-sitting areas. An indoor fountain adds to the peace and tranquility of this former sanctified site. There are five ethereally elegant guestrooms, all containing stories of their frequent spectral visitors. While visiting this unique bed and breakfast, one is just as likely to encounter a phantom guest as a paying one.

One frequent spirited guest is none other than a former minister who has yet to be named. The minister is frequently sighted in the Wisteria Garden Room, primarily by men. The stern-looking gentleman often appears standing in front of the bed and seems to enjoy putting the fear of God in some guests before disappearing. The bedroom is not the only place the preacher is witnessed. Occasionally the elderly man is spotted walking out of the Wisteria Room and follows guests out into the former sanctuary/altar area of the building before vanishing. He is also sighted in the Timeless Treasures Bedroom.

According to owner Richard Bogatch, the minister is the most frequently spotted ghostly guest in the former church. Bogatch reported that a couple staying in the Wistera Room were suddenly awakened to a strange- looking man standing in front of their bed, looking intently in their direction. After a few heartbeats, the man, described unhesitatingly as a minister, just dissolved in front of their eyes. The strange thing is, men are much more frightened of the ministerial vision than women. Another couple claims to have had a ghostly encounter in the room. After the husband had gone to the bathroom, his wife reported that a male figure resembling a preacher had simply materialized and gotten into bed with her. When the husband returned, the man vanished. The woman wasn't frightened, but the husband was a little upset, as can be expected. Fortunately, they stayed the rest of the night in the room without incident.

When the building first opened for business, the Bogatch's reported that several people walked in off the street and upon entering, immediately remarked that the place was haunted, or in their terms, it had a "palpable presence" inside. In the former choir loft, now the Emperor's Room, numerous guests have reported being kept awake by the sound of people singing at all hours of the night. Some guests were spooked enough by the ghostly music to ask for another room. Others simply wanted to rest without having hymns sung by a spectral choir, which by the way, some guests, find very soothing.

The Victorian Rose Room has it's share of activity, including the Bogatch dog barking in front of the door at someone invisible. Other reports from the room include the door knob which sometimes mysteriously rattles as if someone "unseen" is trying to enter. The former sanctuary, now loaded with antiques and a cozy sitting area is also rumored to be haunted by a young woman who reportedly accidentally fell to her death from the choir loft (this has not been substantiated as yet). She is occasionally sighted or felt below the Emperor's Room where the choir loft would have been.

The Fleur-de-lis bedroom was once the site of a strange occurrence. According to Bogatch, two women who were staying in the room were ready to check out when one woman could not find her keys. She knew she had left them in plain sight, but for some reason they had just vanished. She searched around the room, under the bed, in the bathroom, and closet; nothing. She reopened her suitcase and purse and rummaged through everything once again, to no avail. Just as she was about to give up, she heard a noise at her feet. When she looks down, her keys has magically reappeared.

Add to the list of unexplained phenomena, a swinging chandelier, mysterious shadows and voices, a presence in the basement area (the Bogatch living area) and a general feeling of being watched or followed, and you have one haunted inn. None of the reported events suggest anything but friendly spirits inside the inn; besides how could anyone ever be afraid in such a blessed location. Everyone who visits this place, leaves with a feeling of peace and tranquility, and an occasional story to tell about its former occupants who don't want to leave; and who can blame them.

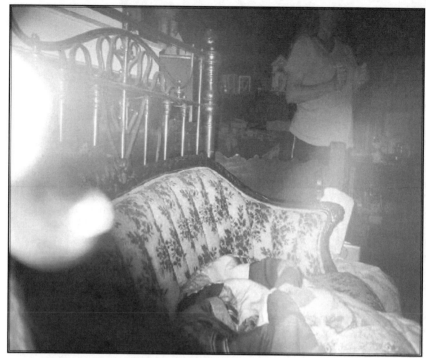
Odd mist forming as San Diego Ghost Hunter Maritza Skandunas is holding dowsing rods

An investigation was conducted by the International Paranormal Research Organization (IPRO) as part of a joint venture with the San Diego Ghost Hunters in 2004. The two groups reserved all the rooms and spent the night photographing and recording inside the church. They also conducted a séance to see if they could make contact with Lynn Mueller and find out what happened the night she died. The dowsing/séance began around 8:00 p.m. and took place near the central-western portion of the sanctuary, in a corner near the Victorian Rose room and the dining table. We all began experiencing a wave of cold pass by us. A small hand-held cassette recorder and a digital voice recorder were placed on a coffee table.

During the séance, numerous pictures of orbs were captured on film and two coughing sounds were picked up on tape with additional Electronic Voice Phenomena (EVP) also discernable as described below.
- Two strange clicking sounds are heard on the tape #406.
- The word "yes" can be heard on tape #436/7. A female voice says "No" on tape #450.
- The group runs through a list for former ministers to try and establish which minister haunts the building. After ten names receive a no response, the dowsing rods cross yes for the name Wade Hamilton. At that point everyone gets chilled to the bone. To the question, "Are you ninety-four years old? … a no can be heard on tape #489. The group sensed that there was more than one minister in the building, so we continued asking from the list of names.
- After the next question, "Are you Reverend Davis? (Two light taps can be heard on the tape #500). The dowsing rods concur by crossing, yes. An investigator

noted that Hamilton 1901 and Davis 1903 served successive terms at the church and would have known each other. Another question was asked, "Did you know each other in life? Reverend Davis... Reverend Davis?" (a female voice says, Oh we are here on the tape #504).

- Another questioned is posited, "You and Reverend Hamilton knew each other, correct? The dowsing rods cross for yes and a faint "Yes" can be heard on tape.
- When investigator Maritza Skandunas states, "That's weird because my maiden name is Davis, a distinct female voice can be heard on tape at #509.
- As the author says "Thank you so very much," a faint voice says, "thank you".
- Numerous clicking sounds and unintelligible voices can be heard throughout the tape including mumbling, whispering voices, a child crying, loud knocks, "I'm sorry," "yes," "killed Lynn," "Jim," "Go back to prison," "It's in a file," you can hear people talking, coughing, and three distinct knocks after we ask for a sign that they are listening.

At the very haunted Victorian Rose, you don't have a prayer of being alone. If it's not a minister watching over you, then perhaps a woman will be singing to you in the choir loft room. Oh, and be sure to say your prayers before going to sleep.

Odd mist forming on couch as San Diego Ghost Hunter Maritza Skandunas is holding dowsing rods

Woodland Hills
Casa de Carlos

Particulars
22901 Ventura Boulevard,
Woodland Hills, CA 91367
Phone: 818-225-8182
Fax: 818-225-8145
Website: www.casadecarlos.com

History

The current restaurant opened in 1961 and has been voted the best Mexican Restaurant in the San Fernando Valley by the Daily News. Prior to its incarnation as a restaurant, the building housed an Italian market and a bookstore.

Hauntspitality

This San Fernando Valley eatery has an added surprise for visitors, Spirits. No, these are not the kind you drink; rather they are benign phantoms who linger on the west side of the building and in the bar. Who are they and why do they remain behind is anyone's guess. There is not just one phantom guest, but according to a psychic who recently visited the place, there are at least two spirits in the building. These are friendly phantom energies that seem to do their own thing while customers take advantage of the delicious food and beverages served inside. Paranormally inclined individuals seem to sense the energies more in the west side of the building and in the bar area where patrons and ghosts actually sit side by side; the only difference is, the living have to pay. There have also been reports from the kitchen area where employees encounter drafts and sense that they are being watched by unseen eyes.

Although no one is sure who the friendly spirits are, they may be tied to the building's past, when an Italian market and bookstore occupied a portion of the current structure. Besides rapidly manifesting cold spots and unexplained footsteps and voices there have been several reports of shadowy figures floating through the walls; perhaps the sightings are a result of too many delicious margaritas? One visitor remarked that while walking through

Orb on the wall near upper left hand corner of the photo (Courtesy of the International Paranormal Research Organization – IPRO)

the western portion of the restaurant, he was suddenly engulfed in a bone chilling draft. Another person took a photograph inside the western area and came home with an orb when he developed his film.

There are other tell-tale signs that this restaurant is haunted, but you'll have to explore the place yourself to find out. The food alone is worth a visit, but the spirits are an added bonus when you dine. Keep a watchful eye when dining and you may see a former occupant keeping an eye on things.

Yosemite National Park
The Ahwahnee Hotel

Particulars
Yosemite National Park, CA
Operated by the Delaware North Company
Reservations 559-252-4848
(Central reservations for all Yosemite lodging)
Website: www.YosemitePark.com

History

During the early 1900's the first director of the National Park Service, Stephen Mather, decided that Yosemite needed a first class hotel, partly to get rich investors and powerful politicians to visit the park and see its beauty firsthand. The Ahwahnee Hotel was designed by architect Gilbert Stanley Underwood, who designed impressive hotels for Zion and Bryce national parks. His original design was for a seven story hotel with a central tower and three wings. The concrete and steel design with granite accents would make it resistant to fire. James McLaughlin was hired to build the hotel at a cost of $525,000.00, and the cornerstone was laid on August 1, 1925. The cost of the hotel almost doubled during construction, but the grand opening took place on July 16, 1927.

Dr. Arthur Pope, and his wife Dr. Phyllis Ackerman, who were Persian rug and tapestry experts, selected the hotel furnishings. Fragments of the original rugs are still part of the decor and some of the original tapestries still hang on the walls. A mural above the fireplace in the Elevator Lobby and the stained glass windows in the Great Lounge are the work of Jeannette Dyer Spencer. Yosemite's Ahwahnee Hotel served as inspiration for Disney's Californian Resort. Over the years the hotel has seen many famous guests, and It has served as a U.S. navy hospital during World War II.

Hauntspitality

Paranormal investigators and "sensitive" individuals know all about the haunted nature of the Ahwahnee Hotel. For years, stories have circulated among staff and guests about cold breezes where there shouldn't be any, disembodied footsteps, shadowy figures that suddenly manifest then just as quickly disappear, lights that turn on by themselves, doors that mysteriously open and close by themselves, unexplained voices, and myriad other events that cannot be readily dismissed as having natural explanations. There are several spirits who reside inside, and a rocking chair that will begin moving back and forth on its own.

Delaware North Companies in 2004 prepared a press release entitled, Ghosts among Visitors at Yosemite's Historic Hotels. According to the press release, the ghost story at the Ahwahnee is that the entire 6th floor is haunted by the ghost of Mary Curry Tressider, who lived on the 6th floor until she passed away in 1970.

People who have stayed in the Tressider Room are convinced that her restless spirit visits those who spend the night inside as well as walks the hallways. Mary has been known to play with the lights in the bedroom and bathroom and stand at the foot of the bed, checking out her room guests. She's not mean spirited, nor does she cause any harm. It's as if she is hanging around, curious and still watching over things. The sixth floor seems to have a certain feel to it that causes people to look behind them as if they are being followed or feel chilled as if someone unseen has just passed through them.

Then there is the parlor of the 3rd floor suite where numerous people have witnessed a ghostly rocking chair move back and forth on its own. On many occasions housekeeping staff have noted a rocking chair in the parlor of the suite when they enter; the only problem is, there is no piece of furniture like that in the parlor. The story behind the phantom chair dates to when President John F. Kennedy occupied the suite. While he was staying there, management placed a rocking chair in the room at his request. When Kennedy left, the chair was removed from the room. From time to time, the phantom chair suddenly materializes in front of startled housekeeping, and then just as quickly vanishes. Why this visitation happens infrequently to some people is anyone's guess.

Guests have also reported hearing phantom children playing in some of the hallways. Their laughter will echo as well as their footsteps for a few seconds before silence is restored. Other times someone will witness a door open and shut in front of them, and hear someone cough or shuffle off, but see no one. There are ghostly parties that reportedly come from unoccupied rooms, and orbs of light that have been recorded by intrepid ghost hunters who love to bring their meters and cameras to investigate this grand hotel.

The Tressider suite on the 6th floor, which was the former bedroom of Mary Curry Tressider when it was the home of the Tressiders, is reportedly haunted. The room constantly felt cold and the photo of Mary Curry Tressider, or more appropriately, the eyes in the photo, followed their every move in the room. Then, later that night, the couple turned the two brass reading lamps above the four poster bed on just because they felt uneasy. When they awoke in the morning, the lamps were both turned off and they were the only ones in the room. Noticeable temperature variations, meter anomalies, orbs, disembodied voices caught on tape, and shadowy figures are all part of the charm of this hotel, where the past and present are separated by the thinnest veil of reality. It's a place where the spirits don't want to leave; and who can blame them. The Ahwahnee Hotel is a slice of heaven with a touch of afterlife ambiance.

Yosemite Lodge at the Falls

Particulars
9004 Yosemite Lodge Drive,
Yosemite National Park, CA 95389
Or P.O. Box 578,
Yosemite National Park, CA 95389
Phone: 559-253-5635

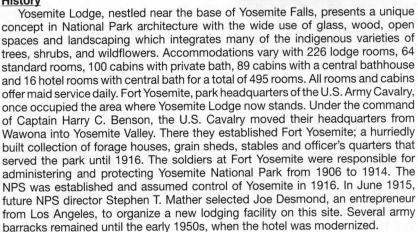

History

Yosemite Lodge, nestled near the base of Yosemite Falls, presents a unique concept in National Park architecture with the wide use of glass, wood, open spaces and landscaping which integrates many of the indigenous varieties of trees, shrubs, and wildflowers. Accommodations vary with 226 lodge rooms, 64 standard rooms, 100 cabins with private bath, 89 cabins with a central bathhouse and 16 hotel rooms with central bath for a total of 495 rooms. All rooms and cabins offer maid service daily. Fort Yosemite, park headquarters of the U.S. Army Cavalry, once occupied the area where Yosemite Lodge now stands. Under the command of Captain Harry C. Benson, the U.S. Cavalry moved their headquarters from Wawona into Yosemite Valley. There they established Fort Yosemite; a hurriedly built collection of forage houses, grain sheds, stables and officer's quarters that served the park until 1916. The soldiers at Fort Yosemite were responsible for administering and protecting Yosemite National Park from 1906 to 1914. The NPS was established and assumed control of Yosemite in 1916. In June 1915, future NPS director Stephen T. Mather selected Joe Desmond, an entrepreneur from Los Angeles, to organize a new lodging facility on this site. Several army barracks remained until the early 1950s, when the hotel was modernized.

Hauntspitality

Considering the history associated with the grounds on which the current building rests, it is little wonder that the building is reportedly home to several spirits. We had heard rumors of ghosts at the lodge for years, but it took our friend and fellow gifted author Antonio Garcez, to thoroughly research the area and provide detailed accounts in his latest book, Ghost Stories of California's Gold Rush Country and Yosemite National Park. The stories are provocative and provide an insight into just how land, imprinted by historical events, can surface in the form of spiritual energy when something is built on hallowed or disturbed ground. We suggest you read his book for the well-written detailed stories. In the meantime, her are some snippets about the haunted lodge.

- Housekeeping has witnessed unexplained reflections in the bathroom mirrors of certain rooms.
- Lights in some of the rooms will suddenly dim or flicker out when entering.
- Mirrors have been removed from the walls only to be relocated under beds or in closets.
- Drawers will refuse to open as if someone unseen is pushing tightly to keep them closed.
- When housekeeping has entered a room to be cleaned, they turn around for a second, then turn back and the bed will be miraculously made up.
- When the beds have been neatly made, sudden impressions or indentations will appear on the linens.
- While staff have been in the process of cleaning certain rooms, their supplies will be moved or vanish.
- Doors will open by themselves and shadowy figures will be seen out of the

corner of people's eyes.

- One spirit, named Mildred who either committed suicide or was murdered on the property has been frequently sighted in the building.

The remodeling efforts seem to have tamed the spirits on the property according to some. However, you'll have to find out the truth for yourself when you stay at this wonderful lodge in one of the most beautiful places on earth; and beyond.

Haunted California References

Associated Press (1997) <u>Guests and Ghosts: Eureka's Mansion a Balance Times.</u> <u>Standard, Travel Section</u>, October 5, 1997.

Auerbach, Loyd (1998) <u>Can True Psychic Phenomena coexist with experimental trickery? Events at the Moss Beach Distillery may let us find out.</u> FATE Magazine, August, 1998

Austin, Paige, <u>Psychic Society Will Seek Out Spirits in Old Towne</u>, The Orange County Register, March 3, 2001

Austin, Paige, <u>Psychics Investigate Old Towne</u>, The Orange County Register, March 8, 2001.

Blackman, Haden (1998) <u>The Field Guide to North American Hauntings</u>. Three Rivers Press, New York.

Bradley Nancy (1998) <u>The Incredible World of Gold Rush Ghosts: True Stories of Hauntings in the Mother Lode.</u> Morris Publishing, Kearney, Nebraska 68847.

Bradley, Nancy Bradley and Vincent Gaddis (1990) <u>Gold Rush Ghosts</u>. Borderland Sciences, Garberville, California.

Burnett, Claudine (1996) <u>Haunted Long Beach.</u> Historical Society of Long Beach, Long Beach, California.

Carrico, Richard (1991) <u>San Diego's Spirits: Ghosts and Hauntings in America's Southwest Corner.</u> Recuerdos Press, San Diego, California.

Ciardelli, Dolores Fox (2000) <u>Favorite Haunts on Main Street</u>. Pleasanton Weekly On Line Edition, September 8, 2000.

Cristallo, Suzanne, <u>Bella Saratoga is popular with all, including a ghost</u>. Saratoga News, November 8, 2000

Cristallo, Suzanne, <u>Bella Saratoga serves up food, music and history: There's even a friendly ghost.</u> Los Gatos Weekly Times, April 1, 1998.

Dalba, Rose (1997) <u>Salon Magazine</u>, September 30, 1997, Mondo Wierdo (ww. salonmagazine.com).

Deffner, Elisabeth (2001) <u>Reporter's Notebook: Shedding Light on Mysterious Goings-on at the Victorian Manor.</u> The Orange County Register, October 25, 2001

Dyer, Jeff (2005) <u>Ghost Hunter's Guide to the San Francisco Bay Area</u>. Pelican Publishing Company, Gretna, Louisiana

Dyer, Jeff (2007) <u>Ghost Hunter's Guide to Los Angeles</u>. Pelican Publishing Company, Gretna, Louisiana

FATE Magazine (October, 1992) Llewellyn Worldwide, 84 South Wabasha, St. Paul, Minnesota.

FATE Magazine (November, 1993) Llewellyn Worldwide, 84 South Wabasha, St. Paul, Minnesota.

Farren, Julie (1999) <u>Bed, Breakfast and Secrets. San Bernardino</u>. The Sun (Living Section) Monday, August 16, 1999.

Barbara Fitzsimmons, Barbara (1987) <u>A Grand Ghostly Night</u>. The San Diego Union, November 25, 1987).

Galasso, Ginny (1996) <u>Sierra Sky Ranch ghosts seem to live on</u>. Sierra Star, Wednesday, October 27, 1999 Online Edition

Garcez, Antonio R. (2004) <u>Ghost Stories of California's Gold Rush Country and Yosemite National Park.</u> Red Rabbit Press, Hanover, New Mexico.

Gibson, Ross Eric (1993) <u>Historical Memories Haunt Brookdale</u>. San Jose Mercury News, October 19, 1993.

Gibson, Ross Eric (1994) <u>The Spirit of Aptos: 116-year-old Hotel to become a Landmark</u>, San Jose Mercury News, April 26, 1994, p.1B.

Graf, Hilber H. (2005) <u>Visiting Haunted Southern California.</u> Infinity Publishing Company, Pennsylvania.

Graf, Hilber H. (2006) <u>Ghost Hunting in Mother Lode Country.</u> Infinity Publishing Company, Pennsylvania.

Hamilton, Sally (1995) <u>Hotel Willow</u>, Book-em Publications, Jamestown, California.

Hart, William (1996) <u>The Spirited Resident of the Cavanagh Inn</u>. Argus-Courier.

Kearney, Syd (2000) Welcome to the Apparit-inn. Houston Chronicle, Travel Section, October 29, 2000.

Haralson, Sari Mitchell (1983) <u>The Brookdale Lodge - Haunted or Haunting?</u> The Valley Times, September 2, 1983).

Hauck, Dennis William (1996) <u>The National Directory: Haunted Places - Ghostly abodes, sacred sites, UFO landings, and other supernatural locations</u> Penguin Books, New York.

Hecht, Peter (1996) <u>"Town argues Hangtown Image."</u> Sacramento Bee, November 30, 1996, Grants Pass Oregon Daily Courier.

Hollywood Hauntings (http://members.xoom.com/Ruthven/sweet.htm.

Jacobson, Laurie and Marc Wanamaker (1994) <u>Hollywood Haunted: A Ghostly Tour of Filmland (1994)</u>, Angel City Press, Santa Monica, California.

The International Society For Paranormal Research (ISPR), P.O. Box 291159, Los Angeles, California 90027 - (213) 464-7827.

Kouri, Michael J. (2001) <u>The Most Haunted Places in Azusa</u>. Tapestry Autum Press, Burbank, California.

Kutz, Jack (1996) <u>Mysteries and Miracles of California: Guide Book to the Genuingly Bizarre in the Golden State.</u> Rhombus Publishing Company, Inc. Corrales, New Mexico.

Lamb, John (1997) <u>Ghost Trackers Newsletter</u> (June 1997 issue - Vol. 16, Number 2).

Lamb, John J. (1999) San Diego Specters: Ghosts, Poltergeists, and Phantasmic Tales. Sunbelt Publications, San Diego, California.

Lathim, Rod (1995) <u>The Spirits of the Big Yellow House: A History of Summerland's Founding Family,</u> Emily Publications, Santa Barbara, California. (Also available at the Big Yellow House.

Marinacci, Mike (1988) <u>Mysterious California: Strange Places and Eerie Phenomena in the Golden State.</u> Panpipes Press, Los Angeles, California.

May, Alan M. (1990) <u>The Legend of Kate Morgan: The Search for the Ghost of the Hotel del Coronado.</u> Elk Publishing, San Marcos, California.

May, Antoinette (1977) <u>Haunted Houses and Wandering Ghosts of California</u>, The San Francisco Examiner Division of the Hearst Corporation, San Francisco, California.

May, Antoinette (1993) <u>Haunted Houses of California: A Ghostly Guide to Haunted Houses and Wandering Spirits.</u> Wide World Publishing/Tetra.

McNulty, Maureen M. (1998) <u>Ghost of the Crystal Rose Inn: A Ghost Child Shares Her Story.</u> Fate Magazine, April, 1998).

Mead, Robin (1995) <u>Haunted Hotels: A Guide to American and Canadian Inns and Their Ghosts (1995)</u>, Rutledge Hill Press, Nashville, Tennessee.

Michaels Susan (1996) <u>Sightings: Beyond Imagination Lie the Truth.</u> A Fireside Book, Simon & Schuster.

Moss Beach Distillery (n.d.). The Distillery News (<u>The Blue Lady From the Past</u>).

Myers, Arthur (1986) <u>The Ghostly Register: Haunted Dwellings---Active Spirits: A Journey to America's Strangest Landmarks</u>. Contemporary Books. Chicago.

Myers, Arthur Myers (1990) <u>The Ghostly Gazetteer: America's Most Fascinating Haunted Landmarks</u>. Contemporary Books, Chicago, Illinois.

Oberding, Janice (2002) <u>Haunted Gold and Silver.</u> Thunder Mountain Productions Press, Reno, Nevada.

Oberding, Janice (2004) <u>Las Vegas Haunted</u>. Thunder Mountain Productions Press, Reno, Nevada.

Reinstedt, Randall A. (1977) <u>Ghostly Tales and Mysterious Happenings of Old Monterey Monterey.</u> Ghost Town Publications, Carmel, California.

Reinstedt, Randall A. (1991) <u>Ghost Notes: Haunted Happenings on California's Historic Monterey Peninsula</u>. Ghost Town Publications, Carmel, California.

Reinstedt, Randall A. (2000) <u>California Ghost Notes; Haunted Happenings Throughout the Golden State.</u> Ghost Town Publications, Carmel, California.

Richards, Rand (2004) <u>Haunted San Franciso: Ghost Stories from the City's Past</u>. Heritage House Publishers, Sn Francisco.

Ritto, Mike (2000). <u>Ghost Story: Does Murder Victim Walk the Halls of Villa del Sol?</u> Fullerton News Tribune, October 26, 2000

Roberts, Denise (1997) <u>The Ghost of the Groveland Hotel</u>, The Modesto Bee, Living Section, October 26, 1997.

Roberts, Nancy (1998) <u>Haunted Houses: Chilling Tales From 24 American Homes.</u> The Globe Pequot Press, Old Saybrook, Connecticut.

Robson, Ellen and Diane Halicki (1999) <u>Haunted Highway, The Spirits of Route 66: Sixty-six spine-tingling tales of ghostly encounters along America's most famous highway</u>. Golden West Publishers, Phoenix, Arizona.

Scott, Beth and Michael Norman (1994) <u>Haunted America</u>. A Tom Doherty Associates Book, New York.

Senate, Richard L. (1986) <u>Ghosts of the Haunted Coast: Ghost Hunting on California's Gold Coast</u>, Pathfinder Publishing, Ventura, California.

Senate, Richard (1992) <u>Haunted Ventura</u>, Charon Press, Ventura, California.

Senate, Richard L. (1993) <u>The Haunted Southland: Ghosts of Southern California (1993)</u>, Charon Press, Ventura, California.

Senate, Richard (1998) <u>Ghost Stalker's Guide to Haunted California</u>. Charon Press, Ventura, California.

Senate, Richard (1998) <u>Ghosts of the Ojai: California's Most Haunted Valley.</u> Charon Press, Ventura,

Shadowlands Haunted Places (www.theshadowlands.net)

Sightings, Paramount Studios, Hollywood, California.

Smith, Barbara (2000) <u>Ghost Stories of California</u>, Lone Pine Publishing, Canada

Smith, Terry L. and Mark Jean (2003) <u>Haunted Inns of America</u>, Crane Hill Publishers.

Steiger, Brad and Sherry Steiger (1990) <u>Montezuma's Serpent</u>. Paragon House, New York, New York.

Teglovic, Antoinette (n.d.) <u>The History of the Hotel Catalina</u>. An unpublished story provided courtesy of Sherrie Walker, Catalina Islander.

Toth, Maria Lynn (1994) <u>Local Haunts. San Bernardino</u>, The Sun (Living Section) Monday, October 31, 1994.

Townsend, Scott (1998) <u>History of Madrona Manor</u> (scott@ serra.com - Serra Systems, Inc., 1998).

Vapor Trails (October 1995 - Hollywood's Ghosts) - http://www/vaoprtrails.com/ USA/USA Features/Ghosts/Ghost.html.

White, Gail (1992) <u>Haunted San Diego: A Historic Guide to San Diego's Favorite Haunts</u>. Tecolote Publications, San Diego, California.

Wlodarski, Robert, Anne Nathan-Wlodarski, and Richard Senate (1995) <u>A Guide to the Haunted Queen Mary: Ghostly Apparitions, Psychic Phenomena and Paranormal Activity</u>. G-Host Publishing, West Hills, California

Wlodarski, Robert J. and Anne Nathan-Wlodarski (1996) <u>Haunted Catalina: A</u>

History of the Island and Guide to Paranormal Activity, G-HOST Publishing, West Hills, California.

Wlodarski, Robert and Anne Powell Wlodarski (2000) The Haunted Queen Mary, Long Beach, California. G-Host Publishing, West Hills, California.

Wlodarski, Robert James and Anne Powell Wlodarski (2000) Dinner and Spirits: A Guide to America's Most Haunted Restaurants, Taverns and Inns. iUniverse.com, Inc. New York.

Wlodarski, Robert J. and Anne Wlodarski (2002) California Hauntspitality: A Ghostly Guide to Haunted Inns, Restaurants and Taverns , Whitechapel Productions Press, Alton, Illinois

Wlodarski, Robert J. and Anne Wlodarski, Ghosts of Old Town San Diego State Historic Park (2006), G-Host Publishing, West Hills, California.

Wlodarski, Robert J. and Anne Wlodarski (2006), Fullerton Ghosts: History and Hauntings in Orange County, California, G-Host Publishing, West Hills, California.

Wood, Ted (1999) Ghosts of the West Coast: The Lost Souls of the Queen Mary and other Real-Life Hauntings (1999). Walker and Company, New York.

Yarbrough, Carolyn J. (1985) Healdsburg Inn Treats a Guest to Special Visitor, Los Angeles Times, Sunday, March 10, 1985.

California Paranormal Contacts

The Bay Area Paranormal Research Society
Fred Speer is the founder of the BAPRS - Their mission is to assist those experiencing a paranormal crisis in a scientific and professional manner. Website: www.rightondesign.com/baprs

California Society for Ghost Research (CSGR)
Chad Patterson (CSGR President and Founder) actively investigates ghosts and hauntings. Chad is a follower of parapsychology and the applications of scientific and socio-scientific study in paranormal research. Website: www.csgr.us

GEIST Web
This Southern California Paranormal Research Group is under the direction of H. James Millora
E-mail: GEISTweb@aol.com/http://members.aol.com/GEISTweb/index.html

Ghost Investigations and Photos
Lori McDonald is a registered IGHS Ghost Hunter/Ghost Researcher who is dedicated to documentation, education, research and investigation of paranormal phenomenon (www.AlienUFOart.com/GhostInvestigationsPhotos.htm - E-mail: Argonaut-Greywolf@home.com

Richard Senate
World famous paranormal investigator and author, Richard Senate is always looking for new investigations to feature in his award winning website: www. ghost-stalker.com and "Ghostwatch" newsletter. E-mail: hainthunter@aol.com

Haunted Places Directory
Dennis William Hauck - Website: www.haunted-places.com - E-mail: Info@haunted-places.com

Haunted Valley Paranormal
The home of the Tri-Valley Paranormal Research Team was established to study paranormal activities in Livermore California and the surrounding area.(http://hauntedvalley.4mg.com/)

Office of Paranormal Investigations
Loyd Auerbach is the Director of the Office of Paranormal Investigations and has been teaching Parapsychology and related topics for several years in the San Francisco Bay Area. Phone: 415-553-2588/Fax: 510-676-5505/www.mindreader.com/E-mail-esper@california.com

The Orange County Society for Psychic Research - OCSPR
P.O. Box 3692, Orange, California 92857 - Telephone: 714-637-5822 - This non-profit organization has been operating in Orange County since 1984 and the group is dedicated to professional investigations of haunted locations throughout southern California.

San Diego Ghost Hunters
Maritza Skandunas, Dawn Gaudette and Vinnie Skandunas form the heart of this intrepid paranormal investigative team based in San Diego. They are excellent at

gathering historical data, genealogy, EVP and taking fascinating spirit photographs. We highly recommend their Website at www.sandiegoghosthunters.com, or E-mail: info@sandiegoghosthunters.com, or by telephone at 619-469-4173.

San Diego Paranormal
Bonnie Vent is a spirit advocate, healer, author and producer who is in charge of San Diego Paranormal. Her mission is to work with experts and regular people who have had extraordinary experiences at the Whaley House, Villa Montezuma, Hotel Del Coronado, Comedy Store and other locales around the world to investigate the paranormal phenomena of the past and present. www.sdparanormal.com or E-mail: bvent@sdparanormal.com

San Gabriel Valley Paranormal Researchers
Founded in 1999 by Diane Melvin, the San Gabriel Valley Paranormal Researchers is a non-profit organization based in the San Gabriel Valley dedicated to investigating paranormal and unexplained phenomenon. Organization members share a common goal in researching, collecting data and documenting paranormal phenomenon for scientific research. P.O. Box 2108, Monrovia, CA 91017 - Website: www.sgvpr.org

Shadowlands: Ghosts and Hauntings
David Juliano has been researching ghosts for over 15 years. Juliano is the co-director and investigator for South Jersey Ghost Research based and a client counselor for another paranormal investigation group. (E-mail: shadowlord@theshadowlands.net-http://hometown.aol.com/shadoland2/ghost)

What should you do if you see a Ghost

1. Don't panic! Just try to relax, and then sit back and enjoy the phenomenon. Concentrate and try to notice every detail you can.

2. As soon as you can after the event concludes, write down exactly what you saw in as much detail as possible. Try to remember if there were any particular smells (perfume, cigar smoke, foul odors), sensations such as cold spots, gusts of air, or feelings of   nausea; music playing or other audible sounds, voices or conversations in the background, or feelings of being watched or touched, etc.

3. Even if you are not the greatest artist, try to sketch what you saw: What the image was wearing, include the style of clothing, shoes, glasses, hats, etc., anything which may   give an indication of a particular time period or era.

4. Draw a diagram or map of where the apparition was sighted, and your location when the event took place. Note the wallpaper (if any), furnishings in the room, types of windows (sash, hinged, pivoted, sliding), flooring (adobe, hardwood, carpeting), or other features in relation to the sighting.

5. Note what time of the day the event took place as well as weather conditions and   temperature, if possible. Also, see if you can locate any nearby vents, or openings, which might help explain away cold spots or drafts.

6. Record general information regarding how the event made you feel (happy, sad, depressed, frightened, exhilarated).

7. Note any unusual circumstances surrounding the event including; storms, high winds, power outages, other people working in the area, construction activities nearby, remodeling being performed, etc.).

8. Note other people present; include any children or animals who might have witnessed the event, or who may have been affected.

9. Attempt to investigate and research the experience further, including who the ghost might have been, or identify a tragedy that may help explain the haunting.

10. Attempt to rule out any explainable or natural causes for the occurrence, or associated noises, or smells. Check for earthquakes, sonic booms, construction, cooking nearby, animals or pests in the house---rule out the obvious.

11. If you are able to summon the courage, talk to the spirit in a sincere manner, and tell it to pass on to the next realm by looking for if it so wishes, and following the white light---prayers to release a trapped spirit oftentimes yield positive results. Never command a spirit to do anything... simply and respectfully provide an option to move on.

12. Always try and surround yourself in protective light when dealing with any energy. It never hurts to say a prayer (generic and non-denominational, or specific based on your religious persuasion). Ask that you not be harmed nor for the energy to attach itself to you when you leave.

The Ghosthunters Kit

Permission to use the following information was granted by Richard Senate. Check out his website (www.ghost-stalkers.com). In the investigations of haunted sites, Senate has put together a collection of tools he has have found useful.

1. 35mm camera loaded with XXX black and white film. A red gel should be placed over the flash unit. This causes the ASA to push into the infrared Spectrum [do not know why it works but using this configuration I have managed to take photographs of ghosts]. A stereo camera is also useful. Take along at least two cameras--one loaded with high speed film for low light and the other with XXX Film.

2. Tape Recorder with a microphone that is external. Use music quality tape and Always use Brand new tape! Never use the Chromium Oxide tape as sometimes a voice might double record. Use the recorded during the walk-though of haunted sites. When you are in a haunted place you may hear nothing! It is only when the tape is played back to spirit voices come out. They have a harsh, whispered quality and they only say one or two words, less than a sentence. This is called EVP for Electronic Voice Phenomena. Take along two tape recorders; an extra one as a back up with regular tape and a built in mike.

3. A good flashlight---but even the best can fail when you enter a haunted site--it seems that ghosts can manipulate electronic units. Sometimes a good kerosene lantern is better or a good old candle and match.

4. Notebook of paper and a pen is one of the best tools to save data. Write down all that you see and feel and record the times when it happened --Keep a journal of your overnight ghost stakeout. Paper is also useful for drawing floor-plans of the haunted site and sketching a likeness of any ghosts you happen to see.

5. A compass can be very helpful in finding your way around county back roads and in mapping out a site. Also, I have found that a compass needle may act strangely in haunted places.

6. A good EM Detector (Or Gauss Meter) is very good tool. Ghosts are found in electro-magnetic fields. We still do not know why, but there is some interesting new research being done on these phenomena.

7. Thermometers are always of help in any ghost hunt. Electronic ones are excellent but ghosts can manipulate them. Any change in the surrounding environment can indicate the presence of a phantom. For countless centuries people have felt an icy cold in haunted places. Some cold spots have a six-degree difference in temperature and in some of the literature twenty degrees are recorded in haunted rooms (I haven't encountered that much of a temperature difference yet!)

8. A silver Cross and a small bottle of Holy Water. (One can never be too careful --- you know, like chicken soup it can't hurt). Over the years silver has been liked to psychic events and I have noticed that women who wear a lot of silver jewelry seem to have more ghostly sightings--Why? I don't know.

9. Dowsing Rods have been used for centuries to find water. But, strange as it sounds they can be used to find areas of psychic disturbances. They seem to react in places of murder and death places where ghosts and poltergeists infest. Almost anyone can use dowsing rods and find lost items, and places where ghosts are found--but be sure you are not just finding buried water pipes! A little practice and you will discover how useful dowsing rods can be!

If you wish to understand more of how ghost hunters seek answers to the riddle of a haunted house read Senate's book **The Haunted Southland**.

Photograph Release Form

If you've experienced anything out of the ordinary, something unexplainable, or an event that might be considered paranormal while visiting a restaurant, tavern, inn, or hotel, we would love to hear from you. You can advise us of your encounter by enclosing this form and the Documenting Your Event form for possible inclusion in revised additions of this book. We would appreciate only first-hand experiences, and if you have them, and photographs taken of the event.

Once again, if you would like your story told, please fill out the enclosed release form, and documenting your event form, and send it to the address below. If your story or photograph is used, we wish to provide proper you with the proper credit. If you wish to remain anonymous, please fill out the forms with the correct information, and then attach a brief note stating if you wish to remain anonymous.

Send to:

G-Host Publishing
Robert Wlodarski and Anne Wlodarski
8701 Lava Place
West Hills, California 91304-2126
Phone/Fax: 818-340-6676
E-mail: robanne@ix.netcom.com

I hereby grant to G-HOST Publishing, permission to reproduce the attached material and/or photographs I have supplied for inclusion in revised editions to West Coast Ghosts, or other subsequent publications dealing with ghosts and the paranormal.

I further consent to the publication and copyrighting of this book to be published in any manner G-HOST Publications may deem fit.

Proper acknowledgment of my photograph(s) material(s) will be provided by G-HOST Publishing within the context of the publication at the publisher's discretion.

Your name: _____

Your address: _____

_____

Your phone number: _____

Date of submission: _____

Signature: _____

Documenting Your California Ghost Encounter

Name_____

Address_____

City_____ State_____ Zip Code_____

Phone (Home):_____ Fax:_____ E-mail: _____

Birth Date:_____ Occupation_____

Married:_____   Single:_____   No. of Children:_____

Number of people residing at the place of the event: _____
Number of people witnessing the event: _____
Name of the person who witnessed the event #1: _____
Relationship:_____   Age:_____
Name of the person who witnessed the event #2:_____
Relationship:_____   Age:_____
Name of the person who witnessed the event #3:_____
Relationship:_____   Age:_____

Other witnesses by name and age:_____
_____
_____

Were there any pets present? (If yes, explain):_____
_____

Date(s) the event(s) took place:_____
_____
_____
_____

Approximate time(s) the event(s) occurred:_____
_____
_____
_____

What were the weather conditions at the time the event occurred:_____
_____
_____
_____

Briefly   describe   the   event:_____
_____
_____
_____
_____

(Continue on the back)

Describe how you felt at the time of the event (Frightened, amazed...)_____

_____

_____

_____

_____

If you can, draw what you saw using the space provided below:

What rooms did the event occur in:_____

_____

_____

Describe the furnishings in the room(s) where the event(s) occurred:_____

_____

_____

Describe the approximate duration of the event(s):_____

_____

_____

Have events occurred before that you know of? (If yes, please elaborate)_____

_____

_____

Have the event(s) increased in frequency (If yes, briefly explain):_____

_____

Do you know the history of the place (If yes, please elaborate):_____

_____

_____

Doyouknowthename(s)ofthepriorowners(Ifso,pleaseprovide):_____

_____

_____

Please return this questionnaire to:

G•Host Publishing
8701 Lava Place, West Hills, California 91304-2126
Phone/Fax: 818-340-6676 - E-mail: robanne@ix.netcom.com

(Thank you for your time and patience in completing this form)

California Ghost Report

If you have a favorite haunted restaurant, tavern, inn, hotel, or bed and breakfast that is not listed in this book, or if you happen to find a haunted establishment while traveling, let us know by mail, fax, or e-mail. Send the following completed form(s) to:

G-Host Publishing
8701 Lava Place
West Hills, California 91304-2126
Phone/Fax: 818-340-6676
E-mail: robanne@ix.netcom.com

Name of establishment:_____

Address: _____

City: _____ State: _____ Zip: _____

Phone: _____ Fax: _____

Toll Free Number: _____ E-mail: _____

Contact Person: _____

Accommodations (If an inn, B&B, or hotel): _____

Amenities (If an inn, B&B, or hotel): _____

Business information: _____

_____

Payment accepted (circle): Visa - MasterCard - American Express - Diners Club

Discover - Carte Blanche - Japanese Credit Bureau - Travelers checks -

Personal checks - _____

For purposes of providing credit in the revised edition

Your name:_____

Your address:_____

_____

Your phone number: _____

Your fax number: _____

Your e-mail address: _____